COMMERCIAL MOTOR TRANSPORTATION

COMMERCIAL MOTOR TRANSPORTATION

By

CHARLES A. TAFF, Ph.D.

PROFESSOR OF TRANSPORTATION

COLLEGE OF BUSINESS AND PUBLIC ADMINISTRATION

UNIVERSITY OF MARYLAND

REVISED EDITION

1955

RICHARD D. IRWIN, INC. · HOMEWOOD, ILLINOIS

REVISED EDITION

First Printing, June, 1955
Second Printing, January, 1956

Library of Congress Catalogue No. 55–9353

PREFACE

▼▼

THE PHENOMENAL GROWTH of commercial motor transportation is one of the most significant economic developments of the twentieth century. The progress of this young, dynamic industry is all the more remarkable when we consider that, for the most part, it has taken place during the last thirty years. Few industries of our time have experienced such rapid expansion in so short a period. Moreover, the industry is continuing to expand at an accelerating pace as more and more shippers and passengers come to rely upon it for convenient and flexible transportation service. Of all the modern means of transportation, that by truck and bus has proved to be the form most easily adaptable to today's multiplicity of needs—so much so, that it now reaches into almost every phase of our daily living.

Despite its mushroom growth the motor carrier industry has now attained a high level of stability. Federal regulation, which became effective with the passage of the Motor Carrier Act in 1935, and state regulation have contributed to this stability as have the efforts of the industry itself.

The first edition of this book was published to meet the need for a complete, analytical, and factual account of commercial motor transportation in both its property-carrying and passenger-carrying phases. During the five years since its publication there have been many new developments in the field and substantial expansion of operations. There is a total of twenty-four chapters in this revision. Eight entirely new chapters have been added. Moreover, the sixteen which comprised the first volume have been rewritten and contain much new material to reflect the changes which have developed during this period.

Part I outlines the scope of motor transportation and of the highway system. The material on highways is greatly expanded and covers such topics as highway administration, toll roads, the benefits of improved highways, and describes the critical need for highway improvements. Because of the importance of highway financing, there is a separate chapter dealing with this subject, which includes methods of allocating highway tax responsibility to different classes of vehicles.

Part II deals with the property-carrying aspects of motor transportation and covers in detail the various phases of trucking management and operations. In motor transportation, there are more diverse types of operations than in any other field of transportation. To provide a better understanding of these operations, both for-hire and private, a new chapter has been added on types of carriers. Another type of operation, that of local cartage, is a big business. A new chapter dealing with this subject analyzes the operations of these carriers. Two new chapters have been added which discuss some of the specialized carriers of property—household goods carriers, tank truck carriers, automobile transporters, heavy haulers, and pipeline stringers. The chapter on the operations of a motor carrier has been expanded into an organization and operations chapter. It includes much new material, as does the chapter on terminal operations and financing. A new chapter on claims and claim prevention has been included. There are separate chapters dealing with motor freight classification and rates and rate making. Two new chapters have been added delineating the Interstate Commerce Commission's policy on such matters as operating authority, mergers, consolidations, control, and rates. Careful attention has been given to the federal and state regulations and restrictions to which the various types of operation are subject.

Part III, which is devoted to the passenger operations of commercial motor transportation, has been brought up to date. It also includes new material on special and charter parties, the transit problem, and private automobiles.

This book is planned as a textbook for courses in commercial motor transportation and as a reference for more general courses in transportation and in traffic management. It should also be of great value to people in the industry or those who are seeking information about the industry. The selection of topics is based upon the author's own experience in teaching a course in motor transportation and upon his practical business activities in the field. Included are all of the topics needed for a thoroughgoing course in the subject.

The author is indebted to many persons for their assistance in supplying information, and the co-operation extended by everyone is deeply appreciated. Particular acknowledgment is due American Trucking Associations, Inc., the American Transit Association, the National Association of Motor Bus Operators, the Bureau of Motor Carriers of the Interstate Commerce Commission, and the Bureau of Public Roads of the Department of Commerce. Among the many motor carriers which have been helpful are: Associated Transport, Jacobs Transfer and Storage Company, Pacific Intermountain Express, Roadway Express, The Greyhound Corporation, and the Trailways Bus System. The encouragement of Dr. John H. Frederick, Head, Department of Business Organization and Professor of Transportation, University of Maryland, is gratefully acknowledged. The author is indebted to his wife, Glatha M. Taff, for invaluable aid in the preparation of this manuscript.

CHARLES A. TAFF

COLLEGE PARK, MARYLAND
April, 1955

CONTENTS

▼▲

PART I. THE SCOPE OF MOTOR TRANSPORTATION AND THE HIGHWAY SYSTEM

PART II. PROPERTY-CARRYING ASPECTS OF COMMERCIAL MOTOR TRANSPORTATION

BIBLIOGRAPHY

INDEX

PART I

The Scope of Motor Transportation and the Highway System

1. MAGNITUDE OF MOTOR
TRANSPORTATION

▼▲

MOTOR transportation is big business, for it is every man's individual mode of transport. One of the most significant developments in the twentieth century has been the growth of automotive transport. It has become an integral part of our transportation system, indispensable to our way of life. It vitally affects every segment of our economy, for through automotive transportation the interchange of ideas and goods has been greatly accelerated, with inestimable benefits to society. In addition, it has virtually revolutionized production and distribution. Its scope is so broad that there is almost no phase of daily living that is not affected by some aspect of this mode of transport. The social and economic effects upon the economy of the nation have been greater than those occasioned by any other single technological development. In the United States, there are about 165 million people and 3 million square miles of land; about 3 million miles of roads and approximately 300 thousand miles of city streets. There is, therefore, a mile of road for every square mile of area and 18 vehicles for every mile of road. In early 1955 there were more than 58 million vehicles registered.

Figure 1–1 shows how the number of motor vehicles has increased over the years and the relative number of automobiles, trucks, and busses in each year. The numbers of trucks, and busses alone now exceed the total of vehicles in 1920. In 1955 the total of trucks and busses was over 10 million. Increases in these larger vehicles now anually recorded are significant beyond their numerical values.

An estimate was made in 1950 by a special study group[1] that motor-vehicle registrations would total 85 million in 1975. However, be-

[1] President's Materials Policy Commission.

3

cause of the rapid increase in vehicles since the end of World War II, the Bureau of Public Roads in 1954 estimated that by 1964 there would be 81 million vehicles.

The annual vehicle-miles from 1920 through 1953 are shown in Figure 1–2. The relative portions of vehicle-miles for trucks, passenger cars, and busses are also given. A little less than 10,000 miles a year is recorded for each vehicle. This adds up to a stupendous total

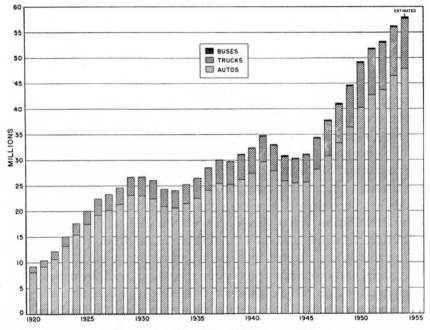

FIG. 1–1. Motor-vehicle registrations, 1920–54.
Source: Bureau of Public Roads.

of vehicular movement which has risen from 302 to 557 billion vehicle-miles between 1940 and 1954.

Automotive transportation is a significant factor in our defense planning. Statistically, there are enough private automobiles alone in the United States to evacuate at one time every man, woman, and child. Much of the success of our productive effort during World War II can be attributed to the availability and flexibility of motor-vehicle transportation.[2] Many manufacturers of tanks, planes, ships, and other essential equipment were operating on the basis of long-distance production lines which often traveled whole states before

---

[2] See Wilfred Owen, *Automobile Transportation in Defense or War*, Defense Transport Administration (Washington, D.C.: U.S. Government Printing Office, 1951).

the final point of assembly was reached. This procedure allowed more direct participation in the war effort by thousands of small plants through subcontracting and by millions of workers who otherwise might have been excluded. Although this procedure took jobs closer to the available labor force and minimized the need for personal transportation, it created additional demands on motor vehicles. The unavailability of other transportation and the convenience

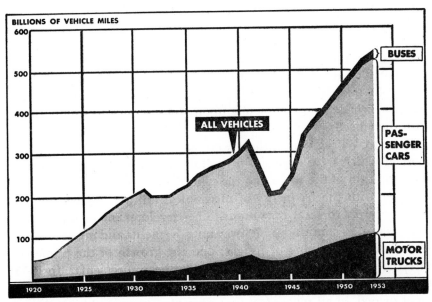

FIG. 1–2. Annual vehicle-miles of travel.
Source: Automobile Manufacturers Association, *Automobile Facts and Figures*, 1954, p. 37.

and flexibility of motor trucks allowed a high percentage of materials and subassemblies to flow between parts of the production lines by motor vehicles.

The decentralization of industry has continued during postwar years and is receiving official encouragement in defense planning as a precaution against any future emergency. It seems, therefore, that automotive transportation will be more essential in any future contingency than it has been in the past.

Automotive transportation has developed largely along two lines —property carrying and passenger carrying. Each of these two types can be further subdivided into private and for-hire operations, the latter being conducted by common and contract carriers. This classification is based upon the nature of the carrier's relationship to the persons or property which are transported. The emphasis in this text will be on the for-hire aspects of both passenger and property-carrying operations. Further discussion of the passenger aspects of motor transportation will be treated separately in Chapters 22–24, inclusive.

PROPERTY CARRYING BY MOTOR CARRIER

There are thousands of communities which are heavily dependent upon truck service for their everyday needs—their bread, meat, milk, groceries, clothing, fuel, ice cream, and movies. There is very little in their day-to-day living which does not come to them at least part of the way by truck. All communities, large or small, depend in some manner upon motor-truck transportation for the satisfaction of their wants. In addition, there are 25,000 communities in the United States which depend completely upon truck service to supply them with their needs.

Prior to World War I, there were approximately 250,000 trucks, most of which were engaged in local delivery service. At that time, the condition of the roads and the solid rubber tires on the vehicles, together with the frequency of mechanical failures, largely limited truck services to local operations. The development of pneumatic tires, as well as continuous highway improvements, did much to stimulate intercity carrying of freight; and the growth of the property-carrying phase of motor transportation has been spectacular. In 1955 there were about 10 million motor trucks, including 413,000 government owned, of all types operating upon the streets and highways of the nation. Figure 1–3 shows the increase by years in truck registrations from 1915 through 1953. Truck registrations have doubled be-

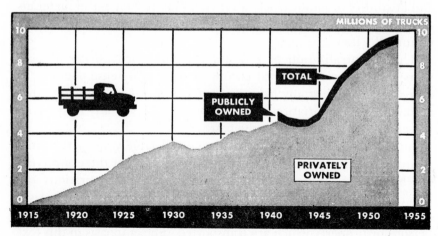

FIG. 1–3. Truck registration by years.
Source: Automobile Manufacturers Association, *Motor Truck Facts*, 1954, p. 20.

tween 1940 and 1953. Data available in 1944 from the Office of Defense Transportation, a wartime agency, indicated that 87 per cent of the trucks were privately operated, that is, by stores, dairies, farmers, and the like. The Bell System, for example, operates a fleet of more than 40,000 trucks. The remaining 13 per cent were for-hire trucks. The percentages today would be slightly different. Excluding government-owned trucks, the estimated breakdown of the truck fleet in 1954 was:[3]

Type	*Number*	*Per Cent*
Private	5,101,000	54.0
Intercity	633,000	6.7
Local	4,468,000	47.3
Farm	2,834,000	30.0
For-hire	1,512,000	16.0
Intercity	567,000	6.0
Local	945,000	10.0
Total	9,447,000	100.0

It has been estimated that on a tonnage basis about three fourths of the tonnage is carried by truck.[4] On a ton-mile basis (a statistical unit using weight and distance—one ton transported one mile is one ton-mile) the situation is different, due in part to the shorter average haul. The estimated volume and percentage distribution of intercity freight traffic, both public and private, in ton-miles by trucks by years were:[5]

Year	Billions	Percentage of Total
1939	52.821	9.72
1940	62.007	10.03
1941	81.156	10.51
1942	59.853	6.44
1943	56.526	5.48
1944	58.047	5.33
1945	66.614	6.49
1946	81.676	9.04
1947	101.663	9.98
1948	115.467	11.05
1949	124.949	13.67
1950	170.184	16.06
1951	182.467	15.56
1952ᵖ	184.106	16.24
1953ᵖ	206.808	17.38

ᵖ Preliminary.

[3] American Trucking Associations, Inc., Research Department.

[4] Office of Defense Transportation, *Review of Highway Transport and Transit Industries during the War* (Washington, D.C., 1945), p. 2.

[5] Interstate Commerce Commission, Bureau of Transport Economics and Statistics, *Monthly Comment on Transportation Statistics*, April 12, 1954, p. 14. 1953 figure furnished by Bureau of Transport Economics and Statistics.

The ton-miles of motor carriers has more than tripled since 1939, and in 1954 it exceeded 200 billion ton-miles. In the intercity for-hire field in 1953, the estimated total ton-miles of the Class I, Class II, and Class III[6] intercity motor carriers of property reporting to the Commission were 65 billion for common carriers and about 8 billion for contract carriers.

The for-hire property carriers which were subject to Interstate Commerce Commission regulation had operating revenues as shown

TABLE 1–1

ESTIMATED REVENUES OF CLASS I, II, AND III MOTOR CARRIERS,
1944–53
(Millions of Dollars)

	REVENUES FROM PROPERTY SERVICE		
YEAR	Intercity Revenues of Intercity Carriers		Total Revenues, Intercity and Local
	Common	Contract	
1944..............	$ 998.9	$ 80.3	$1,351.9
1945..............	1,025.0	80.0	1,406.3
1946..............	1,209.0	87.2	1,654.5
1947..............	1,684.0	114.7	2,213.6
1948..............	2,195.0	155.0	2,698.1
1949..............	2,302.7	169.4	2,911.2
1950..............	3,063.3	199.3	3,737.1
1951..............	3,459.6	226.3	4,169.2
1952r.............	3,602.7	297.9	4,417.5
1953p.............	3,965.6	358.6	4,926.4

r Revised.   p Preliminary.

Source: Interstate Commerce Commission, Bureau of Transport Economics and Statistics, *Monthly Comment on Transportation Statistics*, October, 1954, p. 7.

in Table 1–1. There has been more than a 100 per cent increase between 1946 and 1953 in operating revenues. This gives some idea of the increase in truck transportation which has taken place in a comparatively short period of time. Class I intercity motor carriers received in 1953 about $0.0595 per ton-mile, but there are regional variations from 4 to 8 cents. The average revenue per ton-mile for motor carriers has continued in 1953 as in previous years to be about four times that of the railroads.

The size of the trucking industry may be expressed in the number of people it employs. One estimate is that in 1953 there were 5,737,000 truck drivers in the United States.[7] This figure is derived

---

[6] As classified by the Interstate Commerce Commission for accounting purposes, a Class I motor carrier is one that has gross revenue of $200,000 or more per year; a Class II carrier has from $50,000 to $200,000 gross revenue per year; and a Class III carrier has a gross revenue of less than $50,000 per year.

[7] Automobile Manufacturers Association, *Motor Truck Facts*, 1954, p. 22.

by assuming 0.8 drivers per nonfarm truck, and it includes employees other than drivers of truck transportation companies. The figure widely used by the trucking industry is that in 1953 employment for 6,612,000 persons was directly created by truck transportation. This total includes in addition to truck drivers 240,000 employed in the production of trucks, parts, trailers, tires, and other equipment; 500,000 in truck sales and servicing; 80,000 in petroleum refining; and 55,000 that work on federal and state roads.[8] The trucking industry serves as an important employer of labor.

ADVANTAGES OF TRUCK TRANSPORTATION

The trucking industry has been able to record its rapid advance because of its inherent ability to provide and render advantageous services in competition with other modes of transportation. There are many advantages to motor-truck transportation, but there are four primary benefits: (a) speed; (b) economy; (c) reliability; and (d) convenience.

Speed of service from the platform of the consignor to the door of the consignee is one of the most important advantages possessed by the trucking industry. The shorter transit time by motor carrier has played a major role in increased patronage. This speed of service depends upon the transit time between terminals, the time spent in terminals, and pickup and delivery time. The ability to make expeditious deliveries would not be effective if only occasional service were offered. Frequency of schedule, therefore, is an important part of speed in service. One of the paramount reasons why the trucking industry is able to provide comparatively fast transit time is its inherent flexibility. Operating with a unit of less capacity than the average freight car, the trucker does not have to wait too long to accumulate sufficient freight and usually is in a position to depart immediately after the vehicle is loaded. With the larger share of operations consisting of direct single-line service, the trucker is not delayed by the necessity of making connections in the same degree as a railway. Freight can be collected at its source and delivered to its final destination with a minimum of rehandling. Trucks can be operated over the roads at night when traffic is relatively light. The fixed schedules of trains, on the other hand, often result in early clos-

---

[8] The Department of Labor statistics show employment in establishments primarily engaged in local or long-distance trucking or warehousing to be 724,400 in 1953. This represents the average number of full-time and part-time employees.

ing hours of freight cars and late arrivals at intermediate points and at destination. The speed and flexibility of the truck enables it to substitute for other freight facilities, particularly in the stress of a shortage of rail equipment. During World War II, tank trucks in many instances replaced tank cars in short-haul service. It has been estimated that in 1943 approximately 1,800 tank cars were released from short-haul service and placed in vital long-distance transportation. For one movement, 7 tank trucks and trailers were used to replace 114 tank cars.[9] Operating in 24-hour service, 7 days a week, the trucks were able to speed up greatly their turn-around time.

The economy of truck transportation is not contained solely in rates and charges lower than those available in other modes of transportation. The savings in money that come from better transit time, such as faster turnover of stocks, reduced inventories, and broader market areas, are receiving increased recognition. Generally lower labor and packaging costs and the economy possible in truck transportation in loading and unloading shipments are other factors which are receiving greater attention. The truck driver and helper usually will load and unload truckload shipments; whereas, on rail carload movements, the expense of loading and unloading usually falls upon the shipper or the consignee. Attached to the expense of rail carload shipments, also, but seldom present in truckload shipments, is the cost of delivery of the shipment to and from the railroad freight station when an industry does not have a rail siding. In addition, the truck driver is frequently more competent to load the vehicle than is shipping-room labor, which may represent intangible savings. Also, railroads do not offer pickup and delivery service on less-than-carload shipments at all of their stations; whereas this is the usual practice for all motor-carrier service.

Motor carriers, as a whole, have dependable schedules of shipments and prompt collection and delivery. They have tended to improve and stabilize their standards of service through more efficient operations and to provide relatively careful handling of shipments en route, which is of vital importance to any shipper.

The flexibility of the truck enables the motor carrier to adapt its service to suit the convenience of a shipper if the occasion demands it. For example, a regular shipper can usually arrange to have a truck at his plant almost immediately and at almost any hour of the day or night whenever the tonnage to be shipped or the nature of the serv-

---

[9] Office of Defense Transportation, *War Transportation of Petroleum, Petroleum Products and Other Liquids* (Washington, D.C., 1944), pp. 43 and 45.

ice warrants such special service. The same specialized service can be made available at destination as well. Another advantage of the motor carrier is its ability to provide a more personalized service. Many trucking organizations are fairly small firms and are therefore capable of dealing promptly and directly with the shipper on his trucking problems. The fact that a shipment, in the majority of instances, is in the direct care of a single motor carrier from origin to destination also adds to the element of personal supervision.

Vast technological improvements, coupled with the many advantages inherent in this mode of transport, have broadened the scope of trucking operations. Many commodities which it was thought would not lend themselves to transportation by truck are being moved in increasing quantities. In addition, commodities that formerly were carried only relatively short distances by truck are being moved greater distances. The advantages of motor transportation are unparalleled by any other mode of transportation, and the increased reliance placed upon it by shippers is largely a reflection of its ability to meet any transportation requirement.

QUESTIONS AND PROBLEMS

1. What are some examples of changes in the distribution pattern occasioned by motor transportation? Has this benefited the public? How?
2. Explain why the national-defense aspect of motor transportation is assuming increasing importance.
3. What is the status of the motor transportation industry as an employer? Why are there such wide variations in the estimates of the total number of persons employed in motor transportation?
4. Point out the significance to shippers, highway administrators, and the public of the fact that the total of trucks and busses at the present time is greater than the total of all vehicles in 1920.
5. During World War II a group of experts in highway matters estimated the total number of vehicles that would be on the highways in 1965; yet that number was reached in the early 1950's. What factors accounted for this?
6. Carefully explain the difference between the tonnage carried by motor carriers and the total ton-miles transported by them.
7. What are the inherent advantages of motor-truck transportation? Is there any evidence of a broadening of the scope of trucking operations in regard to commodities carried?
8. As a shipper of general commodities, what advantages possessed by motor transportation would largely influence you in your choice of transportation service? Comment.

9. What evidence is there to indicate that merchants can carry a smaller inventory because of the fact that they are able to replenish their stocks quickly through utilization of motor carriers? Can wholesalers likewise carry reduced inventories because of the speed of delivery by motor carriers? Discuss some of the aspects of inventory policy which may be attributed to utilization of motor carriers.

2. HIGHWAYS

▲▲

AN ELABORATE system of improved highways has been developed in the United States over a period of years, with the majority of the improvements coming during the period since 1920. Many of the early roads were turnpikes of graded, graveled, or broken-stone surfacing which had been built by private companies expecting to profit through the imposition of tolls assessed for traveling upon the road. Prior to the advent of railroads, there was considerable activity, both governmental and private, dealing with the construction of this type of road. In 1830 there were about 27,000 miles of surfaced roads in the United States, most of which were turnpikes in the vicinity of the larger communities.[1]

It is interesting that the development of the bicycle led to an articulate demand in some areas for smooth roads for cyclists. The real impetus for highway improvement, however, did not occur until well after the invention of the first automobile. As ownership of automobiles became more widespread during the early part of the twentieth century, increased attention was given to highway improvement.

Very limited funds were available for highway construction or improvement, and the control of highways was vested largely in cities, towns, villages, and other political subdivisions of the government. An awareness of the need for highway improvement manifested itself in a number of different ways, one of the most significant of which was the establishment in some states of state highway departments. During the years 1900–1920, different state highway departments were first created to administer state grants-in-aid to local units for road improvement, although it appears that they exercised little power as to the nature of the road construction or the location of the roads. The next step in the evolving pattern of state highway depart-

---

[1] Public Roads Administration, *Highway Practices in the United States of America* (Washington, D.C.: U.S. Government Printing Office, 1949), p. 3.

ments was their being given the responsibility for road construction with state funds, supplemented in some cases by local funds. Upon the completion of these roads, they were turned over to local government subdivisions for maintenance. It soon developed that local maintenance was not entirely satisfactory, which resulted in many instances in state highway departments assuming the responsibility for maintenance, as well as construction, involving state funds. The granting of state aid to counties was inaugurated by New Jersey in 1891, and by 1900 six other states had enacted similar legislation. The main routes were those to which the state aid was applied. This practice was adopted by an increasing number of states, so that by 1917 all states were participating to some degree in highway aid. The choice of routes which the state would aid was often made by drawing lines on a map which would connect the larger centers of population.[2] In retrospect, it would appear that, with the limited funds available at that time to implement such a bold program, these planners were truly visionary.

EARLY ROADS

By modern standards, the type of road which was existent in 1900 was very inferior. Prior to 1900, the primary types of surfacing used were gravel and macadam. In 1900, of the 150,000 miles of surfaced rural roads, 72 per cent were gravel, 24 per cent were water-bound macadam, with 4 per cent of miscellaneous materials.[3] The increasing use of highways by automobiles caused the dust binder present in the gravel and macadam roads to be sucked out and blown away, with resulting rapid deterioration of the highways. Engineers devised tar and asphalt binders and, in general, began experiments with different types of road surfacing. The standards in highway surfacing were not high, and it was a common practice to surface a road without much alteration of base grade, curves, or width. The practice of following township or county lines, including the square corners, prevailed in certain sections of the country during the early stages of highway development.

EARLY FEDERAL AID

The interest of the federal government in the development of improved highways in the United States was of very early origin. In

---

[2] *Ibid.,* p. 5.

[3] *Ibid.*

1806, aid by the federal government in the construction of the National Pike from Cumberland, Maryland, to Wheeling, West Virginia, later extended into Illinois (now Route U.S. 40), was indication of such interest. In 1893 the Secretary of Agriculture established the Office of Road Inquiry, which became the Bureau of Public Roads in the Department of Agriculture in 1918. It was transferred to the Federal Works Agency and renamed the Public Roads Administration in 1939. Again, it was transferred in 1949 to the General Services Administration for a few months; and, in August, 1949, the Public Roads Administration was renamed the Bureau of Public Roads and became a part of the Department of Commerce. At the outset, this agency had no funds for actual construction of roads but was to investigate methods of road construction and distribute the information. Shortly after the turn of the century, short strips of highway were constructed with local funds under the guidance of federal engineers in order to demonstrate desirable surfaced roads throughout the United States. From these demonstrations, valuable information was made available concerning the various types of road construction. More tangible evidence of the federal government's interest in road construction developed in 1912 when it authorized $500,000 to pay one third of the cost of improving highways over which United States mail was carried. However, only seventeen states raised the funds necessary to secure the federal assistance. In these seventeen states, 425 miles of road were constructed with an expenditure of $1.8 million.[4]

FEDERAL-AID ROAD ACT

The federal-aid policy for highway construction became firmly established with the passage in 1916 of the Federal-Aid Road Act. This act authorized and appropriated $75 million over a period of 5 years for the improvement of any rural road used in mail delivery and specifically prohibited improvements in towns of more than 2,500 population. Federal participation was not to exceed 50 per cent of the total cost of the roads constructed, provided the total cost did not exceed $10,000 per mile. The states had to match the federal contribution with funds under their control. The $10,000 limit per mile was later increased and then still later removed. This act provided a formula for apportioning the federal funds among the states on the basis of three criteria, each to have equal weight: (a) the area

[4] *Ibid.*, p. 8.

of the state in relation to the total area of the United States; (b) the population of the state in relation to the total population of the United States; and (c) the post-road mileage of the state in relation to the total post-road mileage of the United States. A significant provision of the act was that this federal aid was to be available only to those states with state highway departments which could co-operate with the federal government. Inasmuch as there were only thirty-three states at the time the act was passed with highway departments which met the minimum requirements, those states lacking highway departments took steps toward the immediate formation of departments that would meet federal requirements. Under this act, the obligation of maintenance of highways was placed on the states or their political subdivisions.

Prior to the passage of the Federal-Aid Road Act the principal executive officers of most of the existing state highway departments had joined in the formation of the American Association of State Highway Officials. This organization, which represented the views and desires of state governments on highway matters, was influential in shaping provisions of the act. This influence has been continuously and effectively exerted in all subsequent modifications of the federal highway program.

FEDERAL HIGHWAY ACT OF 1921

The Federal Highway Act of 1921 required the state highway departments to designate a system of interstate and intercounty highways which would be eligible to receive federal aid, the aid being limited to 7 per cent of the total mileage of rural roads in each state. In this manner a federal-aid highway system came into being. Federal funds and matching state funds had to be spent on that system. The act also provided that the state was responsible for maintenance of highways constructed with the aid of federal funds. If a state failed to maintain these highways in proper fashion, the work could be carried out under direct federal supervision, the cost to be paid out of federal funds which otherwise would be available to the state for construction purposes. The War Department at that time was requested to indicate such roads as it considered to be of primary strategic importance and desirable of inclusion in the system. The War Department responded by supplying a map, approved by General John J. Pershing, and all of the highways so indicated were included in the federal-aid system as it was designated.

The original formula governing apportionment of the federal

authorizations remained unchanged in its application to the primary federal-aid system, except by the modification that no state shall receive less than one half of 1 per cent of the total authorized. However, the original requirement of at least equal matching with state funds of the federal contribution to the cost of roads built was modified by the Federal Highway Act, in respect to roads built in any state containing unappropriated public lands exceeding 5 per cent of the total area of all lands in the state, to permit payment of a federal share of the cost up to 50 per cent plus a percentage equal to one half of the percentage of unappropriated public lands in the state. Thus, states having large areas of tax-free federal forests, parks, and lands are compensated by an increase in the ratio of the federal contribution ranging from 54 to 83 cents on the dollar. Thirteen western states currently are in this classification. Some states other than these thirteen contain federal forests, parks, and lands, but the proportion is not large enough to increase the federal contribution.

The Federal Highway Act of 1921 appropriated $75 million for the fiscal year of 1922; but in 1923 the Congress provided for the authorization of federal funds, with specific appropriations to be made as needed. From 1921 through 1932, the federal funds authorized averaged about $100 million per year. When a state had completed and was maintaining 90 per cent of its original federal-aid system of highways, the original limitation of 7 per cent could be increased in accordance with a provision that was passed in 1932. Basically, the federal-aid primary system of a state does not exceed 7 per cent of the entire rural mileage of the state as of 1921. However, when certain conditions are met, a state may increase the designated federal-aid mileage. Two thirds of the states have done this.

During the depression period of the 1930's, the federal-aid policy was liberalized because of the emergency, so that states did not have to match federal funds which were appropriated to provided employment. Furthermore, federal funds could be used for purposes of improvement of the federal-aid highway system through municipalities, as well as for construction of secondary (or farm-to-market) roads. In 1935 an appropriation was made for the elimination of hazards at railroad grade crossings. All of these provisions were later incorporated into federal-aid authorizations.

FEDERAL-AID HIGHWAY ACT OF 1944

The Federal-Aid Highway Act of 1944 authorized $500 million per year for the first 3 postwar years. This act continued the principles involved in the Act of 1921 but also introduced the factor of making funds available for use in the federal-aid system in cities and urban communities of over 5,000 population. In addition, it authorized the spending of federal funds for right-of-way and property damage costs and encouraged participation of local road officials in the choosing of roads to be included in the secondary and feeder-road system. A further provision of this act was the establishment of an interstate system of the more important highways in the United States, which was not to exceed 40,000 miles in length. This has resulted in the establishment of the systems of federal-aid highways in 1954 as shown in Table 2–1.

TABLE 2–1

FEDERAL-AID HIGHWAY SYSTEMS, 1954
(In Miles)

Federal-aid primary highway system:
Rural.. 216,793
Urban.. 17,882

    Total primary....................................... 234,675

Interstate system (part of the federal-aid primary highway system):
Rural.. 33,780
Urban.. 4,020

    Total.. 37,800

Federal-aid secondary highway system...................... 460,002

    Total.. 694,677

Source: Bureau of Public Roads.

The appropriations under the 1944 act were granted as follows: 45 per cent to primary roads in the federal-aid system, which included urban extensions of these primary roads; 30 per cent for expenditures on selected roads in the federal-aid secondary system; and 25 per cent for federal-aid highways in urban areas which had populations of more than 5,000. The criteria used in the apportionment of federal-aid funds among the states continue as established in the act of 1921 for primary roads (area, population, and mileage). For secondary roads the federal-aid funds are allocated to the states in accordance with a formula that gives equal weight to area, rural population, and mileage. It will be noted that the basic difference in this formula from that of the primary roads is the substitution of rural population for total population. The third division of federal-aid allocation to the states for urban areas is based on the ratio which the population in municipalities and other urban communities of 5,000 or more in each state bears to the total population in municipalities and other urban places, of five thousand or more, in all the states as shown by the last federal census. Under the provisions of this act, the federal aid cannot in general exceed 50 per cent of the total construction costs. However, in the case of right-of-way, the federal share cannot exceed one third of the cost involved, though the federal contribution is increased in states that have public lands. Also made a part of this act was the provision for federal funds to be used for the total cost necessary to eliminate hazards at railroad crossings, with the exception that land and property damage costs would be covered by only 50 per cent payment from federal funds and in no event could more than 10 per cent of the federal funds allocated to a state be used for railway-highway purposes.

RECENT FEDERAL-AID LEGISLATION

In 1948 and 1950, federal-aid legislation was enacted which continued, without any basic change, the principles of the act of 1944. For the first time in federal-aid legislation specific funds were authorized in the Federal-Aid Highway Act of 1952 for the improvement of the national system of interstate highways. Heretofore, improvements were made with funds provided for the federal-aid primary highway system, of which it is a part, and for urban highway improvements. In order to accelerate the rate of improvement of the interstate highway system, the 1952 act authorized $25 million for exclusive use on the system for each of the fiscal years 1954 and 1955.

Funds for the national system of interstate highways for the fiscal years 1954 and 1955 were apportioned in the same manner as those for the federal-aid highway system. Funds for the fiscal years 1956 and 1957 are apportioned "one-half in the ratio which the population of each state bears to the total population of all the states, as shown by the latest available federal census: Provided, that no state shall receive less than three-fourths of 1 per centum of the money so apportioned; and one-half in the manner now provided by law for apportionment of funds for the federal-aid primary system." Federal participation for the interstate system was increased to 60 per cent of the cost, except in public-lands states where the 60 per cent may be increased by four tenths of the percentage of the area of the state that is public land.

The Federal-Aid Highway Act of 1954 authorized a 2-year total of $1,932,000,000, which is the largest federal highway program on record. The new legislation also contains broad authority for a research program relating to highway design, construction, financing, and use. In particular, the Secretary of Commerce is directed to make studies of desirable size and weight standards for vehicles using the highways and the feasibility of uniformity in state regulations with respect to such standards and report the conclusions to Congress.

Another provision of this act simplifies the administration of federal aid for secondary roads. At the present time federal funds are used for four federal-aid systems—primary, secondary, urban, and national system of interstate highways.

THE BUREAU OF PUBLIC ROADS

The Bureau of Public Roads in the Department of Commerce is the representative of the federal government in highway administration and has jurisdiction over federal-aid grants to the states. It is headed by a Commissioner of Public Roads, and its staff consists of four divisions and a number of field organizations, as shown in Figure 2–1. Indicative of the liaison work the Bureau undertakes in assisting the states in programming their work is the large percentage of employees of the Bureau who are in the field—approximately 75 per cent.

In addition to federal-aid grants, the Bureau administers annual appropriations for the construction and maintenance of the major highways through national forests and performs a large amount of highway engineering and construction for other federal agencies. In some cases co-operative action with other federal agencies under jointly approved regulations is required by law in the planning of highway systems and programs, with the Bureau in direct charge of all engineering and construction work. At other times the Bureau acts only as an agent in performing such engineering and construction supervision as may be requested for specific projects; or its functions may be limited to review and approval of the location, type, and design of the road, and to general supervision over the construction work. Another important function of the Bureau is its continuous program of research in all phases of highway construction, engineering, financing, legal aspects, and similar activities.

The Bureau of Public Roads establishes technical standards for the various federal-aid road systems (the interstate system, the federal-aid primary system, the federal-aid secondary system, and the federal-aid urban system) and insures that these standards are met. These minimum design standards which guide in the construction

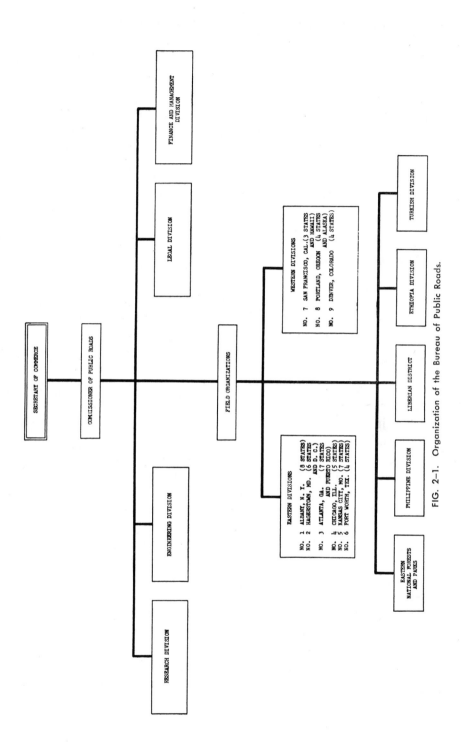

FIG. 2-1. Organization of the Bureau of Public Roads.

of highways are subject to a number of variable factors, such as the daily volume of traffic, whether the terrain is flat or rolling (which affects design speed), the presence of curves, and many other factors. These standards for the same type of highway vary in different sections of the country as well as in the same general area, dependent upon the variable factors listed above. They might be described as flexible standards. The states develop programs of highway construction and improvement which are submitted to the Bureau of Public Roads for its approval within the limitations set forth by the federal-aid statute.

EXTENT OF FEDERAL AID

The participation of the federal government in the early encouragement of road construction and the tangible evidence of such encouragement in the appropriation of federal funds have made an important contribution in the development of our highway systems. In 1921, federal funds expended on highways amounted to $81 million, which represented about 8 per cent of the total revenues for highways for that year. In 1929, federal aid amounted to $93 million, or only 4.3 per cent of the total highway revenues in that year, inasmuch as it was during this period that there were increased state and county activities in road improvements. During the next 10 years, federal funds expended in relation to total revenues for highways increased very greatly, due in part to the abnormal conditions created by the depression. From a high in 1936 of 41.2 per cent, federal aid declined to 23.1 per cent in the prewar year of 1941 and continued downward during the war to 4.2 per cent in 1945. After the war it increased to a high of 11.5 per cent in 1949 and dropped to 9.4 per cent in 1952. It is estimated to be about 9 per cent in 1953 and 1954.

The advisability of broadening federal participation in highway aid, particularly as applied to secondary roads and urban areas, and the recommendation from the Bureau of Public Roads that federal participation in the construction of any highway be increased to more than the present 50 per cent, have been considered. It is felt by some that certain of these activities should be matters for state and local authorities rather than the concern of the federal government.[5]

---

[5] Charles L. Dearing and Wilfred Owen, *National Transportation Policy* (Washington, D.C.: Brookings Institution, 1949), p. 117.

The American Association of State Highway Officials recommended in 1953 that federal contributions be made 75 per cent of the expenditures on the primary system of interstate highways. However, this change can be made only by the Congress. The possibility of increasing the ratio of federal aid to the states might be better accomplished by establishing an aid program on an incentive basis. For example, starting with the present fifty-fifty matching arrangement, it might be provided that for every additional dollar a state would spend beyond its past matching program, the federal government would provide perhaps $1.25. This might serve as an incentive to the states to secure additional revenue to construct needed highways at a faster rate than is presently the case. Such an incentive could be placed on a sliding scale so that a limit would exist as to the amount any one state could secure. An arrangement such as this would have to be provided in new legislation.

DEFINITIONS OF HIGHWAY CONSTRUCTION TYPES

As used in connection with federal-aid construction of highways, the following definitions of highway construction types are given.[6] These are listed with alphabetical designations since the various types of highway construction are referred to in that manner.

NONSURFACED EARTH ROADS:

A. *Primitive Road.* An unimproved route (on which there is no public maintenance), usable by four-wheel vehicles and public, traveled by small numbers of vehicles.

B. *Unimproved Road.* A road using the natural surface and maintained to permit bare passability for motor vehicles, but not conforming to the requirements for a graded and drained earth road. The road may have been bladed, and minor improvements may have been made locally.

C. *Graded and Drained Earth Road.* A road of natural earth aligned and graded to permit reasonably convenient use by motor vehicles and drained by longitudinal and transverse drainage systems (natural or artificial) sufficiently to prevent serious impairment of the road by normal surface water, with or without dust palliative treatment or a continuous course of special borrow material to protect the new roadbed temporarily and to facilitate immediate traffic service.

---

[6] General Administrative Memorandum No. 308, dated August 21, 1946, of the Public Roads Administration (now Bureau of Public Roads).

LOW-TYPE SURFACE:

D. *Soil-Surfaced Road.* A road of natural soil, the surface of which has been improved to provide more adequate traffic service by the addition of (1) a course of mixed soil such as sand-clay, soft shale, or topsoil; or (2) an admixture such as bituminous material, portland cement, calcium chloride, sodium chloride, or fine granular material (sand or similar material).

E. *Gravel or Stone Road.* A road the surface of which consists of gravel, broken stone, slag, chert, caliche, iron ore, shale, chat, disintegrated rock or granite, or other similar fragmental material (coarser than sand) with or without sand-clay, bituminous, chemical, or portland cement stabilizing admixture or light penetrations of oil or chemical to serve as a dust palliative.

F. *Bituminous Surface-Treated Road.* An earth road, a soil-surfaced road, or a gravel or stone road to which has been added by any process a bituminous surface course, with or without a seal coat, the total compacted thickness of which is less than one inch. Seal coats include those known as chip seals, drag seals, plant-mix seals, and rock asphalt seals.

G. *Mixed Bituminous Road.* A road the surface course of which is one inch or more in compacted thickness composed of gravel, stone, sand, or similar material, mixed with bituminous material under partial control as to grading and proportions.

HIGH-TYPE SURFACE:

H. *Bituminous Penetration Road.* A road the surface course of which is one inch or more in compacted thickness composed of gravel, stone, sand, or similar material bound with bituminous material introduced by downward or upward penetration.

I. *Bituminous Concrete, Sheet Asphalt, or Rock Asphalt Road.* A road on which has been constructed a surface course one inch or more in compacted thickness consisting of bituminous concrete or sheet asphalt, prepared in accordance with precise specifications controlling gradation, proportions, and consistency of composition, or of rock asphalt. The surface course may consist of combinations of two or more layers such as a bottom and a top course, or a binder and a wearing course.

J. *Portland Cement Concrete Road.* A road consisting of portland cement concrete with or without a bituminous wearing surface less than one inch in compacted thickness.

K. *Brick Road.* A road consisting of paving brick with or without a bituminous wearing surface less than one inch in compacted thickness.

L. *Block Road.* A road consisting of stone block, wood block, asphalt block, or other form of block, except paving brick, with or without a bituminous wearing surface less than one inch in compacted thickness.

M. *Combination-Type Road.* A road the wearing course of which consists of two or more individual types, each being of such depth as to be classed logically as a part of the traffic-bearing road surface rather than as surfaced shoulders.

FUNCTIONAL TYPES OF HIGHWAY

The Bureau of Public Roads uses the following classification in describing the functional road types:[7]

A. *Arterial Highway.* A general term denoting a highway primarily for through traffic, usually on a continuous route.
B. *Expressway.* A divided arterial highway for through traffic with full or partial control of access and generally with grade separations at intersections.
C. *Freeway.* An expressway with full control of access.
D. *Parkway.* An arterial highway for noncommercial traffic, with full or partial control of access, and usually located within a park or a ribbon or parklike development.
E. *Major Street or Major Highway.* An arterial highway with intersections at grade and direct access to abutting property, and on which geometric design and traffic control measures are used to expedite the safe movement of through traffic.
F. *Through Street or Through Highway.* Every highway or portion thereof at the entrance to which vehicular traffic from intersecting highways is required by law to stop before entering or crossing the same and where stop signs are erected.
G. *Local Street or Local Road.* A street or road primarily for access to residence, business, or other abutting property.

HIGHWAY MARKING

It was common practice some years ago to mark the more heavily traveled routes by painting certain colors on telephone poles at intervals along the highways to aid the traveler. Private organizations interested in improving traveling conditions and road systems often undertook the job of road marking. Today, the main highways are marked by route markers with the initials "U.S." and a route number. This is done through joint action of the state highway departments in order to implement map making and simplify highway travel. Highways running east and west bear even numbers and those running north and south have odd numbers. Most of these routes are a part of the interstate highway system or of the state sys-

---

[7] O. K. Normann and W. P. Walker, "Highway Capacity: Practical Applications of Research," *Public Roads,* Vol. XXV, No. 10 (October, 1949), p. 206.

tems. However, the designation of a highway as "U.S." is without legal or administrative significance.

STATE AND LOCAL HIGHWAY MANAGEMENT

Public highways in the United States are, in general, under the control of the states; and, because of this fact, different methods of management are employed. Because of the varying sizes of the states and the number of miles of highways within the states, the administrative organization necessary to manage properly the respective state highway systems differs likewise. In 15 states, the state highway organization is headed by a single individual, whereas in 5 states these departments have advisory boards or commissions as well as the executive. In 4 states, the state highway executive and the commission have equal authority. In 24 states, the state highway department is controlled by commissions. However, in 10 of these states, the commissions have full administrative control; whereas, in the remaining 14 states, the commissions are policy makers with the actual administration of the state highway departments handled by an executive.[8] In the majority of the states, the state delegates some responsibility for county and local roads to those political subdivisions. However, in 4 states—Delaware, North Carolina, West Virginia, and Virginia (except for 3 counties)—the state has assumed responsibility for local rural roads. In some of the other states, certain of the counties have given the state highway department the responsibility for local roads.

The units below the state level which administer local roads include more than 2,500 counties, about 15,000 rural towns or townships, about 900 special districts and toll authorities, and about 16,-000 incorporated and other urban places. The highway function is administered by approximately 34,000 governmental units, each of which has some degree of responsibility for the administration and support of highways.

An additional 500 counties, rural towns and townships, and special districts are responsible for paying principal and interest on debt incurred for highway purposes, but they have no other highway responsibilities.

State and county highway departments operate under state laws more obsolete than are our highway systems. Because legislators in the past have not given attention to modernization of basic highway

---

[8] Public Roads Administration, *Highway Practices in the United States of America*, p. 23.

laws at the same time they altered the technical and financial provisions, there is a conglomeration of overlapping, uncorrelated statutes that greatly impede highway development. In many instances these laws are of the horse-and-buggy vintage. For example, the control of access and the regulation of land use adjacent to highways as provided now by most states are wholly inadequate. A divided four-lane highway built by a state in 1940 was obsolete by 1952 and was to be replaced by a completely new route by 1955. The original highway was not a controlled-access highway, with the result that commercial establishments and houses were built along the highway. The highway department under the existing statute was powerless to act to prevent this. Instead of a modern highway, the continuous encroachments resulted in a hazardous highway with very limited capacity. States have often constructed community by-passes only to find that failure to control access results in another by-pass being constructed to by-pass the by-pass.

Procedures for the acquisition of right-of-way and the designation of highway systems by administrative bodies, as provided by existing laws, fall far short of what is needed. Highway administrators are compelled to act within the scope of legal authority as set forth in the statutes governing their administration.

Recognition that inadequate highway legislation in numerous states leaves state and local authorities powerless to cope with the problems of highway modernization has resulted in the inception of a study by the Highway Research Board in co-operation with the Bureau of Public Roads, Automotive Safety Foundation, and American Association of State Highway Officials of all state highway legislation with a view to developing the elements essential to model highway laws.

In the postwar period, a large number of states have made studies sponsored by the legislatures, some of which have included the administrative relationships of states and their political subdivisions on highway matters. The recommendations require administrative or legislative action or both.[9]

Many relationships between a state and its counties and cities, and between local units as well, are involved in the planning, improvement, and maintenance of the roads and streets throughout a state. Due to state and federal aid for highways, various intergovernmental

---

[9] See Highway Research Board Special Report 6, *Highway Relationships in Maryland* (Washington, D.C., 1952).

relationships have gradually been established, and in recent years they have expanded. Such relationships range from joint participation in projects to the mere exercise of supervisory control. In many states, however, such development has been sporadic, expanding fragmentarily as specific problems and situations were encountered.

In view of the piecemeal growth of co-operative relationships, it is frequently found in the various states that existing legislative authority is inadequate, that responsibility and authority are not clearly defined and assigned, that policies and procedures are not uniformly executed, and that existing administrative machinery needs revamping. Michigan, for example, as the result of a study completed 3 years earlier, enacted in 1951 a full-scale revision of its laws concerning administration, classification, and finance and fund distribution.

The basic law in Michigan provides for proper reclassification of all roads and streets in the state; for uniform accounting; for advance planning and programming of projects by all highway agencies; for establishment of a single highway fund into which all state motor-vehicle revenues are deposited; and for a new and simple distribution formula for sharing of highway revenues among state and local systems based on needs. At the same time, the principle of local support for roads and streets is emphasized by provisions of the law limiting state participation in such projects to about 50 per cent.

The various requirements of co-operation among the several highway agencies in the state furthers intergovernmental relationships and encourages greater uniformity of standards and good engineering practices among counties and cities.

Another problem of the states and their political subdivisions is with regard to their highway employees. In one state, the statutory limit for the annual salary of the state highway engineer is $7,200. This limit controls the maximum that may be paid to other employees. Of the 48 states, only 19 have merit or civil service systems which are reasonably adequate; 5 states have systems not adequate in their protection and privileges extended to highway employees; and the remaining 24 states have no system at all.[10] The result is that experienced engineers of state, county, and city highway departments are attracted by the higher salaries paid in private employ-

---

[10] Robley Winfrey, Bureau of Public Roads, "To Modernize Our Highways, First Modernize Our Attitudes." Presentation before Annual Highway Conference, University of Tennessee, April 16–17, 1953.

ment. In some instances engineers resigned from public employment to work for consultants at higher salaries on highway plans contracted for by highway departments. Through contracts with consultants, the highway departments paid former employees higher salaries plus a surcharge for overhead.

A problem in many states has been the lack of a yardstick for scheduled improvements. The result has often been that with limited funds available the funds were not spent where there was the greatest relative need. As an engineering tool to show relative conditions of existing highways and as an aid in scheduling highway improvements, a technique known as the "sufficiency rating" has been developed and applied. The sufficiency rating aims to provide a mile-by-mile index of structural condition, of ability to handle traffic, and of driving safety. In using it, engineers establish arbitrary values to define the degree of variation from standard in the several elements of existing roads and streets. For example, structure sufficiency may be judged to be 100 points, service sufficiency 50 points, and safety 50 points.

VARIATIONS IN HIGHWAY USE

Transportation service rendered is not distributed uniformly on highways. It varies widely, both as to volume and character of traffic movement. The streets within municipalities represent less than one tenth of the total highway mileage, yet carry nearly one half of all traffic. Some streets carry as many as 100,000 vehicles daily, as do some rural highways; whereas on others, both urban and rural, the daily traffic is less than 50 vehicles.

A relatively small percentage of the highways in the nation carry the greatest amount of the traffic. As an example, the national system of interstate highways (Fig. 2-2), which was created by the Federal-Aid Act of 1944 and was to comprise 40,000 miles of highways connecting all of the largest cities in the United States, constitutes only 1 per cent of the total mileage of roads and streets in the United States. In the rural areas which it serves, however, it carries 25 per cent of the traffic carried by all rural roads. In the urban areas which this system of highways serves, it carries more than 10 per cent of the traffic moved over all city streets. If a state highway system is examined, it is found that the same situation prevails, that is, that a small portion of a state's highway system carries a relatively large

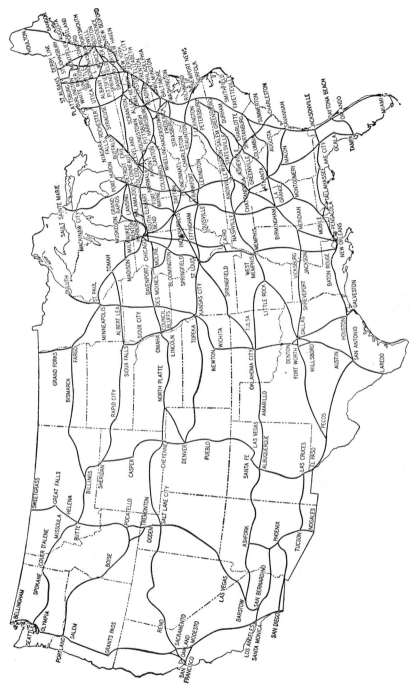

FIG. 2–2. The national system of interstate highways (currently 31,831 miles of rural road and 5,969 miles of urban routes with 2,200 miles reserved for additions to the system.)

Source: Bureau of Public Roads.

amount of traffic. For example, the primary and secondary highway systems constitute some 13 per cent of the rural mileage but carry over 70 per cent of the vehicles.

Figure 2–3 shows the urban and rural mileage and the use which is made of it based on mileage. Particularly to be noted is the fact that rural federal-aid roads make up about 18 per cent of all highway

19% OF ROADS CARRY
81% OF TRAFFIC

		ROAD MILEAGE	TRAVEL MILEAGE
URBAN	ARTERIAL STREETS	1 %	39 %
URBAN	OTHER STREETS	8 %	10 %
RURAL	FEDERAL-AID ROADS	18 %	42 %
RURAL	OTHER ROADS	73 %	9 %

FIG. 2–3. Highway mileage in relation to its use based on mileage.

Source: Automobile Manufacturers Association presentation before House Public Works Committee, 1953.

mileage but carry 42 per cent of all traffic. Urban arterial streets make up about 1 per cent of all road mileage but carry 39 per cent of all traffic.

Relative volumes of traffic on a highway are important indications of the type of facility required and are helpful in indicating priorities of improvements. However, the social or economic importance of a highway to the people it serves cannot be measured solely by traffic volume.

Highways are constructed for the dual purpose of both private and commercial use, and design of major routes must be held to certain standards in the interest of national defense, a factor of vital significance. In addition, state highway engineers have stated frequently that they would construct highways to meet certain standards whether or not there were commercial vehicles operating on those highways, inasmuch as certain minimum standards must be met to take care of the weathering of a highway. Of course, weight and volume of traffic are other factors which are considered. A commercial vehicle does occupy more road space, however, than a passenger car. One commercial vehicle is said to have about the same effect as 2 passenger cars in level terrain and 4 passenger cars in rolling terrain; and in mountainous areas this effect can be as great in relation to highway capacity as 8 passenger cars.[11]

A two-lane highway in level terrain and carrying traffic 30 per cent of which is trucks, for example, will have the same congestion with about 69 per cent of the number of vehicles which the same highway will carry if all vehicles are passenger cars.

DIVERSION OF HIGHWAY-USER REVENUE

It should not be assumed that the total revenues which are secured from highway-user taxes are expended entirely for highway purposes. Highway-user revenue has been used in some states for such nonhighway purposes as mosquito control, state parks, welfare funds, probation and parole commissions, and the like. At the present time, twenty-five states prohibit completely or in part the diversion of automotive tax receipts to nonhighway purposes. In recent years, increasing pressures have been placed upon state legislatures to end diversion of highway-user tax receipts to the general revenue fund. In those states which had no antidiversion laws in 1953, 13 cents out of every highway-user dollar was diverted. Some states divert as much as 50 per cent, whereas others divert as little as one tenth of 1 per cent.

The proponents of antidiversion laws feel that if a gasoline tax is imposed for the express purpose of using the funds to improve highways, it is logical that the receipts from gasoline tax imposts should be required to be expended only for highway purposes. Some of the first state gasoline taxes enacted contained this provision, but other states, in enacting the gasoline tax legislation, did not so provide,

---

[11] House Committee on Public Works, *Highway Needs of the National Defense*, 81st Cong., 1st sess. (Washington, D.C.: U.S. Government Printing Office, 1949), p. 100.

although many people assume that the funds are spent only for highway purposes. The opponents of the antidiversion law feel that such a law places a legislature in a strait jacket since it handicaps the state in applying the revenue of the state to the needs of the state.

HIGHWAY CONSTRUCTION COSTS

Figure 2–4 shows the total cost of federal-aid highway construction, which reflects accurately what has been occurring in the entire

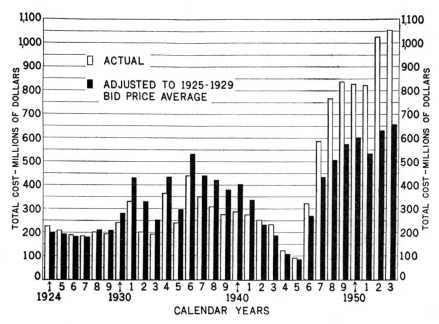

FIG. 2–4. Federal-aid highway construction costs.
Source: Bureau of Public Roads.

highway construction program. The heights of the light bars represent the actual costs in dollars of changing purchasing power. The heights of the adjacent solid bars represent the dollars that would have been required to do the same amount of work at the average prices prevailing during the period 1925–29. Thus the solid bars afford a true comparison of the actual physical volumes of construction involved in the federal-aid program.

From 1928 through 1941, bid prices were lower than the average for the base period. Therefore, the adjusted values (solid bars) are higher than the actual dollar values (light bars). Price increases since 1942 have reversed the relative heights of the bars. Since that year the adjusted values (solid bars) have been the smaller. The solid bars thus reflect the postwar shrinkage in purchasing power of the dollar.

Although 1953's actual expenditure of more than a billion dollars more than doubled the 1936 expenditure of less than $450 million, it produced a construction volume which in adjusted value exceeded the 1936 volume by only about 20 per cent. Between these 2 years, the registration of vehicles increased by about 100 per cent.

The loss of time to the highway improvement program caused by the war and its aftermath has not been generally understood by the public. The construction of federal-aid highway projects was stopped by Executive Order late in 1941 and was in effect until October, 1945, when it was officially lifted. This stop order did not apply to state or local road construction, but other conditions imposed the slowing down of all operations and the abandonment of a major part of the authorized program. The loss of engineering personnel from the highway departments, the disposal of contractors' organizations, the steel shortage, and other similar causes so severely restricted the program of construction that it was not until 1949 or 1950 that the program reached the level of the annual funds provided. Thus, nearly *10 years* of construction and rehabilitation were lost when the major highways had suffered severe deterioration from war traffic and when new traffic was increasing at a rate greater than at any previous time. This is the major reason why there has been an emergency highway condition existing since the war. The modernization of highways was disappointingly slow after the war due largely to the insufficiency of financing. The highway authorities of the states and federal government had planning agencies and engineering know-how but not adequate funds.

A sufficiency analysis of rural portions of the national system of interstate highways, which is the segment of our highway system of greatest significance for service of the nation's transportation needs both in peace and war, shows these highways in 1954 to be variously deficient from state to state (Fig. 2–5). Only 24 per cent of the rural mileage of the system is rated as completely sufficient in its present condition for the service of the traffic it carries. Seventy-six per cent of the mileage is found in need of reconstruction and improvement to correct existing inadequacies, and on 16 per cent of the total mileage the need of reconstruction is critical. A similar situation exists with regard to many other segments.

The national system of interstate highways now carries 25 per cent

PER CENT OF RURAL PORTIONS OF INTERSTATE SYSTEM

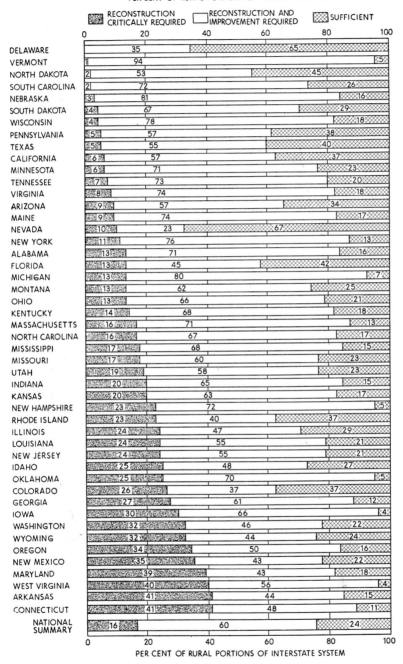

FIG. 2–5. Sufficiency analysis of rural portions of the national system of interstate highways. Arranged by states in ascending order of per cent of critical reconstruction needs.

Source: Bureau of Public Roads.

of the total traffic of the United States but is less than 1 per cent of the total mileage. In order to bring it up to standard and eliminate deficiencies, it would cost approximately $20 billion. One half of all these deficiencies are located in only eight states, and the majority of these areas of deficiency are in the approaches to the cities where approximately one half of all registered motor vehicles are also located, for which reasons any plan which might be developed must recognize the importance of the urban and urban-approach problem.

BENEFITS OF IMPROVED HIGHWAYS

There are numerous studies which show that highway improvements can result in savings not only in time but also in the more tangible form of actual operating costs. A study issued in 1938 by the Bureau of Public Roads gives the average cost of operating a car that traveled 8,000 miles a year as 6.22 cents per mile on earth surface, 5.62 cents per mile on gravel, and 4.63 cents per mile on pavement. The Bureau has stated that it is reasonable to assume that, with the higher costs of today's automobiles and the increasing cost of automotive repairs and fuel, savings effected by improvement in road surfacing would be substantially greater than indicated in earlier reports, operating costs running about 2 cents per mile higher on earth surfaces than on gravel and 2 cents per mile higher on gravel than on paved surfaces. A recent study concludes that gasoline consumption and travel time for trucks vary definitely with the rise and fall of the highway regardless of the length of the section or the number and steepness of individual grades in the section.[12]

Modern expressways and freeways, by eliminating safety hazards, reducing gasoline consumption, and facilitating traffic movement, actually afford substantial reductions in operating costs. Comparative studies of accident experience of various types of roads were published by the Bureau of Public Roads in 1952. The preliminary figures show rates ranging from 0 to 5.7 fatalities per 100 million vehicle-miles for fully controlled-access roads, from 0 to 25.6 for roads with partial access control, and rates as high as 27.1 for roads without any access control.

The Bureau of Public Roads also made a survey of the Shirley Highway in Virginia—a 17-mile, controlled-access, divided roadway bypass—in 1951. The survey showed that commercial operators

---

[12] Highway Research Board, *Time and Gasoline Consumption in Motor Truck Operation* (Washington, D.C., February, 1950), p. 16.

alone are estimated to be saving 311,000 truck and driver hours annually, because forced use of an alternate route would result in much congestion and delay. Coupled with this time factor are the related economies in gasoline, truck and tire mileage, and gross and payload ton-miles.

The amount saved per year would be very close to $2,000,000. Furthermore, if the additional savings to passenger-vehicle operators were also considered, the total economies realized would be tremendous. In addition to the cost advantages, the Shirley Highway has a very low accident rate.

In examining the expressways placed in operation, two facts stand out: the volume of traffic using each expressway is far in excess of the volume estimated during the planning stage, so that the economic benefits of the improvements are far greater than were anticipated; and the effect on value of land adjacent to the expressways was extremely favorable without adverse effects elsewhere. Surveys thus far made indicate that the relief of congestion on old routes from which through traffic was diverted to expressways or other high-type arterials has resulted generally in improved business for those establishments along the old routes that rely chiefly for their business on local trade.

QUESTIONS AND PROBLEMS

1. Trace the early federal highway activity in the period prior to the passage of the Federal-Aid Road Act of 1916. What prompted this federal interest?

2. Compare the formulas used for apportioning federal funds among the states under the Federal-Aid Road Act of 1916 and the Federal-Aid Highway Act of 1944 and 1952.

3. What are the four systems of federal-aid highways?

4. What is the justification for granting a portion of federal-aid funds for federal-aid highways in urban areas?

5. The advisability of broadening federal participation in highway aid, particularly as applied to secondary roads, has been questioned as being a matter for state and local authorities. What is your opinion? Why?

6. List the different highway construction types. How would you distinguish between a low-type and a high-type surface?

7. What accounts for the different methods of highway management employed in the various states? What are the advantages and disadvantages of about 34,000 governmental units each with some degree of responsibility for highway administration?

8. "A relatively small percentage of the highways in the nation carry the greatest amount of the traffic." What are the implications of this statement as far as commercial motor transportation is concerned?

9. "Highways are constructed for the dual purpose of both private and commercial use." What are the advantages of this to the public?

10. "The control of access and the regulation of land use adjacent to highways as provided now by most states are wholly inadequate." Cite some examples of the economic effects which are the result of these factors.

11. List the advantages and disadvantages of antidiversion laws.

12. What has been the trend in highway construction costs? What benefits are derived from our improved highways?

3. HIGHWAY FINANCING

▲▲▲

A BASIC problem of highways in the postwar period has been their financing. Engineers can build highways to any required specifications, but inadequate finances have seriously limited adequate construction for modern highways. The expenditures which are necessary to eliminate the deficiencies in our highway system are tremendous. To raise the required funds and to assign the costs fairly among the different levels of government and the various users of the facilities are tasks which are receiving a great deal of attention. It is a curious fact that of the total expended on highways and vehicles by the public (including items such as cost, insurance, and maintenance), about 90 per cent is spent on vehicles and only about 10 per cent for the provision of highways. Perhaps the willingness of the individual to share in the expenses of providing an adequate highway system has been underestimated.

There have been several methods used in financing highways which are described in this chapter. A part of the problem of highway financing involves the allocation of cost to different classes of vehicles on an equitable basis, which factor is also discussed.

HIGHWAY FINANCES, TAXES, AND REVENUES

During the development of highways in the period prior to 1920, property taxes constituted an important source of revenue for state highway purposes. Although today such taxes are not so important as a source of highway income for the states, they are still a fundamental source of tax revenue for counties and municipalities for use in highway improvement and maintenance. New York led the way in the establishment of a registration fee in 1901 and was followed in this practice by other states. By 1915 all states had registration requirements of some kind, and this was the first of the highway-user charges to be imposed. During the first World War, the practice of registration fees which varied with the weight and capacity of the vehicle was introduced and soon became widely adopted. A number of bases have been employed in the application of a registration fee, particularly for private motor vehicles, such as weight, price, horsepower, flat rate, number of times registered, and combinations of these. In the case of registration fees for trucks, 28 states base them on gross-vehicle weight, 3 states base them on manufacturer's rated capacity, 3 states use owner's declared capacity, 4 states use chassis weight, 1 state uses gross weight per load-carrying axle, and 9 states and the District of Columbia use net or unladen weight figures.

Registration taxes, fees, operators' licenses, and title fees were the primary sources of income received by the states from motor-vehicle owners until 1929. The inauguration in Oregon of a tax of 1 cent per gallon on the sale of motor fuel, the revenue derived therefrom to be used for maintenance of state highways, soon led to the adoption of this second highway-user charge in other states. Since 1929 the gasoline tax has produced the greatest amount of revenue and has been the primary source of highway revenues. Variations among states as to the amount of tax imposed on gasoline ranged in 1954 from 3 cents per gallon to 7 cents per gallon. In 1940 the weighted average gasoline tax in the United States was 3.96 cents per gallon. During the 10 years from 1940 to 1950, the retail price of gasoline, excluding taxes, increased 62 per cent. In this same period the weighted average of gasoline taxes rose by only 12.7 per cent.[1] The weighted average of state and federal gasoline taxes in 1953 was 5.15 cents, a very modest increase in view of the changes in price levels during the same period. In addition to the state gasoline tax, there is also a federal excise tax of 2 cents per gallon on gasoline.

The demand for gasoline is relatively inelastic. This would mean that increases in its price result in a relatively small change in the demand for it. Petroleum companies realize this, and it must not be assumed that state highway departments are unaware of this fact but rather that their recommendations to legislatures to secure more revenue through an increase in this tax are met by formidable opposition, particularly from the petroleum industry at legislative hearings. For example, one state, after considerable study, issued its proposed long-range highway improvement program complete with financing, which included a 1-cent increase in the gasoline tax from

---

[1] E. M. Cope and L. L. Liston, "The Gasoline Tax in Relation to Automobile Operation and Highway Costs," *Public Roads*, Vol. XXVI, No. 8 (June, 1951), p. 157.

4 to 5 cents. At the public hearing, the petroleum industry in this state indicated that the highway improvement program was sound and needed. However, it opposed the increase in gasoline tax to help finance it. It is suggested that the traditional opposition of the petroleum industry to the principle of increasing the gasoline tax might be re-examined in view of the critical need for financing highways and the fact that the petroleum industry is a substantial beneficiary of improved highways. The gasoline tax is often referred to as a "pay-as-you-go" method of highway financing; actually it is a "pay-before-you-go" system, since the tax is paid before the user uses the highways.

The registration fee does not measure highway use to the degree that is true of the gasoline tax. On the other hand, some states have felt that the gasoline tax does not provide a complete measure of highway use, for it is alleged that as the size of the vehicle increases it does not use proportionately more gasoline. Therefore, the states have turned to special taxes on the for-hire carriers of persons and property, which are called "special highway-user taxes." These have not proved to be an important source of highway revenue but have been employed as regulatory devices and have taken the forms of mileage tax, gross receipts tax, ton-miles tax, excise tax, and highway-use compensation tax.

Total highway-user taxes are of such proportions that it is not unusual for a for-hire motor carrier which operates a truck regularly to pay in a single year taxes which approach or exceed the market value of the vehicle.

The federal excise taxes are considered to be general excises and have no legal connection with federal aid for highways. However, there are advocates of what is termed the "linkage" theory in which revenue so received would be earmarked only for highway use, as some states do. A large revenue is secured from tax rates, which on April 1, 1955, were as follows:

Gasoline	2 cents per gallon
Diesel fuel (used in highway-type vehicles)	2 cents per gallon
Lubricating oils	6 cents per gallon
Automobiles and motorcycles	10 per cent on wholesale price
Busses, trucks, trailers, automotive parts, and accessories	8 per cent on wholesale list price
Tires	5 cents per pound
Inner tubes	9 cents per pound

These federal excise taxes paid by highway users total over $2 billion per year. No similar tax is levied against equipment used by any other form of transportation.

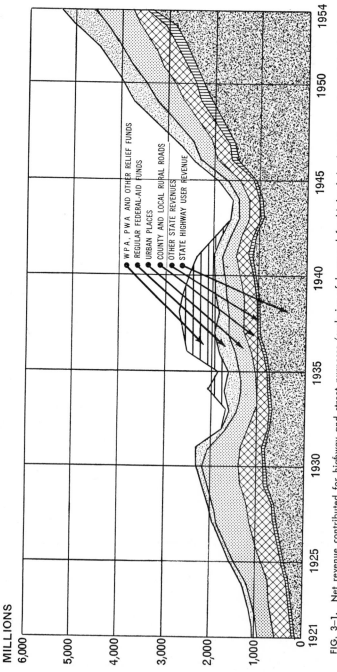

MILLIONS

FIG. 3–1. Net revenue contributed for highway and street purposes (exclusive of borrowed funds) by federal, state, county, and local governments, 1954, estimated.

Source: National Highway Users Conference based on Bureau of Public Roads data.

W.P.A., P.W.A. AND OTHER RELIEF FUNDS
REGULAR FEDERAL-AID FUNDS
URBAN PLACES
COUNTY AND LOCAL RURAL ROADS
OTHER STATE REVENUES
STATE HIGHWAY USER REVENUE

TABLE 3–1

ESTIMATED EXPENDITURES FOR HIGHWAY AND STREET PURPOSES, 1953–54[1]

EXPENDED ON—	1953		1954	
	Million Dollars	Per Cent	Million Dollars	Per Cent
State highways:[2]				
Capital outlay..................	2,276	39.5	2,740	42.8
Maintenance....................	628	10.9	660	10.3
Administration[3].................	130	2.2	135	2.1
Highway police.................	105	1.8	107	1.7
Interest.......................	100	1.7	138	2.2
Total direct expenditures........	3,239	56.1	3,780	59.1
Obligations retired[4]..............	125	2.2	150	2.3
Total disbursements............	3,364	58.3	3,930	61.4
County and other local rural roads:				
Capital outlay...................	463	8.0	488	7.6
Maintenance....................	634	11.0	639	10.0
Administration[3].................	55	1.0	56	0.9
Interest.......................	27	0.5	28	0.4
Total direct expenditures........	1,179	20.5	1,211	18.9
Obligations retired[4]..............	83	1.4	85	1.4
Total disbursements............	1,262	21.9	1,296	20.3
Urban streets:				
Capital outlay...................	422	7.3	434	6.8
Maintenance....................	425	7.3	431	6.7
Administration[3].................	61	1.1	63	1.0
Interest.......................	49	0.8	51	0.8
Total direct expenditures........	957	16.5	979	15.3
Obligations retired[4]..............	125	2.2	130	2.0
Total disbursements............	1,082	18.7	1,109	17.3
Federal expenditures not classified by system:[5]....................	61	1.1	67	1.0
All roads and streets:				
Capital outlay...................	3,222	55.9	3,729	58.2
Maintenance....................	1,687	29.2	1,730	27.0
Administration..................	246	4.3	254	4.0
Highway police.................	105	1.8	107	1.7
Interest.......................	176	3.0	217	3.4
Total direct expenditures........	5,436	94.2	6,037	94.3
Obligations retired...............	333	5.8	365	5.7
Grand total...................	5,769	100.0	6,402	100.0

[1] Federal and state data are for calendar year; local data are for varying fiscal years, 1953 preliminary estimate, 1954 forecast.
[2] Includes expenditures by states on transcity connections of state highways.
[3] Includes engineering and equipment costs not charged to capital outlay and maintenance, and other miscellaneous expenditures.
[4] Redemptions by refunding not included.
[5] Includes funds of other agencies expended directly by Public Roads as well as funds expended by those agencies. Expenditures were principally for capital outlay and are included as such in the totals.
Source: Bureau of Public Roads, Table HF–2, Preliminary, June, 1954.

The growth of revenue for highway and street purposes during the period from 1921 through 1954, shown in Figure 3–1, indicates the trend toward reliance upon highway users for highway funds. Excluding borrowed funds, less than 12 per cent of the total in 1921 came from the highway user, while at the present time about 58 per cent is realized from this source. The decline in the relative importance of general taxes has been from 72 per cent of highway revenues in 1921 to about 24 per cent of the total in 1954. It should be pointed out that the amounts received from state highway-user taxes shown in Figure 3–1 do not include money diverted to nonhighway purposes nor money used for the collection and administration of state highway-user taxes.

In 1954 about 69 per cent of all revenues applicable to highways came from the state governments, 22 per cent from counties and cities, and 9 per cent from the federal government.

Table 3–1 shows the estimated expenditures for highway and street purposes in dollars and percentages as between the different highways and streets. Of the 1954 total, 58 per cent was expended on construction, 27 per cent on maintenance, and the remainder for administration, policing, and debt service.

In 1952 there was a capital outlay expenditure per vehicle-mile of travel of $0.0024 as compared with $0.0010 in 1945.[2]

USER TAXES PAID BY VEHICLES OF DIFFERENT TYPES

Based on nation-wide totals and averages, an estimate has been made of the amounts of state highway-user taxes paid by vehicles of different types and general size groups.[3] Figure 3–2 indicates that automobiles constituted 83.0 per cent of motor-vehicle registration in 1952 and accounted for 64.8 per cent of the user taxes. Busses were approximately 0.3 per cent of the numbers registered and paid 1.9 per cent of the user-tax revenues. Trucks and combinations accounted for 16.8 per cent of the vehicles and 33.3 per cent of the revenues.

A different grouping of vehicles brings out the relations of numbers and payments more clearly. If the values for panels and pickups and other four-tire trucks are added to those for automobiles, this constitutes what may be called the "light-vehicle group." With this

---

[2] Bureau of Public Roads, *Highway Finance, 1945–1952,* (Washington, D.C., January, 1954), p. 3.

[3] Edwin M. Cope, John T. Lynch, and Clarence A. Steele, "Estimate of User Taxes Paid by Vehicles in Different Type and Weight Groups," *Public Roads,* Vol. XXVIII, No. 2 (June, 1954), p. 17.

grouping, it is found that automobiles and light trucks formed 93.4 per cent of the registered vehicles in 1952 and paid 73.6 per cent of the road-user taxes. Medium and heavy trucks and combinations accounted for 6.3 per cent of the vehicles and 24.5 per cent of the user-tax payments. By putting light trucks with passenger cars, the total of the truck contribution is diminished, but the weighting of payments in relation to numbers is increased from less than 2 to 1 to nearly 4 to 1.

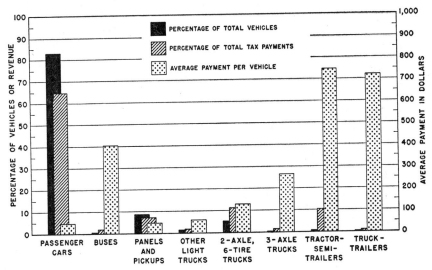

FIG. 3–2. Comparison of registrations and tax payments by vehicle types.
Source: *Public Roads*, Vol. XXVIII, No. 2 (June, 1954), p. 19.

The figures for individual types reveal that two-axle, six-tire trucks amounted to 5.0 per cent of the vehicles, and their tax payments were 11.2 per cent of the total. Three-axle trucks, constituting 0.3 per cent of the vehicles, paid 1.5 per cent of the revenues. Tractor-semitrailers, which added only 0.84 per cent to the vehicle total, paid 10.8 per cent of the total. Truck-trailer combinations constituted 0.08 per cent of the vehicles and made 1.1 per cent of the tax payments. Thus, combinations as a group amounted to less than 1 per cent of the vehicles but accounted for nearly 12 per cent of the revenues.

Comparisons on a vehicle-mile basis are shown in Figure 3–3. It was found that automobiles, which constituted 83.0 per cent of the registrations in 1952, accounted for 80.9 per cent of the traffic volume. If automobiles and light trucks are combined, it is found that this group contributed 89.1 per cent of the vehicle-miles and 73.6 per cent of the revenues. Medium and heavy trucks and combinations accounted for 10.2 per cent of the traffic volume and 24.5 per cent of the revenues. Combinations constituted 0.92 per cent of the vehicles, traveled 3.4 per cent of the vehicle-miles, and provided 11.8 per cent of the revenues.

The average payment of road-user tax per mile of travel by automobiles is 0.49 cent per vehicle-mile, or almost exactly ½ cent. Busses paid 1.64 cents per mile of travel, and trucks and combinations, as a group, paid 1.10 cents. The average for all vehicles was 0.61 cent

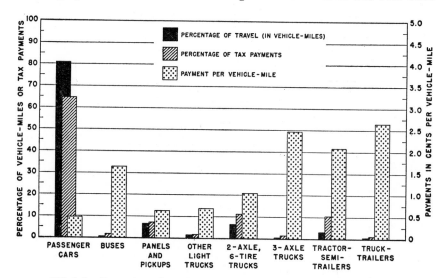

FIG. 3–3. Comparison of travel, tax payments, and payments per vehicle-mile.
Source: *Public Roads*, Vol. XXVIII, No. 2 (June, 1954), p. 19.

per mile of travel. Medium and heavy trucks and combinations, taken as a group, contributed 1.46 cents per vehicle-mile.

Among the general group of trucks and combinations, it is found that two-axle, four-tire trucks paid between 0.6 and 0.7 cent per mile of travel. Two-axle, six-tire trucks paid 1.05 cents per vehicle-mile, and three-axle trucks paid 2.49 cents, the average for single-unit trucks being 0.87 cent. The rate per vehicle-mile for combinations as a group was 2.13 cents; tractor-semitrailers paying 2.09 cents and truck-trailer combinations 2.71.

BOND ISSUES AS MEANS OF FINANCING

Extensive use of borrowing for highway construction purposes has been practiced by counties, municipalities, and states. There has been considerable variation from state to state as to the amount of borrowing for highway purposes.

Some state highway departments have felt that the construction and improvement of highways had to be advanced by means of borrowed funds, inasmuch as construction of highways from operating revenues alone would have been very slow. In some instances, states have had sufficient funds from operating revenues to surface only one lane of a main route, and several years have elapsed before the surfacing of the other lane could be accomplished. Vestiges of this practice are still existent. With borrowed funds, however, the double lane could have been constructed; and it is less expensive to do the complete surfacing of a road at one time.

The most widely used type of bond used by the states for securing funds for highway purposes has been the general-obligation type, which is backed by the credit of the respective states. It is customary to cover the payment of the debt so incurred by the revenue secured from highway-user taxes. The limited-obligation type of bond has been issued by some states; this type does not pledge the general credit of the state but is limited rather to the funds derived from highway-user revenues. A third type is the revenue bond, which is used to finance the construction of a specific facility. The revenue to retire such bonds is dependent entirely, except for insurance, upon that facility. Toll bridges are usually financed in this manner.

In some states the counties were encouraged to issue bonds and turn the proceeds over to the state with the understanding that the state would provide funds for the payment of principal or principal and interest on the bonds. The state used the credit of the local governments to borrow for state highways. This resulted in reimbursement obligations. Although this is not evidenced by state bonds, it forms a fourth type of obligation for highways.[4] The postwar issues have been largely of the first three types, as indicated in Figure 3–4, which shows the types of state highway debt according to security pledged.

There are two general types of provision for the retirement of bonds: the term-issue or sinking-fund method and the serial method. Under the term-issue plan the entire amount borrowed falls due at a certain date fixed when the debt is assumed. A sinking or amortization fund is provided to which annual payments of a fixed amount are made. The plan is so devised that the sum of these payments, plus whatever income is obtained from investing them, will be sufficient when the debt falls due to pay the entire amount.

In recent years the serial method of retirement has become more

---

[4] Hugo C. Duzan and Others, "Recent Trends in Highway Bond Financing," *Public Roads*, Vol. XXVII, No. 4 (October, 1952), p. 73.

popular. Under this plan a predetermined amount of the principal is scheduled to be paid each year, beginning at a certain time after the bonds are sold—usually not less than one year nor more than three. This plan of retirement does not require a sinking fund. The

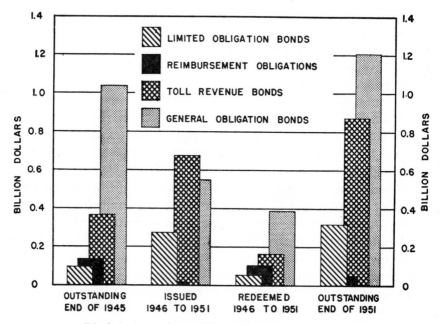

FIG. 3–4. Types of state highway debt.
Source: *Public Roads,* Vol. XXVII, No. 4 (October, 1952), p. 73.

annual principal payments are usually made directly from current income, upon which they customarily have a prior claim.

At the present time, thirty-nine states may incur debt for general or highway purposes, although all but twelve of that number are subject to constitutional limitation of the amount borrowed. Six states authorize borrowing and have no constitutional debt limit. Nine states may borrow only for reasons such as "casual indebtedness" or "failure in revenue." Of this group, eight states have established toll-road authorities or other commissions empowered to issue bonds as a means of circumventing barriers. Constitutional limitations on indebtedness in those states which may borrow take several forms, such as limiting it to a specified percentage of the assessed value of property (for example, 1 percent) of the state.[5]

---

[5] National Highway Users Conference, *State Constitutional Limitations on Borrowing* (Washington, D.C., July 23, 1954).

Borrowing for state highways since 1921 has been characterized by two periods of relatively large-scale activity. The first was during the large road-building program of the 1920's. The depression and war periods saw a lessening of borrowing, although during the early 1930's further state assumption of local debt and revenue bonds used to finance the construction of large toll facilities raised the total outstanding debt for state highways in 1938 to what remained an all-time high until 1951. The bond issue proceeds for highways was 3.2 per cent of the total funds available in 1945 and progressively increased to 12.6 per cent in 1948. This figure was 18.1 per cent in 1952.

TOLL ROADS

The term "toll road" is usually understood to mean any road for which a service charge is collected each time it is used in addition to any general taxes or fees which may be paid by all highway users. In the early part of the nineteenth century, there were developed a number of improved roads on which tolls were charged. Some of these roads were privately owned and operated, whereas others were owned and operated by a state or its political subdivisions. The federal government participated, in a limited manner, in the construction of some turnpikes. The advent and early growth of the railroads were largely responsible for the decline and lack of further development of this type of highway facility.

During the present century in which tremendous strides have been made in automotive transportation, highway development has been characterized by the construction of so-called "free" roads. Although the Pennsylvania Turnpike, on which tolls are imposed, was opened in 1940, it was not until the period after World War II that there has been considerable activity regarding the construction of toll roads. There are about thirty states that are currently interested in roads of this type. In some of these states, toll roads are already in operation. In other states, they are at various stages of planning and development, from states in which exploratory studies are being considered or engineering studies are being conducted to states in which toll roads are under construction.

There are several reasons for the growing interest in toll-road construction. One of these is that the supply of highways is limited in relation to the traffic demand. At the end of 1945, there were approximately 30,000,000 vehicles registered. Between 1946 and the end of 1953 there was an increase in vehicle registrations of 80 per cent and in 1955 there was a total of over 58 million vehicles registered. Highway capabilities have not kept pace with the demands imposed upon them by this substantial increase in vehicles.

Another factor which has accounted for toll-road activity has been the virtual moratorium on highway construction which was necessitated by World War II. Inadequate maintenance during this period due to shortages of labor and materials also accelerated obsolescence of highways. The higher costs of construction which followed the end of hostilities and the backlog of improvements which were necessary combined to make a total which was staggering to many states. The purchasing power of the dollar had shrunk, and many states were unable to finance necessary highway construction. There was the belief in many areas that the cost of construction would drop during an anticipated deflationary period, so badly needed highway construction was often postponed. Although a deflationary period occurred during 1948, there was no appreciable reflection of this in highway construction costs. The combination of postponed highway improvements and higher construction costs have accentuated the interest in toll roads.

With inadequate funds for a pay-as-you-go highway program, states might normally turn to bond issues. In some states, however, there is a constitutional limitation on the amount of bonded indebtedness of the states, which also is a contributing factor to increased toll-road activity. In a state in which the amount of bonds already issued is close to the constitutional limit, the state has to consider some other means of financing needed highways. The establishment of a Turnpike Authority by a state creates a means by which bonds may be issued without regard to constitutional limitations, the security for which is the revenue derived from tolls.

Many states, also, have a limitation on the funds which are available for improving the main arteries due to state statutory requirements which specify that certain percentages of registration fees and gasoline taxes must be returned to political subdivisions of the state, that is, counties, townships, and local governments. In some instances, the amount returned to the local government is as much as 50 per cent. It should not be inferred that the local highway needs do not require this but rather that the state is left with an insufficient amount to bring about all of the required improvements in the heavily traveled highways.

In some of the heavily populated states which are relatively small geographically and are often referred to as "bridge" or "corridor" states, the toll road has had considerable appeal as a means of construction of a modern and adequate facility and getting the out-of-state user to help pay for it. In the case of the New Jersey Turnpike, the out-of-state vehicles range from 60 to 75 per cent of the total traffic, which was an important factor in the construction of this turnpike.[6] In the case of the New Hampshire Turnpike, which is but 14 miles in length, 90 per cent of the traffic is out-of-state vehicles because it is a route that connects southern New England and the Maine Turnpike.[7]

The cost of limited-access highways is appreciable. In many states, the legislators have questioned the feasibility of these undertakings when such facilities could be provided by means of a toll road. In those states also in which the rural interest in the legislature is particularly strong, the disadvantages of limited-access highways to rural residents, with the points of ingress and egress widely spaced, have led to suggestions that such limited-access projects be made toll roads.

The federal government has since 1916 discouraged the building of toll roads and has encouraged the construction of free roads. The manner in which the toll roads have been discouraged is that no money appropriated under the federal-aid highway programs can be spent on toll-road projects. In the Federal-Aid Highway Act of 1916, there is a specific statement that: "All highways constructed or reconstructed under the provisions of this act shall be free from tolls of all kinds." This provision has been carried forward in subsequent acts. The Bureau of Public Roads made a study in 1938 at the request of Congress concerning the feasibility of constructing six superhighways, three east and west, and three north and south. The conclusion of this report, issued in 1939, was that only a small mileage of roads could secure sufficient traffic to be self-supporting if they were improved and operated as *toll* highways.[8]

After World War II, the Bureau of Public Roads reaffirmed its previous statement that (*a*) collection of tolls is expensive and this is passed on to the user as an added burden; (*b*) the points of ingress

---

[6] Statement of Chairman, New Jersey Turnpike Authority before the National Conference on Highway Financing, U.S. Chamber of Commerce, December 11, 1953.

[7] Harmer E. Davis and Others, *Toll-Road Developments and Their Significance in the Provision of Expressways*, Institute of Transportation and Traffic Engineering, University of California, Research Report No. 11 (Berkeley, 1953), p. 16.

[8] House Committee on Roads, *Toll Roads and Free Roads*, 76th Cong., 1st sess. (Washington, D.C.: U.S. Government Printing Office, 1939).

and egress of a toll road are spaced some distance apart which would prevent the use of the toll road for many short journeys that constitute a large portion of highway travel; and (c) the difficulties attendant upon collection make it impractical to operate as toll roads main routes which enter cities. The Commissioner of the Bureau of Public Roads in 1947 indicated that the design standards of a free road must be held substantially lower than those of the toll road if the toll road is to attract the traffic needed for its support.[9] Some modification of this policy is discussed later in the chapter.

In hearings before a House Subcommittee on Public Works in 1953, one of the topics considered regarding highway legislation was a proposal for the extension of turnpikes and toll roads as well as transcontinental superhighways.[10] The feasibility of toll financing and the necessity for superhighway designs were felt by the Commissioner of the Bureau of Public Roads to be matters in which the existence or potential of a substantial volume of traffic as well as other factors have a determining influence. The highways which carry an average of 5,000, 10,000, 15,000, and 20,000 vehicles per day were selected as the exact density of traffic which was necessary to justify such facilities. Most of the roads having over 5,000 vehicles per day are part of the national system of interstate highways.

One of the questions that frequently arises is one concerning the average traffic load necessary to justify a toll road. The answer to this question is that it varies with the cost of construction, which would depend upon topography and other factors as well as the rate of toll collectable.[11] In the case of the Denver-Boulder Turnpike, which in 1953 was carrying less than 5,000 vehicles a day, the tolls had apparently failed to support its entire cost because its funds were being supplemented by expenditure from the state highway department funds.[12] Although roads that carry 5,000 or more vehicles per day may be feasible for toll-road operation it should not be inferred that this is the minimum number necessary to justify a toll road. On the other hand, one of the clues to successful toll-road operation is traffic volume.

---

[9] Letter to Editor of *Sunday News* (Manchester, New Hampshire), dated April 22, 1947. See also "The Case against Toll Roads" presented by Deputy Commissioner of Public Roads at a meeting of the Highway Division of the American Society of Civil Engineers, January 23, 1948.

[10] House Subcommittee on Public Works, *National Highway Study*, Part I, 83d Cong., 1st sess. (Washington, D.C.: U.S. Government Printing Office, 1953).

[11] *Ibid.*, p. 14.

[12] *Ibid.*, p. 14.

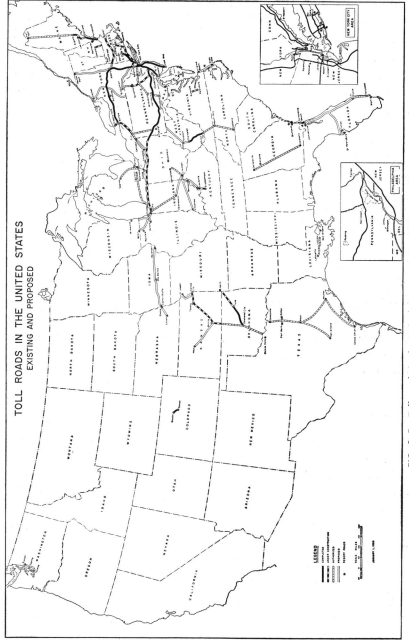

FIG. 3–5.   Toll roads in the United States, existing and proposed.
Source: Bureau of Public Roads.

On March 1, 1955 there were 1,464 miles of toll roads completed, 1,394 miles under construction, 3,273 miles authorized but not financed, and 2,645 miles proposed. Existing and proposed toll roads are shown in Figure 3–5. This is a total of approximately 8,776 miles out of the total of about 3,366,000 miles of highways. On a mileage basis, the future of toll roads would appear to be limited, although they may afford more relief in total dollars than in total percentage of highways. In relation to the total highway needs, or even the limited 40,000-mile interstate system of highways, however, the construction of toll roads will not provide a solution to the total highway problem. In the construction of toll roads, the paralleling free roads still have to be maintained, so there is often the charge that the toll road constitutes a duplication of facilities. On the other hand, substantial improvement of a highway, whether toll or free, usually results in an increase in traffic both by diversion from inferior highways as well as newly generated traffic.[13]

Topography and traffic conditions in the states vary greatly, so that conditions that are considered to be feasible for toll-road operation in one state may not be in another. On the Pennsylvania Turnpike, approximately 60 per cent of the revenues are derived from trucks and busses. Tests made some years ago on U.S. 30 from Carlisle to Irwin, Pennsylvania, which parallels the turnpike, show that because of grade elimination on the turnpike, as compared to U.S. 30, trucks approximating the legal limit in Pennsylvania showed a savings of 16 gallons of gasoline each trip over the 149-mile stretch, with a savings of time of 2½ hours. On the other hand, the truck traffic on the New Jersey Turnpike shows a revenue of only about 14 per cent of the total. The diversion of passenger-car traffic to the New Jersey Turnpike has relieved congestion on the parallel free roads. Therefore, since there is not as great a fuel savings or savings in time as is the case on the Pennsylvania Turnpike, truck use has not come up to toll-road officials' estimates, despite the fact that for 1953 the traffic on the New Jersey Turnpike equaled that of the independent engineers' forecast for 1971, or 18 years later, which was made for the turnpike before its construction. The levels of revenues for this turnpike in 1953 were at the level forecast for 1968; at the end of 1954 it was carrying traffic originally estimated for 1981, and it is now considered necessary to widen the lanes from four to six. The annual revenues on the Turner Turnpike in Oklahoma are at a level suf-

---

[13] *Ibid.,* p. 14.

ficient to pay off the indebtedness in 25 years instead of in 40 as originally planned.

There are four types of toll projects existing or proposed based upon the method of providing the funds. The first is one in which the construction cost is provided from public funds. On completion the service charge is fixed for the use of each section, which is determined to be a fair charge for the service rendered. Another method is for construction funds to be provided by the sale of revenue bonds, with the interest and amortization of the bonds guaranteed by the state. The third method is for construction funds to be provided by the sale of revenue bonds, which are wholly dependent upon the earnings of the project for amortization and interest. These projects are administered by a commission created by the state, but the state does not guarantee the payment of either bonds or interest. This is often termed the "conventional method" of toll-road financing, since there is more of this method of toll financing than any other kind. The last method is for a state by legislative action to grant authority to private interests to build a toll-road project. Texas has such a law, and there are two private toll road companies which expect to build toll roads. Both companies operate on a nonprofit basis. The construction funds are provided by the sale of revenue bonds, and the revenue from tolls is expected to cover the amortization and the interest accruals of the bonds.

Toll roads are usually financed by the issuance of revenue bonds which pledge the tolls, and the rate of interest is usually higher than general obligation bonds which the state might issue to build free roads. Since revenue bond issues can carry "call" privileges for redemption or refinancing which can be exercised after issuance, it may develop that refinancing could be undertaken at rates which would compare favorably with general obligation bonds. In the case of the New York State Throughway and the Garden State Parkway in New Jersey, which, in 1954, were being constructed as toll facilities, the bonds were guaranteed as to principal and interest in each instance by the parent state. Both these projects are expected to be self-liquidating. The pledge of the general credit and taxing powers of these states, if needed, was thought to effect material savings in financing costs.

Since tolls must be collected, such a collection charge is often regarded as being an added cost of this type of facility. The collection costs vary on the toll-road turnpikes now in operation and range from a little over 3 per cent on the Pennsylvania Turnpike to about

15 per cent of the revenues on the Denver-Boulder Turnpike.[14] The operation of toll roads is the responsibility of an independent commission or authority created for this specific purpose. The only compensation the members of such authorities receive is their expenses. As a rule, the commissioner of the state highway department is an ex officio member.

The Pennsylvania Turnpike has often been cited as a successful example of toll-road financing. Successful as it is, there probably are better examples because the cost of building the first section of it was relatively cheap in view of the fact that a portion of the right-of-way and tunnels had been constructed for a railroad.[15] The initial cost of the first section which was built was $71,500,000, of which $29,250,000 was given by a Public Works Administration grant.

The majority of the present turnpikes must be characterized as successful. The current rate of tolls charged for a passenger automobile is from 1 cent to 1.5 cents per mile, which is equivalent to a tax of 15 to 22 cents per gallon. In other words, if an automobile averages 15 miles per gallon and the toll charge is 1 cent per mile, this means that the motorist is willing to pay in addition to the gasoline tax he has already paid the equivalent of an additional 15 cents per gallon to go 15 miles. The weighted average federal and state tax on gasoline is a little over 5 cents per gallon. The toll charges added to this are a form of double taxation, but this could be solved by having the state grant to the Turnpike Authority a fair amount for the gasoline tax earned by operating over the toll road.

Highway users are willing to pay for these toll facilities. This willingness to pay would indicate that perhaps we have underestimated highway users' willingness to pay higher gasoline taxes to provide adequate financing for general highway improvements. An automobile which averages 15 miles per gallon pays a weighted average gasoline tax of a little over 5 cents per gallon, or a tax of $\frac{1}{3}$ of a cent per mile for "free" roads.

One of the most pressing highway problems is the traffic congestion in cities. The most costly highway deficiencies as well as the greatest volume of traffic are in and around our urban centers, an example of which is a 25-mile planned expressway in one eastern state which is estimated to cost $7 million per mile. However, the normal operation of a toll road has thus far not lent itself to urban arterial highways, and toll-road activity has been primarily in the

---

14 Davis and Others, *op. cit.*, p. 29.

15 House Subcommittee on Public Works, *op. cit.*, p. 17.

rural areas. A toll road which skirts a city may relieve that city of the through traffic which has heretofore gone through the city. Although this relieves the city of some traffic congestion, more will be required to solve the urban highway problem.

One of the factors of considerable importance in toll-road operation is that they should be self-liquidating projects. The laws in some states creating the Turnpike Authority stipulate that on the retirement of the bonds, the toll road will be operated free of tolls. In other instances, the statute provides that after the retirement of the bonds for the toll road, the tolls may continue to be charged and the revenues which are derived can be used to finance other toll roads. When the revenue bonds are retired, toll roads should become free roads. If they are not conceived as self-liquidating projects and the general tax revenues or the credit of the states are pledged, the determination of where the toll facility should be built may be based upon political considerations rather than upon economic tests.

Opposition to toll roads has been modified by some organizations. The U.S. Chamber of Commerce feels that financing through the imposition of tolls should be authorized when it has been established that the project cannot be completed within a reasonable length of time by financing from current or prospective tax sources.[16]

The trucking industry's position on toll roads is that it is opposed to the principle of toll financing, but under exceptional circumstances, toll roads should be permitted. However, the toll projects should be surrounded by safeguards to protect the public interest, such as the toll road becoming a free road when the outstanding obligations are retired.[17]

The American Automobile Association favors free highways, but if a toll road appears warranted, it strongly recommends certain safeguards.[18] In 1954 the AAA adopted the policy that the national system of interstate highways should be toll free.

A toll-road study was directed by the Federal-Aid Highway Act of 1954. This study will include the progress and feasibility of toll roads with particular attention to the possible effects of such toll roads upon the federal-aid highway programs. The Secretary of Commerce's report to the Congress, prepared by the Bureau of Public Roads, entitled *Progress and Feasibility of Toll Roads and Their*

---

[16] Highway Policy Statement of the U.S. Chamber of Commerce, adopted April, 1953.

[17] The policy of the American Trucking Associations, Inc., is that of the policy of the National Highway Users Conference, July, 1953.

[18] House Subcommittee on Public Works, *op. cit.*, Part 2, p. 310.

Relation to the Federal-Aid Program, was made in May, 1955. It recommended the continuation of the present law forbidding the collection of tolls on highways constructed with federal-aid funds. However, the present law should be changed to permit inclusion of toll roads as part of the interstate system when they meet the standards for that system and when there are reasonably satisfactory alternate free roads on the federal-aid primary or secondary systems which permit traffic to bypass the toll road.

Some indication of a modification of the federal government's position on toll roads was revealed by the Under-Secretary for Transportation of the Department of Commerce, who earlier stated that a pilot study of the economic potential for toll-road development had been completed and had resulted in the revision of the long-standing federal policy in opposition to toll roads. He stated: "Now toll roads are supported as a sound solution for many of the costly deficiencies on our national system of interstate highways."[19]

The toll-road approach is helpful in relieving the highway problem, but even the most liberal use of this method of financing will not solve our highway problems.

FUTURE HIGHWAY FINANCING

In July, 1954, the President of the United States had presented at the Governors' Conference on his behalf a proposed $50 billion, 10-year highway construction program. The proposal is that the federal government and the states should co-operate closely on the undertaking. One of the points calls for "financing based upon self-liquidation of each project wherever that is possible through tolls or the assured increase in gas tax revenues, and on federal help where the national interest demands it."

On August 30, 1954, the President established the President's Advisory Committee on a National Highway Program consisting of five members of which Lucius D. Clay was chairman. The Clay Committee was a fact-finding group charged with implementing the highway program.[20] In September, 1954, the Clay Committee issued a memorandum entitled "The Highway Problem of the United States,"

---

[19] Address before the National Association of Motor Bus Operators, Chicago, Illinois, September 15, 1954. Under Department of Commerce Order No. 128, issued February 13, 1953, the Under Secretary of Commerce for Transportation exercises general policy guidance over the Bureau of Public Roads, among other activities.

[20] A special Committee of Governors was formed and an Interagency Committee of interested governmental agencies was also established in connection with the President's $50 billion highway program.

which among other things, stated that a preliminary estimate of the total construction needs for all streets and highways through 1964 totaled $101,365,000,000. The estimates were prepared by the state highway departments and submitted to the Bureau of Public Roads for tabulation. They were based upon completion of the highway systems to a standard which would be adequate for traffic demands in 1974 and a population of 200 million. At the present rate of growth the demands of 1974 are expected to be approximately 50 per cent higher than the current levels.

The President's Advisory Committee in seeking views on how enlarged highway construction activity can be financed summed up the problem as follows:

Mileage of all public streets and highways:
1941	3,309,000
1953	3,348,000

Annual vehicle-miles of travel:
1941	333,396,000,000
1954 (estimated)	557,000,000,000
1965 (estimated)	814,000,000,000

Motor-vehicle registrations:
1941	34,894,134
1954 (estimated)	58,129,000
1965 (estimated)	81,000,000

Preliminary estimate of the total construction needs for all streets and highways through 1964....................	$101,365,000,000
Portion of these needs expected to be met with funds estimated to be available through 1964........................	$ 46,800,000,000
Deficit for which recommendation on method for financing is desired..	$ 54,565,000,000

The conclusions and recommendations of the President's Advisory Committee are as follows:

1. A safe and efficient highway network is essential to America's military and civil defense, and to the economy. The existing system is inadequate for both current and future needs. It must be improved to meet urgent requirements of a growing population and an expanding economy.

2. Total construction needs of all highway systems during the next 10 years are estimated at $101 billion, including completion to modern standards of the 37,600 miles of the presently designated National System of Interstate Highways. The present program if continued unchanged would make available for highways during that period approximately $47 billion, leaving a gap of $54 billion.

3. The Committee concurs with the Governors' Conference in recommending to the President that the Federal share of this needed construction program be increased to about 30 percent of the total, with States, cities, counties, and other agencies remaining responsible for financing the remaining 70 percent.

4. The interstate network is preponderantly national in scope and function. Modernization of the presently designated system in 10 years, together with the most necessary urban connecting arterials, is estimated to cost $27 billion. It is recommended that State and local participation be $2 billion of this amount, which would continue the present responsibility of the States for this system.

5. Since roads are a capital asset, it is recommended that the Federal share of interstate construction be financed by bonds to be issued by a Federal Highway Corporation created for this purpose by the Congress. The cost of the interstate system improvement, together with the total authorized funds under the regular Federal-aid highway program to the States, would approximate the revenues which the Federal Government will derive from the motor vehicle fuel and lubricating oil taxes projected at the present rates.

6. The Federal Highway Corporation should have a Board of Directors to be composed of three citizens appointed by the President and confirmed by the Senate with the Secretaries of Treasury and Commerce as ex officio members. On matters involving highway locations, the Secretary of Defense would also serve as an ex officio member. The Commissioner of the Bureau of Public Roads would serve as Executive Director. The Board of the Corporation should be responsible for the development of financial policy. It should serve when necessary as an Appeals Board to resolve major points of difference between the Federal and State authorities which may arise under the program.

7. Toll roads built to acceptable standards and meeting other requirements of the Corporation may be included as segments of the interstate system. However, toll financing is not a satisfactory solution to the full problem of network modernization.

8. Appropriate credit should be given to those States in which adequate sections of the interstate system have been constructed by State or toll financing provided the funds thus made available are used for further highway improvements. Moreover, States that elect to build further toll road sections of the interstate system should be reimbursed for all costs other than financing, provided such funds are used for further highway improvement. Obviously, these funds would become available only after all other Federal funds had been matched as required by law.

9. It is recommended that traditional Federal aid to the States be continued in the amounts authorized by the Congress in 1954 with some adjustments in the amounts for urban areas, and Federal domain roads, omitting the interstate system authorization since this system is provided for in sections 4 and 5 above.

10. In many States the modernization of highway enabling laws is necessary, especially in connection with the acquisition of land for right-of-way, the control of access, and the closer integration of State, city, and county highway managements. States should be encouraged to revise existing statutes where needed to permit expeditious and economical completion of the program. Congress should provide for the use of the Federal right of eminent domain to acquire right-of-way for the interstate

system where it is not feasible to obtain it through normal procedures under State law, and the State so requests.[21]

Basically, the President's Advisory Committee recommends a total construction expenditure by the federal government of $31.225 billion over the next 10 years. Of this total, $25 billion is for the interstate system, $3.15 billion for the remainder of the federal-aid primary system, $2.10 billion for the federal-aid secondary system, $0.75 billion for the federal-aid urban system, and $0.225 billion for forest highways. Financial participation by state and local governments would amount to $2.00 billion on the interstate system including essential urban arterial connections. For the other Federal-aid systems, statutory matching requirements would remain unchanged and would amount to slightly less than the Federal contributions of $6.225 billion. To meet the total estimated cost of $45.005 billion needed to bring these other federal-aid systems (and the forest highway system) up to adequacy in the 10-year period, however, would require a total expenditure by the State and local governments of $38.78 billion in addition to federal funds.

Hearings are being conducted on several bills which have been introduced in Congress regarding the highway program, as there are a number of the recommendations which have become controversial.

Figure 3–6 shows some of the trends in highway development. The construction values are represented to a dollar scale, and the curves of vehicle-miles, gross national product, and depreciated investment represent index values of these different quantities referred to, the value of each in the year 1940 represented as 100. The curve of depreciated highway investment, rising from early low values in the years when the highway system was still largely unimproved, approaches the other two curves during the thirties. This decade was the period when our highways were adequate to their task.

At the beginning of World War II the parallel trends of the three curves diverge abruptly. After the war, gross national product and vehicle-miles converge. However, the curve of depreciated invest-

---

[21] The President's Advisory Committee on a National Highway Program, *A Ten-Year National Highway Program* (Washington, D.C.: U.S. Government Printing Office, January, 1955), pp. v, vi. The Federal Aid Highway Act of 1954 required the Secretary of Commerce to make a comprehensive study of all phases of highway financing. The portion of the study of the President's Advisory Council which deals with financing was based upon data supplied by the Bureau of Public Roads as obtained from the state highway departments. Therefore, it is felt that this meets the requirements for a study of highway financing as required by the Federal Aid Highway Act of 1954. See Committee on Public Works, *Needs of the Highway Systems, 1955–84*, 84th Congress, 1st session (Washington, D.C.: U.S. Government Printing Office, 1955).

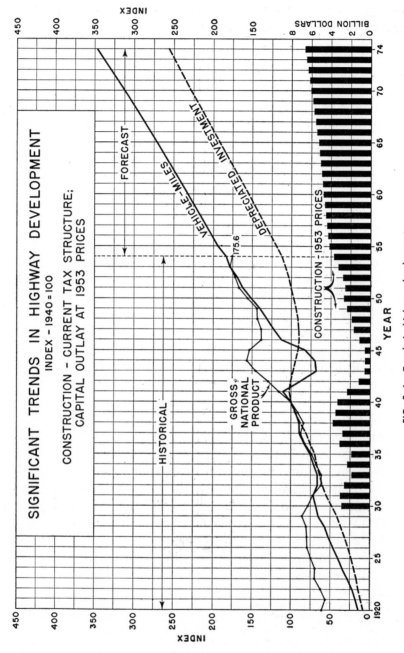

FIG. 3-6. Trends in highway development.
Source: Bureau of Public Roads.

ment, which reflected lessened construction effort, dropped below the other two curves. Based on the capital outlay in terms of 1953 prices, the depreciated investment curve continues much below the vehicle-miles' curve in the forecast period if the collection of highway revenues continues at the current rates of taxation and appropriation.

METHODS OF ALLOCATING HIGHWAY TAX RESPONSIBILITY

One of the most provocative questions in the entire transportation field is that of public aid or subsidy. It is a subject upon which there is much disagreement, and there is danger in any attempt to oversimplify the question. Charges and countercharges are hurled among the various modes of transportation, and accusations are made. The net gain to any party from such performances is doubtful. The curious part of this controversy is the apparent apathy on the part of the public. Although the public is affected by the granting of subsidies to various modes of transportation to a degree greater than it may realize, the effects apparently are so indirect as to cause little concern.

The argument over the question of public aid is basically one of equity of treatment by the federal government of the various modes of transportation. In recent years this problem has become more critical because of the increasing competitive relationships which have developed among the several forms of transportation. The most impartial observers in the field of transportation feel that the users of transportation facilities should pay their fair share of the cost and maintenance of those facilities, with the exception that national-defense requirements might justifiably modify this desired objective to some extent. This appears to be a fair approach to the issue.

With the foregoing approach in mind, let us examine some of the salient facts concerning the highway users' contribution to the construction and maintenance of the facilities they use. This will give us a basis for a better understanding as to whether highway users are receiving any public aid. As has been pointed out earlier, the highways, with but minor exceptions, are owned and maintained by the states and the various political subdivisions thereof. It is further recognized that, through various taxes and assessments, the users of the highway facilities make definite revenue contributions for construction and maintenance. Since there are different types of highways (such as primary and secondary highways, local roads, and city streets) and facilities, as well as different classes of users (such as private automobiles, commercial freight, and commercial passenger users), we must seek to ascertain whether the users of the highways as a whole, as well as the various classes of users in particular, pay their fair share for the use of these facilities.

TABLE 3–2

PERCENTAGES OF RESPONSIBILITY FOR ROAD AND STREET COSTS ASSIGNED TO MOTOR VEHICLES BY VARIOUS INVESTIGATORS

Source	Primary Highways	Secondary and Local Roads	City Streets
Board[1] (period 1940 and later)........	85.0	30.00	40.00
Federal Co-ordinator:[2]			
Period 1921–32.....................	80.0	15–31.50	12–28.50
Period 1933–37.....................	83.0	34.00	30.00
Ennis[3].............................	85.0	85.00	51.00
Duncan[4]............................	82.0	82.00	25.00
Werbitzky[5].........................	90.0	66.00	50.00
Glover[6]............................	90.0	60.00	50.00
Oregon Highway Commission[7].........	80.8	10.90	18.50
Breed, Older, and Downs:[8]			
Period 1921–32.....................	89.9	89.75	48.31
Period 1933–37.....................	90.6	90.60	48.11
Allen[9].............................	100.0	44.00	73.00
New Mexico Highway Commission[10]......	100.0	30.00	15.00
Utah State Tax Commission[11]..........	90.0	60.00	50.00
MacDonald[12]........................	100.0	....	....
Joint Committee[13]..................	100.0	....	....
Dearing[14]..........................	100.0	0	....

[1] Board of Investigation and Research, *Public Aids to Domestic Transportation* (1945), pp. 270–76.
[2] Federal Co-ordinator of Transportation, *Public Aids to Transportation*, Vol. IV (1940), pp. 33, 44–45, 159.
[3] William D. Ennis, *Motor Vehicle Taxation in New Jersey*, report to New Jersey Taxpayers Association at request of Associated Railroads of New Jersey (1935), p. 11.
[4] C. S. Duncan, *Highway Competition* (Association of American Railroads, 1935), p. 8.
[5] H. M. Werbitzky, *Study of Missouri Highway and Street Costs Chargeable to Motor Vehicles* (Missouri State Highway Department, 1937), pp. 20–21.
[6] V. L. Glover, *A Study of Highway Costs and Motor Vehicle Taxation in Illinois* (Division of Highways, Illinois Department of Public Works and Buildings, 1948), pp. 11–13.
[7] Oregon Highway Commission, *An Analysis of Highway Tax Structure in Oregon* (1936), pp. 112–13. Urban extensions are included with primary highways rather than with city streets.
[8] C. B. Breed, Clifford Older, and W. S. Downs, *Highway Costs*, report to Association of American Railroads (1939), pp. 54 and 104. For 1933–37, motor vehicles are assigned 77 per cent of costs of all roads and streets. Percentages for separate road systems, as given above, are derived on same basis used in railroad report for 1921–32 period.
[9] E. D. Allen, *Analysis of Highway Cost and Highway Taxation with an Application to Story County, Iowa*, Iowa Engineering Experiment Station Bulletin 152 (1941), p. 74. Separate percentages are given for primary urban streets (100) and other urban streets (72.3), and for county trunk roads (62.8) and county local roads (36.4).
[10] New Mexico State Highway Commission, *Future Highway Requirements of New Mexico* (1940), p. 61.
[11] Utah State Tax Commission, *Study of Utah Highway and Street Costs as a Basis for. . . . Charges against Motor Vehicles as Compensation for Road Use* (1940), p. 41.
[12] Statements of Thomas H. MacDonald, Bureau of Public Roads, in *Proceedings, Tenth Annual Asphalt Paving Conference* (1932), pp. 7–14; and "Making the Public Roads Pay," *Bus Transportation* (January, 1933), p. 8. No reference is made to assignment of street costs.
[13] Joint Committee of Railroads and Highway Users, *Regulation and Taxation of Highway Transportation* (January 30, 1933), p. 16.
[14] C. L. Dearing, *American Highway Policy* (1941), pp. 154–63. The extent of motor-vehicle responsibility for city street costs is not considered.

Source: Board of Investigation and Research, *Public Aids to Domestic Transportation*, House Doc. No. 159, 79th Cong., 1st sess. (Washington, D.C.: U.S. Government Printing Office, 1945), p. 255; and House Committee on Interstate and Foreign Commerce, *National Transportation Inquiry*, Part 1, 80th Cong., 2d sess. (Washington, D.C.: U.S. Government Printing Office, 1948), p. 134.

There have been a number of studies which have assigned specific percentages of responsibility for highway costs to motor-vehicle users as the amount for which they should be held responsible for road and street costs. As Table 3–2 indicates, there are sharp differences of opinion among the various investigators as to the percentage of responsibility for road and street costs which should be assigned to motor-vehicle users. Since there are three major classes of beneficiaries of highways—(*a*) the property directly served, (*b*) the general public, and (*c*) motor-vehicle users—there is the question of what percentage of the total cost of the highways should be borne by the one class, motor-vehicle users. It can be readily seen that the same basic figures could be used in computation by these various investigators and quite different results obtained because of the differentiation in percentages of responsibility which each had assigned for highway use to motor-vehicle users. It appears likely that some of these investigations may have been prompted by special groups with "axes to grind."

Annual highway costs may be based on an evaluation of the following cost elements: (1) amortization of the investment; (2) maintenance, administration, and operation; and (3) interest on the unamortized investment. Some researchers, using the analogy of the costs of a private facility, have suggested that a fourth element should be included, consisting of the property taxes to which the highway facilities would be subjected if they were privately owned. This is known as a "property-tax equivalent" or "escaped taxes."

Generally, it has been the position of highway engineers and administrators that only those elements of cost which are actually reflected in required expenditures for construction, maintenance, and operation of highways should be included in calculations of annual highway costs leading to the assignment of highway tax responsibility. If this logic is followed, it will be found that the item of interest enters only in connection with the payment of actual interest on debt incurred for highway purposes. When the assignment of highway tax responsibility is determined on the basis of actual required revenues or expenditures, the item of escaped taxes disappears.

ALLOCATION OF COSTS TO DIFFERENT CLASSES OF VEHICLES

Some of the theories which have been proposed for the solution of the problem of graduating motor-vehicle taxes in an equitable manner among vehicles of different sizes will be discussed. Each of the theories has certain shortcomings.

In order to accomplish equity in highway taxation, the theories of the manner in which the tax support should be allocated are based on one or a combination of two basic concepts: (1) the theory that tax support should be allocated among the beneficiary groups in proportion to the highway costs occasioned by each; and (2) that tax support should be allocated in proportion to benefits received which is often termed "value of service."

The *incremental theory* or the *theory of differential costs* uses what is termed the "costs-occasioned" concept. Theories based on benefits received are the *gross-ton mile theory* and the *operating-cost theory*. The *space-time theory* is dependent upon both of the basic concepts.

In making an *incremental study,* there must be a scientific determination of what type of road would be necessary if there were no large and heavy vehicles using it and the highway was built only to withstand the elements and carry light passenger-car traffic. Such a highway would be referred to as a "basic road." Once the cost of the basic road has been determined, the cost of such a road is assigned equally among all motor vehicles (passenger cars, trucks, and busses) on the basis of vehicle-miles operated. The difference in the cost of the basic road and the cost of the roads which are actually built to accommodate all traffic is assigned in its entirety to the heavy vehicles, that is, the additional or incremental costs which are incurred to accommodate these vehicles are assigned entirely to these vehicles.

The use of the incremental theory requires a complex analytical procedure. It also entails many technical problems. There are basic assumptions which must be made, and these must be reasonable assumptions, fairly and realistically made, if the results are not to be distorted. For example, an incremental analysis conducted in California which did not go into great detail assumed that from the standpoint of highway thickness, a highway capable of carrying 8,000-pound axle loads would be adequate; yet the Bureau of Public Roads today indicates that a highway capable of withstanding the elements is adequate to carry axle loads of 11,200 pounds.

In a recent incremental study, it was assumed that if there were no vehicles having axle loads in excess of 4,000 pounds, the roads in the particular state could be constructed to the equivalent of 4 inches of Portland cement concrete.[22] On the other hand, the minimum requirement for the sidewalks in the capitol city of this particular state requires sidewalks of concrete which must be at least 5 inches thick, increasing to 6 inches where a driveway crosses the sidewalk.

---

[22] D. F. Pancoast, *Allocation of Highway Costs in Ohio by the Incremental Method* (Ohio Department of Highways, December, 1953), p. 22.

Some parkways, like the Merritt Parkway in Connecticut and the Outer Drive in Chicago, are designed exclusively for passenger cars, and trucks are prohibited from using them; yet these highways are built 9 inches at the edge and 7 inches in the center.

It can be seen, then, that the basic assumptions in an incremental study are of great significance. Even though in theory the incremental approach to highway-cost allocation possesses merit, the basic assumptions must be reasonable if the results of a study of this kind are to have validity.

The *gross-ton mile theory* is one which assumes that the motor-vehicle tax responsibility for vehicles of every type and size should be measured by multiplying the weight of the vehicle, usually the average operating gross weight, by the miles traveled and distributing the total tax responsibility among all vehicles or all weight groups of vehicles in proportion to this product. The product, weight times distance, is supposed to represent a measure of value of use or value of service which has been rendered to the highway user by the highway facility used.

It has been pointed out that there is no affirmative proof which can be offered that the product, weight times distance, is a measure of value of service. Is the service rendered by a truck filled with sand or one loaded with jet engine parts for an airplane of more or less value than the service rendered by a public-utility truck?

A passenger car weighing 3,500 pounds which travels 10 miles and a truck weighing 35,000 pounds which travels 1 mile will have identical gross-ton miles. However, these two operations are quite different, and different monetary considerations are involved. For various types and sizes of vehicles, the value received from the use of the highways is not proportional to their weight because value of service must be measured in fiscal not in physical terms.[23]

Generally, the use of the gross-ton mile method would impose heavier tax burdens on vehicles in the higher weight groups than other methods. There are numerous shortcomings of the gross-ton mile theory, and it has been authoritatively stated that: "There can be no pretense that the gross-ton mile analysis produces an accurate appraisal of the costs occasioned by vehicles of different sizes and weights.[24]

---

[23] Senate Committee on Interstate and Foreign Commerce, *Study of Domestic Land and Water Transportation*, 81st Cong., 2d sess. (Washington, D.C.: U.S. Government Printing Office, 1950), p. 1051.

[24] *Ibid.*, p. 1029.

Gross weight and ton-miles are not necessarily related to highway costs. In highway construction, engineers consider the weight placed upon individual axles and not vehicle gross weight in constructing highways. What this means in terms of gross weight and axle loads is exemplified in the comparison of two trucks, one with two axles and a gross weight of 26,000 pounds and one with five axles with a gross weight of 86,000 pounds. The smaller truck having one 20,000-pound axle load requires the same standard of highway construction as the larger vehicle which has four such axles. The vehicles have vastly different gross weights, but the axle weights are identical. If the rear axle of the smaller truck were to carry 25,000 pounds, it would actually require a better and more costly highway than the larger truck, although its gross weight would still be only 31,000 pounds.[25]

The incremental theory and the gross-ton mile theory have received by far the most attention. Two governmental studies have been made using these methods—the Federal Coordinator of Transportation[26] or the Eastman report, and the Board of Investigation and Research.[27] Both groups concluded that over the years motor-vehicle users as a whole had paid their fair share for the use of the facilities.

Using the gross ton-mile method, the Board of Investigation and Research allocated the motor-vehicle users' percentage of responsibility which it had assigned and arrived at the conclusion that a number of commercial users, as well as private-user groups, were not paying their share of highway costs; but motor-vehicle users, as a whole, were paying their fair share.

The Eastman report made use of a system of allocation of highway costs among highway users on the basis of the incremental theory. The Eastman report listed twenty-seven different types of motor vehicles and showed that twenty-two of them had more than paid their fair share of highway costs. One of the classes found to have not quite paid its share was the school bus. Three other classes were privately operated trucks, which were found to have made underpay-

[25] *The Basic Problem of Distributing the Highway Tax Burden among the Various Highway Beneficiaries,* prepared by Research Director, American Trucking Associations, 1954.

[26] Federal Coordinator of Transportation, *Public Aids to Transportation* (Washington, D.C.: U.S. Government Printing Office, 1940), Vols. I and IV.

[27] Board of Investigation and Research, *Public Aids to Domestic Transportation,* House Doc. No. 159, 79th Cong., 1st sess. (Washington, D.C.: U.S. Government Printing Office, 1945).

ments, that is, they were not paying their fair share of highway costs. There was only one class of for-hire trucks which was found in the Eastman report to have underpaid, and that was the 5-ton single truck. These figures were for the year 1932. Using 1937 figures, but with less exact detail, the Eastman report found that the preponderance of the classes of motor-vehicle users were more than paying their fair share.

These figures have not been brought up to date. Since the end of World War II, a few states have undertaken comprehensive studies of highway needs for their respective states.[28] As one phase of the studies, some states have attempted to ascertain whether the various classes of highway users were paying their fair share of highway costs. The gross ton-mile method was used in these computations. It is a much simpler method of computing motor-vehicle tax responsibility and, for that reason, will continue to be used in reports less technical than the Eastman report.

The adoption of the incremental theory as the basis of a state analysis has so far had very limited application (Ohio and Minnesota) with the most comprehensive study currently being undertaken in Louisiana.

The trucking industry has felt that of the theories described the incremental theory provides the soundest method to be used in allocating motor-vehicle tax responsibility, providing that the data used as the basis are adequate and that assumptions are fairly made. The trucking industry has developed a method which has become known as the *cost-function method*. A recent study explains the cost-function method.[29] Under this system of highway-cost allocation, the many individual and different items of cost are divided into three categories, with a different yardstick being used in assigning cost responsibility in each category.

The first category embraces certain "stand-by or ready-to-serve costs" which are not affected by either miles traveled or variations in sizes and weights of vehicles. These costs are generally independent of fluctuations or variations in traffic, examples of which are cost for beautification and landscaping. These costs are assigned to the different groups of vehicles on the basis of the number of vehicles in each group.

The second category includes those costs which are affected by var-

---

[28] California, Washington, Oregon, Illinois, New York, Kansas, Nebraska, and others.

[29] Virginia Highway Users Association, *Testing the Equity of Virginia's Motor Vehicle Tax Structure* (June, 1953), pp. 36–66.

iations in sizes and weights of vehicles. These are referred to as "non-weight-use costs" and are essentially the basic highway costs and costs of maintaining and regulating traffic flow. Some of the items in this group would be certain ordinary maintenance costs and certain construction costs. The costs in this category are assigned to the different groups of vehicles on the basis of mileage traveled.

The third cost-function category includes the costs affected both by miles traveled and variations in sizes and weights. These are termed "weight-use costs." The placement of items in the weight-use cost category does not mean that the total cost of the item is chargeable to larger and heavier vehicles but that motor-vehicle weights have some effect on the cost of the item. These costs are assigned to the different groups on the basis of ton-miles operated by each group. However, this method uses ton-miles operated as a yardstick for assigning only those costs which are affected by both weight and distance. In contradistinction to this, the gross-ton-mile theory applies weight times distance in assigning all highway costs.

The cost-function theory contemplates that highway-user tax responsibility should be in the same proportion function-wise as the costs of the highway system. In one study using this method, 13.6 per cent were assigned as stand-by costs, 40.7 as nonweight-use costs, and 45.6 as weight-use costs, and each of the cost categories was allocated among the various vehicle classes on the same basis.[30]

The cost-function method is not considered by its proponents to be the solution to the problem of allocating highway costs. Its primary purpose is to show the fallacy of the gross-ton-mile method and to indicate the large degree of error inherent in the gross-ton-mile method.[31]

There are other theories which have been developed which attempt a solution to the problem of equity in highway taxation. Some of these are: (1) the operating-cost theory; (2) the theory of differential benefits; and (3) the space-time theory.

The *operating-cost theory*[32] assumes that motor-vehicle operating costs rise steadily with the size of vehicle. Therefore, this is an indication of the value of service provided and can be used as the basis for assignment of the highway-user tax responsibility. An example of

---

[30] *Ibid.*, p. 51.

[31] W. A. Bresnahan, "Report to ATA Board of Directors on Truck Taxes," October 29, 1954.

[32] Senate Committee on Interstate and Foreign Commerce, *Study of Domestic Land and Water Transportation*, 81st Cong., 2d sess. (Washington, D.C.: U.S. Government Printing Office, 1950), pp. 1053–1057.

the manner in which the operating-cost theory would apply is where the cost of operation of a passenger car is 8 cents per mile and that of a particular tractor-semitrailer combination is 48 cents per mile; the required tax payment per mile of the combination unit would be six times that of the passenger car. If the annual mileage of the combination unit was three times that of the passenger car, then the former's required annual tax payments would be in the ratio of 18 to 1. The basis of this theory is that the amount of money which is put into the operation of a motor vehicle is a measure of the value of the operation.

There are three bases which may be used in determining what should be included in operating costs. One basis would include only the "running costs," that is, those which vary directly with the mileage traveled. The second method, referred to as "total vehicular costs," would add to the running costs depreciation, insurance, interest, and garage rent or storage. The last method, termed "gross total operating costs," would include all assignable costs associated with the operation of the vehicle, including the drivers' wages, terminal, and overhead costs.

The use of any of these three bases of operating costs would not be as burdensome on the heavier vehicles as is the case with the gross-ton-mile theory. This is because as the size of the vehicle increases there are savings in the cost of operating per ton-mile of goods transported. The primary weakness of the operating-cost theory is that it does not take into account the highway costs occasioned by the use of vehicles of different types and sizes.

The theory of *differential benefits*[33] is one in which an attempt is made to determine the benefits which are derived by vehicles of different types and sizes from the use of the highways by the various users of the highways and to allocate highway costs accordingly to these beneficiaries.

One of the methods used in this theory is to divide the benefits into two categories: (1) the mileage benefits, and (2) time benefits, which together are called the "transportation benefits." The elements of highway improvements from which mileage benefits are secured are as follows: (1) a reduction in the distance between termini; (2) an improvement in roadway surface; (3) a reduction in rise and fall; (4) an improvement in gradients; (5) an improvement in alignment; and (6) elimination of impediments to traffic. Generally, these same improvements result in time benefits as well.

---

[33] *Ibid.,* pp. 1057–1062.

In order to assign the amount of these benefits or savings to each type or size of vehicle, the amount of savings in mileage or time costs which result from a given change or a change of unit magnitude must be computed for all of the aforementioned mileage or time elements. In addition to these transportation benefits, there are certain valuation and other benefits which result from highway improvement. These are determined by subtracting transportation benefits from highway expenditures, the residual amount being the valuation benefits and other benefits.

One method of distributing the benefits or savings would be to allocate them to the road and street systems on a ton-mile basis. Another method of allocating the mileage and time benefits to the road and street systems would be: (1) to establish the relative weight of each of the various improvement elements with respect to the other elements in the production of these benefits, which would take into account the maintenance and operation as well as construction expenditures; (2) for unit value established for each highway improvement element, to establish a tabulation or curve which would show the variation in the amount of savings with the size of the vehicle; (3) to apply the assigned weighting factors and unit benefit factors to the miles traveled by each vehicle type and weight group on the given road or street system. This would result in a number of index factors proportional to the benefits estimated to be derived by each vehicle group from the average annual expenditures. The distribution of the motor-vehicle tax burden for the given system would be among the vehicle groups in proportion to these index factors.

This theory has been used in economic analyses as applied to specific highway improvement projects, in comparing projects involving alternate locations, and in determining priorities of improvement. Although a motor-vehicle tax study using this particular approach has not been tried and in such a study a complex analysis procedure would have to be established, it is felt that there is merit in further study of this approach.

The *space-time theory*[34] is one in which the relative amounts of space occupied by vehicles of different sizes would be used in allocating motor-vehicle tax responsibility. The space on the highway which the vehicle occupies at a given time, plus the speed at which the vehicle travels, together with the number of miles of travel are the factors which would determine the share of highway costs allocated. In this theory, weight is not considered.

---

[34] *Ibid.,* pp. 1062–1065.

Under the space-time theory, a passenger car which operated at a very slow rate of speed, traveling the same mileage as a large tractor-semitrailer combination unit, could have as large a portion of highway costs allocated to it as would be allocated to the combination unit. The only factors considered in this theory which are considered among many factors by an incremental solution are the effects of excess capacity and width requirements of heavy vehicles on the various elements of highway costs.

The weakness of the space-time theory is that space occupancy is not a valid measure of value of service. Although larger vehicles may derive greater benefits, in a monetary sense, than smaller vehicles, the benefits or values cannot be directly associated with the space occupied on the highways by the vehicles.

CONCLUSION

In the present state of development of these theories on the equitable assignment of tax responsibility, each possesses certain defects as well as certain advantages. When states make studies on allocating motor-vehicle tax responsibility among vehicles of different types and sizes, sole reliance should not be placed on any single theory.

It is unfortunate that this problem of highway-user costs has not been resolved; for, as long as it remains a question, there will always be contention among the various agencies of transportation concerning the public-aid question. There is hope that the numerous state studies will form a better understanding of the problem. Commercial highway users have stated that it is their desire always to pay their fair share of highway costs.

QUESTIONS AND PROBLEMS

1. Trace the development of highway-user taxes, and indicate which tax constitutes the largest source of revenue today.
2. "Total highway-user taxes are of such proportions that it is not unusual for a for-hire motor carrier which operates a truck regularly to pay in a single year taxes which approach or exceed the market value of the vehicle." Discuss.
3. What is meant by the statement that the gasoline tax is a pay-before-you-go system of financing?
4. What is the linkage theory concerning the federal excise tax on gasoline? Discuss its advantages and disadvantages.
5. To what extent has the use of bonds been a source of highway financing? What are the different types used?

6. What traffic volume, as one factor, is considered necessary to justify the construction of a toll road?

7. Why do toll roads "afford more relief in total dollars than in total percentage of highways"?

8. Discuss the different types of toll projects based upon the method of providing the funds.

9. Trucks constitute about 17 per cent of all motor vehicles but pay 33 per cent of all highway taxes paid by all motor vehicles. Comment.

10. How is it possible that the same basic figures can be used by various investigators in computing public aid and yet different results be obtained?

11. Explain the incremental theory of highway cost allocation used in the Eastman report. What merit does it possess?

12. What is the gross-ton-mile method of allocation used in the Board of Investigation and Research report? Why is this method used in some of the state studies issued since World War II?

13. For the complex problem of financing highways, what program would you suggest as a state legislator? As a taxpayer?

14. Carefully explain the cost-function and space-time methods of cost allocation to different classes of vehicles.

PART II

Property-Carrying Aspects of Commercial Motor Transportation

4. EQUIPMENT AND ITS FINANCING

▪▪

OUR first trucks were converted automobile carriages with heavier axles and springs and strengthened frames. These appeared around 1900; and, for a period of about 25 years, the preponderance of trucks were 1 ton or smaller and were largely modifications of passenger cars. The differentiation between heavy-duty and light-duty trucks in those early days was marked. The latter were largely standardized and were produced at low cost. The heavy-duty trucks were largely produced to specialized requirements; and, as might be expected, the volume produced was low. About 1929, the passenger-car manufacturers began specialization in light-duty trucks to meet each specific set of operating requirements. The rating of the small trucks was increased from 1 ton to 1½ tons, which caused a greater change from passenger-car design. Today there is almost no such thing as a standard truck, even in the 1½-ton field. Chassis requirements may be standard, but the variety of options is so great that the operator can purchase a truck in the 1½-ton field, as well as in the heavier truck sizes, almost to specifications.

The manufacture of truck bodies is a separate industry in itself. With the exception of the production of a few simple body types, largely of the delivery type, truck manufacturers have not found it possible to standardize trucks for any type of operation. There are special designs which increase in number each year. Manufacturers of trucks have designed and manufactured trucks in a manner that has given them extreme flexibility from unit to unit and that has enabled them to develop better trucks to meet the increasing demand for specialized vehicles resulting from the evolution of motor transportation.

In the early beginnings of the trucking industry, most of the commercial vehicles were built by manufacturers not associated with the passenger-car industry. Passenger-car manufacturers entering the

77

light-truck field reduced the proportion of units handled by the independent manufacturers; nevertheless, the total number of trucks built by the independent companies has steadily increased. The manufacturers who are independent from the passenger-car industry can be divided into two groups: (*a*) those who produce all types of trucks for almost any purpose, and (*b*) those who produce only a few limited and specialized types.

The necessity for individual engineering of one type or another, whether major or minor in nature, characterizes the construction of practically all units except the light-truck units. The truck manufacturer, then, in order to meet specific transportation problems, must have a large number of variations of his truck design. The producer of trucks has a variety of optional clutches, transmissions, and the like which are produced by independent "parts" manufacturers, so that it is possible for him to offer many variations without having to tool up for each completely new unit. Some truck manufacturers provide their salesmen with questionnaires on which are listed all of the factors relating to the specific hauling operations of each potential customer. The truck manufacturer, using each questionnaire as a guide, will select the correct units which will best serve the needs of the individual operator.

A large truck manufacturer may offer about 400 different models which include several thousand variations in bodies and special equipment. The various models which are offered by one truck manufacturer may be made up to include any one of 30 different engines of from 100 to 356 horsepower. Trucks may have as many as 16 forward and 4 reverse speeds. There is a wide range of differences in brakes, springs, frames, axles, and the like. For example, there are 1,000 different sizes and types of brake linings. "New models" among heavier trucks generally appear about every 3–5 years. Some of the manufacturers of specialized equipment redesign about once every 10 years.

The manufacturers of trucks have found that over half of their production falls into three body styles: panel, pickup, and platform.[1] It is common practice for the factory to build these trucks complete. There are a large number of other body styles, however. Figure 4–1 shows the sale of trucks by gross vehicle weights from 1946 to 1953.

Some of the factors that are usually considered in selecting a truck are the type of operation in which it is to be used (whether local or over-the-road), the type of loads, maximum grades encountered and

---

[1] These body types will be described later in the chapter.

the extent of these grades, type and condition of highways and state laws, and desired cruising speed.

Most trucks in use are powered by gasoline engines, although there have been a number of interesting recent developments regarding source of power for trucks. The diesel type of truck engine made its appearance about 1933. Although its use continues to increase rapidly, particularly among the heavier vehicles, it represents but a small portion of the total. Diesel-powered trucks are more widely used in

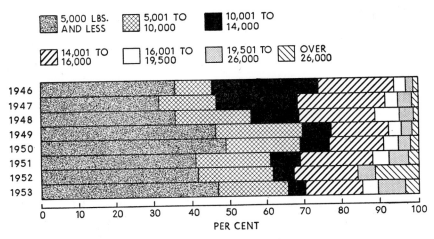

FIG. 4–1. Factory sales of trucks by gross vehicle weight groups.
Source: Automobile Manufacturers Association, *Motor Truck Facts* (Detroit, 1954), p. 5.

the Rocky Mountain and Pacific Coast states and are more popular for long-distance hauling. The higher initial cost and, in the beginning, the lack of service facilities served to retard their development, but by 1953 there were about 76,000 of these vehicles registered. The early problem of controlling exhaust fumes was corrected in later models. Diesels, for equal horsepower, weigh more than gasoline trucks.

Liquefied petroleum gas-powered engines have recently been introduced in intercity trucking. Propane gas and butane gas, so-called "bottled gas," are used. The cost of LPG as a fuel averages about 5 cents per gallon less than gasoline. Reduction in maintenance and operating costs and the elimination of exhaust odor are other advantages. As was true in the early stages of diesel-powered units, there is a limited number of points where LPG is available, but these are rapidly expanding.

Currently, there is considerable experimentation with a gas turbine engine for trucks. A substantial reduction in weight of the power unit is possible with such an engine, but so far fuel consumption is very high.

One company has developed and placed in service what is termed a "steering pusher." This is an independently mounted axle with steering knuckles at each wheel that are steered through drag link and tie rod co-ordinated with the steering of the front axle. It is mounted ahead of the driving axle. Its primary purpose is to increase

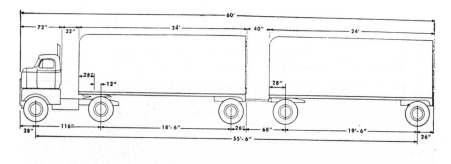

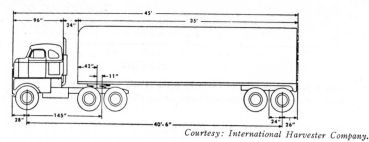

Courtesy: International Harvester Company.

FIG. 4–2. Examples of cab-over-engine units.

the legal allowable load on the driving axle because it makes possible 27,000 pounds rather than 18,000 for a single driving axle tractor.

One of the most significant developments in the postwar period has been the trend toward automatic transmission. This was first started with light-duty models. In the following years, it was used on medium-duty models, and it is now found on the heavy-duty trucks. Heavy-duty tractors with automatic transmissions first appeared in 1954. The savings of time through faster automatic shifting and decrease in driver fatigue are significant advantages of the new automatic transmission. The success of this transmission in the lighter units has led to the optimistic forecast that within a few years as many as 50 per cent of all trucks will be so equipped.

Another important development in tractors has been the growing use of cab-over-engine tractors to improve load distribution and permit use of longer trailers. In about twenty states there are restrictions limiting a combination tractor-semitrailer to 45 feet. The length limit, in nine of these states, of the semitrailer is 35 feet. Thus the power unit can be 10 feet in length. In these states, the cab-over-engine is not necessary unless a sleeper cab is required, since the conventional tractor, which is 102 inches from bumper to back of cab, will fall within the maximum length. Figure 4–2 is a cab-over-engine sleeper cab with a 35-foot semitrailer in a 45-foot limit. Also shown

Courtesy: Pacific Intermountain Express

FIG. 4–3. A dromedary unit mounted back of the driver's cab on the tractor, which adds more pay load. The fifth-wheel coupling is located back of the dromedary for the semitrailer. These units are found in the western states.

is a combination unit of two 24-foot trailers in a 60-foot limit, which is used in the West.

The cab-over-engine possesses particular advantage in those states in which the state law permits a specified maximum over-all length with no restrictions on the length of the vehicles in the combination. When a 60-foot over-all length is permitted, many operators desire a 40-foot semitrailer. Some states impose a limit on the single vehicle length but allow as much as 25 feet in excess of this for over-all length of the combination. The operator may want to use a trailer of standard size for interchange through states which are more restrictive, yet he desires to utilize the potential cargo space on the tractor chassis. This has led to the development of a unit known as a "dromedary" which is on the truck tractor and provides cargo space. The original dromedary carried 4,000 pounds, and tests are currently being made with one which carries over 10,000 pounds. The operator who wishes to get as much cargo space mounted on the tractor as possible will find that the cab-over-engine gives more cargo space. Figure 4–3 shows the dromedary.

There are also some operators who turn to the cab-over-engine chassis in order to place more of the weight of the payload on the front axle. The cab-over-engine can carry on the front axle as much as 10 per cent more of the load imposed on the kingpin than can conventional models.[2]

Courtesy: Illinois California Express

FIG. 4–4. Cab-beside-engine tractor which gives unusual visibility for the driver.

The greater steering effort which is needed as front axle loads are increased to the maximum has met with driver resistance. However, the use of power steering and the placement of more of the chassis overhanging the front axle permit the increase of the pay load from 500 to 1,000 pounds.

An interesting variation of the COE is the cab-beside-engine. This tractor gives the driver unusual visibility, as well as facilitating work on the engine. Figure 4–4 is a cab-beside-engine tractor pulling a semitrailer.

When one truck manufacturer's line complements that of another

[2] Lewis C. Kibbee, "The Need for Dimensional and Operating Characteristics of the COE Chassis," address before the Society of Automotive Engineers, November, 1953.

manufacturer, the two manufacturers producing units which are generally noncompetitive, the manufacturer with nation-wide distribution will handle the other manufacturer's line.[3]

There has been considerable co-operation between carriers and manufacturers of trucks and trailers in an effort to secure sufficient standardization to permit an interchange of tractor and trailer units. Some of the standardization which is in the blueprint stage is a fifth-wheel height of 48 inches, elimination of differences in location of operating instruments, reduction in the number of variations in fifth wheels, uniform electrical connections, distance from front of trailer to center line of kingpin set at 36 inches, as well as a number of others.

TRUCK TRAILERS[4]

Hooking or hitching a two-wheel wagon to an automobile and thus increasing the carrying capacity available to the owner of a small car or truck was the first example of the use of trailers. In the early days, trucks or cars and trailers were hitched together with a loose-hanging clevis made of a piece of metal. The result was that this type of knuckle-steer trailer would weave over the highway. By 1920 there were many organizations in the lumber and building supply business which were using truck trailers. It was at about this time that the problem of attaching the trailer was solved by the development of an automatic fifth-wheel steer and a more satisfactory coupling hook (Fig. 4–5). The fifth wheel is a disk behind the cab of the tractor. The forward end of the semitrailer rests on this disk. By shifting the fifth wheel closer to the cab or closer to the rear axle of the tractor, axle loads can be changed. The fifth wheel makes it easy to couple and uncouple the trailer unit (Fig. 4–6).

The advantages of truck trailers are as follows: (*a*) a relatively large load can be hauled by a small power unit; (*b*) it is not necessary to unload the vehicle to release the power unit for other work; and (*c*) a truck trailer is more easily turned and maneuvered in traffic than a single wheel-base truck of equal capacity.

The tailoring of trailers to suit the requirements of individual operators is as pronounced as in the manufacturing of trucks. Trailers

---

[3] International Harvester Company handles Fageol Van Trucks; and White Motor Company handles Freightliner.

[4] The different types of truck trailers used today will be described later in the chapter.

Courtesy: Fruehauf Trailer Company

FIG. 4–5. Fifth-wheel coupler, showing location on truck tractor.

are designed, as well, to meet various state laws as to size and weight requirements. These factors have combined to make it impossible to produce standard commercial units in any quantity. All trailer manufacturers, however, produce so-called standard models. One large company, for example, produces 6,000 standard models. The materials used in construction may be standard, but the models are not.

Courtesy: International Harvester Company

FIG. 4–6. A truck-tractor unit, showing the location of the fifth wheel on the frame in back of the cab.

An example of a type of operation that calls for different equipment is that of hauling rubber tires. The majority of trailers are of a closed-type van body, but use is also made of an open-type van body in this operation. The tires may be loaded so that they extend above the side wall of the van body. A tarpaulin covering is then tied down. After traveling 25 miles, the tires will have settled so that they are below the level of the side wall, and the tarpaulin will need to be retied.

Although there are about 150 firms engaged in truck-trailer manufacturing, which are geographically located all over the United States, it is estimated that about twelve companies account for 80 to 85 per cent of the volume produced; the two largest companies (Fruehauf and Trailmobile) produce about 50 per cent of all the truck trailers built.

Many truck-trailer manufacturers concentrate their sales efforts in a regional area. Some concentrate on fleet sales, whereas others divide their efforts between fleets and individual operators. One truck-trailer manufacturer has no sales outlets and sells only F.O.B. plant, whereas the larger companies have branch operations. Others have dealer distributors.

It has been estimated by these manufacturers that the production of truck trailers will average about 70,000 trailers each year between 1952 and 1956. Although about 44 per cent of the 1952 output was for the government, approximately 25,000 trailers must be replaced each year due to accidents and over-age. Table 4–1 shows truck-

TABLE 4–1

TRUCK-TRAILER PRODUCTION
(Units)

	Production	Average Value (Shipments)
1946	76,234	2,178
1947	53,112	2,500
1948	44,478	2,980
1949	33,097	3,480
1950	64,617	3,280
1951	67,384	3,790
1952	58,077	3,950
1953:		
Civilian	53,173 ⎱ 97,689	3,075
Government agencies and export	44,516 ⎰	....
1954* (includes 10,000 government and export)	55,000	....

The increase in average value indicates an increase in trailer size, the preponderance of more expensive types such as vans and tanks, and the increasing use of tandem axles with double the number of tires.

* Estimated.

Source, Bureau of Census, *Fact for Industry Series,* M 454, 1954.

trailer production, as well as the average value of shipments. The production of truck-trailer vans constitutes the largest single category of total trailer production. The number of vans produced in relation to total production has varied in the postwar period from a high of 59 per cent in 1950 to 32 per cent in 1953. During this same period, there was an increasing percentage of production of specialized types of trailers. Examples of this type of equipment are tank trailers which have been constructed for the hauling of bulk commodities, such as sugar, flour, salt, and cement. Such trailers have automatic self-unloading equipment. Figure 4–7 is a trailer used in hauling bulk cement. Substantial savings have been effected in handling these bulk items.

Courtesy: Buckingham Transportation, Inc.

FIG. 4–7. A semitrailer used for hauling cement in bulk. It is equipped with a self-unloader which operates pneumatically.

Specialized equipment, such as a truckaway trailer, has also been designed to permit a return haul of freight. This is accomplished by providing side uprights and hinged sections, so that the tracks on which the cars are ordinarily placed are folded out of the way. A semitrailer and trailer designed to haul bulk cement one way and fuel oil on the return is shown in Figure 4–8.

The service life of trailers is usually considerably greater than that of power units, although there are wide variations depending upon the type of equipment. The power unit may have a relatively short service life of 5 years and trailers approximately 10 years.[5] The average number of semitrailers to tractors for Class I intercity motor car-

---

[5] A number of interesting historical articles on the growth of truck and truck-trailer companies appeared in *Motor Transportation* beginning in 1953.

riers in 1952 was 160 to 100 and ranged from 126–160 to 100 during the preceding 10 years. This is due to the fact that the semitrailer can be "dropped" at destination and remain at the dock until unloaded. In the meantime, the tractor can pick up another semitrailer and pull it to its destination.

The shiftable tandem axle is one of the most important recent developments in semitrailers. When different tractors are being used with a semitrailer, the shifting of the rear axles to compensate for the load position can secure proper load distribution. Thus, axles can be shifted to comply with the different state requirements through which the unit operates, and a carrier can standardize on a trailer of

Courtesy: Southwestern Portland Cement Co.

FIG. 4–8. A semitrailer and trailer used for hauling bulk cement one way in compartment built around the tank and for transporting fuel oil in the tanks on the return trip.

one size for its over-the-road operations. Another advantage of the shiftable tandem is that removal of the entire sliding suspension can be made by disconnecting the airlines, removing the pins, and hoisting the body. This allows for the replacing of a unit with an overhauled one in a matter of 30 minutes.

There has been an increasing demand by truck operators for more pay load space or more "cube." This growing demand for increased cubic capacity must be reconciled by trailer manufacturers with state limits on sizes of units. A survey of the dry-freight semitrailer vans sold in 1948 and 1953 clearly shows the trend toward trailers with higher cubic capacity. The 28–30-foot vans in 1948 accounted for 27½ per cent of the business, but in 1953 they accounted for only 3.2 per cent of the total; 30–32-foot vans in 1948 were 23.9 per cent but dropped in 1953 to 10.4 per cent; the 32- to 34-foot vans in 1948 were 16.6 per cent of the total and skyrocketed to 58.7 per cent in 1953. In addition, in 1953, 18.9 per cent of the total was accounted for by the 34–36-foot vans; and 2.4 per cent was over 36 feet.[6]

For those carriers who are particularly interested in "cube," a 2,300 cubic foot trailer is available. What a trailer of this type can mean in terms of cubic capacity is illustrated by the experience of an operator of a large fleet which purchased 380 new trailers of 2,300 cubic feet capacity (see Fig. 4–9) and found that these trailers could haul the same amount of freight as 475 of its old trailers, each having a capacity of 1,900 cubic feet. It is estimated that every additional foot of cargo space of dry freight is worth $50 per year.

Courtesy: Pacific Intermountain Express

FIG. 4–9. A semitrailer with a 2,300 cubic feet capacity equipped with mechanical refrigeration unit.

The additional cubic capacity in new semitrailers has been accomplished by lengthening the semitrailer through the use of cab-over-engine tractors which require less tractor length; reduced clearance of trailers over the tires; lower fifth wheels and fifth-wheel mountings; thinner wall sections; and flatter and thinner roof construction, as well as in a number of other ways.

When maximum cube is desired, it is possible to have a semitrailer with a three-level floor, which has 2,600 cubic feet capacity, if it is assumed that a 12-inch ground clearance between the axles is practicable.

Instead of conventional steel springs, an air suspension has been used on some of the newer trailers. Under this method of construc-

[6] *Traffic World,* May 22, 1954, p. 91.

tion, the load actually rides on an air cushion. As a trailer is loaded, air is automatically pumped to expand the air cushions. When unloaded, the air is released. This makes it possible to maintain a constant height of the trailer. With conventional springs, a trailer must be designed to meet the legal height when empty, and when loaded, sometimes the height is as much as 3 inches lower than allowed.

In order to increase the pay load, there has been greater use of lighter metals in trailer construction, and in 1954 manufacturers made almost twice as many aluminum as steel vans. With lightweight construction material, manufacturers can produce a single-axle dry-freight semitrailer with a weight as low as 6,700 pounds and carrying a manufacturer's standard rating of 25,000 pounds net pay load capacity. This is a pay-load-to-tare weight ratio of a little over three to one.

Plastics have had limited use so far. In some of the new trailers skylight panels of plastic are being placed in the forward part of the roof of the trailer which gives added light for loading and unloading. There have been some plastic sides constructed for trailers, as well as a few tank trailers constructed of reinforced plastic. It appears that plastic will be used when its use is economically sound, but so far it has had limited application.[7]

COMMERCIAL VEHICLE NOMENCLATURE

Throughout the motor-carrier industry, terms are applied to equipment which are only applicable in a particular area. In referring to a piece of equipment, the expression used in one area may have a completely different connotation in another area. These terms become firmly entrenched through usage and are widely found in labor contracts. For instance, a labor agreement in one area may make reference to a piece of equipment called a "jeep." The same term in a labor contract in an area just 500 miles distant may refer to an entirely different piece of equipment. What is referred to as a "double bottom" in Ohio is known as a "train" in another area. A trailer less than 20 feet in length may be called a "pup," and one more than 20 feet long may be called a "dog." Many other examples

---

[7] The difficulties encountered in material allocation for transportation equipment during World War II and the Korean armed conflict indicate that future contingencies of this nature will require an understanding of the essentiality of transportation. In this connection it should be noted that the higher equipment utilization of trailers on a ton-mile basis is a factor to which greater consideration should be given in material allocation.

could be cited. In order to achieve some degree of uniformity with reference to terms and equipment types, it is necessary that use be made of a standard nomenclature which has been established by the Society of Automotive Engineers and the Motor Truck Technical Committee. The adoption of this nomenclature undoubtedly will be slow, but it certainly is desirable.

SAE Standard Commercial Vehicle Nomenclature[8]

A vehicle is any single conveyance on wheels.

Motor Vehicle. A motor vehicle is any vehicle self-propelled or drawn by mechanical power, operated on the highways or natural terrain in the transportation of property or passengers.

Motor Vehicle Chassis. A motor vehicle chassis is a motor vehicle stripped of all essentials necessary for the accommodation of driver, property, or passengers.

4 × 2. A 4 × 2 motor vehicle is a two-axle motor vehicle equipped with four wheels, two of which are driving wheels.

4 × 4. A 4 × 4 motor vehicle is a two-axle motor vehicle equipped with four wheels, all of which are driving wheels.

6 × 2. A 6 × 2 motor vehicle is a three-axle motor vehicle equipped with six wheels, two of which are driving wheels.

6 × 4. A 6 × 4 motor vehicle is a three-axle motor vehicle equipped with six wheels, four of which are driving wheels.

6 × 6. A 6 × 6 motor vehicle is a three-axle motor vehicle equipped with six wheels, all of which are driving wheels.

Note. Motor vehicles designed with other combinations of driving and non-driving axles are defined in the same numerical order.

MOTOR TRUCK

A motor truck is a single self-propelled motor vehicle carrying its load on its own wheels and designed for the transportation of property.

TRUCK TRACTOR

A truck tractor is a motor vehicle designed primarily for drawing truck trailers and constructed so as to carry part of the weight and load of a semitrailer.

Conventional Truck or Truck Tractor. A conventional motor truck or truck tractor is one with the driver's compartment and controls located at the rear of a hood-enclosed power plant.

Cab Forward Truck or Truck Tractor. A cab forward motor truck or truck tractor is one with the driver's compartment and controls located forward of their position on the conventional front-end type of motor truck or truck tractor.

[8] This standard nomenclature appeared first in *SAE Journal,* November, 1948, pp. 22–26, and was incorporated in *SAE 1949 Handbook* (New York: Society of Automotive Engineers, Inc., 1949), pp. 868–71. It will be used throughout the text whenever reference is made to any of the terms contained herein.

Off-Highway Motor Vehicle.   An off-highway motor vehicle is any motor
  vehicle designed primarily for transporting property on natural terrain
  and may be of such size or weight as to be restricted from operation
  on highways by state laws or regulations. (See Fig. 4–10.)

Multi-Stop Delivery Truck.   A multi-stop delivery truck is one equipped
  with a fully enclosed body with driving compartment integral and
  especially designed for quick and easy ingress and egress.

Gantry Truck.   A gantry truck is a motor truck so designed and constructed that it straddles the load to be transported and by means of
  an appropriate mechanism picks up the load and supports it during
  transportation.

Courtesy: Cummins Engine Company and the magazine "Diesel Progress"

FIG. 4–10. Typical of the heavy-duty off-highway trucks is this unit waiting for a 65-ton load
of limestone.

TRUCK TRAILER

A truck trailer is a motor vehicle with or without auxiliary motive power,
  designed to be drawn by a motor vehicle.

Semitrailer.   A semitrailer is a truck trailer equipped with one or more
  axles and constructed so that a substantial part of its weight and load is
  carried by a truck tractor.

Full Trailer.   A full trailer is a truck trailer constructed so that practically
  all of its weight and load rests upon its own wheels.

Dump Trailer.   A dump trailer is a truck trailer provided with a body
  that can be tilted or otherwise manipulated to discharge its load by
  gravity.

Low-Bed Trailer.   A low-bed trailer is a truck trailer equipped with or
  without a platform body, constructed to provide a low loading height
  and designed for the transportation of extremely heavy or bulky property.

134636

Tank Trailer. A tank trailer is a truck trailer designed for the transportation of fluid commodities in bulk.

Passenger Trailer. A passenger trailer is a truck trailer designed primarily for the transportation of passengers.

Pole Trailer. A pole trailer is a truck trailer without auxiliary motive power, designed to be drawn by a truck or truck tractor and attached by means of a reach or pole, or by being "boomed" or otherwise secured to the drawing motor vehicle, and intended for transporting long or irregularly shaped loads such as poles, logs, pipes, or structural members which are capable generally of sustaining themselves as beams between supporting connections.

(Note. Wheel and axle complement: Two wheels are considered the complement of any axle regardless of whether they may be single- or dual-tire equipped.)

Single-Axle Truck Trailer. A single-axle truck trailer is a truck trailer equipped with one axle and two wheels.

Courtesy: American Trucking Associations, Inc.

FIG. 4–11. A trailer-converter dolly. This possesses the necessary parts for converting a semi-trailer to a full trailer.

Two-Axle Truck Trailer. A two-axle truck trailer is a truck trailer equipped with two axles and four wheels.

Three-Axle Truck Trailer. A three-axle truck trailer is a truck trailer equipped with three axles and six wheels.

Trailer-Converter Dolly. A trailer-converter dolly is an auxiliary axle assembly equipped with a lower fifth-wheel half, drawbar, and other necessary parts designed to convert a semitrailer to a full trailer. (See Fig. 4–11.)

(Note. The vehicles defined in this list are used in combinations as illustrated.)

BODIES

Pickup Body or Express Body.   A pickup body is an open-box body with or without flare boards. A pickup body is usually smaller than an express body.

Sedan Delivery.   A sedan delivery is a passenger car sedan-type body adapted to commercial use.

Panel Body or Van Body.   A panel body or van body is a fully enclosed body. A panel body is usually smaller than a van body.

Open-Van Body.   An open-van body is a body consisting of a platform and permanent solid front and sides with or without doors or tail gate and without a permanent top.

Platform Body.   A platform body is a body without raised sides or covering.

Stake Body.   A stake body is a platform body with readily removable stakes which may be tied together with chains, slats, panels, and so forth.

Rack Body.   A rack body is a platform body with slatted sides to contain the load.

Dump Body.   A dump body is a body that can be tilted or otherwise manipulated to discharge its load by gravity.

Tank Body.   A tank body is a body designed for the transportation of fluid commodities.

VEHICLE COMBINATIONS

There are a wide variety of vehicle combinations in use today. The combinations listed on the following pages are by no means

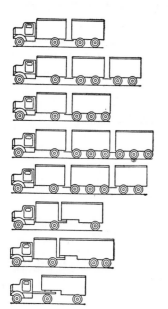

1. Two-axle truck with two-axle full trailer in combination

2. Two-axle truck with two two-axle full trailers in combination

3. Two-axle truck with three-axle trailer in combination

4. Two-axle truck with two three-axle full trailers in combination

5. Two-axle truck with one three-axle and one two-axle full trailer in combination

6. Two-axle truck with single-axle semitrailer in combination

7. Two-axle truck with two-axle semitrailer in combination

8. Two-axle truck tractor with single-axle semitrailer in combination

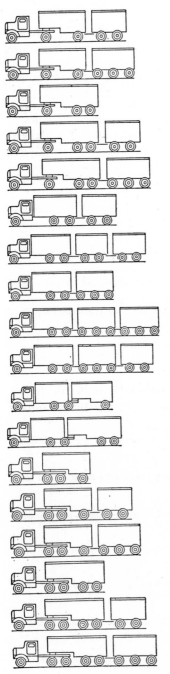

9. Two-axle truck tractor with single-axle semitrailer and two-axle full trailer in combination

10. Two-axle truck tractor with single-axle semitrailer and three-axle full trailer in combination

11. Two-axle truck tractor with two-axle semitrailer in combination

12. Two-axle truck tractor with two-axle semitrailer and two-axle full trailer in combination

13. Two-axle truck tractor with two-axle semitrailer and three-axle full trailer in combination

14. Three-axle truck with two-axle full trailer in combination

15. Three-axle truck with two two-axle full trailers in combination

16. Three-axle truck with three-axle full trailer in combination

17. Three-axle truck with two three-axle full trailers in combination

18. Three-axle truck with one three-axle and one two-axle full trailer in combination

19. Three-axle truck with single-axle semitrailer in combination

20. Three-axle truck with two-axle semitrailer in combination

21. Three-axle truck tractor with single-axle semitrailer in combination

22. Three-axle truck tractor with single-axle semitrailer and two-axle full trailer in combination

23. Three-axle truck tractor with single-axle semitrailer and three-axle full trailer in combination

24. Three-axle truck tractor with two-axle semitrailer in combination

25. Three-axle truck tractor with two-axle semitrailer and two-axle full trailer in combination

26. Three-axle truck tractor with two-axle semitrailer and three-axle full trailer in combination

NOTE 1: Two wheels are the complement of any axle regardless of the number of tires—whether singles, duals, or more.

NOTE 2: Trucks and tractors may be either 4 x 2, 4 x 4, 6 x 2, 6 x 4, or 6 x 6. Additional combinations are possible by other wheel or axle arrangements.

found throughout the United States, because of state size and weight restrictions. These are representative, however, of the various combinations that can be or are being used in various areas.[9]

Some indication as to the trend in the average load carried by trucks and truck combinations can be secured from Figure 4–12. This fig-

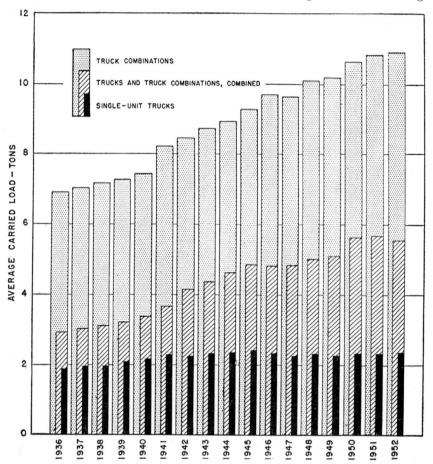

FIG. 4–12.   Average load carried by trucks and truck combinations on main rural roads, 1936–52.

Source: *Public Roads*, Vol. XXVII, No. 11 (December, 1953), p. 241.

ure shows the comparison of the average load carried by single-unit trucks, truck combinations, and trucks and truck combinations combined, covering a 17-year period from 1936 through 1952. The average load carried by truck combinations has steadily increased.

Figure 4–13 shows the number of ton-miles of freight carried by

[9] *Ibid.*

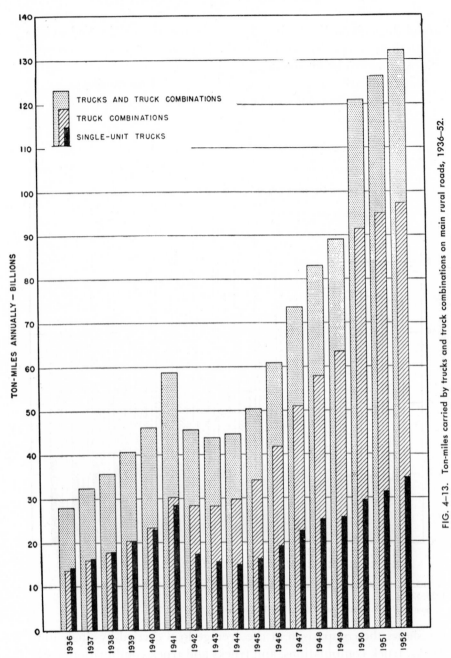

FIG. 4–13. Ton-miles carried by trucks and truck combinations on main rural roads, 1936–52. Source: *Public Roads*, Vol. XXVII, No. 11 (December, 1953), p. 242.

trucks and truck combinations on main rural roads[10] during the same period, 1936 through 1952. In 1936 the truck combinations hauled slightly less ton-mileage than single-unit trucks; whereas in 1952 they hauled almost three times the amount hauled by single-unit trucks. To be noted especially is the increase in the total ton-mileage hauled by truck combinations since the end of World War II.

A comparison of vehicle-miles of traffic, percentage of vehicle loaded, average carried load, and percentage of total ton-miles car-

Courtesy: Pilot Freight Carriers, Inc.

FIG. 4–14. A sleeper-cab tractor and tandem axle semitrailer which is representative of equipment used in over-the-road operations in the East and Middle West.

ried by single-unit trucks and truck combinations on main rural roads in 1952 reveals that, whereas panel and pickup trucks traveled about 33 per cent of the vehicle-miles, they accounted for less than 3 per cent of the total ton-mileage. Truck tractor and semi-trailer combinations traveled about 28 per cent of the vehicle-mileage but accounted for about 76 per cent of the ton-mileage. A typical combination unit is shown in Figure 4–14.

EQUIPMENT FINANCING

The financing of motor-carrier equipment has presented two major problems: (*a*) lack of sources of credit, and (*b*) unfavorable credit

---

[10] All roads outside the incorporated limits of municipalities.

terms in the purchase of equipment. Many financial institutions were wary of loaning funds to the embryonic trucking industry, and certainly this conservative attitude was somewhat justified in view of the record of many early truck operators. The lack of responsibility toward their financial obligations on the part of some motor carriers in the early days of the industry has been a factor in the reluctance of banking institutions to grant applications for motor-carrier equipment financing. Furthermore, prior to 1935, there was not the stabilizing influence in the motor-carrier industry that was introduced with the passage of the Motor Carrier Act at that time and the subsequent placing of the for-hire interstate motor carriers under the jurisdiction of the Interstate Commerce Commission. Even today, banks generally are not anxious to make this type of loan except under terms that many motor carriers feel are too stringent.

VENDOR CREDIT

As a result of inadequate truck equipment financing, some of the truck manufacturers undertook the financing of motor-carrier equipment. This type of credit is called "vendor credit" and is extended or arranged only for the purchase of specific equipment from the manufacturer. This type of credit is not selective and is based primarily on the collateral value of the equipment purchased by the motor carrier. The terms for this purchase are predicated not on the qualifications of the particular motor-carrier purchaser but rather on the value and life of equipment in the hands of *any* motor carrier used under average conditions under average management. Terms of payment are worked out on a statistical average and result in comparatively standard down payments and length of payments. Interest rates on this type of financing are relatively high.

One trailer manufacturer leases new trailers built to customer's specifications. The lease payments are less than actual purchase cost, and the arrangement provides for maintenance by the user with new trailers to replace the old units after 6 years.[11] Under this plan there is no down payment or lease prepayment, as well as other advantages.

SELECTIVE CREDIT

Contrasted to vendor credit is selective credit in equipment financing. This is credit advanced by a lending institution to an indi-

---

[11] Edwards Trailer Company, Centerline, Michigan.

vidual motor carrier based on its individual credit worthiness. This is the type of credit which has presented difficulties both to those supplying credit and those applying for it. The need for understanding of the trucking business by lending institutions and the need for understanding of the banking business by truckers is evident. The promotion of understanding of problems and policies present in each operation will go far to ease credit restrictions.

The financial structure of motor carriers is different from that of other businesses which carry large inventories. Working capital customarily comes first in any analysis of credit worthiness by a financing institution. However, the need for working capital for motor carriers is small. Motor carriers frequently operate successfully with a deficit in working capital.[12] The ratio of quick assets to liabilities is not as favorable in the financial structure of a motor carrier because the motor carrier does not carry large inventories; it has no need to do so, since it sells service and since its inventories are in the form of equipment that is used in the rendition of service.

Usually considered next in any analysis of credit worthiness is the relationship of capital and debt. Here the impressive proportions evidenced in other industries are not necessary. The average motor carrier's normal debt ratio is more than 1 to 1, or a total debt approximately equal to or slightly more than capital. A larger debt proportion can be carried by a highly profitable motor-carrier operation, and frequently is when abnormal replacements are required to rehabilitate truck fleets. There is no set limit to a debt ratio, but a company should have an over-all equity in equipment greater than the collateral margin if its entire debt were secured.[13]

If working capital and debt ratio are not of such great importance in credit analysis for a motor carrier, what is of importance? The ability and integrity of management make up the primary credit requirement.[14] The ability of management is reflected in earnings and in management's profitable operations of the business under reasonable economic conditions. From an analysis of a carrier's income statements can be obtained a reasonably accurate estimate of future available earnings. Such an estimate should include also a survey of the nature of the area served by the motor carrier and the type of

[12] Speech by K. R. Cravens, Vice-President, Mercantile-Commerce Bank and Trust Company of St. Louis, Missouri, before the American Trucking Associations, Inc., Cincinnati, Ohio, January 16, 1946.

[13] William J. Chapman, "Motor Carriers Provide Opportunities for Good Bank Loans," *Banker's Monthly*, June, 1948.

[14] Cravens, *op. cit.*

business solicited by the motor carrier, so that future traffic potentials may be reasonably forecast for several years in the light of past business. A record of stability in management aids a lending institution in estimating future probabilities.

Against revenue trends, the trend of expenses has to be balanced. Managerial ability, again, is of prime importance, with past performance a practical guide. In the eyes of a lending institution, depreciation policy is very important and should be examined thoroughly. Rates of depreciation are examined in relation to service conditions. Maintenance of equipment is closely related to profitable carrier operations; and, in addition, a financing institution depends upon the carrier's maintenance policies to preserve the value of the equipment collateral.

Care should be exercised that the debt matures in amounts that can be handled by the motor carrier without difficulty. Too often, carriers are forced by financing institutions to concentrate too large a portion of their debt maturities within too short a period of time. As a result, revenue operations cannot provide funds for orderly payment. A piece of equipment with a 6-year service life, earning 10 per cent on its average depreciated value, will not pay for itself for more than 4 years. Financed on a 25 per cent down payment, this period can be shortened to a little more than 3 years. For a lending institution to require that such a piece of equipment be financed on an 18-month pay-out schedule is to call for payment of funds other than those produced by revenue. A selective credit analysis for an individual motor carrier should consider, in determining the length of maturities, the life of equipment, management, coverage, and other credit factors. Credit periods of 3–5 years should be justified for heavy equipment, although on a selective basis some carriers may warrant only 2–3 years.

In making loans to motor carriers, the lending institutions must give careful attention to collateral. This is true primarily because loans are repaid out of revenue, not by the liquidation of assets, as in other businesses which have reasonably high accounts receivable and inventory. As has been pointed out also, motor carriers usually have little or no working capital, and their debt ratios are high. Careful attention is given, then, to the life of the equipment in determining maturities. Payments on a monthly basis need not be the same for the life of the loan. If the original credit is based on a variety of equipment—light, medium, and heavy—payments in the early months may be heavier than those of the later months. In that manner, dependence is not placed on light equipment to serve as collateral beyond the middle period of its service life, though such equipment continues to serve as collateral. Also to be considered in such a scheduling of maturities is the fact that lower payments are made in the later stages of the loan, when maintenance costs are higher and collateral value of the equipment lower.

Motor carriers would like to see smaller down payments in equipment financing. However, a piece of equipment operating with average profitability will not completely pay for itself within the time limits of desirable loan maturities unless there is a substantial down payment.[15] On the other hand, a 25 per cent down payment, which is often required, may have a restrictive effect on the current cash position which proper financing is designed to prevent. Some lending institutions have ruled that if a carrier has a substantial equity in the majority of its operating equipment, it is not necessary to require a full down payment. Down payments of 10 per cent to 25 per cent appear desirable, although some carriers receive 100 per cent financed loans by giving a lien on some of their debt-free equipment instead of a down payment.

Trucks, truck tractors, and trailers satisfy all requirements for equipment security better than almost any other commercially used manufactured products.[16] There is a constant market for them which is more stable and broader than the market for most used commercial or industrial equipment; and they are moved easily to the best markets. The service life of such equipment may be estimated very closely, and it seldom has been subject to obsolescence so great as to cut short expected service life. Damaged equipment can usually be put into salable condition, and repair service and repair parts are readily available.

In obtaining any long-term credit from a lending institution, the motor carrier may expect that the institution will require certain warranties, which should cover such conditions as the following:[17]

1. Maintenance of financial condition of motor carrier
2. Restrictions on further borrowing
3. Restrictions on salaries, dividends, withdrawals, and the like
4. Subordination of debt to owners

Naturally, there is some difference in the analysis procedure involving the purchase of a single unit by an individual as compared

[15] Chapman, *op. cit.*

[16] *Ibid.*

[17] Cravens, *op. cit.*

with the purchase of a fleet by a motor carrier. The individual purchase of a unit can be made on quite flexible terms, dependent upon such factors as the purchaser's previous trucking experience, his credit record, the purpose for which the equipment is to be used, and the like. There are many owner-operators who purchase a truck tractor or a truck tractor and trailer unit as individuals and operate such equipment in regular service for a regulated motor carrier, which fact has influence in the granting of credit for the purchase of such equipment.

Lenders often have not distinguished between equipment which is purchased by a motor carrier authorized to operate by the Interstate Commerce Commission and the owner-operator who owns one or more units and leases it, or them, to a carrier. One bank during a 10-year period from 1941 to 1951 loaned more than $35 million for the purchase of motor-carrier equipment. The losses of principal from these loans were less than $20,000, all of which were incurred on loans to individual owner-operators.[18]

Terms of credit for the financing of used equipment must of necessity be more stringent. With equipment serving as collateral, the service life of the equipment will have to be determined. Substantial down payments and short-term maturities would appear to be desirable in financing of this kind.

When it is necessary to refinance equipment loans, the matter of maturities is important. Loans which are refinanced are usually paid on a monthly basis, but, like the original equipment loans, such payments do not have to be uniform for the period of the loan but may be larger during the early months than in the later period. A carrier which has heavy current debts may need refinancing, but most lending institutions are very careful in considering such loans to determine fully the nature and service life of the security which is to be used.

CREDIT CRITERIA

It is difficult to establish specific criteria to meet every situation involving the granting of credit to motor carriers. The consideration of able management is of prime importance. In addition, the following standards receive thorough attention:[19]

---

[18] Regular Common Carrier Conference, *Financing the Motor Carrier Industry* (Washington, D.C., 1952), p. 36.

[19] A summary of a Dun and Bradstreet bulletin appearing in *Transport Topics,* December 19, 1949, p. 23.

1. Consistent record of earnings after all charges
2. Reasonably steady flow of income
3. Normally, a balance replacement program, so that repairs and replacements do not constitute a burden on future operations
4. Sufficient cash together with other liquid assets, including receivables, to meet payroll and other monthly expenses
5. Long-term debt spread over a sufficient period of time so that income after ordinary expenses and taxes, but before depreciation, is sufficient to meet amortization requirements

LEGAL INSTRUMENTS

Equipment notes can be made upon the security of chattel mortgages, conditional sales agreements, or leases, usually with the option to purchase at the expiration of the lease. Lease agreements for purchase of equipment are not uncommon in motor-carrier financing. The form of legal instrument to be used for any financing must be based on consideration of state laws and other circumstances. Because the conditional sales contract gives the lender a title claim instead of a mortgage, it is the most favored instrument in the majority of states for loans on new equipment.[20] It cannot be used for refinancing, and in some states it is not sufficient for collateral purposes because foreclosure requires the cancellation of the debt.

Under a conditional sales contract the buyer makes specific payments and acquires ownership rights in the vehicle. When the payments specified in the contract are completed, the title is vested in the purchaser. In effect, under the conditional sales contract, the purchaser acquires a contingent interest but does not become the full owner until all of the required payments are made.

When the security is a chattel mortgage, the ownership of the vehicle is held by the borrower subject to the mortgage lien. Under a purchase money chattel mortgage, title is held by the borrower but is pledged immediately to the lender until completion of all required payments. A promissory note may or may not serve as evidence of the debt covered by a chattel mortgage. If there is such a note, its payment is secured by pledge of the equipment which is described in the chattel mortgage. The borrower, of course, has possession of the equipment, but his free ownership is limited by the provisions of the mortgage which continues in effect until all of the payments or other requirements in the mortgage have been satisfied.

A bailment lease is another type of lien instrument which may be

---

[20] Chapman, *op. cit.*

used. Even though it is written in the form of a lease, this instrument provides for the title to be passed to the lessee or borrower upon completion of the scheduled payments.

QUESTIONS AND PROBLEMS

1. Trace the early development of the motor truck. Is there any specialization in the production of trucks?
2. Enumerate the advantages of truck trailers.
3. What does the fact that there is a truck-trailer manufacturer which produces 6,000 "standard" models mean (a) to the motor carrier, and (b) to the truck-trailer manufacturer?
4. Define a 6 × 6, a 4 × 4, a 6 × 4, and a 4 × 2.
5. Describe a truck tractor and a semitrailer in conformance with the SAE standard vehicle nomenclature.
6. List the various body types, and define them in accordance with the SAE standard vehicle nomenclature.
7. Assume that you are a banker who has decided to finance motor-carrier equipment. What factors are present today in the motor-carrier industry, as compared with 20 years ago, that might influence your decisions?
8. Define and differentiate between vendor credit and selective credit.
9. List the warranties that the motor carrier may be required to make before obtaining long-term credit from a lending institution for the financing of equipment.
10. What are the standards of credit that receive thorough attention before the granting of credit to motor carriers?
11. What are some of the current trends in power units used in trucks?
12. Discuss the effects of the shiftable tandem axle and the larger cube trailer upon motor carriers? Shippers?

5. TYPES OF CARRIERS

▀▀▀

MOTOR carriers of property can be classified according to a number of different bases. Many of these classifications will be listed and described in order to familiarize the reader with a number of the operations in the motor-carrier industry. The Interstate Commerce Commission, acting under Section 204 (c) of the Motor Carrier Act,[1] adopted the following classification in 1937 after a national investigation:

CLASSIFICATION OF MOTOR CARRIERS OF PROPERTY

I. By type of carrier:
1. Common carriers of property
2. Contract carriers of property
3. Private carriers of property
4. Brokers of property transportation
5. Exempt carriers

II. By type of service in which engaged:
   A. *Regular route, scheduled service.* A regular route scheduled service carrier is any person which undertakes to transport property or any class or classes of property in interstate or foreign commerce by motor vehicle for compensation between fixed termini and over a regular route or routes upon established or fixed schedules.
   B. *Regular route, nonscheduled service.* A regular route nonscheduled service carrier is any person which undertakes to transport property or any class or classes of property in interstate or foreign commerce by motor vehicle for compensation between fixed termini and over a regular route or routes at intermittent intervals and not upon an established or fixed schedule.

---

[1] This section of the Motor Carrier Act of 1935 provided that the Interstate Commerce Commission could establish classification of brokers and carriers as the special nature of the service performed required; this was accomplished in 2 MCC 703 (1937). The Motor Carrier Act was later incorporated into Part II of the Interstate Commerce Act.

C. *Irregular route, radial service.* An irregular route radial service carrier is any person which undertakes to transport property or any class or classes of property in interstate or foreign commerce by motor vehicle for compensation over irregular routes from a fixed base point or points to points or places located within such radial area as shall have been fixed and authorized by the Interstate Commerce Commission in a certificate of public convenience and necessity or permit, or from any point located within such radial area to such carrier's fixed base point or points.

D. *Irregular route, nonradial service.* An irregular route nonradial service carrier is any person which undertakes to transport property or any class or classes of property in interstate or foreign commerce by motor vehicle for compensation over irregular routes between points or communities located within such general territory as shall have been defined geographically and authorized in a certificate of public convenience and necessity or permit, and any other points or communities located within the same general territory without respect to a hub community or a fixed base point of operation.

E. *Local cartage service.* A local cartage carrier is any person which undertakes to transport property or any class or classes of property by motor vehicle for compensation when such transportation is performed in interstate or foreign commerce wholly within a municipality or between contiguous municipalities or within a zone adjacent to and commercially a part of any such municipality or municipalities.

III. By type of commodities transported:
1. Carriers of general freight
2. Carriers of household goods
3. Carriers of heavy machinery
4. Carriers of liquid petroleum products
5. Carriers of refrigerated liquid products
6. Carriers of refrigerated solid products
7. Carriers engaged in dump trucking
8. Carriers of agricultural commodities
9. Carriers of motor vehicles
10. Carriers engaged in armored truck service
11. Carriers of building materials
12. Carriers of films and associated commodities
13. Carriers of forest products
14. Carriers of mine ore, not including coal
15. Carriers engaged in retail store delivery service
16. Carriers of explosives or dangerous articles
17. Carriers of specific commodities, not subgrouped

This classification enables the Interstate Commerce Commission to have a system of identification for any motor carrier. For example, a motor carrier transporting household goods over irregular routes in radial service, which is a common carrier, is classified as a Common Carrier, Class C–2. A motor common carrier transporting new automobiles over irregular routes in radial service is classified as a Common Carrier, Class C–9.

The regulation of interstate for-hire trucking was placed under the jurisdiction of the Interstate Commerce Commission in 1935 with the passage of the Motor Carrier Act. Under this act, all interstate motor carriers are subject to safety regulations, and a number are subject to economic regulation as well.[2] The various states regulate intrastate highway transportation.

CLASSIFICATION BY GROSS REVENUE

The Interstate Commerce Commission also classifies for statistical purposes the motor carriers which are subject to its jurisdiction on the basis of gross revenue. A Class I motor carrier is one that has gross revenue of $200,000 or more per year; a Class II carrier, $50,000–$200,000 per year; and a Class III motor carrier, less than $50,000.[3]

Class I motor carriers of property in 1953 constituted 13 per cent of the total interstate regulated for-hire motor carriers of property. This small segment, however, accounted for about 79 per cent of the total revenue of all regulated motor carriers of property.

FOR-HIRE AND PRIVATE CARRIERS

A workable classification used for differentiating between the various kinds of motor carriers is that of for-hire carriers and private carriers. The for-hire carriers are those carriers which engage in transportation for compensation of one or more classes of freight that is the property of others. The for-hire group embraces the common, the contract, and certain exempt carriers. A brief explanation of each of these groups of carriers follows.

COMMON CARRIERS

The motor-vehicle common carrier is defined by statute as any person which holds itself out to the general public to engage in the

---

[2] Interstate Commerce Commission regulation and state regulation of motor carriers are discussed in a later chapter.

[3] Prior to 1950 a different classification applied under which the division was: over $100,000, Class I; $25,000–$100,000, Class II; and under $25,000, Class III. A comparison of statistics for the periods prior and subsequent to 1950 is not exactly precise.

transportation of property by motor vehicle over regular or irregular routes in interstate or foreign commerce. A common carrier is granted a certificate of public convenience and necessity by the Interstate Commerce Commission which constitutes its operating authority.[4] Common carriers range from the carrier of general commodities to a specialized type of carrier, such as a carrier of household goods. One specialized common carrier is certificated to haul garments from New York City to all points in the United States. This carrier[5] transports soft goods on hangers for new stores, frequently transporting the entire initial stock for a new store, as well as transporting daily shipments to numerous points including Los Angeles and San Francisco. Substantial savings to the manufacturers are made possible through this operation, since it eliminates the use of cartons and the need for pressing and steaming upon arrival. Some of the specialized types of operation are covered in subsequent chapters.

On April 1, 1955, there were 15,686 motor common carriers of property certificated by the Interstate Commerce Commission.[6] The for-hire common carriers constitute the predominant segment of interstate property-carrying for-hire motor carriers which are subject to economic regulation by the Interstate Commerce Commission. The material in this text emphasizes and deals later in more detail with the many aspects of the common-carrier operations in general commodities.

There are two types of common-carrier operation by the general commodity hauler that should be noted. These are distributive operations and key-point operations. The distributive operation is the type in which the motor carrier performs a distribution service in many small towns and communities. This operation is inherently more expensive to conduct because the charges per unit are higher. Such carriers have a network of routes serving local areas where the carrier is engaged in assembly and distribution service. The operator may be unable to secure as much outgoing traffic from a small community as it carries in, and unit charges are higher. Key-point operation is between key points, such as two cities, in which a truckload is dispatched from one key point and continues all the way through to the other key point. This type of operation is one that secures heavy and balanced loads. Moving traffic only between these key points holds costs at a minimum. The operator of a key-point operation

---

[4] Interstate Commerce Act, Section 203 (a) 14.

[5] Gilbert Carrier Corporation.

[6] Section of Certificates, Bureau of Motor Carriers.

charges the same rates as the operator of a distributive type of operation, but the margin of profit should be greater for the key-point operator. Common carriers operate over regular and irregular routes as specified in their certificate. They issue a bill of lading or receipt for goods which is uniform for all shippers served.

CONTRACT CARRIERS

The contract carrier is the second type of for-hire carrier and may be defined as any person that, under individual contract or agreement, engages in transportation for compensation by motor vehicle over any route in interstate or foreign commerce.[7] The interstate contract carrier's operating authority is contained in a permit issued by the Interstate Commerce Commission. The contract carrier makes an individual contract with one or more shippers. It is essentially an independent contractor whose undertaking of transportation service is defined and limited by an individual contract which calls for a service specialized to meet the peculiar needs of a particular shipper or a limited number of shippers and operates to make the motor carrier virtually a part of each shipper's organization.[8] A contract carrier then will pick and choose among shippers those whom it will serve, and this may be done by choosing any particular segment of traffic desired, provided it is within the scope of its operating rights. It may legally refuse to handle any other class of traffic. There were 2,646 contract carriers which had been issued permits and were subject to regulation by the Interstate Commerce Commission by April 1, 1955.[9]

A contract carrier may be any type of commodity hauler. One type may be a contract carrier which performs a distribution service interstate from warehouse or rail terminals to retail outlets. Another type of contract carrier is one that furnishes vehicles and drivers to specific shippers for their exclusive use in the transportation of their commodities between plants of the shipper to the warehouse or jobbers. This is often termed "dedication of the vehicle to the shipper" and is a substitute for private carriage. Other contract carriers may serve different types of shippers but serve relatively few shippers of each type. The vehicles are not used exclusively for any one haul. However, each shipper is guaranteed that a certain number of vehi-

---

[7] Interstate Commerce Act, Section 203 (a) 15.

[8] *Transporation Activities of Midwest Transfer Co.*, 49 MCC 390 (1949).

[9] Section of Certificates, Bureau of Motor Carriers.

cles will be available when needed. Contract carriage of intercity tonnage is becoming increasingly important in the transportation of specific commodities.

There are certain differences in operations which are reflected in operating costs between contract carriers and common carriers. Contract carriers usually have no terminal facilities for platform handling of freight because they make a contract only for volume freight —which means, in effect, truckload lots. They go to the shippers' plants, load the freight, and take it directly to the consignees; and, therefore, they have no need for terminal facilities for freight handling. The documents used may also be different. Figure 5–1 is a form used in lieu of a bill of lading in a dedication of the vehicle to the shipper type of contract carriage.

The revenues per ton-mile received by Class I common and contract carriers is shown in Table 5–1. The average revenue per ton-

TABLE 5–1

REVENUE PER TON-MILE—CLASS I INTERCITY
COMMON AND CONTRACT CARRIERS OF PROPERTY

Year	Common (Cents)	Contract (Cents)
1942.	3.810	3.079
1943.	3.820	3.152
1944.	4.066	3.000
1945.	4.134	3.207
1946.	4.286	3.892
1947.	4.847	3.888
1948.	5.149	3.803
1949.	5.239	4.301
1950.	5.009	4.280
1951.	5.174	4.170
1952.	5.615[r]	4.459[r]
1953.	6.094[e]	4.548[e]

[e] Estimated.   [r] Revised.

Source: Bureau of Transport Economics and Statistics, Interstate Commerce Commission, *Monthly Comment on Transportation Statistics,* July 19, 1954, p. 14.

mile of contract carriers is consistently below that of common carriers because of differences in services and costs.

The contractual terms will have a definite influence on the rate schedule which the contract carrier will charge. A contract may be drawn in which the carrier is relieved of all liability regarding the shipment, in which case the shipper would expect to find this reflected in lower rates. On the other hand, the contract can be drawn requiring the contract carrier to assume full common-carrier liability for the shipments which, likewise, will be reflected in the rates.

Warehouse_____Date Delivered_____Date Loaded_____
Consigned To_____ Truck - Class_____No._____
Location_____R. T. Mileage_____
How Shipped_____ Scale Weight_____
                                                              Trip Time_____
          N. S._____   N. S._____Mty Man Hrs._____
Seals - S. S._____End Door - S. S._____Car Number_____
Pieces Billed_____Date Started_____Refused_____
Pieces Not Del'd._____   Short_____
Pieces Delivered_____Date Finished_____Over_____

| KEY | NUMBER OF PIECES | | | | | TOTAL | C'RGE | CARTAGE |
NO.	GROC.	PROD.	BAKERY	MEAT	TOTAL	WEIGHT	RATE	AMOUNT
TOTAL							XXXXX	

Truckman

Driver's Signature

We hereby certify that the above de-scribed meat or meat food products which are offered for shipment in interstate or foreign commerce, have been U.S. inspected and passed by Department of Agriculture, are so marked, and at this date are sound, healthful, wholesome and fit for human food.

THE GREAT ATLANTIC & PACIFIC TEA CO.

"This is to certify that the above named articles are properly described, and are pack-ed and marked and are in proper condition for transportation according to the regulations prescribed by the Interstate Commerce Com-mission and the Commandant of the Coast Guard".

THE GREAT ATLANTIC & PACIFIC TEA CO.

FIG. 5–1.   Form used in lieu of a bill of lading by a dedication of the vehicle to the shipper type of contract carrier.

The liability of a contract carrier, unlike common carriers, is entirely dependent upon its contractual arrangements with the shipper. The contract carrier may contract under any terms except for total exemption from liability because of its negligence. This right to contract freely is not affected by the Interstate Commerce Act. Thus, dependent upon the contractual arrangements, a contract carrier may be liable for goods in transit merely as a bailee for hire, or, on the other hand, it may be liable to the same extent as a common carrier. As a bailee for hire, it owes the duty only to exercise reasonable care in handling the freight. The carrier would not be liable, therefore, for accidents which were not its fault, but it would be liable if it failed to exercise reasonable care to protect the goods. Actually, the majority of transportation contracts provide for full liability on the part of the carrier. The Commission does not require contracts of contract carriers to include provisions concerning the carrier's liability. It considered this general subject in *Ex parte No. MC–12* and felt that it had no jurisdiction over this aspect of the contract.

If an intrastate movement is involved and there is a question

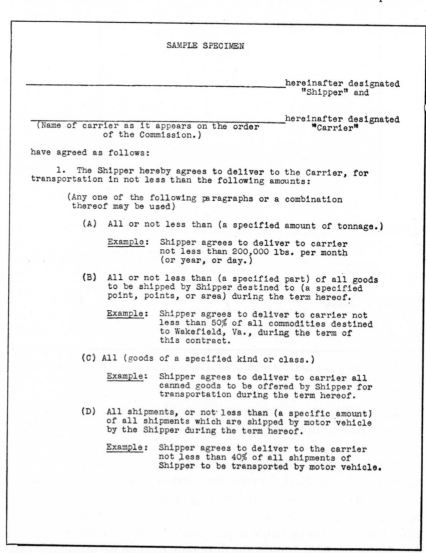

FIG. 5–2. Sample specimen of a contract between the shipper and contract motor carrier.

about the liability of the carrier, the state law would apply. Moreover since there is no overriding federal statute governing the liabilities of contract carriers, state laws would apply to both interstate and intrastate movements. In any particular case, the laws of the state having jurisdiction over the matter would have to be consulted.

A sample form of a contract is shown in Figure 5–2. Characteristics of a contract are: (1) it is bilateral in nature; (2) the shipper should agree to furnish the commodities to be transported by specifying the amount of tonnage to the point, points, or areas named;

- 2 -

2. The Shipper agrees to pay to the Carrier as compensation for such transportation as follows:

Articles or Commodities	Origin	Destination	Rate
:	:	:	:
:	:	:	:
:	:	:	:

(Commodities and territory in contract should conform strictly with those authorized in the order or orders of the Commission.)

3. (Here set forth any rules, conditions or provisions which affect the charges, the value of the service or the extent of the service to be performed.)

4. The Carrier agrees that he will transport said articles or commodities according to the terms, conditions, and for the compensation specified herein.

5. Any shipments in excess of the minimum amount herein specified, which shall be tendered by the Shipper to the Carrier, will be accepted by the Carrier for transportation up to the capacity of his equipment, and charges for such excess shipments shall be at the rate herein specified, and said shipments will be transported in compliance with all of the terms of this contract.

6. It is further agreed that this contract shall continue in force for a period of _____years (or months) from the date hereof, subject, however, to the right of either of the parties hereto to cancel or terminate same upon _____days' (not less than ten) prior written notice to the other party.

The parties hereto have set their hands and executed this agreement in duplicate on this _____day of _____, 19_____.

_____
(Shipper)

_____
(Carrier)

FIG. 5–2 Continued

(3) it provides for a series of shipments within a given period of time; (4) it includes the rates and charges and the method by which the actual amount payable to the carrier can be determined; (5) it contains an agreement by the shipper to pay the specified compensation; and (6) it provides for transportation by the carrier for a particular shipper under the rules, conditions, or provisions which are set forth in the contract. The Commission requires that the contracts must be in writing and copies shall be preserved by carriers as long as they are in force and for one year thereafter. However, one group of contract carriers, those carrying bullion, currency, jewels, and other precious or very valuable articles, does not have to execute contracts. These contract carriers which offer armored-car service do have to file schedules of their minimum rates and charges, however.[10]

The contract should be between the carrier and the party who pays the carrier's transportation charges because the payment of the transportation charge is evidence that the person who pays is the one who controls the transportation.[11] Subsequent to this ruling, the Commission held that, when several consignees pay the carrier, although making no arrangements with it for transportation, these arrangements being made by the consignor who guarantees the charges in case of default by consignee, such a contract is permissible.[12]

The shipper who makes the contract with the carrier cannot offer to others the privilege of shipping commodities under the contract which he holds, although there has been no formal ruling on this matter. When a parent corporation has a contract with a contract carrier and a subsidiary company wishes to ship commodities with the same contract carrier, separate contractual arrangements should be made by the subsidiary.

The contract carrier may add or substitute contracts within the scope of its permit. Therefore, the number of contracts may not be limited.[13]

EXEMPT CARRIERS

The third group of for-hire carriers of property is the exempt carrier group. These carriers are engaged in moving certain commodities for compensation interstate; but, under the provisions of the In-

---

[10] *Contracts of Contract Carriers,* 11 MCC 693 (1938).

[11] Administrative Rule No. 76, February 23, 1939.

[12] *Minnehan Contract Carrier Application,* 26 MCC 533 (1940).

[13] *Butcher Contract Carrier Application,* 1 MCC 485 (1937).

terstate Commerce Act, they are specifically exempt from economic regulation by the Interstate Commerce Commission. These are property carriers using motor vehicles controlled and operated by farmers engaged in the transporation of agricultural commodities or farm supplies; vehicles controlled and operated by co-operative associations, as defined in the Agricultural Marketing Act; vehicles used in carrying livestock, fish, or agricultural commodities; vehicles used exclusively in the distribution of newspapers; vehicles used in the transportation of property incidental to transportation by aircraft; vehicles used in transportation of property wholly within a municipality or zone adjacent to or commercially a part of such a municipality; and vehicles used in casual, occasional, or reciprocal transportation of property in interstate or foreign commerce by a person not engaged in transportation by motor carriers as a regular business.

It is estimated that there were over 50 per cent more exempt carriers operating interstate in 1954 than there were common and contract interstate carriers of property regulated by the Interstate Commerce Commission.[14] They operate about 243,000 vehicles. Most of these exempt carriers are engaged in carrying agricultural commodities, livestock, and fish. Exempt interstate motor carriers are in their operations common or contract motor carriers but are excluded from economic regulation by the Interstate Commerce Act. Therefore, they do not have to secure operating authority in the form of certificates or permits from the Interstate Commerce Commission. They are subject only to safety regulations.

The most important exemption in intercity transportation is the one covering agricultural commodities (not including manufactured products thereof), livestock, and fish. The volume of traffic which moves in exempt transportation has grown substantially, but there are no over-all figures to show what the total volume is. A national survey of the transportation of fresh vegetables showed that a little more than half of such vegetables were moved by truck.[15] A substantial portion of this traffic is transported by exempt carriers.

Much of the transportation of agricultural commodities is over long distances. Figure 5–3 shows a general traffic pattern for transporting vegetables by truck from some of the major producing areas to consuming areas. Apples from the state of Washington move by truck distances of more than a thousand miles. Eggs are moved from Iowa and Minnesota to the East Coast and the West Coast. Lettuce

---

[14] Information supplied by Bureau of Motor Carriers.

[15] Defense Transport Administration, *Transportation of Fresh Vegetables*, 1952.

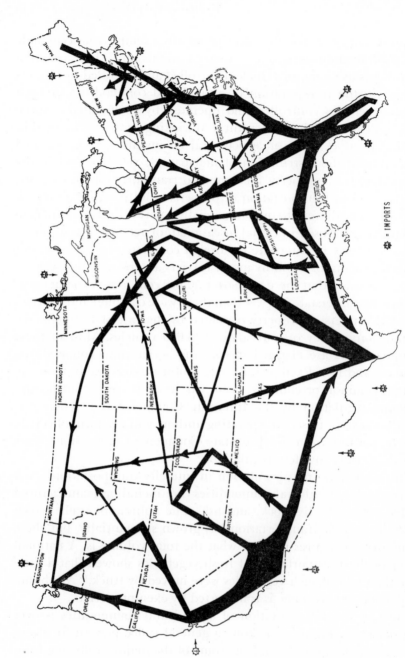

✿ = IMPORTS

FIG. 5–3. General traffic pattern for transporting vegetables by truck from some major producing areas to consuming areas.
Source: Defense Transport Administration, Transportation of Fresh Vegetables, 1952, p. 25.

is transported from California to Chicago, and snap green beans from Florida to Minnesota where they are canned.

There has been a steady increase in the percentage of citrus fruits and vegetables which have moved from Florida by truck. In 1939–40, 21 per cent of the car-lot shipments of citrus fruits moved by truck, whereas in 1952–53, it was 49 per cent. Vegetables for these same years were 40 per cent and 54 per cent, respectively.[16] The majority of these truck shipments are by exempt haulers.

Many of these exempt haulers are owner-operators who own one unit. In other instances, several units may be owned by one individual and operated in this type of service. The arrangements for truck movement of exempt agricultural commodities in Florida are usually made by brokers. These brokers are not subject to regulation by the Interstate Commerce Commission as are brokers of general commodities. The truck operator contacts or calls the broker's office notifying him that he is available for transporting exempt commodities to some particular point. The broker then makes the arrangements with the shipper; and such matters as late arrival, damaged goods, and similar details are handled by the broker with the agricultural hauler.

There are more trucks hired by buyers of citrus products than hired by the shipper, but the arrangements for both of these are usually made through the truck broker.[17] Agreements with some shippers require delivery within a certain number of hours, with the truck operator not being paid if the deadline is not met. The truck broker's fee is usually secured from the truck operator and varies from 5 to 10 per cent of the amount that the trucker is to receive for the haul.

In California truck brokerage has not developed to the extent that it has in Florida. Therefore, truck operators, in many instances, go directly to the prospective shipper and make individual arrangements for the movement of exempt commodities. This has resulted in pickups at a number of points in order to secure a full load.

Some exempt haulers follow a regular pattern of operation, that is, they operate from one general area to another area. There are others, however, which are more migratory in nature. For example, an exempt hauler of agricultural commodities in Michigan carried a load of fresh onions to Florida. Upon finding there was not an

---

[16] *Docket 31342, Proposed Increase Refrigeration Charges,* 1954.

[17] Department of Agriculture, *The Marketing and Transportation Situation,* May 13, 1954, p. 15.

immediate return load of citrus products to Michigan, he carried a load to Washington, D.C., since he wanted to do some sightseeing in Washington. He then leased his unit to a certificated carrier and carried a load of nonexempt commodities back to Florida, and then carried exempt commodities back to Michigan.

The present exempt carriers are considerably more responsible than ones which operated some years ago. In Florida all motor vehicles domiciled there are covered by public liability insurance. Approximately 90 per cent of the exempt truckers carry insurance to protect the owner of the commodities.[18]

Although rates of exempt carriers are not subject to regulation by the Interstate Commerce Commission, there have been several instances in which exempt carriers serving the same general origin and destination points have agreed among themselves to charge not less than a specific rate based on a minimum. However, what has sometimes happened is that some new single-truck operator enters the field who feels that the only way that he can get business and meet the payments on his truck is to make a lower rate, which he does. The other carriers then reduce their rates. However, most of these carriers establish a minimum below which they will not go and explain the fact to the shipper. This minimum which the carriers impose is in order to insure continued operation of the size and type of equipment which they possess.

Approximately 79 per cent of the cattle, 82 per cent of the calves, 85 per cent of the hogs, and 52 per cent of the sheep and lambs move from ranges, farms, and feed lots to markets and slaughtering points by trucks in exempt transportation.[19]

Livestock hauling tends to have a somewhat lower average haul than that of agricultural commodities. In livestock hauling, a conventional bill of lading is not used by most carriers. At the time that the shipment is picked up at the farm no receipt is given to the farmer. The livestock yards, however, provide a form which is a truck consignment (see Fig. 5–4). One of these tickets is filled out for each shipper. This will contain information as to the livestock picked up by the trucker and delivered by him, as well as the rate per 100 pounds and other information.

Livestock haulers are domiciled in the community in which they operate and hold themselves out as common carriers. The rates

[18] House Interstate and Foreign Commerce Committee, *Trip Leasing*, 83d Cong., 1st sess. (Washington, D.C.: U.S. Government Printing Office, 1953), p. 330.

[19] Automobile Manufacturers Association, *Motor Truck Facts* (Detroit, 1954), p. 46.

which they charge one farmer in a community will be the same as they charge another for the same minimum so, although they are free to establish rates which vary, their rates tend to be fixed rates for the same general weights.

TRUCKERS' CODE NO._____

BE SURE THAT ALL CARBON COPIES ARE READABLE

The Union Stock Yard & Transit Company of Chicago

TRUCK CONSIGNMENT

(Make separate ticket for each owner and for each specie, except cattle and calves, before entering yards.)

Date_____ Gate_____ Con. No.

Commission Agency _____

Owner _____ R.F.D._____

Town_____ County_____ State_____

Truckman_____License No._____

Address _____

Trucking cwt.
Rate_____ head

Instructions_____

HOME COUNT		YARDED			UNLOADING COUNT (IF DIFFERENT)		
		BLK.	PEN	DIV.	CRIP.	DEAD	TAG No.
	CATTLE						
	CALVES						
	HOGS						
	SHEEP						

Unloading Count is Correct _____, Truckman

Number of Head Correct _____ Yarded_____

Del'd_____ Rec'd in Good Order_____

Crip. Yarded Blk_____ Pen_____ Div_____ Dead in_____

FIG. 5–4. Truck consignment form used in livestock hauling.

Livestock haulers serving a particular livestock market may secure authority to transport certain specified nonexempt commodities for the return haul. The tendency, however, even if they possess such rights, is to lease their unit on the return from the livestock market to a certificated general commodity hauler, since the livestock hauler does not have a sales force nor the time to solicit business for the return haul. If the livestock hauler has a particularly heavy demand for his service, he may not even lease his truck for the return haul because this ties up his equipment longer, since he has to go to the terminal to load the freight. Therefore, he may make the return trip empty.

Another important commodity which moves in exempt transportation is that of fish. This is transported in refrigerated equipment and, like agricultural commodities, travels substantial distances.

Many exempt carriers maintain no terminals, whereas others, such as livestock haulers, may have a concentration yard which serves as their terminal. When there are but two or three head of livestock to be shipped by one farmer, the stock may be picked up in a small truck and transported to the livestock hauler's loading area, where the stock may be loaded with others in an over-the-road vehicle.

It should not be assumed that all agricultural commodities are transported by exempt carriers. As a result of two court cases,[20] the Interstate Commerce Commission early in 1951 permitted carriers of so-called "nonexempt" items, that is, carriers to which operating authority has been granted, to use their vehicles for transporting agricultural commodities providing the exempt commodities are not moved in the same vehicle at the same time with a nonexempt commodity. Thus, when a regulated carrier finds it to its advantage to move an exempt commodity, perhaps on a return haul, it may do so. A certain amount of this traffic is moved by regulated carriers, but it appears so far to be small.

PRIVATE CARRIERS

Private motor carriers are the second group of carriers in this general classification of for-hire and private carriers. The private motor carrier is a person that transports in interstate or foreign commerce by motor vehicle property of which such person is the owner, lessee, or bailee when such transportation is for the purpose of sale, lease, rent, bailment, or in furtherance of any commercial enterprise.[21] This group requires no operating authority from the Interstate Commerce Commission, since it is not subject to economic regulation but only to safety regulation. Private motor carriers constitute the largest group of motor carriers of property. It is estimated that there were 119,197 private motor carriers of property in 1954 which operated about 767,456 vehicles.[22] There has been a rapid increase

---

[20] *ICC* v. *Dunn*, 166 F. 2d. 116 (1948); *ICC* v. *Service Trucking Co., Inc.*, 186 F. 2d. 400 (1951).

[21] Interstate Commerce Act, Section 203 (a) 17.

[22] Bureau of Motor Carriers.

in private carriage. The number of private trucks used in over-the-road transportation in 1953 was double the number used in 1945.[23]

A merchandising or manufacturing concern which provides its own motor transportation will maintain facilities adequate usually to handle its minimum transportation needs. In other words, if the volume is sufficient to move truckloads with some regularity, the company may decide to undertake private carriage. With the minimum transportation needs met, any additional transportation requirements will be placed by the company upon common carriers.

The final data of the 1947 census of manufactures shows that the industry group which embraced food and kindred products accounted for over half (57 per cent) the total number of trucks owned or leased by manufacturers in private operations. The second largest percentage was accounted for by the industry group embracing lumber and related products, which represented less than a sixth of the number of trucks in the food group and only 9.3 per cent of the total. Together, these two groups owned or leased about two thirds of all the private trucks reported.[24]

Many manufacturing and merchandising firms have become more transportation cost conscious during the past years. For example, a survey was made of a service wholesaler with a $12 million volume handling dry groceries with service to 3,500 customers in a 30-mile radius. This revealed that the annual delivery expense was $150,000, or 1.25 per cent of net sales, which is considered to be a very good average. On the other hand, it was felt that efficient management of delivery expenses would result in a saving of 20 per cent, or $30,000. A saving of this amount would be the equivalent of net profit on $3 million of new business.[25]

There are a number of reasons that prompt business organizations to conduct all or a part of their own trucking operations rather than to rely on for-hire carriers. The use of its own equipment (*a*) assures the ability to effectuate prompt and efficient delivery of rush orders to customers and thereby enhances goodwill; (*b*) assures absence of congestion at loading docks; (*c*) assures the safe arrival of goods not mixed with goods of other shippers and not exposed to extra or inexperienced handling; (*d*) assures on-time deliveries of finished

---

[23] *Traffic World*, December 12, 1953, p. 96.

[24] Bureau of Transport Economics and Statistics, *Monthly Comment on Transportation Statistics* (Washington, D.C., January 12, 1950), p. 10.

[25] Progress Report Number Two, *NAWGA—GMC Trucking Survey*, June 12, 1951.

goods at customers' doors and of raw materials and supplies at their plants; (*e*) makes possible the avoidance of expensive packaging; (*f*) eliminates the 3 per cent payment of excise tax on freight since it is a private operation; (*g*) makes possible the charging for the service of an amount equal to or exceeding the rate of common or contract carriers, thus making private carriage a self-supporting enterprise; and (*h*) provides flexibility through the freedom to operate wherever desired.

Some of the disadvantages of private carriage are: the cost of equipment, the cost of maintenance and difficulty in securing personnel capable of maintaining equipment properly (this may be handled by truck rental or truck leasing), the economic loss occasioned by operating the vehicle empty on return movements, and the burden on management of supervising a motor-carrier operation which is different from the normal business of the company.

A 1953 pilot survey of the Bureau of Census estimated that the volume of commodity movements for distances of 25 or more miles in private and exempt trucks is about 65 per cent of the total ton-miles of truck service.

PROPERTY BROKERS

Another type of operation which is not a carrier operation but which is subject to regulation by the Interstate Commerce Commission is that of property brokers. Brokerage became an incident of motor transportation long before the passage of the Motor Carrier Act in 1935. The preponderance of motor carriers of freight in those days were small operators possessing a limited amount of equipment and without a need for or the means to support an organization that would include salaried salesmen. Many of the carriers offered specialized services—for example, household-goods carriers operating in irregular-route service over a large area. Others operated out of their home base and did not feel that they could maintain even part-time salesmen at all of the points that they served; yet, in order to have efficiency of operation, they sought some way of securing loads between and from these points away from their home base. From these needs developed agencies, independent of both the shippers and the carriers, which were devoted to the solicitation of traffic to be moved by carriers selected by them and from whom they received a fee for their services. These became known as "motor transportation agents" or "brokers." Some states enacted laws regulating the business of these motor transportation agents which were not themselves engaged in transportation but which would make the necessary arrangements for or the selling of transportation. Some of the operations of the brokers in these earlier phases of the development of the motor-carrier industry were beneficial, but there were other instances of irresponsible persons resorting to exploitation of the carriers through excessive charges and certain other questionable practices. The Motor Carrier Act of 1935 set forth regulation of brokers in Section 203 (a) (18) and Section 221.

As defined by the Commission, a "broker means any person as defined in Section 203 (a) of the Interstate Commerce Act not included in the term 'motor carrier' and not a bona fide employee or agent of any such a carrier, who, as principal or agent, for compensation, sells or offers for sale transportation subject to Part II of the Interstate Commerce Act, other than transportation of passengers and their baggage, or makes any contract, agreement, or arrangement to provide, procure, furnish, or arrange for such transportation or shall hold himself out by advertisement, solicitation, or otherwise, as one who sells, provides, procures, contracts, or arranges for such transportation."[26]

The proviso in this definition is particularly important to household-goods carriers because there are many of them which have authority to perform a part of the transportation haul, but they may turn over the shipment at the origin point to a carrier which will take it all the way to destination. The proviso does not require such carriers to secure licenses as brokers. Motor common carriers which surrender to others for compensation shipments the line hauls of which they are not authorized to perform in whole or in part are brokers.

The act provided that the Commission could establish reasonable requirements with respect to licensing of brokers, their financial responsibilities, accounts, records, reports, operations, and practices which became effective in 1952. As of April 1, 1955, approximately eighty-four licenses had been issued to property brokers.[27]

CLASSES OF BROKERS

There are two main classes of brokers of property:

1. Brokers of household goods
2. Brokers of property other than household goods (freight brokers)
   a) Brokers of general commodities or general freight
   b) Brokers of special commodities

---

[26] *Practices of Property Brokers*, 53 MCC 633 (1951, became effective 1952).
[27] Bureau of Motor Carriers.

The majority of licenses have been issued to brokers of household goods. There are some differences that should be noted between the operations of the household-goods brokers and the freight brokers.

HOUSEHOLD-GOODS BROKERS	FREIGHT BROKERS
1. They serve a different type of shipper and deal primarily with householders who move very infrequently, many not more than once or twice in a lifetime.	1. They deal regularly with manufacturing or merchandising firms whose transportation requirements are recurring and who frequently require daily service.
2. Frequently, they perform related accessorial services, such as packing, crating, and storage.	2. They seldom perform accessorial services.
3. The carriers hired by household-goods brokers operate almost exclusively over irregular routes.	3. They employ carriers that operate over both regular and irregular routes.
4. The charges of household-goods brokers (not including those for accessorial services) are always considerably greater than those of freight brokers.	4. Their charges are considerably less than those of household-goods brokers.

There are two classes of so-called "nonbrokerage" services: (1) those which are supplied to shippers, such as warehousing, sorting, storage, preparation of shipments for moving, packing, crating, stenciling, checking freight bills, and handling claims with carriers; and (2) those supplied to carriers, such as arranging for or the leasing of vehicles by or for carriers, maintenance of dock or terminal facilities, performing pickup and delivery service, preparing, arranging, and collecting freight bills, and processing claims.

HOUSEHOLD-GOODS BROKERS

The business of household-goods brokers generally comes from telephone inquiries from shippers, whereupon an estimator is sent to the home of the shipper, where he estimates the space, weight, and charge of the shipment. If he is successful in getting the shipment, he prepares an order for the service or "booking," and the broker will secure a carrier with proper operating authority which can move the shipment at the desired time. There are two levels of rates published for two large groups of household-goods carriers which are available to the household-goods shippers and brokers. Tariffs carrying such rates are referred to as the "low" and "high" tariffs. One broker, who generally knows what carrier will be available to handle particular shipments, bases his estimates of charges on the "low" tariff; if it develops that a carrier operating under those rates is not available on the date of the pickup, the broker notifies the shipper and gives him the option of using a carrier operating under the "high" tariff or waiting until a carrier operating under the "low" tariff is available.[28]

If accessorial services, such as packing, crating, or storage, are furnished a shipper, the household-goods brokers will quote these as an addition to the transportation charge. The broker's charges are usually a percentage of the transportation charges; commissions vary from 20 per cent to 30 per cent, not including accessorial services. On prepaid shipments, the brokers generally deduct their fees and send the balance of the transportation charges to the carriers.

FREIGHT BROKERS

Generally, freight brokers deal with a limited number of carriers under written or oral contracts; and some perform for a flat charge nonbrokerage services, such as checking waybills for shippers, renting terminal space to carriers, and furnishing telephone service and office space to carriers. Some freight brokers own and operate freight terminals where less-than-truckload shipments are received and placed for the carrier to load. Their fees are usually a percentage of the transportation charges. This may be a fixed charge per 100 pounds, or it may be dependent upon the class of traffic or the value of business which is secured for a particular carrier. The freight charges are collected by the carriers, which are billed by the freight brokers for their fees on a weekly or monthly basis.

RULES AND REGULATIONS COVERING PROPERTY BROKERS

The Interstate Commerce Commission has prescribed rules and regulations governing the practices of brokers of transportation of property. A broker may not advertise in any manner to offer his service as a broker without showing in such advertisement his status as a broker in type as large as any other used in the same advertisement.

Brokers may not issue any bill of lading or freight bill in any name except that of a carrier, nor may a broker issue an order for service which does not clearly show the name and address of the

---

[28] *Practices of Property Brokers,* 49 MCC 282 (1949).

broker and the fact that the order is executed as a broker of transportation.

A broker may not charge or receive compensation from a motor carrier for brokerage service performed in connection with any shipment which he owns or in which he has a material interest or the routing of which he controls by reason of any affiliation with or non-brokerage relationship to the shipper, consignor, or consignee. Under this ruling, a shipper is not prohibited from hiring a broker to route all his traffic, but when such a nonbrokerage service is rendered for a shipper, the compensation for it may not be collected by the broker from the carrier. Additional rules are discussed in the chapter on regulation of motor carriers.

AGENTS AS DISTINGUISHED FROM FREIGHT BROKERS

There have been a number of occasions when the Commission has had to distinguish between a bona fide agent and a broker, as those terms are used in the act.[29] In one case, it was pointed out that "every broker is in a sense an agent, but not every agent is a broker. The chief distinguishing feature is that a broker generally acts in a certain sense as an agent for both parties to a particular transaction. Strict agency implies exclusiveness, whereas brokerage involves a holding out generally."[30]

A "bona fide agent," as distinguished from a broker, according to the Commission, is a person who is part of the normal organization of a motor carrier and performs his duties under the direction of the carrier pursuant to a pre-existing agreement with the carrier providing for a continuing relationship between them and precluding the exercise of discretion on the part of the agent in allocating traffic as between the principal and others.

COMMISSION AGENTS

Large motor common carriers have adopted the practice of using the pickup and delivery and platform services of local cartage companies in communities too small to warrant the establishment of a company-operated terminal. In many instances, the traffic is dropped off at the agency station by the over-the-road unit at hours of the day when the consignee's dock or plant is not open. These agents, called

---

[29] *Cain Broker Application,* 2 MCC 633 (1937); and *Copes Broker Application,* 27 MCC 161 (1940).

[30] *Copes Broker Application,* 27 MCC 161 (1940).

"commission agents," are paid for the work they render, such as collection and delivery, platform handling, and billing and collecting, on the basis of a certain compensation per 100 pounds, with the commission per 100 pounds varying with the weight of the shipment;

TABLE 5-2

ILLUSTRATION OF AGENCY CHARGES FOR TERMINAL SERVICE

(Collection and Delivery and Platform)

City or Town	Payments in Cents per 100 Pounds (1945)	Weight of Shipment (Pounds)
A........	8 cents	Any size
B........	8 cents	1–5,000
	3 cents	Over 5,000
C........	10 cents	1–149
	7 cents	150 and over
	3 cents	Truckload
D........	8 cents, with 10-cent minimum per shipment	Any size
E........	8 cents, with 10-cent minimum per shipment	Any size
G........	10 cents, with 10-cent minimum per shipment	Less than truckload
	5 cents	Truckload
H........	7 cents	1–5,000
	5 cents	5,001–10,000
	4½ cents	Over 10,000
I........	8 cents	1–8,000
	3½ cents	Over 8,000
J........	10 cents	1–5,000
	5 cents	Over 5,000
K........	10 cents	1–120
	9 cents	121–5,000
	3 cents	Truckload
L........	10 cents	1–5,000
	5 cents	5,001–20,000
	3 cents	Over 20,000
M........	10 cents, with 10-cent minimum per shipment	Any size
N........	8 cents	1–5,000
	5 cents	Over 5,000
O........	10 cents	1–5,000
	5 cents	5,001–10,000
	3 cents	Over 10,000

Source: Interstate Commerce Commission, Bureau of Transport Economics and Statistics, *Explanation of the Development of Motor Carrier Costs with Statement as to Their Meaning and Significance* (Washington, D.C., 1946), p. 81.

that is, the fee for a 300-pound shipment may be 8 cents per 100 pounds, but for a shipment of over 5,000 pounds, the fee may be 2 cents per 100 pounds. Table 5–2 shows the schedule of payments made by a carrier to commission agents at various points in the midwestern region.

FREIGHT FORWARDERS

The surface freight forwarder holds itself out to the public to provide a through-transportation service from point of receipt of shipment to the final destination in its own name and under its own responsibility. Freight forwarders are common carriers which have other regulated motor, rail, and water common carriers physically move their shipments for them. Therefore, freight forwarders are extensive purchasers of transportation. The over-the-road[31] movement is made in equipment not owned by the forwarder. The function of the freight forwarder is to combine numerous small shipments of individual consignors into consolidated consignments which move in carloads or truckloads, but its tariffs list through less-than-carload or less-truckload rates from origin to destination. The forwarder bears the cost of the transportation it employs, as well as the cost of solicitation, billing, platform handling, loading and unloading, and the investigation and payment of claims performed by it. Freight forwarders have, over a period of years, extensively used the services of motor common carriers.

There are a number of ways in which freight forwarders utilize motor common carriers, but these can be grouped into essentially three classes: (a) the movement of individual shipments from the consignor to the forwarder's terminal (concentration point) and delivery from the forwarder's terminal (break-bulk point) to the consignee prior and subsequent, respectively, to the transportation of such shipments as part of a consolidated consignment; (b) the movement of an aggregation of individual shipments in so-called truckloads between terminals preceding or following the carriage of consolidated consignments in carload by rail; and (c) the movement of an aggregation of individual shipments in so-called truckloads between terminals. It has been estimated that the motor common carriers of commodities receive on the average between 1 and 2 per cent of their revenues from freight forwarders' traffic. Many motor common carriers have agreements with one or more freight forwarders, and a few motor common carriers transport exclusively for the forwarders. The latter carriers are often referred to as "captive carriers," since their entire service can be rendered only on behalf of freight forwarders in accordance with their operating authority.

The basis of compensation has been developed by trial and error over a long period of time and follows no uniform pattern. Contracts between the freight forwarder and the motor common carrier have been negotiated in terms of traffic requirements of the particular service to be rendered, and seldom have these requirements been

---

[31] The term "over the road" is used interchangeably with "line haul" and means the same type of movement, that is, intercity movement of freight using heavy equipment.

the same between any two points. Some of the agreements are oral, and others are memoranda or letters confirming agreements made orally. Motor carriers have agreed to a lower basis of compensation where the freight-forwarder traffic moved in the direction in which the trucks would ordinarily be returning empty or with light loads. Some of the factors that have been considered in individual negotiations are labor costs, amount of light and bulky traffic, volume of movement, traffic flow, and competition among forwarders.

Section 409 was amended in 1950 to prohibit the publication and maintenance of joint rates between freight forwarders and motor common carriers after September 19, 1951, and to permit motor common carriers to perform certain transportation services for freight forwarders under contracts to be filed with the Commission.[32] The Commission issued regulations, effective September 20, 1951, governing the filing of contracts under Section 409 and permitted the acceptance, as substantial compliance with the regulations, of agreements between motor carriers and freight forwarders filed with the Commission prior to September 20, 1951. About 35,000 of these contracts had been filed with the Commission by 1955. One freight forwarder has more than 2,000 contracts on file.

On movements from a concentration point to a break-bulk point under the contract, payment for less-truckload lots may be at less than the published rates over any distance figure. However, payment for truckload lots may be at less than the published rates only when the distance is less than 450 miles.

Another type of rates are assembly and distribution rates published under Section 408. These are published rates in tariff form which are on file with the Interstate Commerce Commission and are not the result of negotiation. They are lower than those applicable at the same time between the same points on nonforwarder traffic. This results in a rate of payment to the motor carriers for the handling of freight-forwarder traffic which is generally below the level of the motor carriers' public local tariff rates.

TRAILER-ON-FLATCAR AND TRAILER-ON-SHIP SERVICE

There has been limited development of a combination service by 21 railroads in which a trailer is loaded at origin and is then physically transported by the rail carrier on a flatcar to destination where a truck tractor is connected to the trailer and moves it to the area

---

[32] Public Law 881, 81st Cong., 2d sess., December 20, 1950.

where it is unloaded. There have been three types of trailer-on-flatcar service which have developed. One is provided by the railroads in their own trailers. Another is that which is provided by an intermediary company that is not affiliated with either a railroad or a motor carrier but owns specially built flatcars and performs certain services such as loading. The third is the moving of the trailers of independent common carriers. A number of questions arose concerning such services which resulted in Commission clarification. It ruled that a railroad was free to transport its own freight in its own trailers and a motor carrier certificate was not needed, including the railroads' pickup and delivery service as part of the over-all performance of trailer-on-flatcar service. Railroads may transport trailers of private carriers because such carriers are shippers, and the same is true of trailers of freight forwarders as shippers and of common-carrier truckers. However, trailers of common-carrier truckers can be transported only under arrangements involving rail-motor joint rates and through routes. Trailers of contract carriers may be carried only to points not served by the contract carrier, with the latter acting as agent for the actual shipper. Thus the contract carrier could haul a trailer to the end of its route and then, acting as agent for the shipper, send the trailer farther on a flatcar.

The use of a well-type flatcar which will carry two 35-foot trailers may facilitate greater use of a combination service.

The development of trailer-on-ship service is one in which trailers are rolled on and rolled off the ship but so far its development has been very limited.

TRADE ASSOCIATION

With its increasing growth, the property-carrying motor-carrier industry developed a need, as have so many other industries, for a national trade organization. The American Trucking Associations, Inc., was incorporated in 1933 under the laws of the District of Columbia. It is the national organization which speaks for all branches of the trucking industry with respect to all matters of general concern to the industry. It encourages those in the industry to seek a solution to their common problems by concerted action. The organization is active in seeking legislation that will advance the interests of the industry and in opposing legislative policies which it feels would be detrimental to the industry.

The membership of this organization is composed of persons and corporations engaged in the transportation of freight, mail, or express by highway vehicles, as well as other persons in allied industries. Any state or local associations of highway-vehicle operators may apply for affiliation with ATA; and, if a state organization affiliates itself with ATA, the members of the affiliated association automatically become members of ATA. There were fifty affiliated associations as of January 1, 1955. A small part of the yearly budget of ATA is secured from the affiliated state associations, which pay one cent per commercial truck registration, other than farm trucks, in the respective states, which amounts to about $40,000 per year. The remainder of ATA General Fund Income revenue is derived from the services it sells and is the primary source of funds. A General Activities Fund to which truck owners, suppliers, and others may contribute is used for publicity and advertising purposes. About one third of the ATA gross income is from this source.

The Board of Directors is composed of seven representatives from each state and from the District of Columbia and one from each of the eleven ATA Conferences. In those states where there is more than one affiliated association, each association sends four representatives to a joint convention, and the latter elect the representatives for the state. One of the seven representatives from each state or territory is normally a regular-route common carrier, one a contract carrier, one a local cartage operator, and one a private carrier. The remaining three may represent any type of carrier or a truck manufacturer or other allied business. An Executive Committee—composed of a president, the past presidents, eight vice-presidents-at-large, four regional vice-presidents, fifty state vice-presidents, eleven conference vice-presidents, a secretary, and a treasurer—serves in an administrative capacity in the organization.

The members of ATA are organized into eleven conferences, according to the nature of the carrier operation in which they are engaged. Each of these conferences has its own meetings to consider problems peculiar to its branch of the industry, and each is governed by its own bylaws. Any carrier whose operations fall within the scope of one of these conferences, whether or not a member of ATA or a member of one of the affiliated state associations, can enroll and participate in the activities of the appropriate conference. However, only carriers who are members of the affiliated state associations have the right to vote in these conferences. The eleven conferences are as follows:

1. Regular Common Carrier Conference
2. Contract Carriers Conference

3. Movers Conference of America
4. Common Carriers—Irregular Route Conference
5. National Tank Truck Carriers Conference
6. Local Cartagemen and Heavy Haulers of America
7. Automobile Transporters Conference
8. Film Carriers Conference
9. Oilfield Haulers Conference
10. Private Carriers Conference
11. Munitions Carriers Conference

A managing director functions under authority from the Executive Committee and the Board of Directors and advises, co-ordinates, and directs ATA activities and programs.

A general manager is responsible for business management, supervision, co-ordination, and direction of ATA staff activities. There are six councils as follows: Council of Safety Supervisors; Customer Relations Council; Equipment and Maintenance Council; National Accounting and Finance Council; National Freight Claims Council; and The Operations Council.

In addition, there are a general counsel, comptroller, highway engineer, and the following departments: Traffic; Safety; Industrial Relations; Public Relations; Research; Law; Field Service; Accounting; and Production and Mailing. The sections are Government Traffic; Freight Claim; Equipment and Operations; and Special Services.

Transport Topics, the national weekly of the motor-freight carriers, is published by ATA. Its editorial columns contain news of interest to the trucking industry and to shippers.

QUESTIONS AND PROBLEMS

1. Differentiate between (a) irregular route, radial service, and (b) irregular route, nonradial service.
2. List the motor carriers of property on the basis of (a) type of carrier, and (b) type of commodities.
3. What type of operation would a common carrier, Class C-2, be? Common carrier, Class C-9?
4. Explain the classification of carriers based on gross revenue. What change has been made in this classification in 1950 and what effect has it had on the number of carriers in the various classes?
5. Define (a) distributive operations, and (b) key-point operations of a common carrier of general commodities.
6. What are the types of contract carriers? How do contract carrier operating costs compare with those of common carriers? Why?

7. What is the statutory difference between a common and a contract motor carrier?

8. "It is estimated that there were 50 per cent more exempt carriers operating interstate . . . as there were common and contract interstate carriers of property." Comment.

9. Enumerate the reasons that prompt business firms to operate their own fleets of private trucks and not to rely on for-hire carriers. What is the trend?

10. Distinguish between household-goods brokers and freight brokers.

11. How can an agent be distinguished from a freight broker?

12. Describe the different ways in which freight forwarders utilize motor common carriers.

13. What need is there for a national trade association in the property-carrying field?

14. Prepare a contract for use by a contract carrier and shipper and identify the primary points covered.

6. LOCAL CARTAGE

▄▄

LOCAL cartage operations are the beginning and the end of every motor-carrier operation in pickup and delivery service, and they represent extensive local operations in motor transportation. The Interstate Commerce Commission's definition of local cartage service, as given earlier, is that a local cartage carrier is any person which undertakes to transport property or any class or classes of property by motor vehicle for compensation when such transportation is performed in interstate or foreign commerce wholly within a municipality or between contiguous municipalities or within a zone adjacent to and commercially a part of any such municipality or municipalities. There are relatively few local cartage carriers which are subject to regulation by the Interstate Commerce Commission, since the majority of such operations fall within the category of exempt carriers under the exemption as defined in the Interstate Commerce Act for vehicles used in transportation of property wholly within a municipality or zone adjacent to or commercially a part of such a municipality.

For the purpose of accounting and the compilation of statistical data, the Commission defines the area of local cartage service as transportation performed within a city or town, including the suburban area contiguous thereto. Local cartage operators would like to have included in local cartage service the area that could be reached and served by them by going out from and back to the local carrier's domicile in the course of a normal working day. This distance would vary, depending upon the type of truck used in the local cartage operation—a lighter vehicle increasing the distance covered and a heavier vehicle decreasing the distance. Another way of defining the area included in local cartage service is that which is contained in some of the labor agreements between local cartage carriers and labor unions; that is, the contract may define local cartage as being

134

service to any of the points within 40 miles of the city hall or the carrier's garage.

Local cartage carriers were the antecedents of for-hire motor transportation. These local operators started by using teams and wagons to deliver local merchandise, to haul coal, and the like. It is from this early beginning in wagons and carts that the term *local cartage* developed. Some of these companies have been operating for almost a century. These organizations vary greatly in size, from one-truck operators in small towns to organizations operating in metropolitan areas which offer many different types of local cartage service and use a hundred or more trucks. Each one operates in a different manner and handles different commodities, although there are many of them which are common carriers.

COMMERCIAL ZONES

As previously stated, there are few local cartage carriers which come under the economic regulation of the Interstate Commerce Commission, inasmuch as their operations are within so-called commercial zones. Even though the operations may be interstate in nature within the zone, they are exempt from Commission economic regulation. For example, a local cartage carrier operating in St. Louis, Missouri, may have operations that cross the river to East St. Louis, Illinois. Such operations are interstate in nature; but, inasmuch as the carrier is operating in a commercial zone of a municipality or contiguous municipalities designated by the Commission, it is exempt from economic regulation as an interstate motor carrier. Such interstate local cartage intrazonal operations are subject, however, to Commission regulation as to qualifications and maximum hours of service of employees and safety of operations or standards of equipment. The limits of the commercial zones are determined by the Commission, and carriers operating wholly within a commercial zone are exempt from economic regulation by the Commission. This exemption does not apply, on the other hand, if the transportation is under a common control, management, or arrangement for a continuous carriage or shipment to or from a point without such municipality. This would mean that if the pickup and delivery at either end of an interstate over-the-road carriage is performed under common control, management, or arrangement for continuous carriage, the carrier would be subject to regulation even though it was operating in a commercial zone. In this manner, some local cartage operators do come under the economic regulation of the Interstate Commerce Commission.

The first commercial zones were established in 1937 after representatives of the Bureau of Motor Carrier's field staff made exhaustive informational investigations as to recommendations for the limits of a commercial zone for a city. Through conferences and field surveys and development of certain other facts, the Commission established the commercial zones for New York City; Chicago; St. Louis, Missouri—East St. Louis, Illinois; Washington, D.C. (see Fig. 6–1); Los Angeles; Philadelphia; Cincinnati; Kansas City, Missouri

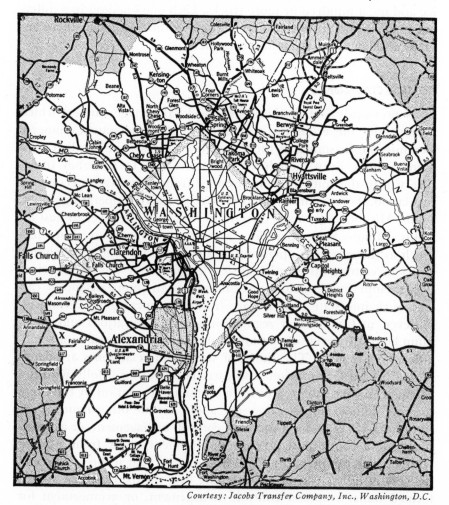

Courtesy: Jacobs Transfer Company, Inc., Washington, D.C.

FIG. 6–1. Map of Washington, D.C., commercial zone which includes, also, the area (light) in Maryland and Virginia adjacent to the District of Columbia. This map is printed by special permission of the American Automobile Association.

—Kansas City, Kansas; Boston; Davenport, Iowa—Rock Island, Illinois—Moline, Illinois; Cleveland; Detroit; Portland; Vancouver; Baltimore; Seattle; Minneapolis—St. Paul; New Orleans; Pittsburgh; Albany, New York; New Jersey points any part of which is within 5 miles of New York, New York; and New York points in Westchester and Nassau counties.

The Commission has also defined by general formula commercial zones not previously established.[1] This report provides for the determination of the commercial zones throughout the United States where specific zones had not been determined by the Commission. The formula used by the Commission in defining such zones is as follows:

1. The municipality itself, hereinafter called the base municipality.
2. All municipalities within the United States which are contiguous to the base municipality.
3. All other municipalities within the United States and all unincorporated areas within the United States which are adjacent to the base municipality, as follows:
   a) When the base municipality has a population less than 2,500, all unincorporated areas within two miles of its corporate limits and all of any other municipality any part of which is within two miles of the corporate limits of the base municipality.
   b) When the base municipality has a population of 2,500 but less than 25,000, all unincorporated areas within three miles of its corporate limits and all of any other municipality any part of which is within three miles of the corporate limits of the base municipality.
   c) When the base municipality has a population of 25,000 but less than 100,000, all unincorporated areas within four miles of its corporate limits and all of any other municipality any part of which is within four miles of the corporate limits of the base municipality.
   d) When the base municipality has a population of 100,000 or more, all unincorporated areas within five miles of its corporate limits and all of any other municipality any part of which is within five miles of the corporate limits of the base municipality.
4. All municipalities wholly surrounded, or so wholly surrounded except for a water boundary, by the base municipality, by any United States municipality contiguous thereto, or by any United States municipality adjacent thereto which is included in the commercial zone of such base municipality under the provisions of (3) of this finding.

In determining distances, airline mileage must be used; and the population for any municipality shall be that shown in the last decennial census.

---

[1] *Commercial Zones and Terminal Areas*, 46 MCC 665 (1946).

The commercial zones of the cities which were individually determined are not enlarged nor reduced by the prescription of the general formula for commercial zones. However, the zones which are determined under the general formula automatically will expand as the population grows or the corporation limits are extended. Commercial zones of United States municipalities which are located at or close to an international boundary have been held to apply only to the United States' portion of the municipality. Carriers would have to secure authority to serve that portion which is not in the United States. When a plant or a government installation is partly within the commercial zone of a city, it is permissible under this exemption to render service to the entire factory or installation, a portion of which is outside the commercial zone if there is a gate which can and is entered within the commercial zone. It also has been held that even though it is necessary to go outside the commercial zone to reach a gate which is inside the zone, this is still within the commercial zone exemption.[2]

The commercial zones of all incorporated municipalities have been determined either individually or by the general formula, although there has been no official determination of the commercial zones of unincorporated communities. It would appear that they are coextensive with the terminal areas of unincorporated communities which the Commission has prescribed by general formula.[3] The limits which are specified therein have ordinarily been considered as the limits of commercial zones of unincorporated communities.

The fact that a local carrier is under common control, management, or arrangement with a line-haul carrier which serves the same city is not, in itself, sufficient to nullify the exemption of Section 203 (b) (8) when there are not joint services or interchange of traffic. However, the common arrangement which would nullify the exemption is one involving arrangement for continuous carriage or shipment between a local carrier and another carrier, either motor, rail, water, air, forwarder, or express. The arrangement may be either oral or written, or in the form of a contract or an agreement. It must be between the local carrier and another carrier for through shipment to or from a point outside the zone to void the exemption.[4]

An arrangement between a local cartage carrier and a shipper or consignee does not nullify the exemption. The local cartage com-

---

[2] *Fleetlines, Inc.*, v. *Arrowhead Freight Lines,* 54 MCC 279 (1952).

[3] *Commercial Zones and Terminal Areas,* 54 MCC 21 (1952).

[4] *Bigley Bros., Inc., Contract Carrier Application,* 4 MCC 711 (1938).

pany, under these circumstances, would establish its own rates and make its own contracts, as well as take its instructions from the shipper or consignee; and it may transport within a zone to or from the docks of line-haul carriers under the commercial-zone exemption.[5]

Most local transportation which does not fall within the commercial-zone exemption is exempt under the pickup and delivery exemption contained in Section 202 (c). Some local transportation does require authority, examples of which are transportation performed for a carrier to or from a point beyond its terminal area or that performed for a carrier not subject to the act, such as a water carrier not subject to Part III.

The Commission has held that no common arrangement exists when the pickup and delivery carrier receives compensation from the line-haul carrier but is employed by the shipper or consignee, such compensation being the line-haul carrier's published collection and delivery allowance.[6]

TERMINAL AREAS

Local transportation which is performed under common control, management, or arrangement is exempt from economic regulation under Section 203 (a) (14). This Section excludes those operations which are already subject to the provisions of Part I of the act, that is, those motor common carriers which are performing collection, delivery, or transfer services which are a part of rail and rail express services. Under Section 202 (c) all transportation by motor vehicle in the performance within terminal areas of collection, delivery, or transfer services by railroads subject to Part I, by water carriers subject to Part III, or by freight forwarders subject to Part IV of the act or for such carriers or for express companies subject to Part I or for motor carriers subject to Part II is exempt from economic regulation except as a part of the line-haul or intercommunity services to which such collection, delivery, or transfer service is incidental.

The terminal area of a motor carrier within the meaning of Section 202 (c) at any municipality the carrier is authorized to serve consists of and includes all points or places which are within the commercial zone of that municipality and not beyond the limits of the operating authority of the carrier. Thus the terminal area of a

---

[5] *Consolidated Freight Lines, Inc., Common Carrier Application,* 11 MCC 131 (1939).
[6] *Jeardoe Common Carrier Application,* 21 MCC 233 (1939).

line-haul motor carrier at any point which it serves is that area within which it performs or has performed for it bona fide collection, delivery, and transfer service. The phrase "collection, delivery, and transfer service" means intracity or intraterminal transportation performed in the picking up, gathering together, or assembling at origin or in the distribution at destination of less-truckload or less-carload shipments prior or subsequent to an intercity or intercommunity line-haul movement and as an incident to such line-haul movement.[7]

The terminal area under Section 202 (c) of any motor carrier at an unincorporated community has been prescribed by a population-mileage formula by the Commission. Using the post office of the community as the central point, the following distances were prescribed: (1) all points in the United States located within the limits of the operating authority of the motor carrier and within $2\frac{1}{2}$ miles of the post office if the community has a population of less than 2,500, within 4 miles if it has a population of 2,500 but less than 25,000, and within $5\frac{1}{2}$ miles if it has a population of 25,000 or more; (2) all points in any municipality, any part of which is within the limits described in (1); and (3) any municipality wholly surrounded or so surrounded except for a water boundary included in (2).[8]

The distances used in defining terminal-zone areas are different from those used in defining commercial-zone boundaries.

IMPLIED AUTHORITY

The Commission has held that terminal areas may not at any point extend beyond the particular carrier's operating authority, including implied authority. Although a terminal point which is authorized to be served may be a city, it is implied that the grant of authority is to serve the immediate community rather than merely the city. In other words, the authority which is implied is that of serving the community and surrounding industry rather than just the city itself.

Although there has been no formal cancellation of Administrative Rules No. 84 through 87,[9] which deal with commercial zones and

---

[7] Commercial Zones and Terminal Areas, 48 MCC 418 (1948).

[8] Commercial Zones and Terminal Areas, 54 MCC 21 (1952).

[9] The Bureau of Motor Carriers has issued ninety-seven Administrative Rules which are considered authoritative in the absence of Commission rulings. In a number of cases, Commission rulings have superceded the Bureau's Administrative Rules.

terminal areas, Rule No. 84 complements the interpretation which the Commission made in the *Commercial Zone* case in that it permits service on both sides of all intermediate point portions of routes when there are no municipalities or communities. Rule No. 87 would appear to be superceded by the liberal interpretation as to implied authority in *Ex parte MC–37*.[10]

Carriers have the same obligation to serve points under implied authority as they have to serve points specifically described in their certificates and permits. This duty is to serve to the extent of the carrier's ability. If it does not want to render service under the implied authority, it can file with the Commission a request to modify its certificate or permit.[11]

STATE REGULATION

Although local cartage is exempt in general from economic regulation by the Interstate Commerce Commission, Oregon, Washington, and Pennsylvania regulate intrastate local cartage operations. In Pennsylvania, common and contract carriers are under the jurisdiction of the Pennsylvania Public Utility Commission. The legislation in this state does not distinguish between local cartage operations and other types of for-hire carriers but includes all types of for-hire carriers under its jurisdiction. In instances where there has been some state or local regulation, it is possible to obtain specific information as to the nature of charges and rules and regulations governing the local cartage carriers in that particular state and thus to gain a better understanding of this phase of the motor-carrier industry.

SERVICES PERFORMED BY LOCAL CARTAGE CARRIERS

Local cartage carriers offer a wide variety of services. Some of these services are as follows: (a) packaged delivery; (b) heavy hauling; (c) pool-car and pool-truck distribution; (d) machinery moving; (e) mobile crane service; (f) packing and crating; (g) merchandise storage; (h) pickup and delivery service for railroads, truck lines, and forwarding companies; (i) furnishing dump trucks; (j) local household-goods moving; (k) leased truck service; (l) general hauling; (m) trash collection; (n) baggage service; (o) refrigerated truck

10 *Commercial Zones and Terminal Areas,* 54 MCC 21 (1952).

11 *Commercial Zones and Terminal Areas,* 54 MCC 21 (1952).

service; (*p*) tank-truck service; and (*q*) armored-car service. A typical type of equipment used in pickup and delivery service is shown in Figure 6–2.

Typical local cartage operations in connection with interstate commerce may be generally divided into three classes as follows:

a) Full carload handling which covers the loading and unloading

Courtesy: Dodge Division, Chrysler Corporation

FIG. 6–2. Typical pickup and delivery type of equipment used in local cartage operations.

of property at terminals, rail sidings, or team tracks and transportation to or from shippers or receivers.

b) Pool-car or pool-truck handling and distribution which covers the assembling or loading of full or partial carloads or truckloads, or the unloading, tagging, marking, routing, sorting, or other such service as a part of the handling of such truckloads or carloads, and the transportation of such property to consignees.

c) Collection and delivery service of less-truckload or less-carload freight within cities and their commercial areas for line-haul motor, rail, or forwarding companies.

The equivalent of (*a*) and (*b*) is also performed from warehouses, warehouse platforms, or similar facilities, and may or may not involve interstate commerce as such.

Services performed under (*a*) contemplate, as a general rule, merely the trucking between the car and shippers' premises. No sorting, checking of kinds, colors, or the like is usually required. Services under (*c*) are a continuation, under original bills of lading, of a movement between terminals and consignees or consignors. Billing is often greatly simplified, based on agreed contract rates under which the local carrier acts as independent contractor for the line-haul carrier or forwarder.

Services under (*b*), however, present an entirely different situation. Shipment in such a pool car or pool truck must be sorted and carefully checked, since all packages may be almost identical in size, shape, or color, but containing an assortment of articles, different colors, quality, and brands. This sorting and checking is a job requiring care, skill, and time. Cartons or containers may not be marked, and the shipper's directions as to segregation and distribution must be carefully followed. Routing of shipments consigned beyond is also an important service. Along with the transportation comes such items as taking proper receipts, making redeliveries, collecting C.O.D.'s, accounting to the shipper for all such items, and, in some instances, storage.

Pool-car distribution is an important function of the cartage industry. It is a departure from the ordinary receiving, transporting, and delivery of carload traffic, of doing or performing many special services for the shipper between the acceptance of the carload of traffic and the ultimate delivery and accounting to shipper, such as providing dock and storage space, since all shipments in the load cannot be delivered immediately, providing sorting, checking, marking, routing, preparing bills and receipts, and then the transporting, handling of C.O.D.'s, and finally accounting to the shipper. The cartage operator is able to consolidate handling with other services and is therefore in a position to give the shipper a complete and economical service throughout an entire metropolitan area. The amount of service to be rendered is generally defined by contract with the shipper.

It is an economical operation for both shippers and receivers to utilize pool-car distribution service in connection with consolidated distribution by a single local cartage operator. The payer of the freight gets the benefit of the carload or volume rate for the line movement and the benefit of specialized handling as a consolidated lot by the cartageman at the destination. This type of service and distribution is an economical one for shippers and carriers because it provides the advantages and benefits of line-haul movement in volume and of specialized distribution by a single local operator at destination. Frequently such operators are making other deliveries to the same consignees or areas at the same time.

Pool-truck distribution performed by many local cartage operators is somewhat similar to pool-car distribution. One of the principal exceptions is that the cartage operator is often required to provide special facilities for handling such pool truckloads or lots.

The charges made by pool-car and pool-truck distributors are usually tailor-made to fit a particular movement. The factors taken into consideration include the type of freight volume involved, weight per shipment and per stop, number of stops, amount of handling needed, the number of separate and distinct services covered, available facilities of consignees, distance traveled in making deliveries, and similar factors. Scarcely any two operations are alike as to service required or cost of handling. Some large manufacturing firms are making extensive use of pool-car and pool-truck services.[12]

Local cartage carriers also perform pool-car and pool-truck distribution out of warehouses and storage facilities which they operate. These warehousemen and cartage operators have regular established charges for handling, sorting and tagging, making bills of lading, routing, and other accessorial services in connection with pool-car or pool-truck handling and distribution.

The Civil Aeronautics Board has found that there are three classes of truckers that provide pickup and delivery service for air freight. The first of these is the airline cartage agent who performs the service offered by the airlines in their published tariffs within the areas and at the rate specified in the tariff. The request for service is made to the airline not the cartage agent, and the shipper or the consignee pays the airline its tariff rate for the pickup or delivery service. The cartage agent is compensated by the airline through Air Cargo, Inc., which is owned by the certificated airlines and performs ground services in connection with air freight.

The second type of pickup and delivery operator is an independent motor carrier engaged by a particular shipper under a contract. He is called a "house trucker" and is paid by the shipper.

Those pickup and delivery operators that do not fall into either of these classes are described as "independent" truckers. They are engaged from time to time by shippers or consignees as the need for the services arises.[13]

In 1953, Air Cargo, Inc., had contracts with 228 local cartage

---

[12] George H. Russel, "Operation Funnels," *American Cartagemen*, September, 1953, p. 16.

[13] *Docket 4850, Local Cartage Agreement Case*, 1952.

companies to perform pickup and delivery service in connection with air-freight shipments, of which they handled 1,022,680.[14]

Another of the services which may be offered by local cartage carriers is that of armored-car service. Armored-car carriers generally operate as contract carriers and perform a variety of services. Their basic service is the collection of customer's receipts for subsequent bank deposit, but there are other services, such as distribution of payrolls to workers and servicing of parking meters, among others. Approximately two thirds of the nation's armored-car fleet is operated by Brink's Express, Inc.[15]

FORM OF CONTRACTS

The local cartage carrier may have a majority of its volume of business coming from but two or three customers with which it will have contracts covering terms and conditions of service. These contracts may be formal documents of great length, or they may be informal agreements confirmed by letter. A formal contract covers one year or a number of years and usually contains an escape clause whereby either party may cancel the contract after proper notice. Even in a long-term contract, it is possible to make it flexible enough to be suitable to both parties. As an example, the contract may be drawn so that it allows for an adjustment of rates should the profit to the local carrier in the contractual carriage fall below a designated minimum or rise above a designated maximum.

Those local cartage companies which are performing freight pickup and delivery service for carriers operating in interstate commerce generally operate under a contract which is uniform. The uniform contract is divided into three parts.

The contractor agrees:

1. To furnish equipment and manpower to move freight between the shipper and the carrier's freight depot
2. If requested by carrier, to collect all charges and C.O.D.'s shown on freight bills
3. To handle bills of lading and receipts in an expeditious manner and deliver such receipts to the carrier
4. To permit an examination by the carrier of all delivery receipts, manifests, and exception reports covered by the operations

---

[14] John R. Pogue, "Partners in Time," *American Cartagemen*, September, 1954, p. 13.

[15] *Wall Street Journal*, March 11, 1953, p. 1.

5. To be responsible as an independent contractor with liability as outlined in this provision
6. To comply with all federal and state regulations and regulations of municipalities applicable to its operation
7. To maintain adequate workman's compensation and public liability and property damage insurance in amounts agreed upon
8. To follow routing instructions of the shipper as shown on the bill of lading and not to give rebates to the shipper
9. That the agreement does not cover the transportation of any freight of which the contractor is the consignor, consignee, or owner thereof

The carrier agrees:

1. To pay the contractor for the preceding month's billing not later than the 20th day of each calendar month at the rate specified in the appendix to the contract

The carrier and contractor mutually agree:

1. That the contractor's liability for freight handled shall be that of an independent contractor
2. That the contractor shall employ persons to operate its equipment, and they shall be employees of the contractor
3. That the agreement is contingent upon approval by such public authority as may be required by law of the tariffs on file and the carrier's election to install and operate service referred to in the tariffs and in the agreement
4. That the agreement shall continue in effect until terminated by either party on 30 days' written notice to the other party
5. That any dispute between the contractor and the carrier which arises out of provision of the agreement which cannot be settled by the parties within 10 days after the dispute arises shall be submitted to arbitration. Either party may request the appointment of an outside arbitrator.

LOCAL CARTAGE RATES AND CHARGES

Local cartage rates are tailor-made. Some of the factors which will affect costs are: (1) the facilities at shipping and receiving points; (2) traffic congestion; (3) point of delivery whether on the dock or inside the building; and (4) special handling. In pricing a cartage job, the time required and the cost of the labor and equipment for the time required are most important.

Because so many cartage jobs are not the same in regard to the service requested, it is very important that the entire cost of the service be computed. The total cost with all types of equipment which the company owns can be computed in a job-price table. A table of this kind shows the miles to be traveled on the left side, while across the top will be the hours required for the job. It is a simple matter when the distance is known in miles to follow the line across until it intersects the column which is headed by the number of hours the job will require. Job-price tables of this sort are used for estimates for specific jobs which are not generally of very long duration.

The rates may be quoted on an hourly basis, which is the rate many of the local cartage carriers prefer; or they may be based on a charge per 100 pounds. The rates may be computed on a per-job basis, or they may be computed on a piece basis. New customers may not desire an hourly rate but may prefer one of the other forms because, being unfamiliar with the service, they often feel that there might be soldiering on the job. It is an established fact, however, that repeat customers have no such qualms about the use of the hourly rate.

In St. Louis, local cartage rates to shippers of pooled shipments range from 10 cents to 60 cents, depending upon the commodity and other factors. Handling charges of 5 cents to 40 cents based upon the service are made in addition. The rates to railroads for delivery of pooled shipments are from 16 to 18 cents.

In Chicago, the rates to shippers are either on an hourly basis or are in cents per 100 pounds and are applicable on all kinds of freight. These rates range from 16 cents to 35 cents.

In addition to the scheduled pickup and delivery service, most contractors provide "special" services at premium rates based upon the day of the week and/or the hour of the day the service is requested. Under this arrangement shipments can be picked up from the shipper or delivered to the consignee on Sundays or holidays or during the night, when no regular service is available, or during a regular business day when a shipment has to reach a consignee before a deadline.

Local cartage companies which are operating within commercial zones not under common control, management or arrangement with intercity carriers do not have to file tariffs with the Interstate Commerce Commission. However, some local cartage companies publish a tariff for their own use and may even distribute it to their customers. The primary purpose of such a tariff is to secure uniformity in the rates charged for similar services.

ORIGINAL
BILL

On COLLECT Order,
Leave as a Receipt For Payment.

On CHARGE Order,
RETURN to Office for Billing.

THE JACOBS TRANSFER COMPANY, INC.
LOCAL FREIGHT HAULING
61 Pierce Street N. E.   Washington 2, D. C.   Telephone DIstrict 7-1124

Date Order Taken_____By_____

Driver_____Truck No._____

Go to_____

Move to_____

Collect From	Charge to			
Name Checked [X] above	This Job To Be Done		C	05100
	PROPERTY OR SERVICE		RATE	CHARGES

ORIGINAL BILL

FIG. 6–3. A job-ticket order.

JOB TICKET

A job ticket is made up when a customer desires to use the services of the local cartage company for local hauling. On this ticket is contained relevant information, such as the name and addresses, commodities to be moved, date and time job is to be done, special directions, the rate and charges, and the person who is to pay the bill. Figure 6–3 is an example of a job-ticket order.

HEAVY HAULERS

One phase of local cartage operations may be that of heavy hauling which may also embrace motor crane service, steel erection, and machinery dismantling and erection. However, heavy hauling may not

LEVEL-DECK SEMITRAILER | DOUBLE-DROP SEMITRAILER

FIG. 6–4. Typical equipment used by heavy haulers.

be confined to just one urban area. Companies of this kind which are engaged in interstate commerce must have operating authority from the Interstate Commerce Commission. Such authority, usually irregular route and involving a territorial grant of states, is granted on such commodities which because of shape, size, form, or weight require use of special equipment or special handling. For example, the carrier may have the rights for heavy hauling between twelve states. Through equipment interchange, heavy haulers can arrange for movements to and from any point in the United States.

A master contract covering equipment interchange has been prepared by the Heavy Haulers, Machinery Movers, and Erectors Section of the Local Cartagemen and Heavy Haulers of America Conference of the ATA. The participants in this master contract do not need to negotiate or exchange a lease on each shipment handled.

The face of the bill of lading of heavy haulers differs considerably from those of common carriers of general commodities. The charges for flagmen with vehicles and without vehicles, the type of vehicle authorized by the shipper, and a certificate of interchange are examples of some of the differences found in this bill of lading.

The equipment which is used by heavy haulers is of special design to facilitate the movement of the items which are transported by such carriers. The gooseneck or lowboy is a common type of such equipment. Figure 6–4 is an example of this type of vehicle. The lowboy may be defined as a vehicle with wheels attached, with the load-carrying bed or platform suspended not more than 36 inches above the road. To facilitate loading and unloading, a tilt deck gooseneck semitrailer has been developed. This is shown in Figure 6–5.

DIFFERENCES BETWEEN LOCAL CARTAGE AND OVER-THE-ROAD OPERATIONS

There are a number of differences between local cartage operations and over-the-road operations. A local cartage carrier frequently finds that dry rot, not wear, is the cause of tire deterioration, whereas

Courtesy: Rogers Bros. Corp.

FIG. 6–5. A tilt deck gooseneck semitrailer used by heavy haulers which facilitates the loading and unloading.

the reverse is the case in over-the-road operations. The investment per unit of equipment for general hauling runs less for the local operator than for the over-the-road operator. The latter operation is a 24-hour operation, whereas local cartage is largely a daytime operation. The accidents experienced in local cartage operations are usually minor in nature, such as smashed fenders; but the accidents in over-the-road operations are more likely to be serious. Therefore, there are differences in insurance premiums between local cartage and over-the-road operations. Over-the-road operators have felt the need for trade associations to promote their interests, but local cartage companies have not felt the need for elaborate trade associations.

The terminals used by local cartage carriers depend upon the type of service engaged in. The local carrier whose business may be contract in character has little need for more than a garage for storage of vehicles. It contracts to pick up a shipment and deliver directly to the consignee, so there is no dock operation involved, as there is in over-the-road operation. The local cartage carrier whose business is like that of a common carrier frequently has warehouse facilities to provide for the transfer and storage of goods when that is necessary, but this type of local operation does not require the terminal facilities which are a part of over-the-road operations.

The number of interstate common and contract carriers may be accurately stated inasmuch as these carriers must secure operating authority from the Interstate Commerce Commission in the form of certificates or permits. Local cartage carriers do not have to secure any form of operating authority from the Commission, however (with the exception noted earlier), and so no record is available on the number of such carriers operating throughout the United States. It is estimated that there are more vehicles and persons engaged in local trucking than in over-the-road trucking.[16]

QUESTIONS AND PROBLEMS

1. Compare the various definitions of local cartage. What reasons are there for these different definitions?
2. What are commercial zones? Of what importance are commercial zones from a regulatory standpoint?
3. How has the Interstate Commerce Commission defined the boundaries of commercial zones? Of what importance are these zones to local cartage operators?
4. List the services that local cartage carriers might offer.
5. An over-all picture of local cartage is difficult to secure. Why?
6. Compile a list of the differences between local and over-the-road motor carriage.
7. How would you differentiate between a commercial zone and a terminal area?
8. What is implied authority? Is it related to the population-mileage formula used in the definition of terminal area?
9. Outline the main points which are covered in a contract between a local cartage carrier performing pickup and delivery service for a regulated common carrier operating interstate.
10. What are heavy haulers? Why are their operations considered to be a phase of local cartage operations?
11. Why are local cartage rates tailor-made? What factors will affect such rates?

---

[16] Linton W. Mason, *Local Trucking* (New York: McGraw-Hill Book Co., Inc., 1951), p. v.

7. SPECIALIZED CARRIERS—HOUSEHOLD GOODS

▬▬▬

VARIOUS aspects of certain specialized carriers are discussed in this and the following chapter because the substantial portion of the book covers the general, rather than specialized, operations of common and contract carriers.

The household-goods carriers constitute one of the largest of the specialized motor-carrier groups subject to Commission regulation. This group of carriers has developed responsive to the needs of the public which it serves. Prior to the advent of the motor van, the transporting of the contents of a household to a new location was performed by rail. This involved cartage of household effects to a warehouse, packing and crating, transportation by the rail carrier, carting to the residence, and unpacking there. The development of household-goods motor carriers made possible transportation from a household to the new location without the extensive crating and packing, rehandling, and longer time in transit.

Many of the early household-goods carriers had performed packing, crating, and local cartage service for railroads. With the improvement in highways and motor-carrier equipment, some of these carriers started rendering service within a limited radius. The success of these carriers led to a broadening of operations, so that at the time of the passage of the Motor Carrier Act in 1935 there was a well-established pattern of household-goods carrier operations.

The extent to which the civilian population of the United States moves each year is not generally realized. Figures compiled by the United States Bureau of the Census from a sample survey show that approximately 20 per cent of the civilian population moved in each year between 1947 and 1952.[1] The number exceeded 30,000,000 in

---

[1] *Washington Post,* December 6, 1953, p. 4R.

the year between April, 1951, and April, 1952. Further, the majority of the persons moving stay within the same community or nearby areas, although vast numbers move across state lines. In the same survey it was developed that nine out of every ten persons who were one year old and over in April, 1952, had moved at least once in their lifetime. Only 2 per cent of the adult population have always lived in their present homes. This is some indication of the potential market of the household-goods carriers.

The busiest months for household-goods movers are from June to September, during which time between 40 and 45 per cent of the total year's volume of business is moved. The largest single shipper of household goods is the Department of Defense, which is occasioned by the rotation of personnel. This accounts for about 35 per cent of all traffic and, in dollars, amounted to approximately $54 million in 1953. The average length of haul for the Department of Defense exceeds 1,000 miles.

NATURE OF OPERATIONS

The household-goods carriers which transport interstate by motor are classified by the Interstate Commerce Commission as irregular-route common carriers of household goods.[2] The nature of household-goods operations lends itself to irregular-route operations, inasmuch as the origin and destination may differ for each and every shipment. The authority to operate over irregular routes enables the carrier to take the shortest practicable route.

RADIAL AND NONRADIAL OPERATIONS

The certificate which is granted may cover operating authority which is radial or nonradial. When the operating authority granted is radial, it authorizes operations only from or to a specified base which may be a city, county, a part of a state, or an entire state or area to specified points or places. An example of this type of certificate is one which reads: "Between points and places in Marshall County, W.Va., on the one hand, and, on the other, points and places in Md., Ky., Ohio, Pa., Va., and the D.C."

---

[2] The author has found one contract carrier with "grandfather" rights to move household goods for employees of the cheese company whose products the contract carrier hauls. *Docket 31466, LCL Transit Co.*

Nonradial operating authority permits the carrier to operate to, from, or between any points within a prescribed area, which may be only two states or may embrace all of the states. There is a relatively small number of certificates which authorize nonradial service to, from, or between all points in the United States. At the present time, examples are those issued to Aero Mayflower Transit Company, Allied Van Lines, North American Van Lines, and United Van Lines. However, there are several other carriers which have large operating territories embracing twenty or more states, examples of which are Atlas Van-Lines, Bekins Van Lines, Burnham Van Service, Greyvan Lines, J. Norman Geipe Van Lines, Howard Van Lines, John F. Ivory Co., and Lyon Van Lines. The radial-type carrier may possess a more limited area of operation. On the other hand, in many instances such a carrier serves as the local agent for household-goods carriers possessing broader operating authority, such as the nation-wide moving companies.

The largest household-goods carrier based on gross revenues is a co-operative nonprofit corporation.[3] It owns no vehicular equipment, and the drivers, helpers, and mechanics engaged in its operations are hired and paid for by its agents. Under hauling-agency contracts, the carriers from which it has purchased operating rights have become its hauling agents. It also has a number of nonhauling agents. The agents of this company, of course, operate for profit.

The corporate organizations of other nation-wide movers are along conventional lines, and they operate for profit, although there is considerable variation in the manner in which they secure their equipment. One company formerly moved about 60 per cent of its traffic in its own equipment but in 1954 placed primary reliance upon leased equipment.[4] Others may operate entirely with equipment which is leased from its agents. Another method is the employment of owner-drivers as independent contractors who perform the service under contract with the carrier. There has been a combination of all three of these types of operation.

Another segment of the interstate household-goods carriers consists of the local moving and storage company which has a certificate covering a limited territory, but their operation is conducted independently of all other carriers in handling shipments within their authorized territory.

---

[3] Allied Van Lines.

[4] Aero Mayflower Transit Co.

CO-OPERATIVE ARRANGEMENTS

There is another group of carriers, the majority of which have limited operating authority, which has combined its service through co-operative arrangements. In this manner, the group handles shipments to and from most sections of the country through interline or interchange arrangements. There are several of these groups of carriers which have made these co-operative arrangements. As a rule, their services are complementary rather than competitive. In some instances, however, the authority which one carrier possesses overlaps that of another in the same group. In one of the groups, there are about forty-eight carriers which have an arrangement whereby they interchange or interline shipments among themselves. A carrier which is a member of one of these groups will turn over a shipment to another, with the originating carrier assuming carrier responsibility to the owner of the goods. These co-operative arrangements are similar to the return-load bureaus which were existent during the 1920's.

AGENTS

The larger carriers make extensive use of agents which they appoint in local communities to represent them. These agents, or agencies, operate under bona fide agency agreements which establish their duties and responsibilities in their respective territories. While the bona fide agency agreements used by various large carriers may vary in detail to fit the particular needs of a carrier's operations, they are much alike in the minimum requirements. Some of the typical responsibilities of the local agent include the solicitation and procurement of business, arranging for helper labor to load and unload, aid in the adjustment of claims, assistance in the dispatch of vehicles, assistance in the collection of charges, the furnishing of accessorial services as required, compliance with the principal's tariffs, the use of only approved advertising, serving as a depository of records, refraining from selling on its own behalf any services for the transportation of household goods beyond the territorial limits of the agent's operating authority, the exclusive selling of the principal's service to all points within the United States beyond the limits of the agent's authority, and the carrying of necessary insurance.

When a bona fide agency arrangement exists, the carrier is obli-

THIS AGREEMENT, made at _____

this _____ day of _____, _____ by and between

AERO MAYFLOWER TRANSIT COMPANY,

of Indianapolis, Ind., hereinafter referred to as Company,

and _____

hereinafter referred to as Agent,

WITNESSETH: That in consideration of the mutual covenants and agreements hereinafter specified, the Company does hereby appoint the Agent as its exclusive Agent in the City of _____,

State of _____, but without limiting the Company's right to transact business within said City, for the purposes hereinafter specified, and for no other purpose, with the privileges herein granted, all subject to the terms and conditions hereof, and the Agent hereby accepts such appointment subject in every respect to the terms and conditions hereof.

THE TERMS AND CONDITIONS OF THIS AGREEMENT ARE AS FOLLOWS:

The duties and agreements peculiar to the Agent shall be:

(1) To faithfully, honestly and properly represent the Company in an active, aggressive and intelligent manner in selling the services of the Company.

(2) To advertise the service of the Company by carrying, at his own expense, a reasonable amount of advertising in the classified section of his telephone directory, and by a general use of other mediums of advertising commonly used in advertising similar services.

(3) To provide or secure helper labor for the Company as and when requested by the Company, at cost, as defined by the Company regulations.

·(4) To assist, under the direction of the Company, in adjusting claims for damage, without charge for such assistance.

(5) To assist, under the direction of the Company, in dispatch of vehicles and to reasonably aid in prompt and efficient accomplishment of the services furnished or to be furnished by the Company.

(6) To furnish necessary accessorial services for the Company at rates to be fixed by the Company.

(7) To assist the Company in making collection of charges.

(8) To endeavor to contract in behalf of the Company for transportation by the Company under its bill of lading and sole responsibility, all shipments as to which the shipper makes inquiry for Company service or designates the Company to be the carrier, whether or not within the scope of the operating authority, if any, of the Agent.

(9) That he will not represent as Agent, or as Agent, endeavor to sell the services of any other motor carrier of household goods while this agreement is in force.

(10) That the Company shall at all times have the sole right to determine and fix the rates to be charged for its services, and the Agent agrees to write all orders for the Company's services in strict compliance with the rates, instructions, rules and regulations of the Company, and the effective and applicable tariffs which the Company has at the time on file with the Interstate Commerce Commission.

(11) (a) To refer any request or order for transportation service, with respect to a shipment proposed to be moved from any city where another agent or office of the Company is located, to such other agent or office, for checking, listing, and estimating, and if such a request is received by the Agent from any other agent or office of the Company, the Agent agrees promptly to check, list, and estimate such shipment and to transmit information resulting therefrom to the inquiring agent or office. In the furnishing of such information to another agent, the Agent agrees to respond by telegram, if so requested, the cost thereof to be prepaid by the Agent.

(b) The Company reserves the right to apportion any commission arising from any shipment among the participating agents or offices in a manner which the Company deems to be fair and equitable based upon the services rendered and the responsibility assumed by them, respectively.

FIG. 7–1. Agency contract between a household-goods carrier and its agent. General provisions are not shown.

gated by and responsible for the acts of its agents within the provisions of the agency agreement and the scope of the carrier's authority. Figure 7–1 is an agency agreement. This agency agreement provides for an exclusive franchised territory which is unusual in agency agreements.

(c) Failure of the Agent to promptly check, list, or estimate any such request or order for service referred to it by another agent or office shall forfeit his right, if any, to any portion of the Commission arising from such shipment. The Agent agrees that he will not solicit or seek to obtain any business for the Company originating in the territory of another agent or office of the Company except in compliance with the foregoing provisions.

(d) To co-operate with other agents and Company offices by exchanging leads or information on prospective moves even when no rights of compensation are embodied therein, and to endeavor to contract in behalf of the Company such leads when furnished by another agent or Company office.

(12) That at all times any authorized representative of the Company, on the Company's request, may be permitted to inspect the Agent's records pertaining to long distance moving.

The duties and agreements peculiar to the Company shall be:

(13) The Company will furnish to the Agent proper forms for the booking of shipments and other Company services, and will keep the Agent promptly informed as to its tariffs, rules and regulations, and will with reasonable dispatch transport lawful or acceptable shipments booked by the Agent.

(14) The Company will carry, at its own expense, insurance on its motor van operations deemed necessary to protect the Company in its operation thereof, including motor equipment leased to it, and to protect the Agent in the performance of his responsibility as Agent in connection with the operation of such motor equipment, whether owned by the Company or leased by it.

(15) The Company will pay to the Agent a commission, to be fixed by the Company, on orders procured by the Agent, or on shipments originating in the territory of the Agent in the servicing of which the Agent has participated, which are accepted and serviced by the Company, the commission to be based upon the charges for the services performed by the Company. Such commission will be paid monthly within ten days following the close of the month for which final accounting is made.

(16) The Company will undertake the collection of advance charges for storage or other services performed by the Agent on his own account on shipments procured by the Agent for the Company for transportation, provided the Agent properly includes such charges in the total bill for collection from the shipper.

The policy of the larger carriers on agency organizations varies. Some carriers appoint only local companies which have household-goods warehouse facilities. Those agents which operate storage warehouses but are not engaged in motor-carrier operations are often termed "nonhauling agents." Others appoint booking agents which have neither warehouses nor vehicles. Thus, there are several common types of agents, *hauling, nonhauling,* and *booking,* as well as combinations of these. The number of agents will vary depending upon the type used. One nation-wide moving company has over 1,000 agents. The majority of the local moving and storage companies which formerly handled their own long-distance moving now act as agents for one of the larger household-goods carriers.

Some companies have branch offices or company sales offices in addition to agents. Greyvan Lines, Inc., for example, has 110 branch offices and over 200 agents. Its use of branch offices is due in part to the fact that for the first 6 months of 1953, 40 per cent of its business was with national accounts and large business firms.[5]

---

[5] *Traffic World,* March 20, 1954, p. 78.

BOOKING

The practice of booking is widespread in the household-goods field and is usually done by agents. It was pointed out in a case before the Commission that 75 per cent of the certificated household-goods car-

Courtesy: Aero Mayflower Transit Co.

FIG. 7–2. A typical moving van used in over-the-road operations.

riers engage in the practice of turning over shipments to others for compensation.[6] Household-goods carriers have felt that when the booking carrier issues the bill of lading in its own name and is responsible to the shipper, the commission which it is paid by the hauling carrier is not in reality a commission but a division of the revenue, since the performance of any service by the booking carrier constitutes participation in the transportation. The Commission, however, has rejected this concept. The Commission has felt that the

---

[6] *Practices of Property Brokers,* 49 MCC 277 (1949).

mere booking of a shipment or even the performance of some accessorial or terminal service in connection with it does not constitute participation in the performance of transportation, so that the booking carrier cannot be classified as a participant in an interline movement and that compensation paid such carrier is not an interline settlement or division.[7]

Household-goods carriers have referred to the practice of the booking carrier turning over shipments to the hauling carrier as "joint carriage." In effect, the booking carrier performs the terminal portion of the joint carriage and the hauling carrier all of the physical transporting of the shipment. Interlining is not common in the household-goods field as it is among the general commodity carriers.

EQUIPMENT

The moving vans which are used in over-the-road operations generally range from 750 cubic feet to 2,000 cubic feet capacity, carrying a load from 5,000 to 15,000 pounds, depending upon the cubical capacity. The semitrailers are of a drop-frame type in order to provide greater capacity. Figure 7–2 is a typical moving van.

Household goods average approximately 7 pounds per cubic foot. The nature of the goods shipped, plus the pads in which they are wrapped, account for the large occupancy of space in relation to weight. It is possible to put the contents of more than one average home in the semitrailer used by the household-goods carriers in interstate moves, but this will depend upon the amount of household goods in each shipment. The furnishings of as many as three average six-room houses may be placed in the larger vans.

Long-distance moving companies seek to consolidate shipments. Some shipments are taken from the home and held at the carrier's warehouse for consolidation with other shipments going to the same general area.

In loading household goods into the van, the load is built up in vertical tiers by following the principle of placing the heavy, bulky pieces at the bottom and the smaller, lighter pieces toward the top. In general, the tiers are from 3 to 4 feet deep and are as many as are needed to fill the van.

Some of the items that are generally carried on a van to handle, protect, and load and unload household effects satisfactorily are pads (180 recommended), mattress covers and cartons, lift straps, floor run-

---
[7] *Ibid.,* 277, 293.

ners, dollies, piano skid, stepladder, and load separator nets. Figure 7–3 shows some of the equipment used to move household goods safely.

PRELIMINARY ARRANGEMENTS FOR SHIPMENT

Except for shipments for the military departments and those made by business organizations, both of which have experience in shipping

Courtesy: Howard Van Lines, Inc.

FIG. 7–3. Interior of a household-goods van, partially loaded, which shows some of the pads, dollies, and other equipment used.

commodities, the household-goods carrier deals with individuals who are wholly inexperienced in shipping. These individuals are not familiar with tariffs and other shipping matters, so that a very heavy responsibility rests with household-goods carriers to deal fairly with such shippers.

The usual procedure for the individual who plans an interstate move is to call one or more carriers. A representative of the carrier will then visit the home in order to determine the number of cubic feet in the shipment, so that the proper vehicle can be dispatched, as well as ascertaining the amount of packing and crating or other additional services which may be desired by the shipper. Since a telephone call to a moving company will bring a representative of a company to a person's address and since people tend to call companies which are listed near the top of an alphabetical list, some of the corporate names of moving companies have been changed in the past so that they will appear first on the alphabetical list in telephone directories. This has been accomplished in some instances through the addition of another word starting with the letter "A" at the beginning of a firm's name, which placed the corporation name as close as possible to the top of the alphabetical list in the telephone directory. In one city, the competitive situation resulted in one company naming itself "AAAAAAA Moving and Storage Company." Not to be outdone others added more "A's" to their names so that each succeeding issue of the telephone directory contained a few more "A's" in company names. This practice was curtailed with the co-operation of the industry itself and telephone companies.

A representative who comes to the person's house will make an estimate of the amount of goods to be shipped together with an estimate of the cost. This information is entered on an "order-for-services" form, a copy of which is given to the shipper. A typical order for services is shown in Figure 7–4. It will be noted that the *estimated* cost of service is shown, the loading date, and the unloading date, the value at which the property is released, and other relevant information. One of the many important items contained in the order for services is a statement that all charges must be paid in cash, by money order, or certified check before delivery, unless other arrangements have been made. Many people assume that a personal check is satisfactory, but this is not the case. The order for services is *not* the bill of lading or freight bill.

The estimated cost of service may be different from the actual cost of service because it is difficult to determine exactly, prior to weighing, the weight of the goods to be shipped. Before motor-carrier regulation was begun in 1935, the estimates generally represented actual charges. After regulation, however, some carriers have estimated costs at a figure as much as one hundred or more dollars less than the actual charge in order to be certain of securing business. Since the estimate was not and is not binding upon the carriers and the charges are ordinarily paid at the time of arrival of the moving van at destination, the shipper too frequently finds himself faced with a bill considerably greater than the estimate quoted him originally. Some of

NATION-WIDE FURNITURE MOVERS **AERO MAYFLOWER TRANSIT COMPANY, INC.** COAST TO COAST SERVICE

General Offices   ORDER FOR SERVICES   Indianapolis, Ind.

Agent_____City_____Date_____

The undersigned shipper hereby orders the above named carrier to furnish the transportation facilities and services described in this order, subject to the contract terms and conditions of uniform household goods bill of lading shown on the back and made a part hereof, and subject to the tariffs of the carrier in effect on the date of the issue of the bill of lading.

Move_____
   Description of Property

If employed by National Account, please give firm name and address, even though charges are to be paid in cash.

For_____

From_____
  Street Address   Floor·

To_____
  Street Address   Floor   City   State

Temporary or Business Address at Destination_____Phone____

LOADING DATE

Loading date desired by Shipper_____

Expedited Service Ordered ☐

UNLOADING DATE

Desired by Shipper_____

Received $_____to apply in prepayment of the charges on the property describud herein.

     Agent or Driver

(The signature here acknowledges only the amount prepaid)

Shippers Are Required to Declare in Writing the Released Value of the Property

(1) When released value does not exceed 30¢ per pound, per article, Transportation Rates shown in Table A of Tariff will apply.

(2) When released value exceeds 30¢ per pound, per article, but does not exceed 75¢ per pound, per article, Transportation Rates shown in Table B of Tariff will apply.

(3) When released value exceeds 75¢ per pound, per article, but does not exceed $1.50 per pound, per article, Transportation Rates shown in Table C of Tariff will apply.

DECLARED RELEASED VALUE

The agreed or declared value of the property is hereby specifically stated by the shipper to be not exceeding____cents per pound, per article.

The shipper hereby declares valuations in excess of the limit set forth above on the following specific articles:

ARTICLE	Excess Value

AERO MAYFLOWER TRANSIT COMPANY, INC.

By_____

AERO MAYFLOWER TRANSIT COMPANY, INC.
INDIANAPOLIS, IND.

ESTIMATED COST OF SERVICE

Actual charges to be collected will be computed by multiplying the actual scale weight of shipment by the applicable tariff rate, where rates are quoted in cents per 100 lbs. Shipper will be furnished record of scale weights.

	Estimated	Estimated
Estimated Van Space Required	Weight per Cubic Foot	Weight of Shipment
Cu. Ft.	Pounds	Pounds

TRANSPORTATION:

        Rate per 100 lbs. Estimated Cost

Estimated weight_____miles_____ @_____ _____

Transportation re: Storage in transit . . . . _____

Wardrobe Service . . . . _____

Extra Pickup or Delivery at_____ _____

Hoisting . . . . _____

Piano Carry . . . . _____

Packing and Unpacking (Itemized schedule attached) . . . . . _____

Storage in Transit at _____ _____

Transit Insurance Premium . . . . _____

Advance charges for the account of (attach itemized invoice) _____

Federal Transportation Tax . . . . _____

All charges must be paid in cash, money order or certified check before delivery unless otherwise indicated below.

Total Estimated Cost _____

BILLING INSTRUCTIONS (Credit extended only to Commercial Accounts under terms of ICC Credit Order, Customer's purchase order, or letter authorizing charge to accompany this order.)

Invoice to_____

Address_____

This order approved by _____

              Shipper

By_____

ORDER FOR INSURANCE

Include $_____ (the total sound value of all goods to be shipped under above Order for Services) TRANSIT INSURANCE under your open policy FT-54147 of the Federal Insurance Company and include premium of $_____ in your charges.

(If no Transit Insurance is desired check here ☐ and sign.) _____
              Shipper

Carrier's Order No.

FIG. 7–4.   Order-for-services form.

these estimates are less than half the ultimate charges.[8] The Commission sought to prescribe regulations which would govern estimating but decided in view of carrier objections not to establish a rule in

[8] Presentation of Commissioner Arpaia before the Annual Convention of Independent Movers' and Warehousemen's Association, March 11, 1953, p. 5.

this regard. Shippers are often partially responsible for the estimated cost of service being at variance with the final cost since they sometimes fail to show the representative of the carrier the contents of closets, attics, and basements.

Prior to loading, a household-goods carrier will make an inventory of the shipment and will record after each item whether it is chipped, marred, or scratched. Until the owner sees this inventory, he may not realize what bad condition his furniture is in; he may wonder after seeing the inventory, whether the furniture is worth the shipping charges. On the other hand, moving companies have found that damaged shipments often become irreplaceable antiques or heirlooms.

Although the order for services usually contains a loading date desired by the shipper, the carrier is not bound to pick up the goods on this date. The shipment may be picked up 1–3 days before the date desired by the shipper or 1, 2, or 3 days later. Every shipment is accepted subject to consolidation with other shipments, unless exclusive use of the van is requested. Delivery schedules are subject to weather conditions, availability of equipment, and other factors. Most carriers have a tariff provision wherein, upon request of shipper, goods weighing less than a prescribed amount will be delivered at destination on or before a date specified by the shipper but will be subject to transportation charges based on a specified minimum weight, which develops a charge greater than if the shipment had been transported at the mover's convenience.

WAREHOUSING

An adjunct of many household-goods carriers is a responsible warehouse service. The agents of some companies are warehousemen and furnish this service for the carrier. Others, however, are warehousemen-carriers. A third group are warehousemen who will provide household-goods storage for any household-goods carriers.

There are several different types of storage that are referred to in the industry, some of which are found in carrier tariffs. Storage-in-transit is the holding of a shipment in the warehouse of the carrier or its agent for storage pending further transportation. Generally, storage-in-transit is limited to 60 days by tariff provision. During the storage-in-transit period, the carrier is responsible for the shipment and its tariff rates apply.

Permanent or regular storage is more complete, since goods are usually wrapped, treated for moth and vermin protection, and placed in a permanent or a regular location from a short period of time to possibly several years. In most states the rates for this service are not under regulation but are determined by the warehouseman in possession. When permanent or regular storage is involved, there are "handling-in" and "handling-out" charges which are usually applied by warehousemen in connection with this type of storage. These charges cover taking the goods from the unloading dock, proper preparation, and placing goods away in permanent location; and removing goods from permanent location, unwrapping, and delivery back to the loading dock.

The liability of the warehouseman is determined by the Uniform Warehouse Receipts Act. A limit of liability per piece or package is contained in the contract terms and conditions of the warehouse receipt.

REGULATION

The Interstate Commerce Act sets forth certain economic and safety requirements with which carriers must comply, which are discussed in later chapters. In addition to this, the Interstate Commerce Commission has prescribed rules and regulations for particular segments of the motor-carrier industry. In the case of household-goods carriers, the Commission originally prescribed eight rules and regulations to govern the practices of all motor common carriers engaged in the transportation of household goods in interstate or foreign commerce.[9] Additional rules have been prescribed so that there are now a total of eleven.[10] The rules which are currently effective provide a framework within which operations can be conducted in a manner beneficial to both shipper and carrier. These rules are as follows:

RULE 1—As used in these rules:

(a) The term "household goods" means personal effects and property used or to be used in a dwelling when a part of the equipment or supply of such dwelling; furniture, fixtures, equipment and the property of stores, offices, museums, institutions, hospitals, or other establishments when a part of the stock equipment, or supply of such stores, offices, museums, institutions, hospitals, or other establishments; and articles, including objects of art, displays, and exhibits, which because of their unusual nature or value require specialized handling and equipment usually employed in moving household goods.

---

[9] *Practices of Motor Common Carriers of Household Goods,* 17 MCC 467 (1939).

[10] *Practices of Motor Common Carriers of Household Goods,* 47 MCC 119 (1947); 48 MCC 59 (1948); 51 MCC 247 (1950); and 53 MCC 177 (1951).

(b) Where any other terms used in these rules are defined in section 203(a) of the Motor Carrier Act, 1935, such definitions shall be controlling. Where terms are used in these rules which are neither defined herein nor in said section 203(a), they shall have the ordinary practical meaning of such terms.

RULE 2—All common carriers by motor vehicle engaged in the transportation of household goods in interstate or foreign commerce shall establish, in the manner and form required by section 217 of the Motor Carrier Act, 1935, and by the regulations of the Commission issued pursuant thereto, rates for the transportation of household goods in interstate or foreign commerce stated in amounts per hundred pounds, and shall not establish rates upon any other basis. All rates applicable to the transportation of household goods established upon any other basis than in amounts per hundred pounds shall be canceled and superseded by rates published in accordance with this rule.

RULE 3—Each such common carrier shall determine the tare weight of each vehicle used in the transportation of household goods by having it weighed prior to the transportation of each shipment without the crew thereon, by a certified weighmaster or on a certified scale, and when so weighed the gasoline tank on each such vehicle shall be full and the vehicle shall contain all blankets, pads, chains, dollies, hand trucks, and other equipment needed in the transportation of such shipment. Each carrier shall retain in the vehicle subject to inspection, a weighmaster's certificate or weight ticket as to each such vehicle showing the tare weight, the date weighed, and a list of such equipment.

After the vehicle has been loaded it shall be weighed, without the crew thereon, prior to delivery of the shipment and the net weight shall be determined by deducting the tare weight from the loaded weight, except that in instances where no adequate scale is located at origin or at any point within a radius of 10 miles thereof, a constructive weight, based on seven pounds per cubic foot of properly loaded van space, may be used. The gross weight, tare weight, and net weight, or the constructive weight, shall be shown on the freight bill.

In the transportation of part loads this rule shall apply in all respects, except that the gross weight of a vehicle containing one or more part loads may be used as the tare weight of such vehicle as to part loads subsequently loaded thereon, and a part load for any one shipper, not exceeding 1,000 pounds, may be weighed on a certified scale prior to being loaded on a vehicle, such part load to be accompanied by a weight ticket evidencing such weighing.

RULE 4—Such common carriers shall establish in the manner prescribed in section 217 of the Motor Carrier Act, 1935, and the rules and regulations issued pursuant thereto, the charges to be made for each accessorial or terminal service rendered in connection with the transportation of household goods by motor vehicle. The tariffs establishing such charges shall separately state each service to be rendered and the charges therefor. The charges so established for packing and unpacking shall be in amounts per container and those for other services shall be separately stated on a unit or hourly basis, whichever is appropriate. No charge so established shall be lower than the cost of performing the service. This rule shall apply only where the line-haul transportation is performed by a motor carrier. The rate for transportation of such goods shall not include the charge for any accessorial service and no such services other than those for which separate charges have been so established shall be rendered by any such carrier.

RULE 5—No discounts of any character whatsoever shall be authorized by tariff provisions or otherwise allowed by any such common carrier and no rates or charges shall be established based upon prepayment of charges.

RULE 6—No such common carrier shall act as agent for any other such common carrier in the solicitation of shipments of household goods in interstate or foreign commerce between points which such agent is authorized to serve and for which it shall have established different rates than those of its principal.

RULE 7—No such common carrier nor any employee, agent, or representative of a carrier shall act as an agent for an insurance company in insuring, under any type of policy, shipments of household goods to be transported by such carrier in interstate or foreign commerce if such carrier, its employee, agent, or representative receives compensation from such insurance company.

RULE 8—No such common carrier shall issue a receipt or bill of lading for household goods to be transported in interstate or foreign commerce prior to receiving such household goods for such transportation, but must issue such receipt or bill of lading when such household goods have been received.

RULE 9:

(a) Liability Restricted. Common carriers by motor vehicle of household goods shall not assume any liability in excess of that for which they are legally liable under their lawful bills of lading and published tariffs.

(b) Insurance policy. Each such common carrier which sells, offers, or procures cargo insurance to or for a shipper of household goods shall deliver to the shipper at or prior to the time of shipment a policy or certificate of insurance which shall show clearly the name and address of the insurance company, the amount of insurance, the premium therefor, and the risks insured against, or the risks excluded, whichever is more appropriate.

(c) Advertisement of insurance. Such common carriers or any employee, agent, or representative thereof shall not advertise or represent to the public that insurance is provided against all risks unless such insurance in fact affords protection to the shipper from every peril to which the shipment may be exposed. When all except certain risks are insured against, this fact shall be indicated in any advertisement of and in any representations to shippers regarding the insurance, and such advertising and representations shall not be such as to deceive or mislead the public or any shipper regarding the scope of the exceptions. Policies providing coverage against specific perils only shall be advertised, represented, and designated as "limited-risk policies," or by some other appropriate designation which will indicate clearly to the shipper that not all risks are covered thereby.

(d) Filing tariffs and evidence of insurance prerequisite to advertising that "all loads are insured." Such carriers, or any employee, agent, or representative thereof, shall not advertise or represent to the public that "all loads are insured" or other similar wording unless such carrier has filed tariffs with this Commission assuming complete liability and has filed evidence of insurance with this Commission providing protection covering all shipments to their full value without limitation and insuring against every peril to which any shipment may be exposed.

RULE 10:

(a) Did not become effective.

(b) Estimate form for shipper's use. Carriers may furnish to shippers or prospective shippers an estimate form which may contain statements of the weights of average pieces of furniture and other household articles of various types, for use by the shipper in making his own estimate of the total weight of his goods. Any instructions necessary to enable the shipper to use the estimate form shall be printed in the form. If cubic foot measurements are used in arriving at the weight, the form shall state that a weight factor of seven pounds per cubic foot shall be used.

(c) Weight of shipment, notification to shipper. After the shipment has been weighed, the carrier if requested by the shipper, shall immediately notify the shipper of the weight thereof and the charges, by telephone or telegraph if requested. The notice shall be at the carrier's expense unless the carrier provides in its tariff that the actual cost of such notice shall be collected from the shipper.

(d) Reweighing. The carrier shall, upon request made by the shipper before delivery and when practicable to do so, reweigh the shipment. A reasonable charge may be established for reweighing only when the difference between the two net scale weights does not exceed (a) 100 pounds on shipments weighing 5,000 pounds or less, and (b) 2 per cent of the lower net scale weight on shipments weighing more than 5,000 pounds. The lower of the two net scale weights shall be used for determining the applicable charges.

RULE 11—Absorption or advancement of dock charges. Motor common carriers of household goods shall not absorb any dock or other charge made by any warehouseman, nor shall any such carrier advance any such charge for the account of any shipper, owner, or other person, except upon the authorization of such person. Whenever such charges are advanced on behalf of the shipper, the carrier shall obtain a receipt therefor from the warehouseman and deliver it to the shipper or the person designated by the shipper at the time the advanced charges are paid.

Rule 1 (a), which became effective in 1939, has since that time been used as a description of the articles which is contained in grants of authority to household-goods carriers. However, the household-goods carriers felt that under the definition they could transport all articles which were shipped uncrated and which required the specialized handling and equipment usually employed in moving household goods. It was felt by household-goods carriers that the test of whether an uncrated article requires specialized handling and equipment usually employed in moving household goods should be the opinion of the shipper. The Commission, however, ruled that the definition of household goods contained in Rule 1 (a) was not unduly restrictive; that it fully covered the proper functions of household-goods carriers and was unambiguous.

Rule 1 (a) is divisible into three parts.[11] Part I relates to a change in the domicile of a householder and does not permit ordinary retail deliveries of new furniture. Part 2 relates to a change in the location of a store, office, museum, institution, hospital, or other establishment. Part 3 relates to the transportation of articles which are of an unusual nature or value and require the specialized handling and equipment of household-goods carriers. The fact that commodities are uncrated does not make them of unusual value or nature. This Part does not necessarily relate, as do Parts 1 and 2, to removals of property due to a change in the location of a householder or an establishment.

Some indication of the differences in commodity descriptions which are contained in certificates issued to household-goods carriers was introduced by a representative of the Household Goods Carriers' Bureau in the case involving the definition of household goods contained in Rule 1 (a).[12] There were excerpts of commodity descriptions from 3,641 certificates. Of these, 1,533 applied only on household goods, 644 applied on household goods and certain other commodities, 1,409 applied on household goods as defined in Rule 1 (a), and 55 on household goods as defined in Rule 1 (a) and certain other commodities. Certificates which have been issued in those proceedings started after the prescription of Rule 1 (a) in 1939 refer to household goods as defined in that rule. Those commodity descriptions which apply without the description under Rule 1 (a) are found in certificates issued prior to the prescription of the definition. The Commission has stated that it does not have authority to amend issued certificates just for the purpose of establishing uniformity.[13]

There were 699 of the 3,641 certificates which authorized the hold-

---

[11] *Practices of Motor Common Carriers of Household Goods*, 53 MCC 177, 182 (1951).

[12] *Ibid.*, 189.

[13] *Ibid.*, 190.

ers to transport certain other articles in addition to household goods or household goods as defined in Rule 1 (a). Some of these articles are new furniture, pianos, used office furniture and equipment, radios and radio parts, bank safes, and many others. The Commission has pointed out that it is more exact to say that when descriptions of additional articles are contained in their certificates, the household-goods carriers are authorized to perform additional *types of service*.[14]

A court case was brought by the Commission against a household-goods carrier which action sought to have the carrier enjoined from transporting shipments of various commodities which allegedly did not fall within the Commission's description of household goods. There were twenty-three representative shipments of commodities which, it was claimed, did not fall within the household-goods commodity description. The court held that the carrier had the authority to transport fifteen of these representative shipments. The court enjoined the carrier from further handling of the other eight types of shipments.[15]

The household-goods carriers have felt that in this decision the court held that each shipment tendered to a mover must be tested under each of the three parts of the household-goods definition and if it qualifies under any one or more of the three parts, then it may be transported by a mover holding authority to transport "household goods" as defined by the Commission in its original report. However, the Commission has felt that each shipment tendered to a mover must be tested under the three parts of the definition considered together and qualify under each of the three parts before it could be transported by a household-goods carrier.

There has been some concern shown by household-goods carriers recently because of the grant of temporary authority by the Commission to automobile haulers to handle and transport valuable automotive show car displays and related exhibit paraphernalia between show display points in specialized van-type equipment. Such displays and related exhibits have often been handled by household-goods carriers under the third part of the commodity description definition. They have protested both informally and formally such grants of authority by the Commission. This would indicate that there are still potential conflicts even between specialized carriers.

A company which enters into over-all contracts to perform com-

---

[14] *Ibid.*, 190.

[15] *Interstate Commerce Commission* v. *United Van Lines, Inc.*, 110 Fed. Supp. 273 (1952).

plete jobs of dismantling, rigging, moving, and setting up all sorts of machinery and structures has been held by the Commission not to require operating authority.[16] Such companies offer in the form of a flat rate, a charge which includes packing and crating of all material where necessary. They physically place it in the carrier's facilities at origin, and at destination they transport it from the carrier's equipment into the plant or office. Under this arrangement, such a company selects a general commodity carrier or carriers and pays them lawful charges for their transportation. The company possesses no certificate, permit, or license, and it is liable to the shipper. Such contractors are competitive with household-goods carriers, since they handle office furniture and similar moves.

The trade association of the household-goods carriers, the Movers' Conference of America, and numerous individual carriers have pointed to the service rendered by household-goods carriers as being different from that of general freight haulers. This difference is said to be due to the special equipment, the use of especially trained personnel, and the fact that movers remove the shipment from the place where the article is originally located, take it to destination, and place the article in the exact location at destination desired by the shipper. It should be pointed out, however, that there are numerous segments of the motor common-carrier industry which operate in a distinct or unique manner different from general commodity haulers, but all of them, without exception, are rendering a common-carrier transportation service, representing a general holding out to the public.

The emphasis upon the importance of the differences of the service of household-goods carriers has led to their pressing for regulatory relief before federal and state regulatory bodies and for taxation relief with some degree of success. For example, household-goods movers domiciled in Ohio in 1953 called on the nominees for the state legislature to accord to movers the same scale of vehicle license fees as was allowed farm truck operators, which tax differential is considerably less than other property-carrying vehicles. A bill was enacted in Georgia which reduced registration fees for trailers and semitrailers used to transport household goods by 50 per cent, which gave movers the same scale of registration fees paid by farmer-owned vehicles.[17]

In a report of the Conference secretary at the annual assembly of

---

[16] *Riggers and Erectors Service Corp. F. F. Application,* 265 ICC 738 (1950).

[17] *Transport Topics,* January 4, 1954, p. 5.

the Movers' Conference of America, it was suggested that household-goods carriers should be exempted from many regulations in a manner similar to haulers of agricultural commodities and should ". . . try to get away from the common carrier stigma."[18]

It is interesting to note, on the other hand, that in regard to rates the household-goods carriers want the Commission to apply the same criterion, that of using the operating ratio as the basis for determining the need for rate adjustment, as that which is applied to the other motor common carriers of property.[19]

RATES

Although household-goods carriers originally published tariffs based on the cubic feet displacement of the goods carried, the dissatisfaction occasioned by such rates due to discriminatory practices resulted in the Commission's prescription of a rule that all rates must be published on a weight basis. The rates, which are published in cents per 100 pounds, are graded in accordance with distance, that is, rates are published by weight brackets and mileage blocks. For example, the rate per 100 pounds would be higher for a light shipment than the rate named for the same distance as applicable on a heavy shipment. The original tariff in which a large number of carriers participated had sixteen weight brackets and many mileage blocks. It also provided three different sets of rates for three classifications of shipments: (a) basic rates which were applied to regular household goods; (b) rates 20 per cent higher which were charged for light and bulky goods, such as millinery items; and (c) rates 20 per cent lower than the basic rate which were charged for office equipment, since the latter traffic was of greater density.

There have been numerous changes through the years, and general simplification in rates. It was found to be unnecessary to maintain three rate classifications, nor was there the necessity for as many weight brackets nor as many mileage blocks. Two of the current major household-goods tariffs provide for but four weight brackets with the mileage blocks going to 4,800 and 5,000 miles, respectively. Inasmuch as almost everyone moves at one time or another, it is desirable to examine in some detail the rates charged by household-goods carriers.

---

[18] *In the Van*, August 15, 1952, p. 3.

[19] Brief of Respondents to examiner in *I & S Docket No. M-4739, Increased Rates on Household Goods*, October 8, 1953, p. 41.

RELEASED RATES

The Interstate Commerce Commission issued a released rate order which permitted the limitation of liability of the household-goods carriers.[20] This order also authorized the payment of an additional amount if the shipper declared the value of the shipment to be higher than the prescribed maximum. The rate of 30 cents per pound per article, as provided in the tariffs, is considered to be the base rate. If the shipper desires to release his shipment at a value exceeding 30 cents per pound per article but not exceeding 75 cents per pound per article, the charge is 110 per cent of the base rate. If the shipment is released at a value exceeding 75 cents per pound per article but not exceeding $1.50 per pound per article, the charge is 120 per cent of the base rate. Tariffs also have excess declared value rates. Such a typical provision is one in which the shipper may declare an excess value on specific articles at a rate of 2 per cent of total excess value declared. Articles on which the shipper declares a value of more than $10,000 will not be accepted. A further order, *MC–No 2B*, issued in 1953, makes released rates applicable not only to the transportation of household goods but also to charges for accessorial services in connection therewith. Prior to this order, there was some question as to the released rates applying to the additional services, such as packing, storage-in-transit, and the like.

A shipper may have the carrier transport the property with the carrier's liability limited only as provided by common law, in which case the rate will be double the rate which is charged for the 30 cents per pound per article released-value rate.

The majority of household-goods shippers release their goods at a value not to exceed 30 cents per pound per article. The effect of such limitation is that many persons take out transit insurance to provide additional coverage. At a valuation of 30 cents per pound per article, the liability of the carrier is inadequate to compensate the shipper for the loss or damage to household goods. To think of any household-goods article in terms of 30 cents per pound per article will demonstrate the inadequacy of such a valuation to a shipper in terms of replacement of the article. Many shippers are not informed by the carriers of the possibility of releasing their household goods at a higher declared value. Also since the declaration of higher values entails the payment of higher rates, many shippers cannot avail themselves of this greater protection. The alternative for the shipper is to

---

[20] *ICC Released Rates Order MC–No. 2A,* January 29, 1948.

take out a transit insurance policy if he wishes to have additional protection.

In 1949 one of the large household-goods carriers secured a released rate order, which action was subsequently followed by a few other household-goods carriers. In May, 1954, the Commission issued *Released Rates Order MC–No. 362* which could be used by all household-goods carriers. This order permits the publication of tariffs on a valuation basis. It provides that the tariff shall contain a base transportation rate when the shipper releases the shipment to a value not exceeding 30 cents per pound per article. If the shipper releases the shipment at a lump sum for the entire shipment, the base transportation rate applies, plus a valuation charge of 50 cents for each $100 or fraction thereof of the declared value.

This order provides that only one of the alternate methods may be employed in determining total liability. This means that if the shipper declares a value in a lump sum and there is loss or damage to his shipment, he is entitled to recover on the weight or value method, whichever produces the greater recovery. The order also provides for a valuation charge of 10 cents per 100 pounds or fraction thereof on storage-in-transit shipments after the first 60-day period of storage. The base storage rate for the first 60-day storage period is applicable. Most tariffs which have been published under the valuation method provide a 360-day storage-in-transit period. To illustrate: If the base storage rate is 50 cents per 100 pounds for each 30-day period or fraction thereof, the storage charge would be $1.00 per 100 pounds for the first 60 days, but for the third 30-day period and each 30-day period thereafter, the carrier would charge its base transportation rate of 50 cents per 100 pounds plus an additional amount of 10 cents per $100 or fraction thereof of declared value.

If the value is not declared in a lump sum but released to an amount not exceeding 30 cents per pound, the additional valuation charge of 10 cents after the first 60 days is computed on value determined on the basis of the actual weight of the shipment multiplied by 30 cents per pound, with a 1,000-pound minimum base provided.

The purpose of the 10-cent charge on the storage-in-transit shipment is to reimburse the carrier for assumption of liability for the longer period of time. When carriers make use of this *Released Rates Order,* it provides a basis for the shipper to declare the actual value of his shipment rather than releasing his goods at 30 cents per pound per article and securing transit insurance to cover the value above the carrier's liability.

Household-goods carriers which have published tariffs on the valuation-charge method have published bill of lading terms and conditions in which they accept liability comparable to that provided by the all-risk insurance policies available to shippers. Carriers which operate on tariffs under *Released Rates Order MC–No. 2B* provide a method for the shipper to obtain additional protection by securing insurance. Such insurance is usually at the rate of $5.00 or less per $1,000 of declared value, and the insurance company receives the premium and assumes the additional liability. Under arrangements of this kind, carriers which sell or procure cargo insurance for the shipper usually hold a master or open policy from the insurance company under which they are given the privilege of issuing certificates or advices of insurance to the shipper binding on the company. Some companies advise the shipper to procure his own insurance in the event additional coverage is desired. Under *Released Rates Order MC–No. 362,* a carrier using this method in its tariff can offer to the shipper greater carrier liability for which the shipper pays 50 cents for each $100 of the declared value of the entire shipment. Thus the charge would be $5.00 for $1,000 of declared value with the carrier retaining this valuation charge.

When the shipper accepts rates based on a released value of 30 cents per pound per article and purchases insurance through the carrier, most claims for loss or damage must be examined in regard to three factors. These are: (*a*) whether or not the loss or damage resulted from a cause covered by the carrier's common-law liability; (*b*) the amount for which the carrier is liable under its common-law obligation; and (*c*) the total damage to property. The cost and delay in securing the necessary information to settle shipper claims was one of the reasons for securing the *Released Rates Order* which permitted the publication of a tariff in which valuation charges could be substituted for the practice of issuing insurance to shippers.

If the released value on the entire shipment is less than the actual cash value of the shipment, the carrier's liability is limited to: (1) that portion of the actual loss or damage represented by the percentage that the released value bears to the actual cash value of the shipment; or (2) the amount of actual loss or damage not exceeding 30 cents per pound of the gross weight of each shipping package or loose article not enclosed in a shipping package, whichever is greater. Only one of the alternative methods may be used to determine the total liability.

The bill of lading and the order for services must carry a statement in boldface type that "unless a different value is declared, the

SECTION II

Rates are in dollars and cents per 100 pounds applied to actual weight (Subject to Rules 5, 17 and 25), on SHIPMENTS when released to a value not exceeding 30 cents per pound per article, and includes loading and unloading and the actual movement or transportation of property from origin to destination, EXCEPT such rates are subject to Item 165 (Additional Transportation) and Item 170 (Overtime Loading and Unloading). Rates in this Section do not include Additional Services.

Break Point indicates weight at which a lower charge develops by use of lowest weight and applicable rate in next higher weight bracket. (See Rule 24)

MILES	1,999 lbs. or less	BREAK POINT	2,000 lbs. to 3,999 lbs. incl.	BREAK POINT	4,000 lbs. to 7,999 lbs. incl.	BREAK POINT	8,000 lbs. and over
1 to 15	2.60	1693	2.20	3637	2.00	6801	1.70
16 to 20	2.70	1704	2.30	3566	2.05	6830	1.75
21 to 30	2.80	1715	2.40	3584	2.15	6885	1.85
31 to 40	2.95	1696	2.50	3521	2.20	6910	1.90
41 to 50	3.10	1678	2.60	3462	2.25	6934	1.95
51 to 60	3.25	1662	2.70	3482	2.35	6980	2.05
61 to 70	3.40	1648	2.80	3501	2.45	6858	2.10
71 to 80	3.50	1658	2.90	3449	2.50	6881	2.15
81 to 90	3.65	1645	3.00	3401	2.55	6903	2.20
91 to 100	3.80	1632	3.10	3356	2.60	6924	2.25
101 to 110	3.95	1621	3.20	3375	2.70	6964	2.35
111 to 120	4.10	1610	3.30	3395	2.80	7001	2.45
121 to 130	4.25	1601	3.40	3413	2.90	7035	2.55
131 to 140	4.35	1610	3.50	3429	3.00	7068	2.65
141 to 150	4.50	1601	3.60	3445	3.10	6969	2.70
151 to 160	4.65	1592	3.70	3406	3.15	6985	2.75
161 to 170	4.80	1584	3.80	3369	3.20	7001	2.80
171 to 180	4.90	1593	3.90	3334	3.25	7017	2.85
181 to 190	5.00	1601	4.00	3301	3.30	7031	2.90
191 to 200	5.15	1593	4.10	3269	3.35	7046	2.95
201 to 220	5.35	1608	4.30	3210	3.45	7190	3.10
221 to 240	5.55	1622	4.50	3201	3.60	7334	3.30
241 to 260	5.75	1635	4.70	3192	3.75	7361	3.45
261 to 280	5.95	1648	4.90	3185	3.90	7386	3.60
281 to 300	6.10	1656	5.05	3209	4.05	7309	3.70
301 to 320	6.30	1667	5.25	3201	4.20	7334	3.85
321 to 340	6.45	1691	5.45	3193	4.35	7357	4.00
341 to 360	6.65	1685	5.60	3215	4.50	7379	4.15
361 to 380	6.85	1680	5.75	3201	4.60	7479	4.30
381 to 400	7.00	1686	5.90	3187	4.70	7576	4.45
401 to 420	7.15	1693	6.05	3207	4.85	7589	4.60
421 to 440	7.30	1699	6.20	3227	5.00	7601	4.75
441 to 460	7.45	1705	6.35	3245	5.15	7535	4.85
461 to 480	7.60	1711	6.50	3231	5.25	7544	4.95
481 to 500	7.75	1704	6.60	3243	5.35	7553	5.05
501 to 520	7.90	1710	6.75	3260	5.50	7565	5.20
521 to 540	8.00	1726	6.90	3276	5.65	7577	5.35
541 to 560	8.15	1731	7.05	3291	5.80	7587	5.50
561 to 580	8.30	1736	7.20	3279	5.90	7662	5.65
581 to 600	8.45	1729	7.30	3289	6.00	7668	5.75

NOTE: For rates to apply on shipments where the declared value exceeds 30 cents per pound per article see Conversion Table herein.

FIG. 7–5. Rates on page 28 of Household Goods Carriers' Bureau Tariff No. 47A.

shipper hereby releases the value to 30 cents per pound for each article.''

Figure 7–5 is a page from the Household Goods Carriers' Bureau Tariff No. 47A. It will be noted that there are four weight brackets

SECTION I

Rates and Charges for Additional Services shown in this Section apply in all territories, and are in addition to all other rates in this Tariff.

ITEM	SERVICE	PER	RATES (In dollars and cents)

20	PACKING AND UNPACKING: (See Rule 27)
	Rates include:
	(1) Packing, unpacking and the use of packing containers and materials, or
	(2) Packing and the packing containers and materials in the event that such packing containers and materials are retained by the shipper or consignee. See Note.
	NOTE:
	    Rates do not include unpacking and containers will be considered to have been retained by shipper:
	    (a) Where shipment is delivered to warehouse (except where delivery to warehouse is for Storage in Transit and delivery is made within the 60-day period as provided by Rule 11); or
	    (b) Where unpacking is performed other than at the time of delivery and at request of shipper.
	BARRELS:
	(Barrel, drum or specially designed fiber container (for use in lieu of barrel or drum) of equivalent standard barrel capacity)......................................
		Each	$ 6.00

	BOXES, WOODEN: Not over 5 cu. ft. .... Over 5, not over 10 cu. ft. .... Over 10, not over 15 cu. ft. .... Over 15, not over 25 cu. ft. .... Over 25, not over 30 cu. ft. .... Over 30 cu. ft. (See Crates)	Each Each Each Each Each	3.50 5.00 5.50 7.50 10.50
	CARTONS: Not over 3 cu. ft. .... Over 3, not over 5 cu. ft. .... Over 3, not over 6 cu. ft. .... Over 5, not over 10 cu. ft. .... Over 6, not over 12 cu. ft. .... Over 10 cu. ft. .... Over 12 cu. ft. including wardrobe cartons.............. Mattress carton.. Mattress cartons, or Bags of heavy Kraft paper or plastic................... Mirror Cartons, Expandable.............................	Each Each Each Each Each Each Each Each Each Cu. Ft. or fraction thereof	1.75 2.50 4.25 4.75 2.50 1.00 (Minimum Charge $5.00 per crate)
	CRATES, WOODEN: Gross measurement of crate...........................	Cu. Ft. or fraction thereof	1.00 (Minimum Charge $5.00 per crate)
30	PAPERING AND PADDING...................................	Cu.Ft.	$ 0.10
40	WARDROBE SERVICE: Use of wardrobe box....................................	Each	$ 5.00
50	LABOR CHARGES: Covers labor services for which charges are not otherwise provided in Tariff when such services are requested by the shipper, per man, per hour or fraction thereof: (a) Except as provided in paragraph (b) below............... (b) When performed before 7 A.M. or after 6 P.M. on weekdays. Saturday, after 12 o'clock noon; or during any hour on Sunday, or legal holiday, national, state or municipal.......................................	Hour Hour	$ 3.25 4.00
60	HOISTING, where necessary: First article.. Each additional article.............................. Applies each time service is rendered.	Flat Charge Each	$20.00 5.00

FIG. 7–6. Additional Services charges on page 18 of Movers' and Warehousemen's Association of America Tariff No. 10.

which are used. The lowest weight bracket is 1,999 pounds or less, but a rule establishing a minimum charge in the tariff specifies that a shipment which weighs less than 1,000 pounds will be accepted only at a weight of 1,000 and at that applicable rate. There are some exceptions to this, usually on short hauls of 50 miles or less, when the minimum charge will be based on 500 pounds. There is a break point shown in the weight brackets. This point indicates the weight at which a lower charge exists through the use of the lowest weight and applicable rate in the next higher weight bracket as provided in one of the general rules in the tariff. For example, Figure 7–5 shows that a shipment weighing 1,632 pounds moving a distance of 100 miles carries a rate of $3.80 per 100 pounds. The charge on such a shipment would be $62.02. However, the lowest weight in the next higher weight bracket, namely 2,000 pounds, moving a distance of 100 miles, can be used, in which event the rate would be $3.10 per 100 pounds, a total of $62.00.

In addition to the line-haul charge, there are rates and charges for additional services.[21] Some of these are the result of requests which the shipper will make to perform a particular service, such as the carrier furnishing barrels, boxes, and cartons for packing; whereas others, such as the charge for moving a piano, have been placed in the tariff because of the additional cost of rendering such service. Figure 7–6 is a specimen page showing some of the additional services and charges provided in the Movers' and Warehousemen's Association of America Tariff No. 10.

For moves wholly within urban areas, the charges are usually computed on an hourly basis or on a per-job basis, and the carriers do not always hold themselves out as common carriers.

There is a difference in services rendered by household-goods carriers and general commodity motor carriers which is reflected in their respective rates. For example, on a shipment of used iron or steel hospital bed ends and bed springs from Medford, Oregon, to Louisville, Kentucky, the rate of a household-goods carrier was $13.70 per 100 pounds and the rate of a general commodity motor carrier was $5.22.[22]

LEVELS OF RATES

One of the requirements of federal regulation is the filing of rates and tariffs which are open for public inspection. This has resulted in the tendency of rates of regulated carriers within a mode of transportation to be identical between specified points on particular com-

---

[21] Common carriers in other fields usually refer to services similar to these additional services as accessorial services.

[22] *Daily Traffic World,* October 31, 1952, p. 1.

modities. The requirement that the tariffs must be open to public inspection has usually resulted in the publication of agency tariffs containing the rates of a number of carriers. This lessens the cost for the participating carriers below that of individual publications. It is not uncommon, however, for individual tariff publications to continue.

An examination of the rate structures of older forms of transportation shows a gradual tendency toward one rate level. The longer the period of time a group of carriers has been subject to regulation, the less likelihood there is of different rate levels, that is, different rates between the same points. There are still basically two levels of rates in the household-goods field which are referred to within the industry as the high level and the low level. Actually, there are more levels than this. The difference in the two basic levels of rates now averages about 7 per cent. The range is from zero on the short distances to 22 per cent for distances over 2,500 miles. The additional service charges also average less. The difference in the two levels was originally as high as 25 and 30 per cent, but it has been narrowed over the years.

The ordinary user of household-goods services is generally unaware of this differential in the rate level. To many people this comes as somewhat of a surprise because they assume that when rates are subject to regulation, there is one common-carrier rate which is applicable. A person who is moving and uses the telephone directory to call two moving companies to come out and estimate the cost of moving his household goods may have chosen a carrier from the high-rate level and one from the low. The estimates therefore may be quite different. The lower-rated carriers usually indicate this fact in their advertising.

RATE BUREAUS

There are two major household-goods rate bureaus—the Household Goods Carriers' Bureau with approximately 1,900 members and the Independent Movers' and Warehousemen's Association[23] with approximately 400 members—as well as a number of others that have smaller membership and are more regional in nature. Each of these

---

[23] The name of the Independent Movers' and Warehousemen's Association was changed in June, 1954, to the Movers' and Warehousemen's Association of America, Inc. The majority of the members of the original independent group were carriers engaged in local or regional household-goods moving which felt that they could operate on a lower level of rates than those charged by the long-distance movers which became members of the Household Goods Carriers' Bureau.

organizations publishes several tariffs. The Household Goods Carriers' Bureau publishes three series of tariffs: Series A which is published on behalf of a majority of its members; Series B which embraces so-called "joint tariffs" published for a minority of its members; and Series C which are individual tariffs.[24] The tariff for Allied Van Lines, Inc., is an individual tariff which is published by this Bureau. Basically, this tariff is the same as the Series A tariffs. The Series B tariffs are on a lower basis than the Series A.

The Independent Movers' and Warehousemen's Association publishes several tariffs which provide for varying levels of rates and differences in packing requirements on household goods for the members which participate in its tariffs.[25]

In addition to the rate tariffs, each of these tariff Bureaus publishes a Scope Tariff, which gives the names of the carriers, parties to the rate tariff, together with a description of the territorial scope of their operations. A comprehensive Mileage Guide is also published by these Bureaus, which contains maps and charts for determining highway distances between all points in the United States. This Mileage Guide is also used by carriers other than household goods carriers.

The procedure for initiation or revision of rates, rules, or regulations to tariffs of the Household Goods Carriers' Bureau is typical of the procedure followed by similar bureaus. Any member carrier, shipper, or receiver of household goods may propose changes. There appears to be no provision for public hearings before the household-goods bureaus. To a certain extent, it may be said that there is a maximum which may be reached in the rates and charges which household-goods carriers can charge the public. That is the point at which individual shippers will dispose of their household goods rather than ship them via household-goods carriers or do the transporting themselves by various methods.

QUESTIONS AND PROBLEMS

1. What is the potential market of the household-goods carriers? Why is there a seasonal fluctuation in household-goods moving?
2. Of what importance is the agent in the household-goods moving field? What are some of his typical responsibilities?

---

[24] *Agreement Relating to Household Goods Carriers' Bureau,* 277 ICC 443 (1950).

[25] *Independent Movers' and Warehousemen's Association, Inc.—Agreement,* 277 ICC 229 (1950).

3. Describe the different types of agents. If you operated a nation-wide moving company, what type would you use? Why?

4. What is booking? What is included in the preliminary arrangements involved in booking?

5. Is the order for services the same as the bill of lading? Is the former document binding upon either party?

6. Compile a list of what you consider to be the obligations of the household-goods carriers based on the regulations prescribed by the Commission.

7. Are the services of household-goods carriers "different"? Are there other regulated common carriers whose services are "different"?

8. Of what importance to shippers are released rates? Why are they used in the household-goods field?

9. Why do shippers often secure insurance on household-goods shipments?

10. How can the existence of two levels of rates in the household-goods field be explained? Have these levels changed through the years?

8. OTHER SPECIALIZED CARRIERS

IN THIS chapter the operations of tank truck carriers, automobile haulers, and oil-field haulers are described as examples of the many specialized carrier operations.

TANK TRUCKS

Tank trucks[1] constitute a specialized type of operation using specialized equipment which is designed for handling a variety of commodities in bulk. The majority of these bulk commodities are in liquid form. The range of these commodities is very extensive, there being more than five hundred, the majority of which are petroleum and chemical products. There are many others, however, such as glue, molasses, milk, fingernail polish, penicillin, liquid latex, ink, and numerous others. About 23 per cent of all the tonnage hauled by Class I intercity motor carriers was hauled by tank trucks in 1953. Based on tonnage, tank-truck carriers are second to the carriers of general commodities.

DEVELOPMENT OF TANK-TRUCK OPERATIONS

The early development of the tank-truck industry was largely in the transportation of petroleum products. During World War II all rail-tank cars, about 18,000, were withdrawn for hauls of less than 200 miles and were placed in long-distance movement to replace ocean tankers. Tank trucks were substituted for tank cars in this operation, which resulted in a tremendous growth in the tank-truck industry. In 1941 it was estimated there were a little over 4,000 over-the-road tank trucks in operation in the United States. In 1943 there

---

[1] This term also refers to semitrailers or trailers.

were almost 15,000, and by 1945 the number had increased to 18,417.[2]

The experience of shippers in World War II in using tank trucks demonstrated that in the short-haul movement (1) tank trucks had faster turn-around time; (2) they required less expensive plant instal-

Courtesy: Cantlay & Tanzola Transportation Co.

FIG. 8–1. Typical western equipment used in hauling petroleum. The tank truck and tank trailer used in combination is often referred to as a "train."

lations and receipts for loading use; (3) delivery could be made directly to service stations and large consumers, bypassing bulk plants; and (4) they provided greater flexibility, since it was no longer necessary to plan movements in keeping with train schedules.[3] During the war it was found that on the average haul of less than 200 miles the turn-around time for a tank truck was between 11 and 13 hours as compared with an average of from 8 to 10 days for tank cars on similar hauls.

The sharp increase in railroad rates after World War II also was a factor in the development of the tank-truck industry. Some tank-truck carriers, after World War II, disposed of part of their equipment because of the uncertainties of future operations, although others felt that what had been accomplished during World War II on a temporary basis was of sufficient advantage to shippers to insure the continuance of a high level of operations.

[2] S. F. Niness, "Tank Truck Industry Post-War Development," *Petroleum Transporter,* September–October, 1952, p. 10.

[3] Petroleum Administration for Defense, *Transportation of Oil* (Washington, D.C.: U.S. Government Printing Office, 1951), p. 12.

The subsequent expansion of the petroleum industry in the chemical field and the expansion of production in the chemical industry led to a greater diversification in tank-truck hauling than previously had been the case. Petroleum products are easy to haul, and the ideal arrangement is to have a volume sufficient to warrant putting specific units in a particular service, since this avoids a mixing of products and possible contamination. However, petroleum products usually constitute a one-way haul. In chemical transportation there is greater possibility of a return haul because the same pound or gallon of chemical is generally hauled three or four times before it is ultimately consumed. Another advantage is that the commodity is heavier.

In the hauling of gasoline, motor carriers have usually confined their operation to a radius of 200 miles, although in the western states there are hauls for distances as great as 600 miles one way. A typical tank truck and tank trailer used in the West is shown in Figure 8–1. In tank-truck movements of chemicals, it would appear that the average length of haul is going to be greater than that of petroleum products.

EQUIPMENT

The equipment which is used in tank-truck operations varies widely, inasmuch as commodities may be moved at temperatures which range from below zero to over 600 degrees above zero. Tank trucks must be constructed to specifications which are issued by the Interstate Commerce Commission.[4] These specifications were prepared in co-operation with carriers, and petroleum and chemical companies. They cover such matters as material, thickness, strength, baffling, valve design, test procedures, and marking. Figure 8–2 is a cut-away of a general-purpose tank semitrailer.

Those tank trucks which are used for transportation of dangerous articles, such as inflammable liquids, compressed gases, and corrosive liquids, have different specifications which have been promulgated by the Interstate Commerce Commission.[5] Figure 8–3 is a MC–310 semitrailer used in transporting corrosive liquids.

Basically tank trucks fall into three types:

---

[4] Specifications for a general-purpose tank truck issued by the Interstate Commerce Commission are MC–300 for mild steel; MC–301 for low-tensile aluminum; MC–302 for high-tensile aluminum; and MC–303 for high-tensile steel. Most tank trucks are of steel construction.

[5] MC–310, MC–311 for corrosive liquids; and MC–330 for compressed gases.

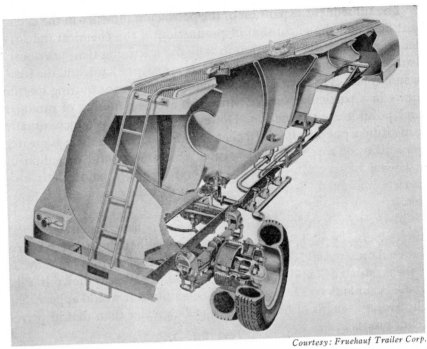

Courtesy: Fruehauf Trailer Corp.

FIG. 8–2. Cutaway of general-purpose tank semitrailer which shows surge plates or baffles, and other details.

1. General-purpose tanks designed to haul noncorrosive liquids, such as gasoline, fuel oil, and similar liquids at atmospheric pressure.

2. Tanks that are designed for hauling corrosive liquids, such as acids and chemicals. This type is constructed of materials that are inert or are lined with materials, such as rubber or phenolic resin coatings to prevent corrosion.

3. Tanks designed for the hauling of liquids under pressure, such as butane, propane, or anhydrous ammonia. These units are designed for working pressure ranging from 18 pounds per square inch to 300 pounds per square inch.

The capacity of tank trucks has increased on the average from slightly more than 3,000 gallons in 1941 to 5,400 gallons in 1951.

The tank truck used in local delivery is an entirely different unit from over-the-road equipment. It is operated by another type of tank-truck business. The equipment used is smaller than over-the-road, consisting primarily of a straight truck with a special individual tank mounted thereon, or a small tank semitrailer with multiple compartments. The operation of these local delivery tank trucks is almost exclusively that of a private carrier. They are owned and op-

Courtesy: Chemical Tank Lines, Inc.

FIG. 8–3. A MC–310 semitrailer used for hauling corrosive liquids. This unit is unloaded through a standpipe running from sump in the bottom of tank to dome assembly through air pressure.

erated by major oil and refinery companies' wholesale and retail facilities, and the independent oil jobber, oil distributor, or retailer operating his own business.

These units are used for delivering petroleum products in relatively small quantities to industrial consumers, homes, and farms. They deliver gasoline and petroleum products to filling stations and fuel oil to homes.

TYPES OF CARRIERS

In 1941 the over-the-road tank trucks in operation were divided evenly between for-hire and private. This was also true in 1945, but in 1951 a survey showed that there were 9,907 tank trucks in proprietary hauling and 15,546 in for-hire service.[6] For-hire trucks are predominant in the chemical tank-truck field. It is reported that about 1,552 are operated by for-hire carriers and 382 in private carriage.[7]

The extent of private carriage in the tank-truck field has always provided strong competition to the for-hire portion. Petroleum hauling has lent itself to the operation of company-owned trucks, and the oil industry has owned or controlled its own transportation facilities in other modes of transportation. Petroleum companies have felt that

[6] *Transport Topics,* September 15, 1952, p. 29.

[7] D. G. Ward, "Opportunities Available in Chemical Transport," *Petroleum Transporter,* July–August, 1952, p. 11.

deliveries from bulk stations to their service stations should be made only in trucks which bear the company name, since an unidentifiable tank truck unloading at a service station might give the patrons the impression that a different brand of gasoline was being unloaded.

The private carrier in over-the-road operations is a company whose primary business is the manufacturing and distribution of petroleum products, chemicals, or other bulk liquids, which operates its own tank-truck transportation system that may consist of large fleets of trucks. In the petroleum field, there are a number of different groups of private carriers: the primary manufacturer and refiner (major oil company) which distributes its own products to its outlets and customers; the manufacturer's agent, who operates one or more of the distributing outlets of the manufacturer from the origin source of supply to its wholesale and retail outlets; and the independent jobber or distributor who owns his own local business, secures his products from either a major manufacturer or refiner or agent of the manufacturer or refiner, and transports these products from his original source of supply to his retail and wholesale outlets.

Because for-hire carriers serve more than one shipper they have an inherent flexibility that private carriage does not possess. For-hire carriers have succeeded when they have provided a better service for the shipper than he can provide for himself, and at a rate which does not encourage private operation. A survey in 1951 showed that there were 1,063 for-hire tank-truck carriers in the United States.[8]

OPERATIONS

Many for-hire operators feel that the best type of operation is one in which they can have 24-hour-a-day loading and unloading. Some shippers have provided keys to permit the for-hire tank-truck operator to unload at night after closing hours. Such so-called "key-stop" operations have advantages to the shipper. For the carrier, it means operations closer to a 24-hour day. The nighttime operations avoid heavy traffic and congested streets. One large tank-truck carrier has over 1,500 bulk plants on key stops.[9]

There are some places where the tank-truck drivers perform the loading and unloading of the unit and serve the customer on a "keep-

---

[8] National Petroleum Council, *Report of the Committee on Petroleum Transportation (Tank Truck Census)*, January 29, 1952, p. 4.

[9] John Ruan, "Improvement Must Come from Within," speech before New England Tank Truck Carriers, Boston, Massachusetts, November 5, 1953.

full" basis. The tank-truck operator watches the customer's storage tanks, and when there is room for additional loads they are automatically added. The majority of petroleum products move on standing orders which may be given to a carrier a week or a month at a time. In chemical transportation there are many specialized individual

P. O. Box 3096 Istrouma Branch ◯	UNIFORM STRAIGHT BILL OF LADING — SHORT FORM Original — Not Negotiable — Domestic **HEARIN TANK LINES, INC.** BATON ROUGE 5, LA. ◯	PETROLEUM TRANSPORTERS

SHIPPER	CONSIGNEE		Shipper's Order No.
SHIPPING ORIGIN	DESTINATION		Meter Ticket No.

This is to certify that the below articles are properly described by name and are packed and marked and are in proper condition for transportation according to the regulations prescribed by the Interstate Commerce Commission.

RECEIVED THE BELOW DESCRIBED PROPERTY IN GOOD CONDITION EXCEPT AS NOTED.

Dray No.

LOADING TIME		UNLOADING TIME	
IN	M	IN	M
OUT	M	OUT	M

Per _____ Shipper
CONSIGNEE

DATE SHIPPED | UNIT Nos | PREPAID | COLLECT

NO. GALLONS	DESCRIPTION OF ARTICLES	WEIGHT	RATE	CHARGES	TAX	TOTAL	Subject to Section 7 of conditions, if this shipment is to be delivered to the consignee without recourse on the consignor, the consignor shall sign the following statement:

The carrier shall not make delivery of this shipment without payment of freight and all other lawful charges.

DO NOT WRITE IN THIS SPACE

Bill Freight to:

(SIGNATURE OF CONSIGNOR)

Company _____

Number _____

City _____ State _____

LOADING TEMP. ° F.	RECEIVED SUBJECT TO THE CLASSIFICATIONS AND TARIFFS IN EFFECT ON THE DATE OF ISSUANCE HEREOF.
SEAL NUMBERS INCLUSIVE	Carrier **HEARIN TANK LINES, INC.** Per _____

ORIGINAL — RETURN TO HOME OFFICE FOR BILLING   **No. 00011**

FIG. 8–4. Bill of lading used by common-carrier tank-truck operators.

loads which require not only special handling but special equipment. Therefore, these shipments do not move on standing orders.

The face of the bill of lading used by regulated tank-truck common carriers is different from that of the motor carrier of general commodities. The number of gallons, meter ticket number, loading time, and loading temperatures are some of the items included on this bill of lading. Figure 8–4 is such a uniform short-form bill of lading.

The terminals of for-hire tank-truck carriers are largely for maintenance purposes and for driver training, inasmuch as the nature of bulk commodities precludes handling or storage by the carrier. Figure 8–5 shows typical driver-training activities of a tank-truck carrier's terminal.

It is particularly important in transportation of chemicals to see that the tank truck is properly cleaned and suited for the product to

Courtesy: Dugan Oil And Transport Co.

FIG. 8–5. Typical driver training at the terminal of a tank-truck operator.

be hauled. At terminals of tank-truck operators, elaborate cleaning systems have been installed which make use of high-pressure steam and hot detergent solutions to clean the tank. It is not unusual to put a man inside the tank to wipe it down.

In for-hire over-the-road operations the entire unit usually carries but a single commodity. Although there are some compartmentized units, their use is usually confined to local operations.

Tank trucks have continued to dominate the short-haul movement. The railroads have sought to regain the petroleum traffic by proposing a rate differential of 1½ cents per hundred pounds lower than tank-truck rates due to the inferiority of rail service. There has been continued litigation regarding this differential.

AUTOMOBILE HAULERS

Whether the carrier is a common or contract carrier depends, in part, upon the desires of shippers. Some automobile manufacturers use contract carriers, and others prefer the service to be offered by a common carrier. Because of the nature and characteristics of the transportation service rendered by automobile haulers, their operating authority embraces areas rather than specific points. About 70 per cent of the new automobiles are transported by carriers of motor vehicles.

Two different types of transporting are used—the driveaway and the truckaway. If the vehicles which are being transported are moved

Courtesy: Howard Sober, Inc.

FIG. 8–6. A truckaway unit used in the East and Middle West.

by motive power which is furnished by one or more of the vehicles, the service is driveaway service. If the motive power is not furnished by one or more of the vehicles being moved, it is truckaway service. Some companies engage in only driveaway service; others in only truckaway; while still others render service using both methods.

TRUCKAWAY

Most new automobiles are transported by the truckaway method. The equipment used in this service is especially designed for this purpose and varies with different carriers. A unit can haul four passenger cars or three cars and a light truck (see Fig. 8–6). Because the state length limit in the West is greater than in the East, truckaway units are used in the West which will carry five and, in some instances, six cars. Also in the West, there are practically no semienclosed units such as are in general use in other parts of the country.

Since the arching height of a truckaway may reach 13½ feet, as compared to approximately 12 feet for most over-the-road equipment, routing of truckaway units poses special problems. Bridges, utility wires, and overhanging limbs are all factors which have to be considered. In dispatching, therefore, specific routes may be assigned.

Although most truckaway units return empty, some trailers of the semienclosed type are converted into units that can be used for hauling certain other commodities, such as shelled corn. This is done by equipping them with steel bottoms, portable sides, and placing a tarpaulin over the top.

DRIVEAWAY

A number of combinations may be used in driveaway service. There is single delivery, which means one car is driven under its own

SADDLE MOUNT DELIVERY   FULL MOUNT DELIVERY

DOUBLE SADDLE MOUNT DELIVERY

3-WAY COMBINATION DELIVERY
(1 FULL MOUNTED AND 1 TOW-BARRED)

TOW-BAR COMBINATION   SINGLE DELIVERY

FIG. 8–7. Different types of driveaway delivery.

power; tow-bar delivery, which is one vehicle driven under its own power and the other towed; saddle-mount delivery, which is one vehicle driven under its own power and another vehicle partially mounted on the first; double saddle-mount delivery; and three-way combination delivery in which one vehicle is driven, one vehicle is completely mounted on the first, and another is towed.

The driveaway method is used primarily in moving new trucks and busses, although there are instances in which the tow-bar method is used for new passenger automobiles. Figure 8–7 shows different types of driveaway deliveries.

An employee who is a driver of a driveaway unit is expected to return to his home terminal by the lowest-cost commercial passenger transportation unless otherwise notified. Some companies maintain a company bus. When a terminal receives a large volume of trucks to be delivered by driveaway service to the same destination, the company bus may be used as the fastest and most economical means of return transportation for the drivers. There are some 16,000 drivers employed by driveaway companies as compared to about 22,000 truckaway drivers.

In both truckaway and driveaway operations, the terminals operated by automobile haulers have greater land area than terminals of general commodity haulers. This is particularly the case at the origin

Courtesy: Fleet Carrier Corp.

FIG. 8–8. Truckaway tractors and semitrailers at a terminal, some of which are loaded and others waiting to be loaded.

terminal because the vehicles are brought there from plants or assembly lines and stored prior to shipment. Figure 8–8 shows truckaway units at a carrier's terminal.

NATURE OF OPERATING AUTHORITY

In the certificates and permits which are issued to motor carriers of automobiles, the terms "initial movements" or "secondary movements" may be found. Initial movement is considered to be the transportation of new motor vehicles from the place of manufacture or assembly to destination, or to a point of interchange with other common carriers. Secondary movement is the transportation of motor vehicles, whether new, used, damaged, or repossessed, between points authorized to be served by the carrier other than the point of manufacture or assembly.[10]

When there is a movement of motor vehicles from the factory to an adjoining parking lot by the manufacturer, the Commission has ruled that this constitutes intraplant movement and does not consti-

---

[10] Administrative Rule No. 75, July 15, 1938.

tute an initial movement. The later movement from the parking lot by for-hire carriers would be the initial movement.[11]

In a situation similar to this when a for-hire carrier transported from the factory to the terminal of another carrier in the same city, this was held to be pickup and delivery service for the second carrier. Therefore, the second carrier's haul would be an initial movement.[12]

A common carrier which has operating authority to transport automobiles in initial movements was permitted by the Commission to purchase or lease a common carrier possessing authority for secondary movements. These authorities could be combined at any point common to both where interchange was possible when the rights were separately owned.[13] However, it has been held that where the combination of initial and secondary authorities will result in a completely new service, there would not be an approval unless there is a definite need for the service, there will be public benefits, and existing carriers will not be seriously affected by the new service.[14]

An individual who acted under a contract as a transport manager for a car manufacturer in transporting new cars was held to be a contract carrier. The drivers secured by the transport manager were obtained through advertisement. The drivers paid their sleeping accommodations, insurance on the car, and a deposit to cover any damage to the car. A part of the deposit was refunded if the car reached the destination without damage. The transport manager paid the car expenses.[15]

OIL-FIELD HAULERS: PIPELINE STRINGERS

An interesting specialized operation is that of the oil-field hauler. This type of common carrier transports oil-field equipment and, in some cases, heavy machinery between nearly all points in the United States. It offers to the oil industry a complete service, such as the erection and dismantling of oil rigs and derricks; the transporting, handling, and spotting of heavy refinery equipment; the picking-up and cleaning of pipelines; and similar services. The equipment possessed by these carriers includes not only motor units but also draglines, bulldozers, and other special facilities. (See Fig. 8–9.)

---

[11] *Payne Common Carrier Application,* 46 MCC 726 (1947).

[12] *George F. Burnett Co.,* 42 MCC 804 (1943), (not printed).

[13] *Clark—Lease—Ronken,* 36 MCC 195 (1940).

[14] *Fleet Carrier Corp.—Lease—Geo. F. Burnett Co., Inc.,* 50 MCC 489 (1948).

[15] *Lord Contract Carrier Application,* 34 MCC 549 (1942).

Courtesy: Autocar Company

FIG. 8–9. The use of a winch on the truck and a full-length roller across the back of the body enables an oil-field drilling rig to be pulled onto the body of the truck. This is typical of the adaptability of trucks in the oil-producing areas of the United States.

A few of these specialized carriers are not oil-field haulers but engage in stringing main trunk pipelines. They take the pipe from a rail car, load it on a truck tractor and trailer, and transport it to the pipeline right-of-way. Special equipment is required for this operation, as it operates over all types of terrain.

QUESTIONS AND PROBLEMS

1. What effect did World War II have upon the development of the tank-truck carriers?
2. Why are specifications issued by the Interstate Commerce Commission for tank trucks?
3. Outline the different types of tank-truck carriers. What are the present trends as to types of carriers?
4. There is a greater possibility of a return haul in chemical transportation than in petroleum products. Why? What does this mean to the shipper? Carrier?
5. Compare the bill of lading of a tank-truck operator with that of a general commodity hauler. What are the differences?
6. Clearly differentiate between the driveaway and the truckaway system of transporting vehicles.
7. What is the difference between initial movements and secondary movements in the transporting of motor vehicles?

8. Is there a solution to the return-haul problem of truckaway operators?
9. Compare the terminal facilities of tank-truck and automobile transporters.
10. What are some of the characteristics of oil-field haulers? Pipeline stringers?

9. ECONOMICS OF COMMERCIAL MOTOR TRANSPORTATION

THE property-carrying commercial motor-carrier industry is composed essentially of small business firms. Of the carriers subject to the jurisdiction of the Interstate Commerce Commission, 26 per cent operated only one truck; 44 per cent, only one or two trucks; 56 per cent, from one to three trucks; and 92 per cent, less than ten trucks. The Class I intercity carriers, which are the largest in terms of gross revenue, operated an average of sixty vehicles, according to the American Trucking Associations, in 1952. There were 2,461 carriers which in 1954 were in the Class I grouping, however; that is, each of these carriers had gross revenue in excess of $200,000 each year. It should be borne in mind, also, that there are some very large intercity motor carriers of property. Of the 10 carriers[1] which were the largest of all motor carriers of property based on gross revenue figures for 1953, 7 were haulers of general commodities. Each of these 10 motor carriers had gross revenue of more than $23 million, and the largest had gross revenue of more than $43 million. There were 100 carriers each grossing more than $6 million in 1953 and over 500 grossing more than $1 million per year. One regular-route general-commodity carrier operates from coast to coast.[2]

The ownership of motor-carrier firms is predominantly individual proprietorship. In 1939, of the intercity carriers of property subject to the general jurisdiction of the Commission, about 70.3 per cent were owned by individuals. Partnerships constituted 12.4 per cent

---

[1] Associated Transport, Inc., $43,000,000; Consolidated Freightways, Inc., $38,000,-000; Roadway Express, Inc., $31,000,000; Allied Van Lines, Inc., $31,000,000; Riss and Co., Inc., $29,000,000; Interstate Motor Freight System, Inc., $26,000,000; Watson Bros. Transportation Co., Inc., $25,000,000; Norwalk Truck Lines, Inc., $25,000,000; Aero Mayflower Transit Co., $23,000,000; and United Parcel Service of New York, Inc., $23,000,000. All of these figures have been rounded.

[2] Denver-Chicago Trucking Company.

and corporations 17.3 per cent. There is a general tendency, as a carrier increases the number of trucks operated, for the corporate form of business organization to be adopted. More than three fourths of the Class I carriers are incorporated. The membership of one of the large interterritorial rate bureaus is composed of 78 per cent corporations and 17 per cent partnerships.

To date, there has been but limited use of financing through public-stock issue. There are, at the present time, ten motor carriers of property which have publicly held stock traded over the counter. It is estimated that this stock is held by about 12,000 to 15,000 stockholders. More than 2,000 of the Class I motor carriers, primarily family corporations, do not average over ten stockholders in each corporation. It is not likely that a carrier will find much of a market for its stock, unless its earnings are sufficient to support a total market value of at least $500,000 in the hands of the public. This means that the carrier probably is not large enough for a public-stock issue un-

TABLE 9–1

DISTRIBUTION OF TOTAL TRAFFIC CARRIED BY COST-STUDY CLASS I
COMMON CARRIERS OF GENERAL FREIGHT, BY WEIGHT OF SHIPMENT

WEIGHT BRACKET (POUNDS PER SHIPMENT)	PERCENTAGE OF TOTAL TRAFFIC CARRIED				
	A		B	C	D
	A–1	A–2			
0– 199........	3.25	3.11	4.80	6.400	7.72
200– 499........	6.27	6.59	8.40	10.964	11.65
500– 999........	7.56	8.02	9.76	12.251	11.27
1,000– 1,999........	8.82	10.47	11.23	14.846	12.60
2,000– 3,999........	11.39	12.04	13.38	15.831	11.69
4,000– 5,999........	6.89	7.85	8.51	8.712	6.75
6,000– 7,999........	4.59	5.02	4.74	4.622	3.79
8,000– 9,999........	2.94	3.45	4.30	3.381	3.52
10,000–11,999........	3.27	3.78	3.79	3.446	2.48
12,000–13,999........	2.29	2.48	3.08	2.606	1.70
14,000–15,999........	1.92	1.66	1.78	2.273	2.02
16,000–17,999........	1.48	1.84	1.98	1.759	2.09
18,000–19,999........	2.32	1.92	2.85	2.736	2.44
20,000 and over......	37.01	31.77	21.40	10.173	20.28
Total..........	100.00	100.00	100.00	100.000	100.00

Code:
  A. *Middle Atlantic Carriers*
    A–1.—New York–Philadelphia carriers for period from July 1, 1945, to June 30, 1946.
    A–2.—Other than New York–Philadelphia carriers for period from July 1, 1945, to June 30, 1946.
  B. Southern interterritorial carriers for year 1943.
  C. Southern intraterritorial carriers for year 1943.
  D. Western trunk-line carriers for year 1944.
  Source: Interstate Commerce Commission, Bureau of Accounts and Cost Finding. *Territorial Cost Scales and Operating Performance Factors in Middle Atlantic Territory* (Washington, D.C., 1948), Exhibit A, p. 133. Interstate Commerce Commission, Bureau of Transport Economics and Statistics, *Territorial Studies of Motor Carrier Costs, Traffic, and Rate Structure* (Washington, D.C., 1947), Statement No. 4723, p. 80; Statement No. 4722, p. 66; Statement No. 4721, p. 281.

less proportionate net earnings, after taxes, are at least $100,000 on that part of the stock sold to the public.

SIZE OF SHIPMENTS CARRIED

There are available data that indicate the size of shipments carried by motor carriers. There have been a number of traffic and cost studies made by the Interstate Commerce Commission which show that Class I common carriers of general freight have a large share of their traffic in the lower weight groups. Furthermore, it is shown in these cost and traffic studies that the size of shipments varies in the different territories served by the sample carriers. Table 9–1 shows the breakdown of size of shipments and the percentage of total traffic accounted for by each weight group.

TYPE OF TRAFFIC

The majority of general commodity hauls are characterized by a single-line haul; that is, the shipments are carried from origin to destination by a single motor carrier. This is true generally throughout the United States, although interline hauls are increasing. Table 9–2 gives the distribution in the Middle Atlantic area of total traffic

TABLE 9–2

DISTRIBUTION OF TOTAL TRAFFIC CARRIED BY COST-STUDY CARRIERS
SEPARATED BETWEEN SINGLE-LINE, INTERLINE RECEIVED,
INTERLINE DELIVERED, AND BRIDGE TRAFFIC

Type of Traffic	Tons	Percentage of Total
NEW YORK—PHILADELPHIA CARRIERS		
Single-line	835,925	86.25
Interline received	71,698	7.40
Interline delivered	60,761	6.27
Bridge traffic	756	0.08
Total	969,140	100.00
OTHER THAN NEW YORK–PHILADELPHIA CARRIERS		
Single-line	1,469,219	82.89
Interline received	154,997	8.74
Interline delivered	138,961	7.84
Bridge traffic	9,439	0.53
Total	1,772,616	100.00

Source: Interstate Commerce Commission, Bureau of Accounts and Cost Finding, *Territorial Cost Scales and Operating Performance Factors in Middle Atlantic Territory* (Washington, D.C., 1948), Exhibit A, p. 134.

among single-line, interline, and bridge traffic. Interline traffic is that traffic which is exchanged between carriers; bridge traffic is that which is transported for the originating carrier by a second carrier to be turned over to a third carrier for delivery to destination. The single-line traffic for the Middle Atlantic area comprises more than 82 per cent of the total traffic carried.

LOAD FACTOR

Motor carriers' loads do not average as high per vehicle-mile as those of the competitive modes of transportation. This is reflected in

TABLE 9–3
AVERAGE LOAD FACTOR BY AREAS AND DIRECTIONS OF MOVEMENT IN
WESTERN TRUNK-LINE TERRITORY FOR COST-STUDY CARRIERS*

DIRECTION	TON-MILES PER VEHICLE-MILE				
	All Areas	Northwest	Northeast	Southwest	Southeast
Eastbound. . . .	7.5	5.5	9.2	6.6	7.1
Westbound . . .	10.3	11.2	10.8	9.4	10.1
Total	8.9	8.3	10.0	8.0	8.7

* Load factors were based on trips for test period in each area. Northwest area is defined as west of a line running from Duluth, Minnesota, via Minneapolis, Minnesota, to Sioux City, Iowa, and north of the Nebraska–South Dakota state boundaries. Northeast area is defined as east of a line running from Duluth, Minnesota, via Minneapolis, Minnesota, to Sioux City, Iowa, and north of the Minnesota–Iowa and Wisconsin–Illinois state boundaries. Southwest area is defined as west of a line running from Sioux City, Iowa, via Kansas City and Springfield, Missouri, to Arkansas City, Arkansas, and south of the Nebraska–South Dakota state boundaries. Southeast area is defined as east of a line running from Sioux City, Iowa, via Kansas City and Springfield, Missouri, to Arkansas City, Arkansas, and south of the Minnesota–Iowa and Wisconsin–Illinois state boundaries.
Source: Interstate Commerce Commission, Bureau of Transport Economics and Statistics, *Territorial Studies of Motor Carrier Costs, Traffic, and Rate Structure*, Part I: *Western Trunk Line Territory* (Washington, D.C., 1947), p. 284.

operations procedures as well as in the rate structure of the motor carriers. Some idea as to the average load factor of certain motor carriers of property operating in the Western Trunk-Line Territory can be secured from Table 9–3, as assembled by the Interstate Commerce Commission. This table shows the ton-miles that are carried per vehicle-mile and indicates that the average load factor is considerably higher on westbound than on eastbound traffic. In the Southern Territory, a recent study found the load factor to average 10.3.[3]

AVERAGE EXPENSES PER INTERCITY VEHICLE-MILE

The average expenses per intercity vehicle-mile for Class I motor common carriers of general freight operating principally with owned

[3] Interstate Commerce Commission, Bureau of Accounts and Cost Finding, *Unit Costs, Performance Factors, Cost Scales and Traffic Data for Motor Common Carriers of General Freight in Southern Territory* (Washington, D.C., 1953), p. 13.

equipment were $0.632 in 1952.[4] Those Class I motor common carriers of general freight operating with owned and leased equipment or purchased transportation had average expenses per intercity vehicle-mile of $0.527. The average expense per intercity vehicle-mile for Class I contract carriers for the same year was $0.355. Although there are substantial differences in services performed by common and contract carriers, the latter's rates generally reflect a close relationship to cost. The average expenses per intercity vehicle-mile of motor common carriers of other than general commodities were $0.354 in 1952.

ELEMENTS OF COMPETITION

Motor carriers of property prior to regulation in 1935 constituted an example of perfect competition in that there were many thousands of small operators, no one of which could influence the price of the service. However, the entire field cannot be so classified today. At the present time the regulated for-hire carriers would constitute the economist's concept of imperfect competition. This is the case since it is necessary that they have operating authority, which is a restriction on their right to enter the business, and they engage in collective rate making through rate bureaus, to mention but two factors which are indicative of imperfect competition. There are such a large number of motor carriers that the regulated for-hire industry cannot be characterized as an oligopoly, but regionally there are a few large firms which predominate.

In analyzing the status of for-hire motor carriers, differentiation should be made between the regulated and nonregulated (exempt) carriers. There are 50 per cent more exempt carriers than there are regulated carriers operating interstate. These carriers are not subject to economic regulation. There is no restriction on entry into exempt hauling, and each may establish any price for its service that it desires. Even in exempt interstate transportation, however, carriers sometimes agree to charge a specific rate between certain origin and destination points. Some exempt carriers publish a tariff, although not required to do so, and charge shippers the same rates for transporting the same quantities. As to whether exempt rates are lower than those of regulated carriers, it is difficult to ascertain, one of the

---

[4] Interstate Commerce Commission, Bureau of Transport Economics and Statistics, *Statistics of Class I Motor Carriers, 1952* (Washington, D.C.: U.S. Government Printing Office, 1954), p. 19.

COMMERCIAL MOTOR TRANSPORTATION

reasons being that the services performed are often not the same.

There are some exempt carriers which have secured operating authority for handling return loads of certain specific commodities and have filed their rates for this traffic with the Interstate Commerce Commission. In some cases, this rate may be 25 per cent less than the carrier which hauls only nonexempt commodities. The lower rate offered by the exempt carrier is often just a "paper" rate, however; it is not used because the provision of facilities for solicitation and other expenses, such as terminal expenses, is not justified, particularly for those exempt carriers which can lease their units for the return haul to regulated for-hire carriers. This supplies a certain amount of revenue and is much simpler. There have been instances during a rail-car shortage in which exempt carriers charged 25 per cent more than the corresponding rail rates.

Upon first examination, it would appear that the exempt carriers, as a segment of the for-hire motor carriers, are an example of perfect competition. Freedom of entry is still existent, and there are thousands of motor carriers which are allowed to set any rates that each carrier or operator wants to set. On the other hand, there are certain rigidities which are beginning to develop, especially in regard to rates, and this development is likely to continue.

RATE OF RETURN

A fair-rate-of-return concept is generally used in the public utility industry in determining the need for rate increases. It bases need for a rate increase upon the rate of return on the investment. When the rate of return on the investment of a utility company falls below a desired level, the company seeks a rate increase in order to obtain a fair rate of return. In industries of this kind, the investment is large, however, in relation to total costs, and the risk is more closely related to the amount of the investment. In the motor-carrier industry, on the other hand, the amount of investment is relatively small in relation to total costs. This is one of the reasons why motor carriers feel that this method of determining the need for rate increases is not valid for their industry. For the year 1946, the net investment of 98 Class I motor carriers operating in one area was $22,389,560. Their operating expenses totaled $84,691,001, or $3.78 of expense for each $1.00 of investment.[5]

In a recent year, all Class I motor carriers of property had $3.08

---

[5] Investigation and Suspension No. M–2723 (1948).

revenue to $1.00 of gross investment in contrast to Class I railroads for the same year of $0.29 of revenue to $1.00 of gross investment. The average investment of Class I intercity property carriers in 1951 was $520,455. Those outside the motor-carrier industry who favor the fair-rate-of-return method of determining the need for rate increases for motor carriers contend that the average operating ratio[6] alone is not conclusive evidence of financial difficulties which require rate relief. They feel that other items should be equally controlling, such as the growth of the industry on past rates, the investment in the industry, and the return on the investment. For example, the rate of earnings of motor carriers based on net worth for individual carriers may be relatively high. The rate of return on net worth for Class I carriers of property averaged about 18 per cent before World War II but fell sharply during the war. After the war in 1946 it averaged 28 per cent and declined in 1949 to 19 per cent of net worth.[7]

OPERATING RATIO

The motor carriers make use of their average operating ratio as a measure of their revenue needs and financial condition. The operating ratio is the proportion which operating expense bears to operating income. Operating expenses divided by operating revenues and multiplied by 100 give the percentage of the operating revenues which are required to pay the operating expenses, this being the operating ratio. An operating ratio in excess of 100 would indicate that the expense of the operation exceeded the revenues derived therefrom. It is desirable to keep the operating ratio as low as possible. Figure 9–1 shows the operating ratios of Class I intercity property carriers from 1943 to 1953 and indicates that the 10-year average operating ratio is about 96.

Motor-carrier operators are in general agreement that stability and serviceability are impaired whenever the individual operating ratio rises above 95 per cent. From the remaining 5 per cent, assorted charges not included in operating expenses must be paid and a profit secured. The danger point for a group of carriers providing service in a given territory is usually reached when the group average rises significantly above 90 per cent. That there is a difference between these operating ratios for an individual carrier and a group of car-

---

[6] This is the method in use, and it will be explained in more detail.

[7] Herbert F. Wyeth, *The Motor Carrier Industry* (New York: Shields & Co., 1951), p. 33.

riers operating in a given area is due to the fact that the operating ratio of the group of carriers will be an average and will be composed of different types of operations, some of which, because of the nature of their operations, are more expensive to conduct than others. However, because of competition, they are operating upon the same rates.

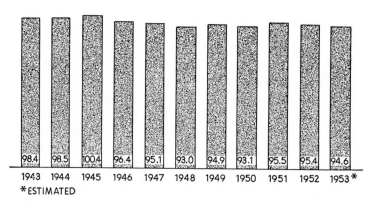

FIG. 9–1. Operating ratio for Class I motor common carriers of general commodities.

Source: American Trucking Associations, Inc., *Trends, 1954.* Based on Interstate Commerce Commission reports.

Motor carriers, in seeking rate adjustment approvals from the Interstate Commerce Commission and state utility commissions, use their operating ratios as the criteria for proving the need for a general increase in rates. For example, Division 2 of the Interstate Commerce Commission, treating one proposal for increased rates which contemplated a 10 per cent increase in less-than-truckload rates and a 4 per cent increase in truckload rates, ruled that such increases would produce an average operating ratio of about 93 per cent, which it believed to be reasonable.[8] Another decision mentioned and used the 93 per cent ratio.[9] Again, in another decision, the granting of a general 10 per cent rate increase was found to be just and reasonable, for it would result in an operating ratio of about 93 per cent.[10]

The need for additional revenue based on the operating ratio alone may have more validity for motor carriers of general commodities than it does for specialized carriers, but it is used for all carriers. For example, a specialized carrier, such as a household-goods carrier, which pays 70 per cent of the gross revenue for the lease of a vehicle

---

[8] *Increased Common Carrier Truck Rates in the East,* 42 MCC 633 (1943).

[9] *Increased Common Carrier Truck Rates in New England,* 43 MCC 13 (1943).

[10] *New England, 1946 Increased Rates,* 47 MCC 509 (1947).

and 20 per cent to a booking agent to solicit traffic has 10 per cent of the revenue left to cover all of the administrative and other costs. These two expenses alone will result in the operating ratio seldom, if ever, being below 90 per cent. If the revenue on a shipment was $100 and the transportation was purchased for 70 per cent of the revenue with an additional 20 per cent commission paid for the solicitation, the expenses would amount to $90. The operating ratio would be 90 per cent. Assume that the revenue is increased on this shipment to $200 and that the transportation was purchased for 70 per cent of the revenue while a 20 per cent commission was paid for the solicitation of the shipment. The increased revenue would then be $200, the expenses $180, and the operating ratio still 90 per cent.

When the Bureau of Accounts, Cost Finding, and Valuation of the Commission has prepared cost studies and when cost comparisons are made with the costs of different agencies of transportation on the basis of revenue need, an allowance of return on investment has been considered. In connection with its recent 1950 study, a 5 per cent return on the motor carriers' depreciated investment for the Southern Territory taken as a whole was found to amount to approximately 1.2 per cent of the carriers' operating expenses, rents, and taxes. If the carriers' allowance for profit was based on this 5 per cent return on depreciated investment, the result would be a profit amounting to about 1.2 per cent of gross revenues. The carriers' operating ratio under these circumstances would approximate 98.8 per cent. The figure of 5 per cent was based on an analysis showing the rates paid on loans by a number of Class I carriers to average between 4 and 6 per cent.

Experience has indicated that 1.2 per cent of gross revenues is not sufficient profit to defray income taxes and to attract capital and business ability to the industry. For this reason, the cost formulas of the Commission provide for computing total revenue need on the basis of an operating ratio of 93 per cent. Although this should not be interpreted as an approval by the Commission of such ratio for any carrier or group of carriers, the objective has been to set forth a procedure whereby an allowance for profit may be included in the cost study. During the period 1946–53, the operating ratios of the motor common carriers of general commodities for the country as a whole averaged approximately 94.8.[11]

[11] Interstate Commerce Commission, Bureau of Accounts, Cost Finding, and Valuation, *Explanation of the Development of Motor Carrier Costs with Statement as to Their Meaning and Significance* (Washington, D.C., 1954), p. 70.

An operating ratio is equivalent to some rate of return if the operating ratio is less than 100 per cent. The operating ratio has been criticized as constituting no standard at all, since the same ratio can provide one company with a substantial reward for its services and not supply another company with an ordinary rate of return.[12]

One of the alternatives to the use of operating ratio is the use of the conventional fair rate of return based on capital necessarily employed in the business and permitting such rate of return to be sufficiently *high* to offset the risk involved.

The Commission has qualified its use of the operating ratio by requiring proof of the accuracy and reasonableness of the charges made to operating expense. It has not indicated that 93 per cent is the breaking point in operating ratio above or below which the operating revenues may be considered as inadequate or adequate, but rather it has indicated that this figure is an approximation of such a level.[13]

Up to the present time, the Commission has shown a preference for the use of the operating ratio as an appropriate standard of measurement for the determination of the general financial condition of the motor-carrier industry. However, it is possible that some refinement in its use may occur. The industry feels that the operating ratio is the only fair and equitable standard by which to assay their financial needs.

SIGNIFICANCE OF OUT-OF-POCKET, JOINT, AND CONSTANT COSTS[14]

Usually, most producers of goods or services offer a multitude of products and services. Their plants, whatever their nature, are actually multiple-purpose facilities, in that they are used in the simultaneous production of several products or services. A factory, although limited to the production of similar articles, may produce many related products in one field, each product having a specific price. A farm may produce several items, such as cotton, cottonseed, livestock,

---

[12] Laurence S. Knappen, "Transit Operating Ratio—Another View," *Public Utilities Fortnightly,* Vol. LI (April 9, 1953), p. 485.

[13] Clyde B. Aitchison, *Fair Reward and Just Compensation, Common Carrier Service* (Washington, D.C.: Association of Interstate Commerce Commission Practitioners, 1954), p. 78.

[14] Largely adapted from Interstate Commerce Commission, Bureau of Accounts, Cost Finding, and Valuation, *Explanation of the Development of Motor Carrier Costs with Statement as to Their Meaning and Significance* (Washington, D.C., 1954), p. 1.

poultry products, and other products, each having a different selling price per unit of output. The truck line may haul a variety of commodities of differing weight density, size of shipment, and value for varying distances, thus providing a very large number of services, each of which must be individually priced. The costs of producing these various products and services fall into two groups: (a) those expenses directly assignable to each separate product or service, and (b) those expenses incurred on behalf of the operation as a whole.

OUT-OF-POCKET OR VARIABLE COSTS

The expenses that can be assigned to any given product or service are termed "out-of-pocket costs" or "long-run variable costs." These include those direct costs for labor, material, equipment, supervision, interest, and so forth, which were incurred solely as a result of the production of the given services. In other words, the assignable expenses include those expenses which would not have been incurred if the service had not been rendered. They include not only those separable items of cost which can be directly measured, such as the labor required to load a truck, but also that part of the otherwise common expenses which varies directly with the units of output, such as the wear and tear on over-the-road equipment as a result of the miles traveled. In the latter instance, the relationship between the units of service rendered (ton-miles) and the added expense incurred for maintenance may not be as obvious as in the former case, but it is nonetheless real. In both instances, added increments of output occasion added increments of expense. Such added increments of expense are directly assignable on a cost-of-service basis to the added traffic which occasioned the added expense.

By observing the effect on the expenses of increasing or decreasing increments of traffic, or by comparing similar operations having a wide range in traffic volume,[15] it is possible to determine within reasonable limits that portion of the expenses which, over a period of time, increases and decreases in direct proportion to changes in output. By dividing the expenses of these out-of-pocket or long-run variable costs by the appropriate units of work or units of service (that is, tons handled, ton-miles, shipments billed, and so forth), there is obtained the out-of-pocket or added-traffic cost per unit of service performed. If the units of service used in handling a given

---

[15] J. M. Clark, *Studies in the Economics of Overhead Costs* (Chicago: University of Chicago Press, 1923), p. 223.

shipment between two given points are multiplied by the applicable out-of-pocket cost per unit, and the products totaled, the aggregate cost obtained constitutes the out-of-pocket expense incurred in handling the shipment. Conversely, the figures indicate the out-of-pocket expense which could have been avoided if the shipment had not

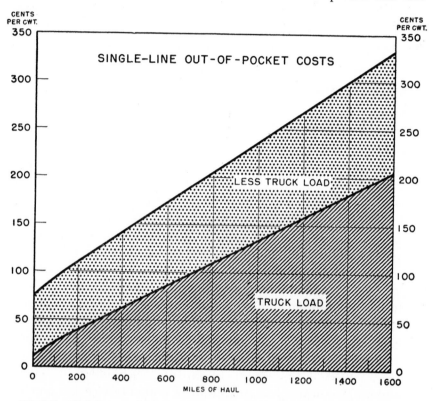

FIG. 9–2. Single-line out-of-pocket costs for Class I motor carriers of general freight in the Southwest Territory, 1953.

Source: Interstate Commerce Commission, Bureau of Accounts, Cost Finding, and Valuation, *Cost Study of Class I Motor Carriers of General Freight in the Southwest Territory—Year 1953* (Washington, D.C., 1954).

been handled. The out-of-pocket costs thus computed are equally applicable to all shipments of a given weight, length of haul, and so on, regardless of whether they represent previously established business or newly acquired traffic. The units of work performed are the same in either case. Figure 9–2 shows the single-line out-of-pocket costs for Class I motor carriers in the Southwest Territory.

Assignable expenses, then, include those expenses which, over a period of time, vary directly with the volume of output. They consist of the long-run variable costs. When such costs are computed for a unit of traffic (per ton, per carload, and so on), they are commonly termed the "out-of-pocket" or "added-traffic" costs. The producer normally will not sell any portion of his output for less than the out-of-pocket costs incurred in producing it. To do so would result in an expense greater than the revenue received. Such losses can be avoided by discontinuing the service. For this reason, the out-of-pocket costs of performing a service normally set the minimum below which prices or rates are not permitted to fall.

CONSTANT COSTS

The constant or indirect costs include the remaining expenses, which are unaffected by increases or decreases in production. Increases or decreases in output are not followed by proportionate increases or decreases in expenses.[16] The constant costs can, in effect, be viewed as consisting of those expenses incurred on behalf of the operation as a whole. They can be avoided only by discontinuing the entire operation or very substantial parts of it. They are not traceable to particular units of output or to classes of customers.[17]

When an operator first starts production, the constant costs are made up of the indirect expenses for that minimum-sized plant with which the business can be started, such as supervision, interest on investment, insurance, and taxes. There is no relationship between such minimum expenses and the units of work performed; therefore, such expenses cannot be attached to any specific units of output on a cost-of-service basis. It is true that, in the long run, the total revenues must be sufficient to recover these constant or indirect expenses; but how much of such expense is attributable to any given unit of output cannot be determined. Constant expenses are unrelated to the separate units of output and continue even though the production of any given unit should stop.

If all the units of output are the same, such as one-pound loaves of bread, the total indirect expenses can be divided by the total of the loaves of bread and a pro-rata cost per loaf of bread arrived at which can be used in fixing prices.[18] Even then the result cannot be truly labeled as the cost for any given unit; rather, it is the statistical apportionment of the constant or indirect expenses over all the units

---

[16] *Ibid.,* p. 1.

[17] J. M. Clark, *Encyclopaedia of Social Sciences* (1937), Vol. XI, p. 511.

[18] Output may have numerous dimensions, such as number of customers, number of sales or deliveries, or weight or bulk of goods and distance delivered. *Ibid.*

of output. If all such units are identical and no discrimination is practiced, the sum of the out-of-pocket costs added to the pro-rata distribution of the constant costs gives a figure that represents a fully compensatory selling price. On the other hand, if the output of the bakery consists of unlike things, such as loaves of bread and assorted cakes, any distribution of the constant costs over the units of output, as pound for pound, no longer can be the only guide in price fixing, unless the value-of-service considerations, that is, the relative demand for bread versus cake, are ignored. If the latter factor is considered, the fully distributed costs, although providing a measure for comparative purposes, nevertheless can be but a beginning point in fixing prices. These unassignable expenses are referred to as the constant costs, indirect costs, fixed costs, overhead costs, or burden.

JOINT COSTS

Joint costs are those costs incurred in the production of two or more products which result from a single, indivisible operation. Examples of joint-cost production most often used are the growing of cotton fiber and cottonseed or the production of hides and beef. The production of the one commodity (or the completion of one or more stages of its production) is inseparable from the production of the other. The two products result, in whole or in part, from but a single operation, the one being the unavoidable result of the production of the other. The expenses for the joint operation are not capable of separation between the jointly produced products on a cost-of-service basis. The basic approach in cost finding of determining the expenses that could be avoided if one or another of the joint products were withdrawn from production is here both unworkable and without meaning. An example of joint costs in the trucking industry is the return movement of over-the-road equipment, a discussion of which follows.

DIFFERENCES BETWEEN CONSTANT AND JOINT COSTS

Constant costs, although like joint costs in that they cannot be assigned to the individual units of output on a cost-of-service basis, nevertheless differ from joint costs in some important respects. When a motor carrier, through successive additions to its staff and plant, reaches that volume of output at which maximum efficiency is obtained, the law of decreasing costs no longer applies, and all costs are variable with output. The out-of-pocket unit costs then equal the over-all average unit costs. Under these conditions, any new traffic whose revenue does not cover over-all average unit costs also fails to cover out-of-pocket costs. Low rates made to encourage traffic when the carrier was operating at much below capacity may need to be examined to see that they are not throwing a burden on other traffic.[19] On the other hand, the joint costs lose none of their characteristics as capacity is approached.[20] Cotton fiber and cottonseed are joint-cost products regardless of the degree to which the productive capacity of the soil is being utilized. In like manner, the return of equipment is as much a joint cost when a truck line is operating at capacity as it was when it was operating below capacity.

A second difference between constant costs and joint costs is that the constant costs constitute only a small part of the trucking expenses. Thus, they can be used to justify only limited discrimination in rate making. Joint costs incurred in connection with the return movement of trucking equipment, although limited to over-the-road running expenses only, relate to a large percentage of the costs and may be used to justify wider spreads in rates as between directions of freight movements than can be justified from a consideration of only the constant costs.

A third difference between constant costs and joint costs is a tendency toward an inverse relationship in the prices for jointly produced products which has no counterpart where only constant costs are involved. Again, using the example of cotton fiber and cottonseed, as the demand for cotton fiber increases, more cotton is grown with the likely result that more cottonseed is made available than the market will take at the existing price. The price for cottonseed, therefore, falls to that price where the demand will take all the seed produced. On the other hand, a fall in the price of cotton fiber will discourage production and lead to a decline in the supply of cottonseed and an increase in its price. Briefly, the prices of joint-cost products tend to vary inversely, the result being the encouragement of a full and complete utilization of the jointly produced products.

The same principle applies in connection with the joint costs existent in the return movement of equipment. A demand for truck transportation in one direction only, from A to B, will necessitate a high rate to cover the costs of round trips. But if a low rate at a level

---

[19] Donald H. Wallace, "Joint and Overhead Cost and Railway Rate Policy," *Quarterly Journal of Economics*, Vol. XLVIII (1934), pp. 597 and 598.

[20] *Ibid.*, p. 585.

somewhere above the out-of-pocket terminal costs will stimulate a demand in the opposite direction (from B to A), it will be offered up to the point where the unused capacity is absorbed. Such a rate structure, however, may be very unstable. Should the high-rated commodity, moving from A to B, cease to move, the low-rated commodity must either pay a much higher rate or cease to move also. Competition among operators for the high-rated traffic, reversals in the direction of traffic flow, or the appearance of high-rated traffic from B to A, thus displacing the low-rated freight, will upset the rate structure as the by-product low-rated traffic finds itself shifted to the classification of principal traffic, upon which full costs must now be secured. Some compromise must be made between the advantages of the long-term stability of rates, on the one hand, and, on the other, the benefits accruing from the greatest utilization of the plant and equipment based on the frequent adjustment of rates to changes.

SEPARATION OF COSTS BETWEEN OUT-OF-POCKET AND CONSTANT

Although the previous explanation of out-of-pocket or variable costs, constant costs, and joint costs has been of a general nature, it will now be applied directly to motor-carrier operations. In the motor-carrier industry, the so-called one-truck operation will find that some of its costs are constant. Although repairs and fuel for such an operator are largely proportional to miles operated, expenses for interest on investment, taxes, and insurance are, within limits, of a fixed character. They are unaffected by whether the carrier hauls part of a load or a full load. However, when its business grows to a point where the carrier must purchase and operate two trucks, these same expenses will become variable to a great degree. When still more trucks are added and operated over a route, it may be seen that, with some lag, the amount of equipment owned and maintained becomes adjusted to the volume of traffic handled. Interest, taxes, and insurance on equipment now vary almost directly with the volume of traffic moved and so become long-run out-of-pocket costs. The operator has now used all unutilized capacity it may have had when it started operations with the one truck. The capacity it now maintains will, over a period of time, be adjusted to the amount of service rendered.

The same result appears if the adjustment of the capacity to the demand is achieved by the appearance of new operators, each owning only one or two trucks. Although the costs for any one operator may be partly of a fixed character, as a group the costs of rendering the service are as variable as if one operator owned and operated all the equipment.

The conclusion may be reached that the costs for the trucking industry over an extended period are very largely proportional to the volume of business moved. This is characteristic of industries where there are a very large number of small producers in the field or where a few big operators perform the service with a plant consisting of a large number of small units (trucks), the number of which, over a period of time, becomes adjusted to the volume of transportation service performed.

The fact that some small portion of the expenses in the motor-carrier industry does not increase in direct proportion to the volume of traffic (that is, behaves as though it were of a constant character and unrelated to the volume of traffic) may be attributed to one or the other of the following: (a) the companies are relatively small and have not fully outgrown the minimum-sized plants with which their operations were started, the result being a less-than-proportionate increase in the expenses as they obtain increased utilization of their original facilities; or (b) the long-run growth of traffic has permitted the gradual introduction of a larger, more expensive, but more efficient, plant which makes possible an operation at a lower unit cost. Industries in which this latter situation exists are referred to as industries of increasing returns or decreasing costs.

Long-run operating costs of railroads are estimated to be between 70 to 80 per cent variable if investment is excluded. This is due to the fact that fixed costs are present in rail maintenance-of-way expenses as well as in capital costs due to the investment in railroad property. In contrast to this, the highway costs for motor carriers are distributed on a use basis through gasoline taxes and license fees. They are proportional to the traffic carried.

It is important to note that the classification of an item of cost as out-of-pocket (variable) or constant may depend upon the period of time under consideration. Some items, such as administrative overhead and property taxes, may remain relatively constant in short-term fluctuations in traffic (week to week or month to month) but become variable with the more permanent changes in traffic volume which occur from season to season or from year to year.

The degree to which the motor carrier's costs are variable is also a function of the volume of traffic handled. When the operation is just beginning and unused capacity exists, the constant costs will constitute a larger portion of the total than will be true when the volume is larger. When the volume of traffic reaches that density per route-mile at which the maximum efficiency of operation is attained and the law of decreasing costs (decreased unit costs with increased volume) is no longer operative, the costs will become wholly variable. It follows, then, that the separation of the expenses between out-of-pocket or variable expenses and those of a constant character will depend in some degree upon the level of traffic attained. Studies of motor-carrier costs indicate that, based on the level of traffic generally experienced in 1943, and over an extended period of time, the operating expenses, rents, and taxes are somewhat between 90 and 100 per cent variable with the traffic volume. Studies made in 1950 indicate that from 82 to 100 per cent of these expenses are variable. Allowances for interest on investment and profit are not included in these operating expenses. Interest charges on a major part of the investment, particularly that related to the investment in equipment, would be a variable cost. The element of profit, over and above interest charges, would have the characteristics of constant costs in that, although it is a "burden" that must be met if the operations as a whole are to have long-term survival value, it cannot be directly assigned to particular kinds of traffic on a cost-of-service basis.

JOINT COSTS IN MOTOR-CARRIER OPERATIONS

Joint costs are present in several phases of motor-carrier operation. The round-trip operation of equipment, as previously stated, has the nature of a joint cost. As all equipment operated in one direction must at some time make the return move in the opposite direction, over-the-road transportation service performed in any given direction inevitably makes available the same over-the-road transportation capacity in the opposite direction. Like the raising of cotton fiber and cottonseed, the round-trip movement constitutes an indivisible unit of production. The only over-the-road costs on a round-trip movement which can be assigned to a given direction are those costs which would not have been incurred if the freight transported in the given direction had not been carried. As such over-the-road costs are limited to that added fuel and wear and tear which can be separately apportioned to the added load, they constitute but a very small portion of the total over-the-road running costs. Therefore, while the total number of round trips operated is closely related to the total volume of traffic handled, and the total running costs for all round trips can be divided between variable and constant, like any other expense, the running costs for any single trip are in a very large measure not separable between the separate parts of the trip. Because of this factor, the joint costs for the round trip are prorated over the total revenue units of traffic hauled on the round trip; that is, they are apportioned over the total round-trip revenue ton-miles. For example, if a truck hauls a 10-ton load from A to B and returns empty, the costs of the round trip are charged to the 10-ton load. If the truck hauls 10 tons from A to B and returns with 1 ton from B to A, the round-trip costs are prorated over the 11 tons, each ton being charged with one eleventh of the round-trip costs. Any attempt to separate the over-the-road running costs by directions, that is, to charge one half to the movement from A to B and one half to the movement from B to A, and then to divide the resulting directionalized costs by 10 tons in the one case and 1 ton in the other, is ignoring the fundamental nature of joint cost. The result is to carry the cost apportionments beyond the point where any differentiation between the rates from A to B and the rates from B to A must be justified by considerations other than differences in the over-the-road costs. When vehicles operate in one direction with truckload traffic and return with less-than-truckload traffic, the round-trip costs are apportioned equally, ton-mile for ton-mile, between both types of traffic.

Two other examples of joint costs in the motor-carrier industry include the vehicle time consumed in running to and from pickup and delivery stops, and the so-called "contact time" on multiple-shipment stops in collection and delivery service. The latter includes the time consumed at the shipper's or consignee's place of business, in starting and stopping the truck, locating the receiver of the freight, receiving instructions as to location of freight, and other miscellaneous delays. The costs here considered are those related only to the number of stops made. They exclude the expenses related to the number of shipments picked up or delivered at the stop or to the size of the shipment picked up or delivered at the stop. The two groups of expenses described here (running to the stop and the contact time at the stop) are of a joint-cost nature insofar as the traffic picked up or delivered at a single stop is concerned. Such costs, when figured for each separate stop, are prorated over the revenue units of traffic (hundredweight) picked up or delivered at such stop.

Still another example of joint costs is found in motor-carrier operation. Vehicles or terminal facilities purchased to meet transportation demands at the peak hours of the day or during peak seasons of the year are available to serve transportation demands coming at off-peak hours or off-peak seasons. The expenses incurred in making the vehicles or facilities available for the handling of traffic at peak periods, such as annual taxes, annual license fees, and those maintenance expenses resulting from the action of the elements, have the characteristics of joint costs in that the capacity thus made available for peak-period traffic is also made available at no additional cost, excluding the wear and tear incurred in handling the traffic, for off-peak traffic. The economic justification for the application of different rates at different times of the year rests on the existence of the "time-jointness."[21] The principle here is that, where traffic varies widely from period to period, the adjustment of the rates to the varying conditions of demand present at different seasons will encourage the maximum year-round utilization of the plant and equipment. The joint expenses of the character here described can be directly separated like other expenses among the various service functions, such as over-the-road running costs, collection and delivery costs, platform handling, and billing and collection. The expenses so separated are prorated over the applicable service units (tons, ton-miles, and so on) without differentiation between traffic handled at peak periods and traffic handled during off-peak periods. The existence of this "time-jointness" in motor-carrier costs has a bearing only when a differentiation in the rates between periods of time is in question. The cost problem then arising is that of determining the limit to which a differentiation in rates can go (that is, the reducing of rates in off-peak periods and the increasing of rates in peak periods) without reducing the rates below the out-of-pocket costs incurred in the off-peak periods.

To sum up the subject of joint costs, there is no justification from a cost-of-service standpoint for distributing any more of these joint costs to any one unit of output resulting from the joint operation than to any other unit of output from the same operation. Furthermore, joint costs do not lend themselves to a distribution on the basis of the directly assignable expenses, for no directly assignable expenses are present in a strictly joint-cost operation.

Regardless of the disposition of the joint costs, there is still the problem of determining that rate structure which will provide the most equitable distribution of the burden of these joint costs, not only as between different commodities but as between different

---

[21] *Ibid.*, p. 613.

weight shipments of the same commodity and shipments moving in opposite directions. The making of the so-called "back-haul" rates is an example. The distribution of the burden of these joint costs is a matter requiring an interpretation of the value-of-service or demand factor by kinds of freight, sizes of shipment, and directions of movement.

SIGNIFICANCE OF CONSTANT AND JOINT COSTS IN FIXING PRICES

The problem faced in the making of rates is similar to that faced by the farmer in selling his cotton fiber and cottonseed. As these are joint-cost products, their costs of production cannot be separated except to a very limited degree as direct expenses which can be assigned to each product on a cost-of-service basis, such as baling, packaging, transportation, and so forth. Although the total revenue received from the sale of both products must in the long run equal their combined cost of production and the price for each should at least cover the direct expenses chargeable to each, the price that will move each of these products in the market depends upon the demand for each.[22] This demand reflects the buyer's opinion of the benefits he can derive from the possession of the product, that is, its utility to him. It is this buyer's demand which ultimately determines the distribution of the constant and joint costs, in other words, the distribution of the "burden." This distribution of the constant and joint costs must consider the value of the service or the conditions of demand. An evaluation of these noncost factors is necessary whenever constant or joint costs are present in the motor-carrier operation.

VALUE-OF-SERVICE OR DEMAND FACTORS

Cost must be governed by utility. The utility of transportation service to the shipper comes not from the cost of producing it but from its ability to satisfy his needs or wants. Difference in degree of utility or in the intensity of demand for the transportation of a certain commodity at a given time and place is measured by the volume of traffic that will be offered for transportation at various possible rates. The results, when listed or charted, are called a "schedule of demand." This demand schedule reflects all the factors that influ-

---

[22] Lewis H. Haney, "Joint Costs with Especial Regard to Railways," *Quarterly Journal of Economics,* Vol. XXX (1916), p. 235.

ence the flow of traffic, including shipper competition, market competition, carrier competition, and the like. It indicates the effect of the rates themselves upon the movement of the traffic. The relationship of the demand schedule to the distribution of the constant costs comes from the economic motive present in rate making that the rate fixed shall be that which, together with the volume of traffic obtainable at such rate, will result in the largest total contribution to the constant or joint costs. This process, which requires at least some conjecture as to the nature of the demand schedule, is commonly referred to as setting rates that will move the traffic or allow traffic to move freely. It implies a fairly accurate forecast of the resulting increase in traffic and gross revenue which will follow any given rate reduction, as well as an approximately correct estimate of the additional expense (out-of-pocket cost) which will be incurred in handling the added traffic.[23]

ADJUSTMENT OF RATES TO VALUE-OF-SERVICE OR DEMAND FACTORS

The practice of adjusting rates to the conditions of demand (value of service) has manifested itself in a number of ways. Some of these are the classification of freight based on other than cost considerations; the establishment of low rates to induce or hold volume traffic for the purpose of maximizing the commodity's contribution to the constant costs; the reduction of rates to meet competition; the establishment of blanket rates from or to large cities; and the charging of a higher rate for transportation in one direction than in the opposite direction on the same or like products.

Value of service or conditions of demand plays a necessary function in the distribution of constant and joint costs. It means, in effect, taking advantage of expansible traffic volume where the traffic will respond to rate reductions. The results are the encouragement of the maximum utilization of the motor carrier's plant and equipment, the distribution of constant costs over a larger volume of tonnage, and the attainment of a lower level of rates on all the traffic, the high-rated as well as the low-rated, than could be realized if differences in rates were limited only to the differences in cost of service. The distribution of the burden of constant costs ultimately rests upon demand factors.

---

[23] Winthrop M. Daniels, *The Price of the Transportation Service* (New York: Harper & Bros., 1932), p. 59.

NORTHERN PACIFIC RAILWAY COMPANY v. NORTH DAKOTA

The decision of the Supreme Court in *Northern Pacific Railway Company v. North Dakota* deals directly with the disposition of constant expenses.[24] The court found that rates fixed by the state of North Dakota on the hauling of lignite coal were confiscatory inasmuch as they did not cover the full cost of the service, including an apportionment of the nonvariable expenses. The court stated:

. . . we entertain no doubt that in determining the cost of the transportation of a particular commodity, all the outlays which pertain to it must be considered. We find no basis for distinguishing in this respect between so-called "out-of-pocket costs," or "actual" expenses, and other outlays which are none the less actually made because they are applicable to all traffic, instead of being exclusively incurred on the traffic in question. Illustrations are found in outlays for maintenance of way and structures, general expenses and taxes. It is not a sufficient reason for excluding such, or other, expenses to say that they would still have been incurred had the particular commodity not been transported. That commodity has been transported; the common carrier is under a duty to carry, and the expenses of its business at a particular time are attributable to what it does carry. The state cannot estimate the cost of carrying coal by throwing the expense incident to the maintenance of the roadbed, and the general expenses, upon the carriage of wheat; or the cost of carrying wheat by throwing the burden of the upkeep of the property upon coal and other commodities.

Although this statement indicates that all costs must be considered in fixing rates, the court nevertheless appreciated the problem of dealing with the constant expenses when it laid down the following rule:[25] "The outlays that exclusively pertain to a given class of traffic must be assigned to that class, and *the other expenses must be fairly apportioned*. It may be difficult to make such an apportionment, but when conclusions are based on cost the entire cost must be taken into account." [*Italics supplied for emphasis.*]

The view has sometimes been taken that under this rule a rate, to be above a confiscatory level, must cover the assignable or out-of-pocket costs as well as some arbitrary apportionment of the constant costs. But, as has been pointed out by economists, the effect would be to give constant costs a significance in law which they do not have in economics.[26] The value-of-service or demand factor is not the same

---

[24] 236 U.S. 585, 596 (1915).

[25] 236 U.S. 597 (1915).

[26] D. Philip Locklin, "The Literature on Railway Rate Theory," *Quarterly Journal of Economics,* Vol. XLVII (1933), p. 211.

for all freight or for all markets. Prices are never based on an arbitrary distribution of the constant or fixed expenses. Indirect expenses never burden all traffic proportionately, ton for ton, regardless of the ability of the traffic to pay.

The meaning of the term "fairly apportioned" is explained somewhat in the following statement from the same decision:

> The legislature, undoubtedly, has a wide range of discretion in the exercise of the power to prescribe reasonable charges, and it is *not bound to fix uniform rates for all commodities or to secure the same percentage of profit on every sort of business*. There are many factors to be considered —differences in the articles transported, the cars required, the risk assumed, *the value of the service,* and it is obviously important that *there should be reasonable adjustments and classifications. [Italics supplied.]*

The court specifically states that value-of-service elements must be considered a factor in rate making. Such elements cannot be a factor in rate making without being a factor in the apportionment of the constant costs, the latter being the only costs remaining after the assignable or out-of-pocket costs are disposed of. The court treats profits as something apart from costs; but profits, whether collected as a fair return on fair value (cost of capital) or as incentive payments to the entrepreneur, are in the long run no different from any of the other costs which must be recovered if the service is to have long-run survival value, except possibly that they have more of the characteristics of indirect expenses than is the case with such items as fuel or labor.

The court stated further:

> With respect to particular rates it is recognized that there is a wide field of legislative discretion, *permitting variety and classification,* and hence the mere details of what appears to be a reasonable scheme of rates, or a tariff or schedule affording substantial compensation, are not subject to judicial review. But this legislative power cannot be regarded as being without limit. The constitutional guaranty protects the carrier from arbitrary action . . . ; and where it is established that a commodity, or a class of traffic, has been segregated and a rate imposed which would compel the carrier to transport it for less than the *proper cost of transportation,* or virtually at cost, and thus the carrier would be denied a reasonable reward for its service after taking into account the entire traffic to which the rate applies, it must be concluded that the State has exceeded its authority. [*Italics supplied.*]

In view of the characteristics of motor-carrier costs, it is thought that the term "the proper cost of transportation," as used here by the court, consists of the out-of-pocket or directly assignable costs plus such contribution toward the unassignable or constant expenses (the remaining revenue needs) as the value of the service or the conditions of demand will permit. Any other concept could not be reconciled with the basic nature of transportation costs.

The foregoing analysis of the nature of costs sets forth the issues which are faced in computing costs to be used for rate-making purposes. The court, in *Northern Pacific Railway Company* v. *North Dakota,* says, in effect, that the expenses that exclusively pertain to a given class of traffic (the out-of-pocket or assignable expenses) must be assigned to that class of traffic and that the other expenses must be fairly apportioned. Such distribution for rate-making purposes must ultimately be based upon the value-of-service or demand factor. From the explanation above of the nature of the value-of-service factors or conditions of demand, it can be seen that an evaluation or economic analysis of these elements is something separate and apart from the computation of the costs.

SUMMARY

Motor-carrier expenses are primarily made up of expenses which, over an extended period of time, vary directly with the volume of traffic handled and thus are directly assignable to particular kinds of traffic. These are the out-of-pocket or long-run variable expenses. Some expenses exist, however, which remain relatively constant or fixed in the face of fairly substantial changes in the volume of traffic. These expenses remain unchanged regardless of whether or not particular shipments or classes of traffic are handled. They are incurred on behalf of the operation as a whole and can be avoided only by the abandonment of the entire operation or, at least, very substantial portions of it. Although such costs are directly assignable to the carrier's operations taken as a whole, they are not assignable on a cost-of-service basis to any particular shipment or class of traffic. The distribution of constant costs on the pro-rata and ton-mile basis serves to limit the differences in the fully distributed costs for different weight shipments to cost-of-service considerations only.

Certain phases of motor-carrier operations, such as the round-trip movement of equipment, are of a joint-cost nature. The expenses incurred in the joint-cost operations cannot be assigned on a cost-of-service basis to the separate traffic units produced in the operation. However, the total costs for the joint operations can be directly assigned to the total output. For example, round-trip vehicle costs cannot be assigned to the traffic handled in each direction. However the total round-trip costs (excluding the constant portion) can be directly assigned to the combined traffic handled in both directions. As there is no justification from a cost-of-service standpoint for assigning more of the joint costs to one unit of output than to any other unit, they are distributed equally, as in the case of constant costs. Briefly, the joint expenses are prorated over the revenue units of service (tons in the case of terminal operations and ton-miles on over-the-road operations).

Since the value-of-service or demand factor constitutes an element to be considered in the ultimate distribution of the constant and joint costs, the distributions of these expenses necessarily constitute only a beginning point in rate making.

There are three levels of motor carriers' costs which, under varying circumstances, are of help in analyzing and testing the compensatory nature of a rate. All three levels are necessary to provide the complete cost picture, and all three are necessary on occasion to explain motor-carrier rates. (a) The first and lowest cost level is that of those one-way out-of-pocket or variable expenses which are separable from the joint expenses incurred in the round-trip movement of the equipment. (b) The second level of cost is that of the out-of-pocket or variable expenses applicable to the operation as a whole. This level embraces those joint expenses such as the round-trip movement of the equipment which, although of a joint nature for an individual segment of the motor carriers' operations, are nevertheless variable with traffic volume when the motor carriers' operations are viewed as a whole. (c) The third level of cost consists of the so-called fully distributed costs which are the out-of-pocket or variable costs plus an apportionment of the constant expenses.

The economic significance of each of these three levels of cost is stated briefly as follows:

(a) The out-of-pocket or variable costs which are separable from the joint expenses incurred in the round-trip movement of the equipment serve as a minimum below which the so-called return-movement rates cannot fall without incurring an out-of-pocket loss. Justification for rates that approach this low level of cost may exist where the value of the service (the conditions of demand) varies widely by directions of movement, the low rates being necessary to obtain a more efficient utilization of the equipment in the direction of the empty return. Under such circumstances, rates may be economically justified at a level slightly above the separable expenses assignable to the one-direction movement, that is, the added cost for pickup and delivery, platform handling, billing, and collection, and some small amount for additional fuel and vehicle wear and tear occasioned by the added weight of the load. Such rates, however, are based on the ability of the remaining traffic handled on the round trip to cover all the joint costs for the trip not recovered from the low-rated traffic. Otherwise, the carrier would incur an out-of-pocket loss for the round-trip movement taken as a whole. The principle at issue is that the revenues secured from the performance of any part of the operations, such as the round-trip movement of a truck, should normally equal the out-of-pocket expense incurred in performing such a segment of the service.

(*b*) The second and broader concept of the out-of-pocket or variable costs, that which is applicable to the operation as a whole, is the one more commonly used. Such out-of-pocket costs provide a minimum below which rates having widespread or general application cannot fall without resulting in an out-of-pocket loss. Inasmuch as such costs reflect the relative amount of transportation service received by the shipment, they provide a measure in cents per 100 pounds of the differences in the rates for shipments of varying sizes, lengths of haul, density, and so forth, which can be justified by differences in the cost of performing the service. Any remaining differences in the rates for the various kinds of traffic must be based on considerations other than cost.

(*c*) The fully distributed costs, based on the out-of-pocket or variable costs plus an apportionment of the constant expenses, provide comparisons of the relative costs of transportation for different regions or territories, separate agencies of transportation, or single carriers, based on total expenses. They also show the extent of the constant costs which are present in the operation and which must be recovered out of the revenues received over and above the out-of-pocket expenses. The comparative showing of the fully distributed costs in addition to the out-of-pocket costs assists in the determination of the limits within which recognition can be given to the value-of-service or demand factor. The fully distributed costs also provide a standard or measure that is helpful in testing the compensatory character of rates and in evaluating the extent to which noncost considerations (value of service or declarations of public policy) have entered into the making of the rates.

The range within which motor carriers can reduce rates below fully allocated costs to meet competition is much narrower than that of railroads. The fact that motor carriers have not always made rates on a cost basis because they are competing with railroads has perhaps caused them to lose sight of the fact that their real competition may be private carriage. The ease with which private carriage may be instituted through the leasing of equipment can mean substantial loss of traffic, particularly truckload traffic, if for-hire service is not priced on a cost basis.

The significance of "cost of service" as opposed to "value of service" in the making of rates may be stated as follows: Cost-of-service considerations go principally to the distribution of the out-of-pocket or long-run variable costs. Value-of-service or demand considerations go to the apportionment of the constant and joint costs. The distribution of the out-of-pocket costs is based on the relative use the traffic in question makes of the carrier's plant and facilities. The apportionment of the constant and joint costs is fundamentally based on an appraisal of the effect the rates themselves would have upon the movement of the traffic and the carrier's revenues. Of far-reaching significance in this latter connection has been the recognition and application of the principle that by reducing the rates on traffic having expansible or elastic traffic volume, the contribution to the constant costs or revenue needs can be increased, within limits, beyond that which can be obtained by limiting rate differences strictly to cost-of-service considerations.

QUESTIONS AND PROBLEMS

1. What facts are there to support the statement that "motor carriers are essentially small business firms"?
2. Identify interline traffic; bridge traffic.
3. Define operating ratio. What is its use in motor-carrier rate cases? Is the fair-rate-of-return concept used in the utility industry also used in the motor-carrier field? Discuss.
4. The motor-carrier industry feels that the operating ratio is the only fair and equitable standard by which to assay its financial needs. Do you agree? Why or why not?
5. Explain out-of-pocket costs. What are variable costs?
6. What are constant costs? Joint costs? List and explain differences between constant and joint costs.
7. "It is important to note that the classification of an item of cost as out-of-pocket (variable) or constant may depend upon the period of time under consideration." Why?
8. Give some examples of joint costs in the motor-carrier industry. Of what significance are joint costs?

9. "The utility of transportation service to the shipper comes . . . from its ability to satisfy his needs or wants." Explain.

10. In what ways has the practice of adjusting rates to the conditions of demand been manifested?

11. State the essence of the decision in *Northern Pacific Railway Company* v. *North Dakota*.

12. Clearly distinguish between the three levels of motor carriers' costs, and point out the economic significance of each.

10. ORGANIZATION AND OPERATION

OF A MOTOR CARRIER

THE development of the motor-carrier industry from its early strug-
gle for recognition as a reliable form of transport to its present ma-
ture and stable position has provided a challenge to management.
Many problems of management in this fast-growing industry were
solved at the time they developed by a management possessing
greater operational knowledge than executive ability. Some of these
"on-the-spot" decisions were valid in the light of good business practices; others were not. Some represented good judgment at the time
they were made but would not stand up under critical analysis today. What is efficient organization for a one-truck business may not
be for a five-terminal business. Nevertheless, there is motor-carrier
management today which is applying much the same methods as it
did when its business was in its infancy, even though its business has
developed into far-flung operations requiring more up-to-date management. Because a motor carrier's business has grown from small to
large during a period when the motor-carrier industry as a whole
has experienced great expansion does not signify that the management techniques of that business cannot be improved. Errors in
judgment are not always evident during a period of rapid expansion.
In any event, no management, however good, can afford in these days
of increased competition, higher costs, and narrowed profits to pass
up the opportunity to analyze its policies, organization, and operation in the light of present conditions.

POLICIES

Regardless of the size of a motor-carrier operation, whether it be
an organization with many branch terminals or one in which the

owner maintains contact with all the personnel, there are certain principles which should be observed in the establishment of a clear-cut company policy, as follows:[1]

1. Statement of any policy should be definite, positive, and understandable to all personnel in the organization.
2. Policies should be translatable into practices and terms and peculiarities of every department or division of the business.
3. Policies should not be inflexible, but they should possess a great degree of permanency.
4. Stability of policies is necessary, for constantly changing policies are fatal to a business.
5. There should be as many policies as are required to cover conditions that can be anticipated but not too many policies to become confusing or meaningless.
6. Policies should be based on fact and sound judgment and should not constitute merely personal reflections.
7. Policies should not prescribe detailed procedure except in few instances.
8. Policies should recognize economic principles, conform with federal and other laws, and be compatible with the public interest.

ORGANIZATION

In every motor-carrier organization, there are certain functions which have to be performed. The assignment of functions to specific departments may vary from company to company, but that is of little significance as long as the functions are properly handled by the departments in charge. In a fast-growing organization, it does happen, however, that departments have been allowed to grow so large as to result in improper performance of component functions. Efficient management may find it wise to re-examine the functions of each department to ascertain if there should be a reallocation of duties.

In addition, top management may find that the organization has expanded to the point where a different type of organizational setup should be employed. In a dynamic industry, the organizational setup must be one in which immediate decisions can be reached and necessary changes effected expeditiously. The financial resources of most motor carriers are not sufficient that they can afford to delay when some particular phase of their activity is losing money.

Of the types of business organization, such as line, staff, and functional, the most common type in the motor-carrier field is line or-

---

[1] L. P. Alford and J. R. Bangs (eds.), *Production Handbook* (New York: Ronald Press, 1948), p. 1383.

ganization. For the small motor carrier, this type of organization fits its needs in a satisfactory manner. If a motor-carrier organization outgrows this type of management, however, top management should not be reluctant to delegate authority and responsibility when efficiency demands such a move. A smooth-working organization and one that builds future management personnel does not place too much reliance upon one individual or several individuals. This is particularly significant in larger motor-carrier organizations, for the greater the size and span of an organization, the greater the need for proper delegation of authority and responsibility.

LINE ORGANIZATION

The line organization (Fig. 10–1) is widely used in business management and is typified by a setup similar to that of a military organization, where there is one person who commands and who alone is responsible for results.[2] This is characteristic of business enter-

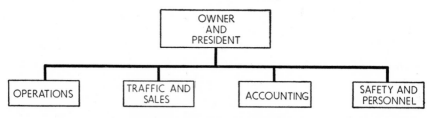

FIG. 10–1. A typical line organization.

prises which can be traced to a small beginning, such as the motor carrier. The owner of a small motor-carrier organization may find that management of his business is a relatively simple matter, for he has complete authority and responsibility, both operational and managerial. In many instances, however, in the motor-carrier field, the small business has grown; and the increased burdens upon the owner require that he delegate some authority and responsibility. Even here, the line organization of management continues, for all of the personnel are subordinate to the owner, who will disseminate downward his decisions and expect compliance therewith. With continuing expansion of his business, he may be forced to delegate further authority because there are not enough hours in the day for him to continue to handle all problems, large and small.

[2] E. Petersen and E. G. Plowman, *Business Organization and Management* (rev. ed.; Chicago: Richard D. Irwin, Inc., 1948), p. 256.

A line organization, then, represents highly centralized management. It is understandable that the founder of such an organization, which has grown and prospered, may find it difficult to relinquish the managerial control which he has maintained since the inception of his organization. On the other hand, what many owners do not realize is that they may retain control of their organizations by the proper delegation of authority and, by so doing, relieve themselves of burdensome details.

STAFF ORGANIZATION

This may give rise to the establishment of a staff, composed of managerial experts, which is expected to relieve the top executive of much of his detail work. It has been pointed out in differentiating between line and staff executives that staff officers are assigned to an authority of ideas, whereas line officers are charged with the authority to command. In general, the staff or the group of managerial experts support the line executive in an informational and advisory capacity. The information or ideas of the staff flow up to a superior; and this executive, possessing authority, may transmit this information or ideas into orders down through the organization.

FUNCTIONAL ORGANIZATION

Some motor carriers have found that the staff organization continues to place too much responsibility upon the top executive as their organizations continue to expand and hence have worked out a functional type of organization. The staff members are given broader responsibility concerning the particular functions of the business they represent. Whereas they formerly functioned in an advisory capacity, they now have authority to command within their own departments. These functional executives and those in lower managerial echelons will have channels established so that there is a free flow and interchange of work of a technical nature between them.

A LARGE MOTOR-CARRIER ORGANIZATION

The manner in which one of the largest motor carriers is organized and the authority and responsibility at the different managerial levels is described in the following paragraphs.

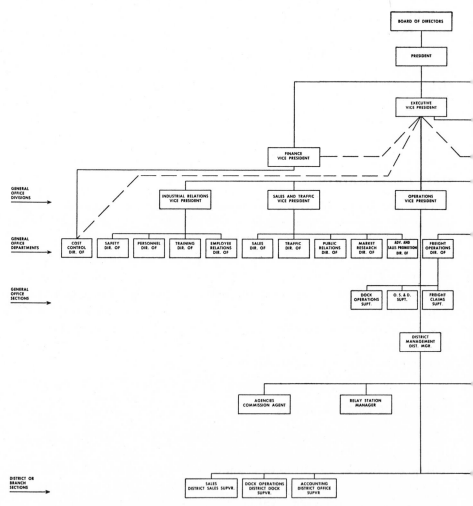

FIG. 10–2. Solid lines on chart show lines of direct authority, including the right to hire, fire, and give direct orders. Dotted lines show administrative control. Each division and department

The organization chart which is shown in Figure 10–2 is divided into the following divisions at headquarters: Industrial Relations; Sales and Traffic; Operations; Transportation and Properties; Accounting and Auditing. The departments are: Cost Control; Safety; Personnel; Training; Employee Relations; Sales; Traffic; Public Relations; Advertising; Market Research; Freight Operations; Interline Operations; Dispatching; Purchasing and Stores; Driving; Fleet Maintenance; Engineering; Accounting; and Auditing. The sections consist of Dock Operations; Over, Short and Damage; Freight

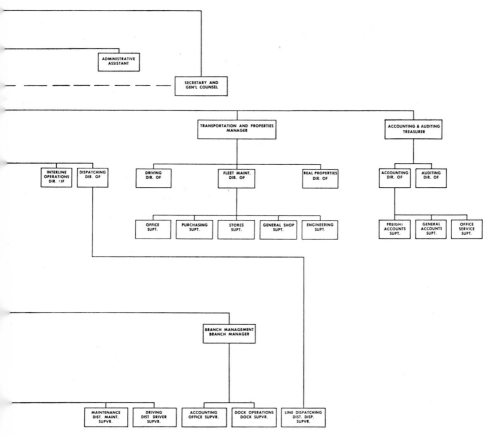

head also carries staff authority and responsibility; he may advise, suggest, recommend, and assist on those matters directly related to his functions.

Claims; Purchasing; Stores; Office (Transportation and Properties Division); Service; Terminal Properties; Freight Accounts; General Accounts; and Office Service. The sections at districts or branches are divided into Sales; Dock Operations; Accounting; Fleet Maintenance; and Driving.

The President is responsible to the Board of Directors and has full authority throughout the company. The general management of the company, however, is the responsibility of the Executive Vice-President, who develops policies and co-ordinates the activities of the division heads. He is responsible for the development of supervisory ability throughout the company and keeps informed of new developments in the transportation and management fields, adapting them, where feasible, to company problems. He also directs the company in negotiation of union contracts and arbitration of labor disputes.

The Executive Vice-President, Vice-President of Finance, and Secretary and General Counsel report to the President. The other Vice-Presidents, the Manager of Transportation and Properties, Treasurer, and Administrative Assistant report to the Executive Vice-President.

The accounting and financial policy is recommended by the Vice-President of Finance. He also furnishes financial information to the President and other executives and prepares forecasts of company cash requirements. He designs special report forms which are used for control purposes throughout the company, such as outbound-inbound tonnage reports and sales quotas. In co-operation with the General Counsel, financial applications are prepared by him to the Interstate Commerce Commission. He recommends the amount of coverage of insurance and negotiates property and liability insurance. His primary function is to serve as financial and economic adviser to the company.

The Secretary and General Counsel has supervision over the company's relations with regulatory bodies. All contracts or other documents dealing with acquisition or sale of assets and the issuance and retirement of securities are handled by him. He arranges for handling legal actions to which the company is a party since he is legal adviser to the company.

The Vice-President of Industrial Relations is responsible for the supervision and co-ordination of the Safety, Personnel, Training, and Employee Relations Departments. Reviews of the wage and salary program and periodic reviews of the organization structure of the company are prepared and recommendations made where necessary. His duties also include the approval of new jobs.

The Vice-President of Sales and Traffic supervises the activities of and prescribes the policies of the Sales, Traffic, Public Relations, Advertising, and Market Research Departments. He directs the programs of these various departments.

The management of terminals as well as the direction of all operations concerned with the handling of freight is handled by the Vice-President of Operations. He establishes and co-ordinates methods and procedures to facilitate a smooth functioning of Freight Operations, Interline Operations, and Dispatching Departments. He has supervision over the districts and branches as well.

The Manager of Transportation and Properties is responsible for the Driving, Fleet Maintenance, and Real Properties Departments. He establishes standard specifications for all automotive equipment and handles the purchase and sale of it. His primary responsibility is the management of the company's motor-vehicle equipment and buildings and property.

The responsibility for establishing and controlling the accounting policies and procedures for the company is that of the Treasurer. It is his responsibility to develop and direct policies concerning the extension of credit. He controls company funds and handles company insurance activities having to do with various specific coverages.

TRAINING PROGRAMS

A number of motor carriers have become very large organizations, and many of the founders of these companies are approaching the age when they must retire from active management. There is a definite need in the motor-carrier industry for the training of qualified personnel to assume future executive responsibilities. The people chosen for further training may be already employed in the carrier's organization, or additional personnel of potential executive capacities may be hired from outside the company. The majority of the top management and junior executives in the motor-carrier industry, thus far, have come from within the industry. Whatever the source of this group of potential future administrators, it is imperative that top management establish a program of training, formal or informal in nature, so that the benefits of well trained personnel may be enjoyed in current operations and an adequate foundation built for the future.

Training may be divided into pre-service, that is, training and instruction prior to the time that the individual becomes a regular employee in the job for which he is being trained, and in-service training for those who are already performing the particular functions for which they are receiving training. The length of the training period is dependent upon the job for which they are being trained and upon the caliber of trainees. Some of them exceed 1 year in length. On the other hand, one company gives rate clerks only 6 weeks of training in the general office before they are assigned to an operating job at a terminal.

A very small number of carriers have established a management training program in which the trainee is rotated through the departments of the company to get a better understanding of the company's organization and management. He must make progress reports and is given tests periodically.

A reservoir of potential management personnel which exists today and which is being tapped to advantage by motor carriers is that being trained by universities, which provide well-balanced business curricula, including comprehensive transportation offerings. When personnel derived from such a source is oriented to the particular procedures of an individual motor carrier, the advantages should soon be manifested.

ORGANIZATION CHART SHOWING FUNCTIONS PERFORMED

Some companies which are not as large as the organization just described publish an organization chart which shows the line of authority and the persons in charge. A functional chart is also prepared which shows for each of the departments the basic functions which are performed by each department. Such a functional chart for a Class I motor carrier grossing less than $5 million a year is shown in Figure 10–3. A number of these functions are discussed in more detail in chapters which follow. The number of departments in a company may be greater or less than shown in the chart. Some of the functions performed by the executive department may be delegated to other or new departments.

There have been too many cases of motor-carrier executives emphasizing those phases of management in which they have had practical experience; i.e., the individual who started as a one-truck operator and has built the company into a fifty-truck operation tends to concentrate his management efforts in operations. If the executive's background has been principally in selling, there is a tendency to emphasize that phase of management. There is a need for a balanced approach to management of the business enterprise and a perspective of the entire organization.

OPERATIONS DEPARTMENT

The operations department is responsible for the handling and movement of all freight. Depending upon the size of the motor carrier, the operations department may be divided into terminal operations and over-the-road operations, but the usual arrangement is to have it all under one department. Since terminal operations are discussed in the following chapter, various aspects of over-the-road operations are covered in this chapter. Leasing, which is also a phase of operations, is discussed in a later chapter.

The operations phase consists not only of handling freight which is moving between points wholly on the company's line but also

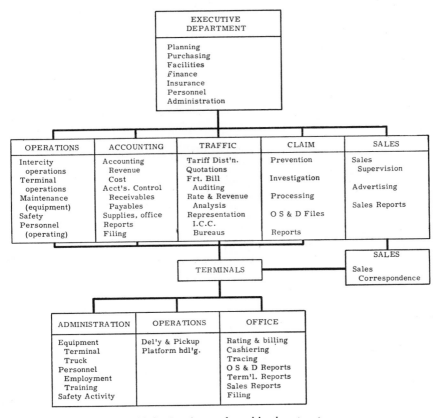

FIG. 10–3. Functions performed by departments.

arranging for the handling of interline shipments. Although the latter function is not as time consuming, it does require careful attention, since frequently the interlined movement is competing with a single-line movement by another motor carrier or by a competitive mode of transportation.

There should be procedures established by the operations department for the handling of freight which will provide uniformity at the various terminals for the purpose of effective management control. Unless there is some degree of uniformity, the handling record at each of the terminals cannot be compared nor improvements made as quickly as should be the case. Some form of a handbook or a pamphlet should be compiled which will describe the correct procedures.

Some operations departments assign individual drivers or driver teams to specific power units, the principal advantage being assignment of responsibility for the particular unit. Others feel that this limits the utilization of such equipment so they do not follow this practice. Inasmuch as maintenance of equipment is an important

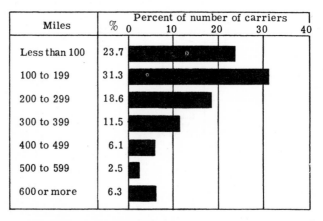

Miles	%	Percent of number of carriers				
		0	10	20	30	40
Less than 100	23.7					
100 to 199	31.3					
200 to 299	18.6					
300 to 399	11.5					
400 to 499	6.1					
500 to 599	2.5					
600 or more	6.3					

FIG. 10–4. Average haul of Class I intercity common carriers of general freight, 1953.
Source: Transport Research, Inc., *Manual of Highway Carriers* (Washington, D.C., 1954).

responsibility of the operations department, the decision regarding assignment of equipment usually rests with it. The operations department generally computes the terminal-to-terminal time on a 30 miles per hour average.

There is wide variation in the average length of haul for Class I common carriers of general freight as shown in Figure 10–4. Almost one third of these carriers has an average haul of 100–199 miles, while 6 per cent has an average haul of 600 or more miles. Some of the carriers with longer hauls have established relay points, whereas others use sleeper-cab equipment, having two drivers take the equipment all the way through to destination. There are proponents of both of these operational methods. Among other things, the relay advocates claim better control over the operation, and the supporters of sleeper-cab operations claim that it is more flexible.

EMBARGOES

If it is physically impossible for carriers to transport freight or there is an unusual accumulation of freight, carriers may impose an embargo. This is an emergency measure and is generally done by the operations department. The imposition of an embargo by motor common carriers requires that they give published notice of the embargo which will specify the date, the reasons, and the length of the embargo, if this is known. A notice of the embargo is sent to the Commission, and copies must be furnished to the District Director of the Interstate Commerce Commission in the district in which the headquarters of the carrier is located. Notice must also be posted in each office of the carrier where the embargo is to be made effective, and notification given connecting carriers.[3]

The same order provides that a motor common carrier which is unable to perform transportation promptly upon request shall notify the person requesting the service of the anticipated delay and the reason for it. Many of the embargo notices are published in the weekly trade newspaper *Transport Topics*.

There have been instances in which carriers have placed embargoes against certain classes of freight which were not desirable to the carrier because of inadequate rates or susceptibility to damage. This, of course, is not the legitimate purpose of an embargo.

LABOR AND PERSONNEL

Motor-carrier operation is a service industry, and the contacts of its employees with the public are many. The role of personnel, therefore, assumes great importance. Effective personnel policies must be formulated not only to serve the public to better advantage but also to bring about closer employee-employer relationships.

CLASSIFICATION OF MOTOR-CARRIER EMPLOYEES

The Interstate Commerce Commission's annual report required from Class I motor carriers establishes the following classification of employees of property carriers:

1. Equipment maintenance and garage:
   Supervisory
   Mechanics (including working foremen)

---

[3] Order of Commission, effective April 15, 1943.

Service employees
Others (including clerical employees)
2. Transportation:
Supervisory
Drivers—Line-haul (over-the-road)
Helpers—Line-haul (over-the-road)
Drivers—Pickup and delivery
Helpers—Pickup and delivery
Others (including clerical employees)
3. Terminal:
Supervisory
Platform employees
Others (including clerical employees)
4. Sales, tariff, and advertising:
Supervisory
Solicitors
Others (including clerical employees)
5. Insurance and safety:
Supervisory
Others (including clerical employees)
6. Administrative and general:
Officers, owners, and partners
Clerical
Others

Many carriers will have individual classifications of employees which will differ from this classification. Furthermore, the classification of employees covered by union contracts varies also from contract to contract and from area to area. For example, one union contract may refer to a freight handler as a "lumper"; another contract may refer to such a worker as a "stacker"; and still another may refer to him as a "platform worker." This lack of uniform terminology can lead to misunderstandings, but it is so prevalent that it is doubtful whether uniformity can be achieved. There is even some carry-over of terminology from horse-and-wagon days, such as the term "hostler," which formerly referred to the man who took care of the horses at the stable and is now used by some carriers to refer to the man who takes care of the trucks at the garage.

The distribution of the Class I motor carrier's wage dollar by type of employee is shown in Figure 10–5. The largest share of the wage dollar goes to transportation employees, that is, those engaged in the transportation of the over-the-road as well as pickup and delivery units. Terminal employees rank next in the amount received as their share of the wage dollar. The amount received by these two groups of employees constitutes three fourths of the entire wage dollar. The importance of wages to gross revenue varies, depending upon the type of service rendered. The wages paid to the employees of common carriers of general freight exceeded those paid by other types of Class I carriers, amounting to about half of gross revenue. Since labor costs constitute approximately one half of total operating

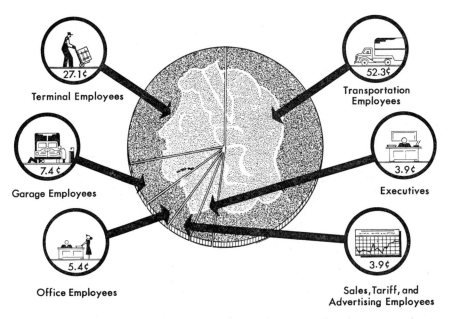

Terminal Employees — 27.1¢

Transportation Employees — 52.3¢

Garage Employees — 7.4¢

Executives — 3.9¢

Office Employees — 5.4¢

Sales, Tariff, and Advertising Employees — 3.9¢

FIG. 10–5. Distribution of the motor-carrier wage dollar by type of employee, 1952, Class I common carriers of general freight. This chart shows how each dollar paid in wages, salaries, and bonuses is distributed among the major employee classifications.

Source: Based on latest available statistics from official reports of Class I motor carriers to the Interstate Commerce Commission, as given in American Trucking Associations, Inc., *Trends* (Washington, D.C., 1954), p. 16.

costs also, and since labor in the industry is represented to a great extent by labor organizations, it appears advisable to consider some of the aspects of the dominant labor organization in the motor-carrier industry, the International Brotherhood of Teamsters, Chauffeurs, Warehousemen, and Helpers of America, AFL, hereafter referred to as the Teamsters' Union.

TEAMSTERS' UNION

The Teamsters' Union comprises the largest international union in the American Federation of Labor with a current membership of 1,300,000, about 30 per cent of whom are truck drivers.

There are three sections of the organization: the international union, fifty-one city and state joint councils, and the local unions, of which there are about a thousand. The international union permits its local affiliates a large amount of latitude. There are also fifteen major trade divisions, such as Beverage, Dairy, Over-the-Road, and others. Contracts are written by the locals, and the only right reserved by the international union is the right to approve the contract proposed and the finished contract to safeguard the union against legal complications. The dues of the locals are not less than $2.00 per month, and the initiation fee is fixed by each local union. For example, one local has the following initiation fees and monthly dues:

	Initiation Fee	Monthly Dues
Over-the-road drivers	$25.00	$2.50
Local drivers	25.00	2.00
Dock workers	5.00	2.00
Cab drivers	10.00	2.00

The local union remits a per-capita tax of 30 cents per month to the international union. If funds in the international union fall below $5 million, each member can be assessed $1.00. In the case of strikes, action may be taken by a vote of two thirds of the local union; but, prior to taking this action, the local must notify the Joint Council of the union. For example, there are twenty-five locals in New York City which are joined together in a Joint Council. The international president then must be notified and will be in charge of the strike in the event such action is taken. The strike benefits which the international union gives to the local are $10 per week per member. Where there is but one local in a city, it usually is a general union which embraces all the crafts coming under its jurisdiction in that city, inasmuch as no one craft in the smaller cities is large enough to support a union of its own. In larger cities, however, a local may be composed of a single craft, such as a milk-drivers' union. Some crafts embrace only driver salesmen, such as soft-drink drivers, and their salaries are usually considerably above those who are drivers only.

A local union may negotiate a number of different contracts. This is because some companies will negotiate with the labor organization individually if they are not members of a trade association. The trade association (local or state) negotiates directly with the local union for contracts for all of its member carriers. There has been a definite trend toward area negotiations for over-the-road carriers. Standard contracts covering large areas are the emerging pattern at the present time. For example, the Western States Conference of Teamsters covers 11 western states; the Southern Conference of Teamsters, 12 southern states; the Central States Conference of Teamsters, 12 central states; and the Eastern States Conference of Teamsters embracing the eastern states. It is apparent that the unions are desirous of negotiating standard contracts in each of these areas, and it is expected that the contracts from all of these areas will be somewhat similar. The President of the Teamsters in 1953 established as one objective future bargaining on a nation-wide basis.

EMPLOYERS' GROUPS

Paralleling the area labor organizations are the employers' organizations. In the southwestern area, the Southwest Operators Associations Negotiating Committee represents carriers in Texas, Oklahoma, Arkansas, and Louisiana. In the southeastern area, the employer group is the Southeastern Area Employers Association, representing carriers in Tennessee, Kentucky, Georgia, Alabama, Mississippi, and West Virginia. In Ohio, the employers are represented by the Ohio Employers Bureau, Inc. The foregoing groups involve about 2,000 motor carriers and 30,000 employees covering a 22-state area. Contracts that were basically the same were made by these groups. It should not be inferred that regional contracts will necessarily be uniformly applied.

There are other similar motor-carrier employers' organizations for the purpose of negotiating with labor on an area basis throughout the United States. Heretofore, the negotiations of these employer groups have never produced the wide area of agreement evident in the contracts just negotiated. The attitude of the National Labor Relations Board toward multiemployer bargaining units is presently to approve such bargaining units only where both parties are agreeable to such arrangements. Employer groups have so far been unable to show the solidarity in negotiations that the labor organizations have, and they have paid for it.

SETTLEMENT OF GRIEVANCES

All contracts provide methods for the settlement of grievances. The following procedure is taken from a contract and is typical:

1. Any employee who has a complaint must first take the matter up with his employer. If not settled, then
2. The employee shall take the matter up with the business agent of his local union.
3. The business agent will take the complaint up with the employer. If not settled, then
4. The complaint is referred to the Joint Committee of the Employers and the Employees Council, which meets once each month. Any grievance so submitted which this group is unable to settle is referred to arbitration on the following basis:
   Two members will be selected by the employers' group, two by the employees, and these four so selected shall select an arbitrator for arbitrating the dispute. The decision of the arbitrator shall be final and binding on both parties. Pending a decision by this Board of Arbitration, there shall be no work stoppage, either by strike or lockout.

POINTS COVERED IN CONTRACTS

Seniority rights prevail in union contracts. For example, if it becomes necessary to reduce the working force, the last man hired shall be laid off first. Seniority also is the primary basis on which various runs are allocated. The method being used may be that of posting the available run, with the man applying who has the most seniority getting the run if he is considered capable of handling it. Rates of pay are "spelled out" in the contracts, specifying the rate to be paid per hours or per mile and differentiating between over-the-road and local rates for drivers. Differentiation is made also in the rate of pay scale between driver personnel and nondriver personnel, as well as on the basis of equipment operated. For example, the driver of a double-axle semitrailer unit receives more per mile (7.7 cents) or per hour ($2.07) than the driver of a single-axle semitrailer unit (7.45 cents per mile or $2.02 per hour).

An example of the provisions for layover pay taken from a contract is that layover pay shall commence following the fifteenth hour after the end of the run. If the driver is held over thereafter, he shall be guaranteed 2 hours' pay even if he is held over just 15 minutes. If he is held over more than 2 hours, he shall receive layover pay not to exceed 8 hours' pay in each 24-hour period, plus comfortable and sanitary lodging. On Sundays and holidays, only meals and comfortable lodgings will be allowed.

Some contracts contain a provision that prohibits an intercity driver, coming into a city in which a union of local drivers has jurisdiction, from making any deliveries except to his company's terminal. Labor organizations may feel that this restriction is a sound practice; but, from the standpoint of flexibility of service, the public may be the loser.

There are many other articles which are covered in an employer-employee contract, such as vacations, meals, rest periods, deadheading, breakdowns or impassable highways, defective equipment, terms of the contract, type of employee, cause for discharge, and the like. In line with the trend in industry generally, an increasing number of motor-carrier labor contracts include health and welfare plans. Such plans may call for any or all of the following benefits: weekly accident and sickness insurance; surgical insurance; group life insurance; and accidental death, hospitalization, or medical insurance.

The provisions of the Labor-Management Relations Act of 1947 (Taft-Hartley) are applicable to motor carriers. Mechanics, office employees, and others in the motor-carrier industry have been organized, but this movement has not been as complete as the organization of the drivers.

LABOR RELATIONS

It is a curious fact that, although Class I operators may be negotiating four to five contracts annually and engaging in the settlement of grievances throughout the year, there are so few carriers that employ a full-time labor-relations executive. Labor costs constitute approximately one half of operating expenses, yet motor-carrier management sometimes postpones preparation for collective bargaining until the present contract is expiring. It should be emphasized that good employer-employee relationships are the aggregate of day-to-day occurrences, such as effective settlement of grievances and the like. In order to maintain an even keel in collective bargaining, motor-carrier management must devote more attention to the labor-relations problem.

At the end of one long bargaining session, an employer is reported to have disgustedly said that the next thing that would happen would be that labor representatives would want holiday pay on their birthdays. The following year this demand was included in the labor representative's proposal. One study of collective bargaining in the motor freight industry has concluded that unions, to date, are in the better bargaining position.[4]

---

[4] M. A. Cohen and M. Lieberman, "Collective Bargaining in the Motor Freight Industry," *Industrial and Labor Relations Review*, Vol. III, No. 1 (October, 1949), p. 31.

For nonunion employees, there should be a wage review conducted annually. This is done by department, division, or section heads, or a review board may be created which will conduct the interview with each nonunion employee. The employee's work should be reviewed and evaluated. Constructive criticisms and suggestions should be made. Where good work has been performed, the employee should be commended for it. As a result of this wage review, the employee should be informed as to any action taken to adjust his salary. In the event that no salary adjustment is made, he should be told the reasons for the lack of action.

SHIPPING DOCUMENTS

BILLS OF LADING

The Interstate Commerce Act does not prescribe a uniform bill of lading for motor carriers, although it does require that receipts for goods must be given by the carrier. Therefore, there is not a particular form of the bill of lading which is used by all carriers. Many of them use the bills of lading, both the straight and the order forms, which are reproduced in the current issues of the National Motor Freight Classifications.

A uniform straight bill of lading serves as a shipper's receipt for the goods and a contract between the shipper and the carrier for the transportation of the shipment. The straight bill of lading is non-negotiable. In other words, it cannot be reassigned or used for the purpose of transacting business between the shipper and the consignee as is the case with the uniform order bill of lading. The majority of shipments move under the straight bill of lading. Under this bill of lading, the delivery may be made upon the proper identification and without the presentation of the bill of lading. The terms and conditions are contained on the back of the bill of lading.

Motor carriers and shippers may use the short-form bill of lading which does not have all of the terms and conditions printed on the back, although all the terms and conditions apply. Shippers often have their own bills of lading printed and are the principal users of the short form. There is little difference between the two forms, but the short form is not used on C.O.D. shipments.

The uniform order bill of lading constitutes a receipt for goods and a contract between the points, and, in addition, constitutes title to the goods. Under its terms, it provides for delivery to the party who possesses the original copy of the bill of lading properly endorsed, that is, signed by the shipper and the origin carrier, upon receipt of the shipment. The endorsement constitutes the signature of the shipper and the signature of the party presenting the bill of lading to the carrier at destination. If the party who presents the order bill of lading is different from the party to be notified, as has been shown on the bill of lading, this would indicate that the order bill of lading has been transferred. Each of the transfers must be recorded by endorsement on the back of the bill of lading. Thus the order bill of lading is a negotiable instrument, and the title to goods may be passed from one party to another by endorsement.

The order bill of lading is usually handled by having the shipper endorse it and forward it together with an invoice and sight draft covering the merchandise to his local bank. The local bank will then forward it to a bank at destination. The party named on the bill as the party to be notified will be notified by the bank at destination, and that bank will make collection from the customer for the amount of the invoice or sight draft and will receipt and surrender the original bill of lading. The customer will then surrender the order bill of lading to the delivering carrier and will receive his goods. The order bill of lading may be endorsed "in blank," that is, it could be negotiated by anyone; and it may be endorsed: "To the order of ......," which constitutes limited endorsement since it cannot be further negotiated. Motor carriers often refer to the uniform order bill of lading as a shipper's order, order notify, or sight draft bill of lading.

When it is not practical to show all of the detailed information on the face of the bill of lading, carriers sometimes issue a check sheet which is attached to the bill of lading, and the bill of lading will refer to attached check list.

HOW TO PREPARE A BILL OF LADING

There is a minimum of three copies of the bill of lading: the original, the memorandum copy which is usually retained by the shipper, and the shipping order copy which is retained by the origin carrier. The carrier's freight bills are issued from the information which is shown on this copy. Many carriers, however, have more copies made of the bill of lading. When there are but three copies of the order bill of lading, the original must be forwarded by the shipper to destination and turned over to the destination carrier before delivery of the goods, the shipper retaining the memorandum

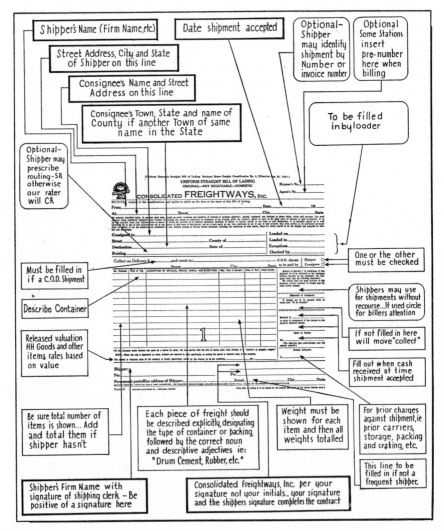

FIG. 10–6. One carrier's method of showing how to make up a bill of lading.

copy, and the shipping order copy being retained by the origin carrier.

The preparation of the bill of lading is very important, and both carriers and shippers have a responsibility for the careful completion of this document. Figure 10–6 shows the method used by a large carrier to instruct its employees on the correct preparation of a bill of lading. In preparing the bill of lading, it must be dated as of the date the shipment is accepted by the originating carrier, and shippers should describe their freight according to classification descriptions.

Carriers may request that the contents of packages be inspected if the bill of lading indicates the shipment may be improperly described. If a shipment is made on a C.O.D. basis, there is a space on the uniform straight bill of lading for the amount of the C.O.D., as well as a space indicating whether the collection fee is to be paid by the shipper or consignee. Generally, the consignee pays this fee. When accepting C.O.D. shipments, a carrier may prescribe that all copies of the bill of lading shall show the following information:

1. The letters "C.O.D." and the amount that the shipper requires to be collected written in large letters and figures in the body of the bill of lading.
2. The mail address of the shipper in the space provided in the heading of the bill of lading.
3. The name and mail address of the party to whom the C.O.D. is to be paid, if other than the shipper, written in space provided. If no space provided, put in body of the bill of lading.
4. The phrase "accept consignee's check made payable to the shipper for the amount of the C.O.D. only" if the consignor in writing or by endorsement on the bill of lading and shipping order authorizes the carrier to accept the consignee's check. In such case the carrier shall not be liable, except for the exercise of due care and diligence in securing and forwarding such check to the consignor.

As a general rule carriers do not accept a C.O.D shipment if a split or partial delivery must be made; if the C.O.D. provides that a discount would be allowed if the shipment is accepted within a specified period; if the bill of lading bears instructions to allow examination or trial by the consignee; or if the shipment is of doubtful or very low value and the shipper and consignee are unknown.

If the shipment is to move on a prepaid basis, this has to be noted on the bill of lading. Otherwise the shipment will move collect. A distribution sheet should be attached to the shipping order copy if a shipment is for pool distribution, and the bill of lading must be so marked. When the pool shipment includes items that are to move beyond the distribution point, the shipper must furnish bills of lading to cover this beyond movement. It sometimes happens that only a part of a shipment is picked up because it is too large to move out on a particular schedule. Under such circumstances, a bill of lading will be issued for the entire shipment with the number of pieces circled. A note in the body of the bill of lading, "balance to follow," will contain a list of those items which were not picked up. When the balance of the shipment is picked up, a bill of lading is issued covering these items with this note on the bill of lading: "part-lot-weight and charges ahead on pro No. . . . ."

On shipments which are reconsigned, diverted, or returned to the shipper, bills of lading must be issued unless tariff regulations provide otherwise. Motor carriers often move shipments which are for their own company without charge, but such shipments are made on uniform straight bills of lading. There are also occasions when there is the movement of employee property or property moved for charitable purposes. In both of these cases, uniform straight bills of lading are issued. All of these movements are without charge, and there is usually a notation placed on the bill of lading indicating that it is "deadhead" freight.

If it is not possible to load a shipment completely on one piece of equipment because of its weight or size, and the balance has to be loaded later, the original bill of lading will show the items actually loaded, as well as the balance which is to follow. This is called a "weight and charges ahead" movement. The billing office makes up a revenue billing covering the total number of items in the shipment and showing the items being forwarded, as well as the number of pieces to follow. A "weight and charges to follow" movement is one in which the bills of lading are not available or there is inadequate information for revenue billing at the time the shipments must move. This is a case in which shipment must move prior to issuance of the revenue bill.

GOVERNMENT BILL OF LADING

In addition to the commercial bills of lading, many motor carriers must be familiar with the government bill of lading. The government bill of lading is issued by the federal government for use in the movement of its property. This bill of lading is nonnegotiable, and the original copy of the bill of lading signed by the shipper and the origin carrier upon receipt of the goods must be forwarded by the shipper to the consignee for execution and surrender to the carrier upon delivery of the shipment. The carrier which seeks to collect the freight charges must have the original bill of lading to present to the proper governmental agency to receive payment.

A government bill of lading serves the same purposes as the commercial bill of lading, but it also serves other purposes. Therefore, it contains additional information. Eight copies of the government bill of lading are necessary for shipping and accounting purposes. There are occasions when a government shipment moves on a straight bill of lading which is marked: "To be converted into a government bill of lading at destination." Motor carriers which handle government shipments generally publish regulations for their employees to follow in handling government shipping documents in order to assure compliance with the requirements.

WAYBILL AND FREIGHT BILL

When freight has been picked up and checked into a terminal, a waybill which is used as a routing document in internal operations by the carrier may be made from the shipping order or bill of lading. From the bill of lading a freight bill (Fig. 10–7) is prepared showing

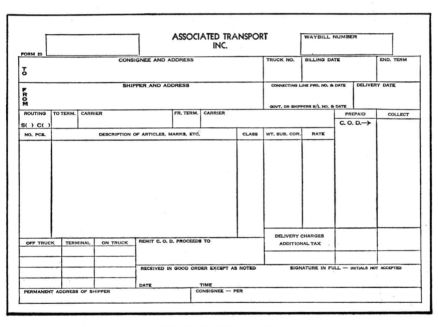

FIG. 10–7. A freight bill.

the total charges that the shipper or receiver is to pay for the shipment.

The carrier assigns to the freight bill a number, which is termed a "pro number." This term is derived from the word "progressive," and it indicates that the freight bills are numbered consecutively. Reference to the pro number is made in correspondence, loss and damage claims, tracing, and the like. If a carrier lists on a load sheet all of the freight bills covering freight loaded on the same truck or trailer, this is termed "scripting."

Care must be exercised in unloading freight both at the carrier's terminal and at the consignee's door. The freight bills are used in unloading the shipments. If there are shipments that have been damaged, notations are made of this fact. Shipments which are received without bills are usually held for receipt of the revenue billing. If freight is delayed which is moving on a prepaid revenue billing, the consignee signs the delivery receipt copy of the freight bill. Carriers generally require a complete signature.

If freight is moving on a collect freight bill, the charges are not collected at time of delivery but the consignee signs the first and second copies of the freight bill, and the motor carrier will submit the freight bill for payment later. If an attempt is made to deliver the shipment and no one is available to accept it, a freight arrival notice to consignee is issued. A duplicate of this is retained and attached to the delivery receipt copy of the freight bill until the delivery is made, or it is otherwise disposed of. These are placed in a suspense file until delivery is requested or until disposal is made in some other manner.

TRUCK MANIFEST

A truck manifest may be used by the operations department for control purposes. On a manifest is recorded each movement of line-haul equipment and its load which is dispatched between cities. Such manifests may be issued regardless of whether the equipment is empty or loaded. Each terminal will have manifests which are numbered with a prefix to identify the terminal. The information shown on the truck manifest includes the name of the consignee, destination, shipper, weight, number of pieces, and pro number, as well as information about the equipment and route. If freight is added at intermediate points, supplemental manifests may be issued. Figure 10–8 is an example of a truck manifest.

SEAL

The line-haul unit must be sealed in order to provide protection for the contents of the truck or trailer. The Congress enacted a law which covers the unlawful breaking of seals or locks on motor vehicles or unlawful entry of motor vehicles transporting property in interstate commerce.[5]

On the terminal-to-terminal loads, the seal, which is a small piece of metal containing a number, is placed on the latch which secures the doors of the body of the vehicle. The seal should be applied by an authorized terminal employee, and the seal number recorded on

P·I·E TRUCK MANIFEST		Original Manifest No. ____ Supplemental No. ____ Supplemental No. ____ Supplemental No. ____					
From	To		Date	Route		Log No.	
Tractor No.	Trailer No.		Driver			Time	
P.I.E. PRO. NO. (Show Station Prefix)	CONSIGNEE	DESTINATION	SHIPPER	WEIGHT	NO. OF PIECES	REMARKS	
						CHECK (√) CUBE UTILIZATION	
						¾ to V. Full	
						½ to ¾ Full	
						¼ to ½ Full	
						Up to ¼ Full	
						No Load	
NOTE: Show sub-total weight for each destination							

FIG. 10–8. Truck manifest.

the manifest. On arrival at the destination terminal, the seal should be removed by authorized personnel and properly recorded on the manifest. If there is a discrepancy, it should be reported.

Some carriers accept shipments on the basis of shipper's load and count, restricting such shipments to straight loads from one shipper to one consignee with both origin and destination on their own line. When the shipper makes exclusive use of a complete trailer, the shipments are accepted on this basis. In this case, the motor carrier

---

[5] Public Law 534, July 24, 1946, 79th. Cong., provides a penalty of 10 years in jail, $5,000 fine, or both.

requires that the trailers be sealed in the presence of the shipper's representative.

The exclusive use of trailers is generally subject to tariff provisions and charges as well as restrictions involving interline movement. The Commission has held that where a notation has provided for the exclusive use of vehicle rule and the notation has been properly made, the charges should be computed in accordance with the rule because of the sealing of the vehicle by the consignor.[6] Even when the shipper orders exclusive use of the vehicle, laxity on the part of the shipper regarding seals has often resulted in the loading of other freight in the vehicle.

SAFETY AND OPERATIONS

The promotion of safety pays in any motor-carrier organization. This may take the form of a well-defined safety program carried out in conjunction with an insurance company, more often as a separate safety program. The usual emphasis in such a program is upon drivers, both over-the-road and pickup and delivery, and it is a most important phase of operations. The responsibility for the safety program is placed directly under the safety director or the safety supervisor, who is responsible to the general manager for the satisfactory functioning of the program. A comprehensive program should embrace the following features: (a) management responsibility and interest, (b) selection of driver personnel, (c) driver training, (d) awards or incentive plans, (e) general safety information, (f) inspections, and (g) road supervision of drivers.

MANAGEMENT CO-OPERATION

The success of a safety program is dependent in large part upon the co-operative attitude of management. Inasmuch as management originates the program, it is necessary that policies be formulated and goals and standards established that can be used to measure progress. It is to the best interests of management to foster actively a well co-ordinated safety program. A good safety program can result in direct money savings and in improved company and industry public relations.

---

[6] *Blass Co.* v. *Powell Bros. Truck Lines,* 53 MCC 603 (1951).

SELECTION OF DRIVER PERSONNEL

Careful selection of driver personnel is of utmost importance in a safety program. Avoidable accidents can be practically eliminated through the use of good judgment and the skill of a truck driver. The general requirements for the selection of driver personnel vary widely, but most companies establish certain requirements such as the following: the driver must be 26 years of age; he must have 2 years of experience on similar equipment and 2 years' employment with one employer; and he must successfully pass the Interstate Commerce Commission's physical examination, as well as driver aptitude and knowledge tests.

The employment procedure for an applicant driver usually begins with an interview with the safety director as well as the personnel supervisor to ascertain whether the driver appears, safetywise, to be a desirable applicant. If the safety director and the personnel supervisor concur, he is given an application blank to fill out. From this completed application form, the company will make a telephone check with the references the applicant has listed. Some companies confine their checks to local references, while others call all references by telephone immediately. For this purpose, a special telephone check list is prepared of questions that the company representative asks concerning the applicant. Upon the completion of the telephone check, another and more detailed interview will be held with the applicant driver, at which time the company representative has before him an interview form with questions concerning experience, schooling, family background, financial and domestic situation, health, special questions about absenteeism and its causes, personal habits, and the like. Some companies supplement this driver interview with a credit report upon the applicant secured from a credit bureau, in addition to checking with the state highway patrol records to determine his accident record.

DRIVER TRAINING

Driver training is given to the newly hired driver while he is making what are called "student trips." These student trips are familiarization training trips which are made in order to acquaint the new driver with the route. He is accompanied on these runs by a regular driver, who observes the new driver's driving techniques.

Any apparent weaknesses are pointed out and ways of correcting them suggested. The new driver is indoctrinated in the driving rules and regulations of the Interstate Commerce Commission, as well as in the individual carrier rules and regulations.

In addition to a specific program for the new drivers, a continuing driver-training program should be conducted for all driver personnel. This may consist of monthly safety meetings, where there are talks by city and state law-enforcement officials, Interstate Commerce Commission representatives, safety engineers, insurance company adjusters, truck manufacturers, and others. Motion pictures and sound slides may also be used effectively at such meetings. Attendance may be stimulated by serving a company lunch and granting points that may be accumulated toward a safety award to each driver who attends the meeting.

AWARDS OR INCENTIVE PLANS

Many different driver award plans have been instituted. One such plan is described in some detail, for it possesses a number of desirable features. This particular plan consists of merchandise awards which are earned through points given for each month's safe driving. The granting of this type of prize has the advantage of support and encouragement of the driver's family. The goal of merchandise coveted by his family makes a vigilant driver, thus cutting down on those accidents which are caused by carelessness. The American Trucking Associations, Inc., offers such an incentive plan to the industry at nominal cost. It is called the S.O.S. or Sights on Safety program.

The first step in establishing this incentive plan is for the individual company to determine the amount of the expenditure to be made for the awards. This must be related to what a decrease in accidents is actually worth. A catalogue that contains over 900 articles of merchandise is given to each driver. Each article in the catalogue is valued in terms of points. The awards that are issued to employees at the end of each month are in the form of certificates, with the amount stated in points. The value of a point is one-half cent, and the driver may use the points to buy merchandise in the catalogue whenever he has accumulated a sufficient number of points for the item he desires.

It is necessary that one person be placed in charge of this program, and the responsibility for accidents must be determined by an Accident Review Board, which decides which accidents are chargeable. There are a number of variations of these point plans, but one of these is to give 1,000 points to each driver who has a safe driving record of 1 calendar month with no chargeable accidents. If a driver has 12 months of accident-free driving, he will have 12,000 points.

The National Safety Council and organizations such as the American Trucking Associations and others provide for a regular mailing schedule of bulletin board material, posters, and information. A carrier can subscribe to these services, which enable it to secure at minimum cost material that deals with safety.

INSPECTIONS

Adequate equipment inspection prior to the operation of each vehicle is an important part of a safety program. This specific responsibility should be assigned so that all potential defects which might jeopardize safe operation of a motor vehicle may be detected. This inspection should include the checking of tires, lug nuts, air-brake hoses and connections, reflectors, windshield wipers, and so on.

The next step in inspection is to have each driver's log properly checked as to accuracy and completeness. The Interstate Commerce Commission prescribes the driver's daily log and requires that these logs be properly maintained. Figure 10–9 is a specimen log, and the following information can be secured from an examination of this log: The driver reported for duty at Washington, D.C., at 6:00 A.M., waited 30 minutes for work, spent 1 hour loading the vehicle, then drove or operated the vehicle for 2 hours, reaching Baltimore, Maryland, at 9:30 A.M., where he stopped 30 minutes for gas and coffee. He left Baltimore and drove for 2½ hours, reaching Havre de Grace, Maryland, where he stopped 30 minutes for lunch. From there he drove for 2 hours, spent 15 minutes on the ferry and reached Camden, New Jersey, at 4:00 P.M., where he spent 1½ hours unloading the vehicle, after which he went off duty for the rest of the calendar day. A stop of 5 minutes at Laurel, Maryland, to make a delivery is included in line 3, "Driving," as the time of the stop was less than the allowable 10 minutes. The two 30-minute stops, at Baltimore and Havre de Grace, and the 15 minutes crossing on the ferry are shown in line 4, "On Duty," as the stops were over the allowable 10 minutes. The total hours for each line show 12½ hours "off duty," 7¼ hours "driving," and 4¼ hours "on duty" for the day covered by the log.

If the motor carrier employs the use of a recorder, such as the Tachograph, the Servis Recorder, or the Speedograph, the charts from this equipment are inspected at this time. To be effective, the charts must be examined daily to check their agreement with the driver's logs, to check whether any driver is exceeding a company or

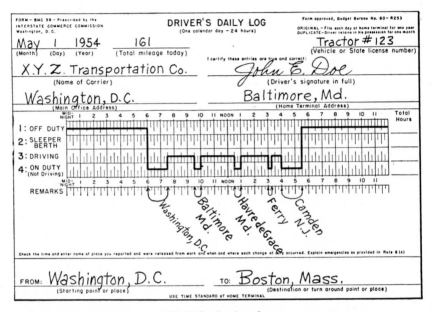

FIG. 10–9. Specimen log.

other speed limit, and to see whether or not the device is being tampered with.

ROAD SUPERVISION OF DRIVERS

Inasmuch as the operation of a truck fleet is conducted over wide areas, it is more difficult to supervise line-haul drivers. The supervision of drivers cannot be considered as the sole method of securing the greatest efficiency from the drivers. An important aspect of operations of this type is to have proper selection and adequate training of drivers in order to create self-supervision in drivers.

There are a number of methods which have been used in supervising drivers—road patrols, check stations, and mechanical-operations records. There is no general agreement as to which is the most effective, since each of them has advantages and disadvantages.

The different types of road patrols will be discussed. The first of these is the *carrier's road patrol.* The road supervisor by direct observation can check the drivers' handling of the equipment as well as checking the equipment. Such a road supervisor will have other duties, such as those of driver training and conducting safety meetings. He also investigates serious or unusual accidents and maintains contacts with law enforcement agencies in the territory in which he operates. He maintains a continuous route survey to report on any unusual conditions on the routes used by his company's equipment. He is also to render assistance to any highway user who is in trouble.

The road supervisors may be furnished with properly marked cars or cars which are unmarked. The advantages of conspicuous marking of the road patrol vehicle far overshadow the disadvantages of marking.

The road supervisor's observation must be of sufficient length to give an accurate report of the operation and condition of the unit. On the open road, from 3 to 5 miles of observation is generally adequate. In urban areas, shorter observations are sufficient. Every effort must be made that the observations are accurate and factual. Although the supervisor has the authority to stop his company's vehicles on the highways, the accident hazard which may be created through such action limits this to a minimum number of cases.

A road patrol report form is used to record the reports. There have been two general types of these reports. One is a check-list type in which the conditions observed are checked as well as other factors, such as the weather, traffic, road surface, and the like. The other method relies upon the observer's narrative description of the conditions. A road patrol form combining both of these methods is shown in Figure 10–10.

Because of the difficulties encountered in attempting to write down the results of the report while driving, some companies have installed dictaphone machines or tape recorders in their vehicles. These reports are then subsequently transcribed to the regular road observation report.

In order for a road patrol to be an effective method of supervision, it is necessary that there be a prompt processing of the road reports and an adequate follow-up with the driver. Both favorable and unfavorable reports should be made. Where there are serious violations, there should be an interview with the driver in order that all aspects of the report can be covered. There have been some instances in the past of road supervisors serving as policemen, which has created a strong antipathy among drivers toward the use of road patrols

REPORT OF ROAD OBSERVATION

Date: _____ Time: _____ M.

COMPANY _____

VEHICLE(S): Truck or Tractor _____ Trailer _____
(Use unit numbers rather than license numbers whenever possible)

OBSERVED: Direction of Travel _____ Route or Street _____

Near _____ Toward _____

Average Speed _____ Top Speed _____ Legal Speed _____ Distance Observed _____

Weather _____ Condition of Road _____ No. of Lanes _____

Traffic Volume _____ Other _____

CONDITION OF UNIT

_____ No Defects   _____ Turn signal   _____ Cab
_____ Headlight   _____ Mirror   _____ Body
_____ Tail light   _____ Brakes   _____ Load
_____ Stop Light   _____ Tires   Safety
_____ Marker light   _____ Wheels   _____ equipment
_____ Clearance light _____ Motor
_____ Reflector   _____ Alighment   _____ Other

OPERATION OF UNIT

_____ Satisfactory   _____ Fails to Keep Right   _____ Improper Turn
_____ Excessive Speed   _____ Straddling Lanes   _____ Traffic Sign
_____ Pass on Hill   _____ Weaving   _____ Traffic Signal
_____ Pass on Curve   _____ Obstricting Traffic   _____ Improperly Parked
_____ Pass at Intersection _____ Follows Too Close   _____ Passenger
_____ Other Improper Passing _____ Fails to Signal
                              _____ Cutting In   _____ Other (Describe)

REMARKS:

_____

_____

_____

_____

FIG. 10–10. Road patrol form.

generally. There should be good relations between the drivers and the road supervisor. An understanding of the road supervisor's job and the benefits to all parties concerned will do much to establish greater confidence.

The cost of a full-time company-operated road patrol has tended to restrict its use to the larger companies, inasmuch as its cost runs from $9,000 to $12,000 per year.

Another type of road patrol is that which is conducted by *insur-*

ance companies which insure motor carriers. Most of the insurance companies have some type of road patrol supervision, although its extent varies among the companies. These reports are furnished to the motor carrier. They provide the insurance company with a degree of control over its risks as well as furnishing motor carriers with a road patrol report from an organization outside their own.

Road patrol service which is furnished by *organizations which specialize in providing this service* is another type of road patrol. These companies usually operate in a regional area and supervise the drivers of a number of motor carriers in that area. They offer their services on a fee basis. The charge may be a set fee per observation; a fee which is determined by the number of carrier's units in the patrol area; or a percentage of the carrier's gross revenue. Such road patrol companies may be able to furnish reports at a lower unit cost than the motor carrier can furnish its own. Companies of this type will furnish any type of coverage that is desired, but it is important that there be an agreement between the motor carrier and the road patrol company as to the latter's responsibilities.

Another type is the *co-operative road patrol* which has been established by more than twenty state or local trucking associations. The co-operative patrols are made up of safety directors employed by the member carriers who voluntarily check each other's equipment as well as their own in the course of their regular duties. The reports are forwarded by the motor carrier to the state or local association which, in turn, forwards them to the carriers whose units were observed. The Department of Safety of the American Trucking Associations has developed a standard co-operative road patrol report form which is not as detailed as the form used for a carrier-operated patrol.

The establishment of a *check-in station* is another method of supervising the line-haul drivers. This may be a designated gas station or diner at which the driver is required to stop and note his times of arrival and departure. This may be accomplished by requiring the driver to punch a time clock or make an entry in a log book. Carriers with a number of terminals may require drivers to check in and out of intermediate terminals on their runs. The check-in stations are generally established at regular intervals, such as every 100 miles, or at points where it is advantageous to refuel.

Check stations can be made more effective if there is a standard driving time established between them. They encourage the maintenance of schedules and provide a point of contact with drivers when the need arises. However, check stations provide only a very limited means of supervision.

A method for identifying all trucks, tractors, and semitrailers must be established because it will simplify many aspects of operations. It can provide an easy means of identification of the different types of units for the dispatcher; for use in maintenance records control; and serves as a means of identifying units for the road patrol. A simple means of identifying semitrailers is to assign the first number as a means of identifying the type of semitrailer. For example, number "2" would signify a single-axle van; "3" a tandem-axle van; "4" a tandem open top; "5" a tandem flat bed; "6" a single-axle open top; "7" a single-axle flat bed; "8" a single-axle refrigerated; "9" a tandem-axle refrigerated; and number "1" reserved for straight trucks.

The second figure can indicate the length of the semitrailer. If the trailer is 32 feet long and it is a single-axle van, the second digit of the 32 feet can be added to the "2" which identifies it as a single-axle van, making the number then "22." A third number should be added to this to identify each of the units of this particular type.

MECHANICAL OPERATIONS RECORDERS

The use of mechanical operations recorders provides a means of road supervision of drivers. In order to give somewhat better control over operations between terminals, motor carriers have made use of recorder devices, such as the Tachograph. This is a mechanism that can be installed in the cab of a truck and connected with the mechanical part of the truck. It will record on a circular chart inside the device information that shows when the engine started, how long the engine idled, when the vehicle was in motion, how fast it traveled, when the vehicle stopped, and the distance traveled between stops. The chart is inserted only by authorized persons prior to truck departure and is marked as to unit, date, destination, driver, and any other pertinent information. The Tachograph clock is set to the correct time and wound. The chart is placed in back of the clock, and a small knife cuts the edge of the chart at the proper time setting. The mechanism is closed and locked. Upon completion of the trip, only a designated person with the proper key can unlock the unit and remove the chart. A recorder which records speed of engine in revolutions per minute is desirable where speed of engine rather than speed of vehicle is the determining economy factor.

The use of this device or a similar one has resulted in benefits to motor carriers. However, the charts must be examined, for these devices can be tampered with. For example, a company may establish 45 miles per hour as its open-road speed limit. There have been cases where a heated pin was pushed through the plexiglass face of the mechanism, causing it to record 45 miles per hour irrespective of the speed traveled by the unit. On the other hand, such tampering is easily detected upon removal and examination of the chart. Instead of the normal jagged edge of the curve ⋀⋁⋀ caused by speed-ups and slowdowns for traffic, the curve comes out perfectly capped ⌒.

There are other ways in which these devices can be tampered with, all of which can be easily detected. From this, it should not be implied that all drivers are averse to the use of such a device, for most drivers feel that it serves as a protection for them. In the event of a controversy concerning speed, for example, they have actual proof of the speed at which they were traveling. Figure 10–11 is a sample of a chart as it appears at the end of a trip. Since this chart is checked against a daily report maintained by the driver (driver's log), it serves as a worthwhile control.

Before mechanical-operations recorders are installed, a survey should be made of all company records, the mileage determined from point of origin to diners, railroad crossings, and the like, for such information will assist in interpreting that which is recorded on the charts.

INTERCHANGE

A phase of motor-carrier operations which must be considered is that of interchange of equipment between carriers. Instead of transferring cargos from the trailer of one motor carrier to that of another, motor carriers have found it much more efficient to interchange equipment. This makes it possible for one carrier to haul a load part of the way and, at a designated transfer point, to turn the equipment over to a connecting carrier, which will complete the haul. The physical exchange of equipment, which is generally confined to trailers, is effected between authorized carriers for the furtherance of through movement of freight over routes each is certificated to serve. In interchange, each carrier has authority to operate in the portion of the haul it performs. Trailer interchange is arranged on several different bases by means of individual agreements

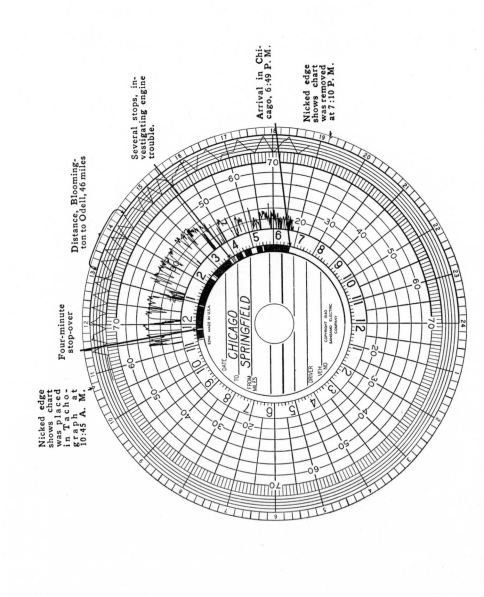

Nicked edge
shows chart
was placed
in Tacho-
graph at
10:45 A. M.

Four-minute
stop-over

Distance, Blooming-
ton to Odell, 46 miles

Several stops, in-
vestigating engine
trouble.

Arrival in Chi-
cago, 6:49 P. M.

Nicked edge
shows chart
was removed
at 7:10 P. M.

CHICAGO
SPRINGFIELD

DATE
TO
FROM
MILES

DRIVER
VEH.
NO.

52341 MADE IN U.S.A.

COPYRIGHT 1940
SANGAMO ELECTRIC
COMPANY

ANALYSIS OF CHART

Distance	TIME	PLACE	REMARKS
0	10:45 A. M.	Springfield	Inserted Chart.
0	11:16 A. M.	Springfield	Left via Route US 66.
16	11:42 A. M.	Elkhart	Stopped 4 minutes, leaving at 11:46.
57	12:54 P. M.	Bloomington	Three minute stop on account of detour.
61	1:14 P. M.	Normal	20 minutes through Bloomington and Normal.
107	2:23 P. M.	Odell	13 minute stop, leaving at 2:36 P. M.
136	3:24 P. M.	Wilmington	Engine begins to heat, causing reduction of speed
144	3:40 P. M.	Highway	Several stops, allowing motor to cool. Note reduced speed.
154	4:21 P. M.	Joliet	9 minute stop, leaving at 4:30 P. M.
162	4:51 P. M.	Highway	17 minute stop for engine cooling leaving at 5:08 P. M.
169	5:26 P. M.	Highway	5 minute stop.
194	6:49 P. M.	Chicago	Arrival.
	7:10 P. M.	Chicago	Removed Chart.

Total elapsed time 7 hours, 33 minutes; actual driving time 6 hours, 26 minutes; average speed 30.3 miles per hour

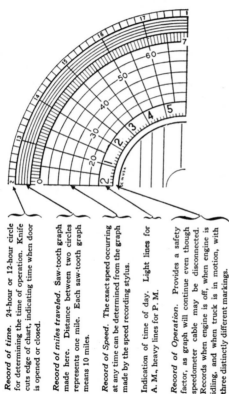

Record of time. 24-hour or 12-hour circle for determining the time of operation. Knife cuts edge of chart, indicating time when door is opened or closed.

Record of miles traveled. Saw-tooth graph made here. Distance between two circles represents one mile. Each saw-tooth graph means 10 miles.

Record of Speed. The exact speed occurring at any time can be determined from the graph made by the speed recording stylus.

Indication of time of day. Light lines for A. M., heavy lines for P. M.

Record of Operation. Provides a safety factor, as graph will continue even though speedometer cable may be disconnected. Records when engine is off, when engine is idling, and when truck is in motion, with three distinctly different markings.

FIG. 10–11. Completed Tachograph chart and explanation.

between carriers. Sometimes completely loaded trailers are interchanged; or, in other cases, a loaded trailer is offered by one of the two carriers in exchange for an empty trailer to be used by the first carrier while the second carrier is completing the through movement.

There is an increasing amount of trailer interchange; but, for motor carriers as a whole, it constitutes a small fraction of traffic volume. Some carriers have established a charge of 3 cents per mile when their trailers are used by other carriers. They, in turn, will pay 3 cents per mile for the use of a "foreign" trailer on their routes. This standard charge for the interchange of trailers, as made by agreement between these carriers, generally provides for cash settlements between the carriers. There are a number of difficulties regarding the interchange of equipment at the present time: (a) nonuniformity of fifth-wheel coupling device; (b) nonuniformity of braking devices; (c) differences in light connections; (d) state restrictions on vehicle weight, length, and width; (e) reluctance of some motor carriers to allow their equipment to be removed from their control; (f) reluctance of some motor carriers to allow equipment bearing their firm name to be operated in a foreign territory; and (g) inability to make suitable agreements covering necessary repairs to a unit while it is in the possession of a foreign carrier.

The lack of uniformity of the fifth-wheel coupling device is in some measure due to the patenting and developing by equipment manufacturers of their own type of fifth wheel. Each manufacturer is anxious to keep his patented type on the market, and the spacing back of the cab varies from manufacturer to manufacturer. Then, too, there are motor carriers which are convinced of the advantages of a certain type of fifth wheel. The fact that each type of fifth wheel is patented would present the problem of arrangements with all manufacturers if one patent type were adopted as the standard.

The reluctance on the part of many motor carriers to engage in interchange of equipment is caused in part by the feeling that their equipment may not be as well taken care of by another carrier. The interchange of equipment that bears the firm name of a motor carrier is of little advertising value to that carrier when it is operated in foreign territory and the motor carrier is using in its stead equipment that bears another firm's name. In addition, necessary repairs to equipment while in the possession of a foreign carrier have been matters of contention. There have been too many instances where equipment turned over to a foreign line is the poorest equipment and is in need of repair at the time of the interchange, or will be in need of repair soon thereafter.

As motor carriers develop additional business and render service over an ever broadening area, it is reasonable to expect that more attention will be given to the economies attendant upon trailer interchange. The elimination of extra handling costs should prove to be a strong incentive for further development of this interchange.

In an effort to improve trailer interchange practices and accomplish a degree of uniformity, there have been a number of recommended trailer interchange practices developed, which are concerned with different phases of equipment interchange.[7]

Before a foreign trailer is accepted in interchange service, it is recommended that the name and trailer number of the offering carrier be printed on the trailer; that there be an interchange agreement between the carriers, parties to the interchange; that there be an inspection of the trailer by an authorized representative of the receiving carrier; that the vehicle and the inspection meet the requirements of any agency having jurisdiction; and that the tires are serviceable.

The owner should accept the return of his trailer from interchange service only after a thorough inspection which shows that the vehicle meets the requirements of any regulatory agencies having jurisdiction; and subject to the responsibility of the carrier which originally acquired the vehicle for any damages noted.

When a trailer in interchange service is unloaded, it must be returned promptly to its owner at the point of original interchange by way of the carriers over whose route it has come to the point of unloading; or in case freight for reloading is not available over that route, it may be returned by other routing that will assure its prompt return to the owner, provided permission is first obtained by the unloading carrier from the carrier initially acquiring use of the trailer from the owner.

In order to facilitate the location of trailers, trailer location reports are recommended. Carriers should maintain an equipment register which contains the trailer number and make. Furthermore, it is suggested that a record should be kept of each trailer in order to indicate its location from terminal to terminal over the system of the owner. When a trailer leaves the owning line, an inspection

---

[7] Developed by the Trailer Interchange Committee of the Regular Common Carrier Conference in 1954. A suggested trailer interchange contract has also been prepared by the Conference.

report should be completed and copies sent to the owner, receiving carriers, and one with the semitrailer. A daily record should be maintained which will show for each carrier with which it conducts trailer interchange, the trailers received from that carrier and the trailers given to it.

At the time of the interchange of the trailer, the tires should be thoroughly inspected to determine any major defects, and to insure that there is sufficient tread for covering safely the round trip. Any deficiencies noted by inspection should be corrected by the owner or the carrier in possession or at the expense of the owner or carrier in possession by agreement. Foreign trailers should be inspected, serviced, and lubricated in accordance with the using carrier's ordinary maintenance program. Such maintenance records should be carried with the trailer.

In the case of repairs, the defects in interchange trailers which are noted at the time of inspection and prior to the acceptance by the receiving carrier will be repaired by the owner; or if authorized by the owner should be repaired by the receiving carrier which will be reimbursed by the owner. Those repairs and other service adjustments which are occasioned by interchange should be absorbed by the user in an amount not exceeding a sum agreed upon in advance by the parties. In the event that repairs are performed by the user, the former should prepare the work orders or job tickets covering the servicing and repairs, with a copy furnished to the owner.

A trailer interchange contract should be used. If there is failure to settle any dispute arising out of the use of such a contract, it should be settled by arbitration. Each side should appoint a member of an arbitration committee who, in turn, should select a third neutral member, with the decision of the committee to be final and binding.

There have been a variety of arrangements governing trailer interchange ranging from oral to written contracts. Because of the many variations in the contracts and the misunderstandings which often arise, a more standard or uniform written contract would be beneficial to carriers which are interchanging equipment.

Effective September 1, 1953, the Interstate Commerce Commission prescribed rules governing the interchange of equipment. When power equipment is being interchanged for any through movement of traffic, there must be a contract which specifies the points of interchange, the use to be made of the equipment, and the consideration paid. The carriers' operating authority must authorize the transportation of the commodities and the service to and from the points where the interchange occurs. Each carrier must assign its own driver to operate the equipment over the route authorized. This latter rule will not apply where authorized common carriers hold certificates of public convenience and necessity authorizing transportation over irregular routes of articles or commodities, which because of their size, weight, or shape require the use of special equipment (heavy haulers) or, until March 1, 1956, of perishable commodities in refrigerated equipment and automobile haulers; under these circumstances, through movements of such articles or commodities on the special equipment may be made without change of drivers at the point of interchange.

Interchanged equipment must be inspected in the manner provided in the leasing rules. Such equipment must also carry a copy of the interchange contract. When using power units of originating carrier, traffic transported in interchange service must move on a through bill of lading issued by the originating carrier, and the rates charged, and the revenues collected, must be accounted for in the same manner as if there had been no interchange of equipment. The rules further provide that when power units are interchanged, they must be identified in accordance with requirements of the Commission's identification rules.

Leased equipment operating in interchange service can be subleased for return to the originating carrier, as well as used in interchange between more than two carriers. A lessee of equipment on a through movement involving more than two carriers shall be considered the owner of the equipment for the purpose of leasing it for movement to destination or return to the originating carrier.

A development that is being watched by the trucking industry is the formation of a freight trailer lease-interchange system called National Trailer Pool, Inc., which was formed by twelve midwestern trucking companies. The plan went into effect in November, 1954. It is anticipated that it ultimately will be nation-wide in scope. There are four types of participation. The stockholder member is one who has turned over his line-haul trailers to the pool for equity in the stock of the company. Such a member will lease all his line-haul trailers from the pool. Any dividends earned from services of the National Trailer Pool are paid to stockholder members.

Another type of member is any common carrier financially responsible which executes a contract with the pool for the leasing of trailers in which it agrees to abide by the pool's interchange rules and charges. Such a carrier may interchange trailers with all stockholder members and other lease-interchange members simply by executing a trailer receipt.

The single-trip participant is another class of member. This is any common carrier which has not qualified itself either as a stockholder or lease-interchange member of the pool, which desires to lease trailers from the pool and to interchange trailers on a single-trip contract with any member who so agrees. The fourth class of membership is any user of trailers who has not qualified himself for any of the interchange privileges of the pool, yet who wants to lease trailers for local purposes from the pool. He cannot interchange trailers with members of the pool.

The companies which initially formed the pool assigned 2,000 semitrailers to it, and the pool company purchased 500 new line-haul semitrailers and 200 city-delivery-type trailers. Ultimately all line-haul semitrailers will be standardized, and a higher utilization is expected from the trailers. Under the lease-interchange plans, trailer charges will be uniform and will be known in advance. It is expected that the economies of group financing and mass purchasing, maintenance, and service will result in lower trailer costs than the conventional method of operation. In most cases the trailers owned by the pool will be covered by insurance policies carried on the truck tractors of member carriers. On single-trip arrangements, overriding insurance coverage of the trailers will be carried by the trailer pool.[8]

ACCOUNTING[9]

For the purpose of prescribing a uniform system of accounts, carriers have been grouped by the Interstate Commerce Commission into three classes, as previously explained in Chapter 5, "Types of Carriers." Class I motor carriers are those with annual gross revenues of $200,000 or more; Class II motor carriers are those with annual gross revenues of $50,000 or over but less than $200,000; and Class III motor carriers are those with annual gross revenues of less than $50,000. The requirements for keeping accounts and filing reports

---

[8] Information supplied by National Trailer Pool, Inc., Minneapolis, Minnesota, November, 1954.

[9] For a more detailed treatment of motor-carrier accounting than is necessary in this text, see H. J. Day, *Motor Carriers Accounting and Cost Control System* (Washington, D.C.: Traffic Service Corporation, 1949).

by Class I motor carriers of property were first instituted in 1938. These motor carriers are required to keep their accounts under a uniform system and to file quarterly and annual reports in a form prescribed by the Interstate Commerce Commission. This regulation initially applied to 1,177 carriers, including a small number of carriers of passengers. By November 1, 1954, there were about 2,624 Class I carriers of property alone which were subject to Commission accounts and reports requirements. The Class II and Class III carriers subject to Interstate Commerce Commission regulation have not had to keep their accounts under the system prescribed by the Commission.[10] Beginning in 1948, however, a simple annual report form has been required from the Class II and Class III carriers, in order that the Commission may obtain information about these classes of carriers. These reports consist primarily of the reporting of revenues, expenses, vehicle-miles operated, tons transported, equipment operated, and some limited information as to the number of employees. The annual report required of Class I carriers, on the other hand, is a 75-page report, with some schedules contained therein to be completed by Class I passenger carriers, the remainder to be submitted by Class I property carriers. A sufficient number of schedules are contained in the report to give a comprehensive picture of Class I motor-carrier property operations.

Because of the wide use made of financial data which are shown in motor-carrier quarterly and annual reports in connection with the fixing of rates, the handling of general revenue proceedings, the handling of applications for the purchase, merger, and consolidation of operating authorities, and the issuance of securities which require Commission approval, it is important that there be close supervision by the Commission of motor-carrier accounting practices. Many dispositions of applications for rate increases have been based principally on the data contained in the quarterly and annual reports of the motor-carrier applicant. The lack of adequate staff in the Section of Motor Carriers of the Bureau of Accounts and Cost Finding (now the Bureau of Accounts, Cost Finding, and Valuation) has caused curtailment in examining and correcting quarterly and annual reports to the point where some reports are given only superficial examination, namely, reports of some local carriers, contract carriers, and haulers of special commodities.[11] Primary attention of

---

[10] Interstate Commerce Commission, *63rd Annual Report* (Washington, D.C.: U.S. Government Printing Office, 1949), p. 73.

[11] *Ibid.*, p. 75.

the Section of Motor Carriers of the Bureau of Accounts and Cost Finding has been directed toward the reports of the general commodities carriers, since this group is principally before the Commission in connection with rate and revenue proceedings.

The Bureau of Accounts and Cost Finding has issued to motor-carrier accountants an Accounting Circular No. MF–1 and supplement, which contains a series of accounting interpretations which represent authoritative explanations regarding certain accounts which appear to conflict or otherwise require clarification. These interpretations, which number over 200, are tentative and provisional in the absence of formal consideration of the subjects but provide a helpful guide for motor-carrier accountants. The Interstate Commerce Commission requires compliance with the regulations for the keeping of accounts and filing of reports; and, through its field staff, which makes investigations of carrier accounts, violations are sometimes discovered which result in the institution of criminal or civil proceedings against the carrier.

The system of accounts prescribed by the Commission has been adopted by twenty state public utility commissions for application to motor carriers operating solely in intrastate commerce.[12] This broadens the base of uniformity of accounting practices and facilitates the organization of comparative data of intrastate and interstate operations.[13]

Authorized Commission personnel, such as special agents, examiners, or accountants, have the right to inspect a carrier's records, including all accounts, records, correspondence, and similar material. This is true even though the records do not relate to transportation. This right of inspection by the Commission has been upheld by the Supreme Court.[14]

CENTRALIZED OR DECENTRALIZED ACCOUNTING SYSTEMS

The accounting system which motor carriers use may be either a centralized or a decentralized plan. Whether a centralized or de-

---

[12] Interstate Commerce Commission, *62nd Annual Report* (Washington, D.C.: U.S. Government Printing Office, 1949), p. 61.

[13] *The Uniform System of Accounts for Class I Common and Contract Motor Carriers of Property* which has been prescribed by the Commission contains essential information and instructions. It is available from the Superintendent of Documents, U.S. Government Printing Office, for a nominal charge.

[14] *U.S.* v. *Alabama Highway Express, Inc.,* 46 Fed. Supp. 459 (1942); 325 U.S. 837 (1945).

centralized accounting system should be used is influenced by factors such as the number of terminals and their geographical location and the size of the company. In smaller companies where there is but one accountant, the accounting system is generally centralized. However, some of the largest Class I carriers also use the centralized system.

The advantages of the decentralized plan are prompt collections, quicker availability of collected funds, records at hand for dealing with shippers, more prompt remittance of C.O.D.'s, better relations with creditors, and use of prevailing wage scales. In the decentralized plan the cashier at the terminal collects accounts receivable.

The advantages of the centralized system are greater uniformity in the classification of transactions; specialization of accounting personnel; greater possibilities for job analysis, evaluation, and production; strict control of costs; closer supervision of accrued items; more current financial statements; and less necessary verification of branch records.

Larger carriers have often adopted machine accounting when this is feasible. The carriers which make use of machine accounting have found that the carrier can develop much statistical information which is useful in cost control forecasting and other activities of the operation. Manual methods, however, still predominate throughout the motor-carrier industry.

INTERLINE ACCOUNTS

An increasing amount of shipments move over two or more main lines, so that interline settlements are assuming greater importance. Some carriers have felt that they should restrict their participation in so-called joint hauls to not more than two connecting carriers. This is due in part to the financial risk if they agree to joint hauls with numerous carriers with which they have little contact.

Where motor carriers have joint rates and one carrier owes another carrier, the collection of the division which is owed is a matter for the carriers to settle or the courts. However, where the Commission by order has prescribed divisions as between carriers or has required retroactive adjustment of divisions, the carriers may base their court actions upon such orders.[15]

Where there is a through joint rate in effect and all carriers participating in the haul are parties to such a rate, the revenue derived is usually divided according to a written agreement through use of

---

[15] Administrative Rule No. 14, August 26, 1936.

one of the following methods, the first four of which are "arbitrary prorate" methods:

1. A flat percentage rate of through gross revenue.
2. A flat rate per 100 pounds which is applicable regardless of any class, commodity, or exception rating.[16]
3. A flat rate per 100 pounds dependent upon the class, commodity, or exception rating used to determine the through rate.
4. A flat percentage rate of net revenue.
5. A mileage prorate. The mileage factors used are generally the short-line mileage between junction points, with reliance upon Rand McNally map distances. The mileage factors are added, and this total is then divided into each mileage factor, having first reduced each mileage factor to percentage by multiplying by 100. The figure secured from so dividing represents the percentage due each carrier.
6. Rate prorate. Determine percentages as in No. 5. However, the factor used is the normal first class rate between junction points.
7. A mileage-rate prorate. This combines No. 5 and No. 6, and the procedure is as follows: The percentages should be determined both by mileage, as in No. 5, and by rate, as in No. 6. Then add the percentage to each line by mileage to the percentage to each line by rate, and divide by the number of lines considered in the computation.

It is essential that interline settlements be made promptly, for it is much easier to make settlements while records are current. Those interline accounts which are outstanding should be reviewed at least once each week; and a definite follow-up procedure should exist, whether by letter, telephone, or personal call. If a carrier's account becomes delinquent, most motor carriers will have specific provisions issued to reroute the freight to a carrier that will settle interline accounts promptly. Furthermore, there is generally a specific procedure in making cash payments to connecting carriers which, in the event of cash payment at the time of delivery, requires that this be done only when previously agreed upon in advance and when there are no charges due from the connecting carrier. In addition, the freight bills will be rechecked for errors, and the amount the driver is to pay the connecting carrier placed on the freight bill. Credit payments which are made to connecting carriers will be remitted upon receipt of a statement from the connecting carrier, after checking to see if there was any error in the extension or division on the freight bills.

In the settlement of interline accounts, a motor carrier deals with two aspects, the so-called collectibles and the payables. The collectibles are amounts that the motor carrier secures from connecting

---

[16] These rates and ratings are explained in more detail in Chapter 16.

carriers and include two categories: (a) shipments that are transferred to a connecting carrier with freight charges collect, which includes that division of revenue from origin to point of transfer; and (b) shipments that are transferred to a motor carrier from a connecting carrier with freight charges prepaid, which includes that division of revenue from point of transfer to destination.

The payables are charges that are due connecting carriers, as follows: (a) shipments that are transferred to a connecting carrier with freight charges prepaid, which means that division of revenue from interchange point to destination; and (b) shipments transferred by connecting carrier to a motor carrier with freight charges collect, which includes the division of revenue from origin to point of transfer at which the motor carrier received the shipment.

CO-OPERATIVE BILL COLLECTION SYSTEM

The collection of freight bills by motor common carriers from hundreds of different shippers can prove most burdensome. Depending on the volume of business, carriers must try to collect from 50 to 3,000 bills a day. The Interstate Commerce Commission regulation requires carriers to bill shippers within 7 days of the time they pick up freight. The Commission thus far has been lenient in enforcing this regulation, but collection of bills has been and is a problem to many motor carriers.

To facilitate the collection of freight bills and the settlement of interline debits between carriers, an organization called Transport Clearings has been formed. It is a nonprofit corporation owned and operated by and for its carrier members and is presently located in St. Paul, Seattle, Portland, San Francisco, Kansas City, Duluth, Salt Lake City, Dallas, and Los Angeles. Transport Clearings was organized in 1942, and an office was established in St. Paul. After an experimental period during which the system was perfected, it was also established in the other cities. Each one of the organizations is separately incorporated and locally run, such as Transport Clearings of Los Angeles and Transport Clearings of the Bay Area (San Francisco). Each one of these co-operative clearinghouses, representing carrier members in its area, buys outright all freight bills submitted by a carrier member which otherwise would be sent directly by the carrier to the shipper. The carrier member, in other words, is paid immediately for all freight bills submitted. Each submitting carrier guarantees that each bill is legal and bona fide in all respects.

Transport Clearings in turn re-sorts the freight bills by debtor (shipper) and submits all bills to the debtors in combined form. This enables the debtors to pay Transport Clearings with one check and one mailing covering bills to all carrier members of Transport Clearings which would otherwise have to be paid to each individual carrier. If a bill cannot be collected, Transport Clearings sustains all the loss; but it will control the carriers' choice of credit customers by advising them that it will accept bills against all shippers except those on a "cash list." This cash list is sent to all carrier members and names the firms which Transport Clearings has learned from experience are unsound credit risks.

A second type of operations conducted is that of interline settlements. Bills submitted against other carrier members are settled or cleared by the co-operative clearinghouse located in the city where the transfer from the line of one carrier to the line of the other carrier takes place. The bills so submitted are charged to and collected from the other carriers by deduction from their settlement check each day. Transport Clearings follows the same system as do banks in their clearinghouse operations, with the exception that banks pay their individual balances whereas Transport Clearings collects by deduction from the money owing to the submitting carriers on all bills submitted.

This nonprofit organization is supported by fees collected from the carrier members. In one city, the fee is 6 cents per bill plus one fourth of 1 per cent on the face of each bill and no charge on interlines. These fees are established to cover only operating expenses and a small reserve to cover bad account losses. The excess of income over expenses is refunded to the carrier members on a prorate basis. The capital needed to start such an organization is put up by carriers plus borrowed funds. Although this organization is of recent origin, it is interesting to note that the Transport Clearings groups collect over $259 million in freight bills a year. In Los Angeles in 1944, the first year of operation for that group, collections were $10 million; and in 1954, they were approximately $74 million.[17]

There are many advantages to a carrier in this type of collection operation, one of the biggest of which is that the carrier's cash is not tied up in accounts receivable. One carrier is reported to have had $230,000 due in freight bills while it owed $170,000 to creditors. It had but $15,000 cash on hand. Upon joining Transport Clearings, the carrier immediately received the $230,000 due it from outstand-

---

[17] Information supplied by Gordon J. Healow of Transport Clearings of Los Angeles, who has been instrumental in organizing Transport Clearings offices.

ing freight bills, less the co-operative's fee for collection; it then paid off the money it owed and had over $70,000 cash on hand.

Shippers, too, like this system of collection, not only because it simplifies their payment of bills to area carriers which are members but also because they are spared the unpleasantness that sometimes arises through misunderstandings over the collection of bills.

BANK INTERLINE CLEARINGS

In addition to the industry-sponsored freight bill collecting system for interline settlements of motor carriers, a number of banks have instituted operations which serve as clearinghouses in much the same manner. The first of the interline clearing houses for motor carriers was organized in 1949 by a Chicago bank. At the present time, there are about twenty such interline houses operated by banks in major cities.

The bank which originally instituted this operation has over one hundred motor-carrier participants. It charges 3½ cents for each collected item regardless of amount and makes no charge for debit items. A one-thousand-dollar balance for each carrier is required, although it has been stated that it is necessary to call daily for reimbursement for overdrafts in some accounts. Daily statements are furnished to carriers. Eighty per cent of the transactions are paid without any difficulty.

Initially all of the banks which instituted the settlement systems confined them to interline accounts. A few banks which operate on an interline clearing system have recently inaugurated a clearinghouse for all common carriers and shippers and receivers. Such an operation, in which both interline settlements and freight bill collections are made, is along the lines of the industry-sponsored freight settlement system.

QUESTIONS AND PROBLEMS

1. List the principles that can result in the establishment of a clear-cut company policy. What need exists for such a policy?
2. What is a line organization? How extensively is it used in motor transportation? Why?
3. Differentiate between the line, staff, and functional organizations.
4. Is there a need for training programs by motor carriers? Why? From what source has top management largely been drawn in the past?
5. In a service industry like that of motor carriers, why are personnel policies of great importance? What is the role of personnel in a serv-

ice industry as compared with that of personnel in an industry manufacturing commodities?

6. Classify employees of motor carriers in accordance with Interstate Commerce Commission Class I annual report requirements.

7. What are some of the labor organizations other than the Teamsters Union in the motor-carrier property-carrying field?

8. Trace the development of the Teamsters Union, and explain its organizational make-up at the present time.

9. Discuss the advantages and disadvantages of the trend toward area negotiations for over-the-road carriers.

10. Outline the points that are covered in a typical labor contract between the employees and the employer.

11. "It should be emphasized that good employer-employee relations are the aggregate of day-to-day occurrences." Comment.

12. What should be included in a comprehensive safety program?

13. Describe an awards or incentive safety plan. What suggestions could you make to improve such a plan?

14. What are some of the difficulties that have arisen where interchange of equipment between motor carriers has taken place?

15. List the advantages and disadvantages of equipment interchange between motor carriers.

16. Enumerate the reasons for the close supervision by the Interstate Commerce Commission over Class I motor-carrier accounting practices.

17. List the reasons why the Interstate Commerce Commission does not require the smaller motor carrier to maintain a uniform system of accounts.

18. Set up a system of motor-carrier accounting for a five-truck operator, using those accounts from the Interstate Commerce Commission uniform system of accounts for Class I carriers which, in your judgment, would be appropriate.

19. Of what importance is cost control in motor-carrier operation?

20. Using the mileage prorate basis, compute the interline division of a joint rate between carrier A, which carried the shipment 40 miles, and carrier B, which carried it 60 miles. The total revenue from the joint haul was $44.

21. Describe in detail the functioning of Transport Clearings. How does this organization benefit the carrier? The shipper?

22. What are the various parts of the bill of lading? Distinguish between the different types of bills of lading.

23. Are motor-carrier bills of lading uniform?

24. Compare the government bill of lading with the commercial bill of lading.

25. What types of road supervision of drivers are used? In your opinion which would be best for a Class I carrier with a 200-truck operation?

11. TERMINALS—THEIR OPERATION

AND FINANCING

▲▲

ADEQUATE terminal facilities have been and continue to be a problem of motor carriers generally. If all shipments made by shippers were of truckload lots, the matter of terminal facilities would not be so great, since an over-the-road truck would be dispatched to the shipper's place of business and loaded at that point for over-the-road shipment. However, intercity common carriers of general commodities find that a large amount of their traffic is composed of small shipments of less-than-truckload quantities which must be consolidated with other small shipments going to the same destination or along the same route. Table 11–1 shows the high percentage of traffic receiving platform handling at origin and destination in studies made by the Interstate Commerce Commission. Central terminals are established by over-the-road operators where these small shipments can be delivered by local trucks and then transferred to the over-the-road vehicle.

The necessity for recognized locations where small lots of freight could be received and handled led motor carriers to lease or purchase whatever room was available. In the early days of the motor-carrier industry, they frequently used vacant lots or small garages. As the extent of their operations increased, they obtained the use of warehouses or other buildings suitable for this purpose. Even today, it can be said that as a rule truck terminals are remodeled structures originally constructed for some other purpose, although there is a trend now toward construction of new terminals built to meet the motor carrier's own needs and specifications. There is little doubt that this trend will continue. Although development of terminal facilities has been somewhat slow in comparison with other phases of the development of the motor-carrier industry, substantial prog-

275

TABLE 11-1

PERCENTAGE OF TONS HANDLED OVER THE PLATFORM AT ORIGIN AND
DESTINATION BY REGION FOR DIFFERENT SIZES OF SHIPMENTS

WEIGHT OF SHIPMENT (LBS.) (1)	SOUTHERN REGION			TOTAL NEW ENGLAND (5)	CENTRAL (6)	TOTAL MIDDLE ATLANTIC (7)	WESTERN TRUNK LINE (8)
	Intra-south* (2)	East-South† (3)	North-South‡ (4)				
100..........	88%	91%	86%	80%	91%	88%	94%
150..........	88	91	86	80	91	88	94
200..........	88	91	86	80	91	88	94
250..........	88	91	86	80	91	88	94
300..........	88	91	86	80	91	88	94
400..........	87	88	86	80	91	88	94
500..........	87	88	86	80	86	88	94
600..........	87	88	86	80	86	88	94
700..........	87	88	86	80	86	88	94
800..........	87	88	86	80	86	88	94
900..........	87	88	86	80	86	88	94
1,000..........	85	83	83	58	77	75	94
1,200..........	85	83	83	58	77	75	94
1,500..........	83	80	80	58	77	75	94
2,000..........	76	76	70	58	57	58	78
3,000..........	76	76	70	58	57	58	78
4,000..........	76	76	70	58	57	44	59
5,000..........	58	62	59	58	30	44	59
6,000..........	58	56	55	21	30	22	32
7,000..........	58	56	55	21	30	22	32
8,000..........	58	56	55	21	30	22	32
9,000..........	58	56	55	21	30	22	32
10,000..........	25	20	31	21	10	7	32
11,000..........	25	20	31	21	10	7	32
13,000..........	25	20	31	7	10	7	28
15,000..........	25	20	31	7	10	7	28
17,000..........	25	20	31	7	10	7	28
19,000..........	25	20	31	7	10	7	28
20,000..........	21	8	13	3	3	2	4
25,000..........	21	8	13	3	3	2	4
30,000..........	21	8	13	3	3	2	4
35,000..........	21	8	13	3	3	2	4
40,000..........	21	8	13	3	3	2	4

* Represents carrier operations principally within the South.
† Represents carrier operations principally between the South and the Middle Atlantic–New England regions.
‡ Represents carrier operations principally between the South and Central regions.
Source: Interstate Commerce Commission, Bureau of Accounts and Cost Finding, *Simplified Procedure for Determining Cost of Handling Freight by Motor Carriers* (Washington, D.C., 1953), p. 17.

ress has been noted in more recent years. Just as the motor truck has been developed along specialized lines to meet differing transportation requirements, truck terminals now are being built to meet the special handling requirements of the motor carrier or carriers for which they are designed. The terminal expense per ton of intercity freight for the Class I common carriers of general freight has risen from 93 cents per ton in 1942 to $3.12 per ton in 1952. This trend in terminal expenses is a matter of concern to motor-carrier

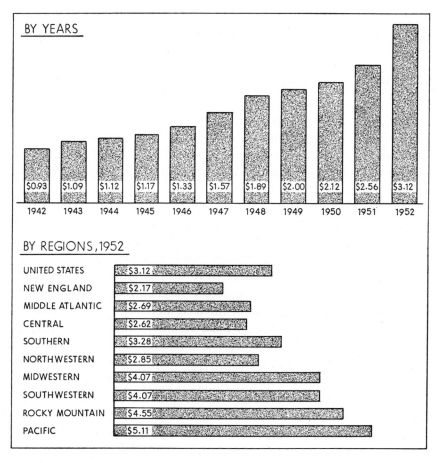

FIG. 11–1. Terminal expense per ton of intercity freight of Class I common carriers of general freight by years and regions.

Source: Based on latest available statistics from official reports to ICC of Class I Motor Carriers listed as "Operating Owned Equipment Principally." American Trucking Associations, Inc., *Trends* (Washington, D.C., 1954), p. 28.

operators. Figure 11–1 gives the amounts per ton by years and regions.

The center of truck operations is the terminal. For many motor carriers, the terminals constitute their general offices, and all activities are concentrated there. For larger motor carriers, the terminals represent branch offices and have accounting, collecting, dispatching, sales, and all other phases of branch operation. Basically, the terminal serves as a consolidation point for LTL traffic, although the larger motor carriers may specifically designate certain terminals as consolidation terminals. This is done when there are numerous smaller intermediate points where LTL shipments are picked up and carried to the designated consolidation terminals.

TERMINAL LOCATION IN THE URBAN AREA

The location of a terminal within an urban area must be selected with a number of factors in mind. These include the present and future needs of the terminal; cost of land acquisition; zoning restrictions; service to customers; accessibility to main highways; availability of power, water, and sewage; traffic congestion; and transportation for employees.

In Chicago a comprehensive survey and recommendations were made in an attempt to solve both terminal problems and traffic problems. The report was made by the Committee on Motor Truck Terminals, whose membership consisted of representative groups. The Committee found that less than 10 per cent of the present buildings were constructed to accommodate mechanized handling equipment or to permit utilization of modern methods of transportation. The lack of terminal space in most terminals caused on-the-street parking of over-the-road trucks around terminals, resulting in greater traffic congestion. The establishment of temporary parking areas to accommodate vehicles was recommended until a comprehensive plan could be implemented to provide adequate terminal facilities.

Since the interpretation of the zoning laws in the past had allowed motor-carrier terminals to be located in industrial, commercial, and manufacturing zones, terminals were widely scattered. The Committee recommended the concentration of truck terminals in four areas, each to be approximately 2 miles apart, the areas to be connected by expressways and to have easy access to main highways. This would be accomplished gradually over a period of years. The survey revealed that 16½ per cent of the volume in weight is interchanged between motor carriers and other forms of transportation. It was felt that 95 per cent of the distance traveled for such interchange could be eliminated by the strategic location of truck terminals.

In some cities, there is a tendency for new terminals to be constructed adjacent to a main highway away from the city's business district. In other cities, they are located within the industrial district but are grouped within a relatively small area. At the present time there is no uniform pattern of terminal location.

TYPES OF TERMINAL DESIGN

A motor carrier does not have terminals at all points which it serves, but it does have terminals in the larger metropolitan areas. The desire of motor carriers to retain their identity and shipper relationships has, in general, caused them to establish their own terminals rather than make arrangements for joint use of terminals. In the construction of new terminals, a much used design has been that of the so-called island-type enclosed dock. The offices and dock form a T shape, with the offices forming the cross of the T. This type of terminal and dock operation is characterized by a cross-dock operation—that is, on one side of the dock, the over-the-road units are loaded and unloaded; on the other side of the dock are the pickup and delivery units. Incoming freight from over-the-road units is moved across the dock to the pickup and delivery units. Conversely, the outgoing freight is unloaded from the pickup and delivery trucks and moved across the dock to the over-the-road units. Although the T design is the most popular, other designs include the I- and L-shaped structures in which the terminal headquarters are placed at one end of the dock. Most of the buildings are single rather than multistory buildings. The island-type design with cross-dock movement of freight has developed in part because of the need for different height loading platforms for the over-the-road equipment and the pickup and delivery trucks. Typical over-the-road semitrailers have floor heights of approximately 52 inches loaded and 54 inches empty, while a van-type city delivery truck's floor height runs from 6 inches to 8 inches lower. For this reason, it has not been possible to set a dock platform height which works equally well for a pickup and delivery truck and an over-the-road semitrailer.

In the construction of terminals as well as in their operation, the dock height is important because savings in freight-handling costs and reduction of damage claims can be secured when the dock is suited to vehicle height or the vehicle body-bed height is suited to the dock. For example, a 4,000-pound fork lift truck with a capacity load will have 10,000 pounds on its front wheels. As it goes into the body of a semitrailer, the body of the vehicle will depress as much as 4 inches.

Two different types of ramps are in common use. One is the ramp from the vehicle body to the shipping platform, which is usually made of sheet metal alloy and is manually placed. The other method of accomplishing a leveling is by mechanical means. One of these mechanical methods is the adjustment of the truck or semitrailer to a line with the platform by means of a lifting platform in front of the dock. The other mechanical method, which is more widely used, is the adjustment of the platform to a line with the truck or semitrailer bed through a power-operated ramp built into the platform. Experience has shown that the volume which can be handled through the use of three mechanically operated ramp-equipped berths is equal to the volume handled through the use of five ramp-equipped platform berths, manually operated.

Whether the ramp is manual or mechanical, the slope should not exceed 10 per cent in order to facilitate loading and unloading.

Many dock offices are located at the center of the dock which serves as a consolidating point for the collection and distribution of bills of lading, freight bills, and other paperwork required for dock operation. The location of dock offices at this point, which is often referred to as a "doghouse," has not been entirely satisfactory. In some of the newer terminals, the dock office is centered on one side of the dock, with a portion of it elevated from 1 to 2 feet above the dock floor. This part of the office is constructed of sliding glass windows which afford a complete view of the dock platform. The dock foreman, city dispatcher, and line-haul dispatcher are located at this point with loud speakers and an intercommunication system for their use. The rating and billing department and OS&D personnel can be located adjacent to them.

Generally, the length of a terminal dock is based on the number of units which must be spotted simultaneously at the dock. To secure this figure, the morning, or inbound delivery phase, and the afternoon, or outbound phase, must be analyzed. The morning phase is found by combining the number of road units to be stripped or unloaded at one time and the number of city units to be loaded at one time. The formula is reversed for the afternoon phase, combining the number of city units to be stripped at one time with the number of road units to be loaded at one time. Four factors will give the basic information. These are: When shall stripping (or loading) begin? When shall stripping (loading) be finished? How many loads will there be to strip (or load)? How long will it take to strip (or load) a unit?

If, for the morning phase, it is found that 10 spots are needed for simultaneous stripping of road units and 13 spots for city unit loading, a total of 23 berths are needed. Assuming that the afternoon phase demands 10 spots for stripping city units and 20 for loading road units, a total of 30 spots are required.

By comparing the morning figure (23) with the afternoon figure (30), the afternoon or outbound phase must govern the dock length. Therefore, the dock must be built to accommodate at least 30 units. Since most units are parked in pairs, with double doors, the dock will be designed to accommodate 32 units, 16 on each side. Allowing 12 feet for each unit, the dock length becomes a minimum of 192 feet.[1]

YARD SPACE

The use of the island-type dock permits a flow of vehicles around the dock, and it is generally felt that this flow should be counter-clockwise around the dock. This permits backing of units from the left side, which is preferred. It is necessary that there be adequate clearance between the dock and the wall or fence enclosing the yard in order to permit the shifting and backing of vehicles. Yard width should be at least twice the over-all length of the vehicle or combination that is going to be backed into the dock platform. The ideal yard width for truck tractor-semitrailer combinations is 100 feet, whereas a van-type city delivery truck requires approximately half this width. This ideal yard width makes for expeditious movement of truck units into and out of truck berths, although many truck terminals have from 25 to 35 feet less space than this ideal figure of 100 feet. One of the reasons for cross-dock operation on the island-type dock is that the separation of over-the-road units from the pickup and delivery equipment means that the side on which pickup and delivery equipment is berthed will not require as much yard space as is necessary for over-the-road equipment. With side-by-side operation in an island-type dock, there must be sufficient yard space on both sides of the dock for shifting and backing of over-the-road equipment.

Because many terminals now in use are remodeled buildings, there are many docks which permit loading and unloading on only one side. This requires use of the truck berths by both over-the-road equipment and pickup and delivery equipment.

FREIGHT TERMINAL HANDLING METHODS

The methods by which freight are handled at the terminal may be divided into two categories—manual and mechanized.

In the majority of the terminals, dock operations are *manual* and

---

[1] *Distribution Age,* November, 1954, p. 35.

involve the use of equipment such as two-wheel hand trucks. A four-wheel flat truck, or a variation of it which has two wheels, two stiff legs, and a roller jack to move the flat truck is also being adopted. This basic type of industrial truck has the advantage of keeping the freight on a flat truck and not placing it on the floor. Its use also cuts down the number of operations involved in loading and unloading. However, some heavy commodities, such as filled barrels or drums, are not as easily loaded on the four-wheel hand truck as they are on the two-wheel hand truck.

Both of these hand trucks are usually rolled into the truck or trailer body for loading and unloading. Generally only one shipment is placed on a four-wheel hand truck, although this is not as closely followed in manual operations as is true when four-wheel carts are used in mechanized operations. The manual method, as far as the equipment cost is concerned, is very inexpensive.

Fifty feet is a typical minimum width for an island-type dock with cross-dock operations using manual equipment. This permits sufficient room for sorting freight, as well as allowing for a free aisle for moving freight. For a dock using manual equipment which handles 100 tons or less of miscellaneous freight daily, the average number of square feet of platform area, including aisles, which is required per ton of miscellaneous freight is 35–45 square feet. In the handling of 100 tons of miscellaneous freight daily, the loading berths necessary will be five over-the-road berths and five pickup and delivery berths.

When an island-type dock exceeds ten truck berths in length, it is considered to be sufficiently large for the economies of operating *mechanized material-handling equipment,* such as fork lift trucks and draglines. Where there is mechanized dock operation, it is desirable for the dock to be somewhat wider than where manual equipment is used. Whereas 50 feet in width is satisfactory for manual dock equipment, the width of the dock for mechanical equipment usage should be approximately 65 feet, and the free aisle should be correspondingly wider than for manual equipment.

During World War II, fork lift trucks and pallets began to appear in motor-carrier terminals. Since that time fork-lift systems have been used in the larger terminals of many motor carriers. The original fork lift trucks in use were of the stand-up type and were gasoline propelled. There has been greater interest and use of the electric fork lifts in recent years, although the initial cost, with spare batteries and charges, is about twice that of a gasoline-engine fork lift truck. There are many factors which should be considered, such as noise, operating cost, and salvage value. Since the fork lift truck on the motor-carrier dock is subjected to frequent stops, starts, and short runs, maintenance is also an important factor. Many other industries use the sit-down-type fork lift truck, but since the driver in a motor-carrier terminal may get on and off the fork lift on almost every load, the stand-up-type is still favored in motor-carrier terminals.

Fork lift trucks may operate directly into the body of the truck or semitrailer, or they may stop at the edge of the dock. Whether it operates into the truck or semitrailer body in both the city trucks and the line-haul semitrailers is largely based on the strength of the floors of the vehicles. To add a heavy floor to carry the load of a fork lift truck will add from 500 to 700 pounds to the tare weight of the vehicle, which reduces its pay load.

When fork lifts are not permitted in the bodies of vehicles, a pallet roller is placed therein. A pallet roller is a steel frame with wide rollers on which a pallet can be placed for rolling backward or forward in a straight line in the vehicle body. Thus, shipments can be rolled on or off the pallet roller in loading or unloading, and a fork lift truck does not enter the body of the vehicle.

Usually only one shipment is placed on a pallet. A 40- $\times$ 48-inch pallet may handle as much as 3,000 pounds. However, if the shipments are very small with two shipments to the same destination terminal, some companies will carry two shipments on one pallet. The reason for handling a single shipment on a pallet is to avoid mixing shipments, which is an important factor in checking freight. Inasmuch as pallets usually are not loaded to maximum capacity under the single shipment rule, it is common practice to tier partially loaded pallets if it is necessary to haul shipments on the dock for a time during the movement across the platform.

Some shippers have palletized and unitized their shipments and handled them with fork lift trucks. Motor carriers with fork lift trucks are therefore in a position to facilitate the terminal handling of such shipments.

Some of the points which will influence whether or not the terminal-handling system should be a fork lift truck and pallet operation are: (*a*) terminal volume, which should be less than 300,000 pounds per day; (*b*) distance of average one-way fork-lift travel, which should be less than 150 feet; and (*c*) volume which is distributed over the working day in such a way that only two fork lift trucks are required normally, and not over three at peak volume.[2]

---

[2] Regular Common Carrier Conference, *Manual for Planning and Operating Terminals,* Rev. No. 6 (Washington, D.C., June, 1953).

The *dragline* is a type of mechanized equipment. It is a conveyor with a powered chain or cable which runs overhead or in the floor and pulls carts from one area on the dock to another. The greatest advantage obtained from a dragline is when it is used for transfer of freight directly from the pickup to the outbound line-haul unit.

In the overhead-type dragline, the chain or cable is attached to rollers which ride in the open sides of a steel channel hung from a supporting structure. The cart has a mast or chain for engaging fixtures attached to the cable. See Figures 11–2 and 11–3.

Courtesy: Merchants Motor Freight, Inc.

FIG. 11–2.   This terminal uses the overhead conveyor system or carrousel. The four-wheel trucks are attached to the conveyor and are moved to the proper locations for loading or unloading.

In the floor-type dragline, the chain is in a trench about 12 inches wide by 12 inches deep. The trench is covered except for a slot a little more than 1 inch wide through which a pin from the cart drops to engage the line. Generally the drag chain is located in the middle section of the dock in a long loop which extends from one end of the dock platform to the other with turn-arounds at the extreme ends of the loop so that the chain goes continuously in one track past the various doors opening on the vehicle-loading berths.

Most dragline conveyors have been put on docks which are more than 60 feet in width and over 450 feet in length. However, there have been draglines installed on old motor freight docks which are neither that long nor that wide. In St. Louis, for example, there is a dragline on a dock which is only 115 feet in length. Some of the older terminals have installed overhead draglines, whereas the trend in the newer terminals is toward the floor type.

The floor-type dragline has several advantages over the overhead type, although it is more costly to install. A floor-type dragline 1,200 feet long is estimated to cost about $22.00 a foot, whereas the overhead type is about $12.00 a foot.[3]

A number of factors that are considered necessary to justify the installation of a dragline are: (a) a dock volume exceeding 300,000 pounds per day; (b) an average one-way travel of handling equipment of more than 150 feet; (c) the need for more than two fork lift trucks to handle normal volume or more than three during peak periods; (d) a wide variation in volume of freight flow from hour to

Courtesy: Merchants Motor Freight, Inc.

FIG. 11–3. Transferring freight from a pickup truck to a four-wheel cart, which will then be hooked to the overhead conveyor.

hour; (e) freight handlers and supervisors which are not too experienced; (f) little hauling of peddle freight; and (g) a large percentage of freight which is fragile or easily damaged.[4]

Under the dragline system, only one shipment is placed on the four-wheel cart, or two small shipments if they are for the same desti-

---

[3] *Transport Topics,* July 20, 1953, p. 41.
[4] *Op. cit.*

nation terminal. When the four-wheel cart is loaded with a shipment, it is pushed out of the vehicle body manually and connected to the dragline. It is given a code number and stays on the dragline until it is removed by the loader at the loading berth or storage spot to which the truck has been coded.

Motor carriers should certainly investigate the possibilities of material-handling equipment because under the right combination of circumstances, substantial economies can be effected through its use.[5] The type of material-handling equipment to be used at motor freight terminals should be chosen only after a careful analysis. Although there are a number of guides, of which some have been given, there are many factors in individual terminal operations which must be considered. For example, a motor carrier whose volume and operations appear to lend themselves to a fork-lift-pallet-type terminal operation has found that the nature of the LTL freight which it handles precludes the use of fork lift trucks.

It is very difficult to select the right freight-handling method for all motor carriers because of the many peculiarities in motor-carrier operations. Some of the factors which are helpful in selecting the correct freight-handling system for individual carriers are shown in Figure 11–4.

METHODS OF FREIGHT CHECKING

There are a variety of checking procedures that are used with different freight-handling systems in truck terminals. This is an important aspect of the control of freight, but there is wide disagreement as to the effectiveness of the different checking systems or the extent to which freight should be checked. On the carrier's docks, there are four different places at which freight may be checked. These are: (a) when the shipment comes off the city pickup truck and is put onto the dock; (b) when the shipment is moved on the dock to the outgoing line-haul vehicle; (c) at the destination city when the freight is checked as it comes off the line-haul vehicle; and (d) when the freight is being loaded onto the city delivery truck at destination.

---

[5] The Terminal Operations Council of the American Trucking Associations, Inc., is active in furnishing the industry with information concerning material-handling activities and has published *Methods of Freight Handling*. There are several trade publications which deal with material handling that are helpful. The meetings of the American Material Handling Society and the Society of Industrial Packaging and Material Handling Engineers, two professional societies, provide much information on material handling.

HANDLING SYSTEM SELECTION FACTORS			
	Hand Trucks	Fork Trucks & Pallets	Dragline Conveyors
System should be used when:	1. Volume is small 2. Hauls are short 3. Storage is not a factor	1. Volume is substantial 2. Freight must be floored	1. Freight is transferred from local to distance carriers 2. Operation is nearly continuous 3. Little freight is floored
Operating characteristics are: 1. Capacity	125 lb per truck	Up to 6000 lb. for shipping operation	420 shipments per hour (avg. size=380 lb.)
2. Speed	200-250 fpm.	500 fpm (approx.)	150 fpm
3. Tiering height	Not over 6 ft.	Up to 15 ft.	Not applicable
4. Aisle Requirements	Side Aisles: 5 ft.; Cross aisles: 3½ ft		
Advantages:	1. Low first cost 2. Requires little aisle space 3. Labor may be unskilled	1. High payload 2. Shipments may be handled as single units 3. Stores freight vertically 4. About 90 per cent of all freight can be palletized	1. Moves continuously 2. High volume capacity 3. Economical for long, fixed-path moves (long docks)
Disadvantages:	1. Low capacity 2. High labor cost 3. Short moves only	1. Fairly high first cost 2. Requires large aisles 3. Operators must be trained	1. High installation cost 2. Precludes storage 3. Path is relatively inflexible
Break-even Points: (Volume Labor)	1. For up to 50,000 lb per day this usually is the economical choice 2. Usually best system if fewer than 5 men are employed on the dock	1. Over 50,000 lb per day if freight is to be floored 2. 50,000-100,000 lb. per day if no freight is floored 3. Hauls must not exceed 300 ft.*	1. Over 100,000 lb per day if no freight is floored

*When hauls are over 300 ft., use trailer trains to supplement fork trucks.

FIG. 11–4.   Freight-handling system selection factors.

Source: ATA Terminal Operator, September, 1953, p. 2.

In the past much of the checking at carriers' terminals was accomplished by assigning one checker to each one or two incoming vehicles. Usually he was given a stand-up desk with pigeonholes or clips for holding papers, which would be located on the dock near the vehicles to be checked by him. The bills of lading would be secured by him from the city pickup driver or the freight bills from the line-haul vehicle which was to be unloaded. The checker would then check the items as they were unloaded and would indicate to the dock workers where to transfer or place the freight. On unmechanized docks, this manual checking of freight is still quite general.

A Class I carrier with sixty terminals, no one of which has an average weight per shipment greater than 600 pounds, handles its freight on its unmechanized docks with four-man crews. Each crew is in charge of a checker who supervises one caller and two rollers. The caller places the freight on a hand truck and tells the checker the name of the consignee, the destination, and number of pieces in the shipment. The checker verifies the information given him by the caller against the bill of lading or freight bill and instructs the caller as to which dock loading zone the shipment is to be taken. The zone number is written on the freight with chalk, and a roller takes it to the zone.

There are a number of variations of this manual checking system. In some instances when the contents are being unloaded by a stripper (person unloading), he will call out to the checker the items which the checker checks against the bill of lading or the freight bill. In other instances, the stripper may also be the checker. Where the freight handling has been mechanized by the use of fork lift trucks and pallets, a manual checking system is frequently used, although the tendency is to establish a centralized checking system when fork-lift mechanization is used.

One of the most widely used types of centralized checking systems is one which is handled by means of two-way telephone communication equipment. Under this arrangement, the checker is usually located near the center of the freight-handling area and is often housed in a glass-enclosed booth which is elevated so that the checker has a clear view of all dock activities. The booth is usually arranged so that the checker has desk space on three sides with adequate room to spread the bills covering several trucks. The checker has a multistation two-way telephone device in the booth, the central unit of which is connected to two-way transmitter speakers hung in each truck or trailer. The stripper can carry a portable microphone station throughout his work area equipped with a call-in switch or button so that he can signal the checker at any time.

The manner in which a central checking system functions may be more easily understood by following the actions that occur on the dock in a typical central checking system. As an over-the-road truck comes in, the bills are sent to the code clerk. He assigns a code number to each bill indicating the parking location for the unit, as well as showing the driver's name, the semitrailer number, the weight, and the number of waybills involved in the particular shipment.

The bill would not show a shipment number if the freight from the particular shipment was to move across the dock to another over-the-road unit already spotted for loading, but it would merely show the loading zone at which the outbound truck or semitrailer was being loaded. Since the floor area would be marked or divided into sections, the bill would show the shipment number with the proper prefix to correspond with the area in which it is to be floored, if the shipment is to be floored.

The floor space that is to be used for interchange freight usually is designated with one or two letters to indicate the name of the connecting line to which the shipment is to be delivered; whereas city delivery freight is usually floored in areas marked to correspond with numbers assigned to the city delivery zones.

When all the waybills or bills of lading for a load have been so marked, they are forwarded to the checker's booth. As the stripper unloads a shipment and places the item on the pallet, the stripper does not report the shipment until the checker specifically asks him to do so in order to avoid confusion. After the shipment is checked out satisfactorily with the checker, the checker assigns a code number to it, marks it on the bill, and gives the number to the stripper, who marks the number with chalk on one of the pieces making up the shipment, thus making it easy for the lift truck operator to carry the shipment to the proper destination point.

The experience of some companies indicates that one checker can work as many as six to ten pickup trucks at one time, which usually results in reduction of manpower. There has been some use made of centrally located recording equipment which is connected to the microphones at the unloading areas. The use of such equipment permits checking at a constant rate after unloading and eliminates the delay during peak periods.

With the dragline conveyor, a somewhat different system from centralized checking is used. A pneumatic tube device carries bills from the dock foreman's office to loading berths. The city delivery truck is located at the receiving side of the platform. The checker, who is located on the dock, has a chart of the loading berths of the trailers assigned to specific destinations. An empty four-wheel truck is pushed to the end of the city delivery truck, and the driver, dock unloader, or stripper will sort and place on the dragline cart one shipment. The checker compares the number of pieces in the shipment as well as the destination shipping tag on the shipment with the bill of lading which has been given him by the driver. If all of these things check, he will mark on the dragline cart placard board the berth number at which the shipment is to be removed from the dragline. On the bill of lading, the identification of the truck and driver which made the delivery are noted after which the bill of lading is rolled into a tight roll and placed in a holder at the side of the dragline cart placard board. That cart is then hooked onto the dragline and travels to the dock space indicated. When it is not possible to place an entire single shipment on a dragline cart, the checker loads the first dragline cart and marks on the placard "1 of 4, MTF (more to follow)." Additional carts needed are similarly marked with the last cart bearing the notation "4 of 4, complete." The bill of lading is then placed in the holder with the final cart. If the shipment on the dragline cart can be loaded directly into the line-haul vehicle, it is pulled to the outside of the dragline chain and loaded.

Shipments on carts that the loader is not ready for may be left connected to the dragline so that the cart goes around several times until the loader is ready to load it into the trailer; or it may be removed from the dragline and put in the center area within the dragline carrousel until wanted.

In some checking systems using the dragline conveyor, the shipment is checked as it is loaded in the trailer, at which time the loader marks the vehicle number and his initials or code number on the bill of lading. It is then sent through a pneumatic tube to the dock foreman's office. The dock foreman or his clerk maintains a cumulative record of the bill of lading weights which are loaded into each vehicle. This enables the dock foreman to determine when the loading of a vehicle should be stopped. After a further check of the bills to see that everything is in order, the dock foreman turns them over to the billing clerk. This process ultimately results in a manifest and freight bills in the dispatcher's office, where they are turned over to the line-haul driver.

In some companies using the dragline operation, the loader does not recheck the shipments when they are loaded into the line-haul vehicles. The bills of lading are removed from the dragline carts as the loader stows the freight in the line-haul vehicles. The loader records the weight on his loading sheet, and the bills of lading are then sent to the billing office through a pneumatic tube system.

At the destination city, the reverse of the method which has been described would be followed in a dragline operation. The stripper or unloader would sort out the shipment according to the freight bills, and a checker would assign the city truck berth spots to the freight bills and to the dragline carts. The city loader may arrange for loading in the order of delivery.

In the different freight checking methods, the checking may be and is done in some companies by persons who do not have the title of checkers. The labor contract at many terminals permits the man who picks up the freight or delivers the freight to load or unload his equipment so that he may be doing some of the checking. The labor contract covering other terminals may provide that a dockman has to do the loading and unloading.

RECEIVING SHIPMENTS

There are a number of different matters that must be covered in some way in order to indicate the conditions under which certain commodities may be accepted because of the destination points or for other reasons. One of these is the matter of points served. Most companies publish a routing guide which will indicate the points served. However, where the shipment has a destination not contained in the routing guide, the operations department will determine whether or not it can be accepted. When the shipments are given to the motor carrier for transportation, they should be accompanied by bills of lading or connecting carrier's freight bills. Most shippers will make out their own bill of lading, but if they have not, the motor-carrier representative accepting the shipment will issue a bill of lading.

Shipments of unusual size or weight may require special equipment. The classification and/or tariff rules of motor carriers will indicate the dimensions of a shipment which are acceptable. Frequently shippers will have a quantity to be shipped which constitutes a full load and will want it to be moved immediately. Such shipments usually are accepted when the equipment is available for its immediate movement.

There are certain points served by motor carriers which are designated as prepay points. Such points are usually those at which there are no terminals of the motor carrier. Therefore, shipments are not accepted to that point unless they are prepaid. The charges are generally collected from the shipper at the time the shipment is picked up. However, if the shipment is of such a nature that the proper description or weight cannot be ascertained, it will be brought to the terminal for weighing, rating, and billing, and held until the shipper pays the charges. Additional requirements of shipments destined to prepay points are that the carrier will not collect on C.O.D. shipments; the shipment will not be shipped on an order bill of lading; the shipment will not require refrigeration or protection from cold; and the bill of lading must show where the shipment is to be unloaded.

When perishable items are accepted, such as frozen meat or citrus juices, the shipper should indicate on the bill of lading the temperature at which the shipment must be maintained. This information is then copied on the freight bills. Fresh meat and poultry which are accepted for interstate movement must conform to existing government regulations and must be accompanied by a government meat inspector's certificate unless the shipment is marked with the government meat inspector's stamp. Some states have quarantine restrictions on nursery stock and fruit and vegetables, and they cannot be accepted unless accompanied by a transportation permit from the horticultural inspector.

In-bond shipments also are treated somewhat differently from the ordinary shipment. Ordinarily in-bond shipments originate at a point of entry into the United States. They are shipments on which United States customs duty has not been paid. They are usually tendered to the motor carrier by a customs broker and released by a United States Customs inspector who furnishes the carrier with a form which it must sign called "Transportation Entry and Manifest of Goods Subject to Customs Inspection and Permit." The carrier's copy of this document is attached to the freight bill or truck manifest and must accompany the shipment. The originating carrier signs in the usual manner a bill of lading or a document serving this purpose. If a full truckload of in-bond shipments is tendered, they can be loaded in one piece of equipment and sealed. Otherwise the shipments have to be individually labeled or tagged.

WEIGHING

The carrier does not weigh all freight that is received at the terminal, but spot checks are made frequently to determine whether the weights on the bills of lading are correct. If the weight is incorrect, the shipper should be notified of the change in weight. Most companies have a form which is filled out termed a "correct weight advice." If there is an increase in the revenue as a result of the discrepancy in the weight, companies often will pay an employee an amount for discovering the discrepancy, such as 10 cents for each 100 pounds up to the first 500 pounds of difference and 5 cents for each additional 100 pounds. If a shipper is consistently careless in showing the correct weights, the carrier may advise the Weighing and Inspection Bureau of the situation.

MARKING AND CHECKING SHIPMENTS

Before shipments are accepted from a shipper or a connecting carrier, all pieces of each LTL shipment should be tagged or marked showing the consignee's name and destination. It is the shipper's responsibility to mark and tag each piece of freight, but if he fails to do this the carrier's representative receiving the freight must mark or tag it.

It is not practical to tag or mark all shipments in the same manner, so there are generally a number of shipping or sticker tags which are used. If shipments are packed in used containers or reshipped in the original container, all of the old marks should be removed. When there is a full load, it is standard practice not to mark or tag each piece which is loaded into a single truck or semitrailer from which there will be no transfer or unloading en route to the destination terminal.

The freight which is received from a shipper or connecting carrier should be checked against the bill of lading or freight bill. This freight check is not merely a counting of the number of pieces but it is a check of the marks and descriptions as well. Overage, shortage, and/or damage should be noted on the bills of lading or freight bill. To facilitate handling of the inbound LTL freight, one checker can be assigned to two loads side by side. When central checking is used, a checker may check a minimum of three and a maximum of eight units at the same time.

DISPATCHING

The operation of the dock in larger motor-carrier organizations is the responsibility of a terminal manager. In smaller motor-carrier organizations, however, the dispatcher is in charge of the dock activities. The dispatcher is a key man in the successful functioning of dock operations. Most dispatchers were at one time truck drivers themselves, so they have an understanding of the problems of operation. It is their responsibility to dispatch the freight properly, so that the units are kept rolling. They make certain that the over-the-road units are properly prepared and swept out before reloading for over-the-road operation. They insure that the freight is checked against the freight bill, piece by piece, before it is loaded. Some dispatchers have separate checkers and loaders, and the checkers' duties are only those of checking the freight against the freight bills. Freight checking is a very important factor because there may be 75 to 100 or more shipments in a single load coming out of a terminal. In loading over-the-road units, rules are established, such as placing all heavy articles on the floor; placing candy in the middle of a unit because it is less subject to heat there; placing carpets on top of all other freight; and many other rules of a similar nature. There are many rule-of-thumb methods for loading over-the-road units which are the result of long experience in the handling of freight. If there are "drop" shipments to be made, that freight must be placed to facilitate its unloading. If a semitrailer has been loaded and there is visible space left, the load must be tapered off gradually in order to avoid tipping and smashing of the contents. If the over-the-road unit goes all the way through to another terminal, it will be sealed at the origin terminal.

Incoming freight must be carefully checked, sorted, and routed for proper distribution. It is the responsibility of the dispatcher to see that there is prompt sorting and routing, and that the activities of the pickup and delivery units are correlated to bringing in shipments for loading and to delivering shipments to local consignees. Since most motor carriers do not have definite, scheduled hours of departure for over-the-road units, the dispatcher must have knowledge of the shipments that are being brought in by pickup and delivery trucks as well as the shipments that are already at the terminal, so that he will know about when to close out a unit and have a driver available. It is not always possible to secure a full load, so that a dispatcher has the responsibility of deciding when a unit should be dispatched. In motor-carrier operations, a shipment cannot be held at the dock beyond a reasonable time or the inherent advantage of short transit time in motor-carrier shipment is negated.

The dispatcher sends out the various pickup and delivery units each day to the points that fall into particular zones within the city which he has established. Drivers of these units then call in after picking up the shipments and receive additional instructions as to where the next pickup should be made in a particular zone or a neighboring zone. It depends upon the amount of freight handled by a motor carrier whether there are separate trucks dispatched to pick up shipments from those dispatched to deliver shipments.

In dispatching loaded less-truckload freight on city delivery equipment, the most widely used method is that of *route loading* or loading in proper sequence, that is, first on, last off. In this system, the city is divided into areas the number of which will depend on the volume of freight to be delivered. These areas are numbered or lettered, and a space is provided on the dock to correspond to each area. Upon the arrival of the inbound line-haul units, the bills are coded by the area to which they are bound.

The advantages of route loading are: (a) it is easier on the driver; (b) loading in sequence is less time consuming which, at present wage scales, is an important factor; (c) there is a saving in fuel cost and wear on the equipment because travel distance, time, and traffic are kept at a minimum; and (d) the reduction in the number of times the freight is handled in the delivery vehicle reduces claims.

There are disadvantages of this system, however. It takes longer to load in proper sequence since most of the freight has to be floored and reloaded which requires more space. More time is taken in the unloading-loading process, and individual shipments may not be delivered as early. The rehandling of the freight, since it is floored and then reloaded, can result in more claims in the terminal, although this is dependent in part upon the freight handling system which is used.

The second method is called *loading by zone*. Under this arrangement, a city is divided into zones. The freight bills which accompany each over-the-road unit to the city are coded by zone according to the street locations of the consignees. The bills are handled by the stripper or checker who sends these inbound shipments to the waiting delivery unit for the proper zone. Since a delivery unit is available for each zone, it is not necessary to floor any of the freight for any zone unless it cannot be loaded immediately without damage to itself or other freight.

Some of the advantages of the zone loading are: (*a*) a greater freight volume can be handled over less floor space in the terminal; (*b*) the total time which is required for unloading line-haul vehicles and loading city delivery vehicles is substantially reduced; (*c*) the incoming LTL shipments do not have to be routed, floored, and rehandled in sequence but the freight goes directly to the vehicle which is being loaded for the zone to which it is destined; and (*d*) delivery vehicles can be out delivering earlier which enables line-haul units to be scheduled for later arrivals and still be quickly handled.

On the other hand, it takes longer to make deliveries under the zone system because it is necessary for the driver to dig through the shipments and sort as he delivers, along with the rehandling and backtracking. There is, also, potential damage to freight due to its numerous handlings in the delivery vehicle.

Which of the two systems is better adapted to a particular carrier's operation depends upon an evaluation of various factors. For example, if dock employees are paid more than city drivers and the total hours of work for dock employees are greater than that of the drivers, the zone loading might appear to be the correct method. However, the potential claims under the zone system would also have to be considered.

A part of the need for better terminal operation is the problem of improving *pickup and delivery production*. The type of trucks used in pickup and delivery service may be a factor in improving operations. Some motor carriers have used the small city-type semi-trailers, that is, 20-foot trailers, in pickup and delivery and peddle-run operations, although heavy reliance is still placed upon trucks. On some downtown streets of certain cities, semitrailers are prohibited for pickup and delivery use. When the vehicles must park at the curb to load and unload across the sidewalk, the truck is preferred equipment. Also, when the shipping or receiving platform can be reached only by backing down the length of a long alley, it is often easier to do this with a truck than a semitrailer. On the other hand, the 20-foot semitrailer is just as easily maneuvered as a straight truck with a 14-foot body. Further, it is possible to get the rear of the semitrailer square against a shipping platform in a loading area which is just slightly wider than the trailer is long. The cubic capacity of the 20-foot semitrailer over the 14-foot truck is more than 40 per cent.

If two semitrailers are used for each truck tractor, one semitrailer can be loaded while the other is on the street making deliveries. The same operation exists for pickups, since a loaded semitrailer may be brought back to the terminal for unloading, an empty semitrailer picked up, and the driver start out to make more pickups.

Whether trucks or trailers are best suited for pickup and delivery and peddle operations depends upon individual situations. The important factor is that an analysis should be made to see the type or types which are best suited. At the present time, there is a trend toward placing more city-type semitrailers in the pickup and delivery fleets than has been done in the past.

It may be that a reduction in pickup and delivery costs can be effected through an analysis of the regular stops on pickup routes. Many carriers have regular stops on their pickup routes where it is assumed that shippers will have daily pickups to be made. Too often, no review is made of these regular stops to determine whether there is freight to be picked up each day or whether the stops are made each day even though there is not freight there to be picked up. One motor carrier making such an analysis found there were 550 regular stops on its routes throughout its system. After discontinuing regular stops for any shipper who did not have freight available at least 4 days a week, the regular stops were reduced to 190, which resulted in a saving in pickup costs.

A study of pickup and delivery operations showed that delay represented over 38 per cent of the total pickup and delivery time, regardless of the type of vehicle unit which was used. The movement of pickup and delivery units in traffic consumed approximately 30 per cent of over-all trip time. Nearly half of the handling time was completely lost due primarily to three of twelve causes. These three were: (1) collection of bills; (2) location of receivers; and (3) unprepared shipments. This study also recommended a number of methods that could be used to improve the problems of pickup and delivery. Some of the matters that require action include zoning, truck loading zones, parking prohibitions, and off-street loading.

There is a distinct need for greater co-operation among shippers and receivers, carriers, and city officials. Delays result in increased costs which are reflected in the rates of carriers. Elimination of some of these delays should benefit both shippers and carriers.

One of the methods of improving the utilization of pickup and delivery equipment, as well as conserving manpower, equipment, fuel, lubricants and tires, has been the use of *two-way mobile radio*. There are a number of radio frequency bands available which are allocated by the Federal Communications Commission. Some of these bands, however, can be used by anyone, which limits the frequencies available to trucking companies. One of the bands on which frequencies are available to truck operators is restricted solely to the contacting of pickup trucks on this band outside the city limits. A petition before the Federal Communications Commission by the motor-carrier industry to permit unrestricted use for pickup and delivery service in the frequencies in this band resulted in an order which became effective March 15, 1955 granting specific frequencies in the 43, 44, and 450 to 460 megacycle bands for use by for-hire carriers.

An estimate of the cost of a two-way radio unit is approximately $8.00 per day, while pickup and delivery truck time has frequently been set at $3.00 per hour. Whether the two-way mobile radio is practicable depends upon the service and cost aspects of such an installation. Some of its advantages are elimination of the use of telephones at shippers' plants for call-ins to dispatchers; reduction of breakdown time on the road; ability to make pickups which otherwise would not be possible; substantial reduction of daily mileage, sometimes as much as 20 per cent; increased productivity; and better control of pickup drivers.

There are a number of different ways of measuring the efficiency of a two-way mobile radio installation, such as productivity per manhour, number of bills handled per day, and tonnage, as well as others. The experience of motor carriers with two-way mobile radio so far indicates that it does not reduce the number of pickup and delivery trucks needed but does permit a greater volume to be handled with a reduction in vehicle and labor costs. Improved service to customers is another result. One carrier which has had successful operation of two-way mobile radio has it at points where the carrier operates fifty units as well as at a point where it operates only twelve units.

It is possible to purchase the equipment outright and have a contract for servicing the equipment, or the motor carrier may lease the equipment. One possibility would be to have a number of motor carriers establish a nonprofit association to render this service.

The dispatcher will also dispatch "peddle trips," which are operated primarily for the purpose of pickup or delivery of freight at the shipper's or consignee's platform at intermediate station points outside a city, town, or commercial zone. Peddle trips usually operate within a radius of from 50 to 75 miles of the terminal and are generally loop runs originated and terminated at one terminal. The principal purpose of peddle runs is to gather and distribute freight en route at the platforms of consignors and consignees, rather than to move it from one terminal to another terminal.

There are some motor carriers which operate certain scheduled hours of departure for over-the-road runs. Others may have only one scheduled departure at a specific time, which is referred to as a "hot-shot" run. A number of carriers which have made use of the "hot-shot" run have found that too many shippers desire all their freight to go on that particular run. Hence, many of the carriers which had instituted this service have discontinued the operation.

A report on the over-the-road schedules which are dispatched is maintained by the dispatcher. Such a report, as Figure 11–5 shows, lists the driver, the loading time, departure time, the equipment, the destination, and other relevant information. This information can be placed on a form which consolidates the schedules dispatched from each terminal. This is usually done by teletype, so that it is possible that the headquarters of the company will have complete information about the status of the equipment and freight dispatched.

The terminals of larger carriers are operated 7 days a week and provide for 24-hour service. However, these carriers are frequently spoken of as being on an 8-day week. This arises from the fact that the maximum number of hours prescribed by the Interstate Commerce Commission for drivers is 60 hours in 168 consecutive hours, or 70 hours on duty in 192 consecutive hours. Many carriers operate under the latter arrangement, which is referred to as an 8-day work-week.

TERMINAL CONTROLS FOR MANAGEMENT

In the past, sufficient measures have not been undertaken to determine the profitability and efficiency of individual terminals. Terminal operation is a significant item in carrier's expenses. Since motor-carrier operations are often conducted over a broad geographical area, it is important in terminal operation that cost-control techniques be used. Such controls, which involve various types of reports, are in and of themselves costly and are impractical unless some action is taken after a review is made of them. These cost controls are of equal importance to the management of the organiza-

P.I.E.

REPORT OF SCHEDULES DISPATCHED

Date

Driver	Call Time	Start Loading Time	Finish Loading or Arrival Time	Departure Time	Tractor	Time Received	Trailer	Time Received	Freight Destination	Total weight—then load breakdown in large marks of 10M or over, available space and oldest bill date

FIG. 11–5. Report of schedules dispatched.

tion at headquarters and the terminal manager of each of the terminals. To company management such reports make possible the efficient management of the organization, while the data which is secured is particularly useful to terminal managers in evaluating the productivity of the terminal. The manner in which cost controls may be applied is to divide the controls into such groupings as platform control, office control, pickup and delivery control, and any additional groupings that are desired for control purposes. Terminal cost controls should develop adequate data on which management can make intelligent decisions.

Platform costs can be compiled in a weekly report showing pounds per man-hour and labor costs per 100 pounds. A monthly report on platform costs would include both of these items plus the over-all costs per 100 pounds. Pickup and delivery costs can be developed in a weekly report and a monthly report, with the costs broken down as was the case for platform costs. The terminal office costs can be developed in a weekly report showing labor costs per bill (shipment) and a monthly report which shows the same information plus the over-all cost per bill (shipment).

The manner in which platform cost procedures are ascertained is given in order to provide a better understanding of terminal cost controls.[6] The three factors constituting platform cost determination are tonnage, man-hours, and labor costs.

1. Compute total outbound tonnage:
   a) Obtain complete billings of previous day.
   b) Check numerical sequence for missing bills.
   c) Total the weight (actual, not billed weight) with an adding machine and insert total weight on Form D–1, line 1, column 2 (Fig. 11–6). Tonnage shown as free astray and as company business shall be excluded from all totals.
   d) Count number of items listed on adding machine tape referred to in "c" above, and insert the number on Form D–1, line 1, column 1 (Fig. 11–6).
2. Compute the amount of outbound tonnage not handled across the platform:
   a) Pickups by line-haul equipment.
      1. Obtain all drivers' pickup records and audit for determination that neither platform handling nor transfer from line-haul to line-haul equipment by platform labor was performed.
      2. Total number of bills and weight and insert on Form D–1, line 2, columns 1 and 2, respectively (Fig. 11–6).

---

[6] This is based upon a report of the Cost Finding Committee of the Regular Common Carrier Conference, issued in October, 1951.

TONNAGE

A. Outbound tonnage—Form D–1 (Fig. 11–6)

DAILY TERMINAL REPORT

TERMINAL_____   DATE_____ 19___.

	PLATFORM		1 NO. OF BILLS	2 TONNAGE
1	TOTAL OUTBOUND TONNAGE			
	TONNAGE NOT HANDLED:		XXX	XXXXXXX
2	PICKUPS BY LINE-HAUL TRAILERS			
3	INTERLINE INTERCHANGE LINE-HAUL TRAILERS			
4	TOTAL TONNAGE NOT HANDLED	(ADD LINES 2 AND 3)		
5	OUTBOUND PLATFORM TONNAGE	(LINE 1 MINUS LINE 4)		
6	INBOUND PLATFORM TONNAGE	(FORM D-2 - COLUMNS 5 AND 6)		
7	TOTAL PLATFORM TONNAGE	(ADD LINES 5 AND 6)		
	MAN HOURS	PAYROLL		

	PICKUP AND DELIVERY	1 NO. OF STOPS	2 NO. OF BILLS	3 TONNAGE
8	CITY DRIVERS - LOCAL EQUIPMENT			
9	CITY DRIVERS - LINE-HAUL EQUIPMENT			
10	LINE-HAUL DRIVERS - LINE-HAUL EQUIPMENT - WITH LABOR COST			
11	LINE-HAUL DRIVERS - LINE-HAUL EQUIPMENT - W/O LABOR COST			
12	TOTAL PICKUP AND DELIVERIES - BY DRIVERS (ADD LINES 8 TO 11)			
13	CARTAGE AND SHIPPERS - CONSIGNEE'S SERVICE			
14	INTERLINE - PICKUPS AND DELIVERIES			
15	TOTAL INBOUND AND OUTBOUND (ADD LINES 12 TO 14)			
	MAN HOURS	PAYROLL		

FIG. 11–6. Daily terminal report.

    b) Interchange of trailers:
       1. Check dispatch records of outbound trailers for determination of outbound tonnage on trailers operated on interchange agreements.
       2. Total number of bills and weight and insert on Form D–1, line 3, columns 1 and 2, respectively (Fig. 11–6).
  B. Inbound tonnage—Form D–1 (Fig. 11–6)
    1. Compute total inbound tonnage:
      a) Prepare inbound unloading record, Form D–2 (Fig. 11–7), for each platform shift.

INBOUND UNLOADING RECORD

SHIFT NO.__________

FROM:_____ A.M. / P.M. TO:_____ A.M. / P.M.

TERMINAL____________________ DATE__________________ 19___

1	2	3	4	5	6	7				8
	MANIFEST			UNLOADED		UNLOADING				
						START		FINISH		
TRAILER UNIT NO.	NO.	TOTAL WEIGHT	TOTAL NO. OF BILLS	WEIGHT	NO. OF BILLS	DATE	HOUR	DATE	HOUR	CHECKER'S NAME

FIG. 11–7. Inbound unloading record.

b) Total columns 5 and 6, Form D–2 (Fig. 11–7), and insert totals on Form D–1, line 6, columns 1 and 2, respectively (Fig. 11–6).

The inbound tonnage as taken from Form D–2 (Fig. 11–7) should automatically include through tonnage unloaded for rehandling and will exclude inbound tonnage not handled. Completion of Form D–1 (Fig. 11–6) computes tonnage actually handled across the platform for the day.

MAN-HOURS

Weekly Terminal Payroll Report, Form W–1 (Fig. 11–8). This compiles:

a) Total hours worked (actual total clock hours, including overtime hours)

b) Overtime hours (for memorandum information only)

c) Overtime penalty (for memorandum information only)

Entries of man-hours and wages paid in appropriate lines and columns on Form W–1 (Fig. 11–8) shall be available from weekly payroll records.

Overtime hours shown on Form W–1, lines 1 through 6, column 4 (Fig. 11–8), shall be hours which are subject to the overtime rate, while lines 1 through 6, column 6 shall contain only amount of wages which are in excess of the amount which would have been paid had no overtime rate been in effect. Example: If column 3 has an entry of 44 hours, 4 of which were subject to overtime rate, the entry in column 4 shall be 4 hours. Assuming a rate of $1.00 per hour for 40 hours and overtime penalty of 50 per cent, the entry in column 5 for the 44 hours should have been $44.00. The difference between $46.00 actually paid and $44.00 (total hours multiplied by regular time hourly rate) shall be entered in column 6.

Carriers whose supervisory and platform foremen and assistant foremen work on other than an hourly basis shall enter on Form W–1, column 3, lines 1 and 2, respectively (Fig. 11–8), the exact number of hours worked each week for such employees.

Pay for hours not worked, such as vacations, guaranteed work day, etc., shall be included in appropriate lines on Form W–1 (Fig. 11–8), but hours not actually worked shall be excluded from Form W–1, columns 3 and 4 (Fig. 11–8).

Those who desire a rough daily comparison of efficiency can have each station report daily on additional lines added after lines 7 and 15 on Form D–1 (Fig. 11–6) the total man-hours worked and the total amount of the daily payroll on the platform, and pickup and delivery work, respectively.

Completion of Form W–1 (Fig. 11–8) to this point compiles hours of work on freight handled across the platform.

LABOR COSTS

Form W–1 (Fig. 11–8) indicates elements of labor cost. Personnel listed in this exhibit may devote part or all of their time to other functions, and if so, a division and segregation in appropriate hours and amounts shall be made on their clock or time cards and allocated to the activity to which their work actually pertains.

1. Element of labor costs:

a) Wages—supervision (including nonworking foremen and assistant foremen).

b) Wages—working platform foremen and assistant foremen.

c) Wages—checkers and dock clerks.

WEEKLY

TERMINAL PAYROLL

REPORT

TERMINAL_____   WEEK ENDING_____19____

1	2	3	4	5	6
		HOURS		AMOUNT	
ACCOUNT NUMBER	PLATFORM SALARIES & WAGES	TOTAL	OVERTIME	TOTAL	OVERTIME PENALTY
1 4340	SUPERVISION				
2 4340	WORKING FOREMEN & ASST. FOREMEN				
3 4340	CHECKERS & PLATFORM CLERKS				
4 4340	FREIGHT HANDLERS				
5 4350	SPOTTERS				
6	TOTAL PLATFORM LABOR				

1	2	3	4	5	6
		HOURS		AMOUNT	
ACCOUNT NUMBER	PICKUP & DELIVERY WAGES	TOTAL	OVERTIME	TOTAL	OVERTIME PENALTY
7 4235	CITY DRIVERS & HELPERS - LOCAL EQUIPMENT				
8 4235	CITY DRIVERS & HELPERS - LINE-HAUL EQUIPMENT				
9 4235	LINE-HAUL DRIVERS & HELPERS - LINE-HAUL EQUIPMENT				
10	TOTAL PICKUP & DELIVERY LABOR				

1	2	3	4	5	6
		HOURS		AMOUNT	
ACCOUNT NUMBER	TERMINAL OFFICE SALARIES & WAGES	TOTAL	OVERTIME	TOTAL	OVERTIME PENALTY
11 4311	OFFICE MANAGER				
12 4312	RATING				
13 4312	BILLING AND MANIFESTING				
14 4312	COLLECTIONS				
15 4313	REVENUE ACCOUNTING				
16 4313	O.S. & D. CLERKS				
17 4313	OTHER OFFICE EMPLOYEES				
18	TOTAL TERMINAL OFFICE LABOR				

FIG. 11–8. Weekly terminal payroll report.

d) Wages—freight handlers (wheelers, loaders, stackers, lift operators and strippers).

e) Wages—spotters (hostlers, jockeys, switchers, yard-birds, etc.). Spotters, etc., are included in platform costs because they are required primarily in the handling of platform tonnage. However, in operations in which spotters, etc., perform services in support of other functions, such as pickup or delivery, maintenance, line-haul, etc., proper division and segregation of hours and wages shall be made and allocated to the activity to which their work actually pertains.

Completion of Form W–1 (Fig. 11–8) to this point compiles actual labor costs of tonnage handled across the platform.

Weekly Platform Operating Report—Form W–2 (Fig. 11–9). Form W–2 (Fig. 11–9) is a compilation of data accumulated on related Forms D–1 (Fig. 11–6), D–2 (Fig. 11–7), and W–1 (Fig. 11–8). Cost factors in handling platform tonnage are: (1) tonnage; (2) man-hours; and (3) labor costs, the interpretation of which results in measurement of performance in terms of: (1) pounds handled per man-hour; (2) labor cost per cwt.; and (3) average weight per shipment.

Data to be filled in columns 2, 3, and 4 will become available as time passes. A simple way to figure a 5-week average is to add together the

WEEKLY
PLATFORM OPERATING
REPORT

TERMINAL_____   WEEK ENDING_____19____.

	PLATFORM		1 THIS WEEK	2 LAST WEEK	3 AVERAGE LAST 5 WEEKS	4 5 WEEK AVERAGE THIS TIME LAST YEAR
1	TONNAGE	TOTAL DAILY FORM D-1, LINE 7, COL. 2				
2	NO. OF BILLS (SHIPMENTS)	TOTAL DAILY FORM D-1, LINE 7, COL. 1			XXXXX	XXXXX
3	MAN HOURS	FORM W-1, LINE 6, COL. 3			XXXXX	XXXXX
4	LABOR COST	FORM W-1, LINE 6, COL. 5			XXXXX	XXXXX
5	OVERTIME HOURS	FORM W-1, LINE 6, COL. 4			XXXXX	XXXXX
6	OVERTIME PENALTY WAGES	FORM W-1, LINE 6, COL. 6			XXXXX	XXXXX
7	COST PER CWT.	LINE 4 ÷ LINE 1				
8	POUNDS PER MAN HOUR	LINE 1 ÷ LINE 3				
9	AVERAGE WEIGHT PER BILL (SHIPMENT)	LINE 1 ÷ LINE 2				

FIG. 11–9. Weekly platform operating report.

figures for five successive weeks, double the total, and point back one decimal place.

Monthly Platform Operating Report—Form M–1 (Fig. 11–10). Data for the monthly report shall be prepared:

1. Add all data shown on line 7, Form D–1 (Fig. 11–6), for all days of the month.
2. Add hours and wages shown on Form W–1 (Fig. 11–8) for all weeks which both begin and end in current calendar month, plus appropriate portion of same data on the weekly Form W–1 (Fig. 11–8) which began in preceding month and ended current month, plus appropriate portion of same data on the weekly Form W–1 (Fig. 11–8) which began in current month and ended in successive month.
3. Entries on lines 10 through 14, and 16 through 23 shall be available from subdivisions by terminals of general ledger accounts.

Completion of Form M–1 (Fig. 11–10) provides a monthly report of platform costs and related data.

Some carriers have felt that an incentive method can be used to cut terminal costs. One Class I carrier has successfully correlated technical design with human appeal to secure efficiently operated terminals. An incentive plan has been established by this carrier in which terminal profits are adjusted to book profits. Twenty per cent

MONTHLY
PLATFORM OPERATING
REPORT

TERMINAL _____   MONTH OF _____ 19___ .

					1	2	3	4
					THIS MONTH	LAST MONTH	THIS MONTH LAST YEAR	LATEST 12 MONTHS AVERAGE
1		NO. OF BILLS (SHIPMENTS)		TOTAL DAILY FORM D-1, LINE 7, COL. 1				
2		TONNAGE		TOTAL DAILY FORM D-1, LINE 7, COL. 2				
3		MAN HOURS		SEE TEXT PAGE 8, ITEM 2				
4		LABOR COST		FORM M-1, LINE 15				XXXXX
5		OVERTIME HOURS		SEE TEXT PAGE 8, ITEM 2				XXXXX
6		OVERTIME PENALTY WAGES		SEE TEXT PAGE 8, ITEM 2				XXXXX
7		LABOR COST PER CWT		LINE 4÷LINE 2				XXXXX
8		POUNDS PER MAN HOUR		LINE 2÷LINE 3				
9		AVERAGE WEIGHT PER BILL (SHIPMENT)		LINE 2÷LINE 1				
10	4340	WAGES - SUPERVISION						
11	4340	WAGES - WORKING FOREMEN & ASST. FOREMEN						XXXXX
12	4340	WAGES - CHECKERS & PLATFORM CLERKS						XXXXX
13	4340	WAGES - FREIGHT HANDLERS						XXXXX
14	4350	WAGES - SPOTTERS						XXXXX
15		TOTAL LABOR COST		ADD LINES 10 TO 14				XXXXX
16	4360	COMMISSION AGENTS						
17	4380	PLATFORM SUPPLIES AND EXPENSE						XXXXX
18	4380	PALLETS & OTHER EQUIPMENT (WRITTEN OFF AS PURCHASED)						XXXXX
19	4380	REPAIRS TO PALLETS, FORK LIFTS & OTHER EQUIPMENT						XXXXX
20	4380	FUEL & OIL FOR PLATFORM EQUIPMENT (INCLUDING TAXES)						XXXXX
21	4540	WORKMEN'S COMPENSATION						XXXXX
22	5060	DEPRECIATION						XXXXX
23	5240	PAYROLL TAXES						XXXXX
24		TOTAL OVERALL PLATFORM COSTS		ADD LINES 15 TO 23				XXXXX
25		OVERALL COST PER CWT.		LINE 24÷LINE 2				

FIG. 11–10. Monthly platform operating report.

of the net profits of a terminal is shared with terminal employees in the following manner: 25 per cent to the terminal manager and his assistants; 25 per cent to the sales force; and 50 per cent to clerical, platform, and pickup and delivery drivers.

Another Class I motor carrier has six freight handling experts called "terminal engineers" who travel among the company's terminals to examine dock procedures, loading practices, and freight-handling techniques. They check out loads and city drivers on the correct operation of freight equipment and indoctrinate new employees with the proper method of delivering and picking up shippers' freight. These experts make reports and recommendations to the terminal managers.

TYPES OF TERMINALS BASED ON OWNERSHIP

The predominant type of terminal in use is the carrier-owned individual terminal. There are, however, other types of terminal operations based on ownership. Among these are the following: (a) the renting of space by a motor carrier to other motor carriers; (b) a co-operative association of motor carriers, with each paying a share of operating expenses;[7] (c) a privately owned terminal company which operates on the basis of leases with carrier tenants; and (d) a terminal operated on a fee basis for each arrival and departure of an over-the-road unit, with a handling charge based on tonnage handled.

The foregoing types of terminal operations are self-explanatory. With one exception, they are slightly different phases of the same operation—joint use of terminals by motor carriers. Some of these terminal operations are referred to as "union truck terminals." The joint use of terminals by motor carriers is looked upon in metropolitan areas as a partial solution to the terminal problem. In a 1954 motor-carrier directory, there are listed sixty common and joint terminals, including union truck terminals. These vary in size from a terminal that serves only four carriers to a terminal that serves fifty-six carriers, including local carriers.[8]

CARRIERS' USE OF JOINT TERMINALS

Motor carriers have shown a reluctance to participate in the union terminal or joint operation. There have been instances where motor carriers have made use of such terminal facilities only until their business has developed to the point where establishment of their own terminals has been possible. Rentals are usually on a per-door basis, and in one very large city they currently range from $55 to $110 per door per month. City traffic experts favor consolidation of terminals, particularly for less-than-truckload mixed merchandise, because they

---

[7] The Seattle Auto Freight Depot is a co-operative terminal which started in 1918 and is still in operation.

[8] *National Highway and Airway Carriers and Routes* (Chicago: National Highway Carriers Directory, Inc., 1954).

feel that it relieves traffic congestion. Many motor carriers, on the other hand, although not favoring joint terminal operations, have eased traffic problems by building their new terminals on sites removed from congested areas. As a result, their less-than-truckload shipments of mixed merchandise will be moved throughout the cities in pickup and delivery trucks instead of in over-the-road units.

It appears that the participation of motor carriers in union or joint terminal operations is not going to increase materially unless at some future time there should be pressure from metropolitan areas for their increased use to relieve congestion in city streets. The experience to date would indicate that the most successful type of joint terminal operation is that in which the carrier tenants perform complementary rather than competitive service.

NEW YORK UNION MOTOR TRUCK TERMINAL

The first publicly financed Union Motor Truck Terminal was formally opened in New York City in November, 1949. This 9-million-dollar Union Truck Terminal was constructed by the Port of New York Authority,[9] just four blocks from the Holland Tunnel, which is the main artery for trucks entering Manhattan from the south and west. The opening of this terminal was expected to reduce by 25 per cent the movement of city over-the-road common carriers which handle less-than-truckload lots.

During its first year of operation this terminal operated at about 37 per cent of its capacity and suffered an approximate loss of $300,-000. At the peak of the terminal's operations, there were twenty-two over-the-road carriers using the facilities. The number of carriers had diminished to just four carriers by the end of the second year of operation, and the 2-year operating loss exceeded a million dollars.

The carriers showed little enthusiasm for the Union Terminal, although the design and utility of the installation were satisfactory. The dissatisfaction of carriers arose from the division of operating responsibility, among other things. The lack of common management in the responsibility for line-haul, terminal, and pickup and delivery operations made it rather difficult to integrate the three operations and maintain a flow of traffic across the platform. Other complaints

---

[9] The Port of New York Authority, a public corporation of the states of New York and New Jersey, was created by treaty between the two states in 1921. It operates projects such as the George Washington Bridge, the Holland and Lincoln tunnels, La Guardia Airport, and certain other facilities.

with its operation were that there were too many handling complications which increased costs, and pilferage was a matter of concern. The recognition of a number of different labor unions, also, created certain labor problems.

The New York Port Authority suspended operations of the New York Union Motor Truck Terminal on March 8, 1952. The Port Authority tried to lease the terminal for 3 years to the Post Office Department, but the latter wanted a 30-year lease so this was abandoned. After a year of suspended operations, the terminal was reopened but with a change in operating procedure. It was leased by five trucking companies which formed the Empire State Motor Truck Terminal Co., Inc. The lease provides for operation of the facility by the trucking companies for 3 years at an initial rate of $170,000 per year, with an option of an additional 2 years at $250,-000 per year. In 1955, over 1,000 tons a day were handled through the terminal.

Under the Port Authority's method of operation, licensed local truckmen performed the local joint delivery operation. Under the new arrangement, the operating agent maintains a common receiving station which enables shippers to bring in their less-truckload freight. This plan also called for establishing a joint store-door pickup and delivery service available to those carriers using the terminal. The Port Authority continues to operate that portion of the terminal building which includes the second and third floor office space, restaurant, bank, and stores that are in the building.

The New York Port Authority also constructed the Newark Union Motor Truck Terminal which was very similar to the New York Terminal except that it was larger. It also incorporated some improvements over the New York Terminal, including an under-the-floor type of chain conveyor system. It was scheduled to have been opened in 1950, but it was never opened as a union truck terminal. In 1948 a clause was inserted in the labor contract of Local 478 of the Teamsters' Union in Newark which restricted the private carrier from transferring freight of more than 5,000 pounds daily to other carriers. This provision would have forbidden the carriers to give the Port Authority terminal any freight over that weight in a single day. Therefore the terminal operation would have been economically unsound. The Port Authority appealed to the officers of the International Brotherhood of Teamsters to modify this clause, but the IBT ruled that government agencies operating truck terminals must abide by contracts in force in local areas. This emphasizes the importance in this type of facility of considering all aspects of operations prior to construction. At the present time, the facility is being used by the Air Force although it may be re-established as a union truck terminal in the near future.

The opposition of motor carriers to union terminals is due to a number of factors: (a) shippers and consignees cannot be given the personal service under a consolidated pickup and delivery system that is possible with individual terminals; (b) possible loss of investment which carriers have in their own terminals; (c) shipper and consignee do not identify the service which is rendered them with the carriers which serve them; and (d) the difficulty in securing cooperation among carriers which is needed for successful, union terminal operation.

Some of the benefits to tenant carriers in a union terminal operation are the possible savings in equipment, gasoline, tires, and labor due to improved freight handling. They have no large investment in terminals and terminal equipment, and line-haul vehicles have shorter turn-arounds. The benefits to shippers and consignees are the elimination of truck congestion at freight docks and reduction of numerous pickups and deliveries by various carriers.

Union terminal projects sponsored by private companies face many difficulties. A privately financed company does not possess the power of eminent domain to secure sites of reasonably large size in urban areas. As it is privately financed, taxes and higher interest rates on borrowed capital must be paid than when the union terminal is a government enterprise. During the initial period of operation, it is necessary that a minimum number of carriers should be using the facility. This would mean that carriers should be contacted and contracts signed with them even before construction starts. Whether publicly or privately owned, however, the financial returns of a union terminal appear to be marginal.

TERMINAL FINANCING

As terminal facilities have been outgrown by motor carriers and there has been greater recognition of the importance of efficient terminal operation to a motor carrier's success, more new terminals are being constructed. For example, a survey of Class I intercity motor carriers of general freight was made in 1951 by ATA which indicated that 287 new terminals were needed and 127 existing terminals should be expanded.

It was estimated that the cost of building these terminal facilities would average $15.00 per square foot, but there was a wide variation geographically in such costs, ranging from $18.97 per square foot in the northeast to $6.81 in the southwest. The average cost of the terminals which were planned under this program, including expansion of existing terminals, was $119,367.[10]

Terminal financing is not the problem that equipment financing is. In terminal financing there is real estate which is considered to be a good security for loans. These loans also are usually made for longer periods of time than loans on equipment. There is, however, the fact that terminals are considered to be special-purpose structures which has, in the past, limited some lenders in this type of financing.

As more information about the motor-carrier industry has become known to lenders, the special-purpose aspect of motor-carrier terminals tends to be of less importance. Whether a multipurpose or single-purpose structure is the basis of a loan, the fundamental factor which is considered by a lender is apparent ability to repay the loan. In financing a new terminal the carrier, before making any commitments concerning the purchase of land or construction, should discuss with a lending source or sources conditions concerning the financing of the proposed terminal. This initial action will save much time and effort and is likely to result in securing a loan on a basis which is satisfactory to both parties. Some of the factors which are considered by lenders are efficient management; excellent service record; adequate earnings; operating rights of the carrier; growth record of the company; company organization; and what the new terminal will accomplish.

The conventional source of capital for terminal financing is a lending institution such as a bank or an insurance company. Loans from individuals who wish to make investments are also available at times. In recent years, there has been an increased amount of capital which has been used to build terminals and lease them to carriers. Under such an arrangement, the builder of the terminal secures an income on his investment from the lease to the carrier. There are advantages and disadvantages to such an arrangement for the carrier, but if a carrier secures all the facts about financing, it should be in a position to determine the feasibility of such a plan.

It should not be assumed that a carrier can secure from lending institutions, such as banks and insurance companies, the full amount needed to cover the construction of a new terminal. States impose

---

[10] *Transport Topics,* February 18, 1952, p. 37.

limitations upon lending institutions regarding the amount that may be loaned on the security of real estate. These limitations vary from 60 to 66⅔ per cent of the appraised value of the security which is offered. Inasmuch as the appraised value is made by the lender's appraisers, it is generally conservative and probably would not be the actual cost of building the terminal.

There may be cases when the appraisal might equal the cost of the land and the terminal, but the limits imposed by states upon lending institutions would mean that the carrier could not secure a loan of more than 60–66⅔ per cent of the total cost. It is possible to supplement this limited amount providing the carrier has a good credit standing by securing from the lending institution an additional amount on regular commercial collateral loan agreements which include a provision that a regular mortgage will be executed when the loan is reduced to the proper amount. If the carrier does not need all of the space in the new terminal for itself, it may lease a part of the space to other carriers. Leases of this kind may be used as collateral on which funds may be borrowed to supplement the amounts received from the lending institution.

QUESTIONS AND PROBLEMS

1. What factors have caused motor carriers to give increased attention to terminal facilities?
2. Describe the island-type terminal. Compile a list of other terminal building types which, in your judgment, would be suitable for motor-carrier use.
3. Differentiate between cross-dock and side-by-side transfer of freight at a terminal.
4. Assume that you had an island-type dock, twenty truck berths in length, on which you were using manual equipment. How would you go about determining the feasibility of mechanizing the dock? Would you use the overhead conveyor, fork lift truck, or other mechanized equipment? Explain why.
5. Of what importance is yard space in the operation of a terminal? What are some ideal yard widths?
6. Describe the work of the dispatcher.
7. What is a "peddle run"? Explain the terms "8-day workweek" and "hot-shot run."
8. List the types of motor-carrier terminals, based on ownership.
9. "Motor carriers have shown a reluctance to participate in the union terminal or joint operation." Discuss. How extensive is the common or joint terminal at the present time?

10. Do you feel that pressure from metropolitan areas may force joint terminal operations in some cities? Why?
11. What are the advantages and disadvantages of the different methods of freight checking?
12. Explain route loading and loading by zone. List the advantages of each system.
13. Why are terminal cost controls so important? What is the trend in terminal costs?
14. How does terminal financing differ from equipment financing? What are some of the sources of terminal financing?

12. LEASING OF EQUIPMENT

THE practice of hiring motor vehicles belonging to others by an authorized common or contract carrier is widespread throughout the motor-carrier industry, but this practice is not generally known to the public. About 40 per cent of equipment of intercity Class I motor carriers of property is leased, as indicated in Figure 12–1, with a

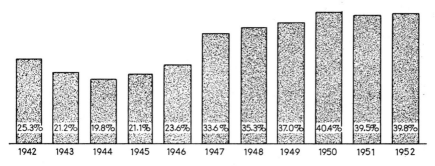

|1942|1943|1944|1945|1946|1947|1948|1949|1950|1951|1952|
|25.3%|21.2%|19.8%|21.1%|23.6%|33.6%|35.3%|37.0%|40.4%|39.5%|39.8%|

FIG. 12–1. Leased equipment, showing the percentage of leased equipment to the total number of vehicles in intercity operation, Class I intercity motor carriers of property.

Source: American Trucking Associations, Inc., *Trends* (Washington, D.C., 1954), p. 20.

sharp increase occurring in the postwar period. This practice came about during the early stages of the development of the for-hire motor carrier, when a shipper might sometimes offer more than could be handled by a particular carrier's available units. Such a carrier, anxious to please a shipper and appear in his eyes to be a dependable and reliable agency of transport, had either to purchase more trucks to handle such occasional situations, which most of them were not in a financial position to do, or to add to their fleets by renting a truck from some individual truck owner or trucks from several owners who could carry the freight for the regular motor carrier without the knowledge of the shipper.

During the early 1930's these lessors or "gypsies," as they were sometimes called, made a business of making one-way trips for any carrier which would hire them, whenever the need arose. Also, some of the for-hire carriers recognized that certain advantages could be gained by employing an owner-operator on a long-term basis with the authorized carrier obtaining the load but with no investment in equipment, which would be furnished by the owner-operator. In this manner, garage and maintenance expense could be avoided as well. Many such arrangements were in effect before the passage of the Motor Carrier Act in 1935. To a great extent, the owners of the vehicles operating today under leasing or renting arrangements either drive the vehicles themselves or hire others to drive for them and are referred to as "owner-operators."

In some instances, authorized motor carriers depend heavily upon other persons to supply them with vehicles to perform the transportation service when they are called upon by shippers to move commodities; an example of this is a company which owns no equipment but leases over 100 units.[1] Another example of heavy reliance upon leasing of equipment is that of an authorized carrier which owns no equipment but leases 600 semitrailers, 200 truck tractors, and 100 pickup and delivery trucks from an affiliated company, as well as additional equipment from owner-operators.[2] Still other motor carriers use equipment that they do not own for certain phases of their operations or over certain routes, during certain periods, or in transporting certain products. There may be periods when a carrier that owns its own equipment cannot meet the peak demand, and it will lease equipment to meet this unusual demand. Particularly is this true of carriers serving seasonal industries. One company which operates irregular routes in the transportation of leaf tobacco in four tobacco-growing states of eastern United States in 1947 averaged 200 truckloads per day during the marketing season of 83 days, as compared to 51 truckloads per day during the remainder of the year.[3] Then, too, in certain areas of the country there is an unbalance in the movement of tonnage by the authorized carriers into an area. Good examples of this are the regular-route carriers of general commodities domiciled in Florida. Their southbound tonnage is much greater than northbound; whereas fresh fruit and vegetable truckers domiciled in Florida carry those products into the northern and eastern cities but feel they cannot afford to return to Florida with

---

[1] *Lease and Interchange of Vehicles by Motor Carriers,* 52 MCC 675 (1951).
[2] *Ibid.*
[3] *Ibid.*

empty units. The regular-route carriers then will lease the vehicles of the fruit and vegetable operators for the return movement to Florida and compensate them for their services.

There are numerous sources from which these motor vehicles can be leased in addition to other for-hire carriers. Exempt carriers, intrastate carriers, and noncarriers, which include truck rental companies and individual owner-operators, are a number of the sources from which equipment may be leased.

TYPES OF AGREEMENTS

For many years there has been a multiplicity of arrangements governing the leasing of motor vehicles, some of which have had to be changed to conform with new Commission rules which became effective September 1, 1953. In the past the most informal of these have been verbal agreements made in person between an authorized carrier or its representative and the owner-operator. In some instances, arrangements were completed by telephone for either a single haul or a round-trip movement. On the other hand, more formal agreements may be drawn up between the parties. A sample agreement is given in Figure 12–2. There may be an agreement covering a one-way or round-trip haul or a long-term leasing arrangement.

The one-way haul or single-haul arrangement is usually referred to as a "trip lease." The trip lease must be a written agreement. The written agreement may cover a single haul (trip lease) or may run for a period of a year and be automatically renewable at that time, with the common proviso that either party may terminate the agreement after proper notice, as stipulated in the agreement. The trip-lease owner-operator has to have a cardboard placard attached to the door of his vehicle identifying his unit as being leased to an authorized carrier, whereas most long-term or term leases provide for the painting of the owner-operator's equipment to conform to company-owned vehicles, including company name. The trip-lease or single-haul owner-operator customarily furnishes all of the equipment to move the agreed shipment; that is, he owns both truck tractor and semitrailer or combination. In many instances, the owner-operator who has entered into a long-term leasing agreement with an authorized carrier may provide only the truck tractor, with the semitrailer being provided by the carrier, although some carriers do require even long-term owner-operators to furnish all their equipment. The

ROADWAY EXPRESS, INC.

EQUIPMENT LEASE

1. In consideration of the covenants of Roadway Express, Inc., herein called LESSEE, the undersigned, herein called OWNER, does hereby lease and deliver to LESSEE the motor vehicles, trucks, tractors, trailers or semi-trailers and all accessories thereto described in Schedule A set forth below and made a part hereof, hereinafter called the Leased Equipment, upon the terms and conditions herein set forth, and covenants and agrees that OWNER will:

1.1 Equip Leased Equipment with all parts, vehicle equipment and accessories required by law and by the Lessee, and at Owner's sole risk and expense service and maintain Leased Equipment in good and safe operating condition in accordance with all Federal, State and Municipal laws, Ordinances, regulations and orders applicable thereto, and safety rules of Lessee.

1.2 At his sole expense and cost procure:

(a) All license plates and identifications required to be procured by the Owner of vehicles by the State in which title is registered; pay all fines or penalties imposed for the negligence or misconduct of the Lessee; pay all taxes, licenses, charge or assessments other than those assumed by the Lessee in Paragraph 2.3 of this Equipment Lease; and

(b) All fuel, oil and supplies necessary for the operation of the vehicle.

(c) Liability insurance with coverage in amounts approved by the Lessee, to protect persons who may be injured or property which may be damaged by the operation of said Leased Equipment while "bobtailing" without trailer or "deadheading" empty, when such operation is not at the written dispatch, direction or order of the Lessee; and when such leased equipment is so operated the Lessee's insurance shall not apply, the Lessee assumes no responsibility for such operation, and the Lessee may, at its option, consider such operation a breach of this lease and may terminate same.

1.3 Assume and bear the entire loss or damage to said Leased Equipment except where said loss or damage is directly caused by the negligence or misconduct of a driver, other than the Owner, assigned by the Lessee to operate said vehicle for a purpose or use for which the Owner would not be compensated.

2. Lessee hereby accepts the lease of the Leased Equipment upon the terms and conditions hereof and in consideration therefor, and of the covenants of the Owner, covenants that it will:

2.1 Pay as rent for the use of said Leased Equipment as follows:

_____

_____

2.2 Operate the Leased Equipment or cause same to be operated in compliance with all Federal, State and Municipal Laws, Ordinances, rules and regulations.

2.3 Assume and pay all the cost of:

Items properly classified as compensation of drivers or helpers as employees; franchise fees or certificates and travel orders; bridge toll, weight and wheel taxes or road and mile taxes levied on roads over which Lessee has dispatched the Leased Equipment; all license plates, permits and identification (except as specified in Paragraph 1.2 (a) above) of said Leased Equipment required by law to be licensed or provided by the Lessee of the vehicle together with all claims, judgments, costs and expense (except as assumed by Owner as specified in Paragraph 1.2 (c) above) for loss or damage to the property of others than the Owner and injuries to or deaths of persons in, occasioned by or incident to the operation by it of said vehicles and not occasioned in whole or in part by any act, failure or fault of the Owner.

2.4 Upon termination hereof, return the Leased Equipment to Owner in substantially the same condition as received except for (1) ordinary wear, tear, depreciation, and (2) loss or damage to the Leased Equipment.

3. Parties mutually covenant and agree that:

3.1 During the term of this lease, the said Leased Equipment shall be in the sole and exclusive possession and control of Lessee and shall be operated exclusively by drivers or helpers selected, directed, appointed and discharged by it, except during such time as the same shall be in the possession of the Owner for the purpose of servicing, maintenance, or repair.

3.2 If Owner is employed as a driver on the equipment leased from him, he shall not be entitled to any compensation as an employee during any period of time in which such Leased Equipment is not available for use by Lessee due to its mechanical or other failure either en route or at a terminal, except, that if during such period Owner, in his capacity as an employee, drives other equipment or performs other services at the direction of Lessee, Owner shall then be paid the compensation due him for such services as an employee.

FIG. 12–2.   A copy of an equipment lease which is used when the equipment is going to be leased for a period of time.

size and the amount of the equipment furnished by the owner-operator will influence the amount of compensation he will receive. Authorized carriers may hold title to the equipment they lease on a term basis and may license the equipment in the name of their companies because the laws of the state in which they operate so require.

METHODS OF PAYMENT

The methods of payment for the use of leased equipment are varied and depend upon a number of factors. One of the methods

3.3 If the Leased Equipment or any part thereof shall be lost, destroyed or damaged so that the same cannot be safely and efficiently operated in motor carrier service, the rent hereof shall abate until the same is repaired by Owner and returned to Lessee in good, safe operating condition, and the Owner covenants that he will either repair or replace such equipment within thirty (30) days after written notice of such loss, damage or destruction is given to him personally or mailed to him by the Lessee.

3.4 The Owner at his cost and expense shall paint such signs, insignia or other information upon said Leased Equipment as the Lessee from time to time shall direct. This does not refer to repainting the entire Leased Equipment.

3.5 Each party hereto shall indemnify and hold harmless the other against all liability, damage, expense or cost of every sort and kind occasioned in whole or in part by the failure of such party fully to perform and discharge each and every of its covenants herein.

3.6 The Owner agrees that upon the termination of this lease he will at his cost and expense remove from said Leased Equipment any and all signs, insignia, identification, permit or license numbers or other material, which indicated that said Leased Equipment was being operated for or on behalf of Lessee, or which had been issued to or on behalf of Lessee, and will forthwith surrender and deliver to the Lessee all licenses, tags, permits, certificates, weight tax tags, name plates, number plates, identification equipment, papers, documents, records and other personal property of the Lessee, and the Owner further agrees that complete compliance by him with the terms of this paragraph is a condition precedent to the payment by the Lessee of any monies due to the Owner for said Leased Equipment at the time of lease termination and the Lessee shall have the right to withhold payment of such monies due to the Owner until the Owner has completely complied with the provisions of this paragraph.

3.7 This lease shall begin on the_____day of_____, 19____, and continue thereafter until terminated, as it may be by either party giving to the other party thirty (30) days written notice, **provided** that the lease shall terminate prior thereto upon one (1) day written notice if either party, after thirty (30) days written notice, shall fail to cure or remedy the breach of any of his or its covenants herein.

Date ....

ROADWAY EXPRESS, INC.

Terminal ....

By ....

Owner ....

By ....

Address ....

Phone...

SCHEDULE A

TRUCK OR TRACTOR	SEMI-TRAILER
Make ....Capacity	Make ....Capacity ....
Year ....Model	Year ....Model ....
Motor No. ....Serial No.	Serial No. ....Type .... (Open, Closed, Refrigerator)
Length .... Gross Weight	Length ....Weight ....
Width ....Height	Width ....Height ....
Size and Number of Tires.................	Size & No. of Tires.................Mud Flaps................. (Yes or No)
Truck Load................. Min................. Max.................	Semi-Trailer Load................. Min................. Max.................
Kind of Brakes................. Stop Light................. (Yes or No)	Kind of Brakes................. Stop Light................. (Yes or No)
License Number................. State.................	License Number................. State.................

FIG. 12–2.—*Continued*

of compensating for the use of equipment is on the basis of time; a second is cost plus mileage; a third is ton-mileage; a fourth is mileage-plus; and a fifth is a percentage of gross revenue. The latter two methods are widely used in the compensation of owner-operators.

An example of payment on the basis of tonnage and mileage is that of a carrier that pays from 17 cents to 25 cents per mile, depending on the tonnage.[4] Other carriers pay 17 cents a mile for 20,000 pounds, with a graduated scale to as high as 50 cents per mile for 59,000 pounds. The percentage of gross revenue, a widely used basis

---

[4] *Ibid.*

for compensating owner-operators for the use of leased equipment, varies greatly among different motor carriers. Some carriers give 85 per cent of the gross revenue to the owner-operator, the company keeping the other 15 per cent. Some grant 70 per cent to the owner-operator with 30 per cent to the carrier, others give 60 per cent to the owner-operator, and still other carriers establish a split of as low as 50 per cent for the owner-operator. The percentage given to the owner-operator depends, in part, upon whether the load is low-rated or high-rated freight. For example, on loads that average 55 cents or less per 100 pounds, 74 per cent may go to the owner-operator and 26 per cent to the carrier; but on loads that average over 55 cents per 100 pounds, 64 per cent may go to the owner-operator and 36 per cent to the carrier. If a return trip is guaranteed, the rate is usually not as great as it is in one direction, i.e., 75 cents per 100 pounds one way but 60 cents per 100 pounds if a return load is guaranteed. The wide variation in the percentage received by the owner-operator depends also on the extent and the type of equipment he furnishes; if only a truck tractor is furnished, he receives proportionately less than if he furnishes a truck tractor and a semitrailer. Similarly, the provision of a two-axle (tandem) trailer, which makes possible a larger pay load, entitles the owner-operator to a greater percentage of the gross revenue. A premium may be paid above the established one-way rate to transport commodities to a certain point, with the proviso that the empty vehicle be sealed on the return trip. Extra compensation is provided for such items as "drop" shipments en route and for mountain mileage—flat amounts being given as $5.00 for each "drop" shipment and $8.00 for mountain mileage. Considered also in the percentage allocation is the company policy toward its own drivers, the provision of insurance, licensing, and the like.

The Commission feels that the rental should not be computed on the basis of a division of the rate or revenue. It is at the present time conducting a rehearing on this matter.

The status of the owner-operators differs from company to company; many of them have the status of individual contractors and are therefore not covered by Social Security or workmen's compensation. These owner-operators must pay their expenses, such as gasoline and oil and personal expenses, while en route. Many carriers which have maintenance crews for their own equipment will service the owner-operator's equipment at cost. If parts are necessary, the carrier will secure them at a company discount and allow the owner-operator to take advantage of such discount. In like manner, gasoline and oil may usually be purchased at company discounts at the company terminals.

Other owner-operators are placed on the payroll as drivers, in which case Social Security and other taxes are deducted from their wages; and their compensation as drivers is fixed separately from that accorded the use of their equipment. Under an eleven-state area union contract in the Middle West, the compensation of drivers is determined separately from that of the use of equipment.[5]

The incentive that exists for an individual owner-operator is the opportunity to become an independent businessman. He can finance his equipment and, if successful in its operation, can pay for the equipment through its operation, which represents an investment of an amount from $4,000 to $15,000, depending upon the unit purchased. Furthermore, the owner-operator does not have to secure a certificate or permit from the Interstate Commerce Commission to operate in this regulated industry; he does not have to maintain a business organization or sell the transportation service.

The net amount received by the owner-operator in the gross percentage allocation, be it 80–20, 70–30, 60–40, or 50–50, may actually be less than these stated percentages, for deductions are made from the owner-operator's share for damage to cargo up to $50. Since the processing of claims takes time, the owner-operator may not have deducted from his earnings a claims damage until several months later, at which time the deduction is made out of current earnings. Some carriers withhold a certain amount of the compensation due the owner-operator for his haul to cover any contingency for which the owner-operator has some responsibility. Some carriers also require the owner-operator to share the cost of a connecting-line transfer, any rate adjustment which might be made, and dock loading and unloading, in addition to damage to freight. It is customary for a term owner-operator to receive an advance for each trip, the amount depending upon the length of the trip.

"WILDCATTERS" OR "GYPSIES"

Some carriers maintain a current list in each of their terminals of those owner-operators whom they can call on a trip-lease basis. These "wildcatters" or "gypsies," as they are termed, are owner-operators who follow the flow of traffic. They will serve any carrier, provided they can obtain truckloads of heavy loading freight. They do not like

---
[5] *Ibid.*

to haul less-than-truckload shipments because of the time consumed and the expense incurred in loading such shipments. An owner-operator of this kind may be domiciled in Detroit, carry a load for an authorized motor carrier to Chicago, and in seeking a load out of Chicago find that it is necessary to go to St. Louis if he wants a pay load; perhaps in St. Louis he will find a load that will work him back to his home base, Detroit. Much like the migratory farmworker who follows the harvesting of crops, the "wildcatter" follows the flow of traffic. It does happen that these "wildcatters" or "gypsies," if anxious to return to their homes, will carry loads for far less than the compensation they normally would receive.

Every carrier which trip leases from owner-operators should maintain a list of those which are approved and disapproved and distribute it throughout its system. A list of disapproved owner-operators is particularly important, since the unsatisfactory owner-operator might be leased again at another terminal in the carrier's system. Some of the experiences that place owner-operators on a disapproved list are: failure to observe federal and state regulations; making unreasonable demands after being loaded; and transporting unauthorized passengers.

DEVELOPMENT OF REGULATION OF LEASING FOR COMMON AND CONTRACT CARRIERS

With a diversity of hiring arrangements already in effect when congressional hearings were held on the bill that eventually became the Motor Carrier Act of 1935, some attention was given to the legal status of the participants to these arrangements within the framework of the proposed bill. There was some question as to whether the owner-operators would be the carriers and anyone hiring their services or leasing their equipment would be a broker or a freight forwarder, or whether the broker or freight forwarder would be the carrier and the owner-operators his agents.

When the Motor Carrier Act of 1935 was adopted, it provided for regulation of the "procurement of and the provision of facilities for" transportation of passengers or property by motor. In addition, the Motor Carrier Act defined a common carrier and a contract carrier, in part, as those which undertake, "whether directly or by a lease or any other arrangement," to transport passengers or property, and so forth. The added language referring to a lease or any other arrangement was eliminated when the Motor Carrier Act was incorporated into Part II of the Interstate Commerce Act of 1940. This was done in the interest of clarity and has been held not to evidence any change in legislative intent.[6]

On August 19, 1936, the Bureau of Motor Carriers of the Interstate Commerce Commission adopted a ruling[7] which remained "tentative" but which provided that the lease or other arrangement by which the equipment of an authorized operator is augmented must be of such character that the possession and control of the vehicle is, for the period of the lease, entirely vested in the authorized operator; that the operation thereof must be conducted under the supervision and control of such carrier; and that the vehicle must be operated by persons who are actual bona fide employees of the authorized operator.

After the issuance of this ruling, Division 5 of the Interstate Commerce Commission referred to it in a few cases without officially adopting or rejecting it and authorized the issuance of certificates to applicants proposing to conduct operations under conditions that met the requirements of the ruling. It therefore became quite generally recognized that "when a certificate or permit holder furnishes services in vehicles owned and operated by others, he must control the service to the same extent as if he owned the vehicles, but he need control the vehicles only to the extent necessary to be responsible to the shipper, the public, and the Commission for the transportation."[8]

Since 1940 the Bureau of Motor Carriers of the Commission has been giving consideration to leasing arrangements of motor common and contract carriers and has held various meetings with representative carriers on the subject. In 1941 a study of the subject was made, and a preliminary statistical report was released in 1943. During World War II, Commission activities were directed toward more pressing problems closely related to the war effort,[9] and leasing practices were bypassed for the time being. The difficulty of procuring new vehicles, as well as Office of Defense Transportation directives and Interstate Commerce Commission orders designed to effect maximum utilization of motor vehicles, in some degree caused leasing to become more widespread during the war. This trend con-

---

[6] *Thomson v. United States,* 321 U.S. 19 (1943).

[7] Administrative Rule No. 4.

[8] *Lease and Interchange of Vehicles by Motor Carriers,* 52 MCC 675 (1951).

[9] Subsequent changes brought about by the war, as well as a later report, have had the effect of making the 1943 report obsolete.

tinued after the war, when many veterans purchased equipment and then leased it to common and contract carriers.

In 1947 the Bureau of Motor Carriers sent a questionnaire to the 19,001 carriers of property which were active and subject to Interstate Commerce Commission regulations at that time. The data obtained were classified into five geographical regions, as follows:[10]

A	B	C	D	E
Maine	Virginia	West Virginia	Minnesota	Montana
New Hampshire	North Carolina	Ohio	Iowa	Wyoming
Vermont	South Carolina	Indiana	Missouri	Colorado
New York	Georgia	Michigan	Kansas	New Mexico
Massachusetts	Florida	Illinois	Nebraska	Arizona
Rhode Island	Alabama	Wisconsin	South Dakota	Nevada
Connecticut	Kentucky		North Dakota	Utah
New Jersey	Tennessee			Idaho
Pennsylvania	Mississippi			Washington
Delaware	Louisiana			Oregon
Maryland	Arkansas			California
District of	Oklahoma			
Columbia	Texas			

The extent of leasing at that time by type of carrier and total number is given in Table 12–1. This table shows that the practice of leasing exists among all types of carriers listed, but the percentage of over-the-road carriers which considered leasing important was

TABLE 12–1

SUMMARY OF EXTENT OF LEASING IN 1947

Type of Carrier and Total Number	Leasing Important	Leasing Un-Important	Did Not Lease
General commodity carriers (5,519)........	27.3%	9.5%	63.2%
Tank-truck operators (457).............	32.6	14.0	53.4
Household-goods carriers (2,611)..........	24.5	6.8	68.7
Heavy haulers (710)...................	21.3	13.2	65.5
Carriers of other special commodities (6,186)	8.3	6.9	84.8
Not classified (2,038).................	50.2	3.7	46.1
Local carriers (1,480).................	7.6	8.9	83.5

Source: *Lease and Interchange of Vehicles by Motor Carriers*, 52 MCC 675 (1951).

greater than the percentage of local carriers which considered leasing important.

More detailed information was secured from those carriers which regarded leasing as being important to their business and is summarized as follows: Class I carriers operating as intercity common carriers of general commodities in Region C leased 51 per cent of

[10] Bureau of Motor Carriers exhibit in *Ex parte No. MC–43, Lease and Interchange of Vehicles by Motor Carriers.*

their equipment, which included over-the-road and pickup and delivery trucks. If the total number of vehicles operated by the intercity common Class I carriers which consider leasing as important to their business in Region C is computed by class of commodity (tank trucks, household goods, and so forth), it shows that 53.6 per cent of the vehicles were leased in 1947. For intercity common Class II carriers during the same period and in the same area, the figure is 58.6 per cent. Region D shows a similar distribution for intercity common Class I carriers, with 50 per cent of the vehicles leased and 36.2 per cent leased by intercity common Class II carriers. In contrast to this, in Region E, of the intercity common Class I carriers which regarded leasing as important to their business, only 14.1 per cent of the vehicles were leased; and 28.3 per cent of the vehicles were leased by intercity common Class II carriers. In Regions A and B, for intercity common Class I carriers, 26.2 per cent and 35.2 per cent, respectively, of vehicles were leased; and for intercity common Class II carriers, the figures are 21 per cent in Region A and 24.6 per cent in Region B.

Some conception of the proportion of different types of leases was secured from those carriers which regarded leasing as important in 1947. There were 38,785 long-term leases, 104,785 round-trip leases, and 394,896 one-way or trip leases. The total number of one-way or trip leases between carriers and owner-operators was about 52 per cent of all such leases used.

In 1947 a set of regulations concerning leasing, which the Bureau of Motor Carriers felt would prohibit undesirable practices that allegedly existed, was discussed with representatives of the American Trucking Associations, Inc., after which the various proposals were discussed at the annual convention of this organization. The carrier representatives at the convention appeared unable to secure unanimity of opinion concerning the proposed regulations, so the Director of the Bureau of Motor Carriers recommended that a proceeding be instituted by the Interstate Commerce Commission to investigate the leasing of vehicles by motor carriers. By order entered in 1948, Division 5 of the Commission instituted on its own motion a nation-wide investigation that is better known as *Ex parte No. MC–43*. The proposals of the proceeding set forth by the Director of the Bureau of Motor Carriers contained four alternative remedies, as well as some other suggestions:

1. Prohibition of use by a carrier of vehicles not owned by the carrier.
2. Requirement that a carrier own a percentage of the vehicles it uses.

3. Prohibition of the use of vehicles not owned or held under long-term lease.

4. Permission to use an unlimited number of vehicles under trip leases, subject to certain requirements.

Hearings in *Ex parte No. MC–43* were held in 1948 at which the field staff of the Bureau of Motor Carriers listed a number of examples of what it felt were undesirable leasing practices, which can be grouped under the following headings:

1. *Informality of Leasing Arrangements.* Because of the informality of arrangements for the use of equipment, questions arise as to liability for accidents resulting in injuries to the public; which insurer is liable at a particular time, the insurer of the authorized carrier or the insurer of the owner; and where the liability of one ends and that of the other begins.

2. *Insufficiency of Control over Operation of Vehicles.* In trip leasing, difficulties arise in establishing responsibility for accidents that occur after the owner-operator has completed delivery. The carrier may deny liability, and the owner may lack insurance after the leased vehicle has delivered the shipment.

3. *Insufficiency of Control over Drivers.* There are complaints that owner-operators may take the most direct route to destination, regardless of the carrier's operating authority; may operate unsafe equipment; and may charge gasoline and tires to the carrier without authorization.

4. *Loss of Contacts with Shippers.* After the vehicle owners have become acquainted with shippers through hauling under lease to a carrier, they may haul for the shipper under lease, without reporting it to the carrier.

5. *Avoidance of Carrier Responsibilities.* Accidents occur to leased vehicles about which no reports are made because the carrier does not know of them; or, by the time the carrier learns of these accidents, the owner-operators involved cannot be located. Where claims are filed after the owner-operators have disappeared, carriers are unable to ascertain essential facts as to liability.

It was also found that many violations of Interstate Commerce Commission regulations, primarily in the field of safety, had taken place. These were discovered through road checks of for-hire and private carriers operating interstate for 6 months prior to September 15, 1948. By establishing the two categories of owned vehicles and leased vehicles and tabulating the violations observed in each group through the road checks, it was found that in all but one region the percentage of leased vehicles violating Interstate Commerce Commission regulations exceeded the percentage of violations in the owned vehicle group.

In addition to violations of the safety and hours-of-service regulations, the use of owner-operators by authorized carriers frequently results in unauthorized operations. These unauthorized operations involve transportation beyond the territory of the authorized carrier by the owner-operator. Authorized carriers sometimes violate the act in permitting other such carriers to perform unauthorized service under the guise of equipment leases. For such transportation, the originating carrier usually paid a toll to the connecting line for allowing its rights to be used. The carriers usually paid a percentage of the revenue for such transportation, so the rates which they were required to charge bore little relation to the cost of performing the service. This also threatened a disruption of sound economic conditions in transportation.

Following lengthy hearings, the Commission in 1951 prescribed regulations intended to eliminate objectionable operating practices in leasing. These regulations established as conditions to the use of leased equipment by authorized carriers that the contract for such usage be in writing; and that exclusive possession of and responsibility for the equipment be vested in the authorized carrier during the period of the contract, which should be for not less than 30 days when the driver is the owner or an employee of the owner of the equipment. Compensation for the use of the leased equipment shall not be measured by a percentage of rates or earnings of the vehicle. The rules also require inspection of the equipment and that it be identified as being in the service of and under the responsibility of the authorized carrier. It is also required that appropriate action be taken by the carrier to assure that the use by it, of a vehicle with the owner or his employee as the driver, will not result in violation of the Commission's motor-carrier safety regulations. The rules established what were considered to be adequate safeguards for equipment used in interchange service by two or more authorized carriers, in order to assure assumption of full responsibility for the operation of such equipment by the authorized carriers during the period the equipment is operated under the certificates of each such carrier.

After these regulations were scheduled to become effective, six suits were instituted in district courts to test the validity of the rules. These were carried to the Supreme Court on appeal in two cases. In January, 1953, the Supreme Court upheld the decisions of the district courts and affirmed the right of the Commission to prescribe the regulations.[11]

---

[11] *American Trucking Associations, Inc.* v. *United States,* 344 U.S. 298 (1953).

Subsequent to this Supreme Court decision, several bills were introduced in Congress which were designed to divest the Commission of the power to regulate the duration of any lease of motor vehicles or the amount of compensation paid for such a lease. These two items have been the ones about which most of the controversy centered. One bill passed the House of Representatives.[12] The Senate was unable to complete action on it before adjournment of that session, however, so the Commission was requested to postpone the effective date of that part of the regulations involved in the legislation until the Congress had time to dispose of the legislation. The Congress did not enact any legislation on the matter, and in late 1953 the Commission reopened hearings on leasing rules to reconsider two provisions. These were its rule against any lease arrangement of less than 30 days' duration and its ban on compensation for leased vehicles which was based on a percentage of the rates involved or on a percentage of the revenues earned by the leased vehicles. The Commission had earlier deferred the effective date of these two provisions to March 1, 1955, and granted an exception from them for motor vehicles owned by farmers or agricultural co-operative associations which haul agricultural commodities or livestock to market and are trip-leased on the return of the vehicle to a point in the state of origin.

SUMMARY OF EFFECTIVE LEASING REGULATIONS

A summary follows of the present status of regulations governing leasing which became effective September 1, 1953.

Exemption from the rules, other than those rules relative to inspection and identification of equipment and equipment rented to private carriers and shippers, is provided for:

1. Equipment leased by one authorized carrier to another for transportation in the direction of a point which lessor is authorized to serve;
2. Equipment to transport railway express traffic or substituted motor-for-rail service, when moving between points that are railroad stations and transporting freight which is on railroad billings;
3. Equipment used solely within municipalities or commercial zones;
4. Equipment for transportation performed pursuant to a plan approved by the ICC in a Section 5 hearing;
5. To the lease of equipment without drivers by an authorized carrier from an individual, partnership, or corporation whose principal

---

[12] H. R. 3203, 83d. Cong., 1st sess., 1953.

business is the lease of equipment without drivers for compensation; and

6. Equipment other than a power unit, provided that such equipment is not drawn by a power unit leased from the lessor of such equipment. This rule is intended to allow the sublease or interchange of trailers or semitrailers between authorized carriers, when such equipment is not drawn by a tractor owned and operated by the lessor. This exemption does not permit common carriers to lease such equipment to private carriers, but does permit shippers leasing such equipment to authorized carriers.

LEASING RULES

The contracts or leases must be in writing, and when covering equipment driven by owner or employee of owner, for not less than 30 days. The 30-day rule is waived in the case of agricultural haulers when they lease to an authorized carrier for a return load over direct routes from the destination of the shipment of agricultural commodities to the place of origin of such shipments. In addition, the 30-day requirement is waived altogether when the equipment is owned and operated by the producer or grower of the agricultural commodities or livestock, or co-operative association of producers or growers, and when the equipment is being returned to a point in the state from which the agricultural products or livestock were transported. When operating under this exemption, the motor carrier must secure a signed statement from the producer or grower or co-operative association which gives the origin and destination of the shipment of the agricultural commodities or livestock and which authorizes the driver of the equipment to lease the vehicle for the return trip.

Contracts covering leased equipment must provide for the exclusive possession, control, and use and for complete assumption of responsibility by the authorized carrier. This provision is interpreted in two ways: (1) As to household carriers, for the transportation of household goods, the control, etc., must be during the period the equipment is operated by or for the authorized carrier lessee; and (2) as to other than household-goods carriers, for the duration of the contract, except provision is made for subleasing to other authorized carriers. Exemption No. 6, just listed, makes these provisions inapplicable to semitrailers and trailers operated under the conditions specified therein.

Contracts must also specify the compensation, which may not be computed on any division or percentage of rates or revenue. However, the provision prohibiting the computation of compensation on a division or percentage of rates or revenue was postponed until March 1, 1955, and in December, 1954, the examiner hearing this case recommended that the 30-day rule and the compensation provision should not be canceled or modified at that time but that the Commission should further postpone their effectiveness for a period of at least 2 years beyond March 1, 1955. In February, 1955, the Commission postponed the effective date of the two rules to March 1, 1956 and further hearings on them are being held. The contracts must be executed in triplicate, one for the owner, one for the carrier, and one to be carried in the vehicle; provision is made for a certificate being carried in the vehicle in lieu of a copy of the lease contract. Receipts must be executed by the carrier when taking possession, and by the owner upon relinquishing possession and control. The equipment must be inspected by the carrier, and the order provides a form for inspection of equipment and certifications of the inspector and the carrier. Identification must be on the power equipment, and if a removable device is used, it must be of durable material and bear a serial number in the authorized carrier's own series for record purposes.

In those cases where the driver is not a regular employee of the authorized carrier, the carrier must make certain that the driver is familiar with the safety regulations and secure a certificate of physical examination; photostatic copies of the original certificate are permissible. The rules also provide for a manifest covering each trip.

The effective date of leasing rules governing household-goods carriers and automobile transporters was postponed to March 1, 1956 and may be further postponed.

The Bureau of Motor Carriers, in 1953, issued two Administrative Rules[13] about leasing and interchange of vehicles which are tentative and provisional in the absence of authoritative decisions on the subject by the Commission. In the first rule it was held that under Section 207.5 (c) of the leasing regulations, a carrier accepting a vehicle under an interchange arrangement may not employ as its own driver the person who brought the equipment to the point of interchange. In the other rule, it was stated that vehicle inspections required under a provision of the leasing regulations of the Interstate Commerce Commission may not be made by the owner or an employee of owner

---

[13] Administrative Rules Nos. 96 and 97, dated September 1, 1953.

of the equipment because such persons could not be considered a bona fide representative of the lessee carrier.

There have also been informal interpretations furnished by the Bureau of Motor Carriers to its field staff regarding various questions concerning the leasing and interchange regulations.

Of the carriers which have been granted operating authority, approximately 800 own little, if any, equipment.[14] There were a large number of carriers which obtained certificates under the "grandfather" clause which did not at that time own trucks. Also there have been certificates granted to carriers since the "grandfather" date which did not own trucks. The Commission has known this at the time that the certificates were granted.[15]

The 30-day period which the Commission prescribed was picked as one which the Commission felt would ". . . make it likely that the carrier would inspect the vehicle, examine the driver, and go through the other proceedings. It was an arbitrary figure picked as a matter of judgment by the Commission."[16]

The attitude of the regulated motor carriers concerning the leasing regulations differs, in large measure dependent upon whether they are already owners of their equipment, in which case they are in favor of the regulations, or whether they lease a substantial portion of their equipment, in which case they are against the regulations. Certainly the Commission's regulations will eliminate some of the malpractices that have existed in connection with leasing. However, the exemptions granted from the regulations may, in the future, lessen the effectiveness of regulation, as has been the case in regard to other exemptions.

STATE REGULATION OF LEASING

Some states have established some degree of regulatory control over the leasing of equipment by motor carriers. In 1954 twenty-five states[17] had regulations affecting this practice. Eighteen of these pro-

---

[14] House Committee on Interstate and Foreign Commerce, 83d Cong., 1st sess., *Trip Leasing* (Washington, D.C.: U.S. Government Printing Office, 1953), p. 454.

[15] *Ibid.*, p. 471.

[16] Statement of Director Blanning, Bureau of Motor Carriers, Interstate Commerce Commission, House Interstate and Foreign Commerce Committee, 83d Cong., 1st sess., *Trip Leasing* (Washington, D.C.: U.S. Government Printing Office, 1953), p. 475.

[17] Arizona, Arkansas, Colorado, Connecticut, Florida, Georgia, Kansas, Kentucky, Michigan, Minnesota, Mississippi, Missouri, Montana, Nebraska, New Mexico, New York, North Carolina, North Dakota, Oregon, Pennsylvania, Texas, Virginia, Washington, West Virginia, and Wisconsin.

hibit or limit trip leasing. A number of other states exercise some control over leasing of equipment through regulations that cover the licensing of the equipment of the motor carrier or the establishment of provisions for special permits for substitution of licensed equipment in emergencies. Some of the states require that the owner or owner-operator of a leased unit must apply for a state license in his own name and that the application must be accompanied by a copy of the lease. The state of Washington, for example, requires that the driver of a leased vehicle must be an employee of the carrier and, furthermore, that trip leases or short-term leases are prohibited. The Department of Transportation must approve a lease; and, to facilitate this, agents of the department are located throughout the state. Household-goods carriers which utilize leased vehicles considerably furnish the Department of Transportation with lists of leased vans which are kept on file at the department. If a listed vehicle of one of these carriers enters the state of Washington, the department is notified and wires permission for the vehicle to operate over the state's highways.

TRUCK-RENTAL COMPANIES

A phase of truck leasing that is particularly significant in local operations and to a lesser degree in intercity operations is that of leasing or renting by truck-rental companies. These organizations are located in all of the metropolitan cities and have equipment available which can be rented or leased under a number of different arrangements. Typical of these is a company that offers for rent passenger cars without drivers on a temporary basis which runs from an hour to several weeks or months; the rental of trucks, also without drivers, for an hour, for a day, or by the week; and last, the leasing of both cars and trucks under long-term contracts which run from 1 to 4 years or longer. In providing the truck on either a temporary (usually referred to as truck rental) or a long-term basis (often referred to as truck leasing) the company furnishes everything except the driver, that is, gasoline, oil, tires, maintenance service, insurance, license, and so forth. For a long-term lease, it will secure the make and model of truck the customer wants and equip, paint, and letter it in accordance with the customer's specifications, giving the customer exclusive use and control of the truck or fleet of trucks during the period of the lease. For example, a distributor of frozen products can secure an insulated body for the carrying of refrigerated products; or a soft-drink distributor can secure the special type of body which is used in the distribution of these products.

The charge for rental units may be based on mileage or may be a combination of time and mileage. The latter arrangement is favored by many truck-rental companies. The rental agreement based on a small truck may be $15.60 a week plus 5 cents a mile.[18] Another company is reported to have rented a truck with a maximum payload capacity of 20,000 pounds at $50 per week plus 18 cents a mile.[19] For a refrigerated truck tractor-semitrailer combination with a 15-ton capacity operating in intercity transportation the charge is about $115 per week, plus 10–11 cents per mile. A grocer in a medium-sized city may lease a small panel truck and pay $18 a week plus 6 cents for every mile over 175 miles. The range is from $15 to $125 a week and 5 cents to 18 cents a mile, depending upon the kind and size of truck, kind of hauling, and terrain. The weekly rate is set to reflect largely fixed costs which do not vary with the operation of the vehicle, whereas the mileage rate represents costs resulting from the operation of the vehicle. The profit these companies secure must be through close cost control and the advantages of a large fleet operation, including discount buying.

The long-term agreements have a number of provisions regarding maintenance and upkeep, cancellation clauses, and an escalator clause, the latter providing for rate increases if the cost of labor and material rises. If a vehicle breaks down, the lessee or driver notifies the company from which it is leased; under the leasing agreement, the company is required to make the necessary repairs within a specified number of hours or provide another vehicle.

The size of these leasing companies varies, but many of them are very large organizations. A company in one city has 4,000 units for rent or lease. Another company, which has 18 sites in 10 cities, has about 800 passenger cars and 1,700 trucks. Domiciled in a single building were about 170 trucks which were leased to 82 customers engaged in 27 different kinds of businesses.[20]

Potential customers of truck-leasing companies are manufacturing producers, distributors, and service firms which own their own trucks, although there has been some development in the leasing of

---

[18] Harris Saunders, "Unit of Equipment Costs for Truck Leasing Operations," *National Association of Cost Accountants Bulletin*, Sec. 1, Vol. XXX, No. 15 (April 1, 1949), p. 894. See also *Wall Street Journal*, October 3, 1952, p. 1.

[19] John J. Casale, Inc., *Contract Carrier Application*, 49 MCC 15 (1948).

[20] Saunders, *op. cit.*, p. 895.

units to certificated common carriers. Many nationally known firms make use of truck leasing from truck-rental companies. The customers of truck-rental companies include beverage distributors, department stores, bakers, florists, grocers, and many others. An indication of the acceptance of the truck rental or leasing idea by business organizations in the securing of their equipment can be ascertained from a comparison of the number of trucks leased over a period of time. It is reported that, in the early 1930's, there were about 1,500 leased trucks belonging to truck-rental companies. By 1940 this number had increased to 18,000; and at the end of 1948 the number had almost doubled to 35,000 vehicles leased from the truck-rental companies, with customers paying $150 million for the use of these units.[21] By 1954 it was estimated there were over 90,000 trucks leased to users by truck-rental companies.

The operators of truck-rental organizations point out a number of advantages of leasing from them as compared with owning a unit or units. These are as follows:[22]

1. The leasing of vehicles permits company executives to devote full time to their own business by freeing them of the details attendant to operating of their own trucks. The truck leasing company takes over management problems, such as purchasing of trucks, fueling and supplies, licensing, insuring, as well as supervision of the maintenance and servicing of the trucks.

2. It is possible to budget costs in advance, since trucks secured on a long-term lease are on a periodical rental basis, plus a mileage rate. From previous operation, truck mileage can be estimated quite closely. Billing may be on a daily, weekly, or monthly basis, and there is only one bill to be paid instead of many to vendors of gasoline, oil, tires, parts, etc., as there would be if the units were owned.

3. Truck leasing eliminates truck maintenance problems. Repairs, washing, fueling, and a myriad of other maintenance details are provided under the leasing agreement.

4. It assures uninterrupted service. Emergencies which arise due to mechanical difficulties are taken care of by the substitution of other leased equipment.

5. It eliminates the capital investment in trucks and frees this capital for other investment. A company which owns its own equipment and changes to leased equipment can sell the owned equipment to the truck rental company at a fair price, thereby liquidating its investment in a satisfactory manner.

6. Attractive well-maintained equipment is a good advertisement for any business firm. Under a truck lease arrangement, the leasing company

[21] *American Cartagemen,* January, 1954, p. 6.
[22] From a brochure of the National Truck Leasing Service, Chicago, Illinois.

replaces trucks with new equipment at pre-determined mileage intervals, as well as taking care of regular washing, polishing, and painting, insuring that the equipment will have a smart appearance.

7. It eliminates surplus equipment. Under truck leasing, equipment needed for normal periods can. be augmented for special peak periods, such as might be needed by a department store during the pre-Christmas season.

The procedure followed by a truck-rental company upon receipt of an inquiry concerning truck leasing is to make a study and cost analysis of the truck user's operation. From this study is developed a proposal to supply leasing service in terms of the user's needs for regular and peak operations, the size of the units, the body equipment necessary, and the weekly rental and mileage charge for each type of equipment. If this proposal is acceptable, a contract is entered into between the truck-rental company and the applicant user. It should be noted that the Commission's leasing regulations exempt corporations whose principal business is the leasing of equipment without drivers for compensation.

NATIONAL ORGANIZATIONS OF TRUCK-RENTAL COMPANIES

There are two national organizations of truck-leasing operators. Of the leasing done by truck-rental companies, these two companies —National Truck Leasing System and Hertz Driv-Ur-Self—account for more than one half of all such leasing. Hertz Driv-Ur-Self owns and operates truck-leasing stations in 28 cities. In 1953 it had over 6,000 trucks under lease and had granted franchises to about 500 leasing firms, in over 400 cities, which operated about 15,000 trucks.[23] These franchised companies pay to the national organization a monthly fee based on the number of vehicles operated for the privilege of being associated with the Hertz system and securing advice on rates, accounting, and purchasing.

The National Truck Leasing System has 52 member companies operating in 150 cities. In 1954 this company had about 20,000 trucks under long-term lease, of which 35 per cent are used by private carriers in over the road service.[24] The National Truck Leasing System assists its new member companies in setting up a rate structure similar to that of organizations already operating under like conditions in a given area. It extends service in facilitating payments

---

[23] *Railway Age,* August 17, 1953, p. 18.

[24] Information supplied by National Truck Leasing System.

to member companies by a business firm lessee with subsidiaries scattered throughout the country, all of which have leasing arrangements for vehicles operated for the subsidiaries by members of the National Truck Leasing System. It allows the parent organization to pay the leasing charges for its entire business structure to the national headquarters of the National Truck Leasing System and forwards the appropriate payments to the member leasing companies supplying the equipment.

There has been a progressive increase in the amount of truck leasing to private carriers by all truck-rental companies over the past few years, as has been pointed out. Their primary area of development has been in providing delivery equipment for local service, although a number of interstate common carriers make use of delivery equipment which is supplied by truck rental companies on a long-term leasing basis. Some of these arrangements have been in existence for more than 15 years. The rental of over-the-road equipment from a truck-rental company, not affiliated with a carrier, has become more important in recent years. One corporation has leased ninety truck tractor-semitrailer and truck units to move its products from Florida plants to markets as far distant as New York and Chicago. However, even though some business organizations have been supplied with the larger equipment necessary for over-the-road hauling of their commodities, the provision of over-the-road equipment to common carriers has been negligible. There are instances where truck tractors and semitrailers have been leased for over-the-road service by common carriers, but the concentration of activities of the truck-rental companies has been and undoubtedly will continue to be in the delivery field.

In the true economic sense whether the equipment is owned or leased the economic cost is borne by the party who uses the equipment. The leasing company's rates, of necessity, include its cost and a profit. A shipper or carrier should carefully analyze the total cost under the owned-versus-leased methods of equipment operation.

QUESTIONS AND PROBLEMS

1. Enumerate the reasons for the development of owner-operators.
2. Identify a trip lease; a term lease. How are these made?
3. List and explain the methods of payment for the use of leased equipment.
4. What incentives are there for the owner-operator?

5. Trace the background of the proposed regulation of leasing by the Bureau of Motor Carriers.

6. Summarize the information secured from the 1947 survey of truck leasing by the Bureau of Motor Carriers.

7. What are the advantages and disadvantages of truck leasing (*a*) to motor carriers, and (*b*) to the public?

8. Explain the rules that have been issued by the Commission to govern truck leasing.

9. What are the advantages to a business firm of securing trucks from a truck-rental company?

10. What are some typical charges for truck-rental units?

11. What are the long-run implications of trip leasing of over-the-road equipment?

13. CLAIMS AND CLAIM PREVENTION

▪▪

THE freight claims procedure used by motor carriers differs among the various carriers, and numerous systems are employed. The essential characteristics of any freight claims procedure should be that it be as simple in its operation as possible, in order to expedite as rapid processing of the claims as is consistent with good business policy. All motor carriers subject to the Interstate Commerce Act are required to investigate carefully all claims before settlement is made.[1] Since a claim is a demand made by a claimant, either shipper or consignee, for restitution for financial loss which was suffered because of the loss of or damage to freight or by application of erroneous rates, weight, or assessment of charges, it is necessary for the claimant to furnish a motor carrier with definite proof of financial loss. An adequately staffed claims department is essential to satisfactory customer relations.

Claims can be divided into two general types: (*a*) cargo claims, and (*b*) claims due to overcharge. Cargo claims are those claims which are filed for freight that the carrier has failed to deliver to the consignee because of the destruction, disappearance, or conversion of the freight, or because of its being damaged by the carrier so as to render its value less to the consignee. Overcharge claims are those which are caused by erroneous application of rates, weights, and assessment of freight charges.

CARGO CLAIMS

Cargo claims are of two varieties: (*a*) those which are attributable to known loss or known damage, and (*b*) those which are attributable to unknown loss or damage.

---

[1] Section 222 (c).

338

STANDARD FORM FOR PRESENTATION OF LOSS AND DAMAGE CLAIM
(Read Instruction on Back Before Filling in This Form)

To: _____
(Name of Carrier)   _____
                                                      (Date)

_____   _____
(Street Address)   (Claimant's Number)

_____   _____
(City, State)   (Carrier's Number)

This claim for $ _____ is made against your company for ☐ Damage / ☐ Loss in connection with the following described shipment:

_____   _____
(Shipper's Name)   (Consignee's Name)

_____   _____
(Point Shipped From)   (Final Destination)

_____   _____
(Name of Carrier Issuing Bill of Lading)   (Name of Delivering Carrier)

_____   _____
(Date of Bill of Lading)   (Date of Delivery)

_____   _____
(Routing of Shipment)   (Delivering Carrier's Freight Bill No.)

If shipment reconsigned en route, state particulars: _____

If shipment moved from warhousing or distribution point, indicate name of initial shipper and point of origin, and, if known, name of prior carrier or carriers and prior billing reference: _____

DETAILED STATEMENT SHOWING HOW AMOUNT CLAIMED IS DETERMINED
(Number and description of articles, nature and extent of loss or damage, invoice price of articles, amount of claim, etc. ALL DISCOUNT and ALLOWANCES MUST BE SHOWN.)

Total Amount Claimed	

The following documents are submitted in support of this claim:

☐ Original Bill of Lading   ☐ Original invoice or certified copy
☐ Original paid freight bill or other carrier document bearing notation of loss or damage if not shown on freight bill.
☐ Carrier's Inspection Report Form (Concealed loss or damage).   ☐ Shippers concealed loss or damage form.
☐ Consignee concealed loss or damage form.   ☐ Other particulars obtainable in proof of loss or damage claimed:

(Note: The absence of any document called for in connection with this claim must be explained. When impossible for claimant to produce original bill of lading, or paid freight bill, a bond of indemnity must be given to protect carrier against duplicate claim supported by original documents.)

Remarks: _____

The foregoing statement of facts is hereby certified as correct.

_____
(Claimant's Name)

_____
(Address)

FIG. 13–1.   Standard form for presentation of loss and damage claim.

KNOWN LOSS OR DAMAGE

The first type of cargo claims is that of freight received with loss or damage visible and with exception at the time of delivery. Claims of this nature usually will be submitted by the claimant on the standard form for presentation of loss or damage claims. Figure 13–1 is an example of this form. These claims should be supported by (a)

Form of Indemnity Agreement to be used when unable to deliver the Original
Bill of Lading or Freight Bill

INDEMNITY AGREEMENT

Date _____ 194___

File No. _____

Whereas, the undersigned cannot supply to the _____ or
(Name of Carrier)

its connections the $\left\{\begin{array}{l}\text{Original Paid Freight Bill}\\\text{Original Bill of Lading}\end{array}\right\}$ covering the shipment hereinafter described,

the undersigned agrees to hold the said carrier and any other participating carrier harmless

and indemnified against any and all lawful claims which may be made against it or them arising

out of the same shipment, and will pay to the said carrier or any participating carrier, all

losses, damages, costs, counsel fees or any other expenses which they or any of them may suffer

or pay by reason of payment of our aforementioned claim without surrender of the said

$\left\{\begin{array}{l}\text{Original Paid Freight Bill}\\\text{Original Bill of Lading}\end{array}\right\}$. The foregoing document(s) cannot be produced for the following

reason: _____

_____

_____

DESCRIPTION OF SHIPMENT

Articles _____

_____

_____

Consignor _____ From _____

Consignee _____ At _____

Date _____ Via _____

Freight Bill Pro. No. _____ Date _____ Issuing Carrier _____

Bill of Lading No. _____ Date _____ Issuing Carrier _____

_____
(Claimant)

_____
(Address)

_____
(By)   (Title)

FIG. 13–2. Bond of indemnity.

the original bill of lading (or bond of indemnity, Fig. 13–2); (*b*) the original destination freight bill (or bond of indemnity); (*c*) the original invoice or certified or photostatic copy; and (*d*) any other particulars which are obtainable to aid in proof of the loss or damage claimed.

STANDARD FORM FOR THE HANDLING OF CONCEALED LOSS
AND CONCEALED DAMAGE CLAIMS.

SHIPPER'S FORM
INFORMATION IN LIEU OF AFFIDAVIT REQUIRED FROM CONSIGNEE IN SUPPORT
OF CLAIM FOR CONCEALED LOSS OR CONCEALED DAMAGE.

SHIPPER'S CLAIM NO............................CONSIGNEE'S CLAIM NO. ....

POINT OF ORIGIN.....................................DESTINATION ....

DATE ....NUMBER OF PACKAGES....................

SHIPPER ....CONSIGNEE ....

COMMODITY ....

INFORMATION REQUIRED	ANSWERS
1 When were the goods packed, if known?	....
(a) Where were the goods packed?	....
2. Were all the articles for which claim is made packed in container in good order?	....
(a) Does your record indicate whether or not the container was packed to its full capacity with the property shipped?	....
(b) If not packed full, what material occupied the remaining space?	....
3. Was the package protected against abstraction of or damage to contents by........ being strapped, sealed, corded, or otherwise specifically protected?	....
(a) If so, how?	....
4. On what date was shipment delivered to truckman?	....
(a) Was the shipment delivered truckman before or after 12 o'clock noon?	....
(b) Was the delivery made to the carrier by your own truck?..........	....
(c) If not, give name of trucking company	....
(d) Give name of driver in either case, if known	....
(e) If not delivered by truck, state how delivered..........	....

I hereby certify the foregoing statement of facts to be true in every particular, to the best of my knowledge and belief

Dated at ....Signature................................

Date .... 19..

In what capacity employed

FIG. 13–3. Standard form for the handling of concealed loss and concealed damage claims—shipper's form.

CONCEALED LOSS OR DAMAGE

The second type of cargo loss or damage, that of concealed or unknown loss or damage, is that freight which is received with no loss or damage visible at the time of delivery and therefore is received without exception. A claim of this kind should be supported by (a) the original bill of lading (or bond of indemnity); (b) the original destination freight bill (or bond of indemnity); (c) the original invoice or certified or photostatic copy; (d) any other evidence which

Standard Form for the Handling of Concealed Loss
and Concealed Damage Claims

CONSIGNEE'S FORM

Information Required From Consignee in Support of Claim for Concealed
Loss or Concealed Damage

Shipper's Claim No. .... Consignee's Claim No. ....

Description of Shipment

Point of Origin .... Destination ....
Date Received .... Number of Packages ....
Shipper .... Consignee ....
Commodity ....

1. When (date and hour) was shipment received at your place of business? ....
   ....
2. Name of truck driver, if known ....
3. If not received by truck, state how received ....
4. On what date was loss or damage discovered? ....
5. On what date was carrier notified of loss or damage? ....
6. Kind of container? ....
7. How was package protected against abstraction of or damage to contents (strapped, sealed, or otherwise)? ....
   ....
8. Was container examined before opening? .... Or after opening? ....
9. If condition of container at time of such examination indicated cause of loss or damage, explain fully ....
   ....
10. If condition of contents or interior packing indicated loss or damage, explain fully ....
    ....
11. If property received did not fill container to capacity, what material occupied the remaining space? ....
12. What condition of container or contents indicated that loss or damage occurred while in possession of carriers? ....
    ....

I hereby certify the foregoing statement of facts to be true in every particular.

Dated at ....
(signature)

Date ....19.. ....
(In what capacity employed)

FIG. 13–4. Standard form for the handling of concealed loss and concealed damage claims—consignee's form.

may be obtainable to prove loss or damage claimed; and (e) inspection report by a carrier representative. If inspection is not made by a carrier representative, the claimant will be required to complete the standard form for the handling of concealed loss and concealed damage claims, shipper's form (Fig. 13–3) or consignee's form (Fig. 13–4), depending upon whether the claimant is a shipper or consignee.

In the motor-carrier rules entitled "Regulations Governing the Inspection of Freight before and after Delivery,"[2] there is the requirement that concealed loss and damage must be reported to a carrier within 15 days of receipt and the merchandise and container held for inspection by the carrier. Many claimants have pointed out that the law and the bill of lading specifically authorize the filing of a claim within 9 months after delivery, or within 9 months after a reasonable time for delivery has elapsed. Motor carriers have felt that there is no conflict between the 15-day provision and the 9-month limitation for filing claims. The 15-day provision merely establishes a basis upon which a seasonably filed claim may be declined, and a carrier has the right to decline a claim which investigation indicates is not its liability. After the declination in writing is made, the claimant has 2 years to bring suit against the carrier in the event he believes the claim is justified.

DAMAGED FREIGHT

The nature of the good shipped, the container used, and the method of packing are all important in safe transportation of goods. Even though the shipper might be at fault, the burden of proof of negligence is upon the carrier after the carrier has signed the bill of lading. This is the case because it is assumed that if the shipment was not properly prepared, the carrier should have rejected it; or if it was quite susceptible to damage, the carrier should have accorded it special handling.

Damaged freight is in a different class from lost freight because, in the latter case, the payment of a claim may be averted if the shipment is found and forwarded to the consignee. Damaged freight, however, represents a permanent injury and one in which the shipper has suffered a monetary loss and expects the motor carrier to compensate him.

Loss and damage freight claim handling procedures vary widely among motor carriers. A suggested loss and damage freight claim handling procedure includes the following points:

1. Make inspections within 48 hours.
2. Acknowledge claim same day received.
3. Give claimant your claim number.
4. Investigate claim immediately; be sure of the facts.
5. Pay claim or deny liability promptly.

---

[2] Established by the National Freight Claim Council discussed later in this chapter.

6. Keep claim files "active"—trace for replies to unanswered correspondence.

OVER AND SHORT FREIGHT

Over freight is freight with or without marks (including articles in excess of quantity on billing) which is found in possession of a carrier at any point without a regular revenue or astray waybill. There can never be an "over" piece of freight without a "short."

Astray freight is understood to be freight which has become separated from the regular revenue freight bill and is covered by an astray freight bill. Freight may be "over" with marks as to shipper or consignee or without marks. In the latter case, it is usually referred to as "dead over." In both of these cases, this freight has become separated from the waybill.

Upon discovery of over freight, an over report is prepared immediately. Figure 13–5 is a copy of an over, short, and damage report. A copy of the report is sent to the transfer and/or the origin or billing point for investigation and determination of the reason for the freight checking out over at the unloading point. The origin or transfer terminal which receives this report should check the various reasons for freight going astray. If the origin terminal cannot account for the overage from its records, the shipper should be asked to help in the matter. The terminal which has the over freight should also request the consignee and shipper for proof of ownership when the origin terminal cannot provide the revenue billing within a reasonable time.

In the case of short freight, the carrier has a bill but no freight or less than the number of pieces called for by the billing. Short freight is a real problem for the carrier has signed the shipper's bill of lading for the freight and the terminal which holds the bill does not know what has happened to it. Because of mismarkings or misdescription by the shipper, the carrier may share the responsibility for short freight. The common causes of such shortages are the failure of carrier's employees to count and pick up the freight signed for, errors made in billing, misloading, and theft, to name but a few.

Over freight which is discovered at an origin terminal should be forwarded to the destination terminal on an astray freight waybill after the original waybill reference has been secured. However, where over freight is found at an intermediate terminal, it is usually forwarded to the destination terminal immediately on an astray

ROADWAY EXPRESS, INC.
AKRON 11, OHIO

OVER SHORT AND DAMAGE REPORT

Original Copy	Akron ☐
First Copy	Akron ☐
Second Copy	Origin ☐
Third Copy	Transfer ☐
Various Stations	☐

Station_____ Date_____ OS & D No._____

Manifest No._____ Station Seal No._____ Intact YES ☐   NO ☐

Name of Account_____ Driver_____

Shipper_____ Consignee_____

Address_____ Address_____

Station Pro No._____ Connecting Line Pro No._____

ORIGINAL DATA SHOWN ON FREIGHT BILL

Number of Pieces	Description	Weight

Number of Pieces — OVER_____ SHORT_____ DAMAGED_____

DESCRIPTION_____

_____ Weight_____

List Notation on Pro if any_____

Disposition_____

Location of Shipment in Truck — REAR_____ CENTER_____ FRONT_____ MIDDLE_____ TOP_____

EXPLANATION OF DAMAGE

POOR LOADING		DOCK DAMAGE	
1 Bumping by hand truck	☐	1 Bumping by hand truck	☐
2 Cartons loaded upside down	☐	2 Cartons stacked upside down	☐
3 Heavy freight loaded on light freight	☐	3 Heavy freight stacked on light freight	☐
4 Loaded atop loose or sharp articles	☐	4 Freight fell over, stacked too high	☐
5 Freight fell over, stacked too high	☐	5 Liquid stacked on top of dry freight	☐
6 Liquid loaded on top of dry freight	☐	6 Leakage from other freight	☐
7 Shifting of cargo	☐	7 Pilferage	☐
8 Leakage from other freight	☐	8 Rough handling while loading, unloading	☐
9 Rough handling loading or unloading	☐	9 Fell off hand truck loading and unloading	☐
10 Damaged before loading	☐	10	☐
11	☐	11	☐

DAMAGE DUE TO FAULTY EQUIPMENT—WET ☐   COLLISION ☐   OVERTURN ☐   FIRE LOSS ☐

REMARKS:

(Use other side for additional remarks)   Name of Checker_____

Signed_____

FIG. 13–5. Over, short, and damage report.

freight waybill and will include the original waybill reference if possible. If over freight is found at destination terminal, it should be held until the revenue waybill reference has been established. A free astray waybill is issued covering freight which checks over from a truck and cannot be applied on revenue billing. The free astray waybill should show the name and address of shipper, weight, description of freight, and at what point and from what vehicle it checks out over.

An over shipment may be delivered upon proper proof of ownership. Typical carrier procedures for making delivery of over freight without benefit of the revenue waybill are:

1. The consignee can furnish the original bill of lading. This document can be attached to the free astray delivery receipt. If the consignee will not surrender the bill of lading, the delivering terminal will take permanent record of the date, shipper, consignee, and the bill of lading number which will be placed on the face or reverse side of the free astray pro; and a full description of the items appearing on the bill of lading against which the free astray shipment is to apply.

2. If the bill of lading is not available, the shipper's invoice may be accepted providing the freight can be identified by case number, stock number, or other means as being covered by the invoice submitted in evidence. If the invoice is accepted as proof of ownership, the delivering terminal should take permanent record on the face or reverse side of the free astray pro of invoice number, date, and description of the item against which the freight is to apply. The consignee's order or the shipper's acknowledgment of the order is also considered to be proper proof of ownership. However, complete information should be recorded for the carrier's records.

3. The consignee's presentation of an original revenue freight bill which carries a previous notation of shortage of the described freight which the carrier is handling on a free astray billing. When the delivery is made to fill an existing shortage, the full pro reference must be made a part of the permanent record on the face or reverse side of the free astray pro in order to close the open OS&D report.

4. Over freight moving C.O.D. "order notify" or for export is not delivered to any consignee without the original waybill reference.

Free astray freight is not delivered to the consignee without the assessment of revenue, except when it fills a shortage on a previously noted revenue waybill, in which case reference should be made to that revenue bill. When the delivery is made on free astray billing, the delivering agent will compute the tariff charges on the scale weight and collect in the usual manner. When the delivering agent cannot determine the point of origin, it uses its best judgment and applies charges accordingly. Any refunds, corrections, or cancellations may be made later upon receipt of the revenue waybill.

When over freight is held without billing for delivery to a consignee served by a connecting carrier, the connecting carrier or carriers serving the point should be contacted. The over freight may be needed to match short freight of the connecting carrier, in which case there can be the establishment of a revenue waybill reference. If the over freight cannot be applied against a shortage of a connecting line, the original waybill reference must be secured before releasing the freight.

Every effort should be made to deliver over freight. After it has been carried on the over report of carriers for 90 to 120 days, however, some carriers then consider the over freight to be salvage freight. Under such arrangements, the headquarters freight claim department may authorize the shipment of the salvage freight to the appropriate department for disposal. When the operations department has exhausted all efforts to dispose of refused or unclaimed freight, it will be shipped to the headquarters claims office for appropriate disposition. Shipments of salvage material to the headquarters are usually handled on a deadhead bill of lading or waybill. If carrier returns salvage to a shipper, it will usually move on a revenue billing, unless the freight claim department authorizes a different procedure.

OVERCHARGE CLAIMS

The second general type of claim is that of overcharge. Claims of this nature are made because of the application of erroneous rates, weights, and assessment of freight charges. An overcharge claim is usually submitted on a standard form for the presentation of overcharge claims. Figure 13–6 is a sample form. An overcharge claim is supported by the following documents: (a) original bill of lading, if not previously surrendered to carrier when shipment was prepaid or when claim is based on misrouting or valuation (or bond of indemnity); (b) original paid freight bill (or bond of indemnity); (c) original invoice or certified copy, when the claim is based on weight; (d) when the claim is based on weight, a weight certificate or a certified statement; and (e) other evidence which can be obtained in proof of the overcharge claimed.

The Commission has differentiated between the procedure in

Standard Form for Presentation of Overcharge Claims.

_____ (Name of person to whom claim is presented)   _____ (Address of claimant)   _____ (Claimant's Number)**

_____ (Name of Carrier)   _____ (Date)   _____ (Carrier's Number)

_____ (Address)

This claim for $_____is made against the carrier named above by_____
         (Amount of claim)   (Name of claimant)
for Overcharge in connection with the following described shipments:

Description of shipment_____

Name and address of consignor (shipper)_____

Shipped from_____ , To_____
              City, town or station   City, town or station

Final Destination_____ Routed via_____
              City, town or station

Bill of Lading issued by_____Co.; Date of Bill of Lading_____

Paid Freight Bill (Pro) Number_____;

Name and address of consignee (Whom shipped to)_____

If shipment reconsigned en route, state particulars:_____

Nature of Overcharge_____
                                Weight, rate, or classification, etc.

DETAILED STATEMENT OF CLAIM

Note.—If claim covers more than one item taking different rates and classification, attach separate statement showing how overcharge is determined and insert totals in space below.

	No. of Pkgs.	Articles	Weight	Rate	Charges	Amount of Overcharge
Charges Paid:						
		Total				
Should have been:						
		Total				

Authority for rate or classification claimed._____
                       (Give, so far as practicable, tariff reference, I. C. C. number, effective date and page or item.)

IN ADDITION TO THE INFORMATION GIVEN ABOVE, THE FOLLOWING DOCUMENTS ARE SUBMITTED IN SUPPORT OF THIS CLAIM*

{ } 1. Original paid freight ("expense") bill.
{ } 2. Original invoice, or certified copy, when claim is based on weight or valuation, or when shipment has been improperly described.
( ) 3. Original bill of lading, if not previously surrendered to carrier, when shipment was prepaid, or when claim is based on misrouting or valuation.
( ) 4. Weight certificate or certified statement when claim is based on weight._____
( ) 5. Other particulars obtainable in proof of Overcharge claimed.†_____

Remarks _____

The foregoing statement of facts is hereby certified to as correct.

_____ (Signature of Claimant)

** Claimant should assign to each claim a number, inserting same in the space provided at the upper right hand corner of this form. Reference should be made thereto in all correspondence pertaining to this claim.
* Claimant will please place check (x) before such of the documents mentioned as have been attached, and explain under "Remarks" the absence of any of the documents called for in connection with this claim. When for any reason it is impossible for claimant to produce original bill of lading, if required, or paid freight bill, claimant should indemnify carrier or carriers against duplicate claim supported by original documents.
† Claims for overcharge on shipments of lumber should also be supported by a statement of the number of feet, dimensions, kind of lumber, and length of time on sticks before being shipped.
Claims based on rates quoted in letters from traffic officials should be supported by the original or copies of such letters.

FIG. 13–6. Standard form for presentation of overcharge claims.

seeking damages for unlawful rates and that which is followed in overcharge claims. When the Commission finds that rates charged by a carrier are inapplicable, it is the duty of the carrier to refund any overcharges without an order or other action on the part of the Commission and without resort to a court.[3]

[3] _Bell Potato Chip Co._ v. _Aberdeen Truck Line,_ 43 MCC 337 (1944).

Unlike Part I of the Interstate Commerce Act under which the Interstate Commerce Commission can issue an order and award directing rail carriers to pay reparation, Part II of the act governing motor carriers contains no such provision. On the other hand, the Commission can review the lawfulness of rates of motor carriers as applied on past shipments. When there are past unlawful motor rates, one method of recovering damages is the filing of a suit against the motor carrier receiving the rate in which it is alleged that there are damages for the collection and payment of the rates or charges which are unlawful because of unreasonableness, discrimination, and undue preference or prejudice in violation of the act. A complaint should also be filed against the motor carrier before the Commission in which the unlawfulness of the rates or charges is alleged and requesting an administrative determination of the lawfulness of the past rates. The complainant, in instituting this action, should notify the Commission of the court action. The court should be petitioned that the case be held in abeyance pending administrative determination by the Commission of the past lawfulness of the rates or charges. The last step is the introduction of evidence in the court of the administrative determination of the Commission to establish the unlawfulness of the rates and charges and to determine the amount of damages.[4]

Prior court action may be waived by the Commission if circumstances warrant. The requirement concerning court action does not appear to be rigidly enforced.

A motor carrier may refund to a shipper the difference between the amount collected for transportation performed and that which has been found reasonable by the Commission after a formal investigation, without waiting for a shipper to institute a court action.

After there is a formal finding that an applicable rate is unreasonable, the carrier does not need to continue its efforts to collect outstanding charges on past shipments in excess of those found reasonable, and it may waive them.[5]

TRACING

Tracing and OS&D's are closely associated, inasmuch as a tracer often means that the freight has gone astray and is covered by an

---

[4] G. Lloyd Wilson, "Steps for Recovery of Damages Based on Unlawful Motor Rates Outlined," *Traffic World,* October 11, 1952, p. 41.

[5] *U.S. Rubber Co.* v. *Associated Transport, Inc.,* 48 MCC 6 (1948).

OS&D report. When a request to trace a shipment is received, particularly one that has been in transit for some time, the OS&D files should be checked on overs and shorts. The trace file should be consolidated with the OS&D file if it is found that the freight is over or short in the hands of the carrier.

Frequently there are requests for information on freight movements which have not been delivered. Although tracers are annoying, carriers are not in a position to judge the importance of a customer's request. It is, therefore, important that each tracer be given prompt and courteous handling. It is desirable to have a tracer form in order that a record may be kept of the action taken. A tracer may be the forerunner of possible trouble in the movement of a shipper's goods, so that a record should be maintained that will be helpful if an overage or shortage of freight should occur.

Carriers with teletype facilities between their terminals may find that this facilitates tracing. However, whether telephone or telegraph is used often depends upon the circumstances in each individual case. If it is a matter of protecting a preferred account, telephone or telegraph is frequently used. A form letter which is sent air mail, special delivery, is also used in tracing.

A tickler file is used to maintain a check on traced shipments. When shippers use tracing for the purpose of expediting, the carrier soon finds that this type of tracer may become quite burdensome, diverting attention from those cases which merit greater consideration.

NATIONAL FREIGHT CLAIM COUNCIL

All motor carriers have the privilege of membership in the National Freight Claim Council of ATA available to them without expense. Although membership is divided into two groups—active supporting members and associate members—they both enjoy the same privileges, the only difference being that the former group voluntarily contributes nominal dues to assist in defraying the expenses of the national organization's claims activities. The National Freight Claim Council has formulated a number of freight claim rules, as well as establishing principles and practices covering loss, damage, and overcharge claims. Motor-carrier members of the Council are pledged to handle claims promptly and efficiently.

The by-laws of the Council provide a procedure for disciplinary action for members who do not observe established claim procedure.

In addition to the National Freight Claim Council, there are a number of regional claim organizations which have been established in recent years. The primary purpose of the original claim conferences is to establish a free interchange of ideas on common problems. Other advantages of such meetings also result from the personal acquaintanceships made among claim agents.

When the first of the regional freight claim conferences was established, it was thought that it could serve as a bureau for matching over and short freight. Experience has shown, however, that the clearance of overs and shorts has best been accomplished through the organization of OS&D personnel at major gateways. Periodic meetings for this purpose are more successful than establishing regional programs through the issuance of consolidated reports of unmatched freight overages.

There has been limited development of shippers' conferences which use the services of motor carriers. The first of these was formed in 1952, at which time discussions of the group were limited to matters of service. The shippers' group is designed to function in the field of shipper-motor carrier relations as a counterpart to a regional shippers' advisory board in the field of shipper-railroad relations which has been operative for many years.

Two of these groups provide that nominal dues will be paid by all members, both shippers and motor carriers. These dues are only enough to cover the expenses of the group. All of these shipper-motor carrier groups which have been formed thus far have been dedicated to the principle of improved procedures and practices. Most of them do not discuss rates and charges.

There are a number of areas in which informal committees of shippers and carriers have been formed for discussion of the feasibility of such organizations.

PRINCIPLES AND PRACTICES FOR INVESTIGATION AND DISPOSITION OF CLAIMS

A number of principles and practices for the investigation and disposition of freight claims have been formulated to secure uniformity among carriers and uniform treatment of claimants in the disposition of claims of like nature. They are also planned to secure better relationships in claim matters among carriers as well as between carriers and their customers. These principles include the time limit for filing claims, the documents required in support of claims, description of claims for deterioration, description of claims for damage by delay, procedure to be followed when two or more claims are presented on the same shipment, and the measure of damages.

Although all of these principles are significant, the one which covers the measure of damages is of particular importance. This reads as follows:

Except in claims involving declared or agreed value, the responsibility of the carrier for loss, damage or injury which is caused to property by the carrier is the full actual loss, damage or injury to such property as suffered by claimant. The maximum liability of the carrier in any event is the destination value in the quantity shipped.

For the purpose of arriving at the correct measure of liability where destination value of the property is a factor (in the absence of a declared or agreed value), any recognized market quotations at destination, or point adjacent thereto, quoting commodity values in the quantity shipped, may be accepted. In the absence of such market quotations or other established market values in the quantity shipped, the bona fide invoice price, plus proportionate freight charges if paid and not included in invoice price, and duty if paid and not refundable, shall represent the reasonable destination value. Brokerage, overhead expenses, percentage above invoice, or other similar items added to the invoice price, will not be paid.

The practice of adjusting claims on non-perishable commodities on the basis of the difference between retail value in good condition and the marked-down value resulting from damage, shipment being sold without repair, is considered to be in the nature of an appraisal of damage and, accordingly, to be a proper practice and in conformity with other expressions regarding measure of damage in connection with property sold in a damaged condition.

In the event of refusal by consignee or owner of shipment not entirely worthless nor so materially damaged as to destroy its value, shipment shall be handled as provided by the bill of lading contract or applicable laws in a manner that will best conserve the interests of all concerned. On claims filed in connection with such refused shipments, carrier liability will be acknowledged only for such damage as appropriate investigation may develop is reasonably chargeable to carriers.[6]

The proper measure of damages is a controversial subject. It involves the determination of what yardstick should be used, after liability has been established, the retail or wholesale price, the market value at destination, or the replacement cost. Ordinarily the law does not contemplate the making of a profit out of a carrier's mis-

---

[6] Freight Claim Section, ATA, *Principles and Practices Covering Loss, Damage and Overcharge Claims* (Washington, D.C., 1953), p. 24.

fortune in losing or damaging goods. On the other hand, it cannot be definitely stated that a claimant should never include any profit in his claim. There are instances in which the profit has been earned. In such cases it appears proper for the claimant to include this earned profit in his claim, although it should be clear that the profit was actually earned and has been lost by the carrier's negligence in losing or damaging the goods.

INSPECTIONS AFTER DELIVERY

After a carrier has delivered a shipment to a consignee, the latter may notify the carrier of a shortage or damage which was not noticed at the time of delivery. Therefore, a notation regarding the shortage or damage was not placed on the freight bill. Such discrepancies often are not discovered for several days after delivery. Upon notification of the discrepancy the carrier should have an inspection made within 48 hours after receipt of the notice, having requested the consignee to discontinue unpacking until the inspector arrives. The carrier requires the consignee to submit the original container, wrapping, packing, and contents as delivered as evidence.

It is advisable for each terminal to maintain a record of requests which are received for inspections. This record should include the date and time of request; nature of request; name and address of the firm or person making the request; and the freight bill number or other reference on the shipment to be inspected. Each record should contain the time, date, and name of the inspector who is notified to make each inspection.

All of this information may be recorded on the reverse side of the delivery receipt copy of the freight bill. Before the inspection is made, the delivery receipt copy of the freight bill for the shipment should be examined to determine whether any exceptions were made at the time of delivery. If exceptions were made that are associated with loss or damage for which an inspection is being made, it is customary for a notation to this effect to be made on the inspection report.

Before the inspection is made, the inspector should secure the consignee's copy of the carrier's freight bill. It sometimes happens that exceptions are placed on the consignee's copy of the freight bill, although the carrier's delivery receipt does not contain the exceptions. If there are no authorized exceptions on the carrier's delivery receipt or the consignee's copy of the freight bill, the inspec-

INSPECTION REPORT OF LOSS OR DAMAGE DISCOVERED AFTER DELIVERY

TERMINAL _____ Date _____ 19 _____ Report Number _____

Shipper _____ Origin _____

Consignee _____ Destination _____

F/B No. _____ Prepaid ☐ Collect ☐ _____ Date Consignee requested inspection _____

Date of Billing _____ 19 ___   Date Delivered _____ 19 ___   Loss or Damage _____ Could loss or damage have been noticed at time of delivery? _____

Date Un-Packed _____ 19 ___   Date of Call _____ 19 ___   Were goods unpacked before the inspection was made? _____ Were containers and packing available? _____

What evidence was there of Pilferage before Delivery? _____

Was there sufficient space in Package to Contain Missing Goods? _____   What material Occupied the Remaining Space? _____

Did Comparison of Check with Invoice or Weighing Package, Verify loss _____   If Released Valuation, Show Weight of Articles Damaged or Short _____

Kind of Container _____ (Carton, Box, Crate, Etc.)   New or Old _____   Wired ☐ Corded ☐ Strapped ☐ Nailed ☐ Sealed ☐

Box Maker's Gross Weight Limit _____   Gross Weight of Loaded Carton _____   If Carton Were Flaps Glued _____   Were Seams or Edges Split? _____

How Were Goods Packed? _____

Do you Consider Adequately Packed or Protected? _____   What condition of container or contents indicated loss or damage occurred with carrier? _____

To prevent comparable damage in the future, how in your judgment should they have been packed or prepared for shipment _____

Did Shipment Have Prior Transportation? _____   If so, Is Merchandise Still Packed in Original Container? _____   Original Point of Shipment _____

No. of Articles	Describe fully nature & extent of loss or damage	Invoice Price
	(If necessary use other side of this form)	

Will there Be Salvage? _____   What Disposition will be made of the Salvage? _____

Consignee _____   Carrier _____

By _____   By _____
                                      Inspector

This Report is Merely a Statement of Facts and Not an Acknowledgement of Carrier's Liability. When presenting claims for loss and damage, attach the following documents:

1. This Inspection Report
2. Original Paid Freight Bill
3. Original Bill of Lading
4. Original Invoice or an exact certified copy showing all discounts
5. Your Bill showing nature and amount of claim
6. Shipper's and Consignee's Concealed Loss and Damage Forms.

Claim blanks and other necessary forms to properly present your claim may be obtained from carriers agent.

FIG. 13–7. Inspection report.

tion report should state "concealed damage" or "concealed loss." In examining the shipment, it is necessary to determine whether the containers and packing are sufficient. Most inspection reports require that if packing is inadequate a statement to this effect should be contained in the report. However, the inspector should show the consignee how damage could have been prevented if better or additional packing were employed. In this manner, the consignee can call the attention of the shipper to the inadequacy of packing so that future shipments can be properly packed.

The invoice should be checked against the freight bill or the bill of lading to determine if they agree. The invoice should also be checked carefully to determine the cost of the shipment. The freight bill, packages, and packing slip should be examined to ascertain where the shipment was packed. The inspection may indicate that the goods have had prior transportation, or that they may have been previously offered for sale.

An inspection report, Figure 13–7, is filled out on which all questions must be answered. The original copy is left with the consignee who will attach it to the claim if it is filed; the duplicate is forwarded to the headquarters claims department after examination by the terminal or branch manager and any notations as to disposition of salvage are made. The third copy is kept by the terminal and attached to the delivery receipt copy of the freight bill.

SALVAGE

As a result of loss or damage to goods, there is the problem of disposing of commodities at their salvage value. If the carrier is responsible for the damage and the damaged goods have no salvage value, the inspector is instructed to dispose of them so that they cannot be used as evidence upon which to file a claim on another shipment. The salvage, in such a case, would be dumped or destroyed immediately. If the carrier is responsible for the damage and the goods have some salvage value, an effort is made to get the consignee to retain them in order that he can get the best possible salvage value from them. Many consignees will not retain damaged goods, in which case the inspector may pick them up and return them to the terminal. Here, a salvage record form is made out, and the matter is handled in accordance with company procedure for such goods. If the inspector cannot take the salvaged goods back to the terminal, they should be labeled with carrier's stickers in order to be identifiable. If possible, they should be sealed.

Where there is doubt as to the carrier's responsibility for the damage, goods are usually not picked up regardless of whether or not they have any salvage value. The inspection report, in this case, should indicate the reasons for not picking up the damaged goods.

A special salvage record form is used for the pickup of the goods. It is important to maintain a continuing record of this type of goods because 30 per cent of the carrier's claim payments may be offset by salvage sales.

LOSS AND DAMAGE CLAIM REGISTER

The maintenance of a loss and damage claim register is recommended. Thus, when a claim is received it can be entered in the carrier's claim register or logbook, as it is sometimes termed, and a complete record made of the claim. In this manner, each claim is given a number and is logged. This expedites the prompt handling of claims which is essential both in maintaining customer goodwill and also in providing for orderly operation of a business. File cards are used in conjunction with this system.

REFUSED OR UNCLAIMED FREIGHT

When a carrier has refused freight on hand, the notice of such refusal should be sent at once. If the freight is perishable, the shipper should be notified by wire. Unclaimed freight should not be held longer than 15 days before giving notice that the shipment cannot be delivered. In forwarding the refused or unclaimed form notice, Figure 13–8, to the shipper and consignee, it is important that the shipper's name and street address be spelled correctly. Questions frequently arise as to whether the shipper received notice when the name is spelled incorrectly or is incomplete.

After the first notice, a follow-up should be made within a reasonable time. In rebilling a refused or unclaimed shipment, the proper storage charges are assessed. The requested disposition of refused or unclaimed freight should come from the shipper, and the consignee's requests for disposition are not acceptable.

RECOOPERING

The recoopering of packages received in damaged condition immediately upon discovery eliminates the probability of theft by extraction from packages and minimizes possible damages which might be incurred if the shipment was allowed to go forward without reconditioning the package. It sometimes happens that several slats in a crate will become broken in shipment or a carton will break open because of pressures upon it, which damage to the crate or carton may not have resulted in damage to the contents. At the time freight

IMPORTANT

NOTICE OF REFUSED OR ON HAND FREIGHT

DATE _____

TO: _____
      Name of Shipper

_____
      Address

_____
   City   *State*

Gentlemen:

Your shipment of _____ covered by our Bill No._____
                        Date

consigned to _____at _____

IS ON HAND at this terminal. Please advise disposition of this shipment at once.

                    (on hand)
The above described shipment is (refused) due to the following reasons:

_____

_____

Collect $ _____   PLEASE REPLY TO

Prepaid $_____   _____
                                              Carrier

C.O.D. $ _____   _____
                                              Address

_____
                    City   *State*

              N O T E

Storage starts _____

Rate_____ cents per cwt. each day first _____ days, _____ minimum.

Rate _____ cents cwt. each day thereafter,_____ minimum

Storage charges become effective____hours after first 7 a. m. after shipment is
      tendered for delivery.

Copies to:

FIG. 13-8. Notice of refused or on-hand freight.

is transferred from over-the-road units to a terminal, these breaks will often be discovered and the freight set aside so that the packaging can be repaired immediately before notifying the consignee that the freight is on hand.

Section 3 of the Bill of Lading Terms and Conditions provides that "except where such service is required as a result of carrier's negligence all property shall be subject to necessary cooperage, packing, and repacking at owner's cost." A motor carrier could perform a recoopering service when the container failure is due to defective or inadequate packing and add such expense to the freight bill, to be collected upon delivery. However, few motor carriers add this charge to the freight bill.

ARBITRATION AND APPEALS PROCEDURE FOR CLAIMS BETWEEN MOTOR CARRIERS

The National Freight Claim Council of ATA provides an arbitration and appeal procedure on claims. When carriers are unable to agree unanimously as to the apportionment of the amount of a claim which has arisen from the transportation of a shipment over the lines of two or more carriers, the bylaws of the Council provide for the use of an arbitration procedure.

An arbitration committee was originally established which consisted of the claims representatives of three disinterested motor carriers. The initial procedure also required that the file describing the elements of the dispute had to be considered by each of the members of the committee. After some experience with this procedure, it was revised to provide for initial arbitration by only one member of the arbitration committee. If any of the parties to a dispute are not satisfied with the decision of the arbitrator, he may file an appeal within 30 days of the ruling. This will then be considered by two additional members of the arbitration committee.

The procedure provides that claims may be submitted for adjudication as to apportionment between carriers and for no other purpose. Before the arbitration committee will consider the claim, the claim file must show satisfactory evidence that payment has been made to the claimant. The parties must also execute an "Agreement to Submit to Arbitration" form before a dispute is submitted for adjudication. When a claim is submitted for arbitration, the claim file is sent to the executive secretary of the Council with a written request for arbitration. A fee of $5.00 is charged for the arbitration of each claim which is handled by one member of the committee. If additional arbitration of the claim requires handling by the other two members, an additional fee of $10.00 is assessed, with the members of the arbitration committee apportioning the liability for the arbitration fee at the time the decision is rendered.

Any carrier participating in an arbitration or appeal proceeding which refuses or fails to carry out the award made by the decision within 60 days after effective date of the award shall be referred to the national committee for investigation. If no justification for the failure to carry out the award is found, the carrier is expelled from membership in the Council.

In some of the cases, the arbitrators have not been able to determine how or where the damage was incurred. Under these circumstances, they have generally ruled that the claim should be prorated among the carriers that handled the shipment. When the evidence shows that there was negligence among several carriers, the claim has usually been prorated among the carriers.

CLAIM PREVENTION

Recommended practices for loss and damage claim prevention are as follows:[7]

1. Each motor carrier should maintain statistics on loss and damage claim payments by causes and commodities on a form approved by the National Freight Claim Council.

2. As a means of identification and protection against misplacement, all over and astray freight should be tagged with an over tag completely filled out at destination, and should be covered with astray freight bill or over report.

3. (a) All over and astray freight not matched at destination must be carefully examined as to contents and marks and accurately weighed and consignee notified when possible. When freight is not delivered within ten days, notice of the overage must be given to the general office of the delivering agent and any others who may be at interest.

(b) The delivery to consignee of over or astray freight (including articles in excess of quantity billed) must be made only upon presentation of the original bill of lading, paid freight bill on which the shortage has been noted, original invoice, definite advice from shipper for forwarding of freight of similar character and quantity or other conclusive proof of ownership carrying with it information as to name of shipper and point of origin. MARKS ALONE ON PACKAGES WILL NOT OF THEMSELVES BE CONSIDERED PROOF OF OWNERSHIP.

(c) When such freight is subsequently delivered notice should be given to all those interested.

4. (a) Deliveries to fill shortages must be recorded on the station record by cross-reference on office copy of freight receipts as well as on OS&D record.

(b) If a shortage is located after claim has been recorded, agent must hold freight and immediately ask freight claim officer for instruction, quoting all file numbers.

(c) When the paid freight bill or bill of lading cannot be produced and delivery is effected upon invoice or other conclusive proof of owner-

---

[7] National Freight Claim Council, ATA, *Freight Claim Rule Book* (5th ed.; 1953), pp. 47–48.

ship, destination agent must secure from agent at point of origin an exact copy of the billing to enable him to complete the record and protect the interested carriers in establishing the correct delivery and collection of revenue.

5. Agents representing lines at common points should, unless otherwise instructed, hold meetings periodically for the purpose of checking reports submitted by carriers to see that over shipments are promptly matched in compliance with Section 3 above.

(a) Any carrier checking freight over with or without marks which it is unable to apply against an existing shortage should handle with consignor, consignee and/or the line or terminal from which received with view of filling shortage with some connecting carrier.

6. To insure proper supervision of the delivery of over and astray freight and the matching of over with short freight at destination, the astray freight billing on destination over reports should be assembled and cleared in the office of a designated supervising officer.

7. Any shortage notation on paid freight bill should be cancelled when shortage is subsequently received and delivered. If necessary, consignee should be called upon to immediately notify shipper of receipt of goods and request return of freight bill for cancellation of shortage notation.

8. At unloading points OS&D reports should be issued at least in triplicate, the original to be sent to Freight Claim Agent of issuing line, a duplicate to the Agent at loading point, and a copy retained as permanent record by issuing Agent.

9. When a loss or damage is noted in transfer or upon delivery which could be attributed to improper packing or the use of inadequate container the Freight Claim Agent should be given the full facts for his handling in an appropriate manner with the shipper in the interest of claim prevention.

10. Loss and damage reports should be analyzed carefully to develop record of any firms which are receiving an unusual number of shipments short or in bad order that the cause producing such condition may be investigated to determine the corrective measures necessary to reduce the loss or damage hazard.

11. Motor carriers should provide a prevention organization which would afford means whereby a systematic study of causes contributing to freight loss and damage might be made and means provided to eliminate those of an avoidable nature, and to exchange helpful information and ideas through the medium of other carriers.

(a) Carriers at their larger terminals should establish organizations to meet periodically and discuss the handling of business at such terminals with view of preventing claims, and making recommendations to the proper supervising officer. Conclusions of meetings of terminal organizations should be published for distribution to interested employees.

12. When a shipment is refused or unclaimed at destination the terminal carrier should send notice requesting disposition direct to consignor with copy to consignee and initial carrier.

13. An Order-Notify shipment must not be delivered to consignee without surrender of the original order bill of lading properly endorsed, except that in the event of loss of the original order bill of lading or on account of its immediate inaccessibility, the destination agent may accept in lieu of this original document a cash deposit or certified check for 125% of invoice value of the shipment.

14. It will not be permissible for a carrier to allow claim correspondence to pass into possession of consignors, consignees, or claimants.

15. Each carrier should provide itself with reliable reference books of the law of loss and damage claims for guidance in the proper adjustment of claims with claimants.

There are many guides for determining the efficiency of a freight claim department. One of the most frequently used is that of the percentage of claims received and settled within a specified period of time. If the carrier settles within 30 days 70 per cent of the claims received, its rating is considered to be excellent. If over 50 per cent is settled, the carrier's rating is considered to be good. Less than 50 per cent is considered to be poor; while lower than 40 per cent is considered to be inexcusable.

There are many factors which affect the claim ratio, such as amount of LTL traffic handled, volume of traffic, amount of interchange, types of commodities handled, number of terminal handlings, freight handling by employees, condition of equipment used, as well as others. The freight claim ratio is expressed as a percentage of revenue. It includes cargo insurance plus cargo loss and damage claims. It is the ratio of net claim payments to gross revenue.

Because of the foregoing factors, it is difficult to compare one carrier's ratio to another's. The average ratio for Class I carriers is above 1 per cent, but it is believed that most carriers can reduce their ratios to 1 per cent or less. Some motor carriers with effective claim prevention programs have reduced their ratio to 0.50 per cent and lower. One Class I carrier has 0.16 ratio.

The following freight claim ratios are based upon a sampling of carriers and are indicative of prevailing conditions in the industry. There has been improvement in the postwar period but much remains to be accomplished.

CLASS I COMMON CARRIERS OF GENERAL FREIGHT
Cargo Insurance Plus Cargo Loss and Damage Claims

	PERCENTAGE OF REVENUE								
	1944	1945	1946	1947	1948	1949	1950	1951	1952
United States..........	2.48	2.46	2.27	2.31	2.19	1.99	1.77	1.85	1.78

It is essential that motor carriers strive for as nearly perfect a shipping record as possible, not only because of the savings that accrue to the carriers from such a record but because of the benefits to the shippers as well. After all, the speediest and most equitable settlement of a claim is at best a poor substitute for prompt delivery of freight in first-class condition. There is an attitude altogether too prevalent among motor-carrier employees that a certain amount of loss and damage is inevitable in the handling of freight. When the loss and damage ratio for a carrier increases, a campaign is usually undertaken to cut down on these claims, but this is a temporary expedient. What is needed is not a sporadic program but a continuous one, in order to minimize loss and damage to freight through the cooperation of everyone concerned.

The maintenance of adequate statistics can be helpful in determining the efficiency of a claims department. This may be done on a commodity basis, shipper basis, or other basis. These statistics should be analyzed and acted upon. The causes of loss and damage claims have been divided by the National Freight Claim Council into the following categories: shortages; theft; improper handling, loading, or stowing; concealed damage; delay; defective equipment; and wreck or fire. The most important single cause, as Table 13-1 indi-

TABLE 13-1

BREAKDOWN BY CAUSES FOR YEARS INDICATED

Causes	1948%	1949%	1950%	1951%	1952%	1953%
A. Shortage	30.84	27.46	25.25	29.68	27.73	30.07
B. Thefts	4.64	3.95	3.10	3.15	5.11	3.97
C. Handling	31.69	35.95	35.15	35.70	35.12	32.81
D. Concealed	15.07	20.99	21.07	17.56	17.38	18.00
E. Delay	0.78	0.81	1.20	0.95	1.22	0.85
F. Equipment	3.10	3.42	3.82	4.16	3.78	4.89
G. Wreck, fire	13.88	7.42	10.41	8.80	9.66	9.41
Total	100.00	100.00	100.00	100.00	100.00	100.00

Source: National Freight Claim Council, ATA.

cates, is that of improper handling, loading, or stowing. This is followed closely by shortages with the third most important cause being concealed damage. These three causes constitute 80 per cent of the total, which gives some indication as to the areas in which claim prevention should be emphasized. The theft figure includes thefts of all kinds. Thefts and petty pilferage of small packages actually account for more of the total than does hijacking.

These statistics can be used by motor carriers to compare their claim program with the industry figures. A large part of these causes of claims are matters over which carriers could exercise a greater degree of control. For example, in bad weather the suction which is created at the rear of a semitrailer as it moves on the highway causes rain and snow to get through even the smallest cracks around the doors and damage the cargo. This often leads to extensive water damage. A most effective means of preventing this is the use of cloth tape which seals all the cracks around trailer doors.

There are many independent testing laboratories and container manufacturer laboratories in which tests are constantly being conducted to develop additional information on containers and improve transit of goods. Carriers, for a nominal fee, can have tests conducted on containers. In some instances, such tests are conducted on containers when the shipper has packed his shipment in accordance with standard shipping practices but the carrier's experience has shown the packing to be inadequate. The shipper is usually more willing to accept the report of an independent testing laboratory rather than the carrier's opinion in this matter.

USE OF IMPACT MACHINES

There are a few motor carriers which have made use of an impact recorder which records on a graph the jolts and shocks to which containers are subject. The use of this device has been helpful in giving the claims department more positive information on where the containers sustain the most shock. There are several different makes of these machines which are small enough to be put in a shoebox.

This machine can be used in claim prevention by placing it in a box and dropping it varying distances, such as 6, 12, or 18 inches. Since the device is exposed, the employees who handle the freight can see the immediate results. Some of the facts that have been developed through the use of the impact recorder by carriers are that the rear section of a semitrailer sustains many more shocks; that there is a definite shock resulting from hooking the tractor and semitrailer; except for accidents, the shocks that are transmitted by line-haul vehicles in transit are not as great as those sustained in the handling of cargo to and from trailers; and spring suspensions on tractors and semitrailers are important in absorption of road shocks.[8]

A lightly loaded vehicle moving at 10 miles an hour when crossing a railroad grade crossing is estimated to transmit a shock to the

[8] *Transport Topics,* March 30, 1953.

lading which is as great as that encountered in shifting boxcars at 15 miles per hour.

TRUCK ALARMS

Since there are numerous cargos of high-value freight, such as textiles, clothing, furs, tobacco, and drugs, which are vulnerable to theft and hijacking, particularly in metropolitan areas, alarm systems have been devised to counteract this danger. There are organizations which install a police-type siren alarm which can be heard for miles and will sound for hours if any unauthorized person attempts to enter, operate, move, or tamper with the protectively wired truck or trailer. These systems of protection have been perfected to the point where a trailer can be protected by the installation of a system that will cause a siren to blow if the trailer is moved in any way by anyone except the authorized operator. This means that the system must not be too sensitive, or it would be set off by street vibration; at the same time, it must be sensitive enough to respond immediately if the trailer is towed away.

This service is not sold to the motor carrier but is leased to it at a set amount for each unit per year. The manufacturer then maintains the equipment. The rental charge for the first year is higher because of the installation charge.

The alarm system has proved to be one of the most effective ways of minimizing pilferage yet devised. Its success is reflected in the lower insurance premiums a carrier secures by having his equipment thus protected, or the carrier may be able to obtain a higher policy limit in the insurance it is carrying as a result of the use of an alarm system.

NATIONAL CLASSIFICATION RULES

There are a number of National Motor Freight Classification rules which, if followed, would constitute a means of claim prevention. Rule 5, Section 1, Paragraph (a), for example, provides in part that "containers must be such as to afford reasonable and proper protection of contents." Paragraph (b) of the same section of this rule provides that "the carrier will refuse to handle any article not in such condition or so prepared for shipment as to render transportation thereof reasonably safe and practicable." The latter provision constitutes a carrier's tariff authority for refusing shipments which because of the nature of their packing would result in claims.

Damage may occur to merchandise in containers which are well engineered due to improperly designed interior packing, or because of the design or construction of the article itself. Rule 5, Section 2, of the National Motor Freight Classification provides that "glassware, articles in glass, or earthenware or fragile articles will be accepted in fiber boxes only under the following conditions:" (which are then listed). The terms of this rule are mandatory upon the carrier to refuse such shipments which are not packaged as required by the rule. If the carrier inadvertently accepts shipments that are not packaged as required by Sections 2 and 3 of Rule 5, it may penalize the shipment by increasing the charges 20 per cent on LTL and any quantity shipments, and 10 per cent on truckload shipments as provided in Section 6 of Rule 5.

Concealed damage, which is a vexing claim problem, could undoubtedly be reduced through greater use by the carrier of one of the classification rules. Rule 2, Section 2, provides that "when carrier's agent believes it necessary that the contents of packages be inspected, he will make or cause such inspection to be made or require other sufficient evidence to determine actual character of the property." A check could be made prior to the acceptance of the merchandise under the provisions of this rule, particularly of those shipments which involve frequent claims.

Rule 33 governing experimental or test shipments makes it possible for manufacturers to test packages which could not be accepted under the existing packaging requirements made in the governing classification.

Rule 3 provides for the nonacceptance of certain specified articles and articles of extraordinary value. The term "extraordinary value" has not been defined by the Commission or the courts. Some carriers have held that the term means a value beyond the normal liability of the carrier. Other carriers have felt that the term is comparative, i.e., an article with an ordinary value of $2.00 per pound when valued at $5.00 per pound would be considered to be of extraordinary value. There are articles under Rule 3 which a carrier should not accept but does.

The reason that there is a lack of adherence to any of these classification rules which could reduce claims is the factor of competition between carriers.

WEIGHING AND INSPECTION BUREAUS

In 1954 the Motor Carrier Weighing and Inspection Bureaus, of which there were about thirteen, formed a nonprofit national organization called the "National Association of Motor Carrier Weighing and Inspection Bureaus." The objectives of this association are: (1) to collect and disseminate information which will be helpful to the Bureaus and the industry generally; (2) to promote co-operation between motor carriers and the shipping public; (3) to publicize the necessity for the work which these Bureaus perform; (4) to encourage educational programs concerning the functions of these Bureaus by the membership and the National Traffic Committee; and (5) to encourage the participation of representatives from the National Classification Board and the National Traffic Committee at each national meeting of the Motor Carrier Weighing and Inspection Bureaus. These bureaus are usually a part of a rate bureau.

Included in an average W & I Bureau's scope of activities are such matters as: determining proper descriptions to be used on bills of lading; checking weights shown by shippers on bills of lading; determining causes of damage; inspecting damaged shipments; recommending improved packing and shipping methods; proposing changes in descriptions for packing in classification and tariffs; checking freight on carrier platform for proper description; testing carrier scales; recommending improved methods of freight handling, loading, and stowing for claim prevention; and assisting in disposing of over, short, and damaged freight.

CLAIMS CORRESPONDENCE

All correspondence in regard to claims from the initial letter until final disposition of the claim should be promptly handled. After an examination of all data regarding a claim, the carrier may decline payment or an adjustment may be made. Whichever course is dictated by the facts developed, all letters should be courteous and factual. Claim declination letters, in particular, should be carefully written. A guide to be followed should be that a letter should not be written that the writer himself would not want to receive. Claim declination letters frequently alienate shippers because of their curtness and lack of explanation.

When claims are paid, the carrier has an opportunity to secure additional goodwill for his company which is often missed. The majority of claim payments are made by check. Too many of these payments are transmitted with a mimeographed letter enclosed which states: "Enclosed is our check No. .... in the amount of .... This is in payment of your claim No. ...., our No. ...."

The payment of a claim is the opportunity to include a selling message. Rather than merely mailing a check in the amount of the claim, the transaction can be personalized by having a motor-carrier salesman deliver the check. If this is not possible, a friendly transmittal letter in which the claimant is informed that the carrier regrets the inconvenience occasioned by the loss and damage and is endeavoring to improve its service by conducting an extensive claim prevention program will leave the claimant with a better regard for the carrier.

QUESTIONS AND PROBLEMS

1. What are the types of cargo claims? What documents must support cargo claims? Why?
2. List the causes of cargo loss and damage claims.
3. What procedure may be followed in delivering damaged freight? What is refused freight?
4. After examining the loss and damage claim ratio for motor carriers, formulate a short- and a long-range program which you feel will reduce that ratio, and explain in detail how you would accomplish it.
5. What tangible benefit could you expect as a motor-carrier operator through the use of an alarm system?
6. What are some of the typical carrier procedures for making delivery of over freight without benefit of the revenue waybill?
7. May motor carriers be required to pay reparations? What is a suggested procedure for handling overcharge claims involving past unlawful motor rates?
8. What is the National Freight Claim Council? Should membership be compulsory?
9. How would you determine the efficiency with which claims are handled by the freight claim department?
10. What are some of the methods of claim prevention which have been successful?
11. In what way do some of the National Motor Freight Classification rules provide a means of claim prevention?
12. How do the activities of motor-carrier weighing and inspection bureaus assist in claims work?

14. INSURANCE

▲▲

INSURANCE plays a vital role in motor-carrier operations. Some of the types of insurance which are used by motor carriers are comparable to those applicable to other business firms, such as insurance on terminals, office equipment, and the like. There has been, however, the development of different types of insurance especially adapted to motor-carrier operations, together with elaborate programs designed to provide comprehensive coverage of all phases of carrier operations.

Various states established minimum insurance requirements before there were any federal requirements as one of the conditions for granting authority to operate intrastate, inasmuch as some of the motor carriers had not shown adequate financial responsibility. Even since the passage of the federal requirements, most state laws still provide for minimum insurance requirements for intrastate operation although in 1954 the Commission requirements were higher than those in thirty-six states on public liability and exceeded the property damage minima in twenty-seven states.

Part II of the Interstate Commerce Act requires that the Interstate Commerce Commission shall prescribe reasonable rules and regulations applicable to brokers and carriers in order to afford protection to travelers and shippers who utilize motor-carrier transportation. As a result of this provision of the act, the Interstate Commerce Commission conducted an investigation and established rules and regulations (*Ex parte No. MC–5*) in 1936, and added further provisions in 1951 and 1955, specifying insurance and surety bond requirements, as well as the requirements for a self-insurer.

Thus, before a certificate or permit may be issued to any person, evidence of security for the protection of the public in the form of insurance, surety bonds, or qualifications as a self-insurer must be on file with the Commission as follows:

1. Cargo liability: Not less than $1,000 on any one motor vehicle for common carriers of property; not less than $2,000 for loss or damage at any one time and place. However, certain low-value commodities, such as coal, lumber, and commercial fertilizer, do not require cargo liability security. Contract carriers of property are not required to file evidence of cargo liability security.
2. Automobile bodily injury or public liability: Not less than $25,000 for injury or death of one person. For all injuries or deaths in any one accident not less than $100,000.
3. Damage to the property of others (excluding cargo): Each accident $10,000.

These minimum requirements are low in the opinion of most carriers which secure coverage of these items in larger amounts than those required by the Commission.

Certain motor carriers (those under Sections 202 (c) and 203 (b)) are exempt from economic regulation under Part II of the Interstate Commerce Act. Therefore, carriers of agricultural commodities are exempt from the requirements of *Ex parte MC–5* regarding security for the protection of the public. The Commission has also exempted from the provisions of *Ex parte MC–5* those common or contract motor carriers which have leased their entire operating rights to others.

In arranging for insurance, carriers request their insurance agents to provide them with the desired amounts of insurance and not less than the minimum insurance specified by the Commission. Carriers must arrange to have evidence of such insurance filed with the Commission by the insurance company in the prescribed form. Most insurance companies are familiar with the Commission's requirements with respect to the procedure to be followed. There are currently about 240 insurance companies listed in Commission files. However, it is the carrier's responsibility to see that the necessary filing is made with the Commission. The insurance must be written by an insurance company or companies legally authorized to transact business in every state in or through which a carrier operates. A carrier may be prosecuted or its certificate or permit may be revoked if the security for the protection of the public is not kept in effect at all times.

Insurance coverage, as filed with the Commission, can be canceled only upon 30 days' notice in writing by a party properly authorized to cancel the insurance.

Surety bonds are filed with the Interstate Commerce Commission and are of two types. There are a few large transportation companies for which the parent corporation acts as a surety. Therefore, if there are claims against the subsidiaries which they are unable to pay, the surety bond furnished by the parent corporation is used to settle the claims. However, most of the surety bonds which are filed

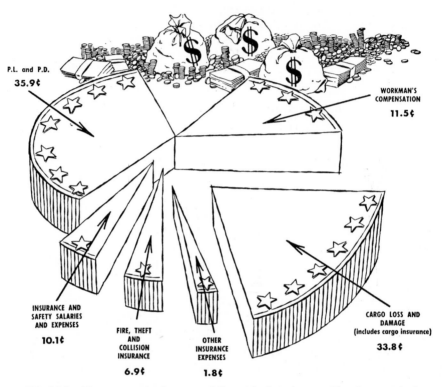

P.L. and P.D.
35.9¢

WORKMAN'S COMPENSATION
11.5¢

INSURANCE AND SAFETY SALARIES AND EXPENSES
10.1¢

FIRE, THEFT AND COLLISION INSURANCE
6.9¢

OTHER INSURANCE EXPENSES
1.8¢

CARGO LOSS AND DAMAGE
(includes cargo insurance)
33.8 ¢

FIG. 14–1. The motor-carrier insurance dollar and where it goes—Class I motor carriers of property in 1952.

Source: Based on available statistics from official reports of Class I motor carriers to the Interstate Commerce Commission. American Trucking Associations, Inc., *Trends* (Washington, D.C., 1954), p. 28.

with the Commission are filed by surety companies, and such a company must be one contained on a list approved by the United States Treasury Department under the laws of the United States and the applicable rules and regulations governing bonding companies.[1]

Out of every dollar of motor-carrier gross revenue over 5 cents is spent in insurance premiums, claims, and other expenditures relative to insurance. The distribution of the motor-carrier insurance dollar, based on the experience of Class I common carriers in 1952, is shown in Figure 14–1. Over one third of each insurance dollar is

---

[1] This list is entitled "Companies Holding Certificates of Authority from the Secretary of the Treasury under the Act of Congress Approved July 30, 1947 (6 USC Sections 6–13) as Acceptable Sureties on Federal Bonds (a)."

spent for public liability and property damage coverage. Cargo loss and damage, including cargo insurance, also accounts for more than one third. The next most important insurance cost is Workman's Compensation.

TYPES OF INSURANCE COMPANIES

There are several different types of insurance which are available from insurance companies which are organized as *stock companies* or *mutual companies.* Some companies specialize in but one type of insurance, such as public liability and property damage, whereas others may handle a more complete line, such as cargo liability and Workman's Compensation. Another source of insurance is self-insurance, which is discussed later.

The stock company in most instances is a corporation that functions with the advantages of a corporation insofar as the buyer is concerned. It limits the carrier's liability to the actual premium charged for the coverage at the time the carrier originally purchased it. It holds no contingencies for any additional expense, nor is the carrier liable in any way in case of any deficit or in case the stock company becomes defunct.

Another type is the mutual insurance company. The policyholders who have mutual insurance own the company. There are assessable and nonassessable types of mutual companies. The policyholders are given a dividend providing the company makes money. A form of the mutual insurance company is the co-operative exchange owned by the members. Insurance is written on a cost basis, plus a small contribution to surplus to insure growth. Such exchanges are composed of companies which specialize in writing certain lines of insurance which have banded together to offer policyholders a full coverage of all lines as well as spreading the risk among the different companies.

Most insurance is available from insurance companies which are engaged in that business, but there are some instances when motor carriers have formed their own insurance company. Probably the best known of these is the Truck Insurance Exchange which was founded in 1935 in Los Angeles by the same group that had, earlier, organized the Farmers Insurance Exchange. At that time there were very few casualty companies in the United States which were interested in covering the hazards of the rapidly growing motor-carrier industry. This limited insurance market was particularly acute in the eleven western states. As a result, a group of prominent western truck operators approached the Farmers Insurance Exchange organization with the request that they organize a company along the same lines as Farmers, which was done. The Truck Insurance Exchange had premiums of over $20 million in 1953. Additional insurance companies have been added from time to time so that many types of insurance are available from this group.[2]

The Commission requires that each insurance company must possess minimum financial resources. The minimum will be determined on the basis of the values of assets and liabilities as shown in its financial statements filed with and approved by the insurance department of the home state of such company, except in instances where, in the judgment of the Commission, additional evidence with respect to such values is considered necessary.

Motor carriers usually secure insurance from agents of insurance companies or from an insurance broker. The latter acts as an insurance buyer for the motor carrier and seeks to secure the best coverage for the carrier consistent with cost. Some state laws define the insurance broker as an insurance buyer. Larger motor carriers tend to deal through a broker or directly with an insurance company.

Some carriers feel that it is desirable to consolidate all coverage with one insurance company if possible, since good experience on one coverage will compensate for a loss on another because the insurance company will look at the over-all picture. Further, adjustment expense, which ordinarily claims about 10 per cent of the premium dollar, may also be reduced by adopting such a plan because many highway accidents involve more than one coverage. It is not infrequent to involve four separate coverages in one loss; that is, Workman's Compensation, when the driver is injured; collision or fire, when equipment is destroyed; cargo, where the load is lost; and bodily injury and property damage liability, when third parties are injured or damaged.

PROCEDURE OF INSURING COMPANIES

There are a number of companies that specialize in the writing of insurance for fleet coverage and provide a comprehensive service.

---

[2] In 1950 a group of operators in the Southwest decided that it would be to their interest to form a stock insurance company (Transport Insurance Co. of Dallas, Texas) that would specialize in serving the needs of the motor transportation industry. The underwriting is restricted to physical damage, liability, cargo liability, and Workman's Compensation exposures on motor-carrier risks for large carriers. During its first 3 years this company wrote premiums in excess of $6 million.

Usually, before such companies will write any insurance, they will have their safety engineers investigate the motor carrier requesting insurance coverage. Safety engineers conducting such investigations check a number of items that have effect upon the safety record of a motor carrier: (a) A check is made of the condition of the carrier's equipment, its age, and other relevant information which would have any influence upon accidents. (b) A thorough investigation is made of the so-called "inside" personnel—that is, the office employees, the dispatcher, and other nondriver personnel—to ascertain attitudes that may have influence on safety records. (c) The territory the carrier is authorized to serve and the routes it is permitted to use are examined because substantial differences are found in operating conditions, both in terms of traffic and terrain, which affect safety. (d) The commodities the carrier is authorized to haul are also examined, since some commodities by their nature are subject to a higher percentage of loss and damage than others; the relative proportions of vulnerable commodities carried is taken into consideration in the establishment of an insurance program. (e) An investigation is made of the records of the owner-operators of equipment for the company, as well as the records of company drivers, to secure the complete picture as to the qualifications of the drivers. In addition, safety engineers will investigate any other factor which they feel is pertinent to the formulation of their reports to the insurance company and the recommendations they will make concerning the feasibility of insuring the risks of the particular carrier.

An insurance company will continue to make available to its policyholders safety engineer services including road patrol reports and recommendations regarding driver selection, as well as many other safety matters.

BODILY INJURY AND PROPERTY DAMAGE INSURANCE

The property damage policy covers loss and expenses arising from claims upon the carrier for damages due to damage to or destruction of property belonging to others by an accident because of ownership or use of the vehicle described in the policy. Liability insurance covers loss arising from claims upon the assured carrier for damages due to bodily injuries or accidental death because of ownership or use of the motor vehicle described in the policy, with minor exceptions. Wise business policy would recommend that amounts substantially greater than the minimum Interstate Commerce Commission requirements of liability and property damage be carried. Many Class I carriers carry at least $100,000 per person and at least $300,-000 per catastrophe, because there have been so many cases which have been carried before juries in which the grants have been as much as $75,000 for an injury.

It is difficult to establish definite limits for general recommendation for bodily injury and property damage insurance, but above a certain point an increase in limits costs comparatively little and the carrier should maintain adequate protection. For example, on bodily injury insurance, using $5,000/$10,000 as a base, a 45 per cent additional premium is required to establish $25,000/$50,000 limits; only an additional 11 per cent to establish $50,000/$100,000 limits; an additional 8 per cent to establish $100,000/$200,000 limits; and an additional 4 per cent to establish $100,000/$300,000 limits. As for property damage, using $5,000 as a base, a 30 per cent additional premium is required to establish a $25,000 limit, and only an additional 7 per cent to establish a $50,000 limit. These rates are stock company rates and apply to average-sized carriers.

A carrier should not be pennywise and pound foolish in establishing adequate bodily injury and property damage coverage.

For intercity operations, bodily injury and property damage insurance is rated on the basis of broad zones, country-wide, there being four zones in all. Zone 1 carries the highest rates and applies to the largest cities. The rates are graded downward, so that those for Zone 4 are the lowest. The applicable rule in the *Automobile Casualty Manual* is so constituted that whenever an intercity trucking risk is rated, Zone 4 is always utilized in developing the premium by averaging the highest-rated zone and the lowest-rated zone into or through which operations are conducted.

Bodily injury and property damage insurance may be purchased on a straight-rate or guaranteed-cost basis. It may also be purchased on a deductible basis, with some companies recommending use of a $100–$500 deductible on property damage only and no deductible on bodily injury due to the fact that personal injury claims are more difficult to settle.

Contracts for bodily injury and property damage are often written on what is termed a "retrospective contract." Retrospective rating is a form of rating whereby the premium is finally determined after the contract has expired by totaling the incurred losses and applying the conversion or cost factors for adjustment of claims, taxes, and a factor for service.

This contract is written by agreeing to a given deposit premium termed a "standard or basic premium" estimated in keeping with the past year's experience. The motor carrier and the insurance company agree, for example, to a 2 per cent rate on gross income ($2.00 per $100 gross) for deposit. The insurance company will further agree to accept a fixed percentage of that deposit for service—a general average being approximately 20 per cent, or the cost of services being predetermined at $0.40. The balance, of $1.60, is reserved for losses which are paid from this reserve. A preagreed adjustment expense, generally ranging from 12 per cent to 20 per cent of the losses, is added to the losses for adjustment services.

This type of contract may be purchased with a minimum premium; generally, the lower the minimum, the higher the maximum. The maximum premium guarantees that the costs will not exceed that certain figure. These contracts are written for limits of $10,000, or a prearranged figure in that range. A separate excess policy is provided for which the motor carrier pays a standard fixed rate.

The primary contract or the retrospective portion of the contract is basically a service contract. The insurance company agrees to take care of the losses and to service the risk. At the end of the accounting year the premium charged equals the losses plus the service charge. In effect, the costs are geared directly to the insured losses. The primary consideration in the selection of such a contract is the ability of the motor carrier to comply with the possible penalty charges between the standard paid in deposit and the maximum premium provided under the policy.[3]

Retrospective contracts are a desirable form of rating for the following types of risks:[4]

1. Risks which are better than the average in their classification but which are not large enough to be entirely self-rated and thus which do not get full credit for their good experience under the experience plan.
2. Risks which may have operated over a period of years under an experience rating credit and which due to a change of ownership must revert to manual rates.
3. Risks which have been self-insured or which are contemplating self-insurance. Retrospective rating permits them to secure the benefits of self-insurance to a large degree but still maintain the advantages of being covered by an insurance carrier.

[3] Insurance Committee of the American Trucking Associations, Inc.

[4] Dwight M. McCracken, Liberty Mutual Insurance Co., in a paper "Retrospective Insurance" presented before ATA National Committee on Accounting, May 19, 1954.

4. Risks which are relatively large and which want their insurance premium for compensation and liability lines handled as a single expense and which feel that the available experience rating plan does not give them sufficient recognition of their good experience, particularly on the general liability and automobile liability lines.

The retrospective method has been recommended particularly for risks which have instituted more effective loss-prevention programs and wish to secure immediate benefit from reduced losses which are expected to result from such a program. It is not considered feasible if the insurance premium is less than $25,000 per year, although there is a trend toward 3-year plans in order to level off the insurance costs from year to year and to make retrospective contracts available to risks which would be too small on an annual basis to lend themselves to retrospective rating.

CARGO INSURANCE

Interstate common carriers carry cargo insurance to compensate shippers or consignees for loss of or damage to property belonging to shippers or consignees. Cargo insurance is inland marine insurance, inasmuch as it is a carry-over of ocean marine insurance to inland transportation. There are two types of cargo insurance contracts. The most common one is a "named peril" policy which provides insurance against named perils of fire, collision or upset, wind or cyclone, floods, and others. This type of insurance covers the causes that result in the majority of claims but leaves the possibility of a claim for some cause not listed as a named peril. Even with the perils named the motor carrier should know just what protection it has. For example, the phrase "collision of the vehicle" is different from "collision of the load."[5]

The other type of cargo coverage is termed a "bill of lading" policy. This provides much broader coverage in that the insurance company guarantees to pay any cargo claim for which the motor carrier is liable for any cause whatsoever. This form should be written on a deductible basis.

Cargo insurance may be bought on a straight-rate basis or on a retrospective-rating plan, but it is usually bought on a straight-rate basis with a deductible in amounts up to the ability of the truck

---

[5] R. O. Stoaks, R. O. Stoaks and Co., Chicago, "Insurance in Motor Freight Transportation," a presentation at Northwestern University School of Commerce, November 28, 1950.

operator to meet claim payments. A $500-deductible provision is quite common, although deductible provisions may be as much as $2,000. However, the premiums on such policies are not as low as might be expected, since the Interstate Commerce Commission requires that the insurance company has the potential responsibility for all loss, including the deductible amount, in the event the motor carrier fails to pay. There is some cargo insurance which is written on a $50-deductible basis, but it is not widely used because of the higher rate.

There is wide variation in the amount of cargo insurance carried, with the range being from $5,000 to $100,000 or more. Generally, not more than $100,000 per vehicle for cargo insurance will be taken by any one insurance company, so that if a special cargo which has a valuation exceeding this figure is to be moved, additional cargo insurance may be secured from other companies. Motor carriers are sometimes called upon to carry cargo valued at more than $100,000. During World War II, a particular motor carrier placed in one semitrailer a shipment that was consigned to a government installation. After the load had been dispatched, one of the employees, who had been in service for a period of time, recognized from the description on the bill of lading that this shipment was radar equipment of unusually high value, worth more than $500,000. He immediately notified his superiors; they were successful in halting the shipment on the outskirts of the city, where it was placed under guard. Four additional truck tractor-semitrailer units were dispatched and the load equally divided among the five units, the risk of loss thereby being spread over a number of vehicles and thus covered by insurance. Needless to say, these units proceeded to their destination with escort. Recently there have been single shipments moved which were valued at as much as $3 million.

WORKMAN'S COMPENSATION

Workman's Compensation coverage is required in all states except one. It is written to comply with the compensation statutes of the states where the motor carrier operates. In most states these rates are established by a rating bureau and are subject to modification based on the past 3–5 years' experience. Coverage may be purchased at bureau published rates without modification or may be purchased in a policy subject to retrospective rating, whereby the published rate is paid and the final premium is not determined until after the policy has expired and the losses have been determined. The premium is then adjusted to the amount of losses incurred for the year.

ADDITIONAL COVERAGES

Fire, theft, and collision insurance is usually referred to as physical damage insurance and is used to cover equipment. The coverage should be adequate to enable the carrier to replace lost equipment. It should also be adequate to cover the concentration of vehicles.

Bodily injury and property damage claims arise from operation of motor vehicles. However, a *comprehensive general liability* policy is needed which will cover all legal liability for claims brought as a result of personal injury or property damage arising out of other causes. Comprehensive general liability covers all contingencies, known and unknown, whereas under a plain liability policy only the known hazards are covered.

Fire insurance policies may be secured in standard form to cover terminals and other real estate. An appraisal of all properties should be made for this coverage. Fire insurance is frequently sold with a coinsurance clause which is an agreement on the part of the motor carrier to carry insurance up to a percentage of the valuation of property insured. The failure to do so makes the motor carrier a coinsurer.

Burglary and theft insurance may be secured. Whether or not a theft of company-owned property or cash in its possession is likely to occur in sufficient amount as to cause any impairment of working capital is a factor to be considered.

Fidelity bonds may also be taken out. The cargo policy should be examined to determine whether or not infidelity of employees is excluded. If it is, and valuable merchandise is transported, it is important that drivers be included in the fidelity bond.

Another type of insurance is what is referred to in the insurance field as *"bobtail"* insurance. Since there are many truck tractors which are owned by individual drivers, or owner-operators, provisions are made for coverage under the carrier policy when the unit is operated in commercial service for the carrier. The "bobtail" insurance provides coverage for the truck tractor after it leaves the carrier's docks and for all nonrevenue driving until it returns to the docks. This covers such driving as going to the owner-operator's home and any other driving which is not for revenue.

COST OF INSURANCE

The payment for insurance may be one of several different types. The *gross-receipts plan* has been widely used by many insurance companies. In the early days of trucking insurance, the carrier might have had to pay the premium on a policy for an entire year, although equipment might be idle for a considerable period of time, unless the carrier wanted to cancel the insurance. Under the gross receipts basis, the insurance premium is based on gross receipts, so that if a trucker's equipment is idle for 10 weeks, there is no insurance premium payable for that period of time. However, there is a minimum premium on policies written on a gross receipts basis. This is usually 20 per cent of the estimated annual policy premium. The premiums paid by carriers for their insurance vary considerably. As a result of the investigations of safety engineers, there is an established "fence" rate, which is predicated upon their findings. After the first year's operation of the assured, it may be that the safety record will be above or below the predictions of the safety engineers; the insurance rate will then be changed accordingly. On the gross-receipts basis, a common rate is 4 per cent, although some carriers pay as low as 1 per cent and others pay above 6 per cent.

Another basis is the *specified-car basis* in which an individual premium is charged for each truck or semitrailer which is insured. The *retrospective-rating plan* explained earlier constitutes a third basis.

SELF-INSURANCE

As a means of effecting savings in their insurance programs, self-insurance plans have long been considered by motor carriers. The type of insurance which involves the most claims against the carriers is cargo insurance. As pointed out in the discussion of this type of insurance, most carriers are insured for the property they carry under some sort of a deductible plan. Under coverage such as this, it has been found that some motor carriers have been expending large sums of money for the settlement of small claims for which they are liable under a deductible arrangement, as well as paying large sums of money for the insurance they must carry for their protection. Insurance programs comprehensive enough to insure that a carrier is not paying the majority of claims itself represent such an expenditure that most carriers do not have such coverage. Many motor carriers believe that the answer to this problem is a program of self-insurance.

The Interstate Commerce Act, under Section 215, permits a motor carrier to qualify as a self-insurer. In order to qualify, however, the motor carrier must establish to the satisfaction of the Commission its ability to pay final judgment recovered against it for bodily injuries to or death of any person resulting from the negligent operation, maintenance, or use of motor vehicles in transportation service subject to Part II of the act; and for loss of or damage to property of others, which includes cargo, coming into the possession of the motor carrier. It must be able, in the judgment of the Commission, to do this without affecting the stability or permanence of its business as a motor carrier in interstate or foreign commerce. The Interstate Commerce Commission for a number of years required that motor carriers which wanted to self-insure must be qualified to self-insure completely. While many motor carriers were qualified and desired to self-insure partially, it was the attitude of the Commission that the Commission did not have adequate funds or staff properly to protect the public interest if it were to grant the applications for partial self-insurance authorization to the many carriers desiring to establish such partial programs.

Until 1949, very few motor carriers had qualified with the Interstate Commerce Commission as self-insurers because of the Commission's restrictive interpretation.[6] The majority of the motor carriers which had complete self-insurance programs approved by the Commission were carriers of passengers; and, of the remaining property carriers, a number were owned by railroads. There were many motor carriers which desired to self-insure for cargo only, but the Interstate Commerce Commission turned down all requests for partial self-insurance programs even though the motor-carrier applicants could show sufficient net worth to handle partial liabilities without endangering their stability or permanency.

In January of 1950, however, the Commission acted favorably upon two applications by motor carriers to establish partial self-insurance programs.[7]

In one of these cases the motor carrier sought to secure the right to self-insure to the amount of the first $10,000 any liabilities arising

---

[6] Less than fifty motor carriers were authorized as self-insurers by the Interstate Commerce Commission on December 31, 1949, according to the Bureau of Motor Carriers, Interstate Commerce Commission.

[7] MC–43038, Commercial Carriers, Inc. (1950); MC–76266, Merchant's Motor Freight, Inc. (1950).

from a single occurrence regardless of their nature, whether death, bodily injury, or loss or damage to property, including cargo; and to secure excess insurance from an insurance company to cover all liabilities over and above the first $10,000 up to the limits of its existing policies. The motor carrier estimated that such a self-insurance program would mean an annual saving of $17,000.

An analysis of the financial statements and other relevant information led to a decision by Division 5 of the Interstate Commerce Commission to approve such an arrangement, contingent upon three conditions:

1. That the motor carrier continue to maintain a sound financial condition.
2. That the motor carrier secure and maintain in effect excess insurance covering any amount in excess of $10,000 which it may have to pay as a result of a single occurrence involving death or bodily injuries to any person, or loss or damage to property of others, or loss or damage to cargo for limits of at least $10,000 to $500,000.
3. That the insurance company or companies providing such excess insurance certify to the Commission that such excess insurance is in effect and will not be terminated except on thirty days' notice to the Commission.

The action by Division 5 in these two decisions gives some indication of a somewhat more liberal view on the subject of self-insurance than it had held heretofore. This should not be interpreted as opening the door to partial self-insurance by all motor carriers, however. Particularly to be noted is the attachment of conditions to the approval of partial self-insurance of the motor carrier insuring all risks to the amount of the first $10,000, one of which was that of continued sound financial condition of the motor carrier. At the present time less than 1 per cent of the motor carriers subject to economic regulation are self-insured, either partially or completely.

Those motor carriers, except those owned by railroads, which have been authorized to self-insure are required by the Commission to file a claims report every 6 months and a quarterly financial report.

The Commission has not established definite criteria for qualification as a self-insurer, but it decides each request upon the merits of the case. Each carrier requesting permission to self-insure receives a letter from the Commission containing the following paragraph:

In reply to your letter of (date), requesting information as to the procedure required of motor carriers to be granted authority to act as self-insurers under the provisions of Section 215 of the Interstate Commerce Act, we are pleased to advise that the Commission has established no set rules governing the qualification of motor carriers as self-insurers; but determines each application for approval of authority to self-insure on its own merits, giving due consideration to the size and extent of the motor carrier operations involved, the nature of the operation, the net financial worth of the applicant, its past record of business success, the experience of the insurance company previously insuring it, its ability to borrow readily and safely to meet all liability obligations which might arise, and all other pertinent matter. In short, each applicant must establish to the satisfaction of the Commission its ability to self-insure without loss of security to the public and without endangering its own stability and the permanence of its business. Because of this the Commission must maintain certain high standards for judging the qualifications of motor carriers as self-insurers.

The last sentence of this paragraph states that high standards must be maintained, but the Commission has not announced any specific standards against which to evaluate the applicant. If, in the opinion of the Commission, the carrier has demonstrated sound management and has the financial resources to cover its liability obligations, it may be permitted to operate as a self-insurer.

Generally, unless a motor carrier has a premium expenditure of at least $150,000 a year, it is not feasible to self-insure. If a carrier's losses are $100,000 a year, normally the premium would be approximately $150,000, since $100,000 must be used to pay the pure losses, and an additional $50,000 to compensate the insurance company for the costs of administration and reinsurance, plus a profit. It is the experience of the insurance industry that the relationship between premium and losses is $3.00 of premium for every $2.00 of losses.

In this illustration, approximately $50,000 above losses would be available under a self-insurance program to provide reinsurance and a claims and safety service. Considering an average public liability and property damage insurance rate of $2.00 per $100 revenue and an average insurance rate of $2.00 per $100 revenue for full coverage cargo insurance, it has been concluded that a motor carrier would require an annual minimum revenue between $4,000,000 and $5,000,000 to provide an adequate premium spread to maintain self-insurance.[8]

Self-insurance is generally considered as applicable to fleets that are in a position to handle their losses up to at least the first $10,000. Before selecting such a plan, however, consideration should be given to the ability to service and supervise losses; the availability of proper supervisory service to direct that work; and the application of han-

---

[8] *Transport Topics*, May 19, 1952, p. 19.

dling losses as it applies to the furtherance of the safety program. Self-insurance may be used in connection with adequate excess insurance, carrying from the amount of losses the motor carrier can handle, on up to the limits necessary to protect properly the financial security of the company.

The fact that the premiums on insurance will vary depending upon the safety record of a motor carrier in itself provides justification for safety programs and any other measures which would insure a better carrier record, since this improved record would be reflected in carrier savings.

QUESTIONS AND PROBLEMS

1. Point out the significance of adequate insurance coverage in motor-carrier operations.
2. List the items that insurance safety engineers will check in investigating a motor carrier which is seeking fleet coverage.
3. How is public liability and property damage insurance rated?
4. Why has the Interstate Commerce Commission required minimum insurance requirements for motor carriers?
5. Explain the deductible provisions found in cargo insurance.
6. What are the advantages of a premium based on gross receipts?
7. "The Interstate Commerce Commission has for a number of years required that motor carriers which wanted to self-insure must be qualified to self-insure completely." Why?
8. What is meant by partial self-insurance? What is the Commission's attitude at the present time on partial self-insurance?
9. What conditions have been imposed on a common carrier of general commodities which has been approved by the Interstate Commerce Commission to self-insure partially?
10. Ascertain and report on the trends at the present time in self-insurance, both complete and partial.
11. What is a retrospective contract? Is it used with all types of insurance?
12. Define named peril; bill of lading policy; mutual companies; and specified-car basis.

15. MOTOR FREIGHT CLASSIFICATION

▪▪

WHEN the Motor Carrier Act was passed in 1935, which established federal regulation of interstate motor carriers, one of its provisions required motor carriers to establish, observe, and enforce just and reasonable rates, charges, and classifications, and just and reasonable regulations and practices relating thereto.

DEVELOPMENT OF MOTOR CLASSIFICATION

In November, 1935, a committee of one hundred motor-carrier tariff men and transportation experts was appointed to formulate a motor-carrier classification. The original issue of the National Motor Freight Classification was filed with the Interstate Commerce Commission in March, 1936, and consisted of two volumes, one containing LTL ratings and the other volume ratings. Upon reissuance, the LTL and volume ratings were combined into one volume, which procedure has been followed since that time.

The freight classification is an index or a list of thousands of articles which shows how those commodities are grouped or classified for the purpose of applying rates or charges. It does not fix the rates in dollars and cents to be charged for transporting the articles. It merely states in which class or rating each commodity belongs. The rates or charges in dollars and cents for the transporting of the commodities are established by each motor carrier and published in tariffs. The freight classification arranges into groups articles with similar transportation characteristics; and to each group is affixed a number or letter, which is called the "rating." Thus, a hundred articles may be grouped, based on their transportation characteristics, into but five groups.

Because of this grouping, rates can be applied to these five groups, whereas in the absence of such classification, there would have to be separate rates on each of the articles. The classification then provides a means of establishing a relationship between articles which are grouped. Each number or letter which is assigned to each class bears a definite percentage relationship to the other numbers or letters. The Class 1 rating is equal to 100 per cent, Class 2 is equal to 85 per cent of Class 1, and so on down to Class 7, which is 27½ per cent of Class 1. Above Class 1 or 100 are multiples, such as Class 1¼, or 125 per cent of Class 1, and on up to 5 times 1, or 500 per cent of Class 1. After the rating is found reference must be made to a tariff, which will give the class rate for the article.

There are many articles which are specifically described in the classification, and through the use of "NOI," which means "not more specifically described," the description is broadened so virtually everything is classified. New articles are manufactured and introduced to the public continually. These commodities are not always properly indexed and listed in the classification, inasmuch as there has been no actual handling of these commodities before that time. The classification contains a rule-making provision for the classification of commodities not specifically indexed called the "rule of analogy." A specific description and rating in the classification for the new item is made by the classification committee in the event it is determined that the current descriptions do not apply.

NATIONAL MOTOR FREIGHT CLASSIFICATION

The National Motor Freight Classification, in general, follows the older rail classification, partly because of the fact that when the Motor Carrier Act was passed—requiring, among other things, that tariffs be filed with the Interstate Commerce Commission—the task of formulating completely new classifications was so formidable that motor carriers simply followed the rail classification. As a result, originally almost all of the entries in the National Motor Freight Classification had descriptions that were the same as those in the railroad classification. Even at the present time it is estimated that over 80 per cent is identical due to the competition between rail and motor carriers.

The National Motor Freight Classification divides the United States into three areas similar to the rail classification. The National Motor Freight Classification areas are East, South, and West. The contents of the National Motor Freight Classification are as follows:[1]

---

[1] A number of interesting articles on the origin and development of the National Motor Freight Classification have appeared in *Transport Topics*, beginning with the March 15, 1954, issue.

1. List of commissions with which the classification is filed
2. Table of contents
3. Participating carriers
4. Index to articles
5. Index to rules
6. Rules and regulations
7. Prescribed forms for bills of lading
8. Explanation of ratings, abbreviations, characters, and reference marks
9. Ratings of articles

Figure 15–1 is a sample page from the National Motor Freight Classification. A brief summary of the sample page follows: The item number on the left side serves to identify the article. The page number on which the article is described is not listed in the index to articles, but the item is numbered so that it is necessary to use the item number in looking up the article. Item 87500 is Corn Stalks, NOI, which means that it is not more specifically described in the classification. If the shipment is in bales not machine pressed or in bundles, the less-than-truckload rating applicable is 1½, or 150 per cent of Class 1 in all three classification areas. If the shipment consisted of 20,000 pounds or more, the volume rating would apply as follows: Class 5 in the East, Class 7 in the South, and Class 5 in the West. Item 87550 shows a differentiation between an article which is SU, or set up, and is rated D1, or double first class (200 per cent), for AQ, any quantity. The same item KD, or knocked down, is rated much lower. Under the volume rating, where the letter F appears, it refers to Class F in the East. Where 37½ appears, it indicates Class 37½, or 37½ per cent of Class 1. Item 87475 under the volume minimum weights shows Ⓦ 12.4 applies on a Ⓣ 2 or truckload rating of Class 2. The minimum weight factor is covered in Rule 34 and is explained later in the chapter. The minimum weights on volume ratings or truckloads are generally higher on some commodities than it is possible for motor carriers to transport. However, there are at present tariff rules which publish, as a whole, lower minimum weights than those found in the classification.

The bulk of the classification in terms of pages consists of a list of participating carriers, index to articles, rules and regulations, and classification of articles. The articles which are classified are listed alphabetically under the noun. If this is not sufficiently descriptive, adjectives are used as well. When any part of the description of an article is indented from the left margin in a position subordinate to the text preceding it, the description must be read with its context

Item	ARTICLES	RATINGS LTL	RATINGS @Vol.	@ Vol.Min. Wt.-Lbs.
	SPRINGS—Continued			
87430	Note—Not applicable on springs constructed of material over .49 inch thick; when exceeding .49 inch thick rate as Springs, Steel, other than Wire, coiled.			
87440	Torsion, steel and rubber combined, in boxes	2	45-5-45	24,000
87450	Sprinkler Heads, Automatic Fire Extinguisher, in barrels or boxes, see Note, item 87460.	2	F-4-4	30,000
87460	Note—Volume ratings also apply on Sound Warning Signals not in excess of 10% of weight on which charges are assessed.			
87470	Squilgees (Squeegees), in boxes or crates	2	F-4-4	20,000
87475	Stairways, Ramps, Platforms, Stands or Chutes, aircraft or ship loading, unloading or service, portable, see Note, item 87476:			
	SU	3tl	3tl	AQ
	KD, in packages	1¼	ⓣ2	ⓦ12.4
87476	Note—Polished or decorated surfaces or other parts subject to damage must be adequately protected.			
87480	**STALKS:**			
87490	Corn, Broom Corn or Sunflower, ground or Shredded, in bags; Vol., loose or in packages	1	5-6-5	20,000
87500	Corn, NOI:			
	In bales not machine pressed, or in bundles	1½	5-7-5	20,000
	In machine pressed bales	1-4-3	5-7-5	20,000
87510	Cotton:			
	In bales not machine pressed, or in bundles	1½	37½-6-5	20,000
	In machine pressed bales	1-5-3	37½-6-5	20,000
87520	Hemp:			
	In bales not machine pressed, or in bundles; also Vol., loose	1½	2	10,000
	In machine pressed bales	3-4-3	5-6-5	20,000
87530	**STANDS:**			
87540	Adding Machine, Cash Register, Typewriter or Card Index Cabinet:			
	SU, in boxes or crates	1½	ⓣ2	ⓦ10.6
	KD or Folded, in boxes or crates	2	ⓣ4	ⓦ30.6
87550	Barrels, Cask, Tank or Vat Supporting, iron or steel:			
	SU	D1	D1	AQ
	KD, taken apart or flat	3	37½-6-5	36,000
87560	Bench plate, lapping plate, layout surface plate or surface plate, steel, SU	2	F-4-4	24,000
87570	Cat or dog feeding, in boxes	2	F-4-4	24,000
87580	Copying Press, in boxes or crates	1	3	20,000
87590	Flower Pot, steel:			
	SU, not nested nor interlaced, in barrels, boxes or crates	D1	1	10,000
	SU, nested or interlaced, in barrels, boxes or crates	1	3	20,000
	KD, in barrels, boxes or crates	2	F-4-4	24,000
87600	Flower Pot, wire:			
	SU, not nested nor interlaced, wrapped, or in boxes or crates	D1	1	10,000
	SU, nested or interlaced, in boxes or crates	1	3	20,000
	KD, in boxes or crates	2	3	20,000
87610	Flower Pot, wooden:			
	SU, wrapped or in boxes or crates	1½	1	10,000
	KD, flat, in boxes or crates	2	F-4-4	24,000
87620	Microphone, Floor, in boxes	2	F-4-4	24,000
87630	Sad Iron, iron, Electric, in barrels or boxes	1	3	20,000
87640	Sad Iron, iron, other than Electric, in barrels or boxes	3	4-6-5	36,000
87650	Sidewalk Sign, iron, KD, in packages	3	5-6-5	36,000
87660	Stands, NOI, other than Furniture:			
	SU, not nested nor interlaced, in packages	1½	2	10,000
	SU, interlaced or nested or KD, other than flat, in packages	1	3	16,000
	Flat, folded flat or KD flat, in packages	3	37½-5-5	30,000
87665	Vending Machine, sheet steel, in boxes or crates	110	ⓣ3	ⓦ14.4
87670	Starch, Arrowroot. See item 33465 for ratings dependent upon agreed or released value:			
	In containers in barrels or boxes	1	5-6-5	40,000
	In bulk in bags or barrels	3	5-6-5	40,000
87680	Starch, liquid, in barrels or boxes	F-4-4	ⓣ5-ⓣ7- ⓣ5	ⓦ40.6
87690	Starch, NOI, in bags, barrels, boxes or pails, see Note, item 87700	F-4-4	6-7-5	40,000
87700	Note—Ratings will also apply when in 5-ply multiple-wall paper bags, total basis weight for all walls not less than 230 pounds, net weight of contents not exceeding 140 pounds, or in 4-ply paper bags, total basis weight for all walls not less than 170 lbs., net weight of contents not exceeding 120 pounds.			
87710	Starch Substitutes, inedible, consisting of a physical mixture of starch made from grain or flour made from grain and chemical constituents, the chemical content not to exceed two per cent, in bags, barrels, boxes or pails, see Note, item 87700	F-4-4	6-7-5	40,000
87720	Starting cranks, internal combustion engine, in packages; also Vol., loose	F-4-4	5-7-5	30,000
87730	**STATIONERY:**			
87740	Book Mailing Corners, metal, paper covered, in boxes	1	3	20,000
87750	Calendars, NOI (including calendars with thermometers attached), Calendar Backs, Calendar Mounts, Date Pads or list finders, in boxes, or in inner containers in cloth bags	2	F-4-4	24,000
87760	Crayons, Artists', in boxes	1	3	20,000
87770	Crayons, School or Marking, in barrels or boxes	3	37½-6-5	36,000

FIG. 15–1. Specimen page from National Motor Freight Classification No. 12.

especially within the preceding heading. For example, in Figure 15–1, Item 87530, Stands, controls Items 87540 through 87665.

There are approximately 200 generic headings contained in each of the classifications similar to the one just cited, some of which have but two or three entries, but the majority are quite lengthy, an example of which is the heading "Machinery and Machines or Parts Named" which covers about 25 pages.[2]

The classification also contains different types of motor-carrier bills of lading. Since the classification has the widest distribution of any motor-carrier tariff, it is felt that this accomplishes greater uniformity in the bill of lading used by motor carriers, since the exact form of the bill of lading for motor carriers has never been prescribed by the Interstate Commerce Commission.

As indicated earlier, the National Motor Freight Classification originally contained practically identical entries to the railroad's Consolidated Freight Classification. Motor carriers soon found that certain of the items contained in the rail classification, particularly those which were light and bulky, could not be moved on a compensatory basis at the existing rating in the classification. Many of the light and bulky articles have been docketed for a change in their classification, so that there are fewer identical entries between the rail and motor classifications than was originally the case.

With the establishment of the railroads' Uniform Freight Classification No. 1, as a result of the Interstate Commerce Commission's action in *Dockets 28300* and *28310* covering rail classification and class rates, which rail classification became effective May 30, 1952, the National Motor Freight Classification No. A–1 was published and became effective on July 10, 1952. Although the Commission issued an order in *Docket MC–C–150* placing motor carriers on notice to effect uniformity of the National Motor Freight Classification, it did not issue a final order in this *Docket*. The National Motor Freight Classification No. A–1 (now A–2) was published to be more competitive with its rail counterpart, the new Uniform Freight Classification No. 1 (now No. 2) with the exception of certain light and bulky articles. There are then at the present time two National Motor Freight Classifications: National Motor Freight Classification No. 12, which corresponds more or less to the railroads' Consolidated Freight Classification No. 20; and National Motor Freight Classification No. A–2, which corresponds more or less to the railroads' Uniform Freight Classification No. 2.

The make-up of the National Motor Freight Classification No. A–2 is similar to National Motor Freight Classification No. 12. However, instead of three ratings for LTL and three ratings for volume for East, South, and West, which are found in many instances in

---

[2] *Transport Topics,* May 17, 1954, p. 75.

National Motor Freight Classification No. 12, No. A–2 contains one rating for LTL and one for volume or truckload in the majority of cases as shown in Figure 15–2. In No. 12, there is uniformity in East, South, and West classification areas for Class 3 and above, but there is no uniformity below Class 3. In A–2, where there is but a

Item	ARTICLES	RATINGS		@ Vol. Min. Wt.-Lbs.
		LTL	@Vol.	
86350	Signals or Signs, Road Traffic or Vehicle, reflector, in boxes or crates			
86360	Signs, cast iron, in boxes or crates	85	55	24,000
		70	45	30,000
86370	SIGNS, OTHER THAN FIGURES OR IMAGES, PREPAID:			
86380	Advertising boards, wooden, in packages			
86385	Advertising boards, wooden, old, used, having value only for reconditioning, in bundles	70	37½	30,000
86390	Electric, neon, secured and suspended in boxes or crates, see Note, item 86400	55	35	36,000
86400	Note—Fibreboard boxes must comply with Rule 5, Section 2. Crates must be lined with double wall fibreboard testing not less than 275 lbs. Glass parts must be so packed so as to provide not less than two inches clearance between such parts and the inside wall of container.	400	400	AQ
86410	Electric, NOI, including electric neon signs without tubing, in boxes or crates (brackets or hangers may protrude)			
86420	Reinforced plywood panels with attached metal treated glass letters or designs, flat, in boxes or crates	125	⑦70	⑧20.6
86430	Roller, car route, in boxes	100	55	24,000
		100	70	20,000
86440	Signs, other than figures or images, NOI:			
86450	Aluminum, brass, bronze, copper or zinc, in boxes or crates, see Note, item 86451	100	⑦70	⑧20.6
86451	Note—Aluminum signs, framed, may be accepted in bundles cleated at each corner or metal strapped.			
86460	Cloth, Oil Cloth or Wire Cloth, mounted on wooden frames, in boxes	100	70	20,000
86470	Cloth, Oil Cloth or wire cloth, not mounted, in packages	100	70	24,000
86480	Cloth, Oil Cloth or Wire Cloth, mounted on solid fibreboard or wooden backs, in boxes or crates, or in cleated bundles			
86490	Concrete, in boxes or crates	100	55	30,000
86500	Fibreboard, iron bound, varnished, in boxes or crates	85	55	24,000
86510	Fibreboard, paperboard or pulpboard, plain, varnished or waxed, NOI, in packages	85	55	30,000
86520	Glass globe, glass, NOI, or glass and metal, wood or synthetic gum or resin compound Combined:	100	55	24,000
	Not flat, KD flat nor nested, in barrels or boxes	150	77½	15,000
	Flat, KD flat or nested, in barrels or boxes	100	55	24,000
86530	Iron or steel covered with celluloid, in boxes	85	55	24,000
86540	Iron or steel, NOI, framed or not framed, in packages	77½	45	30,000
86547	Pulpboard, ground, and plastic combined, molded, in boxes	85	55	24,000
86550	Revolving, NOI, in boxes	200	100	10,000
86560	Wire:			
	Flat in packages	100	70	20,000
	Other than flat, in boxes or crates	200	100	10,000
86570	Wooden, in packages	85	45	30,000
86610	Triple, in boxes	100	70	20,000
86620	Silica Gel, spent, in bags, barrels or boxes	50	35	50,000
86630	Silica, NOI, or Silex, NOI, LTL, in bags, barrels or boxes; Vol., in bulk or in packages	50	35	40,000
86640	Silicon Carbide Briquettes, in boxes, or in packages metal strapped to pallets	55	35	50,000
86650	Silicon Carbide, Crude, LTL, in bags, barrels or boxes; Vol., in packages or in bulk	50	35	56,000
86660	Silicon Carbide, NOI [not Flour nor Grain Abrasive], in lined barrels	55	35	50,000
86670	SILK, Raw, Spun, Schappe or Thrown, including Organzine, Singles, Tram, Warp or Yarns, value declared in writing by the shipper, or agreed upon in writing as the released value of the property, in accordance with the following, see Note, item 86680:			
	If value does not exceed one dollar per pound, in bags, bales or boxes, or on wrapped beams in crates	100	70	30,000
	If value exceeds one dollar per pound, in bags, bales or boxes, or on wrapped beams in crates	150	100	30,000
	If consignor declines to declare value or agree to released value in writing, shipment will not be accepted.			
86680	Note—The value declared in writing by the shipper, or agreed upon in writing as the released value of the property, as the case may be, must be entered on Shipping order and Bill of Lading, as follows: "The agreed or declared value of the property is hereby specifically stated by the shipper to be not exceeding _____per pound." (Ratings herein based on released value have been authorized by the Interstate Commerce Commission in Released Rates Orders MC No. 1 of January 16, 1936, and FF No. 2 of January 19, 1943, subject to complaint.)			
86690	Siphon Bottles (Fitted with siphons), metal, in barrels or boxes	100	60	24,000
86700	Sizing, Casein, in bags or boxes	60	37½	30,000
86704	Sizing, emulsified petroleum, see Note, item 86706, in bulk in barrels or in tank trucks, see Rule 23			
86706	Note—Ratings apply on a mixture of petroleum wax or petrolatum and water, rosin or emulsifying agents, the petroleum wax or petrolatum not to exceed 52% and the rosin or emulsifying agents, singly or combined, not to exceed 15% of the total weight.	55	35	40,000
86710	Sizing, NOI:			
	In containers in barrels or boxes			
	In bulk in barrels, kits or pails; also Dry, in bulk in bags	70	37½	30,000
86720	Sizing, Rosin, in barrels, or dry, in paper or rubber bags; also Vol., in tank trucks, see Rule 23	60	37½	30,000
86730	Skeletons (Anatomical Specimens), in boxes	65	35	40,000
86740	Skewers, steel or wood, NOI, in barrels, boxes or crates	200	100	10,000
		70	37½	30,000

FIG. 15–2. Specimen page from National Motor Freight Classification No. A–2.

single rating, it is applicable, unless otherwise provided by tariff, to the entire United States. Class 1 is considered to be 100 per cent, and the other classes bear a specific percentage relationship to Class 1, or 100 per cent. In No. 12, the classes range from 5t1, or 500 per cent, to Class 7, or 27½ per cent. It has been pointed out that No. 12 is similar to the railroads' Consolidated Freight Classification in that Class 1 is 100 per cent, Class 2 is 85 per cent of Class 1, and so on. However, in the east, Class F is 55 per cent of Class 1.

With the publication of National Motor Freight Classification No. A–1, there were twenty-three classes which were provided. These were: 500, 400, 350, 300, 250, 175, 150, 125, 110, 100, 92½, 85, 77½, 70, 65, 60, 55, 50, 45, 40, 37½, and 35. There were three Class 30, but in A–2, the bottom class is Class 35.

The following is a breakdown of ratings in the National Motor

Ratings	LTL			TL or Volume		
	East	South	West	East	South	West
5t1	2	2	2	2	2	2
4t1	18	18	18	12	12	12
3½t1	11	11	11	1	1	1
3t1	45	45	46	30	30	31
2½t1	36	36	36	7	7	7
D1	440	439	440	16	15	15
1¾	11	11	11	10	10	10
1½	441	441	441	51	51	51
1¼	108	108	108	52	51	51
110	1	1	1	2	2	2
1	2,081	2,063	2,071	288	278	282
92½	....	....	....	2	2	2
2	2,854	2,799	2,827	774	596	607
85	2	2	2	2	2	2
77½	4	4	1	2	26	26
75	....	....	....	7	8	7
70	2	2	2	4	5	151
3	2,902	2,589	2,798	1,524	1,594	1,516
F	672	....	....	1,339	....	....
65	2	2	2	11	13	13
60	13	5	5	5	8	2
4	1,061	984	1,892	1,165	2,197	2.333
57	1	....	....	....	....	....
55	....	....	....	5	6	24
50	....	696	....	11	114	74
45	0	0	1	400	25	1,884
42½	....	....	....	0	0	1
40	1	....	....	1,144	12	38
5	....	198	....	2,572	1,144	3,881
37½	....	....	....	793	255	4
35	....	....	....	2	3	2
6	....	240	....	717	3,053	26
7	....	....	....	0	1,522	0
32½	....	....	....	10	2	0
30	....	....	....	86	2	2
0	14	26	7	20	20	7
Total	10,722	10,722	10,722	11,066	11,066	11,066

Freight Classifications showing the number of ratings assigned to each class used in the classifications. This tabulation of the number of ratings by classes contained in NMFC No. 12 and Supplement No. 1 is divided according to territories.[3]

In No. 12, there are over 33,000 truckload and volume ratings. The majority of these, it will be noted, are Class 3 and below. The total number of LTL ratings in No. 12 is a little over 32,000, and the majority of these ratings is Class 3 and above.

Shown below is the number of ratings by classes contained in NMFC No. A–1, which includes Supplement Nos. 1 to 17:[4]

Ratings	LTL	TL or Volume
500	2	2
400	22	13
350	0	1
300	70	27
250	39	6
200	453	15
175	15	9
150	535	60
125	339	57
110	76	5
100	1,996	253
92½	251	4
85	2,054	793
77½	674	61
70	1,995	1,342
65	508	58
60	531	125
55	538	1,546
50	713	607
45	1	1,965
40	1	1,163
37½	0	802
35	0	2,348
30	0	3
0	6	5
Totals.....	10,818	11,274

There were a little more than 11,000 of these ratings in contrast to those contained in No. 12, more than 33,000. The reduction in the number of ratings simplifies the classification. The majority of truckload and volume ratings in A–1 was Class 55 and below. The total number of LTL ratings is slightly less than that for the truckload and volume. Because of the nature of the service rendered, as well as packing containers and other matters, the majority of the LTL ratings is Class 85 and above. In terms of items in the classifications, there are 9,956 in A–1 and 9,846 in No. 12.

---

[3] *Transport Topics*, May 10, 1954, p. 14.
[4] *Ibid.*

A classification is applicable only when tariffs make specific reference to it. Since National Motor Freight Classifications No. 12 and No. A–2 are competitive with the railroad's Consolidated Freight Classification No. 20 and Uniform Freight Classification No. 2, respectively, the motor carriers will adopt the motor classification which will insure continuing competition. In the Far West where CFC No. 20 is currently used, motor carriers use NMFC No. 12; but in the Southern Territory, east of the Mississippi, where railroads use UFC No. 2, the motor carriers use NMFC No. A–2. NMFC No. A–2 is used by motor carriers in several of the rate territories covering a substantial geographical area.

CLASSIFICATION RULES

Both of the National Motor Freight Classifications contain rules numbered to 34, with Rule Nos. 5½, 12½, and 14½ included, to make a total of 37 rules. Some of these rules are almost identical to the railroad classification rules covering the same subjects, whereas others are considerably different from the rail rules. One important difference between the National Motor Freight Classification rules and the railroads' classification rules is that there are not as many motor classification rules and the packing requirements are not as detailed as is the case with rail classification rules.

Classification rules and regulations have great significance, and the principles contained therein must be learned by the user of the classification. A knowledge of these rules enables the user to look up the ratings for individual commodities without referring each time to all of the more than 30 rules. Certain of these rules are often referred to in other tariffs as having application on shipments subject to that tariff. Thus, in many instances, classification rules and regulations may apply even on articles which are not subject to the classification and class rates.

A careful reading of the rules shows that the phrase "unless otherwise provided" appears in many rules. This indicates that there may be and, in many instances, there are exceptions to these rules. It is possible for so many exceptions to be made to a rule that it has very little effect, such as Rule 12 in which a minimum charge for a single shipment was made. The minimum charge provided in Rule 12 at the present time is not applicable on interstate commerce, and steps are being taken to cancel the rule. The carrier's tariffs must be consulted for the applicable minimum charge. The elimination of Rule

12 would indicate that the rules, like other parts of the classification, are not static.

The rules cover many matters, including acceptance of goods, marking shipments, definitions of shipments, loading or unloading heavy or bulky articles, and articles subject to the bill of lading conditions. A number of classification rules are discussed in other chapters. The operation of Rule 34 is described here in order to illustrate the manner in which a rule is used.

In the description of articles in the National Motor Freight Classification, the extreme right column is headed "Volume Minimum Weight—Pounds." The weight which is shown under this caption is supposed to represent the minimum weight under which truckload or volume weights can be assessed. However, these weights represent those which are contained in the rail classifications for rail boxcar minimum weights. In adopting the railroad classification minimum weights, the motor carriers found that some of the minima exceeded the legal load limit of the states in which they operated. Beginning with the first National Motor Freight Classification, the truck minimum weights were controlled by special rules in motor class-rate tariffs. In 1948 certain light and bulky articles were tested in relation to the carrying capacity of average trailers. The publication of Rule 34 that year established minimum weight factors. Six tables were formulated as follows: Table A which is based on a vehicle with a capacity of 2,000 cubic feet; Table B on one of 1,800 cubic feet; Table C on one of 1,600 cubic feet; Table D on one of 1,400 cubic feet; Table E on 1,200 cubic feet; and Table F on 1,000 cubic feet.

An article under the column titled "Volume Minimum Weight—Pounds" which has a Ⓦ in front of the figure is subject in the classification to a minimum weight factor found in Rule 34. For example, in the current National Motor Freight Classifications "Old, Used Bowling Pins, in bags or boxes" is Ⓦ 36.4. The minimum weight factor in the classification will be found in Rule 34. If a rate tariff carries a provision that "Table D, Rule 34 of the Classification is applicable in determining minimum weights where minimum weight factors are named in the Classification," Table D would be referred to opposite the minimum weight factor of 36.4, and the truckload minimum weight would be found to be 36,000 pounds. If the rate tariff had indicated Table E was applicable, the minimum weight would be 30,900 pounds.

The carrier's tariff must be consulted to determine which table of

RULE 34

APPLICATION OF MINIMUM WEIGHT FACTORS

Sec. 1. The minimum weight factors named in connection with the individual descriptions and ratings herein apply as set forth in tables shown in Section 3 of this rule.

Sec. 2. Carriers' tariffs must be consulted in order to determine the table designating the applicable truckload minimum weight. Where carriers' tariff does not make provisions for application of this rule, Table F, Section 3, will apply.

Sec. 3. Tables of Truckload Minimum Weights:

WHEN MIN. WT. FACTOR IS:	TRUCKLOAD MINIMUM WEIGHT, IN POUNDS, WILL BE:					
	TABLE A	TABLE B	TABLE C	TABLE D	TABLE E	TABLE F
10.0	10,000	8,000	7,000	6,000	5,000	4,000
10.1	10,000	9,000	8,000	7,000	6,000	5,000
10.2	10,000	10,000	8,800	7,700	6,600	5,600
10.3	10,000	10,000	10,000	8,700	7,500	6,000
10.4	10,000	10,000	10,000	10,000	8,600	7,100
10.5	10,000	10,000	10,000	10,000	10,000	8,300
10.6	10,000	10,000	10,000	10,000	10,000	10,000
12.1	12,000	10,800	9,600	8,400	7,200	6,000
12.2	12,000	12,000	10,700	9,300	8,000	6,700
12.3	12,000	12,000	12,000	10,500	9,000	7,500
12.4	12,000	12,000	12,000	12,000	10,300	8,600
12.5	12,000	12,000	12,000	12,000	12,000	10,000
12.6	12,000	12,000	12,000	12,000	12,000	12,000
14.1	14,000	12,600	11,200	9,800	8,400	7,000
14.2	14,000	14,000	12,400	10,900	9,300	7,800
14.3	14,000	14,000	14,000	12,200	10,500	8,700
14.4	14,000	14,000	14,000	14,000	12,000	10,000
14.5	14,000	14,000	14,000	14,000	14,000	11,700
14.6	14,000	14,000	14,000	14,000	14,000	14,000
15.1	15,000	13,500	12,000	10,500	9,000	7,500
15.2	15,000	15,000	13,300	11,700	10,000	8,300
15.3	15,000	15,000	15,000	13,100	11,200	9,400
15.4	15,000	15,000	15,000	15,000	12,900	10,700
15.5	15,000	15,000	15,000	15,000	15,000	12,500
15.6	15,000	15,000	15,000	15,000	15,000	15,000
34.1	34,000	30,600	27,200	23,800	20,400	17,000
34.2	34,000	34,000	30,200	26,400	22,700	18,900
34.3	34,000	34,000	34,000	29,700	25,500	21,200
34.4	34,000	34,000	34,000	34,000	29,100	24,300
34.5	34,000	34,000	34,000	34,000	34,000	28,300
34.6	34,000	34,000	34,000	34,000	34,000	34,000
36.1	36,000	32,400	28,800	25,200	21,600	18,000
36.2	36,000	36,000	32,000	28,000	24,000	20,000
36.3	36,000	36,000	36,000	31,500	27,000	22,500
36.4	36,000	36,000	36,000	36,000	30,900	25,700
36.5	36,000	36,000	36,000	36,000	36,000	30,000
36.6	36,000	36,000	36,000	36,000	36,000	36,000
40.1	40,000	36,000	32,000	28,000	24,000	20,000
40.2	40,000	40,000	35,600	31,100	26,700	22,200
40.3	40,000	40,000	40,000	35,000	30,000	25,000
40.4	40,000	40,000	40,000	40,000	34,300	28,600
40.5	40,000	40,000	40,000	40,000	40,000	33,300
40.6	40,000	40,000	40,000	40,000	40,000	40,000
45.1	45,000	40,500	36,000	31,500	27,000	22,500
45.2	45,000	45,000	40,000	35,000	30,000	25,000
45.3	45,000	45,000	45,000	39,400	33,700	28,100
45.4	45,000	45,000	45,000	45,000	38,600	32,100
45.5	45,000	45,000	45,000	45,000	45,000	37,500
45.6	45,000	45,000	45,000	45,000	45,000	45,000
46.1	46,000	41,400	36,800	32,200	27,600	23,000
46.2	46,000	46,000	40,900	35,800	30,700	25,600
46.3	46,000	46,000	46,000	39,400	33,700	28,100
46.4	46,000	46,000	46,000	46,000	39,400	32,900
46.5	46,000	46,000	46,000	46,000	46,000	38,300
46.6	46,000	46,000	46,000	46,000	46,000	46,000
50.1	50,000	45,000	40,000	35,000	30,000	25,000
50.2	50,000	50,000	44,400	38,900	33,300	27,800
50.3	50,000	50,000	50,000	43,700	37,500	31,200
50.4	50,000	50,000	50,000	50,000	42,900	35,700
50.5	50,000	50,000	50,000	50,000	50,000	41,700
50.6	50,000	50,000	50,000	50,000	50,000	50,000
56.1	56,000	50,400	44,800	39,200	33,600	28,000
56.2	56,000	56,000	49,800	43,600	37,300	31,100
56.3	56,000	56,000	56,000	49,000	42,000	35,000
56.4	56,000	56,000	56,000	56,000	48,000	40,000
56.5	56,000	56,000	56,000	56,000	56,000	46,700
56.6	56,000	56,000	56,000	56,000	56,000	56,000
60.1	60,000	54,000	48,000	42,000	36,000	30,000
60.2	60,000	60,000	53,300	46,700	40,000	33,300
60.3	60,000	60,000	60,000	52,500	45,000	37,500
60.4	60,000	60,000	60,000	60,000	51,400	42,900
60.5	60,000	60,000	60,000	60,000	60,000	50,000
60.6	60,000	60,000	60,000	60,000	60,000	60,000

FIG. 15-3. Rule 34, NMFC No. A-2.

applicable truckload minimum weight applies. If the carrier's tariff does not provide for the application of Rule 34, Table F applies. The figure which precedes the decimal point in the minimum weight factor represents the rail competitive minimum, whereas the figure after the decimal point is the key to the density of the article. The density indicates the maximum theoretical loading which is possible if all of the cubic space of a vehicle is utilized in any of the six sizes of vehicles represented in the tables. The table which is used is the one which reflects the cubical capacity of most of the vehicles operating in a particular rate territory. Figure 15–3 shows Rule 34. There are about 1,065 minimum weight factors contained in National Motor Freight Classification No. A–2 and the same number in No. 12. The new high-cube truck-trailers may affect the present scale of truckload minimum weights in Rule 34.

NEW ENGLAND AREA CLASSIFICATION

There are other motor classifications which are used by motor carriers in addition to the National Motor Freight Classification.[5] In the New England area, there is the Coordinated Motor Freight Classification. The ratings in this classification, which are used in conjunction with class rates, have been established to produce about the same revenue per truckload on all commodities transported. Density or weight per cubic foot of the commodity is the primary determinant of the classification, with value a secondary factor. For example, the ratings and the shipping weight per cubic foot are as follows:[6]

Rating	Shipping Weight per Cubic Foot (Pounds)
Class 4 times 5...............	3 and under
Class 1.....................	3– 6
Class 2.....................	6–10
Class 3.....................	10–15
Class 4.....................	15–20
Class 5.....................	20 and over

Coordinated Motor Freight Classification No. 7 contains eight classes:

---

[5] Associated Motor Carriers Freight Classification, Association of Interstate Motor Carriers, and Lawrence Traffic Bureau Motor Freight Classification.

[6] *Motor Carrier Rates in New England,* 47 MCC 661 (1948).

Class
1
2
3
4
5
1½t1—150 per cent of Class 1
2½t1—250 per cent of Class 1
8t1   —800 per cent of Class 1

In this classification, the multiples of Class 1 are found to a limited extent and are applicable on those articles which have a density of less than one pound per cubic foot. Although density is the primary factor in the construction of this classification, those articles which have unfavorable transportation characteristics, such as a tendency to impregnate other commodities with which they are loaded, or the degree of fragility is such that other commodities cannot be loaded on them, or a susceptibility to theft which would require extra precaution to avoid loss, may be rated higher than the element of shipping density alone would warrant. Figure 15–4 shows the ratings and description of articles in a manner somewhat different from that used in the National Motor Freight Classification. In

ITEM	RAT-INGS	ARTICLES
		ABRASIVES:
5	5	Abrasive Cloth or Paper, including Emery or Sand Paper, in packages
		Alundum, Corundum, Emery or other Natural or Synthetic Abrasive Material consisting chiefly of aluminum oxide or silicon carbide:
10	5	Crude or Lump, in packages
15	5	Flour or Grain, in packages
20	5	Refuse, including broken wheels, wheel stubs or wheel grindings, in packages
25	5	Wheels, other ⌐an pulp grinding
30	5	Wheels, pulp grinding, in packages
		ACIDS:
35	5	Abietic, in barrels
40		Acetic, glacial or liquid:
	3	In carboys
	4	In glass in barrels or boxes
	5	In bulk in barrels
	5	In tank trucks (See Rule 17)
45		NOIBN, Dry:
	4	In glass in barrels or boxes
	4	In cans or cartons in barrels or boxes
	5	In bulk in bags, barrels or boxes
50		NOIBN, Liquid:
	2	In glass bottles, each packed in rattan or willow baskets or hampers
	5	In carboys not exceeding seven (7) gallons (See Note)
	3	In carboys exceeding seven (7) gallons, completely boxed or necks projecting
	4	In glass in barrels or boxes
	5	In bulk in barrels
		NOTE — Carboys completely encased; necks must not project
55	5	Arsenic, fused, in barrels or boxes, or in bars wrapped in paraffined paper in wooden boxes only
60		Arsenic, other than fused:
	3	In carboys
	5	In barrels
	5	In tank trucks (See Rule 17)
65	5	Azelaic, from animal or vegetable fats, in bags, barrels, or boxes
70		Boric (Boracic):
	4	In glass in barrels or boxes
	5	In cans or cartons in barrels or boxes, or in bulk in bags, barrels, boxes or steel pails

FIG. 15–4. Ratings and description of articles in Coordinated Motor Freight Classification No. 7.

comparison with the National Motor Freight Classifications, the New England Classification contains fewer variations in ratings which are dependent upon the way in which a particular commodity is packed for shipment.[7]

After the passage of the Motor Carrier Act in 1935, New England area motor carriers used the National Motor Freight Classification for a time. However, they soon developed the Coordinated and Official Classifications; and the Official was absorbed by the Coordinated on January 1, 1955. The development of their own classifications was partly the result of a cost study and also because there was not the degree of rail competition faced by motor carriers in this area as compared with motor carriers located in other areas in the United States. Therefore, it was felt that there could be a departure from the classification procedure which had largely dictated the formulation of the National Motor Freight Classification, namely competition. The Commission authorized the New England area carriers to use these two classifications. The Coordinated Classification is used largely in conjunction with interstate class rates in New England, but outside of New England, and generally between points in New England and points in other rate territories, the class rates of motor common carriers are those found in the National Motor Freight Classification.

The current Coordinated Motor Freight Classification contains rules numbered 1 through 29.

RAIL CLASSIFICATIONS

In addition to the motor-carrier classifications, there are a number of motor-carrier participants in both the railroads' Consolidated and Uniform Freight Classifications. Some state regulatory commissions have required motor carriers to use the rail classifications for intrastate shipments.

FACTORS INFLUENCING CLASSIFICATION OF ARTICLES

The characteristics of the commodities which must receive consideration in fixing classification ratings are generally as follows:[8]

1. Shipping weight per cubic foot
2. Liability to damage

---

[7] *Motor Carrier Rates in New England,* 47 MCC 657, 662 (1948).
[8] *Motor Carrier Rates in New England,* 47 MCC 660, 661 (1948).

3. Liability to damage other commodities with which it is transported
4. Perishability
5. Liability to spontaneous combustion or explosion
6. Susceptibility to theft
7. Value per pound in comparison with other articles
8. Ease or difficulty in loading or unloading
9. Stowability
10. Excessive weight
11. Excessive length
12. Care or attention necessary in loading and transporting
13. Trade conditions
14. Value of service
15. Competition with other commodities transported

The order in which the foregoing classification elements have been listed is not necessarily the order of their importance. It is necessary to weigh the importance of each factor from a classification standpoint, and this importance varies with each commodity or group of commodities with similar transportation characteristics.

Of course, some elements are given greater weight for particular commodities than is true of others. Often in classifying articles it must be determined if the correct description is applied. For example, the National Classification Board was asked to classify a product being placed on the market which was a dog shampoo. Is it a shampoo, an insecticide, a soap, or a toilet preparation? In this case, it was classified as a liquid soap.

In a proceeding involving a number of light and bulky commodities, the Commission prescribed a table of ratings related to density which was to be used as a guide where density was considered to be the predominant element involved.[9] The Commission indicated that all commodities could not be rated solely on the basis of density and that its scale of ratings should not be construed as an inflexible guide in assigning reasonable classification ratings to all light and bulky articles. However, it ruled that in fixing ratings on articles moving by motor carrier the density of the articles must be accorded more consideration than has heretofore been the case and that other characteristics must also be given appropriate consideration.

The Commission in *Dockets 28300* and *28310* pointed out that the principles underlying the assignment of classification ratings have remained the same, but there has been a change in recent years in the influence of the controlling factors. The policies of the classification committees have been affected by *competition between agencies*

---

[9] *Incandescent Electric Lamps or Bulbs*, 44 MCC 501 (1945); and 47 MCC 601 (1947).

of transportation, so that shipping weight density is now the dominant consideration in determining southern classification ratings. Value is of diminishing importance, and in certain instances, as between like articles, it has disappeared altogether as a factor. The same is true also in the abandonment, to an extent, of differentiation and graduation of the ratings according to the methods or forms of packing.[10]

NATIONAL CLASSIFICATION BOARD

The task of classifying commodities and other matters relating to the contents of the classification are performed for motor carriers by the National Classification Board. This Board is composed of not less than three and not more than five full-time members, one of whom serves as chairman. It considers proposals for changes in descriptions of articles, minimum weights, packing requirements, ratings, and rules or regulations in the National Motor Freight Classifications. It holds public hearings, recommends the disposition of proposals, and instructs the publishing agent of the National Motor Freight Classifications regarding resulting changes in the classifications. In a recent year, which is typical, the Board issued five printed dockets, and twenty public hearings were held on these dockets in four cities. The dockets consisted of 515 subjects, 84 of which were filed by carriers, 203 by shippers, and 228 by the Board; 258 subjects were approved in whole or in part; and 257 were disapproved. There were five appeals during this period from the Board's dispositions, which were filed with the National Traffic Committee. Two of the appeals were remanded by the Committee to the Board for further consideration, two were withdrawn, and Board action was upheld on one.

The National Classification Board holds not less than three public hearings each year, unless there are fewer than five proposals pending in which case the Board may defer its hearing. There have been, however, an average of about 55 subjects per docket in the past. Each hearing lasts from 1 to 3 days.

After public hearings, at least three members of the Board are designated by the Secretary to vote on the disposition of each proposal and issue a notice of the action taken. A majority vote of those designated members governs the action of the Board. If the Board reports a proposal as adopted, and there are no objections within 20

---

[10] *Class Rate Investigation, 1939,* 262 ICC 447, 485 (1951).

days after date of notice of disposition, the Board instructs the publishing agent to publish it. The Board may deviate from the terms of a proposal but may not unduly broaden the issues defined in the published docket.

The Board may reopen or reconsider any docket subject upon which a disposition notice has been issued within 6 months following the date of the initial notice, providing reconsideration shall not be

National Classification Board

1424 SIXTEENTH STREET, N. W. • WASHINGTON 6, D. C. • DUPONT 3200

APPLICATION FOR CHANGE IN
NATIONAL MOTOR FREIGHT CLASSIFICATION

Date **April 23** 19 **53**

INSTRUCTIONS

BE SURE TO ANSWER EACH QUESTION PRECISELY AND FULLY, FURNISHING ADDITIONAL INFORMATION ON SEPARATE SHEET IF NECESSARY.

Give full description of Article and Composition. State whether crude, rough or finished; liquid or dry; if fruit or vegetables, whether green, frozen, dried or canned. Furnish catalogue, cuts or photograph. Supply samples when practicable.

If package is of curved or irregular shape use extreme outside measurements.

To ascertain the "weight per cubic foot" multiply together the three dimensions of the article as packed for shipment, and where the results is in cubic inches, divide by 1728 to reduce to cubic feet, then divide the weight by the number of cubic feet thus ascertained. To obtain the cubic feet of space occupied by a barrel, pail, etc., square the greatest diameter and multiply by the height.

If not separately described at present in Classification, give reference to item number and explanation of how the commodity is now being rated.

Give description EXACTLY as you propose it to be established in the Classification.

Submit two copies of application and each supporting exhibit or statement.

NOTE In order that applications may be quickly processed, complete and correct information must be supplied as to the density and value of the commodity involved.

	L. T. L.			Vol.			Min. Wt. (Pounds)
PRESENT CLASSIFICATION: Item 24500 - by analogy. Silica Gel or Silica Gel Catalyst, LTL in bags, barrels or boxes: Volume in bulk or in packages.	70	70	70	37½	37½	37½	23,000
PROPOSED CLASSIFICATION: Hydregel LTL in barrels or boxes: Volume in bulk or in packages.	50	50	50	27½	27½	27½	25,000

NOTE - Show complete descriptions above, including packing requirements and wording. Arrange the proposed description and ratings exactly as you think they should appear in the Classification. If volume shipments do not require same packing as L.T.L., show differences clearly and explain fully in statement of justification.

KIND OF PACKAGE	OUTSIDE DIMENSIONS OF PACKAGE OR PIECES			WEIGHT AS PACKED FOR SHIPMENT (POUNDS)		WHOLESALE VALUE AS PACKED FOR SHIPMENT	
	Length	Diameter Width	Height	Pkge. or Piece	Per. Cu. Ft.	Pkge. or Piece	Per Lb.
55 gal. drums	21 3/4	29 3/4		274	47 lbs.		4 to 5¢
	20 3/4	33 3/4		179	47 lbs.		4 to 5¢

1. Trade Nomenclature **None** _____ 2. Is commodity fragile? Yes ☐ No ☒

3. Does commodity require refrigeration ☐ , Heat ☒ , Special Handling ☐ ? **No**

4. Is commodity inflammable Yes ☐ No ☒ Explosive Yes ☐ No ☒ Liquid Yes ☐ No ☒ ,
   Paste Yes ☐ No ☒ DRY Yes ☐ No ☒ ?

FIG. 15–5. Application for change in classification.

granted after the effective date of publication in the classification. When the Board reaches its final conclusions, a revised disposition notice subject to all of the procedural rules applicable to initial dispositon shall be issued. The Board cannot reopen any docket subject which was previously appealed and acted upon by the National Traffic Committee.

The appeals procedure provides that if the Board receives written objections with stated reasons within 20 days after its date of notice

---

Rev. April 1952

5. Is commodity SU ☐: KD ☐: Flat ☐: Other than flat ☐: Nested ☐:
   Not Nested ☐: Wheeled ☐: Not Wheeled ☐: Wheels attached ☐: Compressed ☐:
   Not compressed ☐:

If nested are the following requirements met:
   NESTED: Three or more different sizes of the article enclosed each smaller within the next larger, or three or more of the articles placed one within the other so that each upper article will not project above the next lower article more than one-third of its height.

   NESTED SOLID: Three or more of the articles placed one within or upon the other so that the outer side surfaces of the one above will be in contact with the inner side surfaces of the one below and so that each upper article will not project above the next lower more than one-quarter inch.

6. What is average weight loaded in trailer. _27,000_ lbs?

7. Is the commodity double tiered for shipment? _Yes_

8. Materials from which commodity is made _Silicate of Soda, Sulphuric Acid, Alumina Hy-_ _drate_ and _water_

9. Supporting DATA: Photos ☐ Blueprints ☐ Catalogs ☐ Samples ☐ Advertising ☐

10. Area of movement: East ☒ South ☐ West ☐ All Territories ☐

11. Volume of movement for given period: _____ LTL _variable_ TL _200 tons a month_

12. Claim experience? Manufacturer ☐ Shipper ☐ Carrier ☐

   The only claim experience was due to one truckload not being properly
   protected by the carrier from freezing during cold weather.

13. Do you have objection to releasing your name as source of this information? Yes ☐ No ☒

   STATE FULLY WHY CHANGE OR ADDITION IS NECESSARY OR DESIRABLE (If, as justification, applicant refers to ratings of other articles in the classification, complete information as to weight, value, packing, loadibility and other pertinent factors of such comparable items should be given).

   Hydrogel, which is unfinished silica gel or silica gel catalyst, is a gummy like substance which carries a moisture content of approximately 70% and sells for about 4 to 5¢ a pound. Silica gel catalyst has a moisture content of about 17% and its value is 3 to 4 times that of hydrogel.
   Hydrogel is very similar in one respect to spent silica gel or silica gel catalyst in that the value is about the same.
   The variation in the weight of two typical drums used is due to the variation in density of material used, as required by different customers just as there are various grades of our finished silica gel and silica gel catalyst depending on the different uses to which the commodity is put.
   We feel because hydrogel is a semi-finished product with a relatively low value that we are entitled to the same rating as new accorded spent silica gel or silica gel catalyst. Hydrogel will lead heavier because of its very high moisture content.
   We feel that with the publication of Class 27½ on truckloads and Class 50 LTL it will mean increased business for this Corporation and more tonnage for the trucking industry.

Signature of authorized representative:

_____(Title)
   Traffic Manager

Business of Applicant:
Complete Address:
   The Davison Chemical Corporation

of disposition of a proposal from fifteen participating carriers in the classification or from eight members of the National Traffic Committee, the decision of the Board is automatically appealed to the Committee through its secretary. If the Board reports a proposal as having failed of adoption, the proponent may appeal the decision of the Committee within 20 days after date of notice of disposition by the Board by written notification to the secretary of the National Traffic Committee, setting forth the basis for the appeal. The Board may permit additional time for filing appeals by proponents, but not more than 30 days.

The hearings which are held on appeals are made before the National Traffic Committee. A majority of the Committee present decides whether an appealed proposal shall be approved, dismissed, or resubmitted to the Board. Those appealed proposals which are approved by the Committee are published by the publishing agent. All interested parties are given notice by mail of hearings by the Board or of appeal hearings before the National Traffic Committee. The same notice is given to the public by publication in *Transport Topics* not less than 14 days preceding such hearing. The procedure for changes in the National Motor Freight Classification provides the right of independent action so that any participating carrier may publish, cause to be published, or concur in any tariff or tariffs containing exceptions to the classification and any or all provisions thereof.

Since 1945 the National Classification Board has issued a series of principal rulings of which there are twenty-eight series of over 2,000 rulings at the present time. These rulings have been given wide distribution through carrier organizations and weighing and inspection bureaus. They provide clarification of matters on which the Classification Board has been asked for its interpretation.

There are a number of different proposals for changes in the classification which are considered by the National Classification Board, as mentioned earlier. One of these is the addition of a new item to the classification. Proposals are made on forms which are provided by the National Classification Board. An example of a shipper's proposal to add a new item is shown in Figure 15–5. Detailed information about the commodity and the reasons why it should be classified as proposed are given. This proposal was carried in the National Classification Board's *Docket No. 59,* which contained 131 different shipper and carrier proposals, as in Subject No. 75 where the following appears:

SUB. No.	ITEM No.	DESCRIPTION	N. M. F. C. 11			N. M. F. C. A-1		
			LTL	Col.	Min. Wt.	LTL	Vol.	Min. Wt.
75 (S)	....	Add an item: CHEMICALS: Hydrogel, LTL, in barrels or boxes; TL, in bulk or in packages............................	4-50-50	5-7-5	@26.6	50	27½	@26.6
		ⓦIndicates minimum weight factor. (See Rule 34)						

After *Docket No. 59* was heard, the Classification Board voted on Subject 75. Its notice of disposition is shown in Figure 15–6. It will be noted that the shipper's proposal in this instance was recommended for approval with modifications. Inasmuch as there were no objections within 20 days, the recommendation of the Board appeared in a supplement to the National Motor Freight Classifications, which became effective April 20, 1954, as shown below:

SUPPLEMENT No. 6 TO NATIONAL MOTOR FREIGHT CLASSIFICATION No. 12

Item	Cancels item (Original issue, except as noted)	ARTICLES	RATINGS		@Vol. Min. Wt.-Lbs.
			LTL	@Vol.	
*23245	--------	CHEMICALS: Hydrogel, in barrels or boxes; TL, in bulk or in packages.............	F-4-4	Ⓣ5-Ⓣ7- Ⓣ5	ⓦ30.6

SUPPLEMENT No. 22 TO NATIONAL MOTOR FREIGHT CLASSIFICATION No. A-1

Item	Cancels item (Original issue, except as noted)	ARTICLES	RATINGS		@Vol. Min. Wt.-Lbs.
			LTL	@Vol.	
*23245	--------	CHEMICALS: Hydrogel, in barrels or boxes; TL, in bulk or in packages....................	55	Ⓣ35	ⓦ30.6

There have been a relatively small number of appeals from the National Classification Board's actions. During the first 15 years of its operation, there were 2,882 subjects considered and disposed of by the Board with only 24 appeals filed with the National Traffic Committee.[11]

NATIONAL TRAFFIC COMMITTEE

The National Traffic Committee is composed of one hundred elected representatives of common carriers with at least one member from each state and the District of Columbia. The primary duty of this Committee is to investigate, consider, and make recommendations with respect to matters affecting the classification of commodities; and finally to decide, fix, and prescribe the contents, provisions, and ratings of the National Motor Freight Classifications. It considers policy matters affecting the publication of the National Motor

---

[11] *Transport Topics,* October 8, 1951, p. 16.

NOTICE OF DISPOSITION, ISSUED PURSUANT TO RULES OF PROCEDURE.

NATIONAL CLASSIFICATION BOARD

Jos. C. Colquitt, Chairman
N. F. Behme, Jr., Member
H. C. Willson, Member
James E. Bordeaux, Member

Eugene H. Huffman, Secretary

1424 Sixteenth Street, N. W.
WASHINGTON 6, D. C.

Docket 59
Subject 75
P.N. No. 1734
September 30, 1953

Re: Hydrogel

PROPOSAL (S): It is proposed to add an item as shown below:

ADD AN ITEM

Item No.	Description	NMFC #12 LTL	TL	M.W.F.	NMFC #A-1 LTL	TL	M.W.F.
- - -	CHEMICALS: Hydrogel, LTL, in barrels or boxes; TL, in bulk or in packages. . . .	4-50-50	5-7-5	26.6	50	27½	26.6

PROPONENT'S JUSTIFICATION: We feel because hydrogel is a semi-finished product with a relatively low value that we are entitled to the same ratings as now accorded spent silica gel or silica gel catalyst. Hydrogel will load heavier because of its very high moisture content.

DISPOSITION: Approve with modifications.

PUBLICATION: In accordance with these recommendations the Classifications will be amended as follows, but not sooner than 20 days from the date hereof, unless such action is stayed by appeal.

ADD AN ITEM

Item No.	Description	NMFC #12 LTL	TL	M.W.F.	NMFC #A-1 LTL	TL	M.W.F.
- - -	CHEMICALS: Hydrogel, in barrels or boxes; TL, in bulk or in packages. . . .	F-4-4	5-7-5	30.6	55	35	30.6

NATIONAL CLASSIFICATION BOARD

cc: F. G. Freund - Issuing Officer
All Parties of Record

FIG. 15–6. Disposition notice.

Freight Classifications. The Committee also can investigate and recommend with respect to any national traffic problem of general concern to the motor-carrier industry.

The administrative and detail work is handled by eight subcommittees, the membership of which varies from seven to twenty-five members. To qualify for membership on the National Traffic Committee, the individual must be an officer, owner, or full-time employee of a motor carrier which is a party to the National Motor Freight Traffic Agreement, or an officer or full-time employee of an organization, other than the American Trucking Associations, publishing tariffs for the account of carriers (there are currently twelve motor-carrier tariff bureau officials on the Committee), parties to the National Motor Freight Traffic Agreement. Each participating carrier may nominate one qualified person who may be placed on the ballot to represent the state in which the nominating carrier is domiciled.

The schedule of fees for motor carriers which participate in the National Motor Freight Classifications varies depending upon

FIG. 15–7. Organization of the National Traffic Committee.

Source: Section 5a application of carriers participating in the National Motor Freight Classification.

whether the carriers are intrastate or interstate, and whether they are Class I or other than Class I carriers. The fees for Class I carriers are based upon the gross revenue. Figure 15–7 shows the organization of the National Traffic Committee.

The Committee has a formal service agreement with the American Trucking Associations to own and publish the National Motor Freight Classification; to compile and analyze statistics; and to pay the costs in presenting, defending, or prosecuting administrative or judicial proceedings involving these matters. The Director of the Traffic Department of ATA serves as secretary to the Committee and is also the issuing officer of the National Motor Freight Classification. As issuing officer, he has the classification printed, distributes it, and files it with the Commission and those states which require a filing.

In order to comply with a decision of the Commission, the National Traffic Committee in 1955 voted to set up two organizations. One is to be called the National Motor Freight Traffic Association and will handle traffic matters of general concern, as well as compiling, publishing, and collecting fees for participation in the National Motor Freight Classification. The second organization, the National Classification Committee, will handle the joint consideration of classification matters, set the policies and procedures of the National Classification Board, and contract for the publication of the National Freight Classification. Only carriers or carrier representatives will be eligible for membership on this 100-man committee. It is expected that these changes will become effective in 1956.

QUESTIONS AND PROBLEMS

1. Carefully explain the development of the National Motor Freight Classification.
2. What is the purpose of classification? Is classification of greater or lesser importance today as compared to 20 years ago?
3. Describe the composition of the National Motor Freight Classification. Choose an item from NMFC and compare it with the same item as classified in the railroad's Consolidated or Uniform Freight Classification.
4. Compare the two National Motor Freight Classifications. Why are there two?
5. What is the purpose of the classification rules? Are they used only in conjunction with class rates?
6. How would you explain the basic differences between the National Motor Freight Classification and the Coordinated Motor Freight Classification?
7. What are the factors which influence the classification of articles? Is there any one factor that appears to be of more importance than others?
8. What is the composition of the National Classification Board? What is the procedure followed by it?
9. How are the members of the National Traffic Committee chosen? What is its relationship to the National Classification Board?
10. If a carrier proposal fails of adoption before the National Classification Board, what steps may then be taken by the carrier?

16. MOTOR-CARRIER RATES AND RATE MAKING

▼▼

HISTORICALLY, motor-carrier rates have been said to be on a level with the rates of the railroads. When the motor carriers filed their original tariffs in 1936 with the Interstate Commerce Commission, their rates were predicated largely upon those charged by rail carriers. It has been pointed out, however, that there are many rates, both interstate and intrastate, which are commonly believed to be based on rail rates but prove upon research to be rates historically fixed by a particular motor carrier for a particular shipper and thereafter followed first by other motor carriers and then by the railroads.[1]

Prior to the passage of the Motor Carrier Act in 1935, it was customary for motor carriers which handled substantial amounts of interstate traffic to publish and distribute to shippers "rate books" or "rate guides" which quoted rates. Some of these rates applied to movements in which two carriers participated. These rate guides resembled railroad tariffs in form, and the rates in these guides were incorporated in the tariffs that were required to be filed with the Interstate Commerce Commission with the passage of the Motor Carrier Act in 1935.

In rate making, there are a number of theories that are useful in an explanation of particular rates. A practical explanation of the method by which rates are made is the rule of the "Four C's"—Custom, Competition, Comparison, and Compromise. Although regulation has modified the rule of the "Four C's," it has not fundamentally changed this pattern.[2]

---

[1] *Report of the Federal Manager of Motor Carrier Transportation Systems and Properties to the Director of the Office of Defense Transportation* (Washington, D.C., 1946), p. 115.

[2] Board of Investigation and Research, *Relative Economy and Fitness of the Carriers,* House Doc. No. 595, 78th Cong., 2nd sess. (Washington, D.C.: U.S. Government Printing Office, 1944), p. 6.

TRAFFIC DEPARTMENT

Many rate matters are handled by the traffic department. This department usually embraces sales in smaller companies, whereas there will be a separate sales department in larger companies. The traffic department has as one of its important responsibilities the interpretation of the application of classifications and tariffs and the furnishing of such information to salesmen or to the company's customers. It also supervises the distribution of tariffs throughout the company. The traffic department analyzes classification and rate docket proposals and represents the company at such docket meetings in which it has an interest. In rate and classification matters before regulatory bodies, the traffic department represents the motor carrier. In larger companies, this duty is performed in co-operation with the general counsel. The traffic department also establishes government rate quotations.

Tariff files must be maintained in order that there can be expeditious quotation of rates to customers. Shippers and consignees are contacted for consultation regarding traffic problems. The traffic department also establishes divisions of revenues between the company and other carriers and publishes division sheets controlling the divisions. Routing guides showing points served which are on the company's lines, as well as points served through interline agreements, are also prepared by this department.

Research must be undertaken in many rate matters in order to have a sound basis for rate proposals. The traffic department must also settle controversial matters regarding claims for overcharge.

RELATIONSHIP OF SIZE OF SHIPMENTS TO RATES

Motor carriers make a distinction between truckload and less-than-truckload shipments. In order to secure a truckload rate, which is lower than that applied to less-than-truckload shipments, a shipment of minimum weight as established by the carriers must be tendered or the minimum paid. The truckload minimum will be that weight which can be transported in a single vehicle. Any shipment less than this minimum is called a "less-than-truckload lot." In addition to truckload and less-than-truckload categories, motor carriers have established a "volume minimum." This can be described as a minimum weight which is in excess of what can be loaded in a single truck. When a shipper tenders the volume minimum weight of a commodity, the volume rate applies even though it may exceed the carrying capacity of the largest vehicle available and must be carried in two or more vehicles.

Rates on graduated quantities have been established in some areas on quantities of 5,000, 10,000, and 20,000 pounds. If a shipper can tender shipments of 10,000 instead of 5,000 pounds, he can secure a lower rate; and, if he can tender shipments of 20,000 pounds, he can secure a lower rate than that applicable to the 10,000-pound shipment.

Shipments fall into three general classes: (a) shipments loaded at the shipper's door in the over-the-road unit which occupy the entire vehicle and are unloaded at consignee's door from the over-the-road unit; (b) shipments picked up at the shipper's door in the over-the-road unit and carried with other freight for all or a substantial part of the journey, without being handled over the platform of original terminal; and (c) shipments picked up at the shipper's door, delivered to consignee in pickup equipment, and handled over platform at both origin and destination. Truckload shipments or shipments weighing more than 10,000 pounds usually fall in the first category; those weighing between 5,000 and 10,000 pounds, in the second category; and less-than-volume shipments (less than 5,000 pounds), in the third category.

Shipments in the last two categories moved at the same rates until recently. This was an outgrowth of rail rate structure designed long before pickup and delivery service. The Interstate Commerce Commission, in MC–C–518, approved the assessment of an arbitrary charge of 20 cents per 100 pounds on less-than-volume shipments, thus separating for the first time less-than-volume shipments from less-than-truckload shipments. The less-than-volume shipment differs from the less-than-truckload shipment in that it requires relatively more pickup and delivery service and more platform handling, the cost of which operations has increased at a much faster rate than over-the-road costs. Table 16–1 gives the Commission figures on the relative cost of pickup and delivery service, by territories. This shows that in every territory the cost of such service is much greater on the smaller shipments than on the volume shipments.

The Bureau of Transport Economics and Statistics of the Commission has defined small shipments as those weighing 300 pounds or less. A study which it made indicated that Class I intercity motor carriers of general commodities in 1951 handled 8 per cent of all such shipments, which accounted for about 21 per cent of the num-

TABLE 16-1

RELATIVE COST FOR PICKUP AND DELIVERY SERVICE, BY TERRITORIES*

(In Cents per 100 Pounds)

AVERAGE WEIGHT PER SHIPMENT (POUNDS)	SOUTHERN, 1944		WESTERN TRUNK LINE, 1944	MIDDLE ATLANTIC, 1945–46	
	Intraterri- torial	Interterri- torial		New York– Phila- delphia Group	Other than New York– Philadelphia Group
100............	$0.22	$0.27	$0.25	$0.35	$0.47
200............	0.13	0.16	0.15	0.22	0.28
300............	0.10	0.12	0.12	0.17	0.21
400............	0.08	0.10	0.10	0.15	0.17
500............	0.07	0.09	0.09	0.13	0.15
600............	0.06	0.08	0.08	0.12	0.14
700............	0.06	0.08	0.07	0.11	0.13
800............	0.05	0.07	0.07	0.11	0.12
900............	0.05	0.07	0.07	0.10	0.12
1,000............	0.05	0.07	0.06	0.10	0.11
1,200............	0.04	0.06	0.06	0.09	0.10
1,500............	0.04	0.06	0.05	0.09	0.10
2,000............	0.04	0.05	0.05	0.08	0.09
5,000............	0.03	0.04	0.04	0.06	0.07
10,000............	0.02	0.03	0.03	0.06	0.06
15,000............	0.02	0.03	0.03	0.05	0.06
20,000............	0.02	0.02	0.03	0.04	0.05

* Data shown are taken from working papers of the Cost Section used in compiling the motor-carrier costs for various proceedings before the Commission.

Source: Interstate Commerce Commission, Bureau of Accounts and Cost Finding, *Territorial Cost Scales and Operating Factors in Middle Atlantic Territory*, Identification A (Washington, D.C., May, 1948), p. 146.

ber of pieces and 49 per cent of the aggregate weight for this type of shipments moved by all carriers and the Post Office. Motor carriers received about 17 per cent of the total revenue received by all carriers and the Post Office for such shipments.[3]

From the standpoint of cost of service, a small shipment has always presented a special problem. This problem, so far as rates and charges are concerned, derives primarily from cost differences which lie principally in the terminal service. In large part, this situation is due to the fact that much of the cost of picking up, handling, and delivering a small shipment is independent of the weight of the shipment. Certain elements of the pickup and delivery cost, and a substantial part of the general office and terminal clerical cost, being independent of the weight of the shipment, are, therefore, several times as great, per 100 pounds, for a 100-pound shipment as for a 1,000-pound shipment. Small shipments require platform handling to a greater degree than shipments of larger size.

---

[3] Interstate Commerce Commission, Bureau of Transport Economics and Statistics, *Statistics of Small Shipments* (Washington, D.C., July, 1953), pp. 1, 3.

BROKEN STOWAGE

It is recognized in motor-carrier operations that it is impossible, in general, to load shipments to the full width, length, and height of a vehicle. This is termed "broken stowage," because of the existence of spaces unavoidably left unfilled. These unfilled spaces occur on account of irregularities in the sizes of packages in mixing common loads of crates, bundles, boxes, bales, rolls, pipes, barrels, drums, and the like. In addition to the unfilled spaces between packages, the empty spaces at the sides, the ends, and the top of the cargo constitute broken stowage. Thus, waste space may exist even where the packages are uniform in their dimensions. An average over-the-road unit with a van body 7 feet × 7 feet × 30 feet has a loss of 8 per cent of the total cubic space of that body if there is empty space of 3 inches below the roof, 3 inches along one side, and 3 inches between the back of the load and the rear doors. Upon analysis, a number of less-than-truckload loaded vehicles filled with general cargo were found to have a space of 6 inches to 1 foot at the top of the load.[4] In a van body with a height of 7 feet, a space of 1 foot at the top of the load is equal to a loss in total space of 14 per cent. Ordinarily, the horizontal space between packages will amount to from 2 to 5 inches out of the total body width of 7 feet. If an allowance is made for an average loss of 6 inches at the top of the truck and a loss of 2 inches of load space across the width of the truck and a loss of 4 inches between the front end of the body and the rear doors, the total waste space would be slightly over 10 per cent.[5] Terminal managers have estimated that broken stowage for the average over-the-road vehicle runs from 5 to 15 per cent of the space capacity.[6] This element of waste space must be considered in the formulation of rates.

DENSITY

Because the cubical content for the maximum weight-carrying capacity of an over-the-road unit is limited, the influence of density may have a bearing in the establishment of a rate. A standard-size unit of an over-the-road truck has a cubical area capacity of 1,000

---

[4] Interstate Commerce Commission, Bureau of Transport Economics and Statistics, *Explanation of the Development of Motor Carrier Costs with Statement as to Their Meaning and Significance* (Washington, D.C., October, 1946), p. 75.

[5] *Ibid.*

[6] *Ibid.*

cubic feet and a weight-carrying capacity of 20,000 pounds. The shipping-weight density of the standard-size units of vessel, barge, boxcar, and truck is as follows:[7]

Explanation	Vessel	Barge	Boxcar	Truck
Cubical-area capacity (cubic feet).......	598,878	134,695	2,926	1,000
Weight-carrying capacity (tons).........	12,222	2,000	40	10
Shipping-weight density (pounds per cubic foot)......................	41	30	27	20

The division of the cubic feet capacity of 1,000 into the weight-carrying capacity, 20,000 pounds, results in a shipping-weight density of 20 for an over-the-road unit. In other words, 20 pounds for each cubic foot of space would provide a full load based on a maximum weight-carrying capacity of 20,000 pounds. Some commodities, such as frozen orange juice, have a very high density (50 lbs. per cubic foot); and a truck may be loaded to its weight capacity although not over 5 to 10 per cent of its space capacity is used. A bulky commodity, such as household goods, on the other hand, may have a low density (7–12 lbs. per cubic foot); and the entire cubic space of the vehicle may be insufficient for the carrying of 20,000 pounds. The ideal situation would be to carry only those commodities of such density as to fill the cubic capacity and load to the 20,000 pounds. That seldom happens. However, it might be possible to secure this maximum shipping-weight density by having a mixture of low-density and high-density freight, so that the vehicle could be loaded to its weight capacity.

Freight rates are usually quoted on a weight basis; but the amount of weight that can be carried in a truck, except as limited by state laws and the weight-carrying capacity of the vehicle, depends upon the density of the commodity or commodities. The lighter and bulkier articles will, in general, be charged at a higher rate to compensate for the lack of weight, even though they fully load the vehicle's cubic space.

CLASS RATES

A class rate is one that is governed by a rating in a classification. In establishing a class rate, there will be factors similar to those enumerated as receiving consideration in fixing classification ratings

---

[7] Board of Investigation and Research, *Comparison of Rail, Motor and Water Carrier Costs*, Sen. Doc. No. 84, 79th Cong., 1st sess. (Washington, D.C.: U.S. Government Printing Office, 1945), p. 22.

which will have influence. Class rates have a broader application than other rates. There is widespread use of mileage scales, which results in the rate increasing as the distance increases but not in exact proportion to increases in distance. To simplify rate construction, class rates are usually made on a group basis; that is, the principal city in each group is known as the base point, and the rates are published between the base points. However, in some instances, towns in a group are over 70 miles from the base points, so that there may be a lack of uniformity in rates on a distance scale except between the base points. Table 16–2 shows class rates for different-sized shipments based on distances which were found to be reasonable by the Interstate Commerce Commission in one case.[8]

The rate scale used by motor carriers is generally either one which is being used by railroads or one with the necessary modifications. In 1952 the railroads had a class rate scale prescribed by the Commission in *Dockets 28300* and *28310* to be applicable throughout the United States east of the Rocky Mountains.[9] This scale has become known as the *28300* scale. In the Southern Territory this scale was generally adopted by motor carriers. In another rate territory, the basic scale was adopted but with some class rates included which are as much as 35 per cent above the railroads' *28300* scale. The deviation from the class rate scale usually occurs where the competitive situation requires or permits it.

Some class rate tariffs incorporate what is termed a "class-rate stop" or a "minimum-rate stop." This means that, although goods may be rated at a lower class in a classification, the class rate applicable will be the same as on a higher class. In other words, the article may be rated Class 6 in a classification; but, because it cannot be carried profitably at a Class 6 rate, the carriers establish a rate stop at Class 5 in the rate tariff. Anything rated below a Class 5 rating carries a Class 5 rate. The need for the class-rate stop is attributed to the fact that the motor carriers largely adopted the railroad classification but soon discovered that the rail class rates on lower-rated, long-haul traffic were not compensatory to the motor carrier, especially where there was a joint-line movement. The establishment of the class-rate stop was the solution to this problem and is widely found in the tariffs of the motor carriers.

The effect of the minimum-rate stop is to provide a bottom rate on class traffic and to raise the classification rating on all traffic which

---

[8] *Motor Carrier Rates in New England,* 47 MCC 675 (1948).
[9] *Class Rate Investigation, 1939,* 286 ICC 5 (1952).

TABLE 16–2

CLASS 1 RATES IN AMOUNTS PER 100 POUNDS
SOUTHERN NEW ENGLAND

Distance	Under 250 Pounds	250–1,399 Pounds	1,400–2,699 Pounds	2,700–4,499 Pounds	4,500 Pounds and Over
11 miles........	$1.84	$1.57	$1.36	$0.91	$0.73
15 miles........	1.87	1.60	1.41	0.95	0.77
19 miles........	1.90	1.62	1.45	0.98	0.81
23 miles........	1.93	1.64	1.49	1.02	0.84
27 miles........	1.99	1.70	1.53	1.06	0.87
31 miles........	2.05	1.76	1.57	1.10	0.90
35 miles........	2.11	1.82	1.60	1.13	0.93
39 miles........	2.16	1.88	1.64	1.16	0.96
44 miles........	2.21	1.94	1.67	1.19	0.99
49 miles........	2.27	2.00	1.72	1.22	1.02
54 miles........	2.33	2.06	1.77	1.25	1.05
59 miles........	2.39	2.12	1.82	1.28	1.08
64 miles........	2.45	2.18	1.87	1.32	1.11
69 miles........	2.51	2.24	1.93	1.36	1.15
74 miles........	2.57	2.30	1.98	1.40	1.18
79 miles........	2.62	2.36	2.04	1.44	1.21
84 miles........	2.67	2.41	2.09	1.48	1.25
89 miles........	2.72	2.46	2.14	1.52	1.29
94 miles........	2.77	2.51	2.19	1.57	1.34
99 miles........	2.82	2.56	2.24	1.62	1.39
104 miles........	2.87	2.61	2.29	1.67	1.44
109 miles........	2.92	2.66	2.34	1.72	1.49
114 miles........	2.97	2.71	2.39	1.77	1.54
119 miles........	3.02	2.76	2.43	1.82	1.59
124 miles........	3.07	2.80	2.48	1.88	1.65
129 miles........	3.12	2.84	2.53	1.93	1.70
135 miles........	3.17	2.89	2.58	1.98	1.75
142 miles........	3.22	2.93	2.63	2.04	1.80
148 miles........	3.27	2.98	2.68	2.10	1.86
155 miles........	3.32	3.03	2.73	2.16	1.92
161 miles........	3.36	3.08	2.78	2.22	1.98
168 miles........	3.41	3.13	2.84	2.28	2.04
174 miles........	3.46	3.18	2.90	2.34	2.10
181 miles........	3.51	3.23	2.96	2.40	2.16
187 miles........	3.57	3.28	3.02	2.46	2.22
194 miles........	3.63	3.33	3.08	2.51	2.28
200 miles........	3.69	3.38	3.14	2.57	2.33
207 miles........	3.75	3.44	3.20	2.63	2.39
213 miles........	3.81	3.51	3.26	2.69	2.45
220 miles........	3.88	3.58	3.33	2.75	2.51
226 miles........	3.95	3.66	3.39	2.81	2.57
233 miles........	4.02	3.74	3.46	2.87	2.63
239 miles........	4.10	3.82	3.54	2.94	2.69
246 miles........	4.18	3.90	3.61	3.01	2.75
252 miles........	4.24	3.98	3.68	3.08	2.81
259 miles........	4.32	4.06	3.76	3.15	2.88
267 miles........	4.40	4.14	3.84	3.22	2.95
275 miles........	4.49	4.22	3.92	3.30	3.02
283 miles........	4.58	4.30	4.00	3.38	3.09
291 miles........	4.67	4.37	4.08	3.46	3.17
299 miles........	4.76	4.44	4.16	3.54	3.25
307 miles........	4.83	4.51	4.24	3.62	3.33
315 miles........	4.90	4.58	4.32	3.70	3.41
323 miles........	4.97	4.65	4.40	3.78	3.49
331 miles........	5.04	4.72	4.47	3.85	3.57
339 miles........	5.10	4.79	4.54	3.93	3.65
347 miles........	5.16	4.86	4.62	4.01	3.72
355 miles........	5.22	4.93	4.69	4.08	3.79

Source: *Motor Carrier Rates in New England*, 47 MCC 682 (1948).

would move at lower rates in the absence of the rate stop up to a rating equivalent to the rate stop. There are numerous individual minimum-rate stops on less-truckload, single-line movements. Ordinarily joint-line hauls are subject to higher individual stops than single-line hauls. The Commission has felt that the use of class-rate stops "not only results in undue disadvantage to freight rated in the lower classes but in effect to a certain extent constitutes avoidance of the duty imposed by law upon all motor common carriers to afford reasonable transportation service at reasonable rates in all classes of traffic."[10]

However, the Commission felt that motor carriers should be permitted to continue the use of class-rate stops during the emergency of World War II. Since the end of the war, the Commission has re-emphasized the desirability of eliminating class-rate stops. One agency tariff was found to contain individual stops for about 517 carriers, with each carrier maintaining a variety of stops for different movements. For one large carrier, there were 90 statements of minimum-rate restrictions containing about 330 separate minimum rates. In a recent motor-carrier application case for operating rights, the general nonparticipation of motor carriers in through rates in the area in which the applicant proposed to operate and the use of rate stops when through rates did exist caused a proposed finding by an examiner of the Commission that existing service was inadequate. Therefore, the applicant should be given the right to operate.

COMMODITY RATES

The second general type of rate is that of commodity rates, which generally are published to provide for the movement of traffic believed to require a lower rate than is provided in the classification. The commodity rate is usually a point-to-point rate applicable to a specific commodity between certain points and thus has a limited application. This type of rate based primarily on volume and regularity of shipments is widely used by motor carriers. It is possible for a commodity rate to be higher than a class rate, but the reverse is usually the case.

EXCEPTION RATINGS

The publishing of exceptions to the classification in a separate tariff removes articles from the classification and establishes rules or

---

[10] *Minimum Class Rate Restrictions, Central & Eastern States,* 44 MCC 367 (1945).

rates that modify the normal class rates. These are, in general, below the class rates. The exceptions, in effect, might be looked upon as amendments to the classification and are established for a variety of reasons: to meet competition, to accomplish a more restrictive application of particular rates, and to move a considerable volume of traffic of a particular type. These exceptions contain rules and regulations governing the application of rates and practices which are not covered in the classification. Exception ratings and rules in a rate tariff, unless otherwise indicated, take precedence over the classification. The exceptions ratings are used in conjunction with class rates.

No exact figure is known as to the percentages of traffic which move under class rates, commodity rates, or exception ratings for the United States as a whole. Some indication of the tonnage moved under each type of rate is given in a study made in 1945, which indicated that approximately 28 per cent of the tonnage moved on exception ratings, an additional 28 per cent on commodity rates, and 38 per cent on class rates, with an additional 6 per cent on class-rate stops.

OTHER RATES

There are many other types of rates which are published, some of which are discussed in this chapter. There may be arbitraries to an off-line point, or differentials added to the basic rates and rules outlining additional services may apply for which an additional charge will be applicable. These rates are published in tariffs, which in effect are price lists of carriers, in accordance with general tariff circular requirements prescribed by the Commission. There are many different kinds of tariffs, such as class, class and commodity, general commodity, specific commodity, grouping (points around a principal city may be grouped), accessorial charge or allowance, scope of operations (area served by carriers), mileage, and tariff indexes. Local tariffs contain rates which apply between points served by one carrier. Joint tariffs contain rates which apply for two or more carriers; and there are other types of tariffs based on the type of rates which are contained. There are many changes which are made in the rates so that supplements are issued to the tariff. Figure 16–1 shows a tariff and the supplements issued to it in one year's time.

Two levels of rates may be published in a tariff. For example, one level may include all increases that have been made, and the other not include certain increases but published to apply only via certain

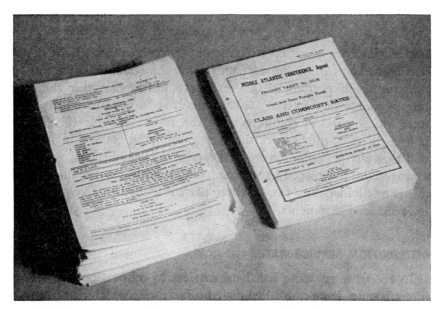

FIG. 16–1. Supplements (left) to a class and commodity tariff (right) issued in a period of one year. The volume of the supplements is about four times that of the original tariff.

carriers which wish to protect the lower level. In one tariff, the lower level is published in Section 2½ of the tariff and the higher level is published in Sections 1 and 2. Section 2½ applies only via carriers and to the extent shown in Item 1321 of the tariff. For this reason these carriers are known as "1321 Carriers." Generally the 1321 carriers are the ones which protect both classification and exception rates in the tariff. Carriers other than the 1321 carriers are those which protect only the exception rates and apply the rates in another tariff on classification-rated traffic.

AVERAGE RATES

In a number of cases, railroads have published dual rail commodity rates which are often referred to as "incentive" or "discount" rates. Under this plan, two rates are published. For example, one is a base rate which is applicable on the first 40,000 pounds in the shipment, and the other is a rate which is 20 per cent lower than the base rate and applies on portions of the shipment which weigh more than 40,000 pounds if the excess amount is loaded into the same car as the initial 40,000 pounds.

Motor carriers, in order to be competitive on such traffic, have established commodity rates which are generally referred to as "average rates." Average rates are made by computing the rate in cents per 100 pounds which would be applicable under the dual rate system of rail rates based on the average weight of a commodity when it is moved by rail. If the average weight of a commodity moved by rail was 50,000 pounds, 40,000 pounds would be moved at the base rate by motor carriers and 10,000 pounds at 80 per cent of the base rate. Motor carriers compute what the rail rate is for the 50,000 pounds, that is, they secure the average rate and make this the rate that they charge. Shipments which exceed the vehicle capacity under average rates are placed in a second vehicle with less-truckload shipments or divided into two or three parts if loaded in a vehicle with less-truckload shipments.

DISTRIBUTION SERVICE RATES

In recent years some line-haul carriers in connection with their intercity rates have published distribution tariffs which provide that truckload or volume shipments may be consigned for distribution by the line-haul carriers. There are both individual carrier tariffs and agency tariffs which contain these rates. These tariffs are generally applicable on freight of all kinds, with certain commodities excepted. These shipments, in effect, are pooled shipments which require numerous separate deliveries at destination.

Local cartage companies also perform distribution at destination for railroads which render pool-car service. Often truck shipments are distributed at destination by local cartage companies.

The distribution rates which are established by the line-haul carrier provide for a small additional charge to be added to the line-haul rate. The carrier will then render multiple split delivery service to a number of consignees. A prior haul by the carrier offering the distribution service is not required in all tariffs. Some require the consignor to furnish a bill of lading for each part of a pooled shipment to be distributed, whereas others require a bill of lading and distribution sheet covering the truckload or volume shipment from origin to destination point. A pooled shipment may require as many as thirty deliveries or as few as five. Table 16–3 shows distribution rates on pooled shipments consigned to the carrier at a specified point as published in a distribution tariff. These are graduated distribution rates based on weight.

In general, these distribution rates have been maintained at about the same level for a number of years, although there have been substantial increases in a number of other rates. The class rates maintained by motor common carriers from Chicago or St. Louis to nearby points are generally substantially higher than the distribution rates charged by some carriers.[11] As an example, the fourth class rate from St. Louis to Websters Grove, Missouri, a distance of 10 miles, is 31 cents. The distribution rates for delivery to Websters Grove, which is within a 23-mile radius of St. Louis, varies from 14 cents to 6 cents, depending upon weight, as shown in Table 16–3. In effect, this is less-truckload service at slightly more than truckload rates.

Distribution rates are generally below those of local cartage carriers which also perform pooled shipment service. These carriers have sought to have the Commission prescribe minimum reasonable rates for distribution rates, but the Commission has declined to do so. It

TABLE 16–3

DISTRIBUTION RATES ON POOLED SHIPMENTS CONSIGNED TO CARRIER AT ST. LOUIS, MO.*

Minimum Weight in Pounds	*Cents*
Under 2,500	14
2,500–4,999	11
5,000–7,499	9
7,500–9,999	7
10,000 and over	6

* The same rates apply to all points in St. Louis, Mo., and also to numerous specified points in Illinois and Missouri located within a 23-mile radius thereof.

Source: *Local Cartage National Conference* v. *Middlewest Motor Freight Bureau, Inc.*, 62 MCC 239 (1953).

has held that there is nothing in the act which specifically prohibits a line-haul carrier from performing a distribution service at a point which it is authorized to serve.[12]

Split delivery means that there can be several deliveries at one destination. Stopping in transit to unload partially means that the service must be performed at a point between origin and destination. It may not be performed within the corporate limits of the destination nor may more than one stop be made at the intermediate point.[13]

Stopping in transit and split deliveries are looked upon as separate services. The provisions covering them should be stated separately in tariffs, and separate additional charges should be specified. There

---

[11] *Local Cartage National Conference* v. *Middlewest Motor Freight Bureau, Inc.*, 62 MCC 239 (1953).

[12] *Ibid.*

[13] *Stopping in Transit at Pittsburgh, Pa.*, 34 MCC 653 (1942).

have been occasions when a tariff rule authorizing two stops in transit was made without additional charge.

ALL FREIGHT RATES

Section 409 (a) provides that if line-haul transportation between concentration points and break-bulkpoints in truckload lots for a total distance of 450 miles or more is performed under contracts, such contracts should not permit payment by freight forwarders to motor common carriers of compensation lower than would be received under rates or charges established under Part II of the act. This amendment to the act became effective in 1951. Subsequently a number of motor carriers filed tariffs proposing all-commodity rates or all-freight rates (merchandise in mixed truckloads) which were to replace former joint rates and divisions with freight forwarders. These rates were suspended. Upon investigation, Division 2 held that truckload rates of motor common carriers in the particular case were unreasonably low. They were below a reasonable minimum level to the extent that they were less than rates which were 45 per cent of the *Docket 28300* Class 1 rates, minimum 20,000 pounds, within the investigative territory or less than rail rates, minimum 30,000 pounds, on all commodities when in mixed carloads to, from, or between the same points when such rail rates are lower than rates made 45 per cent of the *Docket 28300* Class 1 rates to, from, or between such points.[14]

The all-commodity or all-freight rates are patterned to some degree upon the railroads' all-commodity rates. The all-commodity rates of motor carriers do not apply on all commodities because the tariffs contain some classifications of property in which certain commodities are excepted and certain restrictions apply. For example, one tariff provides that the rates apply on a mixed shipment which consists of ten or more commodities, no one commodity to exceed 50 per cent of the weight of the lading or of the minimum weight, whichever is greater. Some of the articles which are excepted include commodities in bulk, explosives, livestock, and perishable freight, as well as others.

One motor carrier which hauls only for freight forwarders maintains its charges in its tariffs in dollars by truck for various stated maximum weights ranging from 20,000 to 24,000 pounds and rates in cents per 100 pounds for "overage," i.e., weight in excess of the

---

[14] *Merchandise—Mixed Truckloads—East, MC–C–1331,* April 22, 1955.

maximum which produces charges relatively lower than its truck-load charges. Some motor carriers maintain all-commodity rates which are available to any shipper who can meet the conditions contained in the tariff, although the primary users of such rates are freight forwarders.

ASSEMBLY AND DISTRIBUTION RATES

Section 408 authorizes motor common carriers to establish for freight forwarders and others who employ or utilize the instrumentalities or services of such common carriers under like conditions less-truckload assembling and distribution rates which differ from their normal less-truckload rates between the same points. These rates apply only *to assembling points and from distribution points.* They cannot cover terminal-to-terminal movements. Individual shippers and shippers' co-operative associations have utilized assembly and distribution rates under similar conditions as those prevailing for freight forwarders. The assembly and distribution rates are usually lower than rates on nonforwarder traffic.

The reasons for assembly rates which were 85 per cent of class rates were cited in one case as being the elimination of solicitation expense, a reduction in the cost of rating, billing, and adjusting claims, and a savings in delivery expense.[15]

In another case, assembly and distribution rates which were approximately 70 per cent of the ordinary rates were found to be reasonable.[16]

ALLOWANCES

Carriers sometimes permit the shipper an allowance when the shipper performs a part of the transportation service, such as picking up his shipment at the terminal rather than having the carrier deliver it to him. Allowances are not made to a shipper or consignee for performing a service unless it is one which the carrier is obligated to perform under its tariffs as an essential part of a transportation service.[17]

Parties who perform pickup and delivery service for rail and motor carriers and freight forwarders may be permitted to receive more

---

[15] *Definition of Freight Consolidators,* 43 MCC 527 (1944).

[16] *Distribution Rates, Newark, N.J., to N.J. and N.Y. Points,* 46 MCC 745 (1947).

[17] *Mid-Western Motor Ft. Tariff Bureau, Inc. v. Eichhootz,* 4 MCC 755 (1938).

than the shipper's allowance in the tariff only under a written contract. The terms of this contract must provide that such a person shall be required to furnish the service as an agent or as an independent contractor of the carrier or freight forwarder and shall be required by such contract to issue, or to accept, in the name of the carrier or freight forwarder, receipts for the goods picked up or delivered by him in such service.[18]

Payments which are in excess of the tariff allowance and not under such contractual arrangements are held to be the giving of an undue and unusual preference and advantage and constitute rebating.[19]

These contracts do not have to be filed with the Commission but are retained by the carrier. They do not have to cover general pickup and delivery service but rather an allowance contract could be made with a number of local cartage companies or an allowance contract with a warehouseman to pick up and deliver only shipments moving to and from that warehouse.

MINIMUM CHARGES

In a case before the Commission dealing with charges on small shipments by motor carriers, a witness for the Commission introduced an exhibit which showed ninety-seven varieties of minimum charges to be in effect in various rate territories. In some of the urban areas, such as New York and Chicago, a minimum charge based on less than 100 pounds is maintained on restricted types of traffic, but generally the minimum charge is stated to be the applicable Class 1 rate for 100 pounds subject to a minimum of $1.00 or more depending upon the rate territory. There are higher minimum charges which are provided for specified services.

When minimum charges are stated as the applicable Class 1 rate for 100 pounds, it is necessary to find a rate scale number of the Class 1 rate in the tariff to which the minimum charge is tied. This number is then converted into the minimum charge or that amount which may be charged on a higher basis according to the class tariffs. It is then necessary to check back against the minimum charge to determine which is higher. To compensate for this, a surcharge of $1.50 is added to the freight charges computed at the applicable weight and rate on all shipments of less than 5,000 pounds in one

---

[18] *Allowances for Pick-Up-and-Delivery at Kansas City*, 272 ICC 331 (1948).
[19] *Ibid.*

rate territory. In this rate territory, it was stated that more than 70 per cent of shipments in excess of 5,000 pounds moved in line-haul from shipper's door to consignee's door, with nearly 20 per cent handled by trailer spotting. Thus, a minimum use of terminal facilities or equipment was involved. In contrast to this, just 12 per cent of the shipments under 5,000 pounds was picked up and delivered in line-haul semitrailers and only 1½ per cent by trailer spotting. Further, it was stated that it cost four times more for pickup and delivery of less-truckload traffic than for a ton of volume or truckload freight.[20] In this particular case, decided in 1955, the Commission ordered cancellation of the surcharge and authorized a minimum charge of $3.00; and increased rates for two weight groups to make up for revenue produced by the surcharge.

However, when motor carriers imposed a surcharge to compensate them for the expense of a weight-distance tax enacted by the state of New York, the Commission found that the surcharge established for this purpose was not just and reasonable. The Commission stated that this tax, like other operating taxes, should be treated as a normal operating expense and be reflected in the rates rather than in surcharges.[21]

The experience of carriers has been that the minimum charge rate structure for the smaller shipments is a method to price a service which consists of weight, distance, terminal, and clerical functions, whereas the rate scale is based on only weight and weight-distance.

NET WEIGHTS

Although most rates are based on the gross weight of the shipment, i.e., the package and its contents, the Commission has approved motor-carrier truckload rates based on net weight of the contents of a package and on the inclusion of the rate of empty containers in the rate for the loaded movement. It also has approved the supplying of containers by the carrier, as well as the interchange of containers for others with consignor and consignee provided there is no discrimination and that the charges collected are reasonable for the entire service performed. In the same case, it was held that tariffs providing for rates of empty containers without additional charge,

---

[20] Brief of Central States Motor Freight Bureau filed in *I and S M-4462 Surcharge on Small Shipments Within Central States*, 1953.

[21] *Surcharges—New York State*, 62 MCC 117 (1953).

even if they can be loaded with other freight and moved back at the carrier's option, are unlawful.[22]

ACTUAL-VALUE AND RELEASED-VALUE RATINGS

Although the Interstate Commerce Act[23] provides that motor carriers are to be responsible for the full value of merchandise transported by them where freight is lost or damaged, it also provides for a limitation of that liability in specific instances where approved by the Commission. Applications to provide such limited liability have been made to the Interstate Commerce Commission to cover certain commodities and have been approved by the Commission. The effect of these approvals by the Commission has been to provide at least two ratings on certain commodities. These are actual-value ratings and released-value ratings. The rating to be applied in some of these commodities where limitations of liability have been approved by the Commission, whether it is to be an actual-value rating or a released-value rating, will depend upon the shipper's designation of the rating in the bill of lading.

The actual-value ratings have been published on commodities where the range of value has been so wide that it is difficult to establish one rating based on an average value. When this rating is used in a bill of lading or on shipping orders, the shipper must designate the use of the rating and certify the actual value of the commodity. An example of a commodity so rated in the National Motor Freight Classification No. A–2 is shown in Table 16–4.

A shipper can specify an arbitrary valuation on certain commodities which may or may not be the actual value of the commodity to be shipped. However, the amount that the shipper specifies in the bill of lading will determine the rating that will apply on the shipment, as well as the estimate of the carrier's liability in the event of loss or damage by the carrier, and is termed the released value of the commodity. Examples of released-value ratings to be found in the National Motor Freight Classification No. A–2 are shown in Table 16–5.

Where a commodity is subject either to an actual or to a released valuation, the value of the commodity should be expressed in the rating in essentially the same manner as indicated in the classification. If the classification provides a rating based on a value in cents per 100 pounds, the value of the commodity on the bill of lading

---

[22] *Iron or Steel in Containers—Central Territory,* 54 MCC 139 (1952).
[23] Section 20 (11).

TABLE 16-4

EXAMPLES OF ACTUAL-VALUE RATINGS OF COMMODITIES IN THE NATIONAL MOTOR FREIGHT
CLASSIFICATION

ITEM	ARTICLES	RATINGS		VOL. MIN. WEIGHT (POUNDS)
		LTL	Vol.	
32525	Binoculars, Field Glasses, Opera Glasses or Telescopes, NOI, see Note, item 32526: Actual value not exceeding $1.00 each, in barrels or boxes..........................	125	Ⓣ85	Ⓦ12.6
32526	Actual value exceeding $1.00 each, in barrels or boxes..........................	300	Ⓣ150	Ⓦ10.6
	Note. Shippers must certify on shipping order and bill of lading the actual value of the property as follows: "Actual value of the...........(insert name of commodity) is hereby stated by the shipper to be 'not in excess of $1.00 each' or 'in excess of $1.00 each,' " as the case may be.			

should be expressed in that manner. If a carrier representative prepares a bill of lading covering such a shipment, the value of the commodity—that is, the value in cents per pound, per 100 pounds, and so forth—must be secured from the shipper. The shipper should be informed that there is more than one rating in effect, depending on the actual or released value of the commodity. In all cases where commodities are accepted at actual-value or released-value ratings, the bill of lading must be signed by the shipper. As discussed in an earlier chapter practically all household goods are moved at released value ratings.

The increased value of commodities due to inflation and technological advances has resulted in greatly increasing liability for motor common carriers. The use, in a few instances, of released rates in which the liability of the carrier is limited to a specified amount per pound or per article has been one method of meeting this problem. It has been suggested that all freight transported by rail and motor carriers could be covered by a general tariff provision based upon a released rate order similar to that issued to the Railway Express Agency. It is estimated that 75 per cent of the freight transported by motor common carriers is worth less than 25 cents per pound, whereas 95 per cent of the freight carried by railroads is worth less than 25 cents per pound.[24] Under this plan a basic value of 25 cents per pound of gross shipping weight would constitute the liability of the carrier. If the shipper elected, he could de-

[24] A. F. Arpaia and C. G. Jensen, "Common Carrier Liability in the Atomic Age," *Michigan Law Review,* Vol. LI, No. 8 (June, 1953), p. 1191.

TABLE 16–5

EXAMPLES OF RELEASED-VALUE RATINGS OF COMMODITIES IN THE NATIONAL MOTOR FREIGHT CLASSIFICATION

ITEM	ARTICLES	RATINGS LTL	RATINGS Vol.	VOL. MIN. WEIGHT (POUNDS)
56950	Leather Scrap, NOI, value declared in writing by the shipper, or agreed upon in writing as the released value of the property, in accordance with the following; see Notes 3 and 4, Items 56960 and 56970:			
	If not exceeding 3½ cents per lb., in packages.....	60	35	30,000
	If exceeding 3½ cents per lb., in packages........	70	37½	30,000
56960	*Note 3.* The value declared in writing by the shipper, or agreed upon in writing as the released value of the property, as the case may be, must be entered on the shipping order and bill of lading, as follows: "The agreed or declared value of the property is hereby specifically stated by the shipper to be not exceeding.......... cents per pound." If consignor declines to declare value or agree to released value in writing, the shipment will not be accepted. (Ratings herein based on released value have been authorized by the ICC in Released Rates Orders MC No. 1 of January 16, 1936, and FF No. 2 of January 19, 1943, subject to complaint.)			
56970	*Note 4.* Ratings apply only on old worn-out leather articles, other than belting, boots, or shoes, or on scraps of old (used) leather, or on tanners' tearoffs or rough roundings, or on leather refuse from the manufacture of leather or leather goods, and do not apply on bellies, heads, shanks, or shoulders, nor on leather cut or stamped into forms, shapes, or strips.			

clare excess value for which a charge of 10 cents per 100 pounds of excess value would be set. Each separate shipping package or piece would be treated as a unit for the purpose of determining liability in the event of loss or damage.[25] The publication of a rule limiting motor-carrier liability to $3.00 per pound is under consideration by motor carriers.

TRANSIT PRIVILEGES

The development of the transit privilege (other than stopping in transit to load or unload partially) has been limited, although an increasing number of carriers have authorized such privileges by tariff

---

[25] *Ibid.*

provisions since the end of World War II. The motor-carrier tariff files of the Commission contain roughly twenty motor-carrier agency tariffs which authorize transit. There are relatively few individual line tariffs covering transit privileges which have been issued.[26]

The storage-in-transit privilege has been the privilege which has been more widely granted by motor carriers than any other. This has been granted on frozen citrus juice concentrates and juices; storage of frozen eggs; storage and repacking, and/or rehandling of dairy products; freezing and storage of foodstuffs; and storage of unfinished fabric.

Other transit privileges that have been granted include fabrication of iron and steel articles; reconditioning of iron and steel pipe; dipping-in-transit on shipments of tire fabric; liquid chemicals for rehandling, further treatment, and storage, which permits mixing of chemicals; and processing in transit of paper and paper products, which permits cutting and trimming of the paper.

When transit arrangements or privileges have been established by motor carriers, there has been very little policing of these arrangements, even though there are tariff provisions for this action.[27]

The reluctance of motor carriers to engage in transit is due to a number of reasons, among which are the empty mileage incurred, the difficulties of interline settlement between motor carriers, and the record keeping required. The motor transit tariff provisions are similar in many respects to rail provisions for this privilege. There is a nominal transit charge, which appears to vary from 3 cents to 15 cents per 100 pounds. The storage period granted by motor carriers in the storage-in-transit privilege is frequently the same as that granted by rail carriers, the figure being 12 months. Most of the tariff provisions governing the rate stipulate that the through rate applies from origin via transit point to destination, as is true in rail transportation.

C.O.D. CHARGES

Frequently, a carrier is called upon by a shipper to collect charges for the commodities at the time they are delivered to the consignee. This is commonly referred to as collection on delivery, or C.O.D. service. The carrier collects a C.O.D. charge for this service. Division 5 of the Interstate Commerce Commission has prescribed rules and

---

[26] Preliminary survey made by Bureau of Inquiry and Compliance, Interstate Commerce Commission, issued September 1954.

[27] *Ibid.*

regulations governing the handling of C.O.D. shipments and collections which require that the carrier must publish, post, and file tariffs that contain the rates and rules governing such service. Briefly, they are required to remit each C.O.D. collection within 10 days after delivery of the C.O.D. shipment to the consignee, and they must keep certain records concerning such shipments. C.O.D. charges are listed in Rule 31 of the National Motor Freight Classification No. A–2.

DETENTION

Motor carriers do not have a system of uniform detention rules as such; but, in a number of tariffs, rules are set forth requiring payment of a charge for the detention of a truck unit beyond 24, 48, or 96 hours. This charge may be assessed on an hourly basis rather than on a daily basis. Table 16–6 shows the free time for loading or un-

TABLE 16–6

WEIGHT IN POUNDS (EXCEPT AS OTHERWISE PROVIDED)	FREE TIME IN MINUTES PER VEHICLE	
	Column A (See Note)	Column B (See Note)
2,000 or less	40	70
Over 2,000 but not over 6,000	60	90
Over 6,000 but not over 12,000	120	150
Over 12,000 but not over 18,000	165	195
Over 18,000 but not over 24,000	210	240
Over 24,000 but not over 30,000	255	285
Over 30,000 but not over 36,000	285	315
Over 36,000 but not over 42,000	315	345
Over 42,000 but not over 48,000	345	375
Over 48,000 but not over 54,000	375	405
Over 54,000 but not over 60,000	405	435
Over 60,000	435	465

Note.
Column A—Applicable on all shipments not covered by Column B.
Column B—Applicable on vehicles when receiving or delivering LTL shipments, or when delivering TL shipments, at piers or wharves in New York Harbor (Note C), Camden, N.J., Gloucester, N.J., and Philadelphia, Pa.

loading freight. If loading or unloading is delayed beyond the free time, a charge of $2.50 per vehicle for each 30 minutes is charged.

DIVERSION AND RECONSIGNMENT

Rules governing diversion or reconsignment of truckload shipments can be found in tariffs that have the rates, but there is wide variation in the wording and charges under the rule. An example of such a provision is shown as follows:

(a) When upon instructions of shipper or consignee a shipment is diverted or reconsigned at destination or at some point intermediate to original destination, such diversion or reconsignment will be effected at a charge of $3.65, and the tariff rate from origin to final destination via the reconsignment point will be applied. In the absence of a joint through rate via the route of actual movement (through the reconsignment point), the lowest combination of intermediate rates will apply.

(b) When a shipment is reconsigned en route and its continued movement involves a backhaul to the original shipping point, or in the direction of the original shipping point over the route of original movement, charges will be assessed at tariff rates to and from the point of reconsignment.

Note A: Carriers do not obligate themselves to divert or reconsign shipment at points short of original destination, but when requested, a reasonable effort to do so will be made.

There are many additional services for which charges are made, but the ones discussed are representative.

ROUTING

There is contained in some tariffs routing that is applicable for the movement of certain commodities. In addition, highway routing guides are issued by an individual carrier, showing the routing to points it serves; and some routing guides have been published for two or more carriers engaged in joint hauls. The publication of a highway routing guide so that a shipment could be routed from point-to-point throughout the United States, however, would be a very difficult task. Many highway carriers have terminal facilities at only a few of their points, which limits them to one-way or inbound service only to the many points where they do not have terminal facilities. Therefore, point-to-point routing is not available with highway transportation except between points having terminal facilities. Terminal facilities are maintained by one or more motor carriers at all the principal points at which freight originates, to which it is delivered, and at which it is interchanged. Many motor carriers maintain terminal facilities at gateway points, through which goods move to terminal junction points for local distribution. Point-to-point routing is possible to the major commercial points, as well as to most intermediate points, through the use of some routing guides which are now available.[28]

---

[28] *National Highway and Airway Carriers and Routes* (Chicago: National Highway Carriers Directory, Inc.; published semiannually). See American Trucking Associations, Inc., *Motor Carrier Directory* (loose-leaf).

Although Part I of the Interstate Commerce Act gives the shipper the right to route his freight via rail, there is no provision similar to this in Part II governing motor carriers. At the time that the Motor Carrier Act was passed in 1935, there were very few through routes involving two or more motor carriers. Furthermore, motor carriers were primarily concerned with the operation of their own routes and did not seek interchange traffic because of the difficulties involved in divisions between carriers.

During the early years of federal regulation, there were a number of cases in which the Commission reiterated that Part II did not empower the shipper to specify routing. However, a careful reading of more recent cases reveals that the shipper's position in routing is receiving greater recognition. The Commission held that although Part II of the act does not specifically grant to shippers the right to designate the routes by which their property should be transported by motor common carriers, such carriers are charged with the duty under Section 216 (b) to establish, observe, and enforce just and reasonable regulations and practices relating thereto. Misrouting is an unreasonable practice according to the Commission.[29] Furthermore, the Commission has jurisdiction to determine whether a shipment has been misrouted.[30]

The question of damages for the misrouting of shipments by a carrier is not a part of the Commission's responsibilities. This question must be determined by the courts. The Commission found that the practice of a motor carrier in transporting shipments over an interstate route when it had available an open intrastate route over which a lower rate was applicable, although the intrastate route was 16 miles longer, was unreasonable.[31]

When the complainant shows that the carrier maintained different rates on the same traffic over two or more open routes, the burden is placed upon the carrier to rebut the presumption that it acted unreasonably in transporting an unrouted shipment over the higher-rated route.[32]

If the initial carrier is unable to carry out a shipper's instructions for movement over an established through route because of the connecting carrier's refusal to handle the shipment, the initial carrier should obtain further instructions regarding rerouting from the

[29] *Metzner Stove Repair Co.* v. *Ranft,* 47 MCC 151 (1947).

[30] *Hausman Steel Co.* v. *Seaboard Freight Lines, Inc.,* 32 MCC 31 (1942).

[31] *Great Atlantic and Pacific Tea Co.* v. *Ontario Ft. Lines,* 46 MCC 237 (1946).

[32] *Ibid.*

shipper.[33] In this same case, the Commission pointed to the parallel situation that had existed prior to 1910 in rail transportation. Prior to that time the act contained no provisions which authorized rail shippers to designate routing, but the Commission found that it was the duty of the initial carrier to obey the routing instructions specified by the shipper. Its failure to do so made the initial carrier liable for misrouting.[34]

On the other hand, if the carrier follows the shipper's routing instructions, the shipper cannot complain that the shipment was misrouted.[35]

It would appear that the motor common carrier does have a specific duty when freight is routed. In a court case it was held that if the motor carrier promises to select the cheapest available rate and route and ship the goods accordingly and fails to do so, the carrier is liable to the shipper in damages for the difference between the rate charged and the cheapest applicable and available rate.[36]

When motor carriers maintain through routes or joint rates and accept a shipment on a bill of lading on which the shipper has inserted a routing, it sometimes is assumed that the carrier has the obligation to observe the routing because in signing a bill of lading the carrier has executed a contract and accepted all of its terms. While the carrier could be sued for contract violation, this action is usually impractical because of the amount involved.

The rate over the route of movement is the applicable rate. Usually a carrier would collect charges based on that rate, and if there was misrouting the shipper would file a claim based on the difference in rates. If the responsible carrier admits misrouting, the charges over the route the shipment should have moved are usually collected at the time of delivery. As a matter of fact, some shippers follow the practice before making payment of reducing the freight bill to the rate applicable via the route specified on the bill of lading.

The cancellation of joint rates does not automatically close the through rate. The Commission has held that this does not preclude the Commission from passing upon the reasonableness of the combination rates which would result.[37]

---

[33] *Eastern Aircraft* v. *Fred Olson & Son*, 47 MCC 363 (1947).

[34] *Ibid.*

[35] *Hausman Steel Co.* v. *Seaboard Freight Lines, Inc.*, 32 MCC 31 (1942).

[36] *T & M Transp. Co.* v. *S. W. Shattuck Chemical Co.*, 148 Fed. 2d 777 (1945).

[37] *Rocky Mt. Lines, Inc.—Elimination of Participation*, 31 MCC 320 (1941); and *East South Joint Rates and Routes, Cancellation*, 44 MCC 747 (1945).

There is much confusion and uncertainty on the matter of the shipper's right to route freight by motor carrier which should be clarified by Commission, congressional, or carrier action.

MOTOR-CARRIER RATE INCREASES

It is extremely difficult to examine the motor-carrier rate structure on a national scale with a view to determining the percentage increase in freight rates which has taken place in the last few years. The reason for this is that motor-carrier rate increases are not filed or established on a national scale. They are largely initiated by the many freight-rate conferences or bureaus on behalf of their carrier members. When increases have been granted, they have been applicable only to the particular territory which requested the increase. The regional nature of rate increases is due to differences in costs and other factors within the various rate territories. Labor costs are a substantial portion of total operating costs for motor carriers. At the present time motor-carrier labor negotiates for wage increases on a regional or area basis. It may well be that if the future brings wage bargaining on a nation-wide scale to the motor-carrier industry it may turn to general proceedings for rate increases as railroads have used for a number of years.

Since all parties to a proceeding may appear before the Interstate Commerce Commission and there is a backlog of cases, there is a lag between the time that an application is filed for a rate increase and its disposition by the Commission. Inasmuch as the rate proposals are only for a particular territory, the time lag is not as great for motor carriers as it is in general rate proceedings for rail carriers, since the latter embrace the entire United States. Table 16–7 indicates the time lag in a number of motor-carrier rate cases.

Railroads in a number of instances in general rate cases have been allowed an interim increase after a hearing. Such an increase represents a temporary increase until final determination is made of the proposed general increase. The procedure followed in railroad cases and in motor cases is different in that the railroads have been under maximum rate orders for many years and must petition the Commission to permit an increase and simultaneously waive the effectiveness of the maximum order or orders. Motor carriers, on the other hand, do not have maximum rate orders issued by the Commission to prevent an increase, with the result that motor-carrier rate bureaus, as a matter of practice, have filed tariffs containing the desired increase in each case without petitioning for a hearing on a proposed temporary increase.

There has been a very substantial increase in the development and use of cost data in rate making by the Interstate Commerce Commission and the motor carriers, placing service primarily on a cost basis. This is a particularly desirable trend, for it enables motor carriers to build a rate structure which will meet present and future competition.

The Bureau of Accounts and Cost Finding of the Commission has developed a simplified motor-carrier cost formula by which motor-carrier costs may be determined.[38] The shortened procedure under this formula applies the relationships, between weight brack-

TABLE 16–7

Case	No. of Carriers	Filed	Decided	"Time Lag"	Percentage Asked	Percentage Granted
Transcontinental and Western increases—1952, I and S M–4416..............	757	8/30/52	4/30/53	8 mo.	9%	9%
Transcontinental and Rocky Mountain increases, I and S M–3950 54 MCC 377....	686	10/24/51	5/9/52	7	6	6
Increases—Pacific N.W., I and S M–3866 54 MCC 125...................	250	8/30/51	3/19/52	6.5	6	6
Increases—Middle Atlantic— New England, I and S M–2949 49 MCC 357....	147	11/29/48	6/17/49	7	10	5
Transcontinental motor rates —increases, I and S M–2833 49 MCC 211....	452	2/27/48	4/11/49	13	9	9

ets, of performance factors obtained by the cost section in past territorial studies to secure allocation of costs between various sizes of shipments.

RATE CONFERENCES AND RATE BUREAUS

After the passage of the Motor Carrier Act in 1935, which required interstate motor carriers to file and publish their rates, rate bureaus and rate-making conferences[39] were developed in the motor-carrier field. These bureaus were patterned after those that had been

---

[38] Interstate Commerce Commission, Bureau of Accounts and Cost Finding, *Simplified Procedure for Determining Cost of Handling Freight by Motor Carriers* (Washington, D.C., August, 1953).

[39] The rate bureaus and conferences will be referred to hereafter as bureaus.

established in the rail field, and today there are more than 100 motor-carrier rate and tariff bureaus. These bureaus provide the rate-making machinery through which a rate change or proposal is formulated. Motor rate bureaus are usually operated by groups of carriers, but there are some bureaus in the motor-carrier field which are operated by individuals. Some of these motor-carrier rate and tariff bureaus limit their membership to common carriers, whereas others permit both common and contract carriers to participate. Other rate bureaus include any type of motor carrier, large or small. Furthermore, some rate bureaus have created rate-making machinery for a specific type of commodity or haulers, such as household goods. Most of the motor-carrier rate bureaus are incorporated as nonprofit organizations and serve their members in the following manner:

1. Aid in preparing, filing, and amending tariffs, schedules of rates, and services.
2. Provide a means for concerted action in handling problems arising under regulatory laws within the areas of business operations of the membership.
3. Disseminate pertinent information to the membership and other interested parties.
4. Serve as a means for interchange of views on technological developments in the motor-carrier industry.
5. Co-operate with other motor-carrier agencies and appropriate government agencies.

Each motor-carrier rate bureau has a Standing Rate Committee composed generally of full-time employees and an Appeal Committee composed of representatives of the carriers. The organization chart of a large motor-carrier bureau is shown in Figure 16–2.

INTRATERRITORIAL MOTOR-CARRIER RATE BUREAUS

Motor carriers in an area or region usually have a bureau to insure a simple and economical method of considering such traffic matters as freight rates and rules and regulations to govern the traffic to be moved. These bureaus act as clearinghouses for the traffic problems which concern the carrier members, as well as the carriers and the shipping public, and the carriers and the Interstate Commerce Commission. Intraterritorial rate bureaus handle and publish rates applicable to points within a defined territory. However, some intraterritorial bureaus also publish rates to points outside the defined territory, in other words, interterritorial as well as intraterritorial rates. The map shown in Figure 16–3 indicates the primary intraterritorial rate bureaus and the areas covered by each.

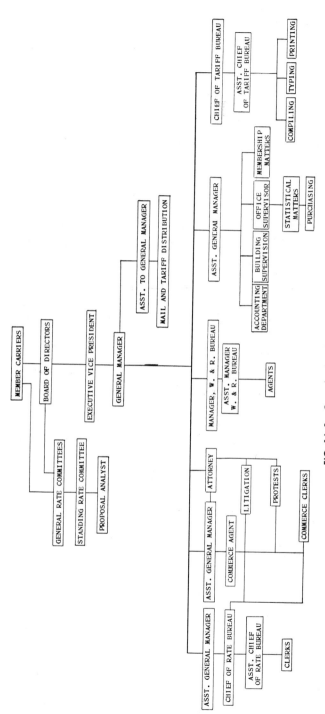

FIG. 16-2. Organization chart of a rate bureau.

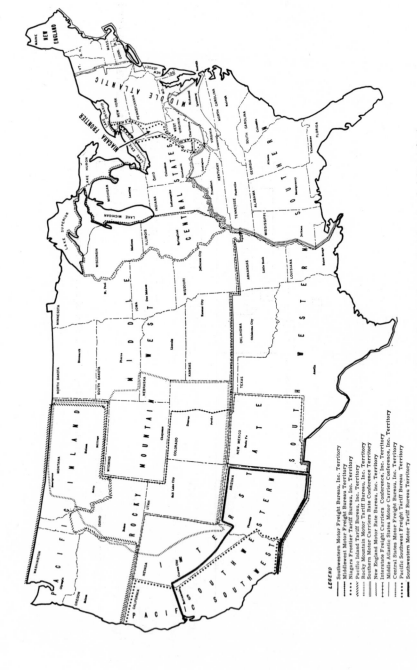

FIG. 16–3. Approximate boundaries of major intraterritorial motor freight territories.

Source: Section 5a filings of Bureaus.

When tariff changes are proposed, the proposals are made through the rate bureaus. The following procedure is typical of that practice in representative motor-carrier rate bureaus. A proposal is made by a shipper or carrier on a form provided by the rate bureau as shown in Figure 16–4. The information submitted on the form must be as

---

MIDDLE ATLANTIC CONFERENCE

D-428
P

DOCKET PROPOSAL FORM
(Submit Three Copies)

| Send Intraterritorial Long Haul Proposals to 2111 E Street, N.W. Washington 7, D.C. | Send M.A.-New England and N.Y. Short Haul Proposals to 254 West 31st Street New York 1, N. Y. | Proponent's File No. 13B-a 28 Date June 7, 1954 |

Proposal originated by....MOTOR FREIGHT EXPRESS...................a...........
(Name of Company)   Conference Carrier
Mail address of proponent.....550 E. King St., York, Pa.   (Shipper or Truck Co.)

1. Nature and purpose of proposed change:....To meet motor carrier competition

2. (a) Proposed Description, Rule or Regulation:

CAUTION - Wherever possible, the description in the National Motor Freight Classification should be used and reference made to the item number. Where the description involves only a part of the Classification description, reproduce only the portion required. If the proposal contemplates a change in a rule or regulation, identify the present rule or regulation by reference to tariff and item number and clearly indicate change desired. If necessary, this information may be shown in an exhibit and made a part of this proposal.

.........See descriptions in Proposals 11170, 11171 and 11172 on
.............various types of floor coverings and sundries.

(b) How packed or prepared for shipment:
(State whether in bags, barrels, boxes or other packages or in bulk)

3. If commodity rate is proposed, are any of the following applicable? (Check appropriate squares)
☐ Shipper to load carrier's vehicle
☐ Consignee to unload carrier's vehicle.   ☐ Other special provision.....................
☐ Subject to Overflow Rule (Rule 62, Tariff 10 or Rule 54, Tariff 15).

4. Basic Detail:
(If necessary, this information may be shown in the form of an exhibit and made a part of this proposal.)
N.M.F. Classification Ratings: Item.......... L.T.L......... T.L................ Min. Wt.,...............
Exceptions Ratings: Tariff........ Item......... A.Q.........L.T.L.......... T.L........ Min. Wt..............

Territory				Present			Proposed			Rail			Other	
From (Unless otherwise indicated)	To	Miles	First Class Rate	Rate or Rating	Min. Weight	% of First Class	Rate or Rating	Min. Weight	% of First Class	Rate or Rating	Min. Weight	Rate or Rating	Min. Weight	
Lancaster Pa.	Washington	108	128	41	26M	32								
	Note 4			38	23M	30								
	D. C.													
				Column 1			40	23M	32					
				Column 2			34	23M	27					

5. Tariff Reference:
(Give complete tariff reference for all rates shown herein. Use separate sheet if necessary).
Middle Atlantic:....Item 1030 Series of Tariff 2-E
Rail:...
Other:........MCTA - Cooper 56-A.............................
(over)

FIG. 16–4. Docket proposal form.

JUSTIFICATION FOR CHANGE

6. How is traffic on which changes are proposed now moving? ....Conference Carrier...........................
(State whether movement is by railroad, motor contract carrier, motor common carrier, water, private truck, freight forwarder, or other mode of transportation.)

7. Give the names of carriers now transporting this commodity between points involved in this proposal.
.......Motor Freight Express...

....

8. Routing:
(a) If proposal covers a commodity rate, will movement be single line haul?. ....   (X) Yes   ☐ No
(b) If joint line service is involved, show names of concurring carriers (Letters of concurrences should be attached)

....

9. Volume: Year
(a) Approximate tonnage in pounds per XXXX.........2,000,000...............................
(b) Present monthly tonnage moving by motor common carriers...Lbs.
(c) Will proposed change attract additional tonnage to motor common carriers?...
    If so, from what source will it be diverted?...

10. Value and Density:
    (Where pertinent, consideration of this proposal may be necessarily delayed unless this information is given)
(a) What is the value of the commodity per 100 lbs. as packed for shipment?...
(b) Density Information:

Type of Package (box, bale, etc.)	Dimension of Package (length, width, depth or height and diameter)	Weight of Package (in pounds)	Weight Per Cubic Foot (in pounds)
....	....	....	....
....	....	....	....
....	...........1500..	....	....

(c) What weight can be loaded in a vehicle of XXXX cubic feet capacity? Excess of legal limit ....Lbs.
(d) What is the weight of the average shipment under proposed rate?....25 to 26,000 lbs.....................

11. If truckload commodity rate is proposed: Yes
(a) Is shipper located on a railroad siding?..... ....
(b) Is consignee located on a railroad siding?......Not involved..

12. If proposal is justified by market or any type of competition, other than carrier, explain.

....
....

13. Additional Justification:
    Furnish detailed statement below outlining reasons why the proposed change should be made. Failure to furnish comprehensive data may result in non-recommendation.

........See letter attached...

....
....
......Desire to make personal appearance at 11 a.m. 6/24/54 in Washington, D. C. ....
....

14. Appearance at public hearing - If proponent desires to appear at public hearing, a request for assignment of time should accompany the proposal wherever possible.
        Signed.....MOTOR FREIGHT EXPRESS.......................................
                              (Name of Company)
                                              G.T.M.
        By.. Title............

complete as possible. Each proposal is placed on a monthly public docket and also published and distributed to members. Wide dissemination of the proposal is achieved through publication in *Transport Topics* and in the *Traffic Bulletin* (transportation journals). The docket is available and open for public inspection. About 10 days after docketing, public hearings are held before the Standing

Rate Committee, at which hearings carriers and shippers appear and argue for or against the proposal. Subsequent to the public hearing, the Standing Rate Committee meets and recommends adoption or the proposal fails of adoption. Appeals may be made to the General Rate Committee. This committee holds monthly meetings which come after a Standing Rate Committee hearing in order that appeals may be disposed of promptly. If the proposal by the General Rate Committee is not acceptable to the carrier making the proposal, the carrier has the right to give notice of independent action, in which case the rate bureau publishes the rate for that individual carrier.

In addition to the regular procedure, the motor-carrier rate bureaus also provide for emergency procedure. Emergency proposals can be received from a carrier member and acted upon by the Standing Rate Committee with or without a hearing within a specific period of time, usually 15 days. The Middle Atlantic Conference defines as emergency proposals those that have as their purpose the following:

1. The meeting, or more nearly meeting, of a reduction made by a competing carrier within the past 45 days, on traffic then being handled, or prior to such reduction was being handled by proponent carrier.
2. The establishment of rates to move traffic for national-defense purposes.
3. The establishment of temporary rates for movement of supplies to relieve injury, damage, or suffering.
4. The establishment of rates on a level heretofore recognized as being proper for the removal of a plant, factory, or other establishment.
5. The meeting of any condition of an extraordinary nature which requires prompt relief and which in the committee's judgment would justify an application to the Interstate Commerce Commission for short notice authority.

INTERTERRITORIAL MOTOR-CARRIER RATE BUREAUS

To facilitate the adjustment of rates between areas, a number of interterritorial motor-carrier rate bureaus have been established. Figure 16–5 is a map which shows the intraterritorial areas to which interterritorial rates are published by interterritorial rate bureaus.

In general, the procedure in presenting interterritorial rate proposals follows the pattern of that described for intraterritorial rate proposals, with the exception that independent action can be taken immediately after a proposal is denied and no appeal is necessary. In both interstate intraterritorial and interterritorial rate proposals

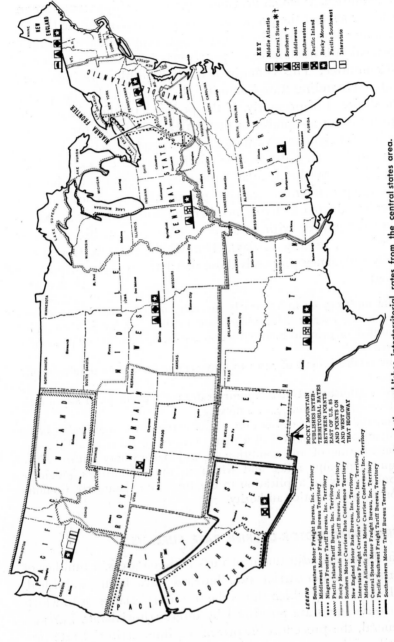

KEY

Middle Atlantic	◧
Central States	◆✳†
Southern	✣
Middlewest	◈
Southwestern	◁
Pacific Inland	◨
Rocky Mountain	⊠
Pacific Southwest	▣
Interstate	□ ▭

LEGEND

▬▬▬ Southwestern Motor Freight Bureau, Inc. Territory
▬▬▬ Middlewest Motor Freight Bureau, Inc. Territory
∿∿∿ Niagara Frontier Tariff Bureau, Inc. Territory
•••• Pacific Inland Tariff Bureau, Inc. Territory
▬▬▬ Rocky Mountain Motor Tariff Bureau, Inc. Territory
▬▬▬ Southern Motor Carriers Rate Bureau, Inc. Territory
▬▬▬ New England Motor Rate Bureau, Inc. Territory
▬▬▬ Interstate Freight Carriers' Conference, Inc. Territory
▬▬▬ Middle Atlantic States Motor Carrier Conference, Inc. Territory
▬▬▬ Central States Motor Freight Bureau, Inc. Territory
•••• Pacific Southwest Freight Tariff Bureau, Inc. Territory
▬▬▬ Southwestern Motor Tariff Bureau Territory

ROCKY MOUNTAIN
PUBLISHES INTER-
TERRITORIAL RATES
BETWEEN POINTS
EAST OF U.S. 85
AND POINTS ON
AND WEST OF
THAT HIGHWAY

* Eastern-Central Motor Carriers Association publishes interterritorial rates from the central states area.

† Central and Southern Motor Freight Tariff Association publishes interterritorial rates between Central and Southern Territory.

FIG. 16–5. Intraterritorial areas to which interterritorial rates are published by interterritorial rate bureaus.

Source: Section 5a filings of Bureaus.

which have been favorably acted upon by the committees after public hearings at which carriers, shippers, and the public have had the opportunity to participate, the proposed rate is filed with the Interstate Commerce Commission for action. In the event of independent action by a carrier, as previously described, the rate proposal involved, if applicable to interstate traffic, must be filed with the Interstate Commerce Commission for its action.

SUPPORT OF INTRATERRITORIAL AND INTERTERRITORIAL RATE BUREAUS

The rate bureaus are supported by dues, assessments, or other revenue contributions, such as the publication and sale of tariffs. There is considerable variation among the bureaus in their means of support, some of them charging dues that are sufficient to cover a major portion of their expenses and depending upon the sale of the published tariffs to augment their revenues. There is generally an admission fee, ranging from $5.00 to $30, and dues paid on the basis of percentage of gross receipts; and, as is to be expected, the by-laws of such bureaus provide a definition as to what constitutes gross receipts. This results in a range of charges from $3.50 to $325 per month in one rate bureau, whereas another bureau has a range of from $5.00 to $40 per month. In addition to being a practical method of formulating rates, the rate bureau procedure is inexpensive for carrier members. In 1944 it cost a Class I carrier less than three tenths of one cent per dollar of gross revenue for all its tariff expenditures.[40] A listing of the different classes of carriers and the schedule of dues which is applicable to interstate revenue for a representative intraterritorial motor rate bureau are presented in Table 16–8.

CONFERENCE METHOD OF RATE MAKING

The method whereby a carrier or shipper originates a rate proposal and submits it to a rate bureau, as previously described, is referred to as the conference method of rate making and was in general use for many years in railroad rate making prior to the development of the motor-carrier industry. Some doubt as to the legality of the conference method of rate making was raised by the Department

---

[40] Senate Committee on Interstate and Foreign Commerce, *Regulation of Rate Bureaus, Conferences, and Associations*, 79th Cong., 2nd sess. (Washington, D.C.: U.S. Government Printing Office, 1946), p. 355.

TABLE 16–8

SCHEDULE OF DUES APPLICABLE TO INTERSTATE REVENUE

	Rate
First $20,000 of gross receipts per month	½ of 1%
Next $60,000 of gross receipts per month	¼ of 1%
Next $120,000 of gross receipts per month	⅛ of 1%
All over $200,000 of gross receipts per month	⅟₁₆ of 1%

MINIMUM $6.00 PER MONTH

Monthly dues to be rounded out to the nearest $5.00 on usual basis for disposing of fractions.

Source: Middle Atlantic Conference Section 5a amended application dated June 2, 1954.

of Justice as a result of investigations questioning whether the operation of a rate bureau is contrary to the antitrust laws. The Department of Justice accordingly brought a criminal suit (which was tried in 1944 and resulted in acquittal) against a number of motor carriers. The questions raised by this suit and a similar suit instituted by the Department against railroad rate bureaus resulted in the introduction of legislation in the Congress to legalize the conference method of rate making. Extensive hearings were held concerning various proposals which would permit rate agreements among carriers. It is significant that there was overwhelming support by shippers' organizations of the bill which was finally passed, and became Section 5(a) of the act, which is known as the Reed-Bulwinkle Act. The effect of the investigations and subsequent congressional hearings has been beneficial to the industry as a whole, for minor abuses were pointed out and corrected.

The amendment exempted from the antitrust laws regulated carriers whose agreements of rates and charges have been approved by the Interstate Commerce Commission. An order issued by the Interstate Commerce Commission on July 6, 1948, stated in detail the rules, regulations, and procedures required for the filing of applications for approval of agreements with other motor carriers covering the establishment of rates. On January 1, 1955, sixteen motor carrier bureaus' agreements had been approved.

The right of independent action is used by the carriers; and, in instances where such prerogative is exercised and the rate in question approved by the Interstate Commerce Commission, succeeding tariffs or supplements thereof often show adoption by other carriers of the rate in question. Shippers and carriers generally are in agreement that the conference method of rate making represents the most practical and orderly procedure for the formulation of rates. With the right of independent action provided and the final disposition, in any event, resting with the Commission, the public is adequately protected in the determination of reasonable motor-carrier rates.

Recently, a motor carrier whose independent rate schedule was suspended by the Commission on the protest of a rate bureau which filed for the carrier challenged the authority of the bureau to protest the schedule. The carrier requested the Commission to vacate its order of suspension and to deny by order the right of the bureau so to act because the bureau, according to the carrier, is the carrier's employee and is not authorized to file the protest.

Many people feel that the motor-carrier rate bureaus exercise more influence on member carrier actions regarding rates than is the case with rail rate bureaus.

QUESTIONS AND PROBLEMS

1. Define the following: class-rate stop; commodity rate; exception ratings; actual-value ratings; released-value ratings; volume minimum; and demurrage.

2. Of what importance is broken stowage in rate making? What is the significance of density in motor-carrier operations?

3. Explain the nature and extent of motor-carrier rate increases in recent years.

4. "There has been a very substantial increase in the development and use of cost data in rate making by the Interstate Commerce Commission and the motor carriers, placing service primarily on a cost basis." Why is this desirable?

5. Explain how motor-carrier rate bureaus serve their members. How are they supported?

6. Describe how a rate proposal is docketed.

7. Enumerate the reasons why the conference method of rate making is the only practical way to formulate rates.

8. What is the essence of the Reed-Bulwinkle Act as applied to motor carriers?

9. How does a class rate scale work? Have motor carriers adopted the 28300 scale used by railroads?

10. What are distribution rates? Average rates?

11. Do you anticipate a greater development of motor-carrier transit privileges? What are some of the problems involved in granting transit privileges?

12. Should the shipper have the right to route motor shipments? Do shippers have any recourse if motor carriers do not follow the routing?

17. MOTOR-CARRIER SELLING, ADVER-

TISING, AND PUBLIC RELATIONS

▪▪▪

SELLING

THE primary duty of the sales department is to sell the services provided by the operating department of the company. In order to accomplish this, a salesman must have a thorough knowledge of the operations of the company. He must know the services which are performed day after day, as well as services which can be rendered by each department of the company when it appears desirable or necessary. The advantages and limitations of his company's interline arrangements should also be a part of a salesman's general knowledge. The salesman must be familiar, then, with the entire operations of the company and the boundaries within which service can be promised and fulfilled. He must understand and be in accord with the policies of the company he represents. The salesman must also have a natural liking for people.

The men who sell transportation service are often called "traffic soliciters." The term that will be used in this text, however, will be that of "transportation salesmen"; because in the present-day competitive transportation era, sales methods, techniques, and effort must be employed to meet the challenge of continuing competitive relationships.

The transportation salesman must maintain contact with the established customers of the company at reasonable intervals dependent upon (a) the value of the account to the company; (b) leads sent in by other transportation salesmen on prospective business; (c) the ability to secure leads for forwarding to other company transportation salesmen; (d) the special service required by the customer; (e) the attention necessary for maintaining goodwill; and (f) the common courtesy owed a customer who is using the service of the company.

All prospective customers should be contacted by the transportation salesman to familiarize them with the services of the company and how these services will benefit the prospective user. The transportation salesman will also handle complaints and try to solve any problems on a fair and equitable basis. In all matters, he must work closely with the operating department, the terminal manager, and other departments in order to meet the service requirements of the customer.

The selling of motor freight transportation represents the selling of a service, which is not a simple matter. The salesman who demonstrates the superiority of a fountain pen has tangible evidence which makes the selling job easier. This is not the case in selling a service. In this type of selling, the salesman has no product to show which can sell itself at the time of the call on the prospect. Rather, it is necessary that the salesman convince the shipper that he should buy a service, the advantages of which he cannot know exactly until he has purchased and used it.[1]

FINDING THE PROSPECTS

Before the motor transportation salesman can sell motor freight service, he must find the prospective shippers, commercial or government. Curious as it may seem, this may prove to be as formidable a task as the actual selling once the prospective shipper is found. Prospects for motor freight transportation can be classified into four groups: (a) those shippers who are already using motor service and therefore are aware of its advantages and know that it meets their transportation requirements; (b) those shippers who make inquiries concerning motor transportation services and charges and who think such transportation service may meet their needs; (c) those shippers who are using a competitive agency of transportation and do not know the advantages of motor transportation; and (d) those shippers who will not try motor-carrier service because they feel that a competitive transportation agency meets their transportation needs. The latter group presents the greatest selling problem.

One of the common methods which is used to locate these prospects is for the transportation salesman to become a member of and attend the meetings of numerous business groups, luncheon clubs,

---

[1] A number of interesting and informative articles on selling freight service have appeared from time to time in *Traffic World* starting in the October 14, 1951, issue. These have been reprinted in booklet form under the title of *Selling Freight Service* and are distributed by *Traffic World*.

Traffic Club affairs, and other organizations where the opportunity to meet businessmen and traffic men exists. The purpose of membership in these organizations, aside from the personal benefits accruing from such participation, is to open a channel through which the motor transportation salesman can make contacts. It has been truly said that much valuable business is obtained through social contacts. After making these contacts, it is possible for the salesman to ascertain whether or not an individual constitutes a logical prospect for a future call. Having met the prospect at one of these informal meetings, it is generally easier for the salesman to secure the interview and establish a friendly basis for the job of selling.

SHIPPING MOTIVES

In this type of selling, the transportation salesman is required to know thoroughly the transportation needs of the shipper, those things a shipper looks for in a transportation service. Some motor transportation salesmen believe that a knowledge of their prospects, their needs, and their problems is of more value even than a knowledge of selling techniques. There are often times when a transportation salesman can make suggestions that will improve packing methods or aid in solving problems in the shipping department.

There are a number of different reasons why shippers choose a particular transportation agency: (*a*) habit, (*b*) economy, (*c*) convenience, (*d*) dependability, (*e*) protection against loss, (*f*) speed, (*g*) extra or special service, (*h*) friendliness or courtesy, (*i*) liability or responsibility, (*j*) reputation, (*k*) trade requirements, (*l*) policy, (*m*) friendship, and (*n*) market competition. These motives, or combinations of them, will influence the choice of a transportation agency by a shipper. It is essential that a transportation salesman, in dealing with a prospect, recognize the motivation that can be effectively used for that particular prospect. Many times a prospect volunteers what it is that he looks for in a transportation service. It should be noted that these motives are largely rational; that is, a traffic manager who is buying transportation service is going to buy on a rational basis, not on an emotional-appeal basis.

IMPORTANCE OF PLANNING

A transportation salesman has to budget his time carefully in order that he can see a sufficient number of prospective shippers. A simple method of accomplishing this is for each salesman to keep a card index of all of his prospects. On each of these cards, he should place pertinent information which will assist him in selling motor-carrier transportation service. Some salesmen may feel that this will include personal information about the prospect, such as his hobbies, as well as business information about the volume of traffic handled, destinations shipped to, and other data of that nature. By recording on a card for each prospect the date of his call and the length of time spent in the call, the transportation salesman has a basis for analyzing whether or not the results he is obtaining are commensurate with the time he spends with each potential customer. In maintaining a card index file on his prospects, it would seem wise for a salesman to arrange a tickler system, so as to insure frequent or regular calls on his prospects to show his sincere interest in securing the business. Furthermore, a salesman should secure from other departments relevant information to be entered in the card index file on the correct cards showing the tonnage and revenue he secured from each shipper; and the status of any damage claims may profitably be recorded on the cards. This enables the salesman to talk intelligently with those shippers he has been serving. Every call should be planned and thought given to the end of accomplishing something. It may be to gain new or additional business or to satisfy a complaint. There is nothing a busy man dislikes more than a call just to say "hello."

TRAFFIC EVALUATION

It is true that in too many cases emphasis has been placed upon tonnage rather than upon the revenue aspects of the traffic. Tonnage of certain types will render a small amount of revenue because of the depressed rates. Unless a salesman watches this carefully, he may find it much easier to sell the tonnage on which his company secures low revenue. One large motor carrier evaluates traffic by the following criteria:

1. *Tonnage.* There must be a proper balance of various classes. Little credit can be given a salesman for securing a lot of tonnage if his average less-than-truckload rating is fourth class. It is necessary that there be a proper balance of traffic of various classes.

2. *Weight Density.* The matter of weight density is very important to all agencies of transportation, but more so to truck transportation than to rail because of less cubical capacity. Therefore, in the solicitation of traffic, it is important that a transportation salesman know the loadability of the freight being handled or solicited.

3. *Risk and Damage Susceptibility.* In an analysis of the value of traffic, consideration must be given to the question of risk of damage, theft, or pilferage. The fact that an article may be rated first class does not mean that this particular traffic is desirable. The matter of risk is not limited to damage to the article itself; consideration must be given also to articles which may cause damage, such as acids or carbon black.

4. *Unit Value.* Thought must also be given to the question of whether the article is of unusual value, which, of course, adds to the risk. Such traffic, too, may require extra care in handling, thus increasing costs. Claims on this class of traffic add unduly to insurance expense or cargo losses.

5. *Size of Shipment and Its Relationship to Cost.* The size, shape, and weight of an article affects the cost of handling and should be considered in analyzing the value of traffic. The quantity shipped should be taken into account; whether the shipments are many and small, or whether they are single shipments of large quantities, must also be considered.

KNOWLEDGE OF COMPANY SERVICES

A well-trained transportation salesman must know his company and the service it offers, and he must apply that knowledge to the needs of individual shippers. He should be able to quote rates and should be conversant with the operating authority, both as to routes and commodities. It is not only important to know the rate structure of his own company but also it is almost of equal importance for the transportation salesman to know what his competitors' price structures are. He should know what service his company is prepared to offer or desires to offer in conjunction with connecting-line carriers. If questions arise concerning matters about which the salesman is unfamiliar, he should always check with his company before giving any information. Although erroneous information may lead to securing traffic one time, it precludes securing future tonnage from that shipper.

SALES DIPLOMACY

It is imperative that a transportation salesman learn very quickly who controls the traffic in a company. There is considerable variation among commercial and industrial firms insofar as the setup of traffic departments is concerned. This means that a salesman must find out who actually controls the traffic. Often traffic is routed from a company's headquarters office far removed from the area the motor carrier serves and an off-line salesman may be assigned to handle this and other national accounts in that city. Some industrial firms have placed in the hands of the purchasing department the control of routing of the goods, even though they have a traffic department. A salesman may find to his chagrin that there may not be complete harmony between the traffic and purchasing departments and lose tonnage because he did not ascertain who actually had the authority to control the traffic. Then, too, within an industrial traffic department, the transportation salesman will find that he often must secure the permission of the general traffic manager before contacting any of the subordinates in the traffic department. It is certainly desirable for a salesman to contact some of the key subordinates in traffic departments, for they may be the traffic managers of the future. A transportation salesman must be diplomatic in his dealing with those who control traffic and also with those who are not in a position to exercise control over the movement of traffic.

SALES TRAINING PROGRAMS

It is a common practice in the motor-carrier field to hire a salesman with a "following"; that is, a motor carrier will hire a transportation salesman who has made a successful record in the employment of another motor carrier, in order that this new salesman will bring with him the accounts that he has serviced with his former employer. This type of "raiding" is expensive; and it is questionable, over a period of time, whether it is wise procedure. It may turn out that the transportation salesman is unable to maintain a large share of his former accounts. What is needed are sales training courses in transportation selling. The attribute of the old-time salesman in the transportation field was largely that of a being a "good fellow." Today, it is necessary that a transportation salesman be a trained individual who is thoroughly grounded in the rudiments of salemanship in order to serve his company and his clients. There has been only a small amount of attention given to the selling of motor freight service. Some motor carriers may find it to their advantage to formulate training courses within their organizations so as to improve the caliber of their salesmen. There are many successful salesmen whose talents could be utilized in establishing these company training programs.[2]

---

[2] The Customer Relations Council of the American Trucking Associations has sponsored several motor-carrier salesmen's training programs. It also has furnished much current sales literature which includes training suggestions to its members. The Regular Common Carrier Conference of ATA has sponsored a helpful individual home-study course on sales training for a nominal charge.

The basic steps in selling need to be emphasized in sales training. These are: (*a*) the preapproach, in which background data is secured about the prospect; (*b*) the approach or interview; (*c*) the demonstration in which the presentation is made of a company's superiority; (*d*) overcoming objections; (*e*) securing the order; and (*f*) following up the sale. The provision of supplementary material on the techniques of selling will also add to the value of such training.

COMPANY SALES FORMS

A *traffic lead form* is sometimes used by a transportation salesman when he finds that a prospect called upon by him does not control the routing of shipments but that the routing is handled by another office which is located nearby and can be contacted by another salesman of the motor carrier. Under these circumstances, a traffic lead form is sent by the first salesman which contains pertinent information which will be helpful to the other salesman in making the call. The name of the shipper and city, the consignee and destination, commodity, present routing, who controls the routing, and any other data which will be of value are supplied. Figure 17–1 is a sample of

ROADWAY EXPRESS, Inc.
TRAFFIC LEAD FORM

Date..

TO.. FROM..

SHIPPER.. CITY..

CONSIGNEE.. DESTINATION..

COMMODITY.. NOW ROUTING..

ROUTING CONTROLLED BY..

PERSON TO CONTACT..

WEIGHT.................... RATE.................... AUTHORITY....................

....

....

REMARKS:..

....

....

....

....

....

BY:..

This copy to one who is to solicit

FIG. 17–1. Traffic lead form.

a traffic lead form. Upon receipt of this form, the receiving office or salesman will follow up the lead and will then make a lead acknowledgment, indicating the action that has been taken.

LEAD ACKNOWLEDGMENT

Date..

TO..FROM..

SHIPPER...CONSIGNEE...

In reply to your lead above be advised that

1. Routing order is attached..

2. Routing is controlled by...you must secure...................

3. Consignee will specify our routing on purchase order..

4. Shipper will use our lines until instructed otherwise...

5. Customer declines to change present routing, which is..

6. Rates unequal, Tariff reference below..

REMARKS:...

....

....

....

....

....

....

....

A *routing order form* is widely used by motor transportation salesmen in selling transportation service. This is a plan whereby the consignee routes practically all the shipments of goods he purchases at the time of the purchase by designating the routing he desires. Therefore, by controlling this routing, he becomes a key man for the motor transportation salesman to contact. If the salesman can convince him of the advantages of shipment via his company, he will furnish the consignee with a routing order form to complete and send to his suppliers. This form, in effect, tells the shipper of the goods to forward all future shipments via this specific motor carrier, since satisfactory arrangements have been completed with the motor carrier for the handling of the shipments. This form may be altered or modified in particular cases by additional remarks.

Accompanying this routing order form is an acknowledgment that has been provided by the motor transportation salesman and sent by the consignee to the consignor. This acknowledgment is returned by the consignor to the consignee and acknowledges receipt of the routing instructions to forward future shipments to that consignee by the specific motor carrier. Figure 17–2 is a sample of the routing order and acknowledgment.

ROUTING INSTRUCTIONS

City_____

Date_____

Gentlemen:

Your cooperation will be appreciated in routing our future shipments, via:

ASSOCIATED TRANSPORT, INC.

We believe our transportation needs will be served best through Associated Transport service.

So that our file may be complete, will you kindly acknowledge these instructions promptly.

_____

_____

BY:_____

- -

ACKNOWLEDGMENT

City_____

Date_____

_____

_____

_____

Gentlemen:

We acknowledge receipt of your shipping instructions to forward your future shipments by Associated Transport, Inc.

These instructions will be complied with.

_____

BY:_____

FIG. 17–2.   Routing order form and acknowledgment.

This sales aid is widely used and favored by many motor transportation salesmen. They feel that, if they can successfully sell their transportation service, the routing order insures a continuing flow of traffic, provided that adequate service is maintained. It should be noted that there is nothing legally binding in this order form insofar as either party is concerned, and the consignee may change his mind and secure the service of another carrier whenever he sees fit.

Another form may be used when a shipment is observed moving adversely by any salesman. Relevant data about the shipment are recorded on a so-called *"hot-tip" form,* as shown in Figure 17–3, and

HOT TIP FORM S17

Date __________

To __________ From __________

At __________ At __________

The following was observed today moving adversely:

Shipper __________

Address __________ St. __________ City __________ State

Commodity __________

Moving By __________

Consignee __________ For Acct. of __________

Address __________ St. __________ City __________ State

Weighed About __________ Lbs. or ☐ LESS TRUCKLOAD ☐ TRUCKLOAD

Remarks: __________

FIG. 17–3. Hot-tip form.

given to the appropriate salesman for action. On the reverse side, space is provided for recording the report of the contact and the results.

The establishment of a *daily sales report* or sales work plan, as shown in Figure 17–4, provides a record which is helpful to the salesman and the sales manager. The number and type of call and brief remarks about the salesmen's call are placed on the form which is sent to the main office of the carrier, with a duplicate kept by the salesman.

An analysis of sales data may be made for management control purposes on a form prepared for that purpose. Figure 17–5 is a *customer record card* which shows pertinent information about the commodities, the points to which they are shipped, and the calls

Service	DAILY SALES REPORT	Courtesy

PREPARE THIS REPORT DAILY. Make contact reports on all C and D calls.
Send original of this report to main office. Retain duplicate in your files.

Representative_____ Date_____

Type Call	Firm Called On	Address
	Firm	
	Remarks	
	Firm	
	Remarks	
	Firm	
	Remarks	
	Firm	
	Remarks	
	Firm	
	Remarks	
	Firm	
	Remarks	
	Firm	
	Remarks	
	Firm	
	Remarks	
	Firm	
	Remarks	
	Firm	
	Remarks	

CLASSIFICATION OF CALLS
A - Soliciting new business
B - General or routine call - everything O K.
C - "GOT THE BUSINESS"
D - Lead furnished other representatives for business to or from this acc't
E - Made contact by telephone

FIG. 17–4. Daily sales report form.

which are made. On the back of this card, Figure 17–6, there is space for the outbound and inbound tonnage and revenue by months. This information, which is placed in a card index, can be very helpful in analyzing accounts not only by the salesmen but also by the sales manager.

There are a number of reports which a company compiles daily which are helpful in sales work for they indicate, to some degree, the success of the sales effort. The *daily terminal report, pickup and delivery report,* and *daily report of truckload shipments* are typical of those which are very useful in the sales effort.

CUSTOMER RECORD CARD

District__________ Terr. No.__________
Date of filing__________

Firm__________ Address__________
City__________ State__________Tel.__________

KEY PERSONNEL:

1.__________ Title__________ 3.__________Title__________
2.__________ Title__________ 4.__________Title__________

Principal commodity__________
Ships to and receives from the following major points__________

Remarks:

CALLS MADE

19		19		19		19	
JAN.-MAR.	APR.-JUNE	JAN.-MAR.	APR.-JUNE	JAN.-MAR.	APR.-JUNE	JAN.-MAR.	APR.-JUNE
JULY-SEPT.	OCT.-DEC.	JULY-SEPT.	OCT.-DEC.	JULY-SEPT.	OCT.-DEC.	JULY-SEPT.	OCT.-DEC.

FIG. 17–5. Customer record card (front).

Mo.	O/B Tonn.	O/B Rev.	I/B Tonn.	I/B Rev.	Total Tonn.	Total Rev.	Mo.	O/B Tonn.	O/B Rev.	I/B Tonn.	I/B Rev.	Total Tonn.	Total Rev.
Jan.							Jan.						
Feb.							Feb.						
Mar.							Mar.						
Apr.							Apr.						
May							May						
June							June						
July							July						
Aug.							Aug.						
Sept.							Sept.						
Oct.							Oct.						
Nov.							Nov.						
Dec.							Dec.						
Total							Total						

YEAR 19							YEAR 19						
Mo.	O/B Tonn.	O/B Rev.	I/B Tonn.	I/B Rev.	Total Tonn.	Total Rev.	Mo.	O/B Tonn.	O/B Rev.	I/B Tonn.	I/B Rev.	Total Tonn.	Total Rev.
Jan.							Jan.						
Feb.							Feb.						
Mar.							Mar.						
Apr.							Apr.						
May							May						
June							June						
July							July						
Aug.							Aug.						
Sept.							Sept.						
Oct.							Oct.						
Nov.							Nov.						
Dec.							Dec.						
Total							Total						

FIG. 17–6. Customer record card (back).

SHIPPERS' VIEWS

A traffic managers' survey was conducted in 1953[3] to which 1,000 shippers replied. This represented an approximate 5 per cent return of the questionnaire form. From the information solicited by the questionnaire, of particular interest here are the principal factors considered by shippers in determining the selection of truck or rail service, the choice of advertising media, and suggestions for improving motor-carrier salesmen and service.

Sixty-one per cent of the shippers indicated that a particular motor service is chosen because of service, whereas 43 per cent chose a particular motor carrier because of rates, and 37 per cent because of reciprocity. In checking the reasons shippers prefer truck to rail service, the respondents selected truck service in preference to rail service for ten of eleven reasons cited. The following tabulation shows the percentage of returns which indicated particular reasons for choosing a transport service:

Reasons for Choosing Transport Service	*Percentage Favoring Trucks over Rail*
Prompt Pickup	92%
Shorter time in transit	98
Direct service	94
Lower rates	44
Less handling	89
Personal and special service	90
Less loss and damage claims	81
Prompt claim and COD settlement	64
Less packing	93
Like salesmen	83
Superior salesmanship	77

In answer to the question as to how motor-carrier service could be improved, the respondents suggested:

1. Improve tracing.
2. Improve pickup and delivery service.
3. Improve driver courtesy and service.
4. Pay claims promptly.
5. Answer correspondence promptly.
6. Follow routing specified on bill of lading.
7. Remit C.O.D.'s more promptly.
8. Have unrestricted interchange and improve interlining.
9. Reduce transfer time at junction points.
10. Improve terminal operations and handling techniques.

---

[3] Prepared by Customer Relations Council, American Trucking Associations, Inc., and by the author, the questionnaire was distributed by the membership of the Customer Relations Council to 20,000 traffic managers.

11. Establish greater uniformity in motor freight tariffs and distribute tariff schedules without cost.
12. Establish less-truckload-lot service comparable to truckload-lot service and accept all freight tendered.

Continuing their analysis of motor-truck transport service, 50 per cent of the shippers replied that they had trouble tracing motor-carrier shipments. Forty per cent indicated that this trouble occurred frequently, while 88 per cent of the shippers said they thought the tracing of shipments could be improved by:

1. Greater teletype coverage
2. Tying teletype service of two carriers together
3. Closer contact with break-bulk points
4. Making operating personnel salesminded
5. Greater co-ordination between connecting lines
6. Better records of shipments

In answer to the question as to which form of advertising used by motor carriers in soliciting traffic is most effective, the respondents stated that the most effective is the routing guide or service guide. A close second choice, but still leading all other types, is the salesman. Following in order of preference are direct mail, trade publication advertising, novelties, newspaper, and radio advertising.

Traffic managers surveyed have very definite ideas concerning motor-carrier salesmen, their approach, actions, preparation, etc. In the section of the questionnaire devoted to suggestions on how to improve the effectiveness of motor-carrier salesmen, they listed twelve major and specific suggestions:

1. Make salesmen better informed about the service they're selling.
2. Give salesmen additional sales training.
3. Select salesmen more carefully.
4. Make certain salesmen know rates, give them rate training, and teach them how to read tariffs.
5. Better understanding of operations, including schedules, "hot-shot" runs, connecting carriers, interchange points, insurance coverage, and operating authority.
6. Give correct information regarding facilities and service, with greater co-ordination between operating departments and salesmen.
7. Sell only service they can provide, with less romancing of their companies and services.
8. Greater co-operation between traffic and operating departments.
9. Know customer's products and needs.
10. Study and prepare data about accounts before making calls (what's being done about claims and tracing, etc.).

11. Know routing and be informed about competition (including other forms of transport service).
12. Notify shippers of embargoes.

In the section limited only to their observation of the actions and presentation of salesmen, however, the respondents showed that:

Description of Salesmen	*Percentage of Questionnaire Respondents Checking This Item*
Just "drop in" to solicit...	67%
Don't know enough about their business.........................	50
Offer some help in routing, packaging, loading docks, other problems (76 per cent replied they could use such expert help)........	47
Arrive with definite prospectus................................	42
Use sales presentations, literature.............................	32
Indulge in too much social conversation........................	20
Sell motor freight industry institutionally.....................	20

No other mode of transportation can do more to satisfy the varying requirements of all shippers. A motor transportation salesman who knows the needs of each shipper upon whom he calls and how his company can best serve those needs and a motor carrier who insures that his salesmen are backed up by co-operative and interested operations personnel will work effectively not only for their own interests but also for the best interests of the motor transportation industry at the same time.

SALES MANAGEMENT

The growth of motor-carrier companies and the increase in personnel necessitates control of the sales functions through sales management. Responsibility for all the sales activities are centralized under a sales manager whose control of these functions governs the degree of effectiveness of the sales department. If the motor carrier is a large firm, there may be regional sales managers as well.

The sales manager's functions include the following: (1) the sales operation which embraces such matters as selection, training, and supervising of salesmen; (2) sales control which includes allocation of accounts (national and local), quotas, and budgets; (3) market research which involves analysis of markets and research on potential tonnage; (4) sales promotion which is primarily the use of advertising as a sales aid; and (5) the establishment of a sales policy consistent with over-all company policy.

The mere appointment of a sales manager does not mean that the aforementioned functions will be performed. Neglect of any or some of these functions may not be the fault of the sales manager. Motor-carrier top management, in too many instances, uses its vice-president of sales or general sales manager for "trouble shooting" purposes, not leaving sufficient time for him to manage the salesmen, which is one of his primary responsibilities. Some companies have also insisted that certain accounts which the sales manager was instrumental in developing be retained and serviced by him. In some instances these accounts are so time consuming that more than half of a sales manager's time is spent with these accounts. Under such circumstances, he is carrying the title of general sales manager but is not performing the functions. There should be a balancing of activities to assure that each receives proper attention.

There remains much to be accomplished in determination of sales costs. Such matters as the cost of selling individual customers, cost of operating regional sales offices, costs of individual salesmen, and the sales costs of truckloads versus less-truckloads are some of the phases of motor-carrier sales management which need further analysis. Although the ratio of selling expense to total cost may be easily ascertained, this figure itself may be a meaningless average. The development of standard or unit costs can result in a figure which can be considered the normal or standard expense of performing a particular function. This standard may be used then as a guide in the comparison of results with the standard which has been set.

The use of sales forecasting has become more widespread and more effective. Many forecasts utilize the quota system under which the sales manager meets with the company's controller to establish a sales figure based on the previous year's business. To this figure is added an arbitrary amount, the total of which is the sales quota. The quota method is vulnerable to changes in economic conditions because of the long period involved. Too, salesmen often become discouraged when the quota has been set too high and have just stopped trying to meet what they feel is an unfair quota.

A shorter-range sales forecast has been adopted with considerable success. A motor carrier may establish thirteen periods of 4 weeks each. These 4-week forecasts can be secured by obtaining individual terminal forecasts from each terminal manager and salesmen. Since their costs are going to be set on the forecast that they make, these individuals know that they should be neither too conservative nor overly optimistic but try to forecast accurately what the revenue will be for the next 4-week period.

The forecasts from all terminals are studied individually. Market data factors are also considered. The forecasts are checked against the volume for the same period in the preceding year to ascertain over-all trends. Larger individual accounts are closely examined for any special circumstances that might affect operations, and the trend of revenue for the current 4 weeks is checked closely. Local and national economic factors must also be considered for which numerous available indexes are useful. These forecast figures are then presented at a meeting of all department heads, at which time the total figure is usually modified. The controller establishes a cost-allowance figure per one thousand dollars of income so that a budget is tied to sales volume.

COMPENSATION

Motor transportation salesmen are usually paid on a straight salary basis, a set amount per week, semimonthly, or monthly. There are two other types of compensation that may be used in paying salesmen —commission and bonus. The type of plan to be used by a motor carrier should be the one that best suits its needs. A combination of salary, commission, and bonus may be used, although a combination of two of these is more likely. Some motor carriers have tried a compensation plan which is a combination of straight salary and commission. Such a plan often establishes a quota in terms of total tonnage; and the salesman receives, in addition to his salary, a commission based on the tonnage of shipments he secures. With a plan of this kind, some motor carriers have found it important to differentiate between tonnage which can be hauled profitably and that which cannot be hauled so profitably. Where there has not been any such differentiation in type of traffic, it has been found that a salesman tends to work those accounts that will deliver the greatest amount of tonnage, which often is that which allows the smallest margin of profit.

A drawing account may be used in conjunction with a commission plan of compensation for salesmen. This is the advancing of a weekly or monthly amount of money to a salesman. It is expected, however, that the salesman's earnings from commissions will exceed the amounts drawn from such an account.

GIFTS

Considered by the transportation salesman as an aid to selling and by others as an advertising expense is the matter of gifts, usually in the form of merchandise of nominal value. Such items as paperweights, key cases, penknives, novelty pencils, pocket flashlights, tickets to sports events, and other similar items may be given by the salesman to the traffic men he serves. Some motor carriers feel that gifts are an indispensable part of a transportation salesman's equipment. However, their effectiveness is questionable. Their use appears due largely to the fact that competitors use them. In addition to these token gifts, it is common practice for shippers to be remembered at Christmas with appropriate gifts which take a more substantial form.

The matter of Christmas gifts to their customers, the shippers and receivers of freight, has developed into one of the troublesome problems confronting the motor-carrier industry. The practice of a simple remembrance at Christmas has developed into a competitive weapon with each carrier trying to outdo its competitors. Although some industrial traffic departments have established a company policy against the acceptance of Christmas gifts from transportation companies, other shippers make a special point of calling a carrier prior to the visit of the salesman with his annual Christmas remembrance to tell the carrier what has already been given him by some other carrier. There is the suggestion, implied or otherwise, that the carrier equal or better its competitor's gift. The result has been an expensive practice which is of doubtful benefit to the carrier.

In sales meetings when there is a discussion of this problem, one salesman may relate that his company had given a gift to a customer which cost $10.00 but one of its competitors gave a gift which cost $25.00. A shipper has even been given a television set by one carrier, and so the salesman for a competing company proposed that the following year his company give that shipper a refrigerator.

A survey dealing with this subject which was sent to 367 motor carriers, from which there was a 25-per cent return, reveals some interesting information about this problem.[4] Of those answering the survey, 77 per cent indicated they expended funds for Christmas gifts and gratuities for customers, whereas 23 per cent did not. As to whether these gifts are essential to the carrier's sales effort, 25 per cent said "yes," 75 per cent said that it was merely a matter of custom, and all said their competitors followed the practice. Throughout the comments on these questions, the factor of competition is foremost.

---

[4] Customer Relations Council, American Trucking Associations, Inc., "Survey on Christmas Gifts and Gratuities," April, 1954.

Asked whether a cessation of the practice would hurt the respective carrier's business, the answers indicated that it would not hurt business if all carriers stopped it at the same time: 30 carriers felt that the funds which are usually expended for Christmas gifts should be available for local charities; 20 carriers felt that the money should be used for scholarships; 10 felt that it should be a combination of charities and scholarships; while 11 carriers felt that nothing of this nature would be necessary or helpful.

There were 19 motor carriers which reported that they did not give Christmas gifts to customers. One company has never followed the practice but has always donated to local charities as well as sponsoring a scholarship program. These expenditures are not related to an amount which might otherwise be spent for gratuities, however. The other 18 carriers had given Christmas gifts at one time, but 6 stopped without any substituting program; 7 adopted scholarship plans; 4 adopted a charity plan; and 1 a combination scholarship and charity plan. Of these 19 companies, 10 of them specifically stated that their policy stand had actually earned them friends and had been a substantial aid to them in their public-relations program.

This problem is one which will have to be solved by both individual and joint action of the carriers themselves. If a carrier decides to give only modest gifts, then it runs the risk of appearing to its customers to be a "cheapskate" in comparison with the other carriers which give much larger gifts. In a case of this kind, a carrier would be just as well off to be giving nothing. The amounts expended for gifts have become progressively larger, as has the amount of time expended in the administrative aspects of this gift giving. The dollar amount in some instances exceeds $15,000 for some companies.

One possible solution would be for carriers to agree to limit the amount which could be expended on individual gifts. On the other hand, the use of these funds in establishing scholarships or for charitable purposes or for both possesses so many advantages for motor carriers. It demonstrates the willingness of the industry to accept its social responsibilities; it furthers the educational possibilities for promising students; and it is invaluable in public relations to individual companies and to the entire industry.

SALES CONVENTIONS

Greater attention could be given to the matter of state or regional sales conventions and sales meetings. Opportunities should be presented for motor transportation salesmen to meet and exchange ideas. Round-table discussions and presentations on the techniques of selling motor transportation are methods of exchanging information which can be of mutual benefit to all. Valuable sales promotion ideas can be secured through the participation of motor-carrier salesmen in such activities.

ADVERTISING

One of the most effective tools of the modern businessman is advertising. The motor-carrier industry could well afford to devote more attention to this aid to selling, for advertising in the motor-carrier field is largely of the hit-or-miss variety. Motor transportation service must be merchandised, and advertising can help to accomplish this task efficiently and at reasonable cost. Many motor carriers believe that a salesman alone should take care of supplying the traffic volume, not realizing that this is an expensive way to do business. Since the salesman is the most expensive item in the selling budget, an advertising program which will increase the productivity of his personal contacts with shippers will result in lower over-all unit selling costs. Advertising is proxy salesmanship which acquaints a shipper with the motor carrier before a salesman's visit. An advertising program correlated to a salesman's activities makes the selling job easier and effects savings in time for the salesman. Savings in time are savings in money for the motor carrier when translated into a greater number of calls made each day by a salesman.

There are a number of advertising media available; and each possesses merit, depending upon the desired objectives of the advertising program. Local newspapers, national advertising, magazines, trade papers, direct mail, radio, and television are some of the most widely used forms of advertising today. Many motor carriers make use of advertising in local trucking directories and national traffic directories which are in the hands of most shippers or traffic men. Certain types of motor carriers, such as household-goods carriers, may keep their name before the public by employing numerous media, including radio advertising, whereas carriers of general commodities tend to aim their advertising to reach a special group. One of the most favored methods of advertising used by motor carriers is that of direct-mail advertising. The effectiveness of this medium of advertising could be increased were it to be of a more personal nature than is found in the ordinary pamphlets, folders, and blotters, although that type of advertising is better than no advertising at all.

The value of advertising is twofold. From it should be secured (a) direct results, measured in traffic, that is obtained; and (b) indirect results in aid to salesmen in making known the name of the company and its service, thereby simplifying the task of selling. It has been pointed out that a salesman of motor transportation service must know where his potential shippers are. An advertising program, likewise, to be effective in increased volume of traffic, must know where potential shippers are and must transmit to those potential shippers through the best possible medium or media the facts about the motor carrier which are of importance to the shippers. The survey in the selling phase of this chapter showed a number of reasons why shippers utilized certain motor carriers or certain modes of transportation service and not others. An effective advertising program for a motor carrier, and one which works with a motor carrier's salesmen, analyzes the shippers' desires and needs and stresses the manner in which the particular motor carrier can fulfil those needs.

Perhaps one of the reasons why advertising is not used more extensively by motor carriers is that too much is expected in the way of tangible results. Motor-carrier operators are very practical men and look for a precise measure of benefit from any expenditure of time and money. The benefits of advertising, however, do not always take a tangible form. Particularly is this true of the advertising of a service such as motor transportation, for much of the result of an advertising program will be indirect. Advertising serves the motor carrier as an inexpensive contact, as well as being a method of creating interest in and preference for a carrier's service. Thus, advertising takes the intermediate steps necessary to the production of an order.

There are some motor common carriers which have published in their tariffs a provision which authorizes the use of a banner or sign which is furnished by the shipper when he orders exclusive use of the vehicle or offers sufficient freight to fill a vehicle. It is used only when the vehicle is designated to that shipper for movement of his goods. A contract carrier can discriminate among its shippers and can arrange with them to carry their advertising on its vehicles. The Interstate Commerce Commission has not exercised control over advertising by carriers, but when advertising would result in the violation of some specific provision or provisions of the act, it undoubtedly could take action. Certain advertising practices of household-goods carriers were found to be unlawful and unreasonable, and the Commission prescribed a regulation to remedy this situation.[5]

Each year the Customer Relations Council of ATA holds an advertising contest for motor carriers in which the best over-all advertising campaign, best advertisement in a publication, and best direct mail piece are chosen. The standards used in judging the 1954 contest constitute a guide as to those features which are considered to be part of effective advertising:[6]

1. Does it "get through" to the traffic manager?
2. Does it get to the point in a way that the traffic manager will stop, read and record?
3. Does it get to the point quickly—is what you say specific and definite?
4. Does it give useful information?
5. Does it make the useful information seem important?
6. Does it call on your prospect in overalls or in a carefully pressed business suit?
7. Is there any continuing purpose seemingly to what you are doing:
   a) Are the shots scattered or concentrated?
   b) Are you putting right appeals to the right people—or are you giving all things to all people?
8. Are you using the most effective media for the job at hand?
9. Does the advertising technique—copy, layout, art, photographs, etc.—compete favorably with others which are seeking the reader's attention and time in the same media?
10. Have you thought through what you are doing, how you are doing it, and why you are doing it?

PUBLIC RELATIONS

A part of the selling program of any motor carrier must be that of public relations. Public opinion is of vital importance to the motor-carrier industry. There must be definite responsibility for the formulation of an adequate public relations program. This task frequently falls to the sales department, since the members of this department have many contacts with persons outside the motor-carrier industry. This is, by no means, a project that should be confined to the sales field, however, but is one that must permeate a carrier's entire organization at every level. All too often, the development of an internal public relations program of proper indoctrina-

---

[5] *Practices of Motor Common Carriers of Household Goods*, 47 MCC 119 (1947).

[6] Developed by G. D. Crain, Publisher, *Advertising Age;* Thomas C. Hope, General Traffic Manager, Montgomery Ward & Co.; and John W. Ladd, President, Ladd, Southward, Gordon & Donald, Inc., Chicago, Ill.

tion for all employees is neglected. It is certainly true that motor-carrier drivers, operating as they do on public highways, are under close scrutiny of the traveling public to a degree much greater than is true of any other intercity property carrier. The result is that the actions of a truck driver on the highway are a decisive factor in the formulation of public opinion concerning the motor carrier he represents, as well as of the industry as a whole.

A good public-relations program emphasizes the importance of every individual in a motor carrier's organization. It starts with the answering of a telephone in the motor carrier's place of business. It is the result of impressions its salesmen make in their contacts with the public, the conduct of its drivers on the road, and the impressions formed by people who call at the carrier's place of business. A good public-relations program is a composite picture of all the elements of a motor carrier's organization. Everyone in a motor carrier's organization should realize that his part in creating good public relations for the company is vital.

ASSISTANCE FROM NATIONAL AND STATE TRADE ASSOCIATIONS

The motor-carrier national and state trade associations bear the brunt of the public-relations program which is carried on in the industry. They are doing a good job of presenting the facts concerning the industry to the carriers themselves and to the public. It is essential that the motor-carrier associations continue to tell their story in the future, as in the past, in terms of *facts*. Many motor carriers rely heavily for information concerning public relations upon these agencies which disseminate information on all aspects of good industry relations. If a motor carrier makes use of the factual information supplied by an industry association and makes certain that the information is transmitted directly to all employees, it has made a start on good public relations.

In 1953 the ATA Foundation, Inc., was created for the purpose of enabling suppliers of the trucking industry to offer special assistance in the public relations problems of the industry. The foundation is planned to be a public relations arm of ATA, but it does not conflict with the basic ATA public-relations program since the Foundation is open only to the nonoperating side of the industry. Each contributor, to the extent of its financial contribution, will have the option of specifying that its own advertising agency specify and place advertising or other projects undertaken on behalf of the trucking industry and underwritten by its contribution. All advertisements, direct mail, publicity, or other public-relations projects of the Foundation, which are financed by the Foundation, are signed "American Trucking Industry—ATA Foundation."

A number of substantial contributions are being made to the Foundation. It is administered by a Board of Trustees consisting of a minimum of eleven members and should be helpful in assisting in the public relations activities of the trucking industry.

COMPANY NEWSPAPER

The publication and distribution of a company paper offers an excellent and informal means of conveying those ideas which a motor carrier wishes to emphasize. Such a paper need not be lengthy. The mimeographing of several pages of "news" about employees, citing examples of good employee public relations, and facts about the company and the industry which can be helpful to employees in meeting the public are a few of the many items which could be included in a paper of this kind. It might even be desirable to have weekly or monthly awards for the best example of good employee public relations. A motor-carrier organization need not be large in order to make effective use of such a builder of company morale and public relations.

Every effort must be made to nurture and expand the goodwill that has been developed toward the motor-carrier industry. To accomplish this successfully, each motor carrier, through its application of a good public-relations program within its company, can make certain that it is adding to, not subtracting from, public goodwill.

QUESTIONS AND PROBLEMS

1. Do you agree that the term "transportation salesmen" is the best one to be used in describing those who sell motor transportation service? Why or why not?
2. What makes the selling of a service difficult?
3. Of what significance is the application of shipping motives in selling motor transportation? What are rational motives?
4. "It is true that in too many cases emphasis has been placed upon tonnage rather than upon the revenue aspects of the traffic." Why is an understanding of this statement important? On what basis or bases would you evaluate traffic?
5. What is sales diplomacy? How would you go about learning who controlled the traffic in a firm? Why?

6. Draw up a list of "do's and don'ts" for motor transportation salesman.

7. Assume you have been hired by a regular-route motor common carrier of general commodities to draw up a sales program for a ten-truck fleet, operating interstate, which has just started business. Describe your program.

8. How are transportation salesmen compensated? Formulate a sound compensation incentive system for the transportation salesmen of a motor carrier employing ten transportation salesmen.

9. Explain the reasons why motor carriers do not utilize advertising to a greater extent as a selling aid. What is your opinion on greater use of advertising?

10. "Public opinion is of vital importance to the motor-carrier industry." Explain. How would you organize a public-relations program for a specific motor carrier?

11. Is the motor-carrier industry faced with a continuing public relations job? Why? What part do the motor-carrier trade associations have in public relations work?

12. In a survey of traffic managers, what suggestions were made as to how to improve the effectiveness of motor-carrier salesmen?

18. REGULATION OF MOTOR CARRIERS

STATE regulation preceded federal regulation in the field of motor transportation. By 1928 property carrying by motor vehicle was regulated in thirty-three states and the District of Columbia, and passenger carrying by motor vehicle was regulated in forty-three states and the District of Columbia.[1] However, there was great variation among the states in the regulatory statutes which were enacted, and many have been modified or augmented. The states undertook regulation for a variety of reasons, which were reflected in the statutes enacted. Some tended to emphasize safety regulation. Others undertook the regulation of the for-hire property and passenger carriers, and still other regulation was undertaken in order to safeguard the highways through the establishment of weight and size limitations. There is evidence that some of the states had statutes enacted in behalf of special-interest groups which sought to restrict the development of motor carriers. Other states, however, had more liberal attitudes, as reflected in the statutes that were enacted to regulate the commercial carriers. Early state regulation of commercial motor transport in many instances was unsuccessful because of the manner in which the statutes were administered.

The states ran into considerable difficulty in attempting to regulate the property-carrying common and contract carriers. In three states, cases before the United States Supreme Court held that state statutes which attempted to regulate motor-vehicle contract carriers were unconstitutional.[2] Until 1925 it had been believed that, in the absence of federal regulation, the state had power, if it desired, to control interstate traffic within the boundaries of the state. The United States Supreme Court in two cases stated that regardless of

---

[1] *Motor Bus and Motor Truck Operation,* 140 ICC 741 (1928).

[2] *Michigan Public Utilities Commission* v. *Duke,* 266 U.S. 570 (1925); *Frost* v. *Railroad Commission of California,* 271 U.S. 583 (1926); *Smith* v. *Cahoon,* 283 U.S. 553 (1931).

the absence of federal regulation the state did not have the right to restrain interstate operations.[3] Another important case which had effect upon the developing pattern of regulation was that of *Stephenson* v. *Binford*.[4] The decision in this case upheld a Texas statute which provided for separate and somewhat different treatment of the contract carriers and common carriers. As was followed later by the federal government in its regulation pattern, Texas statutes required contract carriers to secure permits and required common carriers to secure certificates of public convenience and necessity.

The state regulatory agencies which were given the job of regulating the commercial motor carriers varied in different states; such agencies were variously called the Public Service Commission, the Public Utilities Commission, the Commerce Commission, the Railroad Commission, and the like. These state agencies were already exercising regulatory control over intrastate operations of certain other modes of transportation. Today, the administrative control by state regulatory bodies over intrastate operation is extensive, covering safety as well as economic regulation. All states have these regulatory bodies to regulate property carriers, with the exception of New Jersey and Delaware. Although the latter has the power to regulate, it has never appointed the regulatory body. In a few states, private carriers and local cartage companies are regulated.

The granting of certificates of public convenience and necessity to common carriers or permits to contract carriers enables the state to exercise control over the number of for-hire carriers operating intrastate. The general procedure is to regulate the rates of the common carriers, which must be just and reasonable, and to require the filing of tariffs with the regulatory body. The rates must be made public and must be adhered to. Somewhat similar requirements are imposed upon contract carriers. Certain records must be maintained and reports made periodically to these state commissions. Rules to be followed in the establishment of accounting systems must be observed by the commercial motor carriers. Some of the state regulatory bodies have been empowered to administer the special taxes which are levied upon commercial carriers in their states, such as ton-mile, mileage, and gross receipts taxes. Insurance requirements or the bond requirements for the different classes of carriers are generally stipulated by the state agency. In the safety field, the hours of service are generally regulated for the common and contract carriers but not

---

[3] *Buck* v. *Kuykendall*, 267 U.S. 307 (1925); *Bush* v. *Maloy*, 267 U.S. 317 (1925).
[4] 287 U.S. 251 (1932).

for the private carriers. Relevant data concerning the regulation of commercial motor carriers by the various state agencies can be found in Table 18–1. This table shows that all states except New Jersey require operating authority in the form of certificates for common carriers and that all states except New Jersey and Vermont require operating authority in the form of permits for contract carriers. After the passage of the Motor Carrier Act in 1935, a number of states patterned their state requirements, either through modification of existing statutes or the enactment of new statutes, upon the new federal requirements so that there was a greater degree of uniformity among the states than had hitherto been the case.

However, there is still variation in intrastate regulation because of the numerous problems which exist. For example, in California, regulatory records show that 81 per cent of all revenue for hauling freight and express is received by motor carriers. In regulating motor carriers this state has two laws: one a public utilities code governing regulation of common-carrier trucks operating under certificates of public convenience and necessity; and the Highway Carriers Act of 1935 which governs operation of other for-hire trucks under a permit system. A permit is very easy to secure and requires only the payment of a nominal fee. The result was that by 1954 there were but 411 certificated motor carriers to which 1,320 certificates and permits had been granted, whereas there were 14,050 permitted carriers.

The California Public Utilities Commission, after intensive investigation, has found that the two existing laws for the regulation of different types of for-hire trucks create irreconcilable disharmony. The only feasible solution is remedial legislation. The Commission in late 1954 established a new declaration of policy to enable highway carriers operating under permits to file applications for certificates where they qualify.

DEVELOPMENT OF FEDERAL REGULATION

A Supreme Court decision in 1925 declared that a permit could not be refused an interstate operator.[5] Serious question then arose as to whether the states could control the operation of interstate commercial motor carriers, and the state regulatory bodies became active in the sponsorship of federal regulation. A bill was introduced in Congress in 1925, and in every session thereafter, until the passage of the Motor Carrier Act in 1935. For a period of almost 10 years,

---

[5] *Michigan Public Utilities Commission* v. *Duke,* 266 U.S. 570 (1925).

TABLE 18–1

REGULATION OF COMMERCIAL MOTOR CARRIERS BY STATE AGENCIES
Alphabetically by States

STATE	STATE REGULATORY AGENCY	CLASSES REGULATED			CERTIFICATE OR PERMIT REQUIRED			COM CAR REQUI PRO CONVI A NECI
		Com-mon	Con-tract	Pri-vate	Com-mon	Con-tract	Pri-vate	
Alabama	Public Service Commission	Yes	Yes	No	Yes	Yes	No	Y
Arizona	Corporation Commission	Yes	Yes	Yes	Yes	Yes	No	Y
Arkansas	Public Service Commission	Yes	Yes	No	Yes	Yes	No	Y
California	Public Utilities Commission	Yes	Yes	No	Yes	Yes	No	Y
Colorado	Public Utilities Commission	Yes[1]	Yes[1]	Yes[1]	Yes	Yes	Yes	Y
Connecticut	Public Utilities Commission	Yes	Yes	No	Yes	Yes	No	Y
Delaware	Public Service Commission	Yes	Yes	No	Yes	Yes	No	N
Florida	R.R. & P.U. Commission	Yes	Yes	No	Yes	Yes	No	Y
Georgia	Public Service Commission	Yes	Yes	No	Yes	Yes	No	Y
Idaho	Public Utilities Commission	Yes	Yes[3]	No	Yes	Yes[2]	No	N
Illinois	Illinois Commerce Commission	Yes	Yes	No	Yes	Yes	No	Y
Indiana	Public Service Commission	Yes	Yes	No	Yes	Yes	No	Y
Iowa	State Commerce Commission	Yes	Yes	No	Yes	Yes	No	Y
Kansas	Corporation Commission	Yes	Yes	Yes	Yes	Yes	Yes	Y
Kentucky	Dept. of Motor Transportation	Yes	Yes	No	Yes	Yes	No	Y
Louisiana	Public Service Commission	Yes	Yes	No	Yes	Yes	No	Y
Maine	Public Utilities Commission	Yes	Yes	No	Yes	Yes	No	Y
Maryland	Public Service Commission	Yes	Yes	No	Yes	Yes	No	Y
Massachusetts	Dept. of Public Utilities	Yes	Yes	No	Yes	Yes	No	Y
Michigan	Public Service Commission	Yes	Yes	No	Yes	Yes	No	Y
Minnesota	R.R. & Warehouse Commission	Yes	Yes	No	Yes	Yes	No	Y
Mississippi	Public Service Commission	Yes	Yes	No	Yes	Yes	No	Y
Missouri	Public Service Commission	Yes	Yes	No	Yes	Yes	No	Y
Montana	Board of R.R. Commissioners	Yes	Yes	No	Yes	Yes	No	Y
Nebraska	State Railway Commission	Yes	Yes	No	Yes	Yes	No	Y
Nevada	Public Service Commission	Yes	Yes	Yes	Yes	Yes	Yes	Y
New Hampshire	Public Service Commission	Yes	Yes	No	Yes	Yes	No	Y
New Jersey	Dept. of Public Utilities	No[3]	No	No	No	No	No	N
New Mexico	Corporation Commission	Yes	Yes	No	Yes	Yes	No	Y
New York	Public Service Commission	Yes	Yes	No	Yes	Yes	No	Y
North Carolina	Utilities Commission	Yes	Yes	No	Yes	Yes	No	Y
North Dakota	Public Service Commission	Yes	Yes	No	Yes	Yes	No	Y
Ohio	Public Utilities Commission	Yes	Yes	Yes	Yes	Yes	Yes	Y
Oklahoma	Corporation Commission	Yes	Yes	Yes[4]	Yes	Yes	Yes[4]	Y
Oregon	Public Utilities Comr.	Yes	Yes	Yes	Yes	Yes	Yes	Y
Pennsylvania	Public Utility Commission	Yes	Yes	No	Yes	Yes	No	Y
Rhode Island	Public Utility Administrator	Yes	Yes	No	Yes	Yes	No	Y
South Carolina	Public Service Commission	Yes	Yes	No	Yes	Yes	No	Y
South Dakota	Public Utilities Commission	Yes	Yes	No	Yes	Yes	No	Y
Tennessee	R.R. & P.U. Commission	Yes	Yes	No	Yes	Yes	No	Y

STATE	CONTRACT CARRIERS REQUIRED TO PROVE PUBLIC INTEREST	RATES REGULATED BY COMMISSION		INSURANCE OR BOND REQUIRED			HOURS OF SERVICE REGULATED			HOURS OF SERVICE REGULATED BY:
		Common	Contract	Common	Contract	Private	Common	Contract	Private	
ama........	Yes	Yes	Yes	Yes	Yes	No	Yes	Yes	No	P.S.C. rule
na.........	Yes	Yes	Yes	Yes	Yes	No	Yes	Yes	Yes	Statute
nsas.......	Yes	Yes	Yes	Yes	Yes	No	Yes	Yes	No	P.S.C. rule
ornia.......	No	Yes	Yes	Yes	Yes	No	Yes	Yes	Yes	Statute
rado........	Yes	Yes	Yes	Yes	Yes	Yes	Yes	No	Yes	P.U.C. rules
ecticut.....	Yes	Yes	Yes	Yes	Yes	No	Yes	Yes	Yes	Statute
ware.......	Yes	Yes	Yes	Yes	Yes	No	Yes	Yes	No	Statute
da.........	Yes	Yes	Yes	Yes	Yes	No	Yes	Yes	No	Statute
gia........	Yes	Yes	Yes	Yes	Yes	No	Yes	Yes	No	Statute
o..........	Yes	Yes	Yes[3]	Yes	Yes[3]	No	No	No	No	....
is..........	No	No	No	Yes	Yes	Yes	Yes	Yes	Yes	Statute
na.........	Yes	Yes	Yes	Yes	Yes	No	Yes	Yes	No	Statute
....	No	Yes	Yes	Yes	Yes	No	Yes	Yes	No	Statute
as.........	Yes	Yes	Yes	Yes	Yes	Yes	Yes	Yes	Yes	C.C. rule
ucky.......	Yes	Yes	Yes	Yes	Yes	No	Yes	Yes	No	Statute
iana.......	Yes	Yes	Yes	Yes	Yes	No	No	No	No	....
e..........	Yes	Yes	Yes	Yes	Yes	No	Yes	Yes	No	Statute
land.......	Yes	Yes	Yes	Yes	Yes	No	No	No	No	....
achusetts....	Yes	Yes	Yes	Yes	Yes	Yes	Yes	Yes	No	Statute
igan.......	Yes	Yes	Yes	Yes	Yes	No	Yes	Yes	No	Statute
esota.......	Yes	Yes	Yes	Yes	Yes	No	Yes	Yes	No	Commission rule
ssippi.......	Yes	Yes	Yes	Yes	Yes	No	Yes	Yes	No	Statute
uri........	Yes	Yes	Yes	Yes	Yes	No	Yes	Yes	No	P.S.C. rule
ana........	Yes	Yes	Yes	Yes	Yes	No	No	No	No	Statute
aska........	Yes	Yes	Yes	Yes	Yes	No	Yes	Yes	No	Statute
da.........	Yes	Yes	Yes	No	No	No	Yes	Yes	No	P.S.C. rule
Hampshire..	Yes	Yes	Yes	Yes	Yes	No	No	No	No	....
ersey......	No	No	No	No	No	No	No	No	No	Statute
Mexico.....	No	Yes	Yes	Yes	Yes	No	Yes	Yes	No	Statute
York.......	Yes	Yes	Yes	Yes	Yes	No	Yes	Yes	Yes	Statute
Carolina...	Yes	Yes	Yes	Yes	Yes	No	Yes	Yes	No	U.C. rules
Dakota....	Yes	Yes	Yes	Yes	Yes	No	Yes	Yes	No	Statute
....	Yes	Yes	Yes	Yes	Yes	Yes	Yes	Yes	Yes	P.U.C. rules
oma.......	Yes	Yes	Yes	Yes	Yes	Yes[4]	Yes	Yes	Yes[4]	Dept. Pub. Safety rule
on.........	Yes	Yes	Yes	Yes	Yes	Yes	Yes	Yes	Yes	Statute
sylvania....	Yes	Yes	Yes	Yes	Yes	No	Yes	Yes	No	P.U.C. rules
e Island....	Yes	Yes	Yes	Yes	Yes	No	Yes	Yes	No	Statute
Carolina...	No	Yes	Yes	Yes	Yes	No	Yes	Yes	No	P.S.C. rules
Dakota....	No	Yes	Yes	Yes	No	No	Yes	Yes	No	Statute
essee.......	Yes	Yes	Yes	Yes	Yes	No	Yes	Yes	No	Commission rule

Continued

TABLE 18–1—*Continued*

REGULATION OF COMMERCIAL MOTOR CARRIERS BY STATE AGENCIES
Alphabetically by States

STATE	STATE REGULATORY AGENCY	CLASSES REGULATED			CERTIFICATE OR PERMIT REQUIRED			COMM CARRI REQUIR PRO CONVENI ANI NECESS
		Com- mon	Con- tract	Pri- vate	Com- mon	Con- tract	Pri- vate	
Texas........	Railroad Commission	Yes	Yes	No	Yes	Yes	No	Ye
Utah.........	Public Utilities Commission	Yes	Yes	No	Yes	Yes	No	Ye
Vermont......	Public Service Commission	Yes	No	No	Yes	No	No	Ye
Virginia......	State Corporation Commission	Yes	Yes	No	Yes	Yes	No	Ye
Washington....	Public Service Commission	Yes	Yes	Yes	Yes	Yes	No	Ye
West Virginia...	Public Service Commission	Yes	Yes	No	Yes	Yes	No	Ye
Wisconsin......	Public Service Commission	Yes	Yes	Yes	Yes	Yes	Yes	Ye
Wyoming......	Public Service Commission	Yes	Yes	Yes	Yes	Yes	Yes	Ye

then, prior to the passage of the Motor Carrier Act, there had been pressure upon Congress for the enactment of federal motor-carrier legislation. The state regulatory agencies were joined in seeking legislation by competitive transport agencies, the Interstate Commerce Commission, certain commercial interests, organized labor, and some of the larger motor carriers. The report of the Federal Coordinator of Transportation, recommending the regulation of both common and contract motor carriers, was made in 1934. The recommendations in this report served as the basis for the Motor Carrier Act of 1935.

MOTOR CARRIER ACT OF 1935

The Motor Carrier Act of 1935, later incorporated as Part II of the Interstate Commerce Act in 1940, provided for the safety and economic regulation of interstate motor carriers engaged in the transportation of persons or property in interstate or foreign commerce, which includes those motor carriers engaged in the handling of interstate shipments but operating wholly within the confines of a state. The congressional policy, as set forth in the act, was to preserve the inherent advantages of motor transportation, foster sound conditions in the motor-carrier industry, promote an adequate motor-carrier service at reasonable rates, encourage co-ordination among the different agencies of transport, and facilitate co-operation between federal and state regulatory authorities. The administration of this act was placed in the hands of the Interstate Commerce Commission. There was some feeling in the motor-carrier industry that the Interstate Commerce Commission might be unable to regulate

STATE	Contract Carriers Required to Prove Public Interest	Rates Regulated by Commission		Insurance or Bond Required			Hours of Service Regulated			Hours of Service Regulated by:
		Common	Contract	Common	Contract	Private	Common	Contract	Private	
ıs..........	Yes	Yes	Yes	Yes	Yes	No	Yes	Yes	No	Statute
ı..........	Yes	Yes	Yes	Yes	Yes	No	Yes	Yes	No	....
nont........	No	Yes	No	Yes	No	No	No	No	No	....
inia........	No	Yes	Yes	Yes	Yes	No	Yes	Yes	No	S.C.C. rules
hington.....	Yes	Yes	Yes	Yes	Yes	No	Yes	Yes	Yes	Statute
: Virginia....	Yes	Yes	Yes	Yes	Yes	Yes	No	No	No	....
onsin.......	Yes	Yes	Yes	Yes	Yes	No	Yes	Yes	No	M.V. Dept. rule
ming.......	Yes	Yes	Yes	Yes	No	No	Yes	Yes	No	Statute

Designated as "common carriers," "private carriers" and "commercial carriers," respectively.
Contract carriers operating over regular routes or between fixed termini are regulated—other contract carriers are not regulated.
Board has jurisdiction over motor carriers of passengers only.
Applicable only to carriers which are operated by owners for the transportation of their own property who collect from the receiver h property for transportation or delivery of same.
urce: Association of American Railroads and Association of Western Railways, *Digest of State Laws Pertaining to the Regulation and on of Motor Vehicles* (1954), p. 167.

motor transportation in a manner that would benefit the industry because of the Commission's long experience in regulating competitive transport agencies. The membership of the Commission is divided into the following five divisions: Division 1—administrative; Division 2—rates, tariffs, and valuation; Division 3—rates, service, and safety; Division 4—finance; and Division 5—motor carrier. Since three members of the Commission serve on each of Divisions 2 through 5, some members serve in more than one division. The total complement of the Commission is eleven. (July 1, 1955, Division 1 was abolished and Division 5 was renumbered Division 1. Division numbers used in the following pages are those prior to July 1, 1955.)

Most motor-carrier cases are handled by Division 5, although finance cases may be handled by Division 4 and certain cases will be heard by the entire Commission. Such matters as applications for permanent operating authority may be set for formal hearing, after being properly docketed, before an examiner (lawyer) of the Commission. He can issue a proposed report which will be subject to exceptions within 20 days after being served. If no exceptions are filed or the order is not stayed by the Commission, the proposed report and recommended order becomes the order of the Commission. Division 5 has jurisdiction over the proposed reports which it reviews, and it issues a final report approving or disapproving the proposed report. The report of Division 5 is subject to motions for reconsideration and for oral arguments before becoming effective.

Appeal may be made for argument before the entire Commission and then the Commission's decision may be further appealed to the courts. The Commission also engages in rule making and conducts investigations on its own motions.

The administrative organization to aid the Commission and the motor carriers is the Bureau of Motor Carriers, which is one of the nine bureaus in the Interstate Commerce Commission.

BUREAU OF MOTOR CARRIERS

The organization chart of the Bureau of Motor Carriers within the Interstate Commerce Commission is shown in Figure 18-1. The

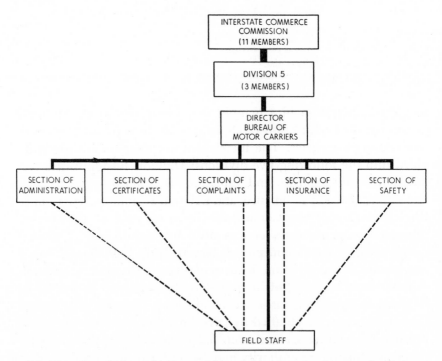

FIG. 18-1. Organization of the Bureau of Motor Carriers, Interstate Commerce Commission.

Director of the Bureau has direction, co-ordination, and supervision of the work dealing with applications for operating rights by motor carriers and brokers; determination of reasonableness of rates of motor carriers; safety of operation by all interstate common, contract, or private motor carriers; filing of certificates of insurance; enforcement of the law and regulations applying to motor carriers; interpretation of the statute, regulations, certificates, and other orders of the Commission; gathering of information concerning the condition of motor carriers and the national business conditions which affect motor transportation; and origination of policies and procedure affecting the regulation of motor transportation.

The Section of Administration is responsible for maintaining a system of property accounting, furnishing information to the general public, maintaining files of various service lists, distributing orders to the various sections, routing all letters and complaints, maintaining all payroll records, preparing Division 5 and other division minutes concerning motor-carrier matters, and maintaining personnel records, as well as other similar activities.

The Section of Certificates is responsible for reviewing, recording, and filing applications for certificates of public convenience and necessity, permits, licenses, and certificates of registration; for work connected with the preliminary handling of applications that are required to go to formal hearing; for the determination, for approval of the Commission, of the disposition to be made of applications for certificates, permits, and licenses which do not require a formal hearing; for the drafting of all final certificates, permits, licenses, and certificates of registration approved for issuance; for reviewing petitions for revocation of certificates, permits, and licenses; for determination, for approval of the Commission, of the disposition to be made of applications for substitution, transfer, or lease, and notifications of transfers of operating rights; and for the determination, for approval of the Commission, of the disposition to be made of applications for emergency authority not otherwise specified in the act.

The Section of Complaints makes plans and establishes policy for execution of work entailed in handling the Commission's motor-carrier formal docket and deals with the public on procedural and other matters; assigns for hearing and hears all motor-carrier matters requiring formal hearings; prepares all recommended, proposed, and final reports; prepares memoranda and makes recommendations to the Commission on all petitions filed in matters handled by the Section of Complaints on all temporary authority applications and shortened procedure rate matters; handles all requests for changes in time or places of hearings, extensions of pleading filing dates, and other procedural questions in formal motor-carrier matters; and recommends to the Commission the institution of general investigations where situations arise suggesting the necessity for such investigations. It maintains complete records on all matters and makes periodic and special reports to the Commission and others; arranges the itineraries of motor-carrier examiners; handles all matters pertaining to joint boards; arranges for hearing rooms throughout the United States for most hearings; and trains motor-carrier examiners, some of whom conduct hearings and submit reports and recommendations to the Commission. The Section of Complaints also has many other similar activities.

The Section of Insurance of the Bureau of Motor Carriers performs work pertaining to the furnishing of insurance or other security by motor carriers and brokers for the protection of shippers and the public, including the preparation of recommendations to the Commission for determination of applications to self-insure, the approval or disapproval of certificates of insurance, and passing upon the qualifications of insurance and bonding companies. This section also performs for the Bureau of Water Carriers and Freight Forwarders work similar to that described above.

The Section of Safety performs work in connection with the promulgation of regulations pertaining to safety, hours of service of employees, and standards of equipment; the obtaining and examination of reports of accidents; the investigation of accidents; and the administration of regulations. This section formulates programs for the execution of the field staff, makes recommendations with respect to administrative or punitive measures to be taken against recalcitrant motor carriers, and, in general, acts in a supervisory and advisory capacity with respect to the safety activities of the field forces. Its activities extend to consultations on safety matters with numerous agencies, governmental and otherwise, including engineering and technical societies, particularly in the development and application of engineering techniques to safety problems, and other activities in the field of safety.

The field staff of the Bureau of Motor Carriers furnishes information and interpretations of the law and the Commission's rules and regulations to motor carriers and the general public, including safety of operations, insurance for the protection of the public, rate matters, and operating authorities. It handles complaints against motor carriers from the public and other carriers and is responsible for enforcement of the law and the Commission's rules and regulations. It advises the Commission of conditions in the motor-carrier industry and conducts special and general investigations on which specific recommendations are submitted. The fourteen districts of the Bureau of Motor Carriers are shown in Figure 18–2.

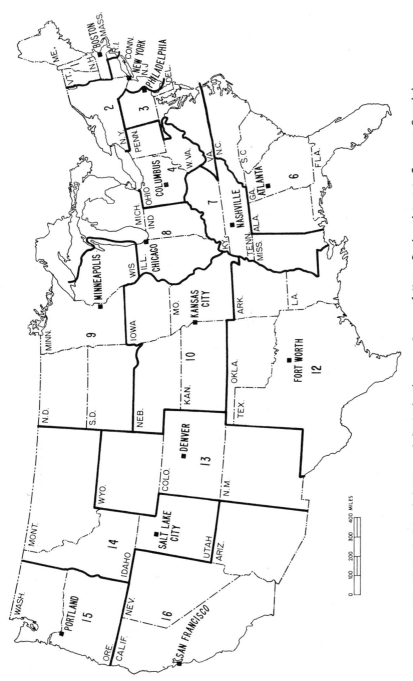

FIG. 18–2. Outline of districts and district headquarters, Bureau of Motor Carriers, Interstate Commerce Commission.

The Bureau of Motor Carriers annually handles about 11,000 informal complaints. An additional 4,000 of a more serious nature are received and handled, of which 600 or 700 are investigated for possible prosecution. The field force makes recommendations on more than 1,400 applications a year covering transfer or lease of operating authority, of which 60 per cent are disposed without hearings. The field staff also investigates and makes recommendations on more than 850 revocations of operating rights and about 2,000 applications for temporary authority each year. The work of the field staff is divided among the following subjects in the percentages shown: operating authorities, 14.68; safety, 31; enforcement, 34.32; rates and tariffs, 3.93; accounts, 2.84; insurance, 8.12; and administration, 5.11.

From July 1, 1953, to July 1, 1954, the Bureau of Motor Carriers handled 2,439 application cases, 271 finance cases, and 985 rate cases, not including petitions for rehearings or temporary authorities.[6] Because of the backlog of applications for motor-carrier operating rights and purchase of authorities, an additional specific appropriation was earmarked in 1954 by the Congress for the Section of Complaints of the Bureau of Motor Carriers to make possible a reduction in the backlog.

Late in 1952 a management study was made of the Interstate Commerce Commission by an outside organization for the Senate Committee on Interstate and Foreign Commerce. This report, which recommended the reorganization of the Commission along functional lines, was adopted in principle by the Commission. Since then there has been a reduction in the number of Commission bureaus from fifteen to nine, as well as other changes, some of which were made by the Commission itself before the report was completed. About 220 employees in various sections of the Bureau of Motor Carriers have been transferred to other bureaus in what motor carriers describe as a process of erosion of the Bureau which was specifically established to handle matters involving motor carriers. Where consolidations have occurred, these have been done primarily to secure co-ordinated and more efficient handling of the types of problems, such as accounting and tariffs, which can be given similar treatment in the various fields of transportation. It appears that consolidation of staff work along functional lines should not affect the interests of a particular group of carriers, inasmuch as separate motor-carrier entities have been preserved. There may be further organizational changes along functional lines made by the Commission.

---

[6] *Traffic World*, August 14, 1954, p. 24.

In 1941 there were 1,402 employees in the Bureau of Motor Carriers. On April 1, 1955, there were 567, of which 243 were in the field. This substantial personnel decrease has occurred when during the same period the number of trucks has almost doubled; their ton-miles have more than tripled; and the regulatory problems have become more complex.

By 1943 the Bureau of Motor Carriers had issued ninety-five administrative rulings. These rulings stated the Bureau's view of the correct application and interpretation of the act in the absence of authoritative decisions on the subject by the Commission. Two additional ones were issued in 1953; and, although many of these rulings are still being followed by the Bureau, some of them have been superseded by Commission decisions.[7]

Examiners of the Bureau of Motor Carriers conduct hearings and submit reports and recommendations to the Commission on motor-carrier matters. An approximation as to the percentage of examiners' recommended reports which are followed by the Interstate Commerce Commission in rate cases is about 50 per cent where the reports are uncontested. In instances where exceptions are filed to the examiners' reports and there are additional hearings, the examiners' reports in rate cases are followed about 85 per cent of the time. In cases that involve operating authority, the Interstate Commerce Commission follows the examiners' reports about 60 per cent of the time when the reports are uncontested. When exceptions are filed to the examiners' reports in operating authority cases and additional hearings are held, the examiners' reports are followed in about 80 per cent of the cases.[8]

MOTOR CARRIER BOARD

In order to relieve members of the Commission of as much detail as possible, a Motor Carrier Board consisting of three Commission employees was established in November, 1953. This Board has the power to act initially (a) on requests by applicants to dismiss applications under Sections 206, 207, 208, 209, 210, and 211 in proceedings which have not involved the taking of testimony at a public hearing; (b) on applications under Section 210a (a) for temporary authority; (c) in incontested motor-carrier revocation proceedings under Section 212a which have not involved the taking of testimony at a public

---

[7] Status of Administrative Rulings, July 1, 1949, Bureau of Motor Carriers.

[8] Information supplied by the Bureau of Motor Carriers, January 1, 1955.

hearing; and (*d*) on applications under Section 212 (b) relating to transfer of certificates or permits which have not involved the taking of testimony at a public hearing. The proceedings of the Board are informal. It can certify any matter to Division 5 for decision. Division 5, in respect of all initial actions of the Board, serves as an appellate division of the Commission.

JOINT BOARDS

To aid in the administration of the Motor Carrier Act, now Part II of the Interstate Commerce Act, certain types of cases involving not more than three states can be referred to joint boards by the Commission. The Commission may also at its discretion refer cases of a kind not specified which may involve more than three states to joint boards for action. The membership of these joint boards consists of one member from each state within which the motor-carrier operations are conducted or proposed. Their decisions are binding, although appeal may be made to the Commission. The members of the joint boards are usually members of state regulatory commissions or individuals nominated by the governors of the respective states. These joint boards are an unusual administrative device; but, inasmuch as the members have knowledge of the state regulatory patterns, some measure of benefit can be expected. Of all motor-carrier cases, one third to one half are initially issued to joint boards. In many instances, an examiner of the Commission will conduct the joint board hearings. Members of the field staff of the Bureau of Motor Carriers represent the Commission on more than one thousand joint board hearings annually. The reports of the joint boards are accepted unless an exception is made to a report, in which case Division 5 of the Commission will issue a report on that proceeding.

EXTENT OF REGULATION BY THE INTERSTATE COMMERCE COMMISSION

There were 19,730 motor carriers authorized under the Interstate Commerce Act to engage in transportation in interstate or foreign commerce for compensation on April 1, 1955. Of this number, there were 18,332 carriers of property, the remainder being carriers of passengers. This property-carrying group of motor carriers which hold authority under the Interstate Commerce Act operates an estimated total of 346,000 vehicles. Another segment of interstate motor-carrier transportation of property is performed by an estimated 33,000 carriers with an estimated 243,000 vehicles which transport "exempt" commodities exclusively, primarily agricultural commodities and fish. There were also an estimated 119,197 private carriers operating an estimated 767,456 vehicles which were used to transport property bought or sold by them incidental to their manufacturing or mercantile business.[9] Approximately 40 per cent of the Commission's work deals with motor carriers.

ECONOMIC REGULATION

All motor carriers transporting property in interstate or foreign commerce for compensation are subject to some portions of the Interstate Commerce Act and to some regulations of the Commission. There are two broad fields of regulation—economic and safety. The so-called "regulated for-hire" motor carriers are subject to both economic and safety regulation, whereas certain other carriers are subject only to safety regulation. Private carriers of property and some classes of carriers (exempt) which transport property for compensation are subject only to the provisions of the act and the regulations pertaining to safety which cover qualifications and maximum hours of service of employees, standards of equipment, and safety of operation.

If a motor carrier's application for operating authority is granted, the prospective carrier must comply with the Commission's tariff and insurance requirements before a certificate or permit will be issued. Further, no operations may be lawfully conducted until a certificate or permit is actually issued by the Commission. If operating authority is granted to a motor carrier, the carrier must file with the Commission the name and address of some person (an individual may name himself) to whom notices and orders of the Commission are to be sent; and also the name and address of a resident of each state in or through which operations are to be conducted upon whom may be served court process in any legal proceedings. The names and addresses of these persons named as statutory agents must be kept current by the carrier as well as the carrier's legal address.

Before a certificate or permit may be issued to any person, evidence of security for the protection of the public in the form of insurance, surety bonds, or qualifications as a self insurer must be on file with the Commission. A carrier may be prosecuted or its certifi-

[9] House Committee on Appropriations, *Independent Offices Appropriations for 1955* (Washington, D.C.: U.S. Government Printing Office, 1954), p. 575.

cate or permit may be revoked if the security for the protection of the public is not kept in effect at all times. The other requirement after Commission authority is granted and before a certificate or permit will be issued is that a common carrier must file tariffs with the Commission containing rates, fares, rules, and regulations in conformity with tariff instructions issued by the Commission. A contract carrier must file a schedule of minimum charges and bilateral contracts between itself and each shipper. Common carriers are issued certificates of public convenience and necessity, and contract carriers are issued permits. These permits and certificates constitute the operating authority of those carriers which meet the requirements of the act as interpreted by the Interstate Commerce Commission. A certificate is granted to a common carrier only if required by public convenience and necessity. The contract carrier's permit can be issued if it is consistent with the public interest and the National Transportation Policy. These operating authorities serve to control the availability of motor transportation service. Under the provisions of the act, a "grandfather clause" enabled those carriers which had bona fide operations and operated continuously except in circumstances beyond their control as of June 1 (common carriers) and July 1 (contract carriers) of 1935 to secure their operating authority without proof of public convenience, public necessity, or public interest.

The regulation of business practices (economic regulation) for common carriers includes the following: (a) certificate requirements, as outlined above; (b) requirements of reports and prescription of a uniform system of accounts for Class I carriers; (c) publication of rates and observance of rates, which must be reasonable and nondiscriminatory; (d) prescription by the Interstate Commerce Commission of maximum and minimum rates can be exercised; (e) requirement of 30-day notice for changes in rates; (f) suspension of proposed rates for a period not to exceed 7 months; (g) requirement of insurance or surety bonds, including public liability and property damage and cargo loss and damage; (h) requirement of approval of the Interstate Commerce Commission for security issuances of over $1,000,000; and (i) requirement of Commission approval of consolidations and mergers, as well as other forms of control (not applicable if total number of vehicles is less than twenty).

The regulation of business practices of contract carriers, in addition to those regulations already listed for common carriers which affect accounts and reports, consolidations and acquisitions of control, and security issuances, includes the following: (*a*) prescription of minimum charges only; (*b*) filing of schedules of minimum charges, which are open to the public; and (*c*) requirement of surety bonds or insurance, not including cargo loss or damage.

A report issued in April, 1955, and prepared by the Presidential Advisory Committee on Transport Policy and Organization, which consisted of a number of Cabinet members chairmaned by the Secretary of Commerce, contained a number of recommendations designed to strengthen common carriers, among which was one to increase competitive forces in rate making and another to revise the National Transportation Policy. ATA has indicated strong opposition to a majority of the recommendations.

EXEMPTIONS TO THE MOTOR CARRIER ACT

There are a number of exemptions to the Motor Carrier Act, now Part II of the Interstate Commerce Act, at the present time. Some of these exemptions are discussed in other chapters. These exempted groups are subject to the safety regulations which the Commission prescribes, such as the qualifications and maximum hours of service of employees, standards of equipment, and safety rules. Specifically excluded are school busses; motor vehicles owned or operated by hotels; trolley busses; motor vehicles incidental to air transportation; motor vehicles under the authority of the Secretary of the Interior which are used in transporting persons in national parks and monument areas; motor vehicles controlled and operated by farmers to transport agricultural products from the farms and transport supplies to the farms; motor vehicles controlled and operated by co-operative associations or federations of co-operative associations as defined in the Agricultural Marketing Act of 1929; motor vehicles used principally in carrying livestock, fish, or agricultural commodities, not including manufactured products thereof; motor vehicles used exclusively in the transportation of newspapers; vehicles operated exclusively on rails; and motor vehicles used by railroads or express companies, freight forwarders, or persons as incidental to rail transportation pickup and delivery service, since this is already subject to regulation by the Interstate Commerce Commission under Part I of the Interstate Commerce Act.

The second group of exemptions are those that are termed conditional in that the Commission may continue these exclusions from the act to the extent that it finds necessary to carry out the National Transportation Policy of the act. The conditional exemptions included the transportation of persons or property wholly within a municipality; between contiguous municipalities, or within a zone adjacent to and a part of a municipality or municipalities; and casual, occasional, or reciprocal transportation for compensation by any person not engaged in transportation by motor vehicle as a regular occupation or business.

The reason why a number of these exemptions were given was to ease the problem of regulation, inasmuch as certain exempted carriers were essentially local in their operations. Careful examination of these exemptions frequently gives rise to the charge that certain of them cover special-interest groups, and therefore it is questionable whether or not such an exempt status should be permitted to continue for such groups. It would appear that it would be extremely difficult to change the status of these exempt carriers after permitting them such a long period of freedom from regulation.

The language in the exemptions which are contained in Section 203 (b) is not uniform regarding the use of vehicles. Some of the exemptions are more stringent than others regarding this matter. The hotel and newspaper exemptions require that the vehicles be "used exclusively" in the exempt transportation. The school children exemption contains the restriction "employed solely," whereas the national parks exemption uses "operated . . . principally." The agricultural commodity, livestock, and fish exemption applies only if the vehicles "are not used in carrying any other property, or passengers, for compensation." The farmer, co-operative association, and taxicab provisions exempt certain motor vehicles but do not contain language which might be interpreted to restrict their use at other times. The commercial zone, casual or occasional, and aircraft exemptions refer to transportation and make no mention of the use of vehicles.

The transportation of newspapers is an exemption which requires that the vehicles have to be used exclusively in the exempt transportation. The Commission has interpreted this to mean that the vehicle can only be used in the transportation of newspapers if it is to be exempted.[10]

The comic supplements or illustrated supplements are considered to be a part of the newspaper. Ordinary magazines, however, are not. Newspapers may be transported under this exemption in the same

[10] *Elliott Extension of Operations,* 6 MCC 578 (1938).

vehicle and at the same time as United States Mail moving under contract with the Post Office Department.[11]

The casual, occasional, or reciprocal exemption is a conditional exemption which is applicable to transportation which is casual, occasional, or reciprocal by any person not engaged in transportation by motor vehicle as a regular business. An example of this exemption is that of a farmer who might occasionally carry his products or his neighbor's products to a market area. This exemption might apply to persons who now and then carry property but do not do so regularly.

The incidental to transportation by aircraft exemption has been defined as that confined to the transportation in bona fide collection, delivery, or transfer service of shipments which have been received from or will be delivered to an air carrier as part of a continuous movement under a through air bill of lading covering, in addition to the line-haul movement by air, the collection, delivery, or transfer service performed by the motor carrier.[12]

Prior to this decision, there had been earlier determinations by the Commission in which varying distances between cities and outlying airports were used in determining the exemption. Intercity motor common carriers had urged the Commission to prescribe the commercial zone of a city as being the limit of the exemption. However, the Commission recognized that a reasonable terminal area for an air carrier at particular points may be different from that for a surface carrier. The terminal areas published by the air carriers in their tariffs on file with the Civil Aeronautics Board are considered to be the area within which the exemption applies. The Commission in using the terminal area of the air carrier assumed that the Civil Aeronautics Board would not hesitate to reject any publication which would result in an unreasonable enlargement of the air carrier's terminal area.

Section 203 (b) (6) provides an exemption for motor vehicles used in carrying property consisting of ordinary livestock, fish (including shell fish), or agricultural commodities (not including manufactured products thereof), if such motor vehicles are not used in carrying any other property or passengers for compensation.[13]

---

[11] *Blau Common Carrier Application*, 61 MCC 705 (1953).

[12] *Kenny Extension—Air Freight*, 61 MCC 587 (1953).

[13] For an account of the background of the agricultural commodities exemption see Charles A. Taff, *Operating Rights of Motor Carriers* (Dubuque, Iowa: Wm. C. Brown & Co., 1953).

This exemption is a very important one because it is estimated that there are over 50 per cent more carriers engaged in the hauling of exempt agricultural commodities than there are regulated carriers, about 33,000 such carriers operating more than 200,000 vehicles. The Commission has indicated the meaning of "agricultural commodities (not including manufactured products thereof)" to be "products raised or produced on farms by tillage and cultivation of the soil (such as vegetables, fruits, and nuts); forest products; live poultry and bees; and commodities produced by ordinary livestock, live poultry, and bees (such as milk, wool, eggs, and honey), but not including any such products or commodities which, as a result of some treatment, have been so changed as to possess new forms, qualities, or properties, or result in combinations."[14] In this case, the Commission listed fourteen groups of commodities which fall within the exemption. By later legislation, horticultural commodities (not including manufactured products thereof) were added to this list of commodities which were exempt under Section 203 (*b*) (6).

The term "fish (including shell fish)" used in this exemption includes frozen, quick frozen, and unfrozen fish, and shell fish in the various forms in which it is shipped, such as live fish, fish in the round, beheaded and gutted fish, filleted fish, beheaded shrimp, and oysters, clams, crabs, and lobsters, with or without shells, including crab meat and lobster meat, but excluding fish and shell fish in hermetically sealed containers and fish and shell fish which have been otherwise treated for preserving, such as smoked, salted, pickled, spiced, corned, or kippered.[15]

The Commission at one time relied upon the "channel of commerce principle" as being a practical basis for limiting the extent of this exemption with regard to fish. Under this principle, a commodity was considered to be exempt only when shipped in the form customarily provided by the producer and was an exempt product only until it entered the ordinary channels of commerce. Thus, shipments from the fishermen to a fish broker or wholesaler would be exempt, but shipments from the broker to wholesalers or retailers would not be exempt since the product had entered the ordinary channels of commerce when it reached the broker. The same channel of commerce theory was urged upon the Commission for its adoption

---

[14] *Determination of Exempted Agricultural Commodities,* 52 MCC 511 (1951).

[15] *Monark Egg Corp. Contract Carrier Application,* 52 MCC 576 (1951). This is based on a court decision in *ICC* v. *Love,* 172 Fed. 2d 224 (1948) which broadened the Commission's interpretation of this exemption.

by regulated motor carriers to be applicable to agricultural commodities, but the Commission rejected the channel of commerce theory since it had earlier lost a court appeal in which it supported the channel of commerce principle.

Since February, 1951, the Commission has followed the decision of the courts in two cases, in which it was held that a vehicle may be used for transportation under the exemption in Section 203 (b) (6), even though at other times it is used for intrastate or interstate transportation for compensation of commodities not mentioned in the exemption.[16] However, a vehicle may not at the same time be used for transportation of commodities under the exemption and transportation of commodities not covered by the exemption. Thus, a certificated carrier authorized to transport certain commodities in one direction may, without authority, transport exempt commodities on the return trip.

There has been an expansion of commodities held to be exempt under the agricultural exemption. In two recent court cases (*ICC* v. *Kroblin* and *Frozen Food Express*) it was held that dressed poultry was an agricultural commodity and therefore exempt.

There are two provisions in the act which apply to motor carriers which operate physically intrastate but are transporting goods in interstate commerce. The first of these is the second proviso of Section 206 (a), and the second is the certificate of exemption.

Those carriers which can qualify under the provisions of the second proviso of Section 206 (a) (1) of the act do not have to secure operating authority from the Interstate Commerce Commission even though they are operating in interstate commerce. There are three basic requirements for operations under this proviso: (1) the carrier must be a common carrier lawfully engaged in operations solely within a state; (2) there must be a board in such state having the authority to grant or approve certificates of convenience or necessity authorizing intrastate operations; and (3) the carrier must have secured such a certificate from such a board.

Therefore, an intrastate operator can transport passengers and property in interstate commerce between points covered by its intrastate certificate without having to secure a similar certificate from the Interstate Commerce Commission. The intrastate operations under this proviso are subject to the limitations as to commodities, points, and territory which are provided in the state certificates. The

---

[16] *U.S.* v. *Dunn,* 166 Fed. 2d 116 (1948); *ICC* v. *Service Trucking Co., Inc.,* 186 Fed. 2d 400 (1951).

burden of proof for establishing that its operations fall within the terms of the proviso is upon the carrier which files under the second proviso of Section 206 (a) (1).[17]

The part of the proviso which refers to the phrase "within any state" has been given a rather strict construction. For example, an intrastate carrier operating wholly within one state could not qualify under the proviso if it conducted interstate operations in other states not physically connected with the one-state operation.[18]

The purpose of the other exemption, the certificate of exemption, which is contained in Section 204 (a) (4a), is to permit transportation in interstate or foreign commerce when it is of such character or volume as to be of little, if any, consequence in effectuating the National Transportation Policy by carriers engaged in intrastate operation solely within a single state in conformity with the laws thereof without imposing upon such carriers the burden of federal regulation. The phrase "solely within a single state" which is used in this exemption precludes the issuance of a certificate of exemption to one who conducts any operations outside the one state, even those exempt carriers hauling agricultural commodities under Section 203 (b) (6).[19]

BROKERS

The operating authority of a broker is a license which is issued by the Interstate Commerce Commission, and eighty-four licenses for property brokers had been issued by April 1, 1955. The Commission prescribed rules and regulations, which became effective in 1952, governing the practices of brokers of transportation of property. The rules require that each broker must keep and retain for a period of 3 years an exact record of each transaction in which he participates. He is required to keep open for public inspection at each place of business which he maintains a schedule stating the maximum charge for each brokerage service which he holds out to perform, and he cannot collect any more than that amount. Schedules stating the minimum charge for nonbrokerage service to shippers, consignors, and consignees and the maximum charge for such service for carriers must be kept open for public inspection. The

---

[17] *Refrigerated Transport, Inc., Eligibility Second Proviso*, 54 MCC 625 (1952).

[18] *Texas & P. Motor Transport Co. Common Carrier Application—Louisiana*, 10 MCC 525 (1938).

[19] *Grubbs Exemption Application*, 30 MCC 561 (1941).

Commission did not establish what the minimum or maximum charge should be.

Brokers cannot give money or other things of value, except inexpensive advertising specialties, to any shipper. This rule was aimed primarily at brokers who through gifts secured the privilege of routing traffic which in turn was given to the highest bidder. The duties and obligations of brokers are prescribed in one of the rules, such as protecting the interest of the shipper; not charging or accepting compensation from both a shipper and a motor carrier on the same shipment without advising both parties; the exercise of diligence; and the payment in full of all freight charges collected by a broker by the carrier or carriers employed by him. The carrier must have the authority to perform the types of service arranged for by the broker, either to destination or to a normal point of interchange with a connecting carrier.

Brokers are not required to make an annual report, nor is a uniform system of accounts prescribed by the Commission for them. However, one rule governing accounting requires the segregation of broker accounting from that pertaining to any other business and the allocation of common expenses on an equitable basis.

The rules prescribe that a broker's license may be transferred if approved by the Commission. There is also no prohibition against a person holding a license as a broker and a certificate or permit as a carrier, and there are some instances when such a dual status has been authorized. The license may be restricted in order to exclude from its scope transportation which the person is authorized to perform as a carrier. However, in other instances, such as in the case of household-goods brokers also authorized as carriers, such restrictions may or may not be included.

A broker's license will indicate the point or points at which he may conduct his business and from which he may arrange transportation to other points or areas. There are a number of household-goods brokers' licenses which authorize service ". . . to all points in the United States."

A licensed broker may lawfully arrange for exempt transportation unless the license restricts this.[20] Exempt transportation may be arranged for by brokers who do not hold authority. Thus the brokerage rules and regulations do not apply to brokers of transportation who arrange for hauling exempt commodities under Section 203 (b).

---

[20] *Copes Broker Application,* 27 MCC 153 (1940).

The regulations do apply to brokers of transportation performed under the second proviso of Section 206 (a) (1).

SAFETY REGULATION

The Interstate Commerce Commission has prescribed rules and regulations governing qualifications of employees and safety of operation and equipment of all motor carriers operating interstate, including exempt carriers. The common and contract interstate operators had safety rules prescribed first, and regulations to promote the safety of operation of all other interstate carriers have been in effect since 1940. All of the for-hire motor carriers which hold operating authority from the Commission were notified that they were subject to safety regulation by the Commission.

In 1954 there were more than 100,000 exempt or private carriers which had never formally been advised that they were subject to safety regulations. It is estimated that nearly 35,000 of those carriers have been notified, and that 2,500 a year are being notified. At the present rate, it will take about 40 years to complete serving official notice on all of the private and exempt carriers.[21]

There is a general misunderstanding of the safety work of the state and local governments, on the one hand, and the federal government, on the other hand, in their effort to reduce accidents upon the highways. The goal of all highway safety programs is the prevention of death or injury to persons and destruction of property. The accomplishment of this goal is approached by these two groups in different ways. The state and local police are primarily concerned with traffic control. This involves the direction of traffic in such a manner as to obtain the most orderly flow possible under prescribed minimum regulations governing speed, driving practices on the highways, use of signal devices, and size and weight limits. The principal function of the field staff of the Bureau of Motor Carriers, on the other hand, is the institution of programs to assure safe operating and maintenance practices and qualifications of drivers in the operation of truck and bus fleets to insure that passengers and the public will not be injured or killed upon the highway.

The safety work performed by the Commission does not duplicate that performed by the various states. This has been attested to by state officials who are charged with highway safety because it had

---

[21] Interstate Commerce Commission, *67th Annual Report* (Washington, D.C.: U.S. Government Printing Office, 1954), p. 125.

been suggested that there was a duplication of effort. Eighty-two officials from forty-one states addressed letters to the Commission stating that there was no duplication.[22] States with regulations on the transportation of dangerous commodities usually pattern them after the ICC regulations.

A complete revision of the Motor Carrier Safety Regulations became effective July 1, 1952. This revision contained important changes in regulations relating to the minimum qualifications of drivers, the standards of equipment and accessories necessary for safe operation, and in requirements relating to inspection and maintenance of vehicles. A number of modifications of these regulations were made subsequent to their issuance.

At the present time these safety regulations which have been prescribed by the Commission are a very important part of the work of the Bureau of Motor Carriers in the promotion of safety by all possible means. Safety regulations are divided as follows:

Part 190.   General (definitions)
Part 191.   Qualifications of drivers
Part 192.   Driving of motor vehicles
Part 193.   Parts and accessories necessary for safe operation
Part 194.   Reporting of accidents
Part 195.   Hours of service of drivers
Part 196.   Inspection and maintenance
Part 197.   Explosives and dangerous articles

Requirements concerning qualifications of drivers deal with mental and physical condition, driving experience and skill, age, knowledge of regulations, and the like. The Commission prescribes that a physical examination be taken before a driver enters the employment of a motor carrier. The driver must be re-examined every 36 months after January 1, 1954. The certificate of physical condition must be maintained by the carrier, and the driver must have a copy with him while on duty.

The driving of motor vehicles embraces many requirements, such as maintaining a reasonable speed limit, good physical condition while driving, the proper distribution and securing of a load, and certain requirements concerning the stopping of certain vehicles at all railroad grade crossings (vehicles transporting inflammable liquid —cargo tanks), special care in overtaking or passing, placement of emergency signals for disabled vehicles, duties of the drivers in case of accident, and that all equipment shall be in good working order.

[22] *Transport Topics,* March 22, 1954, p. 1.

Emergency equipment which is required in every bus, truck, or truck tractor is prescribed.

Beginning in 1937, the Interstate Commerce Commission required every common and contract carrier operating under authority granted by the Commission to secure an identification plate for each vehicle. There was a fee of 25 cents for each metal plate, and it was required that such a plate be attached to the rear of each motor vehicle. Effective January 3, 1955, the use of such identification plates was prohibited, and each carrier is required to display its name or trade name and Interstate Commerce Commission certificate, permit, or docket number assigned to such operating authority on both sides of each power unit operated.

The parts and accessories required on motor vehicles are specified. This refers to the number and placement of lighting devices and reflectors on every bus, truck, truck tractor, semitrailer, and full trailer; the requirements as to the adequacy of brakes and brake performance on all vehicles and combinations of vehicles; use of safety glass on all vehicles; and miscellaneous parts and accessories, such as windshield wipers, defrosting devices, coupling devices, and others. Motor vehicles which are used in driveaway operations are required to have specific parts and accessories which the Commission has prescribed.

Every motor carrier which has operating authority from the Interstate Commerce Commission is required to report to the Commission every accident in which a motor vehicle operated by it is involved and from which there results an injury to or the death of any person or property damage to any and all vehicles, cargo, or other property involved to the extent of $100 or more. Specific forms are prescribed for filing these accident reports. These must be filed as soon as possible and, in every instance, within 15 days after the accident. The reports are made to the district field director.

The hours of service of drivers are prescribed and stipulate that no driver shall drive or operate for more than 10 hours in the aggregate in any period of 24 consecutive hours unless such driver be off duty for 8 consecutive hours during or immediately following the 10 hours' aggregate driving and within the stated period of 24 consecutive hours. In case of adverse weather conditions, the aggregate 10 hours of driving may be increased to 12 hours, so that a driver may complete his run. These maximum hours of service were established after thorough studies of driver fatigue had been conducted by the United States Public Health Service. The drivers of sleeper-cab equipment may drive for 5 hours, rest 4 hours in the sleeper cab, and then drive another 5 hours; and continue this until the driver has completed 60 hours. The work week for drivers of motor vehicles is limited to 60 hours in 7 days or 168 consecutive hours, or 70 hours in 192 consecutive hours. A driver log must be kept by the driver, and this log is maintained in duplicate for each day of the month. Operators of farm trucks do not have to maintain driver's logs. The original of these records is retained by the motor carrier for one year and furnishes the basis for necessary reports to the Interstate Commerce Commission. The driver keeps his copy for one month.

Inspection and maintenance regulations require that every motor vehicle shall be maintained in safe operating condition. This covers such items as lubrication, inspection of damaged vehicles, and the driver's trip report concerning any discovered defect or deficiency. In addition, there are recommended practices regarding daily or weekly inspection, wiring inspection, and forms.

Special safety regulations have been prescribed governing the transportation of explosives and other dangerous articles by motor vehicle. There are many such regulations, such as the markings to be placed on the motor vehicle, precautions while loading and unloading, and specific directions to drivers concerning precautions to be observed in such operations. During World War II, the application of safety regulations to cover the transportation of explosives and other dangerous articles was broadened to include common, contract, and private motor carriers not only in interstate and foreign commerce but also in intrastate commerce. The application of regulations to intrastate operations for the transportation of these explosives and dangerous articles was limited to the duration of the war and 6 months thereafter.

One phase of the work of the Safety staff of the Bureau of Motor Carriers is educational in nature. It includes participating in instruction in schools having to do with instruction of fleet operators, drivers, and maintenance personnel, and with instructing various groups concerning special subjects which pertain to highway safety. The promotion of safety through education of fleet owners and operators is an important function of the Safety staff. They cooperate with many agencies which are concerned with safety, such as the National Safety Council; and members of their staff serve on a number of committees, including the Federal Safety Council and the President's Highway Safety Conference. The latter two agencies were created by executive order of the President.

The Section of Safety of the Bureau of Motor Carriers holds conferences with manufacturers to acquaint them with unsafe designs as revealed by accident analyses. The Safety Section of the Bureau also works closely with the industry and other agencies in the promotion of safety. It has also engaged in developing recommendations for the safe transportation of iron and steel articles, tests of new types of braking devices, and development of specifications for new types of tank motor vehicles. After extensive field inspections, recommendations have been made concerning corrective measures in the construction of tank motor vehicles. A number of states have adopted the recommendations resulting from the investigations relating to such matters as shifting of lading on steel hauling trucks and construction of tank motor vehicles.

Where administrative action has proved ineffectual, prosecution for violation of safety regulations has been undertaken. An examination of the Interstate Commerce Commission's annual reports will show that there have been prosecutions during each year for violations of safety regulations. The motor-carrier violations consist principally of permitting or requiring drivers to remain on duty for excessive hours, failure to have on file physicians' certificates of physical fitness of drivers, employment of drivers not meeting the qualifications prescribed, failure to maintain equipment properly, and failure to report accidents.

The safety aspects are of great importance in motor-carrier operations. The Interstate Commerce Commission, in determining applications for certificates of public convenience and necessity, has given special consideration to the matter of the fitness of the applicants from the standpoint of highway safety. Where some doubt exists, the Commission has reopened application proceedings for further hearings on this matter. In some instances, it has denied applications on finding that, in view of its record of willful violations of Interstate Commerce Commission safety regulations, the applicant is unfit to engage in the proposed operations.[23]

Particular attention has been given to applications from motor carriers for operating authority covering the transportation of explosives, as well as applications for transfer of such authority. The safety records of these applicants are closely examined, and applications have been denied where it appeared from the evidence that

---

[23] Interstate Commerce Commission, *61st Annual Report* (Washington, D.C.: U.S. Government Printing Office, 1948), p. 60.

the carrier had not demonstrated fitness to perform this hazardous work on the highways.[24]

The active promotion of safety regulations by the Bureau of Motor Carriers appears to be increasingly effective, for each year several hundred more reports of accidents are received from carriers which have never before reported accidents.

QUESTIONS AND PROBLEMS

1. Trace the development of state regulation of motor carriers, and cite the pertinent court decisions pertaining thereto.
2. Enumerate the duties of the following: the Director of the Bureau of Motor Carriers; Section of Certificates; Section of Complaints; and Section of Safety.
3. What factors prompted the passage of the Motor Carrier Act? Why are joint boards an unusual administrative device? Do you feel that their use is sound? Why or why not?
4. List and explain the exemptions listed in the Motor Carrier Act. Which exemptions, in your opinion, are justified at the present time? Explain your answer.
5. Outline what is included in the regulation of business practices for motor common carriers.
6. Carefully differentiate between a common and a contract motor carrier based on the statutory definition and Interstate Commerce Commission decisions. Why is this important to shippers? To the public?
7. Why has the Interstate Commerce Commission prescribed safety regulations for all interstate motor carriers—common, contract, and private?
8. It has been suggested at times that we should eliminate economic regulation of motor carriers by the Interstate Commerce Commission and allow competition to serve as the regulator of rates and services. What are some of the consequences that might be expected if this proposal were followed? Do you feel it would benefit the public?
9. What is the purpose of the Motor Carrier Board? Give some examples of the organizational changes in the Commission.
10. Is there an overlapping of safety regulation between the states and the federal government?
11. Compare the regulations governing interstate motor common carriers and brokers and indicate what differences, if any, exist.

---

[24] Interstate Commerce Commission, *63rd Annual Report* (Washington, D.C.: U.S. Government Printing Office, 1949), p. 50. See also *67th Annual Report*, 1954, p. 123.

19. COMMISSION POLICY ON OPER-
ATING AUTHORITY

▲▲▲

COMMON AND CONTRACT CARRIAGE

Although the Motor Carrier Act and, later, Part II of the Interstate Commerce Act define a common and a contract carrier, it has not always been easy to draw a line between the two types of carriage. The entire Commission in one case set forth the distinction between the two.[1] In this case, the essential line of demarcation between common and contract carriage was the presence or absence of an offer or the holding-out to serve the public generally. The Commission found that the holding-out to serve the public does not necessarily consist in public declarations or advertisements but can be established through a series of actions. The ultimate test of common carriage is the fact of holding out or not holding out to serve the public generally. The secondary test which is applied by the Commission in determining whether an operation is common or contract, where a public holding-out is in issue, obscured, or difficult to ascertain, is that of specialization, either as to the nature of the physical operation or in respect of the shippers served. Specialization in respect of service is a characteristic of contract carriage and may be evidenced by the following: (a) use of special equipment required by commodities transported or adapted to the convenience of the shipper; (b) transportation only of certain commodities or of commodities the transportation of which requires the use of special equipment, equipment accessories, or especially trained personnel; and (c) the strict observance of shipper loading and unloading hours or other similar practices.[2] Specialization in respect of shippers served is evidenced or negatived by the following: (a) the number of ship-

[1] *Craig Contract Carrier Application,* 31 MCC 705 (1941).
[2] *Transportation Activities of Midwest Transfer Co.,* 49 MCC 396 (1949).

pers served; (b) the apparent ease or reluctance with which new contracts by shippers are added, either to replace lost accounts or in addition to accounts already served; (c) the allocation of specific vehicles to the exclusive use of certain shippers; and (d) placing of shipper advertising on the vehicles used in the shipper's service.[3] A common carrier status is acquired by a holding-out to serve the public generally without discrimination. The contract carrier, on the other hand, will pick and choose among shippers those whom it will serve and will render a specialized service not available to the public generally but confined instead to the service of a limited number of particular shippers and designed to meet their individual or peculiar needs. In order to keep the line of demarcation distinct between common and contract carriage, Division 5 of the Commission has stated that the contract carrier must stand aloof from the lure of public calling.[4]

A contract carrier is specifically limited in adding contracts to those contracts which are within the scope of its permit. A permit may be subject to the so-called "keystone" limitation, which restricts operations thereunder to those performed under contracts solely with persons who operate wholesale and retail food business houses or food-processing plants.[5] Since a permit authorizes operation only as a contract carrier, Division 5 of the Interstate Commerce Commission has held that, when the number of shippers served or contracts held is such, either alone or with other considerations, as to show a common-carrier operation, it is empowered to require that the unlawful operation be discontinued even though this necessitates among other things a reduction in the number of contracts held by the contract carrier.[6] However, in early 1955 a federal court held in the Contract Steel Carriers case that the number of customers was arbitrary as a basis for finding the contract carrier had unlawfully converted to common carriage.

Those contract carriers which are a substitute for private carriage and dedicate specific vehicles for the exclusive use of the shipper do not tend to convert to common carriage. However, contract carriers which do not operate as a substitute for private carriage often tend, over a period of time, to convert to common carriage. This tendency poses numerous problems.

---

[3] *Transportation Activities of Midwest Transfer Co.*, 49 MCC 397 (1949).
[4] *Transportation Activities of Midwest Transfer Co.*, 49 MCC 390 (1949).
[5] *Keystone Transp. Co. Contract Carrier Application*, 19 MCC 475 (1939).
[6] *Transportation Activities of Midwest Transfer Co.*, 49 MCC 404 (1949).

The Commission has set forth the principles upon which a conversion application, that is, an application to convert from contract to common carrier operations, should be based. These are:

1. Each applicant in a conversion case must accept in full the burden of proving that public convenience and necessity require its operation as a common rather than a contract carrier.
2. A contract carrier should outline its present authority under which no substantial operations have been conducted within the preceding six months or year.
3. The carrier should make a complete statement showing its past operations for some substantial period so that the Commission can verify the carrier's claim of such past use of the authority which it seeks to convert.
4. The carrier should produce such shipper testimony as it can to prove that public convenience and necessity require its operation as a common rather than a contract carrier.[7]

A contract carrier which was ordered to desist from common carriage adjusted its operations to conform to Commission suggestions in order for it to operate as a contract carrier. These changes included a reduction in the number of contracts; a reduction in commodity categories; introduction of greater specialization in service through dedication of particular vehicles to exclusive use of shippers; and through furnishing special types of equipment; guarding against acceptance of unauthorized shipments; acceptance of "keystone" restrictions in its permit; and extensions only when needed by presently served shippers.

Contract carriers cannot interchange traffic with each other,[8] nor can they interchange traffic with common carriers.[9] However, contract carriers may receive shipments from a common carrier or deliver shipments to a common carrier for completion of the transportation haul if this is done in the name of the shipper. Thus the shipper employs the contract carrier as his agent to arrange for transportation beyond points to which the contract carrier is authorized to serve. The bill of lading issued by the common carrier should show the shipper as the consignor rather than his agent, the contract carrier, because the contract carrier cannot furnish service beyond its own line in its own name.[10]

The Contract Carrier Conference in 1953 petitioned the Commis-

---

[7] *Fischbach Trucking Co.,* 61 MCC 539 (1952).

[8] *Luper Transportation Co. (Kansas)—Purchase—McCarter,* 38 MCC 263 (1942).

[9] *Barton—Robinson Convoy Co. Ext.—Moffett, Oklahoma,* 19 MCC 629 (1939).

[10] *Ibid.*

sion to institute an investigation relative to the need for legislative amendments affecting contract carriers. This proceeding was instituted in *Ex parte MC–46, Recommendations Re Legislation—Motor Contract Carriers.* The contract carriers have felt that restrictions have been imposed upon them so that their growth has been retarded. They are requesting clarifying legislation which would include changes in definitions and liberalized permit standards.

DUAL OPERATIONS

The act prohibits dual operations, that is, the holding of a permit as a contract carrier and a certificate as a common carrier, unless specifically approved by the Commission. The Commission may permit dual operations if it is shown that there is good cause. The principal objection to dual operations is that they can result in a particular shipper being given common-carrier service at the lower contract-carrier rate, thereby discriminating against other shippers. The tendency of the Commission has been to permit dual operations where the services are of such different nature as to be noncompetitive or where they are between different points or in different areas.[11] There are no tabulated figures showing the number of dual operations approved by the Commission, although some indication exists in a study where carriers with rights as both common and contract carriers were counted twice and the total number of carriers was therefore said to be "about 100 to 250 too high to represent the actual number."[12] The number is small in relation to the total number of certificates and permits issued by the Commission. However, there appear to be more instances of dual operations in which intrastate authority exists for one and interstate for the other.

COMPETITION

The Commission has felt that there should be adequate competition to serve as a spur to the development of new types of service. On the other hand, it has also recognized that competition should not be unlimited and allowed to run riot, since it feels that it is the Commission's duty to prevent unfair or destructive competitive practices.[13]

---

[11] *McCormick's Exp. Inc., Common Carrier Application,* 12 MCC 632 (1938).

[12] Interstate Commerce Commission, Bureau of Transport Economics and Statistics, *Revenues, Ton-Miles, and Passenger-Miles of Class I, II, and III Motor Carriers, 1940, 1941 and 1944–1948* (Washington, D.C., January, 1949), p. 14.

[13] *Pan-American Bus Lines Operations,* 1 MCC 190 (1936).

When there is sufficient traffic available to permit it, the Commission has held that competition should be encouraged. In cases involving property carriers, the question of monopoly has seldom arisen. The Commission has stated that whether the competition comes from within the motor-carrier field or from other modes of transportation will have a bearing on the granting or denial of authority by it. In numerous cases the Commission has indicated that merely because a point had adequate rail service was not justification for denying motor-carrier service because shippers were entitled to adequate service by both modes of transportation. It appears that the Commission has sought to promote reasonable competition.

PUBLIC CONVENIENCE AND NECESSITY

The Commission may issue certificates to motor common carriers under Section 206 (a) if the service is required by the public convenience and necessity. The meaning of the phrase "public convenience and necessity" is considered by the Commission to be more than the mere adequacy or availability of transportation agencies but less than an acute need.

The standards for determining public convenience and necessity are found through the answers to a number of questions:

1. Will the new operation or service serve a useful public purpose responsive to public demand or need?
2. Will the public purpose be served as well by existing lines or carriers?
3. Can the public purpose be served by an applicant with the proposed new operation or service without endangering or impairing the operations of existing carriers contrary to the public interest?
4. Will the advantages to those of the public using the proposed service outweigh the disadvantages, real or potential, that may result to existing services?[14]

Public convenience and necessity has been judged to exist in operating economies and factors which will result in a greater degree of safety, expedition, and more efficient operations.

FIT, WILLING, AND ABLE

Under Section 207 a certificate may be issued to a qualified applicant if, among other things, the applicant is found to be fit, willing,

---

[14] *Pan-American Bus Lines Operations,* 1 MCC 190 (1936); and *All American Bus Lines, Inc., Common Carrier Application,* 18 MCC 755 (1939).

and able properly to perform the proposed service. Therefore, the question of the carrier's "fitness" is a very important matter.

The Commission has felt that past violation of the act is a factor to be considered in determining the fitness of a carrier but is not an absolute bar to the grant of operating authority. There have been numerous cases in which there were unauthorized operations which have been termed "inexcusable," although the applicant has been held to be fit. However, when operations have been deliberately conducted without authority over a long period of time with the full knowledge that they were unauthorized, the Commission has held the applicant to be unfit.[15]

In determining the fitness of a carrier with regard to violations of safety regulations, the Commission has generally not denied applications of carriers of general commodities for this reason when the service was needed by the public. Carriers of dangerous commodities, such as munitions, are assumed to have a higher degree of responsibility, and the Commission has denied applications by finding the applicant unfit due to violations of safety regulations.

An applicant was unwilling to accept a grant of operating authority to provide a needed service unless additional territory was given to it. There was no need shown for the service in this territory which was already adequately served by other carriers. The application was denied on the basis that the applicant had not established that it was willing to conduct the proposed operation.[16]

The Commission has held that a carrier was not fit and able properly to perform the service proposed because it expected to provide service with vehicles owned by and leased from a noncarrier affiliate.[17] Subsequent to this decision, a bill was introduced in the Congress which would remove from the Commission's consideration in carrier application cases the question of whether the carrier owns its equipment and other facilities. The Commission reversed itself on its original decision after the bill had been introduced in the Congress and ruled that the carrier was fit. However, the Commission did point out that it felt that an applicant should own directly the vehicles proposed to be operated and indicated that this should be the subject matter of a proceeding in which carriers, shippers, and others would have the right to participate. The propriety of instituting such a proceeding was to be considered by the Commission in

---

[15] *Trioli Extension—Brick,* 53 MCC 212 (1951).

[16] *Lusha Extension—Michigan Points,* 53 MCC 677 (1951).

[17] *Lemmon Transport Co., Inc., Extension—North Carolina,* 54 MCC 635 (1952).

due time. One of the concerns of the Commission in this matter is that affiliates not subject to Commission control may drain off operating revenues. If excessive charges are levied against the carrier for equipment furnished through a partner company the job of determining reasonable rates is made difficult. In the central states area some operators conduct their business through as many as eighteen companies. The Commission has no way of determining actual operating costs under such circumstances. There is also divided responsibility for continuous and adequate service.

An applicant whose only submitted evidence relative to its financial fitness and ability consisted of generalized declarations by its representative to the effect that the applicant had always realized an operating profit and that the proposed operations could be conducted at a profit was held not to be fit and able financially since the evidence submitted was insufficient. Something more substantial in the way of specific financial data is required to meet the fundamental requirement of financial fitness and ability.[18]

A more precise position regarding an applicant's fitness, willingness, and ability to perform the proposed service was set forth by the Commission in 1952. At that time the Commission ruled that the applicant's past failures to comply with the act and Commission rules and regulations as well as the gravity of certain past offenses, despite penalties and admonitions, warranted the conclusion that the applicant failed to show that it was fit and willing properly to conduct the proposed operations.[19]

OPERATING AUTHORITY BASED ON DURATION

The Interstate Commerce Commission grants to qualified motor common and contract carriers two primary types of authority based on duration: *permanent operating authority* and *temporary operating authority*. Temporary certificates and temporary permits are not issued—merely temporary operating authority as referred to in the act. Most operating authorities are of a permanent nature. Temporary authority may be secured from the Commission under Section 210a to provide service for such period of time as the Commission shall specify but not more than a total of 180 days. This authority

---

[18] *Producers Transport, Inc., Extension—Benzol,* 54 MCC 621 (1952).

[19] *Mathews Trucking Corp. Extension—Maine and New Hampshire, 1952,* 53 MCC 737 (1952).

may be granted without hearings or other proceedings, providing there is an *immediate* and *urgent* need for the service and there is no carrier service presently operating which is capable of meeting the need.

During World War II the 180-day limitation was eliminated under the Second War Powers Act. This act was extended and the portions covering temporary authority continued until March 31, 1947, at which time temporary authorities were extended by the Commission for an additional 180 days, to expire September 27, 1947. Section 210a specifically states that such temporary authority ". . . shall create no presumption that corresponding permanent authority will be granted thereafter." Those carriers which have been operating under temporary authority and apply for permanent operating authority to operate as a common carrier are obligated to prove public convenience and necessity in the same manner as any other applicant, according to the Commission. However, the numerous extensions of temporary operating authority by the Commission have provided many of the elements which are necessary in securing permanent operating authority. During the war and postwar period many carriers operating under temporary authority filed for permanent authority. By orders issued by the Commission, their temporary operating authority was continued until determination of their application for permanent authority.

When temporary authority is issued, the carrier is subject to all provisions of the act and the rules and regulations of the Commission just as is true of the carrier which holds permanent operating authority. From 1935 to January 1, 1955, 45,509 temporary authorities have been issued.

Section 210a (b) states that when the Commission has pending before it for determination a consolidation or merger of two or more carriers, it can grant temporary approval for the acquiring carrier to operate the entire property involved in the merger application for a period not to exceed 180 days. This insures continued operation of the motor carriers involved pending a Commission determination of the merger application.

It appears that the Commission is adopting a stricter policy regarding temporary operating authority. Beginning in 1954, the Commission has attached a statement to orders granting temporary authority in motor finance cases which informs the parties that the temporary authority should create no presumption that final approval will be given the application. Whether the Commission has authority to extend temporary operating rights beyond 180 days was carried to the Supreme Court in November, 1954.

LIMITED-TERM CERTIFICATE

There are also what are termed "limited-term" certificates. These certificates are issued to expire at a specified time. Such a limited-term certificate might be granted to a lessee who applied for an extension, the certificate being conditioned to expire with the termination of the lease. Thus, when the circumstances indicate that the public interest would be served by such action, this type of certificate may be issued.

REGULAR AND IRREGULAR ROUTES

The operating authorities granted to common and contract carriers which prescribe the highways to be followed are termed "regular-route" authorities. If highways are not specified in the operating authority, the carrier may operate over irregular routes. Operating authorities of irregular-route carriers are futher divided into *radial* and *nonradial* operations. Generally the permits of contract carriers contain authority to operate over irregular routes, while common carriers may be either regular- or irregular-route carriers.

The Commission has not been able to prescribe a general rule by means of which the regular- or irregular-route nature of all operations can be determined, although it has listed eight practices to serve as criteria in the determination of the nature of an operation, whether regular or irregular. These practices are:

1. Predetermined plan. Regular route operation is repetitive and is according to a predetermined plan. This is in contrast to operations strictly on call, as demanded, and where demanded.
2. Character of traffic. A large number of shippers are served and aggregated lots of miscellaneous truckload shipments are carried.
3. Solicitation. Full time solicitors are employed at principal points to secure less-truckload and truckload shipments.
4. Terminals and call stations. Regular route carriers usually maintain terminals at principal points for the handling of less-truckload shipments.
5. Fixed routes. Regular route carriers habitually use certain routes.
6. Fixed termini. Regular route carriers always have fixed termini.
7. Periodicity of service. Regular route service is repetitive in nature so as to become fixed in pattern but it does not depend upon the interval between offerings.

8. Schedules or their equivalent. Regular route carriers observe fixed published schedules of departures and arrivals.[20]

The Commission has stressed that none of these criteria standing alone is conclusive except possibly that of definite published schedules.

There are several types of irregular-route operations: (*a*) one is a carrier of specific commodities or class of commodities which originates freight at one or a limited number of origin points and distributes the freight at all points in a defined destination territory; (*b*) a carrier of general commodities which receives such freight in truckload quantities and distributes to numerous consignees in a defined destination territory; (*c*) a carrier which transports a particular class of commodities between certain points and serves no intermediate points; and (*d*) a carrier which transports products of a limited base area to all destination points in a broad destination territory and returns with general merchandise and supplies that are used in the limited-base area.[21]

The operations of irregular-route carriers which have authority to transport general commodities tend to evolve into regular-route operations, whereas the operations of the majority of irregular-route carriers which render specialized services do not tend to do so. A common carrier may combine a regular route with an irregular route to provide through service, but the separate nature of the regular- and irregular-route service must be preserved. When a single radial grant of authority has been made between a base area and a specified radial area, the Commission has held that a holder of a single grant of radial rights is not authorized to perform service between any two points in the radial area even if the operation is through the base point.[22]

Irregular-route common carriers and contract carriers may cross states for which they have no interstate operating authority in order to join their authorized origin and destination points or areas. Such states are called "traversal" states. In 1952 the Commission issued interpretative rules regarding such traversal states. These rules provide that when no traversal states are named in the operating authority the carrier may operate through any state that provides a

---

[20] *Transportation Activities, Brady Transfer & Storage Co.*, 47 MCC 23 (1947).

[21] Senate Committee on Interstate and Foreign Commerce, 81st Cong., 2d sess., *Study of Domestic Land and Water Transportation* (Washington, D.C.: U.S. Government Printing Office, 1950), p. 1503.

[22] *Jack Cole Co., Inc., Common Carrier Application*, 32 MCC 199 (1942).

direct route. If a certificate or permit names traversal states, the carrier may operate through them or any other state which affords a direct route, unless the naming of particular traversal states is a restriction against operating in any state other than those specified. Traversal states will ordinarily not be found in certificates or permits which have been issued since 1952.

The Commission has issued rules which govern deviation from regular routes which may be occasioned by repairs, floods, earth slides, and similar obstructions. Carriers are authorized to operate over suitable detour routes in order to continue to serve their authorized points, but they cannot serve any point or place as a result of the detour which they are not authorized to serve. The deviation from the authorized route is not to be continued in excess of 30 days, unless the carrier notifies the Commission in writing and supplies certain information indicating the nature of the condition, the period of time, and the detour route.

In a number of general orders the Commission has also authorized common and contract carriers which have authority to operate over regular routes paralleling certain turnpikes, such as the New Jersey Turnpike, to use the turnpikes as alternate routes without securing additional authority. When this is done, the carrier must indicate to the Commission by letter its desire to do this, in which event there are certain conditions imposed.

The Commission has also issued two general orders authorizing common and contract carriers which have been using a particular ferry to use the bridge that replaces the ferry as well as the additional highways necessary in traveling via the shortest practical route between the highways and the bridge.

In order to avoid congested places while transporting explosives or other dangerous articles, the regular-route motor carrier is authorized in a rule prescribed by the Commission to deviate from its authorized routes. The use of the bypass cannot shorten the route by more than 10 miles according to the Commission. Two motor carriers which are interchanging explosives inside a municipality may perform such interchange at any place within 10 miles of the municipality.[23]

The Commission has noted that about five thousand motor carriers hold more than one authority. The Commission's staff is not sufficient to go through all these authorities and include in single certificates all rights granted to an individual carrier. As a result

___

[23] Order dated October 19, 1953.

there is a great deal of confusion concerning the operations of a carrier which are the result of combining operating authorities in different certificates, such operations not being authorized in any single certificate.[24]

The proposal has been made by the Commission to the Congress, with an appropriation requested for the purpose, that an inventory and classification of motor-carrier operating rights should be conducted. Under the present system of filing these authorities numerically, the Commission cannot readily determine which carriers or how many carriers it has authorized to transport any commodities between any two points or within any territory. The Commission has issued more than 100,000 certificates or permits to some 18,000 motor carriers of property, and few certificates are identical as to the operating authority contained in them. More than 200 applications for additional rights are received each month, and the Commission has no practical or expeditious way to determine whether or not it has already authorized one or more carriers to perform the desired service. The result is that it must depend for such information upon protests which may be filed by carriers which have heard of the new application.[25]

OFF-ROUTE POINTS

A regular-route carrier may desire to serve a point that is off its regular route, which is referred to as an off-route point. The off-route point is usually considered to be one which can be served by making a short side trip with over-the-road equipment, which then returns as soon as possible to its regular route and schedule. There is no prescribed distance which constitutes an off-route point. Distances of 5 miles have been considered to be off-route points, as well as one of 25 miles but not one of 100 miles. In 1952 the Commission permitted deviation from regular routes in delivering or picking up United States Mail within 10 airline miles of the authorized routes.

Regular-route scheduled service may be performed to and from such points. Carriers may also have terminals at such points and may interchange at these points. Service may be performed between two off-route points incident to the same route only when such service

---

[24] Interstate Commerce Commission, *65th Annual Report* (Washington, D.C.: U.S. Government Printing Office, 1952), p. 139.

[25] Interstate Commerce Commission, *67th Annual Report* (Washington, D.C.: U.S. Government Printing Office, 1954), p. 59.

is performed in connection with and as an integral part of a good faith operation of that route.

The Commission has held that authority to serve all off-route points within 25 miles of Pittsburgh, the regular route of this carrier being between Syracuse, New York, and Pittsburgh, does not permit cross-haul operations between any two off-route points within 25 miles of Pittsburgh.[26]

Figure 19–1 shows a map of a motor carrier's regular-route and off-route points.

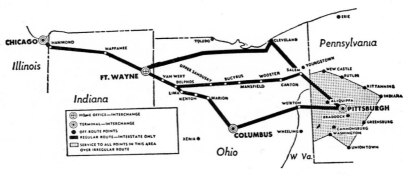

FIG. 19–1.   A motor carrier's regular-route and off-route points.

ALTERNATE ROUTES

Carriers sometimes seek alternate routes which may be granted if there is evidence that shows that the use of the alternate route will result in operating economy and efficiency; that a more expeditious or economical service will result; or a safer operation may be conducted. If the alternate route does not amount to a new or different service which would materially affect other carriers already supplying adequate service, the application for an alternate route may be granted. If it does amount to a new or different service, the carrier must prove public convenience and necessity.

The Commission has established three concurrent requirements which must be affirmatively met before authority can be granted for an alternate route solely on the basis of operating economy and convenience. These are: (1) applicant must presently operate between both termini under appropriate authority over a practical and feasible route; (2) applicant must be in competition with the present carriers operating between these termini by reason of handling a

---

26 *Ferguson Ft. Lines Inc., Modification of Certificate*, 62 MCC 261 (1953).

substantial amount of traffic; and (3) the competitive situation must remain unchanged if the authority is granted.[27]

FOLLOW THE TRAFFIC

For a number of years the Commission ruled that a carrier could be allowed to follow traffic of certain shippers to new origin points when the traffic was of such importance as to have a substantial effect on the carrier's revenues or ability to continue its over-all operations. A more stringent policy in this regard has recently been effected by the Commission which indicates that in the future no carrier will be granted authority to follow traffic if the existing service at the new point is adequate, regardless of the effect on the carrier that is losing the traffic.[28]

The Commission has provided, however, that when a carrier's service is limited to a particular type of service, the carrier's commodity description may be broadened. For example, truckaway service was granted to a carrier to enable it to retain the traffic of a shipper who was discontinuing the use of driveaway.[29]

"TACKING" RIGHTS

The Commission has not permitted contract carriers to render a through service by "tacking" or combining operating grants of authority contained in separate Interstate Commerce Commission permits. The Commission feels that there is no provision in the Interstate Commerce Act for the establishment of through routes or joint rates with other contract carriers or with common carriers. The Commission has allowed a contract carrier to arrange for interchange of traffic with a common carrier, provided the contract carrier acted as an agent for the shipper in a capacity apart from that as a contract carrier in arranging the transportation beyond the point it was authorized to serve,[30] but this practice is not extensive among contract carriers. In addition, the Commission has felt that a single contract carrier cannot render through service between points specified in separate authorities held by it. For example, a contract carrier is is-

---

[27] *Hayes Freight Lines, Inc., Extension—Alternate Routes in Michigan,* 54 MCC 643 (1952).

[28] *Smith & Solomon Trucking Co., Extension—Camden, N.J.,* 61 MCC 748 (1953).

[29] *Blain Drive-away System, Inc., Extension—Truckaway,* 62 MCC 199 (1953).

[30] *Holmes Contract Carrier Application,* 8 MCC 391 (1938); and *Barton-Robinson Convoy Co. Extension,* 19 MCC 629 (1939).

sued a permit to operate from A to B and is later issued a permit to operate from B to C. The two authorities granted in separate permits do not allow the contract carrier to provide through service from A through B to C.[31]

Since Section 209 (b) of the act provides that the Commission shall specify in a permit the business of the contract carrier covered thereby and the scope of that business, to authorize the establishment of through service by means of "tacking" together separate operating authorities would exceed the scope of the business operations covered in the separate permits and thus has been denied by the Commission.

COMMODITY DESCRIPTIONS

One of the difficult regulatory problems has been the interpretation of commodity descriptions which are contained in certificates and permits. Since under the "grandfather" provisions of the act, the carriers themselves described the articles which they were moving at the time regulation was imposed there was little uniformity in the wording of the descriptions used. There have been many individual determinations made by the Commission as to the interpretation of commodity descriptions. Such determinations are important since operations must be conducted within the scope of the certificate or permit.

Railroads, because of availability of all types of equipment, hold themselves out to transport all types of freight. This is not the case with motor carriers for which they have often been criticized. Prior to the Motor Carrier Act, the motor common carrier rendering interstate service had no legal duty to transport all of the traffic tendered to it. Therefore, its holding out fell into a well-defined channel. It transported only such commodities as would readily load into its equipment without damage to other lading or to equipment, and which would not exceed the carrying capacity of its vehicle. Thus, motor common carriers of general commodities, not being equipped to handle commodities moving in bulk, dangerous articles, and others, simply did not solicit this business. With the passage of the Motor Carrier Act, motor common carriers were permitted to continue such operations as they had been conducting with the result that the exceptions now, as then, reflect the self-imposed limitations of the carriers of general commodities.[32]

---

[31] *Longshore Extension—Salem—Youngstown, Ohio,* 43 MCC 759 (1944).

[32] *Descriptions in Motor Carrier Certificates,* 61 MCC 209 (1952).

Based on the commodity descriptions in operating authorities, common carriers of property may be divided into two groups. The first is that of carriers of general commodities with the usual exceptions, which are dangerous explosives, commodities of unusual value, household goods as defined in *Practices of Motor Common Carriers of Household Goods*,[33] commodities in bulk, and those requiring special equipment. The second category is that of common carriers of property authorized to transport special commodities either by name or under generic headings.

In the past, certificates to common carriers have been issued under such general descriptions as the carrying of automotive parts. It is extremely difficult to define specifically a term like "automotive parts." Similarly, a certificate has been issued for the hauling of commodities sold in retail chain stores. This, too, is subject to different interpretation. When the term "general commodities" is used without any exceptions, it has been interpreted to include even products in bulk.

A contract carrier whose permit authorized it to transport "manufactured or prepared foods" felt that it was entitled to transport fresh meats and packing-house products. In this instance, the Commission ruled that the motor carrier could not transport these items under the manufactured or prepared-foods commodity description. This was upheld by the Supreme Court.[34]

It has been stated that the restriction against special equipment when that term is included in a general commodity certificate applies to the over-the-road vehicle and not to mechanical devices used in loading or unloading freight. The special equipment restriction is designed primarily to prevent general commodity carriers from transporting commodities of unusual size, shape, or weight, thus preventing the general commodity carrier from invading the heavy-hauler type of service.[35]

When the term "special equipment" is used in the certificates of heavy haulers, it describes a special type of service but limits such specialized carriers to the movement of commodities which because of size or weight require special equipment. Heavy haulers cannot transport commodities which are loaded and unloaded by winches, cranes, and other power-driven equipment furnished and operated by the consignor or consignee, the carrier not being required to

---

[33] 17 MCC 467 (1939).

[34] *Transport Topics*, October 25, 1954, p. 2.

[35] *St. Johnsbury Trucking Co., Inc., Extension—Heavy Hauling*, 53 MCC 277 (1951).

furnish and use winches, cranes, or other power-driven equipment for loading or unloading of the commodity or to use special-type vehicles for the transportation thereof. Conversely, a carrier holding general commodity authority which contains an exception against the transportation of commodities requiring special equipment is not authorized to transport commodities which require the furnishing of or use by the carrier of winches, cranes, or other power-driven equipment for loading or unloading the commodity or the use of special type of vehicles for the transportation thereof, but may transport commodities which are loaded and unloaded by winches, cranes, or other power-driven equipment furnished and operated by the consignor or consignee if they do not require the use of special type vehicles for the transportation thereof.

In an effort to clarify the scope of motor common-carrier commodity descriptions to be contained in certificates issued in the future, an investigation was undertaken by the Commission in 1949. The order of the Commission regarding this investigation became effective in 1952. It provided commodity lists under class or generic headings and commodity descriptions to be used in filing applications for certificates of public convenience and necessity after that time, as well as describing the commodity scope of such certificates. The lists established were primarily for specialized common carriers, although not every type of specialized service was covered by the commodity groupings. There were fifteen basic commodity groupings with numerous subdivisions. Thus, commodity descriptions in new certificates are now uniform which measurably improves the situation.

REVOCATION AND SUSPENSION

Motor-carrier operating rights can be revoked only in accordance with the procedure established in Section 212 (a) of the act. This Section provides that ". . . certificates, permits, and licenses shall be effective from the date specified therein, and shall remain in effect until suspended or terminated as herein provided. Any such certificate, permit, or license may, upon application of the holder thereof, in the discretion of the Commission, be amended or revoked, in whole or in part, or may upon complaint, or on the Commission's own initiative, after notice and hearing, be suspended, changed, or revoked, in whole or in part, for willful failure to comply with any lawful order, or with any term, condition, or limitation of such certificate, permit, or license."

The procedure of the Commission is to enter an order which directs the carrier to cease violations within a period of not less than 30 days. If during that time the carrier does not comply with the order, the Commission must secure evidence of this failure to comply and an additional hearing is held. If it can be proved in this hearing that the carrier willfully violated the first order of the Commission, the Commission may issue an order of revocation. It should be noted that the revocation or suspension can occur only for *willful* failure to comply with the act or an order of the Commission.[36] There is one exception to this. When fraud or misrepresentation are involved, an operating authority may be revoked without proceeding under Section 212 (a).[37] If an operating authority is issued inadvertently as a result of typographical errors or similar occurrences, corrections can, of course, be made. It is also possible to secure reinstatement of a revoked certificate.[38]

When an order of compliance is issued, it is issued under Section 204 (c). Such an order remains in effect until its expiration date or until terminated by the Commission. It is not terminated merely by the carrier's compliance with the requirements of the order. During the effectiveness of the Section 204 (c) order, the Commission may proceed under Section 212 (a) to revoke, if there is willful violation, without further notice and hearing.[39]

The Commission procedure in revoking operating authority is one in which the burden of proof is upon the complainant. Since the act specifies that the holder of operating authority is to be given not less than 30 days to comply with an order of the Commission, this period of time is adequate to comply with any Commission order. It usually happens, therefore, that even when proof is submitted, the Commission gives the carrier a specified time in which to comply with the order of the Commission, with the result that compliance follows in most cases.

In 1953 about 443 Class II and III carriers had their certificates or permits revoked for failure to file required annual reports for the calender year 1951. Although Class I motor carriers have been

---

[36] *Smith Bros. Revocation of Certificate,* 33 MCC 465 (1942).

[37] *Ibid.*

[38] *Black & Sons Common Carrier Application,* 53 MCC 572 (1951).

[39] *Pennsylvania Greyhound Lines, Inc.* v. *American Bus Lines,* 52 MCC 117 (1950).

fined for failure to file reports within a prescribed period, there has been no revocation of their operating authorities for failure to file reports.

The Commission also has authority under Section 212 (a) to suspend operating authorities. There have been numerous proceedings involving the fitness of carriers in which the Commission has required compliance with Commission orders or suspension would follow. However, like revocation, the number of suspensions has been relatively small. If the carrier wants to comply with the Commission's orders, it is given the opportunity to do so. The effect of suspension is a temporary interruption of operations which can be resumed upon compliance with the Commission's requirements. Suspension does not carry the finality that revocation does. Revocation is a cessation of operations with the likelihood of resumption remote.

Under the second proviso of Section 212 (a), an operating authority may be suspended upon notice of not less than 15 days but without hearing for failure to comply with Section 211 (c), (brokerage rules and regulations), Section 217 (a), (filing of tariffs by common carriers), and Section 218 (a), (filing of schedules of contract carriers).

ABANDONMENT OF ROUTES

The Commission was not given the power under the act to compel a motor carrier operating in interstate or foreign commerce to continue in business if it desires to discontinue operations entirely. The relatively small investment required for operations was a factor which influenced Congress in permitting the motor carrier to cease operations any time that it wanted to do so. However, as long as the carrier holds a certificate authorizing it to conduct certain operations it is under the Commission's jurisdiction to the extent provided by the act and must comply with any lawful requirements which the Commission may establish with respect to continuous and adequate service if the carrier wants to continue its operations.[40] The Commission has permitted the abandonment of portions of an operation when they were not profitable, and there was little public need for their continuance even though the carrier's operations as a whole were in sound financial condition.[41]

---

[40] *Towns of Bristol and Hill, N.H.* v. *Boston and M. Transp. Co.*, 20 MCC 581 (1939).
[41] *Massachusetts N. E. Transp. Co.—Abandonment of Routes,* 51 MCC 573 (1950).

A carrier with broad territorial rights did not transport shipments to all of the destinations it was authorized to serve. It interchanged many shipments with connecting lines, although occasionally it operated its own equipment all the way to destination. In other instances, the carrier used leased equipment. There was no complaint of the service by the public, but the complaint was filed by competing carriers. The Commission held that the carrier was rendering reasonably continuous and adequate service.[42]

In a later case involving a 240-mile regular route over which the carrier was authorized to serve all intermediate points, the facts showed that during 14 months the carrier served only one intermediate point regularly itself. Of 434 shipments consigned to other intermediate points, it turned over to the competing complainant for delivery all but six. This was held to be a failure to render reasonably continuous and adequate service. The carrier was ordered to institute direct service to the points within 60 days.[43]

RAILROAD OPERATION AND CONTROL OF MOTOR CARRIERS OF PROPERTY

Railroads engage in motor transportation directly as well as through noncontrolled motor carriers[44] and through their own subsidiaries. Operations of the two former types are auxiliary or supplemental to train service.[45] Operations of the controlled motor carriers (those in which a railroad has a greater than 50 per cent interest) by railroads may be of the auxiliary or supplemental type or, in some cases, are independent of rail business.

In 1948 property operations by or for railroads constituted 2.3 per cent of the intercity vehicle-miles of all Class I motor carriers of property, although in 1944 they were 3.9 per cent.[46] During this same period there was an increase in vehicle-miles of but 0.5 per cent, although the vehicles used by or for railroads increased 42 per

---

[42] *Akers Motor Lines, Inc.* v. *Safety Transp. Corp.,* 52 MCC 395 (1950).

[43] *Red Ball Motor Freight, Inc.* v. *Herrin Transp. Co.,* 52 MCC 453 (1951).

[44] A noncontrolled carrier is a motor carrier whose course of action the railroad did not have the ability to determine, other than through contractual arrangements for the performance of service for the railroad. Interstate Commerce Commission, Bureau of Transport Economics and Statistics, *Motor Operations by or for Class I Railroads, 1944,* Statement 4829 (Washington, D.C., September, 1948), p. 8.

[45] Interstate Commerce Commission, *62nd Annual Report* (Washington, D.C.: U.S. Government Printing Office, 1949), p. 54.

[46] Interstate Commerce Commission, Bureau of Transport Economics and Statistics, *Motor Operations of Class I Railroads* (Washington, D.C., 1953), p. 7.

cent from 2,826 to 4,019 vehicles. Those motor carriers which are controlled by railroads showed an 8 per cent increase in vehicle-miles in 1951 over 1948.[47] In 1948 there were seventy-one railroads which had motor-carrier operations. Based on vehicle-miles about half of such operations are conducted by six railroads—the Santa Fe, Rock Island, St. Louis–San Francisco, Pennsylvania, St. Louis–Southwestern, and Missouri Pacific.

The Interstate Commerce Commission has felt that Section 5 of the Interstate Commerce Act requires that a railroad or its affiliate seeking authority to acquire control of a motor carrier shall be required to show that the proposed transaction will be consistent with the public interest and that it will enable such railroad to use service by motor vehicle to public advantage in its operations and will not unduly restrain competition. Under Section 207 of the act, railroads may file applications for grants directly to them of authority to initiate new motor-carrier operations. The Commission has, almost without exception, conditioned the grants of certificates under Section 207 so as to restrict the authorized motor operations to service that is auxiliary to or supplemental to rail service.[48]

Similar restrictions as to future operations were not consistently imposed in approving acquisitions of existing motor carriers by railroads or their affiliates prior to a decision by the Commission in 1946.[49] In some of the early cases, Commission approval specified that the proposed acquisition was made subject to such conditions as the Commission might in the future find necessary to impose in order to make certain that future service would be limited to that which is auxiliary to or supplemental to rail service. It has been pointed out that some railroads misconstrued the restrictions of their operating authorities or took advantage of the lack of specific restrictions attached to purchase authorities and render directly or through an affiliate substantial all-motor services at motor rates in direct competition with their own rail services and with independent motor carriers.[50] In a number of instances, following the provisions they have made in their tariffs, the railroads have been hauling motor traffic by rail and rail traffic by motor; and, where rail-

---

[47] *Ibid.*, pp. 2, 9.

[48] *Kansas City Southern Transport Co. Common Carrier Applications,* 10 MCC 221 (1938); *Kansas City Southern Co., Common Carrier Application,* 28 MCC 5 (1940).

[49] *Rock Island Motor Transit Co.—Purchase—White Line M. Frt.,* 40 MCC 457 (1946).

[50] Interstate Commerce Commission, *60th Annual Report* (Washington, D.C.: U.S. Government Printing Office, 1946), p. 44.

road rates were lower, shippers desiring motor-carrier service have offered the traffic on railroad bills of lading to secure the advantage of the lower railroad rates.[51]

Two important proceedings, the *Rock Island Motor Transit Case* which involved acquisition proceedings under Section 5 and Section 213 and the *Texas and Pacific Motor Transport Case* which involved certificates for new routes under Section 207, were carried to the Supreme Court. The Supreme Court upheld the order of the Commission in both of these cases which imposed limitations or restrictions which would insure that the rail operations of motor-carrier service would be conducted in a manner which was auxiliary, supplemental, or incidental to train service.[52] After this decision of the court, Rock Island Motor Transit secured limited temporary authority and applied for permanent authority without the usual restrictions. The entire Commission in *MC–29130,* Sub. 70, in November, 1954, held that the evidence clearly established that public convenience requires less-truckload peddle operations by Motor Transit; that other motor carriers have not cared to render such service and that some hold no intrastate rights in Iowa such as are possessed by Motor Transit; and that Motor Transit's peddle service is based on interstate, intrastate, and rail-billed traffic enabling it to provide better service than others.

In addition, the Commission stated that there was some evidence of public need for truckload services proposed by Motor Transit, but it was not as convincing as that with respect to peddle operations inasmuch as other motor carriers usually have provided satisfactory truckload service. However, the Commission felt that there was sufficient basis to warrant a complete grant of authority.

The permanent rights granted have attached only the conditions of (1) a reservation that such limitations may be attached from time to time as public convenience and necessity may require, and (2) that all contractual arrangements between Motor Transit and the parent railroad shall be reported to the Commission and if it is found necessary they will be revised to be fair and equitable to the parties. The Commission stated that this grant does not mark a departure from established policy of restricting trucking operations of railroad affiliates.

------

[51] *Texas and Pacific M. Transport Co., Common Carrier Application,* 41 MCC 72 (1943).

[52] *United States* v. *Rock Island Motor Transit Co.,* 340 U.S. 419 (1951); *United States* v. *Texas & Pacific Motor Transport Co.,* 349 U.S. 450 (1951).

The conditions which are usually imposed on rail operations of motor-carrier service are as follows:

1. The service by motor vehicle shall be limited to service which is auxiliary to or supplemental of rail service of the railroad involved. This condition requires that the traffic be that of the railroad moving under rail responsibility on rail billing and on rail rates. Unless limited by the third condition explained later, the first condition permits all-motor movements of rail traffic. However, it does not permit all-motor movements on motor billing and motor rates.

2. An applicant shall not serve or interchange traffic at any point not a station on the railroad. The terminal area of the railroad station is the area which is meant by the word "point" and not merely the station.

3. The shipments transported by the carrier shall be limited to those which it receives from or delivers to the railroad under a through bill of lading covering in addition to movement by applicant a prior or subsequent movement by rail. The through bill of lading which is referred to is a rail bill of lading. Often this condition has been revised by the establishment of a key-point system in which case the condition is that no shipments can be transported by the railroad as a common carrier by motor vehicle between any of the following points or through, or to, or from, more than one of said points (with the points being named). The establishment of a key-point condition was instituted in order that local shipment or ex-forwarder traffic or ex-pool-car traffic could be handled by motor carrier. In some instances, there has been a combination of the prior or subsequent rail haul and the key-point system.[53]

4. All contractual arrangements between the motor carrier and the railroad shall be reported to the Commission and shall be subject to revision as necessary.

5. The Commission reserves the right to impose further specific conditions as it may find necessary in order to restrict the motor-carrier service to that which is auxiliary to or supplemental of rail service.

The imposition of restrictions on railroad operation of motor carriers does not apply to those operations which are conducted by the railroads under "grandfather" rights.[54]

When a certificate has been issued without any of the usual con-

---

[53] *Southern Pac. Transport Co. Common Carrier Application,* 51 MCC 695 (1950).
[54] *Pacific Motor Trucking Company,* 34 MCC 249 (1942).

ditions or a statement is contained in the certificate that the Commission reserves the right to impose conditions in the future, the Commission has held that until such time as restrictions are added, the holder may render direct motor-carrier service under the motor-carrier bill of lading, charging all-motor rates, or have joint rates and through routes with other motor common carriers.[55] Subsequently, conditions were added to this particular operation.[56]

The Commission has denied the authority to operate as a motor carrier in lieu of the railroad peddler service, although the new motor service was more desirable for the shippers. It was held that this grant would not be made when existing motor-carrier service was adequate.[57]

Where there are unusual circumstances, the Commission has permitted a railroad or its affiliate to conduct motor operations to a nonrail point, but this is usually due to the fact that the point or route involved would lack reasonably adequate service by motor carrier, which service no independent motor carrier was able or willing to furnish.[58] Railroads which have been authorized to operate motor carriers have usually been required to utilize regular routes.[59]

The primary purpose of the policy of imposing restrictions is to prevent the railroads from acquiring motor operations through affiliates and using them in such a manner as to unduly restrain competition of independently operated motor carriers. This policy, the Commission feels, was and is sound and should be relaxed only when the circumstances clearly establish (1) that the grant of authority has not resulted and probably will not result in the undue restraint of competition; and (2) that the public interest requires the proposed operation, which the authorized independent motor carriers have not furnished except when it suited their convenience.

PRIVATE CARRIAGE

Inasmuch as private carriage by motor vehicle does not come under the economic regulation of the Interstate Commerce Commission, the interpretation by the Commission of what constitutes private carriage is very important. The Interstate Commerce Com-

---

[55] *Campbell Sixty-Six Exp., Inc.* v. *Frisco Transp. Co.*, 46 MCC 222 (1946).

[56] *Frisco Transp. Co.—Extension—Joplin—Miami*, 62 MCC 367 (1953).

[57] *New York Central R. Co. Ext.—Congers, N.Y.—Jersey City*, 61 MCC 457 (1953).

[58] *Frisco Transp. Co. Extension—Springfield Airport*, 47 MCC 63 (1947).

[59] *Willett Co., Extension—Gary, Ind.—Chicago, Ill.*, 46 MCC 35 (1945).

mission uses as its basis for determination of the status of a motor carrier the primary business test; that is, whether a motor carrier is a private operator or a for-hire carrier is determined on the basis of the operator's primary business, not on the basis of compensation received for the transportation performed. This follows a Commission decision in an earlier case, the Woitishek case,[60] which reconsidered the issue of for-hire versus private carriage. In the latter case, the Commission traced two lines of cases which sought to distinguish between these two phases of motor-carrier operation.

In a number of cases in which it was apparent that the furnishing of transportation for compensation was the operator's real business as distinguished from some bona fide merchandising or manufacturing enterprise, the operator was found in each case to be a for-hire carrier. In one case which was representative, the Commission found that, even though there was some semblance of a trade enterprise, the controlling consideration was the primary business in which the operator was engaged, that of furnishing transportation service.[61] In this case, the owner of a small truck was engaged in the hauling of milk from farms on a particular route to a creamery. He finished the milk haul early in the day, after which he occasionally would haul agricultural commodities and feed intrastate for farmers, or coal from an adjacent state to consumers, principally farmers, on his milk route. When he received an order for coal, he would go to the mine, buy the coal with his own funds, and carry it to destination and deliver it to the customer at a fixed amount in excess of the cost of the coal at the mine. In spite of the fact that he owned the coal while in transit and other factors which suggested private carriage, it was held that this operator was engaged primarily in the transportation of property for compensation; and, since his transportation services were available to anyone, he was found to be a common carrier by motor vehicle.

In another line of cases[62] the Commission has found the operators to be primarily engaged in some business other than transportation, such as manufacturing or merchandising, to which the transportation performed was bona fide incidental, although such transportation in some instances earned unplanned profits. In the Woitishek

---

[60] *Woitishek Common Carrier Application,* 42 MCC 193 (1943).

[61] *Carpenter Common Carrier Application,* 2 MCC 85 (1937).

[62] *Congoleum-Nairn, Inc., Contract Carrier Application,* 2 MCC 237 (1937); *Swanson Contract Carrier Application,* 12 MCC 516 (1939); *Youngson Common Carrier Application,* 21 MCC 625 (1940); *Dugan Extension of Operations—Nebraska Points,* 26 MCC 233 (1940).

case, the Commission emphasized that persons engaged primarily in the operation of transportation for compensation and with a purpose to profit from the transportation charge have been found to be for-hire carriers in spite of the fact that each was the owner of the goods transported while in transit and was transporting them for the purpose of sale and may have had some other characteristics of a merchandiser; whereas persons who are primarily engaged in a merchandising or manufacturing enterprise have been found not to be for-hire carriers, although as incidental to their primary business and without intent to profit therefrom, they perform certain transportation for which they receive compensation, which is so identified and, in some instances, includes a measure of profit. This has meant that the finding for or against a carrier for-hire status in each such case has turned upon the sole question of fact as to the primary business of the transporter.

The primary business issue was again brought into focus in the Lenoir and Schenley cases,[63] decided in 1949 by the entire Commission in which it upheld the primary business test.

Thus, if the facts establish (1) that the primary business of an operation is the supplying of transportation for compensation, then the for-hire carrier status is established even though the operator may be the owner of the goods at the time the goods are transported and may be transporting them for the purpose of sale; and (2) that if the primary business of an operator is found to be manufacturing or some other noncarrier commercial enterprise, then it must be determined (a) whether the motor operations are in bona fide furtherance of the primary business, or (b) whether they are conducted as a related or secondary enterprise with the purpose of profiting from the transportation performed. If the latter (b) is found to be the case, then the operator will be found to be engaged in other than private carriage. The Commission stated further that a private carrier is not precluded from realizing an incidental profit in the conduct of its motor-carrier operations without forsaking or endangering its private carrier status. The primary business test has been upheld by the Supreme Court.[64]

The Commission has expressed concern about the development of so-called "buy and sell" activities of some private carriers. Manufacturers and mercantile establishments which deliver in their own

---

[63] *Lenoir Chair Co. Contract Carrier Application,* 51 MCC 65 (1949). This also embraced *Schenley Distillers Corp. Contract Carrier.*

[64] *Brooks Transportation Co., Inc.* v. *United States,* 340 U.S. 925 (1951).

trucks articles which they manufacture or sell are reported to be purchasing merchandise at or near their point of delivery and transporting such articles to their own terminal for sale to others. Such transportation is performed for the purpose of receiving compensation for the otherwise empty return of their trucks and is said to be increasing. Sometimes the purchase and sale is a bona fide merchandising venture. In other cases, arrangements are made with the consignee of such merchandise for the "buy and sell" arrangement in order that the consignee may receive transportation at a reduced cost.

There are also a number of truck owners engaged in so-called "merchandising" exclusively, transporting in both directions freight which they have purchased for sale at destination. Generally, the "sale" price of the merchandise is the cost at origin plus an amount equal to or slightly below the transportation charges of authorized carriers, either rail or motor. Usually it is difficult, if not impossible, for the Commission to determine whether such transportation is a bona fide merchandising venture or is a subterfuge intended to provide transportation for hire without the required certificate or permit and, of course, without payment of the transportation tax.[65]

An informal study by the Bureau of Motor Carriers has indicated that of 143 instances of "buy and sell" operations, 88 were either definitely unlawful or highly questionable, and that many others were generally near the line. Only 13 appeared free of suspicion.[66] Many of these activities are performed over very long distances.

DUAL STATUS, PRIVATE-PUBLIC

Private carriers have often requested authority to operate also as a for-hire carrier. This usually happens when a private carrier has a one-way haul and seeks to overcome this disadvantage by securing operating authority for the return haul. The Commission has felt that a combination of public and private operations of this type is not desirable and has denied many such applications.[67]

There have been a few cases involving small operations in which there was not much possibility of detrimental results, such as favoritism, discrimination, and unfair competitive practices, when the

[65] Interstate Commerce Commission, *67th Annual Report* (Washington, D.C.: U.S. Government Printing Office, 1954), pp. 55–56.

[66] *Transport Topics*, November 1, 1954, p. 16.

[67] *Geraci Contract Carrier Application,* 7 MCC 369 (1938).

Commission has approved public-private operations. Another exception to the principle of the Geraci Case has been when authority has been granted for public-private operations but conditions have been imposed to prevent undesirable practices. The usual conditions are that (*a*) public operations should be conducted separately from the applicant's other activities; (*b*) separate accounting systems be maintained; and/or (*c*) there be no admixture of property in both the public and private carriage at the same time in the same vehicle. One or more of these conditions is usually imposed, and frequently all three are imposed.[68]

Since private carriers can and often do lease their equipment to certificated carriers for return hauls, the prohibition against public-private operations does not work a real hardship on private carriers.

CONCLUSIONS

A study of Commission decisions and Commission policy regarding operating rights of motor carriers of property concluded that the regulation of motor carriers by the Commission could be divided into three periods.[69] The years from 1936 to 1941 constituted an experimental period in which much of the regulation was educational in nature due to the newness of regulation and the many thousands of carriers involved. The launching of regulation and the numerous problems which confronted the Commission resulted in a subordination of policy matters to attention to operating details during this period. The war period constituted the second period in regulation. At the beginning of this period the Commission, with a background of experience and knowledge in motor-carrier regulation, was in the process of examining some of the broad problems of the industry. This work was of necessity postponed to enable the Commission to assist in the prosecution of the war. Since the end of World War II, the third period, that of implementation, has been transpiring. The issues are much more complex, but the Commission is seeking through investigative action to establish policies in numerous areas. As the problems of motor-carrier regulation become more complicated, the need for the establishment of broad principles is apparent. Such principles would be helpful to both the Commission and motor carriers.

---

[68] *Juliano Bros. Common Carrier Application,* 48 MCC 747 (1948).

[69] Charles A. Taff, *Operating Rights of Motor Carriers* (Dubuque, Iowa: Wm. C. Brown & Co., 1953), pp. 224–26.

There have been infrequent suggestions made that reliance should be placed upon competition as an alternative to economic regulation of the motor-carrier industry; and the free play of competitive forces should be permitted to determine such matters as rates and services offered. Such suggestions would include the elimination of operating authority, thereby allowing complete freedom of entry into the industry.[70] This does not appear to be a practicable course of action. The advantages of regulation outweigh the disadvantages.

QUESTIONS AND PROBLEMS

1. How extensive is railroad operation and control of motor carriers of property? What restrictions has the Interstate Commerce Commission imposed on these railroad operations?

2. What are the principles upon which an application to convert from a contract to common carrier should be based?

3. How can "public convenience and necessity" be proved? Does this differ from the phrase "consistent with the public interest"?

4. Explain the different types of operating authority.

5. What criteria are used by the Commission in determining whether the carrier is a regular- or irregular-route operator?

6. Define: off-route points; follow the traffic; and alternate routes.

7. What is the meaning of "fit, willing, and able"? Are there any standards used to measure it?

8. What is the procedure for suspending or revoking operating authority? Is it effective?

9. Has the problem of commodity descriptions contained in certificates and permits been solved?

10. Why is regulatory control over abandonment of routes by motor carriers different from that for railroads?

11. What problems may exist under dual operations? Public-private operations?

---

[70] National Resources Planning Board, *Transportation and National Policy* (Washington, D.C.: U.S. Government Printing Office, 1942), pp. 216–37; Dudley F. Pegrum, "The Economic Basis of Public Policy for Motor Transport," *Land Economics*, Vol. XXVIII (1952), p. 244; and Department of Commerce, *Issues Involved in a Unified and Co-ordinated Federal Program for Transportation* (Washington, D.C.: U.S. Government Printing Office, 1949), p. 33.

20. COMMISSION POLICY ON CONSOLI-
DATIONS AND RATES

▀▀

The subject of consolidations, mergers, and control is a particularly important one in view of the vast number of certificates and permits which have been issued and the growth aspects of the industry. As the assets of property carriers have grown, further expansion through acquisition of the operating rights of other carriers often appears desirable because it may be less difficult to purchase rights than to secure a new grant of authority from the Commission. Further, persons outside the motor-carrier industry are seeking to acquire operating rights through purchase. The determination by the Commission of what constitutes control of a carrier is also of great significance.

CONSOLIDATIONS, MERGERS, AND CONTROL

There has been a gradual reduction during the past 10 years in the number of operating rights which are outstanding, although it appears that the greatest activity in consolidations and mergers is yet to come. The policies of the Commission in transfer, or "finance cases" as they are termed, are of interest not only to carriers but also to shippers and the public since there are many aspects, such as service and competition, which are included. The move toward consolidation is much further advanced in the passenger field than in the property field.

The majority of transfers involve certificates rather than permits. This undoubtedly is due largely to the fact that contract carriers cannot render a through service by "tacking" the rights which they acquire.[1] In the transfer of operating rights, there are two broad

---

[1] Charles A. Taff, *Operating Rights of Motor Carriers* (Dubuque, Iowa: Wm. C. Brown & Co., 1953), p. 79.

groups of transfers, those provided for under Section 212 (b) and those covered by Section 5.

Section 212 (b) of Part II of the act states that, except as provided in Section 5, any certificate or permit may be transferred pursuant to such rules and regulations as the Commission may prescribe. This particular section deals with transactions between small motor carriers operating less than a total of twenty vehicles or between a carrier and a noncarrier in which the transaction involves operating rights only. This section does not apply when the proposed transfer involves only the sale of equipment or the lease of equipment; while Section 212 (b) approval only is required when a person who is not connected with a carrier purchases or leases the rights of a motor carrier.

Section 5(2) of Part I of the act embraces all consolidations, acquisitions, and mergers of two or more carriers when a total of more than twenty vehicles is involved. A person not connected with a carrier can acquire control of a corporate motor carrier through stock holdings. When there is no change in the record holder of the certificate or permit, this requires no Commission approval under either Section 5 or Section 212 (b). Similarly, a person not connected with a carrier or one in control of a carrier can acquire control of one or more corporate carriers through stock ownership which does not require Commission approval providing the twenty-vehicle exemption is not exceeded and a railroad or other carrier, as defined in Section 1(3) of the act, is not a party. With these exceptions, motor-carrier operating authority can change hands only if Commission approval is granted, since under Section 5(2) approval and authorization by the Commission is required while a transfer under Section 212 (b) is covered by one of the rules issued by the Commission which provides that no attempted transfer of any operating right shall be effective until the Commission has approved the transfer as explained later in this chapter.[2]

Division 4 handles the transfer cases under Section 5, and Division 5 handles the transfer cases involved under Section 212 (b). The ascertainment of Commission policy on transfer cases involving the two sections of the act will be discussed separately. A proposed transfer under Section 5 is required to be consistent with the public interest. Further, there are additional requirements as well when a rail carrier or affiliate is an applicant in a case involving a motor carrier.

[2] Rule 2(d)(1), issued December 1, 1943, 8 Fed. Reg. 12448.

SECTION 5(2)

INTERPRETATION OF WHAT CONSTITUTES CONTROL

There have been numerous cases in which the question of control has been discussed. In an early case, the phrase "control or management," which is mentioned in Section 5, was held to include all forms and types of control or management.[3] The manager of a carrier who superintended all its operations, as well as determining matters of policy subject to the supervision of the Board of Directors, would acquire control of the carrier within the meaning of Section 5, it was held by the Commission.[4]

On the other hand, the terminal manager of a motor carrier who did not participate in policy matters, was not an officer or director of the corporation, and performed duties which were primarily of an operational nature was held not to control or manage the carrier within the meaning of Section 5.[5]

When there is actual division of the stock, it has been held that this results in control by both parties.[6] There may be negative control, as well, when a stockholder holds 50 per cent of the stock.[7]

The ownership of a majority of the stock is not necessarily an indication of control. In one instance, 25 per cent of the capital stock was acquired under an agreement in which many of the basic corporate powers and functions were restricted in favor of the purchaser. This was held by the Commission to result in control passing to the purchaser.[8]

It has also been held that the power to repossess vehicles, to grant or withhold supplies and services, and largely to control the routing of traffic are sufficient to show control regardless of the stock holdings.[9] When it is clear that the power to control has been acquired, it is not necessary to show actual use of that power.[10]

There may be control or management in a common interest of two or more carriers due to the relationship between the persons involved. Sons, whose fathers controlled and managed several other

---

[3] *John Colletti—Control—Comet Freight Lines,* 38 MCC 95 (1942).

[4] *Ibid.*

[5] *Brada Cartage Co.—Purchase—Great Lakes Trucking Co.,* 45 MCC 51 (1946).

[6] *New England Greyhound Lines, Inc.—Purchase—New England,* 15 MCC 536 (1938).

[7] *Capitani—Control—Jersey City Keansburg Transit Lines,* 25 MCC 478 (1939).

[8] *Pacific Greyhound Lines—Control—Oregon Motor Stages,* 55 MCC 321 (1948).

[9] *Pacific Greyhound—Control—Geronimo,* 56 MCC 415 (1950).

[10] *U.S. Freight Co.—Investigation of Control,* 39 MCC 623, 636 (1944).

motor carriers, in one of which the sons were minority stockholders
and officers, controlled and managed a motor carrier. The Commission ruled that the sons' company was controlled and managed in
a common interest with those of the parents.[11]

However, in one case, two men who were officials in companies
of the Greyhound Bus System sought to acquire certain sightseeing
and charter rights of two non-Greyhound Companies by forming
two new corporations in which they were president and vice-president and their wives were the sole stockholders. Here, the evidence
did not justify a finding that the new corporations would be controlled or managed in a common interest with the Greyhound Companies, it was decided.[12]

The Commission has authorized control through management
only when each of the individuals was already in control of one of
the carriers and was permitted, in addition, to control through management the carrier fully controlled by the other.[13]

It is possible to acquire joint control because it has been held that
those in joint control of a carrier may, under Section 5, acquire
joint control of another carrier.[14] In another case, joint control of a
carrier by five persons was approved. Two of the five persons were
carriers and the other three controlled carriers.[15]

Four applicants acting together sought to acquire the stock of a
motor carrier, which stock was to be divided among them in proportion to their contributions. Only one of the applicants was
affiliated with a carrier. The acquisition would place the four persons in control of this carrier, and it was held that this constituted
a joint acquisition of control.[16]

A person who is not a carrier but controls a carrier may purchase
another carrier under Section 5,[17] although the creation of complex
interlocking interests in motor carriers has been given as the reason
for the denial of a control application.[18]

[11] *Casser—Control—Bingler,* 55 MCC 696 (1949). See also *Arkansas Motor—Control and Merger,* 56 MCC 665 (1950).

[12] *Gray Line New York Tours Corp.—Purchase—Gray Line Motor,* 50 MCC 339 (1948).

[13] *Ratner and Grimpas—Control—Hayes and Southwest,* 57 MCC 312 (1951).

[14] *Minardi—Control—Coast Line Truck Service, Inc.,* 15 MCC 412 (1938).

[15] *Best Motor Lines—Purchase—Highway Motor Freight Lines, Inc.,* 38 MCC 199 (1942).

[16] *Jessup—Control—Safeway Trails, Inc.,* 39 MCC 233, 239 (1943).

[17] *Suddarth—Purchase—Pettyjohn,* 37 MCC 185 (1941).

[18] *Arrow Transp. Co.—Control—Texas—Arizona Motor Freight,* 58 MCC 155 (1953).

FACTORS AFFECTING APPROVAL OR DENIAL

There are numerous factors which are considered in determining consistency with the public interest. There are, however, certain factors which under Section 5(2)(c) must be considered, among which are: (1) the effect of the proposed transaction upon adequate transportation service to the public; (2) the total fixed charges which will result; and (3) the interest of the employees affected.

The term "public interest" as used in this section has a direct relationship to adequacy of transportation service, to its essential conditions of economy and efficiency, and to appropriate provision and best use of transportation facilities. To meet the test of consistency with the public interest does not require consideration of specific matters but rather the broad considerations in the preceding sentence.[19]

It is absolutely necessary that there be a showing of consistency with the public interest. Serving the interest of the vendee only is not enough, it has been ruled in a recent case.[20]

The effect of the proposed transaction upon adequate transportation service to the public is one in which the competitive aspect is very significant. As interpreted by the Commission, the term "public interest" which is found in Section 5 includes the interest of competing carriers.[21]

The loss of traffic and revenue by competitors was held to be insufficient to justify the disapproval of a transfer as long as the loss would not be so serious as to cause a curtailment of operations.[22] In another case, it was held that single-line service by the vendee would not necessarily make large inroads into the traffic of well-established competitors which were rendering two-line service.[23]

The entire Commission in one important case denied a transfer which would have resulted in a single-line transcontinental motor-carrier operation. The inherent advantage of rail transportation on volume movements of transcontinental traffic was noted, and the fact that essential rail transportation would be adversely affected

---

[19] *Conklin Truck Lines, Inc.—Purchase—Bushroe*, 37 MCC 467 (1941); and *Associated Transport, Inc.—Control and Consolidation—Arrow Carrier Corp. et. al.*, 38 MCC 137, 146 (1942).

[20] *Ringsby Truck Lines, Inc.—Control and Merger*, 58 MCC 739 (1952).

[21] *Shein's—Purchase—Central New Jersey*, 59 MCC 534 (1953).

[22] *Buckingham—Lease—Wiederspan*, 39 MCC 367 (1943).

[23] *Super Service—Purchase—Hayes*, 57 MCC 715 (1951).

by diversion of high-rated traffic.[24] Prior to this proposal, the two motor carriers had interchanged insignificant amounts of traffic at their common point of Chicago. It was felt by the Commission that the combination of these two carriers would result in a new service which would be competitive with existing carriers for which no need had been shown. Upon reconsideration, the entire Commission denied the proposed merger on the basis of the adverse effects which the arrangement would have on competing motor carriers.[25]

There was a great deal of motor-carrier criticism of the action of the Commission in this case, the *P.I.E.* case. Since its decision in this case, the Commission has stated that this decision is not controlling in every situation where a new through service would result.[26] Also, since the *P.I.E.* decision Division 4 has stated that evidence of the nature and scope of the service which has been rendered under the rights proposed to be purchased is necessary in order to appraise fully the effect of unification.[27]

The manner in which the rights are to be used after purchase has a bearing on whether or not the transfer will be approved or denied. The Commission has held that the use of rights by the vendee in a different manner from that which was followed by the vendor, if it results in essentially a new operation constitutes grounds for denial of a transfer.[28] In this connection, it was held that when the vendor had not handled interchange traffic for a number of years but entered into such arrangements with the vendee after a purchase agreement had been executed, such through service was entitled to little weight in a transfer case.[29]

Most of the cases dealing with monopoly have to do with passenger transfer cases, but it is evident that the Commission will not foster a monopoly. At the time approval of Associated Transport was sought, there were nine large property carriers which were brought under common control and eventually were consolidated. In this case, the entire Commission held that there were many car-

[24] *Pacific Intermountain Express Co.—Control and Purchase—Keeshin Freight Lines, Inc., et al.,* 57 MCC 341 (1950).

[25] *P.I.E. Co.—Control & Purchase—Keeshin Freight Lines, Inc., et al.,* 57 MCC 467 (1951).

[26] *Ringsby Truck Lines, Inc.—Control—Northern Transp. Co.,* 58 MCC 594 (1952).

[27] *Consolidated Freightways, Inc.—Purchase—Arrowhead,* 58 MCC 165 (1953).

[28] *Central N.Y. Freightways, Inc.—Purchase—Gorea's Motor Exp., Inc.,* 55 MCC 390 (1948); *Shein's Exp.—Purchase—Stillwell,* 56 MCC 711 (1950), affirmed in *Shein v. U.S.,* 102 Fed. Supp. 320 (1951).

[29] *Central Motor Lines, Inc.—Purchase—Term. Transfer, Inc.,* 58 MCC 389 (1953).

riers in the territory. The mere "bigness" of the applicant would not smother the competition.[30]

EFFECT ON CARRIER EMPLOYEES

One of the provisions that must be considered in a transfer case under Section 5 is its effect on carrier employees. When the Commission felt in a particular case that future developments might affect employees, it reserved, for 2 years, jurisdiction to add conditions regarding employees.[31] It has also held that when the transaction includes intrastate rights, the effect of approval on the intrastate employees has to be considered.[32]

A long-term employment agreement at high salaries which was proposed to be entered into between the buyer and some employees of the seller was found to be undesirable and not in the public interest.[33] It should not be inferred that employment agreements are not permissible. If they are true employment contracts and are not merely a means of increasing the consideration to vendors, such contracts have been held to be not subject to the Commission's jurisdiction under Section 5.[34]

SALE PRICE

One of the factors that is considered in transfer cases is the price which is to be paid for operating rights. The Commission has made a reduction in price to be paid a condition to approval in an early case when the amount to be paid for stock was required to be reduced from $450,000 to $250,000.[35] When important new points are added to the vendee's rights, this may justify a high price.[36]

Some of the elements which influence price are the value of the operation as a going concern, the number of years of development, the right to operate, and the extent to which the public is aware of

---

[30] *Associated Transport, Inc.—Control and Consolidation—Arrow Carrier Corp., et al.,* 38 MCC 137, 150 (1942).

[31] *Schaefer et al.—Control; Transit, Inc.—Purchase—Tyson-Long Co., R. Howerter and W. R. Schaefer,* 50 MCC 433 (1948).

[32] *Hudson Bus Lines, Inc.—Purchase—Boston and Maine Transp. Co.,* 58 MCC 73 (1951); and 58 MCC 133 (1951).

[33] *Transport Co.—Control—Arrow Carrier Corp.,* 36 MCC 61 (1940).

[34] *Rogers Cartage Co.—Control and Merger,* 55 MCC 145 (1948).

[35] *Public Service Interstate Transportation Co.—Purchase—Healy's Special Tours,* 5 MCC 735 (1938).

[36] *Consolidated Freightways, Inc.—Purchase—P.I.E. Co.,* 38 MCC 577, 585 (1942).

the service rendered. In one case, the payment of $100,000 to an affiliate for rights which had been operated for a substantial period of time at a loss was held not to be in the public interest.[37] The mere fact that the vendee is able to pay does not in itself warrant approval of an exorbitant purchase price, the Commission has held.[38]

A finder's fee of 28 per cent of the purchase price was found to be unreasonable. This was ordered to be eliminated from the purchase price by the Commission.[39]

Sale of operating rights for speculative purposes has not been condoned by the Commission. When it appeared that the vendee did not plan to conduct operations under the rights sought but was interested in the rights for resale purposes, the transaction was denied as not being in the public interest. Operating rights are granted for the purpose of authorizing service to the shipping public, according to the Commission.[40]

Large amounts for intangibles, into which category operating rights are usually placed, have been frowned upon. However, it was pointed out that the objective of the act would be defeated if the Commission were to permit payment of purchase prices equal only to the book value of a carrier's physical property. Operating rights are indispensable to operations and are permanent. The purchase price proposed should not be viewed abstractly and apart from all other elements of a transaction, the Commission ruled.[41]

More recently, the amount of $70,000 of a total of $155,000-purchase price was to be paid for intangibles, which included $30,000 as the value of the operating rights. Division 4 denied the transfer application on the basis that the purchase price was greatly in excess of the fair value of the physical property.[42] This case has been appealed.

FITNESS

In a Supreme Court case, it was indicated that the Congress expected the Commission to judge and examine a transferee's fitness in the same manner as it does in granting an original operating au-

---

[37] *Wright et al.—Control; Queen City Coach Co.—Purchase—Smoky Mountain Stages, Inc.*, 57 MCC 779 (1951).

[38] *DeCamp Bus Lines—Purchase—Atlantic Transp. Co.*, 58 MCC 667 (1952).

[39] *Red Star Exp. Lines of Auburn, Inc.—Purchase—Seifert*, 59 MCC 447 (1953).

[40] *G. S. Fraps, Jr.—Purchase—L. Q. Lindley*, 38 MCC 703 (1942); *Silver Ball Trans., Inc.—Lease—Spear Trucking Corp.*, 49 MCC 249, 258 (1949).

[41] *Southeastern Greyhound Lines—Purchase—LeVan*, 55 MCC 543 (1949); and 56 MCC 82 (1949).

[42] *Graves Truck Line, Inc.—Purchase—Whitworth*, 59 MCC 370 (1953).

thority, although this strict interpretation does not appear to have been followed by the Commission.[43]

Fitness is one of the important elements involved in determining consistency with the public interest. The Commission has held that such matters as the number of safety violations, operating beyond authority, and the failure to keep records are elements considered in determining fitness. Actions such as these have been the basis for denial of purchase.[44] The practices in which an exempt freight forwarder engaged were also considered in determining the forwarder's fitness to acquire a motor carrier.[45] It should be noted that lack of experience in transportation is not in itself a sufficient reason to deny an application to acquire control.[46]

In the early stages of regulation, there was occasionally an unlawful consummation of a purchase before it had been approved by the Commission. In these few instances, the Commission usually did not withhold its approval of a transaction on this particular ground due to the fact that the parties concerned were not familiar with all the provisions of the act regarding transfer. However, in the period since the war, the Commission has become more strict in this respect.[47] The only reason for denial in one case was prior consummation without approval. There were no mitigating circumstances in this particular case.[48]

When unlawful consummation was affected by a person who later died and, after his death, his heirs applied for approval, the Commission held that the application should be considered on its merits notwithstanding the violation of the law.[49]

An exchange of rights has been authorized when it would result in a more efficient operation and a more nearly complete service could be rendered by the two carriers concerned.[50]

LEASING OF RIGHTS

Frequently a lease of operating rights is sought with a view toward ultimate purchase of the rights. The Commission's attitude has been

---

[43] *United States* v. *Resler*, 313 U.S. 57 (1941).

[44] *Powell—Purchase—Rampy*, 57 MCC 597 (1951).

[45] *Abco Moving & Storage Co., Inc.—Purchase—Dierking*, 47 MCC 557 (1947).

[46] *Weinstein—Control—Capital Transit Co. and Montgomery*, 56 MCC 127 (1949).

[47] *Tornetta—Purchase—Rittenhouse*, 40 MCC 339 (1945).

[48] *Welch—Control—Montreal—New York Exp.*, 56 MCC 505 (1950).

[49] *Royal Blue Coaches, Inc.—Merger*, 56 MCC 617 (1950).

[50] *Ratner—Control—Emery Transportation Co.—Control and Merger—Great Lakes Cartage Co.*, 50 MCC 43 (1947).

that these leases should be limited to short or trial periods no longer than necessary to secure an appraisal by the lessee of the operation. In one case, a 5-year period was not approved but a 1-year period was authorized.[51]

A request for a 2-year renewal of a lease of rights which had been leased for a 7-year period was denied. A 1-year extension was authorized during which time it was felt that the lessor could decide whether to operate the rights itself or dispose of them. It was implied that there would be no further extension of the lease.[52]

Even when most of the traffic was intrastate and the lessees had made substantial investment in equipment and a terminal on the assumption that the lease would be renewed indefinitely, the Commission indicated that only a limited extension would be permitted.[53]

The Commission has said that approval will not be given to a lease when there is not the intention to acquire the rights.[54] The proposed purchase of operating rights for the sole purpose of leasing them to another carrier is frowned upon by the Commission.[55]

Sometimes the Commission is asked to approve the purchasing of operating rights under the terms of a contract. One in which a 13 per cent down payment was made with monthly installments for the remainder of the amount over a 7-year period, secured by a chattel mortgage on the rights, was approved. However, one of the Commissioners in a dissent stated that this was merely a long-term lease.[56]

The Commission has held that a 6-month lease of rights for the purpose of permitting the lessee to perform a single pipe-stringing operation was not consistent with the public interest. Temporary authority under Section 210a (a) was available if there was an emergency need for such service, it was stated.[57] Section 210a (b) provides that while the determination of an application which has been filed with the Commission for approval of consolidation or merger of two or more motor carriers or of a purchase, lease, or contract to operate one or more motor carriers is in progress, the Commission may grant temporary approval for not more than 180 days of the operation of the motor carrier which is sought to be acquired if the failure to

[51] *Auto Convoy—Lease—Automobile Shippers, Inc.,* 55 MCC 683 (1949).

[52] *Clark—Lease—Santa Fe Trail Transp. Co.,* 56 MCC 20 (1949).

[53] *Northern Transportation Co.—Lease—Terminal Truck Lines,* 56 MCC 259 (1949).

[54] *Wheaton Van Lines, Inc.—Lease—House,* 58 MCC 703 (1952).

[55] *Hancock Transp. Corp.—Purchase—Middlesex Transp. Co.,* 49 MCC 433 (1949).

[56] *Jenkins et. al.—Control; Chesapeake Motor Lines, Inc.—Purchase—Capitol Motor Lines, Inc.,* 57 MCC 249 (1950).

[57] *Willet—Lease—W. B. Thomas,* 50 MCC 1 (1947).

grant temporary approval would result in injury to or destruction of the motor-carrier properties to be acquired or would interfere with their future usefulness. However, the Commission has permitted the lease period under Section 210a (b) to be extended pending its further order to prevent disruption of service where the purchase application could not be determined in time because of the question of legality of control.

Some of the other factors which have been considered in unification proceedings under Section 5 are a reduction in the cost of transportation,[58] the elimination of duplicate operations over a congested route,[59] and more efficient use of combined resources.[60]

OTHER MATTERS AFFECTING PUBLIC CONVENIENCE AND NECESSITY

When the issuance of operating authority greater than the sum of the operating rights of the transferee and the transferor is desired, a Section 5 application should disclose in particular the additional authority which is sought, the proposed manner of operation thereunder, and include a petition for issuance of such authority.[61]

Thus, it is possible in a Section 5 transfer case to seek additional operating authority. In this connection, it has been held that the proof required is of the same degree of character as that required in an application filed under Section 207 which has no connection with a Section 5 proceeding.[62]

It may happen that the authority requested bears no direct relation to the purchase authority sought. In such a case in which the additional authority constituted an entirely new service it was ruled that the request was one which properly should be considered by an application under Section 207 and not under Section 5.[63]

The removal of a restriction upon operating authority may be considered within the scope of a Section 5 proceeding if the removal would result in better co-ordination, after unification, of separate operations. However, when the need for modification of the restric-

---

[58] *Associated Transport, Inc.—Control and Consolidation—Arrow Carrier Corp. et al.,* 38 MCC 137, 146 (1942).

[59] *Eastern Michigan Motor Buses—Control—Great Lakes Motor Bus Co.,* 5 MCC 120 (1937).

[60] *Consolidated Motor Lines, Inc.—Purchase—Simpson Transportation Lines, Inc.,* 5 MCC 109 (1937).

[61] Administrative Rule No. 94, May 12, 1942.

[62] *Novick—Purchase—Fischetto Trucking Co., Inc.,* 38 MCC 477 (1942).

[63] *Bonacci et al.—Purchase—Meyer,* 38 MCC 361 (1942).

tion existed regardless of the proposed unification and did not arise as a result of the proposed unification, this was a matter for proceedings under Section 207.[64]

The Commission can and does impose conditions in acquisition cases. For example, it has required the acquiring carrier to amortize by charges to income over a specified period, or write off immediately where surplus is sufficient, the amount assigned to a specific account by which the purchase price exceeds the value of the physical property acquired.[65] Another example is that of a restriction imposed against the joinder of purchased common carrier rights with those already held by the vendee.[66]

DORMANT RIGHTS

A motor carrier may cease to operate and the service that it was formerly rendering may be absorbed through the expansion of facilities by other motor carriers. Unless the operating authority possessed by the carrier that has ceased to operate has been revoked, it may begin to operate again at some future time under its dormant rights. These dormant rights pose a problem, for "any substantial interruption of one carrier's service tends to result in expansion of other facilities to meet the continuing needs of shippers and thus to cause over-crowding if the suspended service is resumed."[67] The present policy of the Commission in regard to dormant operating authority is that as long as a motor carrier actually holds itself in readiness to perform the service the Commission will refrain from action to require operation or revocation unless there is reason to believe that the dormant operating authority is being held solely for purposes of profitable sale. There must, however, be readiness to perform the service, and insurance must be maintained and filed with the Commission.

Where an authorized motor carrier has discontinued operations without surrendering its operating authority and fails to keep its insurance in effect, the Interstate Commerce Commission institutes proceedings with a view toward cancellation of the operating rights. The entire Commission ruled that when there was a total discon-

[64] *Hayes Freight Lines, Inc.—Purchase—Whitney,* 38 MCC 375 (1942); and *Bonacci et al.—Purchase—Meyer,* 38 MCC 361 (1942).

[65] *Skeel—Purchase—Kuhns and Grays Harbor Lines, Inc.,* 40 MCC 318 (1945).

[66] *Commercial Carriers, Inc.—Purchase—Canfield Drive-away Co.,* 59 MCC 29 (1953).

[67] *Gregg Cartage and Storage Company* v. *United States,* 316 U.S. 74 (1941).

tinuance of service for 5 years, the practical effect of its approval of a transfer would be a new operation rather than unification of existing operations. Therefore, it was disapproved.[68]

In another case, there had also been no service on the routes for 5 years. A proposed purchase of these routes was not opposed by existing carriers, but the Commission disapproved. The purchase was approved of one route on which there had been but a 1-year interruption of service.[69] When no operations have ever been conducted under the operating authority, there has been disapproval of lease or purchase of such operations.[70]

There are some instances in which the rights which are held have not been used very much or operations have been somewhat limited. For example, only one or two shipments had been transported on a regular route in a period of 2 years. The authority to transfer these rights was denied.[71]

A vendor may find that operations between two points are unprofitable due to heavy competition and curtail service sharply between these two points. The Commission has stated that he is not authorized to sell that segment of his rights on the grounds that it had no real going-concern value. Resumption of local service between these two points would, in effect, constitute a new operation.[72]

When irregular routes in which the rights have not been used very much are involved in transfer cases, the Commission has turned down the contention that a distinction should be made between regular- and irregular-route operations in dormant right transfer cases. It stated that in a particular area of the vendor's operation of his irregular-route authority, the operations were of little importance and were not required by the shipping public. The application for their sale, therefore, was denied.[73]

The entire Commission has held that when transportation has been sporadic or negligible with no genuine effort being made to develop traffic, and the vendor is not a competitive factor in the territory, the detrimental effects upon the existing carriers out-

---

[68] *Transcon Lines—Purchase—Anderson Motor Service Co.,* 50 MCC 749 (1948); and 56 MCC 521 (1950).

[69] *Hancock Truck Lines, Inc.—Purchase—Anderson Motor Service Co.,* 55 MCC 115 (1948).

[70] See, for example, *Smith—Lease—Service, Inc.,* 55 MCC 47 (1948).

[71] *Central N.Y. Freightways, Inc.—Purchase, Gorea's Motor Exp., Inc.,* 55 MCC 390 (1948).

[72] *LaMere and Conroy—Purchase—Ziffrin Truck Lines, Inc.,* 55 MCC 501 (1949).

[73] *Robertson—Purchase—Standard Freight Lines, Inc.,* 56 MCC 597 (1950).

weighed the advantages that would accrue to the vendee. The application was denied.[74]

It should be noted that findings in other proceedings concerning continuity of service are not controlling in a Section 5 proceeding.[75]

MEANING OF TWENTY-VEHICLE EXEMPTION

In Section 5, the twenty-vehicle exemption has application only when the parties to the transaction are motor carriers subject to Part II. When one of the parties to a Section 5 transaction is a railroad or other carrier, or a motor carrier controlled by or affiliated with a railroad or other carrier, the twenty-vehicle exemption does not apply. The make-up of the total number of vehicles owned, leased, controlled, or operated by all of the parties to a Section 5 transaction involving only motor carriers subject to Part II has been strictly interpreted. In one instance, vehicles which were used solely in the vendee's intrastate operations were counted as part of the total because the record did not indicate that the vehicles were not available if they were needed for use in interstate operations of a carrier which was controlled by the vendee.[76]

On the other hand, one of the parties in a transfer case owned a piano-selling business in which he operated four piano display trucks which were especially fitted for demonstration purposes. These trucks were not counted, since they were not of a type and construction to be readily available for use in transportation subject to Part II.[77]

It may happen that the number of vehicles in service fluctuates. In an instance of this kind, the number which is normally operated is used. For example, a vendor at the time of the sale agreement operated twenty-one vehicles but disposed of a portion of his rights. He abandoned certain operations, and on the date of application to sell, he was operating but two and the vendee was operating seven. The Commission held that this transaction was not subject to Section 5.[78]

By Commission order, the Commission has prescribed the method for computing the vehicles involved in unifications under the pro-

---

[74] *Auclair Transp. Inc.—Purchase—Moore,* 57 MCC 262 (1950).

[75] *P.I.E. Co.—Purchase—Browning Freight Lines,* 58 MCC 629 (1952).

[76] *Hayes Freight Lines, Inc.—Purchase—Service Freight Line, Inc.,* 40 MCC 210 (1945).

[77] *King—Purchase—Marshall,* 52 MCC 483 (1951).

[78] *Wooten—Purchase—Columbia,* 49 MCC 586 (1949).

visions of Section 5. Any one tractor may be paired with any one semitrailer and the two counted as a single vehicle, but any tractor or semitrailer in excess of those so paired is computed as one motor vehicle. The term "semitrailer" as used does not include a pole trailer or a single motor vehicle transported in driveaway operations by means of a saddle mount.[79]

In driveaway operations, the determination of number of vehicles is based on the aggregate daily average number of motor vehicles transported in driveaway service.[80]

If a number of vehicles were operated by a predecessor of the vendor but these vehicles were not acquired by the vendor, they do not need to be counted in the subsequent sale of the rights.[81]

SECTION 212 (b)

The basis of Section 212 (b) is to make possible the transfer of rights under that section in the most simple manner possible with the least expense to the parties involved. The Commission has adopted "Rules and Regulations Governing Transfers of Rights to Operate as a Motor Carrier in Interstate or Foreign Commerce" for transfers under Section 212 (b). These rules and regulations do not require a hearing, and the applications are handled informally. There has been a very large volume of these applications. From 1935 through 1954, there were 32,254 applications, 28,559 of which were approved, 3,369 denied, and 326 in process.[82]

To secure approval of a Section 212 (b) transfer, an application is filed with the Bureau of Motor Carriers. In the past, the Section of Certificates determined the disposition of the applications subject to the approval of Division 5. However, since November 16, 1953, these applications have been handled by a three-member Motor Carrier Board, composed of Interstate Commerce Commission staff members, which has the power and acts on a number of matters including applications under Section 212 (b) which have not involved the taking of testimony at a public hearing. Division 5 serves as an appellate division of the Commission on the Motor Carrier Board matters.

---

[79] Order of Interstate Commerce Commission, "Combination of Motor Vehicles," dated July 14, 1947.

[80] *Fleming—Purchase—Service Drive-away Corp.*, 35 MCC 607, 611 (1940).

[81] *Dean and Dove—Purchase—Dean*, 51 MCC 376 (1950).

[82] About 70 per cent of transfer applications filed under Section 212 (b) required correspondence with the parties or the Commission's field staff had to supply deficiencies according to a statement by Commissioner Cross before the American Trucking Associations' annual meeting October 29, 1953.

Although the rules and regulations which apply on transfer cases under this section do not require hearings, there is a hearing, in some cases, if it is not known whether the case is a Section 5 or Section 212 (b) case at the time the application is made. Applications are acted upon, and notification is usually given within 30 days after the receipt of the application. Copies of the applications are sent as a matter of information by the Commission to the state regulatory authorities in those states in which either the transferor or the transferee will operate. It is assumed that the state regulatory bodies will have more knowledge of any matter that might disqualify either of the parties. This is unlike Section 5 proceedings in which the proposed transferor or transferee must notify his present or future competitors.

If there is denial of a Section 212 (b) application, there can be appeal to the courts. Some concern about securing judicial review has been expressed since no transcript and findings exist on which the refusal has been based. However, since the Commission requires that there be an application, the appeal would be on the record of the application and its declination.

Some of the more important regulations are given in the following paragraphs. Where appropriate to aid in an understanding of these matters, a brief explanation is also given.

Sec. 179.2 (c) General basis for approval—(1) Except as may otherwise be provided herein, the proposed transfer described in any such applications shall be approved if it appears that the proposed transaction is one which is not subject to the provisions of section 5, Interstate Commerce Act; that the proposed transfer will not result in unlawful ownership or control of a motor carrier; and that the proposed transferee is fit, willing, and able properly to perform the service authorized by the operating rights sought to be transferred, and to conform to the provisions of the Interstate Commerce Act and the requirements, rules and regulations of the Commission thereunder. Otherwise the application shall be denied.

Under this section, it is required that the proposed transferee must be fit, willing, and able properly to perform the service authorized. In one case, the questionable operating practices of the applicant and the lack of frank and complete disclosures were held to make the applicant unfit.[83]

Again when there had been numerous violations of safety regulations and the failure to keep records, an application was denied even though the applicant had been prosecuted for the violations.[84]

---

[83] *Federal Storage Warehouses, Inc.—Purchase—Shafer & Son,* 43 MCC 673 (1944).

[84] *Casiglio—Purchase—Love's,* 52 MCC 777 (1951).

Sec. 179.2 (c) (2) The transfer of any operating rights under which operations are not being conducted at the time of the proposed transfer and have not been performed for a substantial period will be approved only upon a showing that the cessation of operations was caused by circumstances over which the holder of the operating rights had no control.

Even before this rule was prescribed, the Commission had refused to permit a corporation which had purchased rights but never operated them to lease the rights to another corporation.[85] This rule provides a means by which the sale of operating rights which have not been used for some period of time can be limited. However, when there is a showing that a cessation of operations was caused by circumstances over which the holder of the operating rights had no control, the Commission has permitted the sale of rights under these circumstances.[86] The transfer, under such circumstances, of dormant operating rights applies only to Section 212 (b) transactions and not to Section 5.[87]

Sec. 179.2 (d) General basis for disapproval—(1) No attempted transfer of any operating right shall be effective except upon full compliance with these rules and regulations and until after the Interstate Commerce Commission has approved such transfer as herein provided. The mere execution of a chattel mortgage, deed of trust, or other similar document, does not constitute a transfer within the meaning of these rules, and does not require the approval of the Commission, unless it embraces the conduct of the operation by a person other than the holder of the operating right. A proposed transfer of operating rights by means of the foreclosure of a mortgage or deed of trust or other lien upon such rights, or by an execution in satisfaction of any judgment or claim against the holder thereof, shall not be effective without compliance with these rules and regulations and the prior approval of the Commission.

Operating authority under the provision of this rule may be mortgaged, and the mortgagee can secure a lien upon the operating rights without Commission approval.[88] The mortgagee may foreclose on a carrier's operating rights, but the purchaser cannot start carrier operations until there has been Commission approval of the transaction.[89] In this same case, a Section 212 (b) purchase approval was vacated because of the failure to disclose and misrepresentation of certain facts regarding the sale of the rights in a foreclosure.[90]

---

[85] *Silver Ball Trans., Inc.—Lease—Spear Trucking Corp.*, 49 MCC 249 (1949).

[86] *Atwood's Transport Line—Lease—Clarke*, 52 MCC 97 (1950).

[87] *Kenosha Auto Transport—Purchase—Curtis Keal*, 57 MCC 443 (1951).

[88] In re *Rainbo Express, Inc.*, 179 Fed. 2d 1 (1950).

[89] *Metropolitan Trailways, Inc.—Purchase—Emery's Motor Coach Lines*, 52 MCC 321 (1950).

[90] *Ibid.*, 321 (1950).

Sec. 179.2 (d) (2) A proposed transfer of operating rights will not be approved if the Commission finds that the transferee does not intend to, or would not, engage in bona fide motor carrier operations under such operating rights, or if the Commission finds that the transferor acquired such operating rights for the purpose of profiting therefrom and has not engaged in bona fide motor carrier operations under such operating rights.

It is the intention of the Commission in this section to insure that operating rights are used to render service and not held or sold for speculative purposes.

Sec. 179.2 (d) (3) An application for transfer of operating rights by sale and purchase thereof will not be approved if the Commission considers and determines that the purchase price to be paid would be excessive and contrary to the public interest.

The language of this section is broad. There has not emerged, as yet, a specific method or formula for determining the reasonable value of an operating authority in transfer cases.[91]

One aspect of this matter has been the transferee's ability to purchase the rights and still have adequate capital to operate successfully without passing on to the shippers in the form of higher rates the costs of the rights.

Sec. 179.2 (d) (4) The Commission will not approve a transfer of operating rights to a person who controls or who is controlled by, or who is under common control with another person who is the holder of operating rights which duplicate, in whole or in part, except to an immaterial extent, those proposed to be transferred.

The Commission has held that when two or more regular-route operating authorities are acquired by one person, the duplicating routes merge and become but one right.[92] This is also true of duplicate irregular routes, but when regular routes and irregular routes authorize duplicate operations, they do not merge.[93]

This section appears to prevent a carrier from purchasing its competitor. It may well be that if there is not economic justification for duplicative service that this section might be amended.

Sec. 179.2 (e) Division of rights—An operating right may be divided as to routes or territories, and part thereof transferred, provided such routes or territories are clearly severable and the division thereof does not permit the creation of duplicate operating rights. No division of operating

---

[91] *Maurer—Control—Brashear Freight Lines, Inc.,* 58 MCC 647 (1952).

[92] *Southwestern Transp. Co.—Purchase—Johnson,* 35 MCC 437 (1940).

[93] *Geo. F. Alger Co.—Purchase—Kirk Transportation Co.,* 38 MCC 342 (1942).

rights based on the class or classes of property authorized to be transferred will be approved, unless it appears to the satisfaction of the Commission that the part of the operating right sought to be transferred is, because of a difference in the nature or type of the service rendered, clearly distinguishable and severable from the remaining operating rights.

One operating right may be divided into two rights following a sale, under the provisions of this section which deals with a division of operating rights. In the preceding section, on the other hand, it was noted that when two rights had existed previous to the sale, one exists after the transfer. It was held, in one case, that the carrier had but one operation between two points regardless of how many routes or series of highways it operated over between the points.[94]

Most requests for a division of radial irregular-route operations have not been approved because the portion to be sold is usually not held to be clearly severable under the transfer rules. However, in one instance, a district court recognized the severability, although the Commission had not. The Commission was directed to approve the transfer.[95]

The language of Section 179.4 (b) governs transfers for limited periods. A lease or a trial period must be of short duration, although there is no specified period. The essence of this section is that the lease period should be no longer than that required for an appraisal by the lessee of the operations with a view to their permanent acquisition or their retention by the owner.

Section 179.4 (d) governs rental charges. Like an earlier section dealing with purchase price, Section 179.2(d)(3), this section specifies that a rental charge is not to be excessive. These rules appear to be well formulated, although it is doubtful, in the case of a denial under this section, whether the parties realize that such a decision may be appealed.

In a court case, the general public interest standards of Section 5 were held to apply also to a Section 212 (b) transfer.[96]

In some instances, the decisions of Division 4 under Section 5 of the act and those of Division 5 under Section 212 (b) differ. Section 212 (b) applications are generally decided without hearing and under specific rules, whereas Section 5 applications are generally heard, with the facts developed in the hearing indicating the action which is in

---

[94] *Cosentino—Purchase—O. K. Motor Service, Inc.,* 46 MCC 815 (1946), (not printed in full).

[95] *Stearn* v. *United States,* 87 Fed. Supp. 596 (1949).

[96] *Ibid.*

the public interest. This is one of the reasons for some of the differences which have occurred, although there have been different interpretations of policies by the two divisions. Further, Division 4 in Section 5 applications may make findings of public convenience and necessity in matters which are related to the Section 5 proceeding. Therefore, Division 4 may grant rights which duplicate in whole or in part those which are sold. Division 5 has pointed out that the Commission may not, in effect, legislate the provisions of Section 5 into the transfer regulations under Section 212 (b).[97] It had earlier been held that Section 212 (b) decisions are not controlling in Section 5.[98]

A carrier may mortgage its operating authority provided the mortgagor continues to operate the rights. If a transfer application is filed by the mortgagor, the Commission does not notify the mortgagee. Under the transfer rules, approval cannot be withheld because of the existence of a mortgage.[99]

RATES—COMMON

Prior to the development of intercity motor carriers, the rate structure of railroads reflected the influence of the value of service consideration in existing rail rates. Generally rates were relatively high on desirable traffic, as well as on shorter hauls, since such traffic could pay the higher price. With the railroads being virtually the only means of transportation for such traffic, the higher rates did not cause the loss of much volume of this traffic. The revenue derived from these rates enabled railroads to establish low rates on traffic when this was virtually mandatory if there was to be movement of goods.

The rail rate structure was very vulnerable to the competition engendered by the growth of motor carriers because the relatively high rail rates made it possible for motor carriers with a faster, as well as a more complete, service to render such service at the same or lower rates.

The railroads have somewhat belatedly recognized that the nature of their rate structure has lent itself to the development of competitive motor-carrier services. Rail carriers have reduced rates to hold or to regain traffic in a number of instances. Frequently the su-

---

[97] *Atwood's Transport Line—Lease—Clarke,* 52 MCC 97 (1950).

[98] *Hubert—Purchase—Service Freight Lines, Inc.,* 45 MCC 717 (1947).

[99] In re *Rainbo Express,* 179 Fed. 2d 1 (1950); and *Breeding Motor Freight Lines, Inc.* v. *R.F.C.,* 172 Fed. 2d 416 (1949).

periority of motor-carrier service has restrained shippers from returning their traffic to railroads.

REASONABLENESS OF RATES AND RATE COMPETITION

The Commission has held that rates lower than those of other carriers in the same general territory are not necessarily unreasonable. It has been stated that the rates of the other carriers would have to be found just and reasonable before the rates of the first carrier could be condemned.[100]

Although Part II of the act contains no long-and-short-haul clause as is found in the Fourth Section of Part I, the Commission has ruled that when the charge for a short haul exceeds that for the long haul such rates are prima facie unreasonable.[101]

Some of the tests applied to rates which have been established to meet competition are: (a) they must be reasonably compensatory so they will not cast a burden upon other traffic; (b) they must not be lower than is necessary to meet competition; and (c) they must not result in a violation of any section of the act. Where the Commission has required the rates of one transportation agency to be raised to or near the level of rates of another agency, such action was prompted in order to prevent actual or potential destructive competition.[102]

There are numerous recent examples of rate competition of which the following is given to indicate some of the problems involved. Beginning in 1950, the railroads proposed a number of rate cases to establish a rate differential of 1 to 1½ cents per 100 pounds under the rates of motor tank-truck carriers for distances under 75 miles. In some instances, the Interstate Commerce Commission ruled that these rates should be 1 to 1½ cents lower than tank-truck rates to be on a competitive basis, and it prescribed a scale of rates which it felt would produce this result. Because of such differences as rail mileage compared with highway mileage and the different levels of truck rates, the application of the scales prescribed by the Commission did not result in the differential that was prescribed. The scales when applied to short-line rail mileages were in some instances higher and in others lower; in still others the same as truck rates.

Later there were several cases in which the railroads proposed a 1 and 1½ cent differential rail rates under tank-truck rates for distances of more than 75 miles. In one of these cases a district court and

---

[100] *Fifth Class Rates between Boston and Providence*, 2 MCC 530 (1937).

[101] *Hausman Steel Co. v. Seaboard Freight Lines, Inc.*, 32 MCC 31, 39 (1942).

[102] *Eastern—Central Motor Carriers Association v. U.S.*, 321 U.S. 194 (1944).

the Supreme Court upheld the Commission's order prescribing such a differential.[103]

The argument of the railroads has been that their service is not equal to that of tank trucks. Therefore, the differential is necessary in order for them to be competitive. Motor carriers have consistently challenged the differential and have secured rate parity in a number of cases. They state that their costs justify their level of rates, but there is not a cost justification for rail rates to be differentially below their rates.

The competition which motor carriers face is not only that from other modes of transportation but from other motor carriers as well. This has frequently led to the establishment of motor-carrier rates which are noncompensatory. These rate wars have resulted in the Commission's prescribing minimum rates in a number of rate territories in order to stop the practice. The first of these was decided in 1937. Since that time minimum rates have been prescribed in a number of other territories.[104]

The large number of motor carriers, the nature of their operations, and the ease with which volume shippers can engage in private motor carriage have been factors which have tended to keep motor-carrier rates in the lower zone of reasonableness. In those instances when minimum rates have been prescribed by the Commission, such rates often became, in practice, maximum rates because they are the rates which are charged. There have been some instances in which rate proposals have been made by the rate bureaus to increase rates, which action would not be followed by a number of carriers belonging to the respective bureaus. This has made it necessary for the Commission to prescribe a higher minimum.

The establishment of minimum rates may be the only method for securing stability of rates in competitive areas. The Commission was requested by one rate bureau to investigate on its own motion the rates of general commodity haulers, both common and contract carriers, in a given area. Minimum rates had been set in this area in 1950, but by the middle of 1953, the competitive situation had become more acute. For example, in the preceding 12 months, the number of proposals filed by rate bureau carriers for reductions was

---

[103] *I & S 5853, Petroleum from Colorado and Wyoming to Western Trunk Line Territory* (1954).

[104] *Middle Atlantic States Motor Carrier Rates,* 4 MCC 68 (1937); *Central Territory Motor Carrier Rates,* 8 MCC 233 (1938); *New England Motor Carrier Rates,* 8 MCC 287 (1938); *Trunk Line Territory Motor Carrier Rates,* 24 MCC 501 (1940); and *Midwestern Motor Carrier Rates,* 27 MCC 297 (1941).

214, of which 107 were approved by the bureau. Twenty-seven independent action notices were filed between April 1 and July 31, as compared with thirteen in the preceding 8 months.

The number of tariff suspensions by the Commission has increased greatly in recent years. In 1947 there were 97 investigation and suspension cases but 1,235 in 1954. There are over 69,000 motor tariff publications annually filed with the Commission.

VOLUME MINIMUM

The conditions under which shipments are moved in motor transportation are not favorable to volume minimum rates which exceed the capacity of a vehicle. The Commission has not found that it is less expensive to move two or three truckloads from a factory in one day than to move one load. There are numerous motor classification ratings which apply on minimum amounts of 50,000 pounds or more, although in some territories there are no such ratings. In the case of commodity rates, there are few which provide for minima above the capacity of the vehicles.

The Commission does not condemn the minimum above vehicle capacity, as such, but it has examined the reasonableness of the revenue per truck-mile or per ton-mile when the minimum is above the vehicle capacity.

THROUGH ROUTES AND JOINT RATES

Motor common carriers of property may but are not required to enter into through-route and joint-rate arrangements with other such carriers or with common carriers in other fields of transportation. There are many arrangements between common carriers of motor vehicles; but, except in special cases, motor carriers of property and railroads have not been parties to these voluntary arrangements. There have been more arrangements of this type involving motor common carriers of property and water carriers.[105]

ICC EXAMINATION OF RATES

The majority of the protests received by the Commission in motor-carrier rate dockets that are against reduced rates come from motor carriers which are opposed to reduced rates proposed by individual

---

[105] Interstate Commerce Commission, *62nd Annual Report* (Washington, D.C.: U.S. Government Printing Office, 1949), p. 57.

carriers. There are three formal procedures available for handling rate cases before the Commission. These are: (1) the hearing procedure which has been generally employed; (2) the shortened procedure in which the parties present the facts and arguments in writing; and (3) the modified procedure which is a combination of the hearing and shortened procedures. The records made in cases handled under the modified procedure in many instances are as good as, if not better than, those made at a hearing. Due to the many advantages of the modified procedure, the use of the shortened procedure in motor-carrier cases has been greatly reduced. In two thirds of the cases handled under modified procedure, no exceptions are filed to the examiner's recommended order and report. Only rarely is an examiner's recommended order stayed by a division of the Commission on its own motion.[106]

RATES—CONTRACT

The schedules of motor contract carriers must contain the minimum rates or charges actually maintained and charged. Thus, if a contract carrier has a contract with but one shipper, the schedule which is filed with the Commission must contain the rate which is actually charged this shipper.[107]

When the contract carrier serves more than one shipper, for example eight, at least one of the shippers (usually the largest one) served must be charged the minimum rates which the carrier has on file with the Commission. The other shippers may be charged in accordance with whatever agreement they make with the carrier but not a rate lower than the minimum rate filed with the Commission. Such agreements must be in writing and copies filed with the Commission.

The Commission has held that there can be but one actual minimum rate or charge on a given shipment from and to given points.[108] In a particular case, the carrier had more than twenty schedules on file in which there were so many duplications and conflicts it was almost impossible to determine the minimum rate actually maintained and charged without examining the contracts. There have been instances in which conflicting minimum rates have been filed with the Commission at different times by the same contract carrier.

---

[106] *Traffic World*, May 30, 1953, p. 18.

[107] *Auto Transports, Inc., Suspension of Permit*, 51 MCC 600 (1950); and *Auto Transports, Inc.* v. *U.S.*, 343 U.S. 923 (1952).

[108] *Emery Transp. Co., Minimum Rates*, 53 MCC 783 (1952).

The Commission has held that the rates in the latest published schedules are the legal minimum rates.[109]

If a new schedule is filed and becomes effective, the rates and charges which it contains must be used. This is true even if the contract with the shipper calls for a different scale of rates or charges. It would appear that this matter constitutes a breach of contract and would be a matter for settlement by the courts.[110]

The contract carrier's schedule must show the extent of the service which is included in the rate which is filed. The Commission has held that when additional services are provided, such as split pickups, the charges for such services should be shown.[111] When a contract carrier's schedule provides mileage rates or charges, a definite means of determining the mileages must be specified. There are a number of motor-carrier agency mileage guides which are used for this purpose.

A contract carrier may begin service immediately upon the signing of a new contract if the schedule on file covers the movement as to commodities, rates, rules, and similar matters, the only required change being the addition of the shipper's name. The contract has to be filed within 20 days, and, at the same time, the shipper's name must be added to the schedule by issuing a supplement or a reissue. If a contract is entered into which calls for a lower charge than those specified in an effective schedule, it appears that Section 218 (a) prohibits the use of the lower charge until an amended schedule is filed on 30 days' notice or the Commission permits a grant of lesser time.

Schedules and any amendments to them are required to be open for public inspection, so that the minimum rates and charges which are filed by the carrier can be examined by competitors, shippers, or others. On the other hand, the Commission may not make public contracts which are filed with it except as a part of a formal proceeding when it considers such disclosure to be in the public interest or to disclose discrepancies with the carrier's schedule of rates.[112]

The Commission has also held that contracts with no definite formula for the rates and under which periodic adjustments are made to assure that neither party will have undue profits or losses are not acceptable.[113]

---

[109] *Petroleum Products, Wyoming Points to Missoula, Mont.,* 32 MCC 453 (1942).

[110] *Bottemueller v. Wilson and Co.,* 57 Fed. Supp. 766 (1944).

[111] *Dairy and Packing House Products—Iowa, Nebr.—Chicago,* 51 MCC 77 (1949).

[112] *Glass Milk Bottles, Elmira, N.Y., to Md., Pa., and W.Va.,* 29 MCC 191 (1941).

[113] *United Parcel Service of Pa., Inc., Filing of Contracts,* 43 MCC 689 (1944).

REASONABLENESS OF RATES

The reasonableness of the minimum rates which are established by contract carriers has been held by the Commission to be determined by consideration of the cost of the service rendered by contract carriers and the effect of these rates upon the movement of traffic by other contract carriers. The reasonableness of the contract carrier's minimum rates is not to be determined by relating them to the rates or operating costs of competing motor common carriers.[114]

Reasonable rates may be prescribed, even though there is the lack of cost-of-service data.[115] However, the Commission has stated that where cost-of-service data were not available, the protestants might show unreasonableness by comparison with other rates of the carrier.[116]

THROUGH RATES

Contract carriers usually transport the goods from origin to destination, although there have been occasions when the question has arisen regarding contract carriers participating in through rates which are published by common carriers. This has been denied.[117]

QUESTIONS AND PROBLEMS

1. What constitutes control under Section 5 (2)? Is this determined on the basis of percentage of stock?
2. Under Section 5 (2) what factors must be considered in determining whether the transfer is consistent with the public interest?
3. Of what importance is fitness in transfer cases under Section 5 (2)?
4. What is Commission policy on the leasing of operating rights? Do you feel that leasing should be more restricted?
5. What problems are posed by dormant rights?
6. Under Section 5 may a person not affiliated with a motor carrier purchase a motor carrier without Commission approval?
7. How does a transfer under Section 212 (b) differ from one under Section 5?
8. Could an application under Section 212 (b) which was denied by the Commission be appealed later?

---

[114] *New England M. Rate Bureau, Inc.* v. *Lewers and McCauley*, 30 MCC 651 (1941).

[115] *Malt Beverages, Containers from Milwaukee to Cleveland,* 54 MCC 200 (1952).

[116] *Middle Atlantic Conference* v. *Hamblet's Exp., Inc.,* 54 MCC 189 (1952).

[117] *Chicago and Wisconsin Points Proportional Rates,* 17 MCC 573 (1939).

9. List and discuss five of the rules which apply to Section 212 (b) applications.
10. What are some of the tests applied to rates which have been established to meet competition?
11. Contract carriers must file a schedule which contains the minimum rate actually maintained and charged. Exactly what does this mean?
12. Does the determination of the reasonableness of rates for common carriers differ from that for contract carriers?

21. RESTRICTIONS ON INTERSTATE MOVEMENT OF GOODS

▪▪

AN INTERNAL trade barrier is a restriction imposed by a state or municipality in the form of a law, regulation, ordinance, or administrative order which discriminates or unreasonably obstructs, whether intentionally or unintentionally, the free flow of legitimate interstate commerce. One of the unsolved problems of interstate property carrying by truck is the lack of uniformity in the restrictions imposed by the various states. The primary restrictions are those involving size and weight limitations; taxation, licensing, and registration requirements; and miscellaneous restrictions. The commercial users of the highways point out that in a few of the key states through which their units must pass, there are such restrictions upon size and weight limits as to negate economical operation of vehicles, at the same time creating uneconomical loading. The states, on the other hand, declare that they must protect their highways and bridges from destructive loads or loads that are considered to be destructive; that they must conserve the resources of their states and build only those highways and bridges which meet the needs of their states; that they wish to promote safety and minimize nuisances in road use; that they want to equalize the tax burden between local and outside carriers; and that they seek to advance the interests of the states through the control of competition among the modes of transportation. Some measure of uniformity has been achieved in the state size and weight limitations; but progress has been slow, and there is little likelihood of acceleration of this movement toward uniformity. This problem possesses such importance, due to its effect upon carriers, shippers, and the public, as to warrant a more thorough examination by public officials. The costs of these barriers are borne by one or all of the groups depending upon economic circumstances.

DEVELOPMENT OF TRADE BARRIERS

A chronological development of trade barriers was compiled by the Board of Investigation and Research which shows that four states had state-wide size and weight limitations in 1913.[1]

An examination of this problem indicates that by 1920 forty states had established restrictions of some type on weights of vehicles and generally sought through police powers to regulate weights. This early action can be traced, in part, to the loads that were carried during World War I on solid-tire units without regard for the surfaced roads, with resulting deterioration in some of the roads. By 1930 only ten states had common standards of weight limitations, and no two of these states were adjoining. It is alleged that special interests were instrumental in establishing statutes that sought to retard motor-carrier development. For example, there was at one time a Texas statute which permitted trucks to carry a pay load of only 7,000 pounds when operating over the highways but allowed twice that amount for trucks hauling freight to or from a railroad station. This statute was later changed but is illustrative of the difficulties that were encountered within various states.

The complaints of truck operators, as well as shippers, about the lack of uniformity of weight limits and the low maximum weights permitted in many states resulted in action by Congress in 1941 to investigate the problem with a view toward standardization. This was undertaken by the Interstate Commerce Commission, which pointed out the many aspects of this problem. It recommended that provision be made for the entertaining and disposition of complaints filed by a responsible party against a state or political subdivision thereof attacking its limitations as they apply generally or to a particular location; that the Commission be given the authority to fix size and weight standards as need arises, securing a technical report from the federal agency most concerned with road matters, now the Bureau of Public Roads, and from the highway department of the state concerned; and that appropriate consideration be given and public hearings be held. There has been no further development of these Commission recommendations, however.

The acute nature of this problem can be better understood when it is pointed out that in 1941 the maximum permissible gross weight

---

[1] Board of Investigation and Research, *Interstate Trade Barriers Affecting Motor-Vehicle Transportation*, Sen. Doc. No. 81, 79th Cong., 1st sess. (Washington, D.C.: U.S. Government Printing Office, 1945), pp. 5–8.

limits ranged from 18,000 pounds in Kentucky, where combinations were not authorized, to 108,000 pounds in Louisiana. This represented a range between the lowest and the highest maximum of 45 tons. There was some evidence of uniformity within certain geographical regions of the United States. In the southern states, the greatest differential appeared.

During the national emergency of World War II, with the need for flexibility in the movement of war traffic, the existence of restrictions on weight and size in effect in some states would have been detrimental to the war effort. The President called a federal-state conference in May, 1942, at which time the Commissioner of Public Roads proposed minimum limitations for adoption by the states. This proposal became known as the emergency formula and provided for the following:

1. Outside width of vehicle or load . . . . 96 inches
2. Extreme height of vehicle or load . . . . 12 feet 6 inches
3. Over-all length of single vehicle . . . . 35 feet
4. Over-all length of combination of vehicles (no combination to consist of more than 2 units; a truck-semitrailer combination to be considered as 2 units) . . . . 45 feet
5. Total load on any single wheel . . . . 9,000 pounds
6. Total load on any single axle (except that when any pair of axles is less than 10 feet apart the total load on either axle should not exceed 18,000 pounds, and the total load on both axles should not exceed 32,000 pounds) . . . . 18,000 pounds
7. Total gross weight of any vehicle having 2 axles . . . . 30,000 pounds
8. Total gross weight of any vehicle or combination of vehicles having 3 or more axles . . . . 40,000 pounds
9. Vehicles and loads not conforming to specifications listed above to be permitted to operate under special certificates subject to gross load limitation according to formula:
   $W = C(L + 40)$ in which
   W = gross weight in pounds
   L = distance, in feet between front and rear axle in any group of 2 or more axles
   C = 750, where L is greater than 18; 650, where L is 18 or less

It is interesting that this emergency formula was similar in most respects to the standards that had been proposed by the American Association of State Highway Officials 11 years previously. By May 30, 1942, all states had indicated that they had adopted this formula.[2] Compliance with the formula was achieved by law in some states, by executive proclamation in others, through an administrative body, or by nonenforcement of existing state regulations.[3]

---

[2] Office of Defense Transportation, *Civilian War Transport, 1941–1946* (Washington, D.C.: U.S. Government Printing Office, 1948), p. 146.

[3] Office of Defense Transportation, *A Review of Highway Transport and Transit Industries during the War* (Washington, D.C., November, 1945), p. 70.

Some progress was made after the war toward liberalizing the weight limits in some states. The range on combinations now between the lowest and highest gross weight limits is 50,000 pounds and 111,000 pounds, which shows a slight improvement in the situation. There is still ample room for further improvement in this respect. Within geographic areas, many adjacent states allow identical gross weights on the largest vehicle combinations but between geographic areas, there is considerable lack of uniformity. The lowest maximum weight allowances for these larger vehicles tend to be concentrated in the South, the highest in the West.

A list of the size and weight restrictions throughout the United States is given in Table 21–1. Substantial uniformity has been achieved in width limitations, 96 inches being almost standard, except in Arizona, Connecticut, and Rhode Island. The width limitations are not shown in Table 21–1, since for all practical purposes an 8-foot limit is standard. Height is substantially standard, as Table 21–1 indicates, at 12 feet and 6 inches, with a considerable degree of uniformity in the length permitted for single units of 35 feet. In many states, maximum gross weight depends on a formula or a table in which the deciding factor is the length from the center of the first axle to the center of the last axle, that is, the over-all wheel base of the vehicle or combination of vehicles. In preparing Table 21–1, certain assumptions were made. In this case, it has been assumed that the overhang, front and rear, totals 6 feet, that is, approximately 3 feet from the front bumper to the center line of the front axle and 3 feet from the center of the rear axle to the rear of the body or body bumper. Many trucks and trailers have more overhang than this, especially in the rear. Most two-axle trailers have substantial overhang in the rear, yet some are designed for maximum legal capacity under the formula and are built with the rear tires just barely ahead of a vertical line from the rear of the body to the ground. Five-axle tractor-semitrailers may readily come within the 6-foot overhang allowance.

The laws of most states do not differentiate between front and rear axles in limiting maximum axle loads. It is, however, impractical to load the front axle beyond a certain point which, in the formula calculations for Table 21–1, has been assumed to be 9,000 pounds. For example, if the law allows only 18,000 pounds per axle, the practical gross load on a two-axle truck tractor and single-axle semitrailer would be 9,000 pounds on the front axle, 18,000 pounds on the rear truck-tractor axle, and 18,000 pounds on the semitrailer axle, or a total of 45,000 pounds.

TABLE 21-1

STATE SIZE AND WEIGHT RESTRICTIONS
JULY 31, 1954

STATE	HEIGHT	LENGTH			Maximum Axle Load in Pounds	Tandem Axles 4 Apart	Maximum* Gross Weight in Pounds		Combinations	FORMULAE** and TABLES
		Single Unit	Tractor Semi-Trailer	Other Combinations			Tractor Semitrailer Single Axle	Tractor Semitrailer Tandem		
Alabama	12'6" A	35 B-1	45	N. P.	18,000 S	36,000	45,000	55,300	N. P.	700 (L+4C)
Arizona	13'6"	40	65	65	18,000	32,000	45,000	68,000***	76,800	Table
Arkansas	12'6" A	35 B-1	50	50	18,000	32,000	45,000	56,000***P	56,000 P	Table
California	13'6"	35 V, B-1	60 T-2	60	18,000	32,000	45,000	68,000***	76,800	Table
Colorado	12'6"	35 V, B-1	60	60	18,000	36,000	45,000	67,200***	75,200	800 (L+40)
Connecticut	12'6"	45	45	N. P.	22,400	36,000	50,000	60,000	N. P.	....
Delaware	12'6" A	35 B-3	50	60	20,000 S-1	36,000	49,000	60,000	60,000	Table
Dist. of Col.	12'6"	35	50	50	27,000	38,000	53,000	63,890	65,400	Table
Florida	12'6" A	40 V	50	50	20,000 S-2 M-1	40,000	49,000	64,650	64,650	Table
Georgia	13'6"	35 B-1	45	45	18,000	36,000	45,000	55,300	55,300	700 (L+40)
Idaho	14'	35 B-D	60	65	18,000 S-3K	32,000 K	45,000 K	67,500***K	72,000 K	Table
Illinois	13'6"	42	45	45	18,000 S-3	32,000 AA	45,000	59,000 AA	72,000 AA	......
Indiana	12'6" A	36 B-1	50	50	18,000 S-3	32,000	45,000	72,000***	72,000	Table
Iowa	12'6" A	35 V, B-1	45	N. P.	18,000	32,000	45,000	65,478	N. P.	Table
Kansas	12'6" A	35 V, B-1	50	50	18,000	32,000	45,000	63,890***	63,890	Table
Kentucky	12'6"	35	45	N. P.	18,000 S	36,000	42,000	42,000	N. P.	....
Louisiana	12'6" A	35 V, B-1	50	60	18,000	32,000	36,000 P	64,000***P	68,000 P	....
Maine	12'6" H	45 H	45 H	45 H	22,000 S	32,000	50,000	50,000	50,000	Table
Maryland	12'6" A	55	55	55	22,400	40,000 I	53,800	65,000	65,000	850 (L+40)
Massachusetts	N. R.	35 B-D	45	N. S.	22,400 S-3	36,000	50,000	50,000	N. P.	....
Michigan	12'6" A	35 B-1	55	55	18,000 S-1	26,000 J	45,000	67,000***D	111,000 D	......
Minnesota	12'6"	40	45	45	18,000	28,000	45,000	65,000***	66,500	Table
Mississippi	12'6" A	35 V, B-1	45	45	18,000 S-4	32,000 D	45,000	55,980 D	55,980 D	Table
Missouri	12'6"	35 B-1	45	45	18,000 S	32,000	45,000	60,010	60,010	Table
Montana	13'6"	35 B-1	60	60	18,000	32,000	45,000	63,890***	76,800	Table
Nebraska	12'6" A	35 V, B-1	50	50	18,900 M	33,600 M	45,000	64,650***	64,650 M-3	Table
Nevada	N. R.	N. R.	N. R.	N. R.	18,000	32,000	45,000	68,000***	76,800	Table
New Hampshire	13'6"	35 B-D	45	45	22,000	30,000	50,000	50,000	50,000	....
New Jersey	13'6"	35	45	50	22,400	32,000	53,800	60,000	60,000	....
New Mexico	12'6"	40	65	65	18,000 S	32,000	45,000	63,000***	76,800	Table
New York	13'	35 B	50	50	22,400 S-3	36,000°	53,800	65,000	65,000	34,000+(LX850)
North Carolina	12'6" A	35 V, B-1	48	48	18,000 M-2	36,000	46,200 M	58,800 M	58,800 M	....
North Dakota	12'6"	35 V, B-1	47'6" Q	47'6" Q	18,000 S-2	30,000	45,000	59,250	59,250	Table
Ohio	12'6"A	35 V, B-1	45 T	60	19,000 S-5	31,500 W	47,000	69,200***W	78,000 W	38,000 + (Lx800)
Oklahoma	13'6" A-1	35 B-2	50	50	18,000 S-5	32,000	45,000	60,000***	60,000	Table
Oregon	13'6"	35	58 T-3	50 C	18,000 S	32,000	45,000	73,000***L	76,000	Table
Pennsylvania	12'6" A	35 B	45	50	20,000	36,000	45,000	45,000	62,000	......
Rhode Island	12'6"	40	50	50	22,400 S-3	32,000	50,000	60,000 Z	88,000 E	......
South Carolina	12'6"	40 V 1	50	50	20,000	32,000	50,900	63,890	63,890	Table
South Dakota	13'	35 V, B-1	50	50	18,000 S	32,000	45,000	64,650***	64,650	Table
Tennessee	12'6"	35 B-1	45	45	18,000	32,000	45,000	55,980	55,980	Table
Texas	13'6"	35 B-1	45	45	18,000 S-5	32,000 R	45,000	58,420	58,420	Table
Utah	14'	45	60 T-1	60 T-1	18,000	33,000	45,000	71,400***	79,900	Table
Vermont	12'6"	50	50	50	N.S.-S.	N.S.-S.	50,000	50,000	50,000	....
Virginia	12'6" A	35 B-1	45 F	45 F	18,000 D-1	36,000 D-1	40,000 D-1	50,000 D-1	50,000 D-1	....
Washington	12'6" A-2	35 B-D	60 T-2	60 T-2	18,000 S-6	32,000	45,000	65,000***	72,000	Table
West Virginia	12'6" A	35 V, B-1	45	45	18,900	33,600	46,800	63,840 M	73,280 L-1	Table
Wisconsin	12'6" A	35 B-1	50	50	19,500 S-3X	32,000 X	48,000 X	68,000***X	68,000 X	Table
Wyoming	13'	40	60	60	18,000	32,000	45,000	68,000***	73,950	Table

FOOTNOTES:
*—Maximum Practical Gross (see third paragraph General Remarks).
**—Computation based on 6' over hang.
***—3-axle tractor with tandem axle semitrailer.
A—Auto transporters allowed 13½'; A-1: 13'; A-2: 12'10" allowed on 10:22 tires.
B—Buses with 3 axles permitted 40'.
B-1—Buses permitted 40'; B-2: 45'; B-3: 42'.
C—State Highway Department may permit 60'.
D—On designated highways.
D-1—16,000 lb. axle limit and 35,000 lb. maximum gross limit on all but "Heavy Duty Highways".
E—3-axle truck with 3-axle trailer.
F—Exclusive of coupling.
G—Includes 10% tolerance.
H—Height and Length subject to 1'6" tolerance.
I—36,000 lb. if axles spaced less than 48" apart.
J—On designated highways one tandem per combination permitted 32,000 lb.
K—Plus 3% tolerance on axle weight and 8% tolerance on gross weight; also certain allowances between 28'-31', and log & pole hauling.

L—Permit required for gross weight over 60,000 lbs.; L-I—Permit required over 63,840 lbs.
M—Includes 5% overload tolerance.
M-1—Plus 10% tolerance.
M-2—Plus 1000 pounds tolerance; M-3—Plus 3% Tolerance.
N. P.—Not Permitted.
N. R.—No Restriction.
N. S.—Not Specified.
Q—Includes 5% tolerance.
R—36,000 lb. if axles do not have common point of suspension.
S—Subject to 600 lb. per inch tire requirements; S-1: 700 lb.; S-2: 550 lb.; S-3: 800 lb.; S-4 on tires 7:75 and larger; S-5: 650 lb.; S-6: 600 lb.
T—Trailer limited to 35'; T-1: 45'; T-2: 40'; T-3: Semi-trailers 40', comb. 58' by permit.
V—Vehicles over 35' must have 3 axles.
W—With tandem axles spaced more than 4' apart.
X—Includes 1,500 lb. tolerance single axle; tandem, 2,000 lb.
Y—With permit.
Z—Not less than 10:00 x 20 tires; not less than 25' between extreme axles.
AA—Double tandems 30,000 lbs. each, 68,000 lbs. total.

Source: Truck-Trailer Manufacturers Association, Inc.

In figuring the maximum gross for two-axle (tandem) trailers in Table 21–1 (third column from the right), the figures are based on three-axle truck tractors and two-axle (tandem) trailers wherever the greater total allowed by this arrangement of axles would be within the maximum gross allowable load. In figuring the total gross for two-axle (tandem) trailers, it has been assumed that the practical maximum length of a truck tractor-semitrailer is 50 feet. Thus, if the formula is $750\ (L + 40) = W$, where L is the distance between the first and last axle, the value of L would be 44 feet (that is 50 feet less 6 feet overhang), and the computation would be $750 \times 84 = 63,000$. The second column from the right shows the maximum gross load with any combination of axles or vehicles permitted in each state.

A single tractor and semitrailer loaded in Florida and destined for Cleveland, Ohio, within the legal limits permitted by Florida, in order to transport its maximum load in each state, would be compelled in 1955 to revise the vehicle's length and loading in the various states as follows:

Cut five feet from length and unload 4,000 pounds in Georgia;
Add back five feet and reload 5,900 pounds in South Carolina;
Cut off two feet and unload 4,700 pounds in North Carolina;
Cut off three more feet and unload 6,200 pounds more in Virginia;
Leave length as is and reload 6,800 pounds in West Virginia;
Leave length as is and add 200 pounds in Ohio.

It is known that size and weight limitations influence the choice of operating equipment today, as in the past. The most efficient type of equipment may not always be employed because of state restrictions, and this influences the determination of rates charged the public for the carrying of commodities.[4]

RECOMMENDED CODE OF AMERICAN ASSOCIATION OF STATE HIGHWAY OFFICIALS

For many years prior to World War II, the American Association of State Highway Officials had attempted to find a satisfactory basis for uniform regulation of sizes and weights of motor vehicles. This association had at intervals offered recommendations concerning limits suitable for adoption, the successive recommendations differing mainly in consistency with the change of vehicle tire equipment from the early solid rubber to the later pneumatic type. After World War II, the Association renewed its consideration of the matter of uniform regulation of the size and weight of vehicles and by majority vote of its state highway department membership adopted as a policy in 1946 the following recommended limits:

---

[4] See House Committee on Interstate and Foreign Commerce, *Federal Regulation of the Sizes and Weight of Motor Vehicles,* House Doc. No. 354, 77th Cong., 1st sess. (Washington, D.C.: U.S. Government Printing Office, 1941), p. 153.

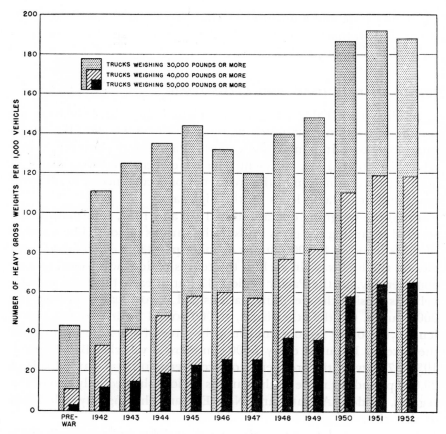

FIG. 21–1. Number of heavy gross weights per 1,000 trucks and truck combinations (empties included) in the summers of 1942–52 and a prewar year.

Source: *Public Roads*, Vol. XXVII, No. 11 (December, 1953), p. 243.

frequencies has been checked several times during the period covered. However, the current frequencies are much larger than those found in 1946. Frequencies of vehicles weighing 30,000 pounds or more in 1952 were 1.4 times as great as in 1946, and over 4 times as great as in the prewar year; those weighing 40,000 pounds or more in 1952 were twice as great as in 1946, and about 11 times as great as in the prewar year; while vehicles weighing 50,000 pounds or more in 1952 were 2.5 times as great as in 1946, and almost 22 times as great as in the prewar year.[7]

Figure 21–2 shows the frequency of axle loads of 18,000 pounds or more, 20,000 pounds or more, and of 22,000 pounds or more for

[7] T. B. Dimmick, "Trends in Traffic Volumes, Vehicle Types, and Weights," *Public Roads*, Vol. XXVII, No. 11 (December, 1953), p. 241.

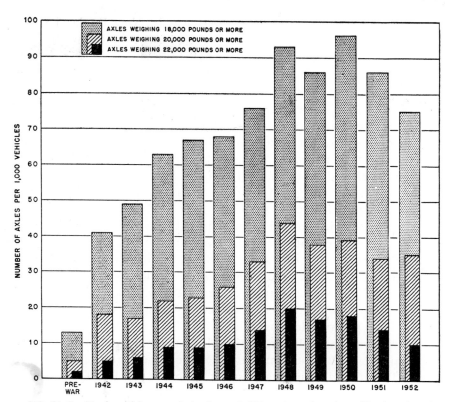

FIG. 21–2. Number of heavy axle loads per 1,000 trucks and truck combinations (empties included) in the summers of 1942–52 and a prewar year.
Source: *Public Roads,* Vol. XXVII, No. 11 (December, 1953), p. 243.

the years from 1942 to 1952, inclusive. The frequency of these heavy loads increased year by year from the prewar period through 1948. Since 1948, however, the trend apparently has been reversed, for with the exception of 1950, the data seem to indicate a definite downward trend. Such a trend may indicate the results of better enforcement of legal limits[8] and of attention given to better load distribution.

The greatest frequency of heavy axle loads was in the Middle

---

[8] The weighing of vehicles by states both at weighing stations and by means of portable scales, has become widespread. Violations have been found in both private and for-hire carriage. A graduated scale of fines, which becomes progressively larger, has been a deterrent to noncompliance with size and weight limits. The Supreme Court in *Illinois Atty. Gen. Castle* v. *Hayes Freight Lines* in 1954 held that a state which sought to bar an interstate carrier from the use of its highways for one year due to violations in weight could not do so. The state could appeal to the Interstate Commerce Commission to have the carrier's certificate revoked, suspended, or changed. Until 1952 the Bureau of Internal Revenue permitted fines for such things as overloading to be deducted as a business expense.

Atlantic region and the next greatest was in New England where moderately low frequencies of heavy gross loads were found. In these two eastern regions, the relatively high frequency is due mainly to the higher legal axle-weight limits in effect in some of the states, and the large number of two-axle truck tractors pulling one-axle or two-axle semitrailers. The relative infrequency of heavy axles in the Pacific region, in the presence of a large proportion of heavy gross loads would indicate a better general distribution of the loads over a larger number of axles.[9]

Well-developed mathematical theories have guided the design of bridges, but the design of road surfaces and their foundations is largely an empirical process. Thus, it is held to be impractical to describe, except in general terms, the effects of heavy-vehicle traffic on either the specifications or the construction costs of highways.[10]

The Commissioner of Public Roads has indicated that while generally the effects of heavy loading on road surfaces "are recognized or suspected, there is a paucity of determined fact upon which to base reasonably precise estimates of the effects of particular loadings on particular types and designs of highways."[11]

In order to supply this recognized lack, three major road tests have been sponsored by the Bureau of Public Roads, the Highway Research Board, and a number of states. The first test was conducted in 1950 on an existing concrete road in southern Maryland. According to the Commissioner of Public Roads, the Maryland test produced only partial answers to the difficult questions about which the Bureau and states are concerned. The testing of a bituminous surfaced road specifically built for testing, with sections of various design, was started in 1953 in Idaho. The third test planned to begin in 1955 in Illinois is the most complete one which will be undertaken. The Commissioner has indicated that it is impossible to draw satisfactory conclusions concerning the physical and economic problems until all these road tests are completed and the data compiled and interpreted.

ECONOMIES OF MOTOR-VEHICLE SIZE AND WEIGHT

Over-all costs of freight transportation by highway include the costs of owning, maintaining, and operating trucking equipment, and

---

[9] Dimmick, *op. cit.*

[10] Statement of Commissioner of Public Roads before House Public Works Committee, April, 1953.

[11] *Transport Topics*, April 20, 1953, p. 1.

such costs of constructing and maintaining highway facilities as may properly be assigned to freight vehicles. From limited partial studies there are indications that as the load capacities of bridges and pavements are increased, the costs of highway construction and maintenance increase, but the degree and trend of such increased costs per unit of freight transported have not been fully developed. Other partial studies indicate that as the size and weight of truck combinations are increased their operating costs per unit of freight transported decrease.

The Highway Research Board has established a Committee on Economics of Motor Vehicle Size and Weight which is to make a study to determine what maximum sizes and weight specifications for motor carriers of property, with corresponding maximum weight specifications for pavement and bridge construction, will result in the most economical over-all highway transportation costs for commodities and freight.

In order to develop a range of truck and truck combination size and weight limits that will result in the lowest over-all cost of highway transportation per unit of freight transported, data is being secured on operating costs of various types of freight vehicles by increments of gross weights for various types of freight service; costs of providing highway facilities by increments of axle loads and frequency of traffic; and relation of total tonnage of commodities hauled to shipping densities of the commodities, in order to judge which commodities should not occupy all of the space in the cargo body of highway freight vehicles.

TAXES, LICENSING, REGISTRATION, AND OTHER FEES

Commercial vehicles are subject to numerous taxes and fees. Usually, interstate vehicles must pay a registration fee the same as intrastate vehicles. In some instances, an interstate vehicle is not required to pay the registration fee; therefore, other taxes are imposed. In addition, the commercial carriers may be subject to other taxes such as gross receipts and mileage taxes, certificate fees, plate fees, and the like. Theoretically, states are justified in establishing systems of taxation which will secure revenues in proportion to the use made of their highways. Actually, the cumulative effect of taxes levied by a number of states upon an interstate carrier creates a restrictive burden. Registration fees, in particular, may result in discriminatory practices. As an example, it is reported that a commercial motor carrier operating from Alabama to South Carolina would have to pay a $400 registration fee in Alabama, $400 in Georgia, and $300 in South Carolina on a 5- or 6-ton truck, which would total $1,100.[12] This may be an extreme case, but it indicates the prohibitive and discriminatory aspects of registration fees which do not measure accurately the use made of the highway by interstate carriers. This practice is to some degree mitigated by reciprocity agreements between the states, although the extent of such agreements is limited. Even where employed, they do not cover all aspects and are constantly subject to change by succeeding state political administrations.

A comparison has been made showing the total state taxes paid by a 1½-ton truck, a 5-ton truck, and a 10-ton truck tractor and semitrailer combination operated by a common, a contract, or a private carrier in each state.[13] By making basic assumptions regarding number of axles, maximum gross weight, annual mileage and revenue, horsepower, value of each unit, and annual gasoline consumption, it was possible to secure a comparison of state truck taxes (excluding personal property tax) and certificate and filing fees for each unit. For the truck tractor-semitrailer operating in West Virginia, the following taxes would be paid on each common, contract, and private unit, assuming they all operated the same mileage. It is widely recognized that the common carriers average a much higher mileage per year than either the contract or private carriers, so that the range here indicated would actually be much greater.

Explanation	Common	Contract	Private
Registration fee.............	$ 519.00	$ 597.00	$298.50
Carrier license fee..........	37.50	37.50	....
Ton-mileage tax............	562.50	....	....
Gross receipts tax..........	231.66	231.66	....
Motor fuel tax.............	562.50	562.50	562.50
Total..................	$1,913.16	$1,428.66	$861.00

In Florida, for the same size unit with the same basic assumptions, the taxes are as follows:

---

[12] Office of Defense Transportation, *Civilian War Transport, 1941–1946,* p. 144.

[13] Association of American Railroads and Association of Western Railways, *Digest of State Laws Pertaining to the Regulation and Taxation of Motor Vehicles* (1948), pp. 152–58.

Explanation	Common	Contract	Private
Registration fee............	$ 721.25	$ 721.25	$ 180.00
Maintenance tax..........	....	....	50.00
Mileage tax.............	450.00	450.00	....
Motor fuel tax...........	787.50	787.50	787.50
Total................	$1,958.75	$1,958.75	$1,017.50

The registration fee for the common and contract carrier unit is much higher than that of the private carrier, on the basis that the common and contract carriers should pay more because they are using the highways for commercial purposes. Many of the common carriers pay over $3,000 in taxes per year per unit and some over $4,000.

Approximately 33 per cent of the total state motor-vehicle fees was paid by trucks, which constitute approximately 17 per cent of the vehicles. If all of the trucks except tractor-semitrailers and truck trailers are eliminated, they constitute about 1 per cent of the vehicles and pay approximately 12 per cent of the state motor-vehicle revenue. A recent study of eleven types of vehicles including trucks showed a wide variation among the states of state road-user taxes and personal property taxes. The national average tax for a farm pickup truck was found to be less than that for a light passenger automobile. On the 40,000-pound, three-axle tractor-semitrailer in private operation, the registration fee varied from $45 to $640.[14]

The restrictions that arise from the taxation of motor fuels prove to be burdensome upon commercial motor carriers, that is, the imposition by one state of a tax on fuel for which such a tax has already been paid in another state. This practice developed because the states that levied higher motor fuel tax rates than neighboring states found that, unless there was legislation enacted specifying the amount of motor fuel that could be brought into the state without payment of the state motor fuel tax, the carriers would load their gas tanks in a neighboring state and try to go through the higher motor fuel tax state without purchasing gasoline. The majority of states had enacted legislation of this kind by 1942; and it was not uncommon for the state laws to stipulate the limit that could be brought in, such as 10, 15, or 20 gallons. The so-called "bridge states" imposed regulations of this type in order to secure from interstate

---

[14] Edwin M. Cope and Richard W. Meadows, "Road-User and Property Taxes on Selected Motor Vehicles 1953," *Public Roads,* Vol. XXVII, No. 7 (April, 1953), p. 127.

commercial users of their highways some compensation in gasoline tax for the use of those highways. It is possible for a trucker to fill his gas tank in Pennsylvania and go across a bridge state, such as Maryland, without purchasing any gasoline; yet he makes use of the highways.

Another potential barrier is the taxation of motor fuel by counties or local governments. However, the application of this to date has been limited, although it might be expanded in the future.

The special taxes and fees which are imposed by states upon motor carriers may be classified as (a) regulatory charges, and (b) measures of highway use. Under regulatory charges are certificates or permit fees, identification plate fees, and franchise taxes, except where these are graduated according to weight, capacity, or earnings. Under the measure of highway-use classification are gross earnings taxes, mileage taxes, and weight and capacity taxes. These can constitute a barrier for interstate commerce where there is a pyramiding of these charges through operation in various states. There are other fees which are more in the form of nuisances than barriers, such as weighing charges and inspection fees.

MISCELLANEOUS RESTRICTIONS

The third general category of restrictions upon interstate carriers is that of miscellaneous restrictions. One of these is the port of entry, which was established in 1933 by Kansas in order to check evasion of the state motor fuel tax law. Later, the functions of enforcement of the state gross ton-mileage tax law, the enforcement of the state prohibition law, and the investigating of vehicles and operators for compliance with the safety laws of Kansas were added. Bordering states quickly retaliated with similar measures, and this spread to other states throughout the United States. Different regulations were applied; the general purpose was to enforce the laws of the various states concerning the operation of commercial motor vehicles, nonresident registration fees, and other carrier taxes, size and weight laws, and safety laws and regulations. In some instances, the ports of entry were given more comprehensive functions. In a report made on this subject, the conclusions regarding the port-of-entry device have been well summarized as follows:[15]

1. It appears that the port-of-entry device does provide a relatively effective means of enforcing State laws and regulations against non-resi-

---

[15] Board of Investigation and Research, *op. cit.,* pp. 48–49.

dent motor-vehicle owners and operators, and it may be the only practical means of achieving that end in some States.

2. The question of the profitability of ports of entry to the States through the collection of fees should not be a deciding factor in answering the general question of their justification. It must be granted that the ports frequently are effective as law-enforcement devices; the mere fact that their process of checking law compliance is well known and that tax evasion at the ports by nonresidents is all but impossible, discourages would-be evaders. Therefore, the operations of ports increases a State's income to a much greater extent than is indicated by port records alone by facilitating an otherwise burdensome and costly collection process. But the arduousness and expense of collecting a tax does not excuse laxity in collections—that would discriminate against those who pay in good faith. If a tax is so costly and difficult of collection that the levying agency is unduly burdened, that tax should be repealed—provided that an efficient method of collection cannot be devised and that the tax is not designed solely as a regulatory measure.

3. Analysis of many of the complaints made against the port-of-entry device reveals that they are actually complaints against the laws and regulations that the ports are designed to enforce and not against the port-of-entry scheme itself. If relief from these restrictions could be brought about through individual State action, cooperative action by groups of States, or action resulting from the imposition of some form of Federal authority, the causes for complaint would be removed—as also might be the need for the ports themselves.

4. Some of the complaints made, however, stem directly from the operation of the ports. Delay, inconvenience, and embarrassment to interstate highway traffic occasioned by the failure of States to operate sufficient ports, to man them adequately, to operate them efficiently, or to keep them open at all times cannot be charged to any extraneous source. The same would hold true also in the case of difficulties arising from the inability, negligence, or disinclination of port employees to perform their duties properly and expeditiously. Operation of the ports could be improved to remedy such situations, thereby removing much of the complaint that is raised against them.

5. The operation of ports of entry undoubtedly causes some retaliatory measures, but such measures would probably be taken anyway if State laws were as rigidly enforced by other means.

6. The term "port of entry" has acquired an unfavorable connotation. This idea, associated with the inconveniences experienced with port operations, causes some traffic and, consequently, some business to bypass port-of-entry States.

The ports of entry represent only a temporary solution to the problems of interstate highway commerce. Until there is a desire on the part of the states to create uniform laws and regulations governing interstate traffic on the highways and to eliminate multiple taxation, there can be no real solution to the problem of trade barriers.

RECIPROCITY

In its broadest form reciprocity means that a state permits vehicles from other states to operate in and through the first state providing a similar privilege is given to vehicles domiciled in the first state and operating in and through other states. Reciprocity was originally secured by agreements between states regarding passenger cars. The relative ease of accomplishing reciprocity for passenger vehicles did not continue with regard to trucks because more complex factors were involved. Reciprocal agreements would do much to alleviate some of the restrictions which presently exist.

Reciprocity is a privilege and not a right. Therefore, it may be granted or removed unilaterally. Full reciprocity on all matters between any two states is the rare exception for the trucking industry, but there have been many agreements entered into which have facilitated the free flow of commerce between the states. Historically, reciprocity has dealt with two structures of taxes, namely the registration fee or license fee and motor fuel taxes. Some of the agreements between states have been informal, whereas others have been formal and have provided for reciprocity on license fees or on motor fuel taxes or both.

A few states have imposed so-called "third-structure" taxes, which are commonly known as ton-mile taxes, mileage taxes, axle-mile taxes, gross-receipts taxes, and others, which kind of tax is imposed only on trucks. The imposition of the third-structure taxes has posed a great threat to reciprocity. When states adopt such taxes and apply them to out-of-state vehicles, the reaction is usually either to impose the same type of tax on trucks from the state which originated the third-structure tax or to terminate the existing reciprocity agreements. For example, after New York instituted a ton-mile tax requiring payment from out-of-state vehicles, Virginia required that New York vehicles must pay a 2 per cent gross receipts tax as long as Virginia vehicles are subjected to the ton-mile levy in New York. Virginia had had the 2 per cent gross receipts tax which applied to Virginia-registered vehicles but, through reciprocity agreements, this tax had previously not applied to vehicles from other states. As long as Virginia vehicles are subjected to the ton-mile levy in New York, New York vehicles must pay the Virginia tax when they operate in Virginia.

Ohio enacted a third-structure tax which became effective in 1954 in the form of an axle-mile tax. Other states retaliated by imposing various types of taxes upon trucks domiciled in Ohio. The rate of the new tax was such that fifteen Class I carriers changed their corporate organizations and moved their operating headquarters from Ohio in order to reduce the number of units subject to the tax and to avoid the retaliatory measures of other states on vehicles bearing Ohio license plates. It is estimated that about twenty other smaller carriers have also moved out of the state.

Reciprocity has taken on a regional pattern. The North Atlantic states deal largely in informal agreements. Ten southern states have had a reciprocal agreement since 1949 which is known as the Southwide Agreement. In the Middle West, there is only one state which cannot grant full reciprocity on all fees. In the eleven western states, there is wide variation as to the authority to grant reciprocity and one state cannot grant any reciprocity to trucks. There are at the present time twenty-six states that have given their officials authority to enter into reciprocal agreements on all fees and registrations.

Since reciprocity may be granted on a unilateral basis, there are sometimes rather unusual grants which are extended. For example, Pennsylvania granted trucks with Delaware licenses the privilege of carrying 60,000 pounds gross weight to and from Pennsylvania, as compared with a 45,000-pound weight limit for Pennsylvania trucks and trucks from other states. This was granted in 1938 and was in effect until 1952, when it was canceled after individual truck operators complained that Delaware trucks were permitted to carry heavier weights through Pennsylvania than trucks licensed in Pennsylvania.[16]

The American Trucking Associations in early 1954 issued a nine-point statement of policy adopted by its executive committee concerning taxation of interstate trucks. This statement outlined the principles of proportionate distribution among the states of first- and second-structure taxes.

TYPICAL EFFECTS OF INTERSTATE BARRIERS

There are a number of economic effects of trade barriers. In some instances their effect may be primarily upon the public; in other instances upon the motor carriers; and in still other instances upon both groups, some of which have already been described.

One study of state motor-vehicle regulations which restrict movement of agricultural commodities concluded that such laws "may

---

[16] *Transport Topics*, April 21, 1952, p. 25.

distort the economy of a region to a greater extent than other laws and regulations, such as quarantines, which may completely prohibit interstate movement."[17]

Another effect of the restrictions is that the equipment which is used will not necessarily be the most economical for the truck operator, since the equipment may be purchased to conform to the most restrictive state through which the operator's units travel. Truck operators may, instead of standardizing their equipment, purchase units which will meet the varying requirements of particular states. Therefore, they have to carry larger parts inventories because of the lack of uniform equipment. Any of these matters which increase operating costs are usually passed on to shippers in higher rates.

A study in the hauling of fluid dairy products in Wisconsin found that the Wisconsin regulation which was more restrictive than that of Illinois placed the Illinois producers in a more favorable position in the competition for the Chicago market. The competitive price for milk is the delivered price, and milk can be transported more economically in larger trucks which were permitted in Illinois but not in Wisconsin. The practical maximum gross weight of vehicles permitted in Wisconsin was 66,000 pounds, while Illinois permitted 72,000 pounds.[18]

SOLUTIONS TO TRADE BARRIERS

There are a number of proposals which have been advanced as possible solutions to the trade-barrier problem. Since it is such a complex issue, perhaps there is no single proposal which will solve the problem, and the ultimate solution may rest in a combination of proposals. It should not be inferred that a solution means the elimination of the size and weight limitations but rather that a solution would represent a realistic approach to uniform regulations.

One possibility is that of conditioning federal grants in aid to the states upon the adoption by the states of uniform requirements on those highways which are constructed with federal funds. This would be primarily in regard to size and weight limits. It is true that federal-aid highways constitute only a small portion of the highways,

---

[17] J. S. Hillman and J. D. Rowell, *Barriers to the Interstate Movement of Agricultural Products by Motor Vehicle in the Eleven Western States* (Tucson, Ariz.: University of Arizona, 1953), p. 3.

[18] Department of Agriculture and University of Wisconsin, *Regulations on Weight of Motor Trucks* (Washington, D.C.: U.S. Government Printing Office, 1952), p. 7.

but this is an important portion, and would be a step toward uniformity.

The prescription of federal standards could accomplish a greater uniformity, but under such an arrangement the state highway departments would recommend, where necessary for the protection of highways and highway safety, an adjustment in the standards.

Federal regulation of sizes and weights of motor vehicles with a limited amount of federal control is another proposal which has been made. Under this suggestion, the Interstate Commerce Commission would regulate the sizes and weights of motor vehicles engaged in interstate commerce. The Commission could act upon the complaint of shippers, carriers, or others to investigate alleged obstructions to interstate commerce. After hearings, the Commission could prescribe maximum standards necessary to remove the obstructions. Similarly, a federal regulatory body could be given jurisdiction to determine whether any state or local tax levied upon for-hire interstate carriers imposes an undue burden upon interstate commerce or discriminates against any such carrier.

Another proposal is to establish a firmer basis for reciprocity. The initiative in reciprocal matters should not be left to the states but rather motor carriers should encourage reciprocity by assisting the states in working out equitable distribution between the states of the fees and taxes involved.[19]

QUESTIONS AND PROBLEMS

1. Describe the development of state trade barriers to motor-carrier operations.

2. Would you agree that "the Commission be given the authority to fix size and weight standards as the need arises"? What are the practical advantages or limitations to such a procedure?

3. What reasons are there for the wide variations among the states on maximum gross weights?

4. Explain the AASHO code. Why has it not been adopted by all the states? What is the attitude of motor carriers toward this recommended code?

5. What trends are evident in axle loads? Gross loads?

6. Cite specific examples of how "the cumulative effect of taxes levied by a number of states upon an interstate carrier creates a restrictive burden."

---

[19] See Committee on Interstate and Foreign Commerce staff report, *State Taxation of Interstate Trucking and the Reciprocity Problem,* 84th Cong., 1st sess. (Washington, D.C.: U.S. Government Printing Office, 1955).

7. Why do "ports of entry represent only a temporary solution to the problems of interstate highway commerce"? Assume that you are the top state highway official. Would you favor the establishment of a port of entry? Why or why not?

8. The establishment of trade barriers between the states is often referred to as an effort to Balkanize the United States. Do you agree? Explain the effect of such Balkanization (*a*) upon the motor carrier; (*b*) upon the shipper; and (*c*) upon the consumer.

9. Formulate a practical program, equitable to all parties, which in your opinion would eliminate the state restrictions now imposed upon motor carriers.

10. What is reciprocity? Has it been successful in overcoming the restrictions on the interstate movement of goods?

11. List some of the economic effects of trade barriers. What are some suggested solutions?

PART III

Passenger-Carrying Aspects of Commercial Motor Transportation

22. INTERCITY PASSENGER OPERATIONS

LINKING thousands of communities today and forming an integral part of the passenger transportation system is the intercity motor bus operation. Paralleling to a great extent the improvements in our vast highway system, intercity bus operations have developed so rapidly that it is little short of phenomenal. The services rendered by these companies have become the accepted standard for thousands of passengers each year. The origin of intercity bus operation was humble. Most of today's operations had their origin in short-route sedan automobile service which in some cases was originally a side line of a local livery man. Some began as operations of automobile dealers who were unable to find purchasers for their busses. Others were instituted by railroads in order to permit the abandonment of expensive rail service to rural points which produced low revenues. Still others represented efforts of electrical interurban railways to economize in their operations, as well as to provide a more flexible service.

An example of the difficulties encountered in intercity bus operations even as late as 1937 is that of the Boise-Winnemucca Stages,[1] operating between Boise, Idaho, and Winnemucca, Nevada. This company had equipment which consisted of one 1935 Ford sedan and later, in the spring of 1938, two 1938 seven-passenger Dodge sedans. After the acquisition of this new equipment, a daily schedule was started. Road conditions were very poor, except for 74 miles in Nevada which had been paved. The next 28 miles in Oregon were graded gravel of poor construction. The following 93 miles in Oregon were entirely country road which wound through the desert and over lava beds. This particular road was at least a foot deep in dust during the summer months and, in the spring and winter, was

---

[1] Transcript, MC–C–550, National Bus Fare Investigation of Class I Common Carriers of Passengers, p. 1478.

nothing more than a series of mudholes. It was practically impossible for a car to make a trip without getting broken spring leaves, spring shackles, and hangers. After 6 months of operations, there was hardly a spot on the body or frame of any of the cars which had not been welded or patched. Furthermore, tire mileage of 3,000 miles was considered to be very good. On this account, it was necessary to maintain spare tires at every town along the road, since it was often necessary to change tires three or four times in one trip because of blowouts. In 1938, when 30 miles of graveled road in Oregon were finished, the bus line was able to cut 1 hour off its previous 12-hour schedule. There were still many days during the slack season when cars ran in both directions without passengers and with very little express. The road continued to be muddy during the winter and spring. At times, the road would be flooded entirely in a certain spot so as to be impassable. In these cases, the northbound and southbound cars would meet at the mudhole, transfer their passengers either by building a bridge or by putting them on a dump truck, if one was available, or by having the drivers carry them across on their backs. Despite these early trials and tribulations, this carrier now has a successful passenger operation.

However, the operational problems and difficulties experienced by this carrier were greater than most. The growth of intercity bus common-carrier operation has been very rapid and appears to have reached a stable basis more quickly than the property-carrying aspect of highway transportation. This has been due, in some degree, to the fact that passenger operations are somewhat more simple than freight operations, since passengers assemble at a terminal and are discharged en route or ride on through to a terminal.

The members of the intercity bus industry are in general small business organizations, with a few outstanding exceptions. Excluding the rail-affiliated bus companies, practically all bus companies originated as individual or partnership enterprises. The stock in most of the companies today is owned by only a few individuals. In the case of carriers with annual gross revenues of less than $200,000, there is an average of slightly in excess of 3 owners per company; in the revenue group from $200,000 to $500,000, an average of 6 owners per company; in the revenue group above $500,000, the average is 53 owners per company, largely because of the influence of one company which has a public issue.[2] The small-business nature of the

─────────

[2] *Ibid.*, pp. 3829–31.

TABLE 22-1

Intercity Passenger-Miles

(In Billions)

Year	Total Intercity Travel	Private Automobiles	Public Carriers				
			Total	Rail-roads*	Intercity Buses†	Air Lines‡	Water-ways
1929	186.6	154.3	32.3	24.2	6.8	. . . . . .	1.3
1930	189.4	160.9	28.5	20.2	7.1	0.1	1.1
1931	192.3	168.6	23.7	15.9	6.7	0.1	1.0
1932	175.6	156.4	19.2	12.0	6.3	0.1	0.8
1933	176.2	156.5	19.7	12.0	6.4	0.2	1.1
1934	190.4	168.1	22.3	13.9	7.1	0.2	1.1
1935	201.8	178.3	23.5	14.4	7.6	0.3	1.2
1936	226.6	197.4	29.2	18.2	9.2	0.4	1.4
1937	261.9	228.4	33.5	21.5	10.3	0.4	1.3
1938	255.2	226.3	28.9	18.7	8.2	0.5	1.5
1939	266.0	234.7	31.3	19.6	9.5	0.7	1.5
1940	279.1	245.8	33.3	20.8	10.2	1.0	1.3
1941	307.6	264.3	43.3	26.5	13.6	1.4	1.8
1942	274.6	199.6	75.0	50.3	21.4	1.4	1.9
1943	261.2	147.1	114.1	84.6	26.0	1.6	1.9
1944	275.4	151.3	124.1	92.2	27.4	2.3	2.2
1945	300.9	179.8	121.1	88.1	27.5	3.4	2.1
1946	349.1	253.6	95.5	60.4	26.9	5.9	2.3
1947	346.3	273.0	73.3	40.8	24.6	6.1	1.8
1948	355.6	287.4	68.2	36.0	24.3	6.2	1.7
1949	379.1	316.7	62.4	30.5	23.3	7.2	1.4
1950	396.9	337.3	59.6	27.5	22.3	8.6	1.2
1951	445.8	379.3	66.5	30.4	23.4	11.4	1.3
1952	477.6	410.3	67.3	30.0	22.5	13.5	1.4
1953	498.0	432.1	65.9	27.5	21.3	15.6	1.5

* Commutation passenger miles not included.
† Estimated passenger miles of charter travel included, beginning with 1939.
‡ Estimated domestic passenger miles of travel by irregular air carriers included, beginning with 1948.
Source: Interstate Commerce Commission; 1953 data estimated. (Courtesy of National Association of Motor Bus Operators.)

great majority of the carriers is an important characteristic of the passenger-carrying industry.

The Class I intercity motor carriers of passengers in 1946 (at that time those having gross revenues of $100,000 or more)[3] were tabulated by ownership and the following analysis made:[4] The largest class, comprising 35.1 per cent of the total number, consisted of carriers owned by several individuals or by family groups. These carriers, however, accounted for only 14 per cent of the operating revenues. Next in number were carriers owned by individual families,

[3] The Class I, Class II, and Class III motor carriers of passengers are explained later in this chapter.

[4] Transcript, MC–C–550, pp. 135–36. This proceeding was instituted by the Interstate Commerce Commission on its own motion on July 1, 1946, for an investigation of bus fares of Class I common carriers of passengers subject to the Interstate Commerce Act.

which represented 18.1 per cent of the total number and 5.8 per cent of the total revenue. More than 10 per cent of the carriers were owned by sole proprietors; their operating revenues totaled 1.6 per cent of the total. Rail carriers owned 6.9 per cent of the carriers, and these carriers contributed 12.3 per cent of the revenues. Another 1.1 per cent of the carriers, with 4.6 per cent of the revenues, were owned by railroads and bus lines. Greyhound Corporation and its subsidiaries owned 4.7 per cent of the carriers, which contributed 13.3 per cent of the revenues. Greyhound in conjunction with rail carriers

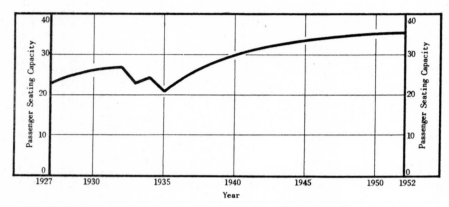

FIG. 22–1. Average seating capacity per intercity type of bus manufactured.

Source: National Association of Motor Bus Operators, *Bus Facts* (22d ed.; Washington, D.C., 1953), p. 16.

and others partly owned an additional 6.2 per cent of the carriers, accounting for 29.3 per cent of the revenues.

An indication of the size and growth of intercity motor bus operations can be secured from an examination of total intercity passenger-miles[5] performed by all passenger agencies of transportation, as shown in Table 22–1. In 1953, of the 65.9 billions of passenger-miles operated by public carriers, 21.3 billions, or about 33 per cent, were accounted for by intercity bus operations. In a 24-year period, busses have increased their passenger-miles from 6.8 billions to 21.3 billions, or more than tripled the passenger-miles from 1929 to 1953.

An examination of the number of busses operating in intercity bus transportation provides further evidence of the growth of bus transportation.[6] In 1932 there were 26,706 busses in intercity bus

---

[5] A statistical unit which is the sum of the mileages traveled by all passengers.

[6] Department of Commerce, *Domestic Transportation* (Washington, D.C., February–March, 1946), p. 34.

operations; this number had decreased by 1954 to about 23,800. The increase in seats made available in intercity bus operations is greater than a number of years ago, inasmuch as the seating capacity in busses has increased. The National Association of Motor Bus Operators pointed out that in 1937 only 35.9 per cent of busses used in intercity traffic had a seating capacity of more than 36 passengers. In 1940, 67.8 per cent had over a 36-passenger capacity, with that trend continuing.[7] The trend in the size of all intercity-type busses manufactured from 1927 to 1952 is shown in Figure 22–1. This figure represents the average seating capacity of all intercity busses which have been manufactured during those years. A tabulation of the three most popular bus sizes for each year from 1936 through 1954 is given at the right below:[8]

INTERCITY			
1st	2d	3d	
36	21	33	1936
37	21	35	1937
37	25	30	1938
37	25	29	1939
29	27	25	1940
29	25	37	1941
33	37	29	1942
29	33	37	1943
33	37	29	1944
37	29	33	1945
33	37	29	1946
37	33	29	1947
37	29	41	1948
37	29	41	1949
37	41	29	1950
37	41	36	1951
36	29	41	1952
41	29	37	1953
41	45	29	1954

ADVANTAGES OF INTERCITY BUS TRANSPORTATION

Convenience is a very significant factor in the choice of a carrier, and therein lies part of the success intercity busses have experienced in securing a share of the passenger market. The routes of intercity busses are projected into the most convenient city areas. Dependent upon operating rights, they may pick up or discharge passengers at almost any point on their route which the passenger desires. Intercity bus operators have provided service to thousands of intermediate communities between major cities; in addition, they have rendered service to sparsely populated areas which have been without public transportation.

Closely associated with its accessibility to passengers is the advantage given to passenger convenience by the frequency of schedule. The relatively small size of the intercity bus as compared with a train makes it much more simple to adjust schedules to the needs of the traffic. Some indication of scheduled frequency of intercity bus operations can be secured from the Greyhound Corporation operations. In 1943, they were rendering service equal to about six round

---

[7] *Ibid.*

[8] *Bus Transportation,* 33rd Annual, Review of Industry Progress, February, 1955. p. 33.

trips per day over their entire system. Additional evidence is available as to traffic flow on nine selected routes, each over 225 miles in length, of certain Greyhound companies during a test week in 1943. Each of the routes had terminal cities which were multiple market centers, with one or more retail market centers as intermediate points. The average of the nine routes showed a percentage of terminal-to-terminal passengers of 5 per cent, and intermediate points to terminal passengers of 37.9 per cent, and an intermediate point-to-point passenger average not touching either terminal of 57.1 per cent.[9] The high percentage of intermediate point-to-point passengers can be traced in some measure to the convenience provided by inter-city bus operations.

An analysis of the 1947 schedules of 216 Class I intercity carriers, as shown in *Russell's Official Motor Coach Guide,* was introduced in MC–C–550 in 1950. The 1,775 routes embraced an average of 7.4 daily schedules each way per route, varying from 11.7 average daily schedules each way per route in New England to 5.5 average daily schedules per route in the thinly populated North Central Territory. Eighty per cent of the routes shown had a schedule frequency of 3 or more daily schedules each way, 46 per cent had a daily schedule frequency of 6 or more each way, 19 per cent had a daily schedule frequency of 12 or more each way, and 8 per cent had a daily schedule frequency of 18 or more each way. This is even more impressive when it is realized that only schedules useful for interline information are included in *Russell's Official Motor Coach Guide.* Many of the very frequent short-distance schedules are omitted. The frequency with which busses operated over each mile of route per day averaged 9 busses in 1952.[10]

Progressive steps have been followed through the years for improvements in the comfort accorded intercity bus passengers. Rapid strides have been made in a relatively short period of time from the days of the bus with body and chassis made separately and equipped with hard rubber tires to the integral construction of the present day with balloon tires, well-cushioned reclining seats, and air conditioning. Comfort was and still is an important item influencing the choice of an agency of transportation by a passenger for his journey. Bus equipment improvements are being made constantly to provide inducement for travel by bus.

The element of speed influences the choice of carrier by a passen-

---

[9] *Investigation of Local Feeder, and Pick-up Air Service,* 6 CAB 1 (1944).

[10] Burton B. Crandall, *The Growth of the Intercity Bus Industry* (Syracuse, N.Y., 1954), p. 242.

ger. A study of about 1,500 scheduled services between more than 150 pairs of major terminal points showed intercity bus operators in the South and West to have scheduled speeds of 5 to 12 per cent faster than in the East.[11] The range in scheduled bus speeds averaged less than 5 per cent from the low to the high speed, as contrasted to speed variations of as high as 100 per cent for railroad service.[12] Furthermore, the highway mileages of the bus routes were generally shorter than the rail distances in the studied services. For distances over 500 miles, it was found that, although the running time of busses and railroads were comparable, the total elapsed bus time was not equal to rail because of meal and comfort stops.

Cost to the traveler influences his choice of passenger agency to a degree. In this respect, the intercity bus has offered fares that average somewhat below those of the other commercial passenger carriers; and the disparity has increased since the end of World War II. A passenger traffic study based on 1939 fares reveals that round-trip bus fares were about 76 per cent of the round-trip rail coach fares based on about 350 origin and destination points.[13] A similar general trend was noted in comparing one-way fares by bus and railway coach. The tendency has been for the fare per mile to decrease the longer the journey in intercity bus operation, with some shorter trips bearing a charge comparable to the rail coach fare. Intercity bus operations which are competitive between two points do not adhere to the same fare, and this practice is common in intercity bus operations. Solely on a cost basis to the passenger, the advantage in intercity travel rests with the bus. A comparison has been made of 7,025 bus fares, both intraterritorial and interterritorial, between principal points in the various rate regions as of 1940 and 1948, respectively, with corresponding rail coach fares between the same points as of the same dates.[14] This study shows that, as of 1940, the bus fares on the average were 78 per cent of the corresponding rail coach fares; but, as of 1948, bus fares were only 64 per cent of the corresponding rail fares. This drop was primarily due to the fact that, by 1948, rail fares had increased 36 per cent over 1940 levels, whereas bus fares had increased only 11 per cent during that same period.[15] As between individual fares within any territorial group, however, there is no

---

[11] Board of Investigation and Research, *The National Traffic Pattern*, Sen. Doc. No. 83, 79th Cong., 1st sess. (Washington, D.C.: U.S. Government Printing Office, 1945), p. 133.

[12] *Ibid.*, p. 134.

[13] *Ibid.*, p. 137.

[14] Transcript, MC–C–550, pp. 4030–36.

[15] *Ibid.*

uniformity whatever in the relationship between rail and bus fares in either period.

In 1953 the average revenue per passenger-mile for Class I rail and motor carriers was:[16]

```
Air coach (scheduled)........................................4.12 cents
Rail parlor car and sleeping car (rail tickets only)..............3.38 cents
Rail coach....................................................2.53 cents
Motor bus....................................................2.04 cents
```

The intercity bus operations on a price basis appear to be in a good position to hold their own in securing a good share of the commercial intercity passenger traffic.

CLASSIFICATION OF PASSENGER OPERATIONS FOR STATISTICAL PURPOSES

The Interstate Commerce Commission classifies motor carriers of passengers into three groups for statistical purposes, in the same manner as that of property carriers. Class I passenger carriers are those with annual gross revenues of $200,000 or more; Class II, from $50,000 to $200,000; and Class III, under $50,000. Under Interstate Commerce Commission regulations, a motor carrier's revenues must average in excess of $100,000 for a period of 3 years before this carrier is placed in Class I. A better perspective of the relative importance in terms of number and revenues of the three classes can be secured by examining some motor-carrier traffic statistics. Revenues for the Class I carriers have been compiled annually since 1938 by the Interstate Commerce Commission. Data have not been available on Class II and Class III carriers except for special surveys made in 1939, 1940, and 1941, although beginning in 1948 annual reports have been required from Class II and Class III motor carriers. To fill this void in statistics, the Bureau of Transport Economics and Statistics of the Interstate Commerce Commission has issued a study that establishes a technique for constructing estimates on the unreported traffic and revenues of the Class II and Class III motor carriers.[17] Relying on the procedures developed in this study, Table 22–2 shows the percentages and revenues of the Class I, Class II, and

---

[16] Interstate Commerce Commission, Bureau of Transport Economics and Statistics, *Monthly Comment on Transportation Statistics* (Washington, D.C., June 14, 1954), p. 12.

[17] Interstate Commerce Commission, Bureau of Transport Economics and Statistics, *Revenues, Ton-Miles, and Passenger-Miles of Class I, II and III Motor Carriers, 1940, 1941, and 1944–1948,* Statement No. 490 (Washington, D.C., January, 1949).

TABLE 22–2

CLASS I, CLASS II, AND CLASS III MOTOR CARRIERS OF PASSENGERS

YEAR	NUMBER OF CARRIERS			REVENUES		
	Class I	Classes II and III	Total	Class I	Classes II and III	Total
1941............	13.62%	86.38%	100%	83.51%	16.49%	100%
1944............	19.35	80.65	100	89.20	10.80	100
1945............	23.10	76.90	100	90.88	9.12	100
1946............	23.66	76.34	100	91.13	8.87	100
1947............	23.19	76.81	100	90.92	9.08	100

Source: Interstate Commerce Commission, *Revenues, Ton-Miles, and Passenger-Miles of Class I, II, and III Motor Carriers, 1940, 1941, and 1944–1948*, Statement No. 490 (Washington, D.C., January, 1949), p. 29.

Class III motor carriers of passengers, by years. In 1947, the preliminary estimate showed that 23.19 per cent of all intercity carriers were Class I and accounted for almost 91 per cent of the total revenue of all intercity carriers of passengers. The remaining 76.81 per cent were Class II and Class III carriers and secured less than 10 per cent of the total revenue. The proportion of the total revenue which the Class I passenger carriers have been receiving has followed an upward trend, and in 1952 the Class I intercity carriers comprised 6 per cent of the carriers and received 62 per cent of the revenue.

In intercity bus operations, the majority of operators render essentially passenger service. However, there are some joint carriers of passengers and property. In 1953 there were nineteen such carriers.

TYPES OF PASSENGER OPERATIONS

There are a number of variations in types of operations. Some bus operations are long-haul trunk-line operations with almost no intrastate or short-distance traffic. Others are trunk-line carriers with extensive branch-line or local or intrastate operations and traffic. Still others are bridge carriers which enjoy volumes of long-distance through traffic, as well as substantial local traffic and revenue. Some provide frequent short-journey, home-and-work service closely resembling mass transportation operations. Others conduct a diffused or radial type of short-distance operations over routes none of which are trunk lines or main traffic arteries, and many of which traverse thinly populated rural areas. For some carriers, the geographical locations of the major cities and the various minor points served have created operating and traffic problems peculiar to those operations.

The differentiation of the (*a*) local, (*b*) city, (*c*) suburban, and (*d*)

intercity carrier is not an easy task. The Interstate Commerce Commission classified passenger carriers as local carriers if their average fare per passenger is 20 cents or less. Furthermore, those carriers that engage exclusively in charter, sight-seeing, or special service are classified as local carriers, regardless of the average revenue per passenger; and revenue and number of passengers so carried are not used in computing the average fare per passenger. Local and suburban passenger service is defined by the Commission as service performed within a municipality and within the trading and suburban residential area adjacent thereto. Intercity service constitutes all services operated beyond the limits defined for local and suburban service, and this interpretation of intercity service as defined by the Commission is the one used in this text.

The periodical *Bus Transportation,* in its annual review issues, uses the following classification:

City. Operates exclusively within the confines of the city proper.

City-Suburban. Operates in city confines and runs some service to suburban areas surrounding the city proper.

Intercity, Short-Haul. Operates between two or more cities and averages a fare under 35 cents.

Intercity, Long-Haul. Operates between two or more cities and averages a fare of 35 cents or more.

In the 3 years prior to World War II, Class I intercity carriers carried a little over 9 per cent of their passengers in local operations, but in the postwar period they have averaged carrying about 20 per cent in local operations. In the postwar period, the average intercity bus trip per carrier has increased and was 57 miles in 1952, but it has not reached the prewar high of 77 miles in 1939.

SERVICE DIFFERENTIATION

With the development of intercity bus transportation, there has been experimentation with various standards and types of service. Sleeper busses, express service, free meals, and free pillows have been some of the innovations used to differentiate service, although the overwhelming portion of service has been and still is what might be termed standard.[18]

---

[18] There was the development of some second-class bus service in which rates were as much as 30 per cent below the standard first-class bus rates; there were no terminal facilities, with the loading at a designated point on a street; and older equipment was used. However, the low cost to the traveler of the first-class or standard bus service has resulted in the elimination of the second-class service. See 51 MCC 87 (1939).

In 1929 sleeper bus service was started between Cleveland and Buffalo, via the Great Lakes Line, with sleeping accommodations for 18 persons and seats for 4 in the smoking compartment. In 1929, Pacific Greyhound Lines started a Los Angeles to San Francisco "nite coach" service; and sleeper service was operated between San Francisco and Medford, Oregon, in 1932. The Columbia Pacific Nite Coach Line inaugurated sleeper service between Los Angeles and San Francisco in 1934; and, by 1939, Santa Fe Trailways had started service between these two points, using equipment with sleeping accommodations for 25 persons. A charge of $1.00 for a single berth and $1.50 for double berth was made on the latter service. Considerable experimental work has been conducted with sleeper busses; but the limited nature of sleeper bus utilization to date would seem to indicate that because of restricted passenger capacity, its revenue-generating possibilities are not sufficiently great to encourage bus-line operators to adopt it. By 1945 there were no busses with sleeping accommodations in operation.

Generally, the longer the trip via bus, the greater the disadvantage in terms of speed as compared to rail coach travel, although new limited access highways will minimize this disadvantage. To offset this, some intercity bus operators have introduced express service on certain heavily traveled routes and have been able thereby to provide express schedules comparable to rail schedules. The use of such express bus service reportedly is from 5 to 18 per cent faster than the ordinary intercity bus service.[19] Southeastern Greyhound Lines started with one schedule between Cincinnati and Jacksonville, Florida, in December, 1938, and this has been expanded to six daily scheduled trips. Extension of this "limited" bus service from Chicago to Jacksonville, and from Detroit to Jacksonville, with connections for limited service on to Miami, has been made possible by exchange agreement with other Greyhound carriers, so that limited busses travel straight through.

Two daily round trips between Jacksonville and New Orleans between Teche Greyhound and Southeastern Greyhound have been established by interchanging equipment with only four stops en route. The limited schedule from Jacksonville to New Orleans is 15 hours and 19 minutes, as compared with the regular schedule of 19 hours and 30 minutes.

Even this de luxe service appears to be further refined. One car-

---

[19] Board of Investigation and Research, *The National Traffic Pattern*, Sen. Doc. 83, 79th Cong., 1st sess. (Washington, D.C.: U.S. Government Printing Office, 1945), p. 124.

rier has limited schedules on which all seats are reserved and a 10 per cent extra fare is charged. The bus has lavatory facilities, free pillows, a buffet, and a steward; whereas express schedules do not have reserved seats, these extra facilities and services are not provided, and no extra fare is charged. The limited service provided is supposed to tap a new segment of passenger travelers, and a survey by Southeastern Greyhound among 2,500 bus passengers who used their limited busses show these patrons highly in favor of the 10 per cent extra fare, as it tends to keep the service exclusive.

There has been an expansion and improvement of through bus schedules involving both express and limited service in line with the trend toward longer trips by bus. It is possible to go from coast to coast via Continental American Trailways without change of bus, and Greyhound has through busses covering trips up to 2,300 miles.

Some intercity bus operators have found that the establishment of a limited service has achieved success during the summer season only. One such company, in view of its experience, has no extra fare and provides limited service by stopping at only a few important terminals, so that the time en route is much less. Another firm providing limited services requires reservations to be made for the seats, provides a pillow for each passenger, charges extra fare, and uses the newest equipment with a schedule that provides very few stops. Neither of these services is of the de luxe limited type, yet each represents a differentiation in service from that found in other forms of passenger transport.

The successful establishment of a nonstop, reserved seat, extra-fare luxury service schedule has been instituted for a route as short as 40 miles. Apparently, relatively short hauls offer exploitation potentialities under the proper circumstances.

The establishment of de luxe limited service is not a new idea. There are numerous instances prior to 1938 of such innovations as extra-fare schedules, installation of lavatory and running water, reserved seats, nonstop service, complimentary refreshments en route, and even guarantee of hotel reservations at the destination point. The increased use of this type of service represents a desire to make attractive the long-haul journey by bus. Some bus operators appear to have been more successful than others in such operations, but public acceptance and patronage of this type of service appears to be great enough to assure the expansion of limited or express through bus service.

RAILROAD PARTICIPATION IN INTERCITY
PASSENGER OPERATIONS

Railroad participation in intercity bus operation has been extensive. The railroads' interest in this field dates back to 1924, at which time the Boston and Maine Railroad substituted motor coach service for rail passenger service between Ashburnham and South Ashburnham, Massachusetts.[20] Although, in other areas of the United States, railroads were giving increasing attention to the use of busses, the early movement appears to have taken place in New England. By 1929 the railroads were convinced that bus operations were no longer of an experimental nature, and approximately 1,450 busses were being operated by railroads at that time.

Busses have been used by the railroads for intercity passenger transportation for a number of reasons. Among these are the supplementing of rail service, replacement of train service on branch lines, provision of feeder service to the railroads, extension of bus service into independent areas, and sight-seeing or a part of all-expense tours.

A study issued in 1953, based on data secured from 131 Class I railroads (those with gross operating income of $1 million or more per year), shows that 57 railroads were furnishing motor passenger service during the test week.[21] Based on the number of vehicle-miles operated, 87 per cent of these bus operations are found to be in the category of motor operations in addition to train service. This service is in addition to rail passenger service between points on the lines of the railroads. Over 60 per cent of this service, based on vehicle-miles, is between main-line points, with most of the remaining service between main-line and branch-line points. This might be interpreted as an attempt on the part of the railroads to augment their share of the total intercity passenger volume of traffic, inasmuch as it has been pointed out that in many instances inability to coordinate train and bus schedules and rates has limited the possibilities of purely substitutional and supplementary services.[22]

There are a variety of means by which the railroads conduct mo-

---

[20] Association of American Railroads, *Highway Motor Transportation* (Washington, D.C., 1945), p. 147.

[21] Interstate Commerce Commission, Bureau of Transport Economics and Statistics, *Motor Operations of Class I Railroads*, Statement No. 5321 (Washington, D.C., June 1953).

[22] Board of Investigation and Research, *op. cit.*, p. 125.

tor-carrier operations. However, the usual procedure is for railroads to conduct motor-carrier passenger operations through subsidiaries. Direct operations are negligible. Where railroads do enter directly into bus service, the runs are very short.

The railroads have furnished an important section of bus passenger service, and it is appropriate to ascertain what percentage of the total for-hire motor passenger operation they do furnish. An estimate based on vehicle-miles indicates that in 1948 motor passenger operations by or for Class I railroads was 25.1 per cent of the independent Class I motor-carrier passenger mileage of the United States.[23] The Class I railroad book value investment in motor carriers of passengers in 1948 was $47,752,596.[24]

There is somewhat of a concentration of railroad-furnished motor-carrier passenger operations on the part of a few railroads. Three railroads—Southern Pacific, Union Pacific, and Santa Fe—account for 58 per cent of the total based on vehicle-miles and 13 of 57 railroads reported 85 per cent of the total.[25]

In the Eastern District two railroads—Boston and Maine and Pennsylvania—accounted for 55 per cent of the total in that district; while in the Western District the Southern Pacific and Union Pacific had 64 per cent of the rail vehicle-miles operated by or for railroads in the Western District.[26]

To passengers, the co-ordination of passenger services by the various modes of transportation appears highly desirable, and certain advantages to the carriers effectuating co-ordination appear to make such a move practical. There is substantial opportunity for improvement in the co-ordination of rail and highway passenger services. The greater number of railway-bus co-ordinated operations have been the result of the substitution of busses for curtailed railway service. About 11 per cent of motor passenger operations by Class I railroads in 1948 represented the partial or entire replacement of train service as a type of service, based on the number of vehicle-miles operated.[27] Railroads in the West have utilized co-ordinated motor-rail services to a greater degree than the important long-distance railroad-controlled bus lines in the East, which continue to operate independently and in competition with the railroad serv-

[23] Interstate Commerce Commission, *Motor Operations of Class I Railroads*, p. 98.

[24] *Ibid.*, p. 8.

[25] *Ibid.*, p. 58.

[26] *Ibid.*, p. 59.

[27] *Ibid.*, p. 3.

ices.[28] The classic example in the West was the rail-bus service provided by the Santa Fe Railroad between Los Angeles and San Francisco. Busses carried the Santa Fe passengers from the bus terminal in San Francisco across the bay to Oakland. From Oakland to Bakersfield, streamlined rail equipment carried the passengers to where direct connections were made by bus for the journey to Los Angeles. The Santa Fe's all-rail distance from Los Angeles to Bakersfield was 282 miles, as compared with the highway distance of only 112 miles. This joint bus-rail co-ordinated service made it possible for the Santa Fe to establish a schedule that compared with the fastest all-rail schedules between these points.

The publication of through fares for joint rail-bus travel has not had widespread application, and it has been suggested that such arrangements be made mandatory. Greater acceptance has been achieved in the West for choice of either bus or rail coach travel when the passenger has purchased a rail ticket. Under the honoring arrangements used by the primary western railroads, railroads such as the Rock Island and Missouri Pacific sell the rail coach service to an individual at the regular railroad fare and then give the passenger the option of using bus service for part of his trip over bus lines which the railroads own or control. Passengers who travel into the West via other railroads are given the same option as the local passengers on the western railroads and bus lines, namely, that of using bus service. It is reported that, because of a lesser amount of ownership or control of bus lines by railroads in the Eastern and Southern territories, there are relatively few cases where optional use of bus service is offered, as compared with that in the West. Although the number of vehicle-miles operated has continued high, some railroads have indicated a desire to drop their passenger services entirely.

The utilization of motor operations by the railroads is an important aspect of our commercial passenger traffic. For some railroads the furnishing of bus service has proved profitable and indispensable to their total operations.

GREYHOUND LINES

As stated earlier, there are many small intercity motor carriers of passengers. However, there are a number of very large organizations, the largest of which is The Greyhound Corporation, consisting of a number of incorporated operating companies. This organization was

---

[28] Board of Investigation and Research, *op. cit.,* p. 126.

operating 96,010 route-miles at the end of 1953 and 6,469 busses in the forty-eight states and Canada. The following is a list of associated Greyhound bus companies in 1954.

Atlantic Greyhound Corportation
  Clinch Valley Transit Company, Inc.
Capitol Greyhound Lines
  Capitol Greyhound Lines of Indiana, Inc.
Central Greyhound Lines, Inc. of New York
Eastern Canadian Greyhound Lines, Ltd.
Indiana Greyhound Lines, Inc.
New England Greyhound Lines, Inc.
Northland Greyhound Lines, Inc.
Pacific Greyhound Lines
Pennsylvania Greyhound Lines of Indiana, Inc.
Pennsylvania Greyhound Lines of Virginia, Inc.

Richmond-Greyhound Lines, Inc.
Southwestern Greyhound Lines, Inc.
Western Canadian Greyhound Lines, Ltd.
The Greyhound Corporation
  Pennsylvania Greyhound Lines
  Dixie Greyhound Lines
  Florida Greyhound Lines
  Great Lakes Greyhound Lines
  Northwest Greyhound Lines
  Overland Greyhound Lines
  Southeastern Greyhound Lines
  Teche Greyhound Lines
  Greyhound Central Revenue Bureau
  (Divisions of The Greyhound Corporation)

There are other companies associated with Greyhound, such as terminal, garage, and building companies, Greyhound Motor & Supply Co. and Greyvan Lines, Inc., a household-goods carrier. The Greyhound Corporation operates these companies in its own right and through subsidiaries, some of which in turn control other subsidiaries.

The Greyhound system had its beginnings prior to 1926, but it was in November of that year that a $10-million holding company was formed to take over some of the interstate bus lines operating in the Middle West. One company that joined the group that became the Greyhound system used a racing Greyhound dog as its trade mark. Patrons of that company referred to it as "the Greyhound line." Although the firm name was entirely different, this was the name adopted by the entire system.

In the early stages of development, Greyhound confined its operations to Illinois, Michigan, Indiana, Wisconsin, Minnesota, Ohio, Kentucky, Missouri, and Texas. The ensuing years, however, saw it spread in all directions through purchases and mergers, so that it soon reached both coasts and had routes from border to border. For example, in 1933, Southwestern Greyhound Lines was organized by merger of Southland Greyhound, a part of Western Greyhound

Lines, and Southwestern Transportation Company, in an attempt to prevent further financial losses by these three companies. The Southland Greyhound Lines had been built up through the purchase and consolidation of about twenty operations, consisting of companies, individual owners, and even individual operators. One route of Southland Greyhound operation was originally owned by twenty-four individuals, and each had a certificate to operate one schedule between San Antonio and Corpus Christi, Texas. Nearly all of the lines that Southland Greyhound purchased, operated, and consolidated were within the state of Texas and were generally from Dallas south and west. Western Greyhound Lines was built up through purchases and consolidations of about twenty-five various companies. Acquisition of control of other bus companies has continued since federal regulation was imposed with the passage of the Motor Carrier Act in 1935. Since that date, it has been necessary to secure the approval of the Interstate Commerce Commission for such mergers.

In the early development of The Greyhound Corporation, several railroads formed partnerships with it in the operation of certain bus lines. As a result, bus operations of some of the larger railroads were merged into the Greyhound system. In this development, these railroads relinquished operating management but retained substantial minority interests in a number of Greyhound subsidiaries. The Greyhound companies in which railroads participated to some extent have accounted, in the past, for over 50 per cent of the route-miles operated. The partnership contributed materially to the growth and expansion of Greyhound, since it reduced rail opposition to its expansion.

However, divided ownership made it necessary for Greyhound to operate the properties as separate corporations. In the interest of greater economy and efficiency, it appeared to Greyhound management that its policy should be directed toward the establishment of operating divisions wholly integrated into a single transportation system. The Greyhound Corporation, over the past few years, has purchased the railroad interests in a number of Greyhound affiliates. Greyhound has applications before the Commission to purchase the interest of the Pennsylvania, Great Northern, and Southern Pacific railroads. If these are granted, the Richmond-Greyhound Lines, which is 49 per cent owned by the Richmond, Fredericksburg and Potomac Railroad, will be the only Greyhound line with a rail interest.

Although each of Greyhound's operating companies functions

independently, there is close correlation of all activities, which makes for passenger conveniences, operating economies, and profitable operations. Ordinarily, Greyhound uses a product of the Truck and Coach Division, General Motors Corporation. Standardization of equipment is very complete throughout the entire system. In intercity service a diesel-powered, 41-passenger bus termed the "Highway Traveler" and the 43-passenger Scenicruiser (see Fig. 22–2) are

Courtesy: The Greyhound Corporation.

FIG. 22–2. The 43-passenger Scenicruiser with elevated rear deck 90 per cent enclosed by picture windows.

the two currently used which are standard. There are cases, however, where a different make of bus has been purchased for a particular short-haul service. Transit-type busses are used on suburban runs.

In an effort to secure an increased amount of the all-expense tour market, Greyhound has developed its subsidiary, Greyhound Highway Tours, Inc., which sells the packaged tour, with hotel accommodations, bus transportation, and sight-seeing services included in the charge. By 1954, seventy-four Greyhound travel bureaus had been established to sell such service, and Greyhound's tour business amounted to $6⅔ million.

A Sleep-Over Service by which long-distance travelers may enjoy sight-seeing in daylight hours while stopping overnight in Greyhound approved hotels was inaugurated on a limited basis in 1954.

Their charter business in 1953 was $9,906,676. The tour and charter business is looked upon as ideal traffic by bus operators, since it uses idle equipment.

In order to improve rest-stop facilities, a subsidiary, Greyhound Post Houses, Inc., was formed to develop restaurants and improved rest rooms. Some stations are owned and operated by this Greyhound subsidiary, whereas others are operated on a franchise basis whereby control of standards set by Greyhound can be maintained. There were 149 Post House units in 1954.

As further evidence of the desire of Greyhound to secure its share of the commercial passenger market, it established sales offices abroad in 1932, although this project, of course, was interrupted by the war. In 1946, Greyhound sales agencies were re-established on a more extensive basis; and, by 1949, there were more than 600 such agencies abroad. Foreign travel agents have been utilized also by Greyhound as its representatives with steamship lines and airline operators. The agent is paid 10 per cent of the purchase price of the foreign transportation order. Thus, Greyhound seeks to sell foreign travelers to the United States before they arrive in the United States.

The trend of the load factor (ratio of passenger-miles to seat-miles) for The Greyhound Corporation as a national system is shown in Figure 22–3. Prior to the war, the average for the entire system was just over 50 per cent. Beginning in 1941, the load factor rose rapidly, reaching a high of almost 80 per cent in 1944. Since the end of the war, the load factor has declined to reach a level by 1949 of about 55 per cent, or about 10 per cent above the prewar average.[29] The load factor for Greyhound has been felt to be higher than the national average for the Class I motor carriers of passengers.[30]

The Greyhound system faces competition from other bus companies as well as other modes of transportation. Southwestern Greyhound, for example, made a check to ascertain how many of the fare points it served were not served by any other bus company.[31] It was found that there are only 304 points that are not served by at least one other bus company. Of this total, 156 points, or more than half, had a population of 100 or less; 117 had a population of over 100, but less than 1,000; 19 had a population between 1,000 and 2,000; 7 had a population between 2,000 and 3,000; and only 5 had a population of over 3,000. Of the 5 points with a population of over 3,000,

---

[29] Exhibits 944 and 947, MC–C–550.

[30] Transcript, MC–C–550, p. 945.

[31] *Ibid.*, pp. 2768–70.

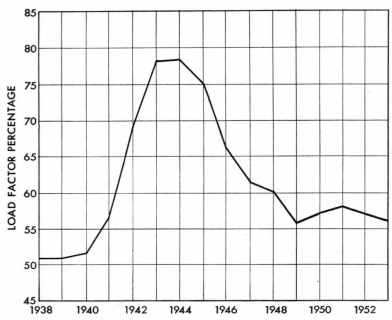

FIG. 22–3.   Load factor. Percentage of occupied seat-miles—Greyhound Lines as a single system.

Source: Brief of intercity motor carriers represented by the National Bus Traffic Association, Inc., filed in MC–C–550, January 16, 1950, and annual reports.

3 were in the 3,000–4,000 group, 1 had a population of 5,021, and the remaining point had a population of 8,297. In spite of the competition faced, The Greyhound Corporation grossed 45 per cent of the total gross revenue received by Class I intercity bus carriers in 1953.

The Greyhound Corporation has been characterized by a very progressive attitude. Its system has shown rapid growth and profitable operations and doubtless will continue to merit traveler acceptance and patronage.

TRANSCONTINENTAL BUS SYSTEM, INC.

Transcontinental Bus System, Inc., is the second largest operator in the United States and grossed 7.5 per cent of the revenue for Class I bus operators in 1953.[32] Transcontinental is a newcomer to the field, having been organized in 1947, with operations starting in March, 1948. It purchased the operating rights and property of the Dixie Coach Corporation and the passenger-carrier operations of the

---

[32] *Wall Street Journal,* May 11, 1954, p. 16.

Santa Fe Trail Transportation Company, as well as acquiring control of the Continental Bus System, Inc.[33] It has acquired control of other carriers, including the West Coast Bus Lines, Ltd., doing business as the Continental Pacific Trailways, and the Continental Southern Lines, Inc.

The name, Continental Trailways, is the trade name used by the companies operating under the corporate parent company known as Transcontinental Bus System, and its operations are mainly in the southern half of the United States. Its principal stockholders are the individuals who controlled the carriers that went into the Transcon-

Courtesy: Continental Trailways.

FIG. 22–4. Typical equipment used by Transcontinental Bus System. The New York Port Authority Bus Terminal in the background is the largest municipal bus terminal.

tinental Bus System. In 1953, American Buslines, Inc., a transcontinental operator from New York to San Francisco by way of Chicago and St. Louis which commenced operations in September, 1935, under the name of All American Bus Lines, Inc., was purchased by the Transcontinental Bus System. This added 14,600 route-miles to bring the T.B.S. total to 42,255. This system has a modern, up-to-date fleet (see Fig. 22–4) and has gained wide traveler acceptance.

---

[33] *Transcontinental Bus System, Inc.—Control—Continental*, 50 MCC 193 (1947); *Transcontinental Bus System, Inc.—Control—Continental*, 50 MCC 305 (1948).

TRAILWAYS BUS SYSTEM

The Trailways Bus System was organized in 1936 with five member companies as a nonprofit association to co-ordinate schedules and services of independently owned operations into a nation-wide bus system. The management of the association rests with the Board of Directors of twelve, which are elected, and with other committees, such as Traffic and Advertising, Schedule, Finance, Safety, Promotion, Business, By-Laws, Interline Auditing, Purchasing, Uniform Paint and Equipment, which implement top policy action. Four meetings a year are held, and at the annual meeting financial requirements are decided upon and assessments levied on the members to meet this budget.

By 1955, forty-two member companies operating 73,368 route-miles in forty-four states were functioning under the bylaws of the association. The companies comprising the system are as follows:

Arkansas Motor Coaches, Ltd., Inc.
Atlantic Stages, Inc.
Boston and Maine Transportation Co.
Brooks Bus Line
Capital Motor Lines
Capitol Bus Company
Carolina Coach Company
Carolina Scenic Stages
Colonial Trailways
Consolidated Bus Lines
Continental Bus System, Inc.
Continental American
Continental Central
Continental Crescent, Inc.
Continental Dixie
Continental Pacific
Continental Panhandle
Continental Rocky Mountain
Continental Southern
Continental Tennessee
Continental Western
Dahlonega-Atlanta Stages
De Luxe Motor Stages, Inc.
Denver–Colorado Springs–Pueblo Motor Way, Inc.
Evergreen Trailways
Frisco Transportation Company
Georgia-Florida Stages
Indianapolis and Southeastern Stages, Inc.
Jacksonville Bus Company
Maine Central Transportation Company
Modern Coach Corporation
Pacific Trailways
Queen City Coach Company
Safeway Trails, Inc.
Service Coach Line, Inc.
Smoky Mountain Stages, Inc.
Southern Stages, Inc.
Tamiami Trail Tours, Inc.
Trailways Motor Tours of Colorado Springs
Union Bus Lines, Inc.
Valley Transit Lines, Inc.
Virginia Stage Lines, Inc.

More than 3,000 pieces of equipment were licensed in 1954.[34] The standard paint design, consisting of cream and crimson colors, is well

---

[34] "National Trailways—an 18 Year Success Story," *Bus Transportation* (September, 1954), p. 40.

recognized in most parts of the United States today, although the area east of Chicago and north of the Mason-Dixon Line, which has high passenger traffic potential, is served to a limited degree by the Trailways system. The Trailways organization is relatively strong in the southeastern section of the United States, as well as along the Atlantic seaboard extending into New England. This system has grown rapidly and today offers services that are comparable with those of the other progressive lines.

INDEPENDENTS

Most of the larger intercity motor bus operators are associated in one way or another with a transcontinental system. Representative of the independent intercity bus operators (those not affiliated with the Greyhound or Trailways systems) is the Jefferson Transportation Company, with headquarters in Minneapolis, Minnesota. This is a north-south operator with its northern terminus in the twin cities of Minneapolis and St. Paul, where its principal connecting carrier is the Northland Greyhound Lines, and its southern terminus in Kansas City, Missouri, where it serves as an independent carrier to a number of lines, such as the Southwestern Greyhound Lines, the Burlington Transportation Company, the Missouri Pacific Transportation Company, and the Crown Coach Company. As an "independent" operator, this company has endeavored always to treat other carriers impartially in its exchange of business, whether or not the latter were themselves competitive to the Jefferson Transportation Company.

The Jefferson Transportation Company in 1954 was operating over 1,566 route-miles or about the same amount, except for slight modifications, as it has been for the past 25 years. The adaptability of the management of this company may be demonstrated by its purchase, in the late 1920's and early 1930's, of several passenger automobiles which were used on the dirt road detours while portions of the main highway were being improved. The regular bus would travel to the detour; there the passengers would be transferred to the four or five automobiles to continue their way through and connect at the end of the detour with a regular bus. Possessing fifty-five busses in 1953 as compared to a prewar size of thirty-five units, it operated 4,516,848 bus-miles in 1953 and carried 978,445 passengers.

The average passenger-miles per passenger were 79.4 miles in 1953, and the average revenue per passenger was $1.73. It is of interest to note that, in addition to the regular schedule of six busses each way on the 99-mile run between Minneapolis and Rochester, Minnesota, nonstop scheduled limousine passenger service with all seats reserved is operated on four round trips per day. The latter service

Courtesy: Jefferson Lines.

FIG. 22–5. Equipment typical of that used by an independent bus operator.

costs about 4 cents per mile one way and is ultra service in every respect.

Operators such as the Jefferson Transportation Company are typical of the many independent companies which have rendered excellent service with excellent equipment (See Fig. 22–5) for a great many years to the communities which they have since become certificated to serve.

TERMINALS

Terminal facilities provided by bus operators for passengers have improved materially during the past years, yet there appears to be room for further improvement in supplying better accommodations through the construction of modern terminals. The bus terminal movement is said to have received its impetus in the West, where the need for adequate terminals was recognized and action taken to provide such facilities. In 1926, modern bus terminals were provided by Pickwick Stages, Inc., of California, which, at that time, operated the largest route under one ownership in the United States. Recognition of the importance of bus terminals to their operations was not lacking on the part of many early bus managements; rather, there was a reluctance to commit themselves financially during a formative stage when one of the keys to success was low operating cost. It was felt that the inadequacies of the so-called "terminals" and the inconveniences to the passengers were more than offset by the low fare.

The advantage of modern bus terminals is based in part on experience to date which shows that bus lines which offer terminal facilities to passengers have less fluctuation in their traffic because of seasonal and weather conditions. It is becoming increasingly evident that terminals can generate not only passenger-related revenue but nonpassenger-related revenue as well. There are several methods whereby a company can provide its own terminal. One is for the motor carrier itself to purchase and build the terminal property. Another is to lease the property and construct the building. Another method is to form a terminal company.[35]

In hundreds of small communities, an intercity bus operator will arrange with a local merchant, such as a drugstore, filling station, beauty shop, or cafe, to act as agent on behalf of the bus company in selling tickets; the merchant's store, in effect, provides the terminal. Under such an arrangement, the agent typically receives a commission of 10 per cent on the one-way or round-trip tickets, 5 per cent on commuter tickets, and 5 per cent of any charter sales he makes.

In the larger communities, facilities are commonly provided by the bus companies, individually or collectively. For the United States as a whole, Class I intercity terminal expenses were 17.76 per cent of total expenses.[36] In June, 1943, the Greyhound Lines operated 359 company-owned and operated stations, with an additional 13 terminal companies which were operated jointly by two or more operating companies, which included Greyhound and non-Greyhound companies.[37] Since 1946 Greyhound has made substantial expenditures for new terminals, including a $10 million one in Chicago which was opened in 1953. Table 22-3 shows that, in 1947, 120 Class I intercity passenger carriers, which accounted for 89 per cent of the revenues of Class I passenger carriers, had a total of 7,242 carrier stations, with 74 per cent of their revenue coming from these sta-

---

[35] Transcript, MC–C–550, pp. 3514–15.

[36] *Ibid.*, p. 3670.

[37] 6 CAB 1 (1944), p. 39.

tions; and that there were 13,291 agency offices in commercial establishments, providing 21 per cent of the revenue.[38] The motor bus industry either maintains a passenger station or a ticket agency in virtually every town of 1,000 or more. As a rule, it is not economical for a carrier to operate a passenger station in towns of less than 5,000 population. However, it is sales volume and not population which determines the feasibility of a carrier's station.

TABLE 22–3

PERCENTAGE OF PASSENGERS AND REVENUES, BY TYPE OF SALES AGENCIES, 1947

Item	United States	New England	North-east	South-east	South Central	North Central	West
Number of agencies:							
Carrier stations...........	7,242	282	2,228	1,637	1,268	627	1,200
Commercial establishments..	13,291	529	3,198	2,635	2,812	2,357	1,760
Total agencies............	20,533	811	5,426	4,272	4,080	2,984	2,960
Percentage of passengers ticketed:							
Carrier stations...........	59	53	60	60	51	58	63
Commercial establishments..	27	23	25	24	44	29	29
Cash fares...............	14	24	15	16	5	13	9
Percentage of ticket revenue:							
Carrier stations...........	74	64	77	75	63	75	76
Commercial establishments..	21	24	17	19	36	21	21
Cash fares...............	5	12	6	7	2	4	3

Source: Exhibit 923, Schedule 2, MC–C–550.

Tickets sold at commercial establishments are for about half the distance of those tickets sold at the carrier stations.[39] Travel bureaus which sell bus tickets, as well as tickets for other transportation companies, sell essentially long-distance tickets, the average journey of tickets sold in this manner being greater than that of any other type of agency.[40] The bus lines do not concentrate only upon the major sources of traffic, although their major traffic volume originates at or is destined to the major metropolitan centers. The nation-wide traffic test conducted by 120 Class I intercity carriers in MC–C–550 reveals that, during the typical test week, 59 per cent of the passengers and 74 per cent of the passenger revenue originated at metropolitan centers of sufficient importance to warrant maintaining terminals. Furthermore, during the test period, 27 per cent of the

---

[38] "The I.C.C. Fare Case," Bus Transportation, Vol. XXVII, No. 12 (1949), p. 56.
[39] Transcript, MC–C–550, p. 3724.
[40] Ibid.

passengers and 21 per cent of the passenger revenue originated at points whose size was not sufficient to warrant large terminals but was large enough to permit the operation of commission agencies; whereas 14 per cent of the passengers and 5 per cent of the passenger revenue originated at rural roadside pickup points.[41]

Figure 22–6 shows graphically the proportion of total passengers represented by the various types of sales agencies. The classification "operated by another carrier" includes railroad stations and other bus stations. Other bus stations as referred to in this figure are large commission agencies which are actually bus terminals. The difference

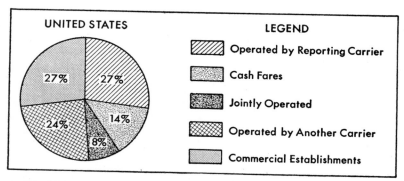

FIG. 22–6. Percentage of total passengers represented by various types of sales agencies, 1947.
Source: Exhibit 932, MC–C–550.

between them and commercial establishments is that, insofar as commercial establishments are concerned, at those particular places the sale of bus tickets is incidental to another type of business. Figure 22–6 shows the relatively high percentage of commercial establishment agencies in the industry. The average for the United States as a whole is 27 per cent, and certainly the maintenance of the large number of these commercial establishments as bus ticket agencies is very desirable from the public standpoint. The average ticket sales of these commercial establishments is $12 per day.[42]

The development of rest stops and meal-stop facilities has presented one of the major problems of intercity motor bus operations. Meal stops originally were governed to some degree by the drivers. Whoever gave the drivers free meals received the business from them when they came through the town. In metropolitan centers, ade-

---

[41] *Ibid.*
[42] *Ibid.*, pp. 3722–23.

quate rest-stop facilities are arranged; but in the smaller communities, it is customary to make an arrangement with the owner of a highway restaurant to take care of this phase of the bus industry's service. Larger bus operators have adopted a program of building and operating meal-stop and rest-stop facilities at key points.

When a terminal is constructed by an organization such as Greyhound and then other bus companies utilize that terminal, one method by which the latter contribute their share to the expenses of the terminal is by turning over an amount equal to 15 per cent of their ticket sales at that terminal. If the total terminal expense is less, then the percentage that the tenant lines will pay under such an arrangement may be 13½ per cent. Usually, noncompeting connecting carriers enter into an agreement with Greyhound for the use of the latter's terminals. However, such a generalization is subject to qualification. A competitor will not find the Greyhound-owned terminal available for use. However, that same terminal may be used by a bus line which is competitive over certain segments of Greyhound routes. The Department of Justice has filed action in the courts against carriers alleging terminal control has been used to restrain competition.

The union bus terminal possesses many advantages to the passenger, especially where he finds it necessary to change to another line. The general organization for this type of terminal is that each of the companies that expect to utilize it will contribute financial aid for its construction. Expenses for running the terminal are on an agreed prorated basis. The New York Port Authority Bus Terminal is the largest municipally owned union bus terminal.

QUESTIONS AND PROBLEMS

1. "The origin of intercity bus operation was humble." Explain this statement. Cite an example of the difficulties encountered in starting an intercity bus business.

2. "The members of the intercity bus industry are in general small business organizations, with a few outstanding exceptions." Explain. What is the ownership distribution of Class I intercity motor carriers of passengers?

3. Enumerate the advantages of intercity bus transportation. Of what importance is schedule frequency to the public? To the carrier?

4. What are the types of motor passenger operations? How does the Interstate Commerce Commission classify motor passenger carriers? How does the magazine *Bus Transportation* classify motor passenger carriers?

5. Trace the development of railroad participation in intercity bus operation. What reasons have prompted railroads to use busses?

6. How does railroad participation in intercity bus passenger operations compare with its participation in intercity truck operations? What reasons can you give for this difference?

7. What would account for "a concentration of railroad-furnished motor-carrier passenger operations on the part of a few railroads"?

8. List the reasons for or against co-ordination of passenger services by the various modes of transportation.

9. Describe the Greyhound organization. What is Greyhound Highway Tours, Inc.? Cite examples of what you would consider progressive developments by the Greyhound Corporation.

10. Summarize the facts concerning the following: (*a*) Transcontinental Bus System, Inc.; (*b*) American Buslines, Inc.; and (*c*) Jefferson Transportation Company.

11. What is the Trailways Bus System? In what areas is it particularly strong? What advantages does membership in such a system possess?

12. What are the salient facts regarding early bus terminal development?

13. "It is sales volume and not population which determines the feasibility of a carrier's station." Comment.

14. What are the usual arrangements for the joint use of a bus terminal? Are union bus terminals desirable from the standpoint of the public?

15. What is service differentiation? Why does it exist? Trace the development of the intercity sleeper bus.

16. Define the following: "limited" schedules; express schedules.

23. INTERCITY PASSENGER OPERATIONS
(Continued)

▬▬

IN MOST states, legislation affecting intercity bus operators was initiated for safety purposes. Later, state statutes were enacted for the economic regulation of fares, tariff publications, and certificates of public convenience and necessity. By 1928, forty-three states and the District of Columbia regulated the transportation of passengers by motor vehicle, with all states but Delaware having some regulatory control over transportation of passengers by 1932.[1]

Phases of the pre-federal regulation period have been traced in Chapter 18, on regulation of property carriers, and are equally applicable to passenger carriers. It is worth noting that intercity bus operators are said to have asked for federal regulation for several years prior to 1935. The Motor Carrier Act of 1935 became effective in 1935, and carriers subject to the act are regulated by the Interstate Commerce Commission. The regulation prescribed by this act of interstate motor common carriers of passengers is substantially the same as that prescribed for interstate motor common carriers of property.

FEDERAL REGULATION

Since 1935, a common carrier of passengers engaging in interstate commerce has been regulated as follows: (a) it must secure a certificate of public convenience and necessity to operate; (b) a uniform system of accounts is prescribed for Class I carriers; (c) rates and fares must be reasonable and nondiscriminatory, with publication of rates required; (d) the Interstate Commerce Commission can prescribe

---

[1] *Motor Bus and Motor Truck Operation,* 140 ICC 685 (1928).

maximum and minimum rates and, in addition, possesses rate-suspension power; and (*e*) consolidations and mergers are subject to approval by the Commission. The foregoing is a partial but representative list of the Interstate Commerce Commission's regulatory powers over interstate motor carriers of passengers. In addition, it has regulatory safety control power since maximum hours of service are set and qualifications of employees are prescribed, as well as other matters relating to safety established by the Commission. Most bus common carriers render a regular-route service between fixed termini, about 95 per cent of the service being of this type. In 1955 there were 1382 common carriers.

The permission for an intercity bus common carrier to carry express and newspapers must be secured by specific grant from the Interstate Commerce Commission, whereas mail may be carried without such specific authorization. Baggage is a part of all passenger operations, and a common weight allowed on an adult ticket is 100 pounds.

A motor carrier of passengers can be authorized to transport baggage in a separate vehicle, but newspapers or express must be transported in the same vehicle as the passengers. However, the transportation of baggage in the separate vehicle is not authorized unless there is a need shown for such service.[2]

There is not the requirement of proving a need for the service as far as baggage is concerned, but this is necessary for the movement of newspapers in conjunction with passenger service.

The financial responsibility of common and contract carriers must be established to the satisfaction of the Interstate Commerce Commission through the filing of adequate insurance policies to cover liability or by acting as self-insurers. The Interstate Commerce Commission minimum requirement for motor passenger carriers for bodily injury and property damage is $10,000 limit for bodily injuries to or death of one person and $5,000 limit for loss or damage in any one accident to property of others. The limit for bodily injuries to or death of all persons injured or killed in any one accident varies from $30,000 for passenger equipment with seating capacity for seven or less passengers to $100,000 for equipment with seating capacity for thirty-one passengers or more.

Reasonable through rates are to be established with other common carriers by the bus common carriers. Section 216 (a) requires car-

---

[2] *Kirk Common Carrier Application,* 24 MCC 431 (1940).

riers to establish reasonable through routes. However, the rate may be a joint one or it may be a combination of locals if the carriers agree. Through routes and joint rates which have been established by an order of the Commission cannot be canceled without securing the permission of the Commission. If such routes and rates have been established voluntarily, they may be canceled on 30 days' notice or less if short notice permission is secured, subject to suspension.[3]

Contract carriers of passengers are issued permits for interstate bus operation by the Commission. However, the number of such carriers is so small as to be unimportant. During World War II, some industrial plants, because of the stringent gasoline and tire rationing problems applicable to motor vehicles, used busses on a contract or private basis in order to insure an adequate labor force. However, this was an emergency expedient. By 1955, seventeen permits had been issued under Section 209. Passenger brokers are required to have licenses from the Commission, as is the case for property brokers.

The degree of maturity possessed by intercity bus operations by 1935 largely accounts for the relative freedom from problems which often accompanies the imposition of regulation. No difficulties were encountered in determining the legal status of operations, as there were practically no contract or private operations; and determination of the relationship of federal to state authority over bus operations presented no particular problem. Tariffs for passenger operations are relatively simple, and the industry was well prepared to file them with the Commission. Accounting and statistical requirements incident to federal regulation occasioned little trouble, largely because of the experience of the passenger carriers in reporting to the states. The securing of compliance with the regulation has called forth little in the way of educational work on the part of the Commission.

There has been a relatively greater degree of consolidation and mergers among Class I bus operations than there has been among regulated property-carrier operations. Intercity bus transportation possesses attributes which, in the absence of regulatory checks, tend toward monopolistic operations, and the industry presently might be characterized as an oligopoly. The Commmission has fostered competition by authorizing additional long-haul motor carriers, such as Transcontinental Bus System, and by granting bridge-route

---

[3]Administrative Rule No. 8, August 19, 1936.

extensions, particularly to member carriers of the Trailways system, in order to provide competition on through routes. Although The Greyhound Corporation has been authorized to acquire numerous carriers which often has lessened competition, the Commission in many such cases has felt that the improved service to the public justified the grant. In following a policy of regulated competition, the question has been raised whether there is a need for two large nation-wide bus systems, which fact appears to result in unwarranted duplication of service and facilities.[4]

PASSENGER-CARRIER EXEMPTIONS TO ECONOMIC REGULATION

The Motor Carrier Act, now Part II of the Interstate Commerce Act, provides certain exemptions for passenger operation. School busses, taxicabs, motor vehicles owned or operated by hotels exclusively to transport hotel patrons between hotels and local common-carrier stations, motor vehicles for exclusive use in the transportation of persons when incidental to transportation by aircraft, and transportation of persons in national parks or monuments by motor vehicles under the control of the Secretary of the Interior are carriers exempt from the Motor Carrier Act. Motor vehicles controlled and operated by a co-operative association, as defined in the Agricultural Marketing Act, are also exempt.

Two conditional exemptions are the transportation of passengers wholly within a municipality or between contiguous municipalities or within a zone adjacent to and commercially a part of any such municipality; and secondly, the casual, occasional, or reciprocal transportation of passengers by motor vehicle.

Commission rulings which serve as guides in the determination of the scope of the exemptions are briefly cited.

Motor vehicles owned or operated by hotels used exclusively to transport hotel patrons are exempt. At the time that the act was passed, it was common practice for hotels to furnish local transportation between the hotel and local common-carrier stations. Free transportation was used as a means of securing business for hotels during the depression of the 1930's. Most of such transportation has been discontinued. The Commission pointed out in an early case that this exemption applied for local transportation only.[5]

---

[4] Burton B. Crandall, *The Growth of the Intercity Bus Industry* (Syracuse, N.Y., Syracuse University, 1954), pp. 264–65.

[5] *Shores and Brown Common Carrier Application*, 26 MCC 243 (1940).

The transportation of persons in national parks or monuments by motor vehicles under the control of the Secretary of the Interior is exempt under the act. Where there were bus operations limited to passengers traveling between the railheads and Yellowstone Park, although much of the operation was outside the Park, it was held to be within the exemption.[6]

Although a similar holding was made as to Yosemite Park, a 173-mile operation from the Park to the Lake Tahoe resort area, which was not a railhead but an additional point of scenic interest, was held to be not within the exemption.[7] This exemption applies only to carriers moving passengers.

The *school bus exemption* applies to motor vehicles employed solely in transporting school children and teachers to and from school. "Solely" is interpreted by the Commission to mean "employed at the time solely," so that at other times it is possible for the vehicles to be used in nonexempt transportation without affecting the exemption. When there are official functions of the school sponsored and paid for by the school, such as athletic games or field trips, the exemption applies. In 1954 there were over 130,000 school busses as compared to about 23,780 busses operated by regulated intercity bus operators.

When a summer sight-seeing tour is made in a bus owned and operated by a public school or bona fide parochial or private school, such operation if actually an occasional one is exempt under Section 203 (b) (9). However, if the bus is owned by a person operating during the school year under contract with the school, neither the casual or occasional nor the school children exemption applies.[8]

Taxicab operations which are exempted by Section 203 (b) (2) are essentially local operations conducted within a municipality and its environs. What constitutes the mileage limitation within which taxicabs must operate in order to be within the exemption has not been prescribed, but where the transportation is to points beyond 25 miles from a city, it is not usually considered to be local in nature. When transportation was performed in taxicabs and sight-seeing limousines which sometimes carried two or more groups together, the vehicles having a capacity of not more than six passengers, this was held to be a bona fide taxicab service where it extended within the Washington, D.C. commercial zone to points as far distant as 18 miles.[9]

[6] *Yellowstone Park Lines, Inc., Common Carrier Application,* 7 MCC 195 (1938).

[7] *Yosemite Park & Curry Co. Common Carrier Application,* 49 MCC 522 (1949).

[8] Administrative Rule No. 80, May 23, 1939.

[9] *Motor Carrier Operations, Washington, D.C., Mt. Vernon, Va.,* 51 MCC 197 (1949).

The service provided by taxicabs which were used to transport athletic teams in several states was held by the Commission to be a chartered party service and was not within the exemption.[10]

The *casual, occasional, or reciprocal exemption* does not apply when passenger travel is arranged by a travel bureau for compensation.[11]

The transportation by a worker of one or more of his fellow workers to and from work on a share-the-expense basis where the transportation is over routes and in vehicles which would be used if the worker traveled alone falls within this exemption.

In interpreting the exemption of *transportation incidental to transportation by aircraft,* the Commission has indicated that distance is not the controlling factor but rather the essential character of the traffic. Another consideration is whether the motor operations between a city and an airport are designed for the use of customers of the airlines which serve that city.[12]

When weather conditions caused passenger flights to be diverted to an alternate airport and a motor carrier moved the passengers in what would ordinarily be construed as line-haul transportation at the airline's expense, it was held to be within the exemption. This was true even though the distance was approximately 90 miles between Chicago and Milwaukee because such operations were sporadic, irregular, and emergency in nature, serving as a substitute for air operations and not as a complement thereto.[13]

The motor carriers in the exemption categories, although not subject to economic regulation, are subject to safety regulation by the Commission.

SPECIAL OR CHARTER PARTY SERVICE

Charter service involves the transportation of groups, such as athletic teams, bands, lodges, or other similar groups, which have been assembled by someone other than the carrier who collectively contracts for the exclusive use of certain equipment for the duration of a particular trip or tour to transport charter parties to any point. All regular-route operators have charter authority, whereas a few carriers have certificates for only charter or special service. Charter rates are at tariff rates per bus-mile.

---

[10] *Peters Common Carrier Application,* 23 MCC 611 (1940).

[11] *Exemption of Casual, Occasional or Reciprocal Transp.,* 33 MCC 69 (1942).

[12] *Picknelly Extension of Operation—Bradley Field,* 47 MCC 401 (1947).

[13] *Graff Common Carrier Application,* 48 MCC 310 (1948).

Special service generally contemplates that such service will be rendered on week ends, holidays, or other special occasions within defined territorial limits to a number of passengers which the carrier itself has assembled into a travel group through its own sales activity. Each passenger has a ticket covering a particular trip or tour which has been arranged by the carrier.[14] Passengers are assessed the tariff fares per individual passenger, whether special tour movement rates or the standard fare for special party service.

Irregular routes may be granted to conduct a special or charter party operation, even though the carrier has no regular-route operation.[15] In an early case, it was held that service to family groups which were transported in sedan-type vehicles in a nonscheduled door-to-door service over irregular routes between New York City and certain mountain resorts was a form of special operation.[16]

In one case, there was scheduled daily service from the railhead to Carlsbad Caverns, New Mexico, over the same highway, which was the only highway available. This was held to be special operations. The reasoning was that inasmuch as the service was one devoted to sight-seeing and pleasure tours, the frequency and regularity which were due to the large volume of business did not convert the operation into a regular route.[17]

Passenger brokers, of which there were 114 in 1955, may use the services of carriers which hold charter authority, either (1) specific authority or (2) incidental authority. Those carriers that have received certificates specifically authorizing transportation of charter parties of irregular routes within designated territories possess specific authority. Incidental authority is possessed by those motor carriers which hold certificates authorizing some regular-route operations which by reason of such regular-route rights hold the incidental right under Section 208 (c) of the act to transport charter parties from points in the territories served by the regular routes to any point in the United States, for the transportation of groups of persons assembled and dealt with by the broker on an individual basis subject to the following conditions: (1) the transportation is a conducted all-expense tour; (2) that a written contract is entered into between the broker and each tour patron wherein the latter agrees or designates the broker as agent of the tour group for the purpose of arranging transportation; (3) that the contract for transportation ar-

14 *Fordham Bus Corp. Common Carrier Application,* 29 MCC 293 (1941).

15 *Regulations, Special or Chartered Party Service,* 29 MCC 25, 30 (1941).

16 *Nudelman Common Carrier Application,* 22 MCC 275 (1940).

17 *Resler* v. *Hunter Clarkson, Inc.,* 41 MCC 665 (1943).

ranged by the broker, as agent, with the carrier shall be one between the tour group and the carrier; (4) the carrier is to be paid its full published charter fares; and (5) the broker arranging transportation as agent for a tour group shall not receive any commission from the carrier.[18]

If these conditions are not met, the passenger broker in dealing with patrons on an individual basis cannot use the services of a charter carrier and must use either regular-route service or the services of a carrier with special authority. Likewise, these conditions would not apply where a broker acts as an intermediary between a charter carrier and a spokesman for a club or similar group who wishes to charter a vehicle in his own name for his group.

The regulations which have been established to govern the transportation of special or charter parties, authorized under Section 208 (c), have been prescribed by the Commission. They define special or charter parties, specify the origin and destination territory, specify a tariff provision regarding deadhead mileage and separate transportation rates and charges in connection with all-expense tours, limit the frequency of operation so that it will not amount to a regular service, prohibit the sale of individual tickets, and prohibit seasonal carriers from operating other than seasonal operations.[19]

One of the rules in reference to origin territory specifies that the charter service can be rendered ". . . at any point or points within the territory served by its regular route or routes." This has been rather liberally interpreted. For example, a point 23 miles from the carrier's nearest regular route was held to be within the territory served by its regular route.[20]

A number of problems have arisen, especially since 1949, regarding charter or special party carriers whose operations are in competition with regular-route intercity bus carriers. These matters have resulted in litigation.[21]

STATE RESTRICTIONS ON INTERCITY BUS OPERATIONS

State limitations were imposed by Maine and Massachusetts in 1913 through a prescribed maximum for gross weight of vehicle, as

---

[18] *Tauck Tours, Inc., Extension—New York, N.Y.,* 54 MCC 291 (1952).

[19] *Regulations, Special or Chartered Party Service,* 29 MCC 25, 47 (1941); and *Regulations, Special or Chartered Party Service,* 48 MCC 521 (1948).

[20] *Indiana Motor Bus Co. Extension—Charter Parties,* 41 MCC 577 (1942).

[21] See brief of *National Bus Traffic Association, Inc. and Hudson Transit Lines, Inc. v. United States of America and the Interstate Commerce Commission,* filed in U.S. District Court, District of New Jersey, February 20, 1954.

TABLE 23-1

RESTRICTIONS OF COMMON CARRIER MOTOR BUSSES AS FIXED BY STATE LAW

	Maximum Width (In.)	Maximum Height (Ft. In.)	Maximum Length (Ft.)	Maximum Gross Weight Four Wheels Pneumatic Tires	Maximum Speed State Roads
Alabama................	96	12–6	40	..... (a)	NS
Arizona................	96	13–6	40	..... (b)	..... (c)
Arkansas...............	96	12–6	40 (d)	..... (b)	55
California..............	96	13–6	40 (d)	..... (b)	55
Colorado...............	96	12–6	40	30,000	60
Connecticut............	102	12–6	45	32,000	..... (e)
Delaware...............	96	12–6	42	30,000 (f)	50 (g)
District of Columbia....	96	12–6	35 (h)	..... (b)	25–30
Florida................	96	12–6	40	24,000 (i)	50–60 (j)
Georgia................	96	13–6	40	..... (k)	55
Idaho..................	96	14–0	40 (l)	..... (b)	55–60 (m)
Illinois................	96	13–6	42	36,000	45
Indiana................	96	12–6	40	36,000	55
Iowa...................	96	12–6	40 (d)	..... (n)	50–55 (o)
Kansas.................	96	12–6	40 (p)	..... (q)	60
Kentucky...............	96	NS	NS	NS	50–60 (j)
Louisiana..............	96	12–6	40 (d)	..... (r)	55
Maine..................	96	12–6	45	32,000	45
Maryland...............	96	12–6	55	..... (s)	50 (g)
Massachusetts..........	96	NS	40 (d)	36,000	40
Michigan...............	96	12–6	40	..... (t)	40–50 (u)
Minnesota..............	96	12–6	40	..... (v)	50–60 (j)
Mississippi.............	96	12–6	40 (d)	..... (b)	55
Missouri...............	96	12–6	40	..... (b)	50
Montana...............	96	13–6	40	..... (b)	NS
Nebraska...............	96	12–6	40 (d)	..... (b)	50–60 (j)
Nevada................	96	NS	NS	..... (b)	NS
New Hampshire.........	96	13–6	40 (w)	30,000	50
New Jersey.............	96	13–6	35 (x)	30,000	50
New Mexico............	96 (y)	12–6	40	..... (a)	..... (z)
New York..............	96 (aa)	13–0	40 (d)	36,000	50
North Carolina........	96	12–6	40 (d)	..... (ab)	55
North Dakota..........	96	12–6	40 (ac)	..... (a)	50–60 (ad)
Ohio...................	96	12–6	40 (d)	..... (ae)	50
Oklahoma..............	96	13–6	45	..... (b)	55
Oregon................	96	12–6	35	..... (b)	55
Pennsylvania...........	96	12–6	40 (af)	..... (ag)	50
Rhode Island..........	102	12–6	40	32,000	..... (ah)
South Carolina........	96	12–6	40 (d)	..... (b)	55
South Dakota..........	96	13–0	40 (d)	..... (b)	50–60 (j)
Tennessee..............	NS	NS	40	42,000	NS
Texas..................	96	13–6	40	..... (ai)	55
Utah..................	96	14–0	45	..... (b)	50–60 (j)
Vermont...............	96	12–6	50	30,000	45
Virginia...............	96	12–6	40	..... (aj)	55
Washington............	96	12–6	40 (ak)	..... (b)	50
West Virginia..........	96	12–6	40 (d)	..... (b)	55
Wisconsin..............	96	12–6	40	..... (b)	55–65 (al)
Wyoming..............	96	12–6	40	..... (am)	60

(a) Weight equals 650 (L plus 40) where L (distance in feet between first and last axles of a vehicle) is less than 18 feet; 700 (L plus 40) where distance between axles is 18 feet or over. (b) Weight dependent on distance in feet between first and last axles. (c) Reasonable and prudent under existing conditions but not in excess of 45 m.p.h. during nighttime on other than state highways and 50 m.p.h. during daytime on other than state highways and during nighttime on state highways. (d) Buses in excess of 35 feet must have not less than 3 axles. (e) As indicated by traffic signs. (f) Limitation applies to 2-axle vehicle equipped with pneumatic tires and power brake on each rear hub. (g) 55 m.p.h. on dual lane highways. (h) Director of Traffic permits operation of 40 foot buses. (i) 30,000 lbs. when equipped with air brakes and dual rear wheels with pneumatic tires. (j) Nighttime, 50 m.p.h.; daytime, 60 m.p.h. (k) Weight equals 700 (L plus 40); L equals distance in feet between first and last axles. (l) 3-axle, 40 foot buses may be operated upon such highways as may be designated by Idaho Board of Highway Directors. (m) Nighttime, 55 m.p.h.; daytime, 60 m.p.h. (n) 32,000 to 65,478 lbs. according to axle spacing and subject to axle weight limitation of 18,000 lbs. (o) Nighttime, 50 m.p.h.; daytime, 55 m.p.h. (p) Except when used in local urban transit operations buses in excess of 35 feet shall have not less than 3 axles. (q) 32,000 to 63,890 lbs. according to axle spacing and subject to axle weight limitation of 18,000 lbs. (r) Wheel and axle weight dependent on size of tires; gross weight governed by tire limits. (s) Weight equals 850 (L plus 40); L equals distance in feet between first and last axles. (t) Weight dependent on type of tires and axle spacing. (u) Speed dependent on width of highways. (v) 28,000 to 66,500 lbs. according to axle spacing; maximum for 2-axle vehicle, 36,900 lbs. (w) Operation of 40 foot buses, having 3 axles and axle load of not more than 18,000 lbs. permitted on highways specifically designated by Commissioner of Motor Vehicles. (x) Operation using certain highways permitted to operate 40 foot buses between points in New Jersey and New York Port Authority bus terminal. (y) State Highway Commission, after engineering investigation, may designate highways or sections of highways on which buses 102 inches in width may be operated. (z) 70 m.p.h. on highways in open country and 60 m.p.h. in other locations during daytime; 60 m.p.h. on highways in open country and 45 m.p.h. in other locations during nighttime. (aa) Public Utilities Commission authorized to permit buses a width of 102 inches on highways 20 feet or more wide. (ab) Limitations on buses fully equipped for operation are: 22,500 lbs. for 2-axle, 35 foot buses and 30,000 lbs. for 3-axle, 40 foot buses. (ac) Buses in excess of 35 feet in length must have 3 axles and be equipped with drinking water and toilet facilities. (ad) Nighttime, 50 m.p.h.; daytime, 60 m.p.h., or as zoned. (ae) 38,000 lbs. plus an additional 800 lbs. for each foot of distance between first and last axles. (af) 2-axle buses limited to 35 feet and 3-axle buses to 40 feet except that 2-axle ,40-foot buses may be operated over routes wholly within munici-

well as a limitation on weight per inch of tire width. In the same year, Washington and Pennsylvania pioneered with weight limitations. From that time to the present, the number of states with size and weight limitations has increased steadily. In the intercity passenger-carrying field, the limitations that have applied to single-unit trucks have been applicable, as a rule, to busses. The restrictions fixed for busses by the various states which were in effect in 1954 are found in Table 23–1.

There is evidence that the state size and weight limitations influence the selection of equipment. Thirty-four Class I motor carriers of passengers so indicated in 1940.[22] Furthermore, these carriers were desirous of securing changes, such as greater length and greater axle width. The trade association of the intercity bus operators (National Association of Motor Bus Operators) has on numerous occasions proposed changes that would make for greater uniformity of the state laws regarding size and weight. As an example, in 1941, it pointed out that the most modern 37-passenger equipment could not be used in Tennessee and legally could carry only 10 passengers in North Carolina and South Dakota; 20 in Georgia, Mississippi, and Texas; 25 in Arizona; 30 in 16 states; 35 in South Carolina; and a full load in 25 states. More recently, on behalf of the industry, the trade association has advocated increasing the width limitation to 102 inches in order to permit greater width of seats and aisle, and increasing the length limit, which in most states is 35 feet, an additional 5 feet. Bus design changes, such as moving the engine to the rear, have increased passenger and baggage capacity in some cases by as much as 30 per cent. However, benefits such as wider seats and aisles, more leg space, toilets, and air-conditioning equipment now rest in large measure with changes that might be made in state size and weight limitations. Other advantages that might accrue to the intercity bus operator would be a reduction in the cost per seat-mile, the possibility of cutting down the number of extra sections, and more flexible equipment.

palities, with consent of such municipalities, and over regular routes which traverse more than one political subdivision, with approval of Public Utility Commission. (ag) Except when operated within municipalities or in business or residence districts, 2-axle buses limited to gross weight of 30,000 lbs., with not more than 20,000 lbs. on any axle; 3-axle buses limited to 40,000 lbs. gross weight, with not more than 20,000 lbs. on any axle, and two rear axles shall be parallel and not less than 36 inches apart. (ah) Rate of speed greater than 35 m.p.h. is presumptive evidence of a rate of speed unreasonable or improper. (ai) Texas Highway Laws provide for licensing of buses of a gross weight of 28,000 lbs. and up. (aj) 2-axle vehicles with six wheels permitted 35,000 lbs. (ak) Buses in excess of 35 feet in length must have 3 axles and operation of such buses limited as determined by Director of Highways. (al) Nighttime, 55 m.p.h.; daytime, 65 m.p.h. (am) 32,000 to 73,950 lbs. according to axle spacing and subject to axle weight limitation of 18,000 lbs.

Source: National Association of Motor Bus Operators, *Bus Facts* (23rd ed.; Washington, D.C., 1954), p. 63.

[22] House Committee on Interstate and Foreign Commerce, *Federal Regulation of the Sizes and Weight of Motor Vehicles*, House Doc. No. 354, 77th Cong., 1st sess. (Washington, D.C.: U.S. Government Printing Office, 1941), p. 158.

The degree of enforcement of the state size and weight limits varies. Generally, whether intercity passenger motor busses operate intrastate or interstate, they are subject to these state restrictions. The statutes which establish these limits have been enacted, in general, for the same reasons as those enumerated in the restrictions on property carrying. These include the desire on the part of the states to promote safety, to protect highways, and to control competition among the different agencies of transportation. The influence of these limitations has had considerable effect on the development of intercity passenger motor carriers in many phases of operation.

Sizes and weights of intercity busses are subject to regulation by incorporated cities and towns to a limited degree. It is reported that 31 states delegate to local authorities certain powers concerning regulation of sizes and weights of motor vehicles, whereas 13 states do not mention extension of such powers.[23] Of the other 4 states, one stipulates that its size and weight restrictions do not apply within incorporated cities and towns; another state sets limits for cities over 75,000 only; the third makes its height and width limitations applicable in cities and towns; and the fourth stipulates that neither cities nor towns can make any ordinance by law or resolution regarding sizes and weights.

The trend has been slow toward an adjustment of state size and weight limitations which are alleged to be discriminatory against intercity busses, as has been the case for intercity property carriers. The recommended code of the American Association of State Highway Officials for height, length, width, and axle load of vehicles is given in Chapter 21. As applied to busses, the recommendations are as follows:

Height	12 feet 6 inches
Width	96 inches
Length, single bus (2 axles)	35 feet
Length, single bus (3 axles)	40 feet
Axle load	18,000 pounds

The diversity of regulations relating to economic and safety aspects of intercity bus operation from state to state has led to the creation in all states and the District of Columbia of state officials who negotiate with other state representatives to secure reciprocity agreements concerning such items as licenses, taxes, regulatory laws, and similar matters. As might be expected, the privilege of reciprocity has not been granted by all states in all aspects. It is reported

---

[23] *Ibid.,* p. 258.

that free reciprocity is provided for common-carrier busses which operate exclusively interstate by 23 states, with 15 states permitting free reciprocity for common carrier busses operating both interstate and intrastate, whereas the District of Columbia gives free reciprocity to all states in all aspects.[24] If no reciprocity is granted, it is common practice for the nonresident owners to pay the same license fees as resident owners.

Since most interstate bus operations are also intrastate operations, complete and unrestricted reciprocity did not apply to them under generally existing laws. The result was that vehicles operated by interstate carriers are now assessed an average of at least two full registration fees; in some cases as many as eight are required.

The most common types of third-structure taxes are vehicle-mile, passenger-mile, seat-mile, and gross-revenue taxes. Twenty states and the District of Columbia levy third-structure highway-use taxes on busses. The proportions of total highway-use taxes that are levied on this basis range from an estimated 13 to 66 per cent and for the states levying such taxes average approximately 42 per cent of the respective totals. Some of these taxes are levied for highway purposes, like the third-structure taxes on property carriers, while others are for general revenue. Six states specifically designate the use of these taxes for other than highway purposes.

The three principal types of licensing and registration requirements in an eleven-state area on the Atlantic seaboard are as follows: (*a*) the license or registration fee; (*b*) the registration of the vehicle with the regulatory commissions in each state; and (*c*) title fees and, in some states, sales or use taxes on busses. The problem of properly licensing and registering equipment in these eleven states for one operating carrier requires the full time of one man.[25]

PASSENGER-CARRIER OPERATING COSTS

A study by the Bureau of Transport Economics and Statistics of the Commission indicates that as the capacity of the bus increases, the operating cost per seat-mile decreases, and operating expenses do not increase proportionately with bus size.[26] The use of larger

---

[24] Association of American Railroads, *op. cit.*, p. 140.

[25] Transcript, MC–C–550, pp. 1909–11.

[26] Interstate Commerce Commission, Bureau of Transport Economics and Statistics, *Operating Costs of Intercity Motor Carriers of Passengers*, Statement No. 452 (Washington, D.C., 1945), p. 2.

intercity bus equipment has taken place in part because experience has shown that increased bus size has brought about no material change in operating costs per vehicle and has definitely reduced the weight and operating expense per passenger carried.[27] However, it was found that areas of operation have great influence on operating expenses, and there was a difference of as much as 5 cents per bus-mile due to area of operation.[28] Vehicle age, on the other hand, has little effect on operating expense, being accountable for a range in operating expense of about 1 cent per bus-mile.[29] Gross vehicle weight, it was shown, has very significant effect, for vehicle weight resulted in differences of almost 20 cents per bus-mile. The latter factor has been a strong incentive for increased use of lightweight metals, as well as improved methods of bus construction.

Figure 23–1 shows the distribution of the major items of the expense dollar over a period of years. That portion spent for wages and salaries has shown an almost constant increase during the period from 1939 to 1952. As a result of rising wages, 35.2 per cent of operating expenses were expended for labor costs in 1939 and increased to 45.6 per cent in 1952. A rise of 10 per cent in wages today requires a fare boost of almost 5 cents on the dollar just to meet expenses, even if there are no increases in the cost of equipment, operating supplies, license fees, or any of the various other items required for bus operation.

Other expenses, although also greater, represent declining proportions of total expenses. Materials, supplies, and other nonlabor costs included in operation and maintenance expenses were down from 38.8 per cent of expenses in 1939 to 36.2 per cent in 1952, and similar declines occurred in the remaining types of expenses, namely, depreciation costs, operating taxes and licenses, and rents.

Of the total wage bill, drivers' wages constitute about half of the wage bill. Slightly more than 85 per cent of all Class I bus operator drivers are paid for most or all of their work on a mileage basis. The remainder of the work is paid for by the hour, by the trip, or at a specified salary. While the 35-mile speed limit for all commercial vehicles was in effect during World War II, a reduction in speed meant an increase in hours of work for many drivers. Many of the

---

[27] Board of Investigation and Research, *Technological Trends in Transportation*, Sen. Doc. No. 76, 79th Cong., 1st sess. (Washington, D.C.: U.S. Government Printing Office, 1945), p. 57.

[28] Interstate Commerce Commission, *op cit.*, p. 4.

[29] *Ibid.*, p. 4.

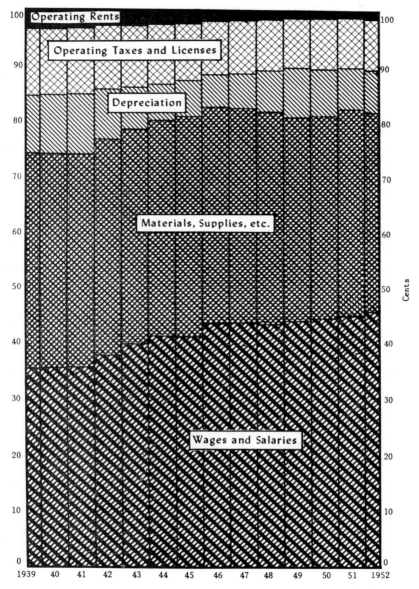

FIG. 23–1. Distribution of the major items of the expense dollar.
Source: National Association of Motor Bus Operators.

larger carriers negotiated what was termed a "slowdown bonus," varying from 7.5 to 10 per cent of the drivers' normal earnings at over-the-road rates. These bonuses, as a rule, expired at the time the wartime limitation of speeds was lifted. Driver costs on a bus-mile basis was 8.4 cents in 1952. The drivers are organized to a higher degree than any of the other segments of the bus labor force and are represented by the Amalgamated Association of Street Electric Railway and Motor Coach Employees of America, American Federation of Labor.

The increased number of intercity busses powered with diesel motors has had some effect on the relationships between the various items of operating expense, and the trend is toward such units. The bus manufacturer which in recent years has produced about 50 per cent of the entire industry output has indicated that about 95 per cent of its production is now diesel and 5 per cent gasoline.[30]

One basic fixed expense is depreciation which is about 8 per cent of the total operating expenses of the Class I intercity bus operators. Generally, Class I bus operators depreciate their equipment on an 8-year basis, although the bus may not be retired at the end of that time. Some operators prefer the use of the vehicle-mile for computation of depreciation. Good business practice has been to retire a bus when the maintenance costs added to the annual amortization of the investment will be greater on the old bus than on a new one. Some typical depreciation rates are as follows:

25   per cent per year over a 4-year period, no salvage
12½ per cent per year over an 8-year period, no salvage
4   cents per vehicle-mile
2   cents per vehicle-mile

Table 23–2 clearly shows the trend in expenses, as well as revenues, per bus-mile for the intercity Class I bus carriers. Since World War II, the margin between revenue and expenses has narrowed to the point where rate adjustment appears necessary if the public is to continue to receive adequate bus service and if the carriers are to remain solvent.

A salient factor characterizing intercity bus operations is that the traffic volume varies so greatly from season to season, day to day, and hour to hour. It is customary for a carrier to maintain 25 per cent or more of its fleet for the sole purpose of meeting the peak season demands. It is not unusual for the bus operator to have over 100 per cent more passengers during the summer months than during the winter season. A long-distance carrier may have to double its service on a week end, as compared with a weekday. A carrier operating between a city and a surrounding rural area has a large outbound

---

[30] Transcript, MC–C–550, p. 3222.

TABLE 23–2

DEVELOPMENT OF THE CLASS I SEGMENT OF THE INTERCITY BUS
INDUSTRY

Year	Number of Carriers	Operating Revenues per Bus-Mile	Expenses per Bus-Mile
1939	165	$0.236	$0.205
1940	154	0.233	0.205
1941	156	0.262	0.216
1942	163	0.353	0.235
1943	189	0.413	0.261
1944	225	0.414	0.276
1945	263	0.405	0.289
1946	287	0.364	0.291
1947	283	0.346	0.301
1948	280	0.354	0.314
1949	280	0.356	0.328
1950	194	0.363	0.328
1951	187	0.387	0.342
1952	179	0.402	0.355
1953	179	0.405	0.364

Source: National Association of Motor Bus Operators.

movement from the city before a week end or holiday and a heavy inbound movement at the end of that period. Carriers may experience
directional fluctuations as well, for the revenue per mile going in one
direction may be double that going in the opposite direction. The
industry establishes basic year-round schedules and augments these
schedules with extra sections or establishes new schedules to meet the
peak demands. These directional and peak demands necessitate a
large amount of empty or deadhead miles which normally equals
about 16 per cent of the total mileage operated, based on a test week
for a large number of carriers.[31]

FARES

Historically, the most important factor influencing the bus fare
structure has been competition. A bus company is generally a competitor of the railroad. However, the motor bus meets its greatest
competition from the private automobile, for the latter possesses the
advantage of complete flexibility in time, direction, and place of
movement. In these respects, the bus is at a decided disadvantage.
The advantage that the bus has in this competition is the lower cost
to the passenger. This competition places an effective ceiling on the
fares of bus carriers which assures reasonable rates to the public.[32]

[31] Transcript, MC–C–550, pp. 621, 883, 968, 1243, and Exhibits 38, 96–99.
[32] *Ibid.*, p. 3760.

The present fare structure is not the result of any scientific planning. It is the result of the operation of several compelling influences, such as the competition of the private automobile, rail competition, competition within the industry itself, and the ability of the traffic to bear the charges. The latter element is particularly important in the case of long-haul traffic.

Prior to federal regulation, there were many instances of changes in fares almost from hour to hour. At one time, when the standard charge from St. Louis to Kansas City, Kansas, was $7.00, one carrier charged only 75 cents.[33] Fares varied as quickly as agents could change "blackboard" prices in shop windows. Agents of some bus companies were sold a book of twenty-five tickets from Chicago to Los Angeles for $16 per ticket, and they would dispose of these tickets for any price above $16 that they desired.[34] The passage of the Motor Carrier Act eliminated these fluctuating fares. There were, however, and still are many instances of two or more lines operating between competitive points and charging different fares. This gives rise to variations in the rate per mile which a carrier charges throughout its system, as represented in Table 23–3. The rate per mile varies on

TABLE 23–3

RATE PER MILE ON DIFFERENT ROUTE SEGMENTS OF A MOTOR BUS CARRIER

Fare Points	Fare	Miles	Rate per Mile
Moultrie–Adel..............	$0.45	21	$0.0214
Moultrie–Nashville.........	0.70	35	0.0200
Moultrie–Lakeland.........	0.90	54	0.0157
Moultrie–Valdosta..........	0.90	79	0.0114
Adel–Nashville.............	0.25	12	0.0208
Adel–Valdosta.............	0.45	50	0.0090
Nashville–Lakeland.........	0.30	20	0.0150
Lakeland–Valdosta.........	0.35	18	0.0194
Adel–Lakeland.............	0.55	23	0.0239

Source: Exhibit 435, MC–C–550.

one segment from $0.009 per mile to other segments that range up to $0.0239 per mile.

The pressures of mounting costs and the increased competition from the private automobile since cars have become more plentiful again has caused many intercity bus operators to experience a diminishing profit margin. In 1953 the Class I motor bus operators with annual revenues from $200,000 to $750,000 had an operating ratio (the percentage of operating revenues which are absorbed by operat-

---

[33] *Ibid.*, p. 2350.

[34] *Ibid.*, p. 2350.

ing expenses) of 96.2, and those with revenues over $750,000 had an operating ratio 89.2 per cent. Table 23–4 shows the estimated reve-

TABLE 23–4

INTERCITY CLASS I BUS OPERATIONS
ESTIMATED REVENUE PER PASSENGER-MILE

1934	$0.0250	1946	$0.0166
1939	0.0155	1947	0.0170
1940	0.0146	1948	0.0175
1941	0.0146	1949	0.0185
1942	0.0165	1950	0.0189
1943	0.0169	1951	0.0195
1944	0.0165	1952	0.0203
1945	0.0164	1953	0.0206

Source: National Association of Motor Bus Operators.

nue per passenger-mile in 1934 and from 1939 through 1953. To be noted especially is the fact that from 1939 through 1951 the revenue is less than 2 cents per passenger-mile.

The excise tax which was originally imposed during World War II to discourage riders from using public carriers and as a revenue measure is currently at the rate of 10 per cent. This tax has been particularly burdensome to passenger carriers, including bus operators, for among other things it gives a substantial cost advantage to private transportation.

Intrastate fares are characterized by many inconsistencies, partly because of carrier policy and partly because of state regulatory policy. The intrastate fare structure is of vital importance to intercity bus operations, inasmuch as in the United States as a whole intrastate passengers comprise 82 per cent of the passengers and produce 50 per cent of the revenue, with the average length of journey being 21 miles and the average revenue of one-way fares about 2 cents per passenger-mile.[35]

Intercity bus fares are subject to the tapering principle, which means that the longer the journey the lower the fare. A 10-mile trip may cost 3 cents a mile, whereas a 1,500-mile trip may cost only 1½ cents per mile. The manner in which this tapering fare principle works is reflected in the amount of revenue the bus carrier receives per passenger-mile by length of journey. Figure 23–2 used in the MC–C–550 *Investigation of Bus Fares,* shows the range for Class I intercity carriers in the various rate territories and the average for the United States, by length of journey. The United States average

---

[35] "The Evolving Fare Picture," *Bus Transportation,* Vol. XXVIII, No. 2 (February, 1949), p. 53.

for trips up to 9 miles was over 2¾ cents per passenger-mile and dropped to 1½ cents shortly before 500 miles.

As a result of an industry-wide fare investigation of Class I intercity carriers of passengers which was instituted by the Interstate

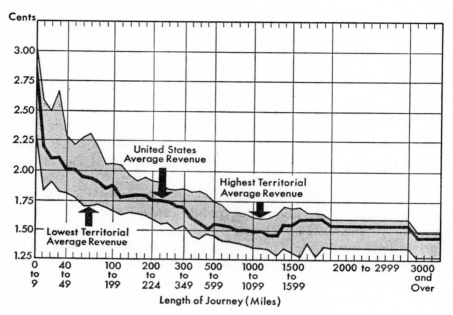

FIG. 23–2. Range of average revenue per passenger-mile by length of journey (on one-way traffic basis).

Source: Exhibit 932, Schedule 4, MC–C–550.

Commerce Commission in 1946, there was an endeavor on the part of the industry to bring about greater uniformity in bus fares. However, it was found that the intercity fares and charges of the carriers were, on the whole, lower than those in effect in 1934, prior to federal regulation, and did not require uniform fares. The Commission further ruled that fares and charges of the carriers, except for transportation in special, charter, and certain local mass transportation services, were not unreasonable or otherwise unlawful.[36] The average fares covering all types of intercity service in various sections of the country for The Greyhound Corporation in 1952 ranged from 2.10 cents to 2.16 cents a mile in the northeastern region; from 1.91 to 2.00 cents a mile in the southeastern region; and from 1.82 to 1.85 cents a mile in the western region.

In 1947 the one-way tickets of 120 Class I carriers constituted

---

[36] *Investigation of Bus Fares,* 52 MCC 332 (1950).

about 56 per cent of the total tickets, with round-trip tickets accounting for about 27 per cent of the total. The remaining percentage represents reduced rate tickets, such as those extended to the clergy, children's fares, excursion tickets, military tickets, employee reduced rate, and commutation tickets. Scheduled intercity service accounted for 86.3 per cent of 1952 revenues of the Class I carriers, and local riders accounted for 4.1 per cent.

MISCELLANEOUS REVENUE

Charter and special-service revenues, which have been growing steadily in importance during the postwar years, amounted to 4.8 per cent of total revenues in 1952 as compared with 1.8 per cent in 1946. Except for the war years, the revenue per bus-mile operated in charter and special service is above regular scheduled service. Since 1950 it has been about 6 cents per bus-mile more. Among the miscellaneous services which accounted for 4.8 per cent of revenues in 1952, the most important was transportation of express, an increasingly important item which accounted for 2.4 per cent of operating revenues in 1952 as compared with 0.8 per cent in 1946.

It might be noted that, originally, in express shipments by bus, the necessary arrangements were made by the shipper with the driver, who pocketed the revenue. Because of the threat to the bus companies of being held liable for loss regardless of whether they were parties to such agreements, as well as the threat of loss of potential bus revenue, intercity bus managements began offering to carry express for their own account. The service so provided to many communities is invaluable. An example is that of prescriptions that are filled and sent to outlying areas in response to doctors' requests. Delivery of automotive repair parts constitutes another example of the indispensable service rendered by intercity busses. A portion of intercity bus express service is operated by motor carriers under contract with the Railway Express Agency. Most of the package express rates are on a weight-mileage basis, although some are a percentage of the passenger fare. The newer busses with enlarged baggage space have facilitated the development of package express.

The rapid delivery of newspapers into suburban and rural areas reached by intercity busses has done much to improve circulation of newspapers in such areas. The exploitation of this medium of delivery has been developed particularly in the Middle West. The ease of handling and assurance of this regular income has made for a relatively low rate for this service. The revenue secured by intercity bus operators from this type of service is second in importance to express revenues.

Ranking behind express and newspaper revenue are the charges collected by intercity bus operators for carrying mail. This service is provided generally in instances where utilization of the intercity bus would expedite the movement of first- and second-class mail, as well as service into areas lacking rail service. The Post Office Department grants a blanket contract to certain operators which requires them to carry all mail offered. Another type of contract stipulates that only a certain number of first-class mail pouches are to be carried on one trip, with the remainder to be handled on succeeding trips.

On January 1, 1955, there were 134 routes operating in 33 states, 106 under contract and 28 operated by the government's Highway Post Office Service, which was set up to supplement the Railway Postal Service. The private contractor's vehicle must be completely dedicated to carrying the mail, although there are a few railroad-operated busses which have space for a few passengers. The average rate per scheduled mile of those carriers under contract is $0.2844 per mile, and those operated with government vehicles $0.3300 per mile.[37] It is expected that eventually all of the government-operated routes will be converted to private operations. The conditions imposed upon private operations are:

1. The carrier must operate in the county or adjoining county in which the highway contract will operate.
2. Equipment must be new and conform to specifications laid down by the Highway Post Office Service.
3. Under the contract, the carrier must operate on a specified, definite route on a posted schedule.
4. The contract runs for 4 years, and a bid bond equal to 5 per cent of the amount bid which guarantees execution of the contract and a performance bond equal to 50 per cent of the annual pay must be posted for each route operated under contract.
5. The carrier forfeits the revenue for any trip which is not run.

A minute portion of nonpassenger revenue is secured from charges for baggage in excess of the minimum of 100 pounds per adult fare and 50 pounds per half-fare. These minimums are not universal, and there is considerable variation in the permissible weight limitations.

As previously indicated, the nonpassenger revenues constitute a small but essential portion of total revenue. The ability to render

[37] *Traffic World*, August 14, 1954, p. 22.

these services is of great value to intercity bus operators. The benefits gained by such service, although difficult to measure, unquestionably redound to the carriers' advantage in performing community and passenger service.

NATIONAL BUS TRAFFIC ASSOCIATION

The tariff-publishing activities for intercity bus operators are handled primarily by the National Bus Traffic Association, which was formed in 1932. The members of the board of directors are from different regions and are elected by the membership. The board appoints all committees. Representative committees are the Uniform Tariff Committee, the Finance and Auditing Committee, the Uniform Schedule Committee, and the Baggage Committee. The Association has approximately 380 members, and rates are published for over 300 carriers which are not members. With some few exceptions, the National Bus Traffic Association publishes all of the interterritorial tariffs and all of the intraterritorial tariffs involving interline fares. In addition, in some territories, it publishes interdivision fares, and, in a few instances, the local fares of its members. The five rate territories are shown in Figure 23–3. There are approximately 96,000 fares published in the interterritorial tariffs, 57,000 in the intraterritorial tariffs.[38] A basing-fare tariff names fares to about 23,000 points throughout the United States, so that an agent can construct a fare from any point in the United States to any other point in the United States served by a participating carrier in the tariff.

Proposed rate changes involving a rate between a point on one carrier's line to a point on the lines of one or more other carriers are filed with the chairman of the National Bus Traffic Association, who studies the proposal and submits the proposed rate and his study to interested member bus carriers for their views, at a regular or special meeting. Where the carriers are not in agreement, the carrier proposing the rate change has the right of independent action; but, before such right is exercised, the chairman consults all interested carriers again to see if they wish to go along with the proposed change.

Each interstate carrier usually fixes its own rates between points on its own line and files changes with the National Bus Traffic Association and with the Interstate Commerce Commission.

[38] *Ibid.*, pp. 3704–5.

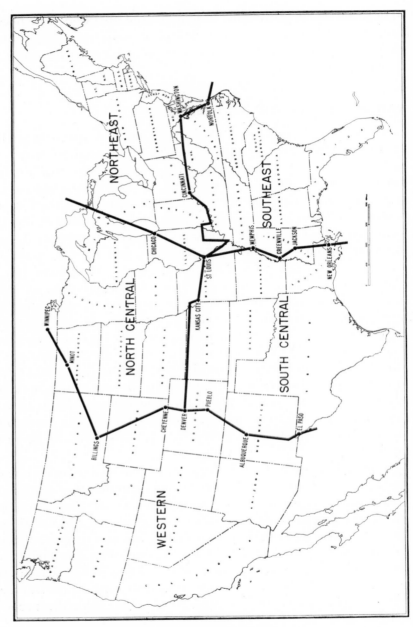

FIG. 23–3. Motor bus rate territories.
Source: National Bus Traffic Association.

TRADE ASSOCIATION

The trade association of motor bus operators is the National Association of Motor Bus Operators. NAMBO has operated as an organization since 1931, although there were antecedent organizations. Representative of the activities of NAMBO in behalf of its members are the following: consideration of legislative proposals which would affect bus operation; compilation of statistical data; bulletin services concerning actions of regulatory agencies; problems involving wages and working conditions; maintaining co-operative relationships with public officials and business organizations; and working for equitable taxation and greater uniformity in size and weight limitations.

The board of directors is composed of a representative from each of eleven regions, augmented by thirteen directors-at-large. A president, a vice-president, a treasurer, a secretary-manager, and a general counsel, and seven associate member directors, comprise the remaining group. Standing committees are as follows: Legislative, Labor Relations, Research and Planning, Safety, Reciprocity, Insurance, Accounting, Minimum Standards of Bus Design and Construction, Advertising and Public Relations, and Airline Operations.

QUESTIONS AND PROBLEMS

1. How does the determination of the legal status of the intercity bus operator as to private, contract, or common carrier compare with that of property carrying?
2. List the exemptions for passenger operation under Part II of the Interstate Commerce Act. At the present time, are all of these exemptions valid, in your opinion? Why or why not?
3. Explain the primary items of operating expense for intercity busses. What effect has vehicle age on operating expense?
4. What is meant by a "slowdown bonus"? What basis is primarily used by Class I operators for compensating drivers? Why?
5. Enumerate the problems occasioned by variations in traffic volume.
6. Trace the evolution of the intercity bus fare structure prior to federal regulation. What influence have rail fares and the private automobile had upon bus fares?
7. "At one time, when the standard charge from St. Louis to Kansas City, Kansas, was $7.00, one carrier charged only 75 cents." Does the public actually benefit by such a condition? Justify your conclusion.

8. Describe the intrastate bus fare structure. Of what importance is the intrastate fare structure to interstate fares?

9. What is the tapering principle?

10. How important is passenger-related service revenue to the bus operator? How important are these services to the public? Comment.

11. What conditions have been imposed by the Highway Post Office Service in granting a contract for the hauling of mail by bus?

12. List the state restrictions on intercity bus operations. What are the reasons for these restrictions? In your opinion, are the reasons justified from the point of view of the public? Why or why not?

13. The problem of properly licensing and registering equipment for a carrier operating busses in an eleven-state area requires the full time of one man. What are some of the questions raised by this fact?

14. What trends are apparent with respect to reciprocity? In your opinion, is reciprocity a right or a privilege? Discuss.

15. Describe the work of (*a*) the National Association of Motor Bus Operators, and (*b*) the National Bus Traffic Association.

16. How would you define special party? Charter party?

24. URBAN PASSENGER TRANSPOR-
TATION

▪▪▪

URBAN transportation involves the movement of people, as distinguished from that of vehicles, and is mass transportation (generally defined as transportation by a public carrier during a year of passengers equal to the population of the city served). Transit operations include public passenger transportation which is provided by local motor bus lines, electric street railways, elevated and subway lines, interurban electric railways, and trolley bus lines.[1] These types of transit operations are treated here in a manner designed to describe the relative position presently held by each in urban transit operations, with a general description of the factors present in today's passenger transit industry.

Early transit operations were carried on with horse-drawn streetcars; later, cable cars were developed in some cities. The growth of the American cities provided a sufficiently dense traffic to necessitate a faster mode of transportation than that of the horse-drawn streetcars, and the average speed of passenger service was increased by the use of electric traction. With the utilization of electric power, the transit industry took shape, and electric traction lines were developed in many cities. As the larger metropolitan areas continued to grow, the resulting congestion led to the introduction of subway and elevated railways in some areas. The next vehicle to appear on the transit scene was the motor bus, which was in use before World War I, although the expansion of this means of transport came after that war. The trolley bus[2] was primarily developed in the late 1920's, there being only forty-one such busses in service in 1928.

For many years, the only source of transportation to work, shop-

---

[1] Taxicabs, suburban railroads, sight-seeing busses, and school busses, which are phases of local passenger operations, are not treated in this text.

[2] A trolley bus is a motor bus electrically powered from overhead wires.

ping, and recreation centers for the great majority of the urban population was the transit line. Many transit lines owned amusement parks and provided transportation directly to the parks on week ends. A 5-cent ride across the city in a streetcar and a day spent at an amusement park was a very popular diversion during this period, and transit lines enjoyed unusually profitable operations.

The investment of the surface, subway, and elevated railways has always been appreciable. The subway and elevated provide their own roadbed; and the surface street railways are required to provide their roadbed, which includes the property extending 18 inches on each side beyond the car tracks. This roadbed has to be maintained, and property taxes must be paid on it by the transit company. Transit companies operate under franchise, some franchises covering periods as long as 50–75 years. In the larger cities, these franchises were often coveted in the earlier days; political aspects frequently entered into the granting of these operating rights, awarding, as they did, the exclusive right to operate within a city. A transit line still operates under a franchise from the city, although there are some instances where the state has assumed regulatory jurisdiction over local services. In the beginning and for many years, most of the transit companies were subsidiaries of local utility companies which furnished electric service. Although many transit companies are still operated by local electric companies, the trend over the past years has been toward independently owned and operated companies.[3] The most important competitor of the urban transit lines has been and is the private automobile. With the increasing use of automobiles in the late 1920's, the favorable financial position of transit companies materially changed.

TRENDS IN EQUIPMENT AND ITS USE

Transit management, in an endeavor to maintain present traffic and attract lost traffic, began rehabilitating equipment in the 1930's. Some companies adopted the new P.C.C. streetcar,[4] which was

---

[3] During the depression National City Lines was formed by five brothers. They purchased numerous transit properties from electric utility companies and rehabilitated the properties with new busses. A 5-cent fare was generally charged. By 1939, National City Lines was operating in thirty-seven cities. There were subsequent additions as well as substantial investment in some of the larger city transit systems, making a total of more than forty wholly owned urban transit companies by 1954.

[4] This streetcar was developed by the Electric Railway Presidents' Conference Committee, consisting of the heads of some twenty-five electric railway companies, who, with manufacturers of cars and equipment, subscribed approximately $1 million to develop this new model of streetcar.

brought out late in 1935. The greatest change, however, for the United States as a whole was the widespread adoption of motor bus equipment. Table 24–1 shows the trends in transit passenger equipment in the United States from 1938 through 1954. The number of railway cars has steadily decreased during this period, both for surface and for subway and elevated. On the other hand, the number

TABLE 24–1

TRENDS OF TRANSIT PASSENGER EQUIPMENT IN THE UNITED STATES

CALENDAR YEAR	RAILWAY CARS			TROLLEY COACH	MOTOR BUS	GRAND TOTAL
	Surface	Subway and Elevated	Total			
1938	31,400	11,205	42,605	2,032	28,500	73,137
1939	29,320	11,052	40,372	2,184	32,600	75,156
1940	26,630	11,032	37,662	2,802	35,000	75,464
1941	27,092	10,578	37,670	3,029	39,300	79,999
1942	27,230	10,278	37,508	3,385	46,000	86,893
1943	27,250	10,255	37,505	3,501	47,100	88,106
1944	27,180	10,219	37,399	3,561	48,400	89,360
1945	26,680	10,217	36,897	3,716	49,670	90,283
1946	24,780	9,429	34,159	3,916	52,450	90,525
1947	21,607	9,370	30,977	4,706	56,917	92,600
1948	17,911	9,456	27,367	5,708	58,540	91,615
1949	14,859	9,869	24,728	6,366	57,035	88,129
1950	13,228	9,758	22,986	6,504	56,820	86,310
1951	10,960	9,644	20,604	7,071	57,660	85,335
1952	9,700	9,476	19,176	7,180	55,980	82,336
1953	7,990	9,244	17,234	6,941	54,700	78,875
1954	6,600	9,160	15,760	6,650	53,590	76,000

Source: American Transit Association, *Transit Fact Book* (New York, 1954), p. 14. 1954 estimated.

of motor busses has steadily increased during this period and in 1954 amounted to three times the number of the total railway cars in operation. The number of motor busses in operation was about 60 per cent of the grand total of all types of equipment in operation in 1954. Although the trolley bus has increased also during this period, the number in operation is relatively small in comparison with the other types of equipment in use. The trolley bus does possess many advantages, such as curb discharge, no odors in operation, comfort, and quiet. Furthermore, it has greater flexibility than the streetcar but, not having a separate power plant, is not as flexible as the motor bus.

Motor busses operated about 69 per cent of the total revenue vehicle-miles accounted for by all public transit vehicles in 1954. This is in sharp contrast to the situation that existed in 1938, when motor busses accounted for a little more than one third of the total revenue vehicle-miles. In that year, motor busses operated only slightly more revenue-miles than the surface railways, whereas in

1954 they operated six times the amount accounted for by the surface railways. Table 24–2 shows the number of revenue vehicle-miles operated by the various types of transit vehicles for the years from 1938 through 1954. The subway and elevated railways showed a decrease over the period which is particularly sharp starting in 1950,

TABLE 24–2

REVENUE VEHICLE-MILES OPERATED IN THE UNITED STATES BY EACH TYPE OF TRANSIT VEHICLE

(In Millions)

CALENDAR YEAR	RAILWAY			TROLLEY COACH	MOTOR BUS	GRAND TOTAL
	Surface	Subway and Elevated	Total			
1938.............	922.3	457.4	1,379.7	67.9	986.4	2,434.0
1939.............	878.3	469.4	1,347.7	74.9	1,047.4	2,470.0
1940.............	844.7	470.8	1,315.5	86.0	1,194.5	2,596.0
1941.............	792.2	472.8	1,265.0	98.4	1,313.0	2,676.4
1942.............	850.4	469.6	1,320.0	115.7	1,612.0	3,047.7
1943.............	978.0	461.7	1,439.7	129.7	1,693.0	3,262.4
1944.............	977.9	461.0	1,438.9	132.3	1,713.3	3,284.5
1945.............	939.8	458.4	1,398.2	133.3	1,722.3	3,253.8
1946.............	894.5	458.9	1,353.4	143.7	1,807.2	3,304.3
1947.............	839.3	462.3	1,301.6	155.1	1,885.7	3,342.4
1948.............	699.3	458.1	1,157.4	178.0	1,975.7	3,311.1
1949.............	555.4	460.0	1,015.4	200.0	1,968.2	3,183.6
1950.............	463.1	443.4	906.5	205.7	1,895.4	3,007.6
1951.............	387.6	424.0	811.6	208.8	1,893.0	2,913.4
1952.............	321.2	400.4	721.6	215.2	1,877.7	2,814.5
1953.............	273.7	391.1	664.8	211.7	1,819.0	2,695.5
1954.............	213.0	376.2	589.2	196.9	1,746.0	2,532.1

Source: American Transit Association, *Transit Fact Book* (New York, 1954), p. 11. 1954 estimated.

and the trolley bus showed a substantial increase. On the other hand, surface railway revenue vehicle-miles in 1954 were about one third of the amount operated by them in 1938. The increase in the proportion of revenue vehicle-miles operated by motor busses is impressive in total vehicle-miles during this period.

The transit equipment which is used in a particular city varies somewhat with the size of the city. All of the subway and elevated railway cars are found in cities with populations of 1,000,000 or more. There are none in use in smaller cities. The preponderance of surface railway cars are in cities of 250,000 or more, with only a small number in use in any smaller cities. Motor busses, on the other hand, are found in cities of all sizes. For example, in 1948 there were 18,400 motor busses in cities of more than 500,000 population and 7,100 in cities of less than 50,000.[5]

The seating capacity of the different types of transit equipment

---

[5] American Transit Association, *Transit Fact Book* (New York, 1954), p. 14.

varies, with the streetcar, as a rule, having the greatest seating capacity. The newer equipment in use on the subway and elevated lines has a seating capacity of from 44 to 56 persons. Streetcars have a seating capacity of from 49 to 61; trolley busses, from 40 to 48. Of the new busses which were delivered in 1953 for urban transit use, the seating capacity of almost 80 per cent was 40 or more.[6] In general, the restrictions on size and weight limitations which are applicable to intercity motor busses do not apply to urban transportation. The trend is toward motor busses with greater seating capacity (see Fig. 24–1).

Courtesy: General Motors Corporation, Truck and Coach Division.

FIG. 24–1.   A 55-passenger city-type bus used in mass transportation.

Double-deck busses, which have an average seating capacity double that of the conventional city-type bus, have been in use in some of the larger cities; however, none of these units have been produced in recent years. These busses have three axles, with two of the axles in the rear (tandem).

The most popular bus size in 1936 was a 23-passenger bus. Since that time, the seating-capacity trend has been upward, until in 1954 the most popular bus size in city-type busses was one with a seating capacity of 51. The three most popular sizes in city-type busses, by seating capacity, for the years from 1936 through 1954 are as shown in the following tabulation:[7]

---

[6] *Ibid.,* p. 12.

[7] *Bus Transportation,* 33rd Annual, Review of Industry Progress, February, 1955, p. 31.

	CITY		
	1st	2d	3d
1936	23	32	21
1937	25	21	23
1938	25	24	31
1939	29	27	41
1940	27	40	36
1941	27	40	31
1942	45	27	40
1943	27	29	41
1944	27	40	36
1945	27	29	41
1946	27	36	45
1947	41	45	27
1948	45	44	40
1949	45	36	31
1950	45	36	51
1951	45	31	36
1952	45	51	36
1953	51	45	58
1954	51	45	52

There are a variety of reasons for the adoption of busses in transit operations, among which are the following: (a) flexibility in traffic; (b) individual power supply; (c) ability to pass each other; (d) through service to off-route locations; (e) ability to combine routes, with one vehicle rendering the service; (f) low initial cost; and (g) curb discharge.

The investment in the transit industries as of December 31, 1953, was $3.9 billion. More than $3 billion of this investment is represented by the surface railways and subway and elevated railways, so that, although the number of motor busses in operation in 1953 was over twice the number of railway cars, the investment in motor bus operation was only slightly more than one fifth of the investment in railway operations.[8] The difference in investment represented by the two types of operation has certainly influenced the trend toward motor bus operation. The factor of low initial cost also has contributed to greater ease in financing motor bus equipment for urban use.

Another standard for assaying the relative position of the various types of transit operations is by reviewing the number of passengers carried by each type of urban passenger service. Table 24–3 shows the total number of transit passengers in the United States, by types of service. The trend for this period indicates the dominant position achieved by the motor bus in transit service. The number of passengers carried by motor bus exceeds the total number carried by all other public carriers in urban transportation.

[8] American Transit Association, *op. cit.*, p. 2.

The transit industry has provided a larger market for motor busses than has the intercity field. Transit-type busses have been produced in greater numbers than intercity-type vehicles, except for 1 year

TABLE 24–3

TOTAL NUMBER OF TRANSIT PASSENGERS IN THE UNITED STATES, BY TYPES OF SERVICE
(In Millions)

| CALENDAR YEAR | RAILWAY | | | TROLLEY COACH | MOTOR BUS | GRAND TOTAL |
	Surface	Subway and Elevated	Total			
1938.....	6,545	2,236	8,781	389	3,475	12,645
1939.....	6,171	2,368	8,539	445	3,853	12,837
1940.....	5,943	2,382	8,325	534	4,239	13,098
1941.....	6,081	2,421	8,502	652	4,931	14,085
1942.....	7,290	2,566	9,856	899	7,245	18,000
1943.....	9,150	2,656	11,806	1,175	9,019	22,000
1944.....	9,516	2,621	12,137	1,234	9,646	23,017
1945.....	9,426	2,698	12,124	1,244	9,886	23,254
1946.....	9,027	2,835	11,862	1,311	10,199	23,372
1947.....	8,096	2,756	10,852	1,356	10,332	22,540
1948.....	6,506	2,606	9,112	1,528	10,728	21,368
1949.....	4,839	2,346	7,185	1,661	10,162	19,008
1950.....	3,904	2,264	6,168	1,658	9,420	17,246
1951.....	3,101	2,189	5,290	1,633	9,202	16,125
1952.....	2,477	2,124	4,601	1,640	8,878	15,119
1953.....	2,036	2,040	4,076	1,566	8,260	13,902
1954.....	1,555	1,912	3,467	1,421	7,504	12,392

Source: American Transit Association, *Transit Fact Book* (New York, 1954), p. 7. 1954 estimated.

over a 30-year period. The ratio of production of city-type to inter-city-type busses has been approximately two city-type busses for each intercity-type bus.[9] The trend in recent years for the city-type busses has been the hydraulic drive or torque converter rather than the mechanical shift. This is particularly true on the larger-size units which are used primarily in heavy traffic, as this simplifies driving.

PASSENGER POTENTIAL

The rides per capita of urban population by all types of urban transit in 1953 were 153. This is less than the 176 rides per capita in 1940, but less than half the high of 312 rides per capita during a war year, 1945.[10] The private automobile, of course, is providing much of the transportation, which is reflected in the decrease in per-capita rides since the end of World War II.

Dependence upon public transit systems increases with the size of the city. The range of home-to-work transportation reliance on

[9] *Bus Transportation*, 32nd Annual, p. 32.
[10] American Transit Association, *op. cit.*, p. 7.

public transit in cities of less than 50,000 was 17 per cent; 50,000–100,000 was 25 per cent; 100,000–250,000 was 27 per cent; and in cities over 250,000, it was 43 per cent.[11]

The urban transit systems certainly are in a position to carry a great many more passengers than they are carrying, as they proved during World War II. This war caused great increases in the number of passengers carried by public transit systems, in many instances resulting in over a 100 per cent increase.

FACTORS IN OPERATIONS

There are operational factors in the transit industry which sometimes present problems. The transit industry is subject to traffic peaks in the morning and in the afternoon, as well as a falling-off of traffic on week ends. To meet the peak traffic demands, it is necessary to maintain equipment in excess of that which otherwise would be needed. These peak periods add to schedule difficulties, also. During the peak period, the schedule may call for a transit vehicle over a particular route every 2 or 3 minutes; whereas, during the off-peak period, a vehicle every 10 or 12 minutes or less often may be adequate.[12] This necessitates a certain amount of split shifts for drivers, who may work, for example, 4 hours in the morning, with 3 hours off, and 4 hours again in the afternoon. The splitting of shifts has always been a matter of contention between transit management and transit employees, with the latter contending that there should be extra compensation for the time between shifts. During World War II, the staggering of working hours at industrial plants and of store and office hours increased the carrying capacity of the existing transit vehicles by spreading the peak hours and so effecting greater utilization of existing equipment.

A factor in transit operations increasingly being used is that of the express run, which has fewer stops and thereby appreciably cuts down on running time. It is estimated that the time for boarding and alighting is about 13 per cent of scheduled running time, so the elimination of stops can speed up the run. During the war, the Office of Defense Transportation requirements established fewer stops as a war expedient, which practice has been continued by many transit

---

[11] Automobile Manufacturers Association, *Automobile Facts and Figures* (Detroit, 1954), p. 62.

[12] A comprehensive and valuable source of information on transit operations, as well as other related transit matters, is Frank H. Mossman (Ed.), *Principles of Urban Transportation* (Cleveland, Ohio: Western Reserve University Press, 1951).

companies. The elimination of a number of stops reduces operational expense, since the many stops in urban operations cause a large amount of maintenance of equipment and makes for a much higher consumption of gasoline and oil than is found in intercity passenger operations.

One of the advantages in city operations is the flexibility of the motor bus. However, its flexibility does make for many requests for additional routing or rerouting. When the bus serves outlying areas, residents frequently contact their local city officials to petition that the bus route come down their street. The traffic potential in outlying areas is limited, but it is difficult to convince residents of that fact.

Transit operators establish a reserve for injuries to passengers, such as 1½ per cent of gross revenue per month. This is augmented by other types of insurance carried with regular insurance firms. The depreciation reserve which is used depends upon the type of equipment. A 45-passenger bus may be depreciated on the basis of 300,000 miles at so many cents per mile, or in about 5 years. The smaller busses are depreciated on the basis of the same mileage but at a cent per mile less, depending on company policy.

It is customary for city transit firms which operate with busses to make a mileage contract with a tire company. The latter supplies the tires and maintains them during the life of the tire-mileage contract. The transit company pays on the basis of a fraction of a cent per mile for the tires, the exact amount per mile being stipulated in the mileage contract. This arrangement has resulted in lower cost for tires and has been utilized by some intercity carriers as well. It is estimated that approximately 80 per cent of the urban transit companies operate under such tire-mileage contracts.

Approximately 55 cents out of each transit dollar goes to employees.[13] Both the drivers and the maintenance workers of the transit companies are organized and are primarily represented by the Amalgamated Association of Street Electric Railway and Motor Coach Employees of America, American Federation of Labor. Runs are allocated on a seniority basis, and the employees are paid on an hourly basis. Most labor agreements call for a minimum guarantee if an employee is asked to report for duty and no work materializes. In 1953 the average number of employees in the transit industry was 220,000, half of whom were motor bus employees. The average annual earnings per employee were $4,150.[14]

---

[13] American Transit Association estimate.
[14] American Transit Association, *op. cit.*, p. 12.

FARES

Since the end of World War II, the factors of increased costs and increased competition from the private automobile are combining to narrow the margin between operating revenues and expenses for transit companies. The operating ratio for all transit operations was about 82 per cent in 1938. This decreased to a low of approximately 72 per cent in 1943, because of high traffic density; but since that time the operating ratio has been increasing, and it has varied from 89 to 91 in the years since 1947, which is extremely high. These operating ratio figures include those of all surface and subway and elevated railway operations, which have a much lower operating ratio than motor bus operations. In 1953 operating income was but 2.96 per cent of operating revenue, and the financial plight of the transit industry was critical.

A basic difficulty of transit operations has been the rigidity of the fare structure. A riding public which becomes accustomed to a certain fare does not take kindly to any proposed increase, regardless of the need of the transit company for such an increase. Many franchises specifically state what the fare shall be. Under such circumstances, transit companies have had to figure out ways to secure adjustments and yet leave the basic fare unchanged, such as charging one cent for each transfer, soliciting greater revenue from advertisements in their vehicles, and the like. A transit company proposing a fare change may find that there may be political repercussions. It is easy for citizens to contact their councilmen, and the evident impact on family budgets of a fare increase sometimes operates to make such increases hotly contested issues.

There are a number of fares which are used in transit operations: cash fares, tokens at slightly less than cash fares for a specific number, children's fares, school fares, zone fares, and weekly passes. The cash fare has long been favored by many companies, inasmuch as it is the simplest fare under which to operate. When a 10-cent cash fare is used in combination with tokens and/or weekly passes, the tokens may sell three for 25 cents. Where the savings on token fares are appreciable, token fares may constitute 95 per cent of the total fares. The principle involved in the higher cash fare is that the cash fare is used by the occasional rider and therefore costs him somewhat more than for the rider who uses the transit system regularly, such as the purchaser of tokens or the weekly pass. In the postwar period there has been a trend toward more cash fares and the elimination of the weekly pass.

There have been a greater number of adjustments in fares since the end of World War II than in any similar period. More than two thirds of the nation's cities had transit fare increases by 1950.[15] By the middle of 1953, there were 42 cities in the 25,000-or-more population class that charged a 15-cent transit fare. There were only 17 charging that much in September, 1950, and only one at the start of 1949. Eight transit systems had moved up to 20 cents.[16] In 1952 there were fare increases in 266 cities and over 100 in 1953. The transit companies have been caught in a squeeze between falling passenger traffic and increasing costs. Further, it is estimated that for every 3 per cent increase in transit fares, there is a 1 per cent loss in passengers.

One of the problems faced by many of the transit companies has been the changing pattern in the average length of ride. For example, one company had a ratio of short rides (½-mile or less) to long rides in the earlier days of 1 to 6. Today, this company experiences one short ride for every 24 long rides, or a ratio of 1 to 24. This has given rise to increased consideration of the use of a zone-fare system, which to date has been relatively uncommon in this country but is widely utilized in Europe. The basic idea of a zone fare is to have an inner zone centered in the business district, which constitutes Zone 1; then concentric circles of radii of 1 mile, 2 miles, or 3 miles (whatever the predetermined zonal dimensions) will be established. In this manner, it is possible to set up a graduated fare structure by zones which more closely reflects the distance traveled. There are difficulties attendant to the establishment of a zonal system, however, one of which is the collection of fares.

There are a few zone systems which depart from the central zone idea, and there are flat fare systems which incorporate zoned service. The latter type of system is one in which certain routes from the center of the city out into the suburban areas are set up with express, limited, and local service, operating different distances for different fares, premium fares being charged for the express and limited service. Under the zone system, those individuals who from choice or accident live 2 or 3 miles or less from their place of employment will pay less for their daily commuting rides than those individuals who live 5 or 7 or more miles from where they work. In other forms of transportation as well—taxi, private automobile, suburban bus line, or commuter service on a railroad—distance is the determinant. In 1951 there were but twenty transit systems with the zone system.[17]

---

[15] "Four Years of Fare Increases," *Mass Transportation*, Vol. XLVI, No. 1 (January, 1950), p. 36.

[16] *Wall Street Journal*, July 20, 1953, p. 1.

[17] "To Zone or Not to Zone," *Bus Transportation*, July and August, 1951.

MUNICIPAL OWNERSHIP

The overwhelming number of transit operations are conducted by private companies, a total of 1,565 in 1953 as compared to 40 municipally owned transit systems. A study that was recently made of all transit companies whose revenues exceeded $1 million annually and on which operating information was available indicated that there were 137 private companies and 6 municipally owned companies in this category. These municipal systems were in New York, San Francisco, Boston, Detroit, Cleveland, and Seattle.[18] The conclusions of this study were as follows:

1. The claims by the proponents of municipal ownership that such ownership will provide a lower fare level are not borne out by the facts; where differences in the fare level do exist between private and municipal ownership, they are in favor of private operation.
2. Municipal systems on a cost basis compare unfavorably with private systems, and this factor accounts for the deficits present in municipal ownership.
3. There is very little difference between the two types of ownership in the amount of service given.

Even in a smaller city of 25,000, municipal ownership with its tax advantages was found to be costlier than private operation.[19]

Municipal operation of urban transit lines does not provide the solution to any transit problems, whether financial or otherwise. Probably no other industry is subject to as much criticism by it patrons as the transit industry. There is hardly a rider who lacks some suggestion about how the system should be operated. On the other hand, municipal ownership seems to be subject to just as much criticism from the passengers as private ownership. Municipal ownership, which was supposed to solve all the problems, is not the panacea to transit problems which its advocates had averred it would be.

POSSIBLE SOLUTIONS TO THE TRANSIT PROBLEM

The provision of an adequate urban transportation system in our urban communities has been considered to be essential. However, the increased use of private automobiles, including car-riding pools; the increase in the number of new and modern shopping centers

---

[18] "What Are the Facts about Municipally-Owned Transit?" *Bus Transportation*, Vol. XLVI, No. 1 (January, 1950), p. 2. The Chicago Transit Authority, which grosses over $1 million, was not included for lack of operating data.

[19] "Why We Found Public Ownership Is More Costly," *Bus Transportation*, December, 1953, p. 32.

built in residential suburbs, eliminating the need for so many trips downtown into the centers of cities; and the increased traffic congestion, which has materially slowed up streetcars and busses in most cities causing a greater expenditure of fuel and labor time without any corresponding increase in services or passenger revenues are some of the factors which have combined to jeopardize the future of the transit industry.

There are several possible solutions which involve city officials, business organizations, the transit companies, and the public. One measure is a city traffic plan which would embrace the transit system. It would include such matters as parking regulations, one-way streets, and possibly the assignment of the curb lane to transit vehicles. For example, a government-sponsored parking survey made in St. Louis showed that the transit company carries more than 41 per cent of the people who enter the shopping district between the hours of 8 A.M. and 6 P.M., and this is done with less than 3½ per cent of the total vehicles. If these transit riders used private automobiles, they would have needed 72,000 cars—a 70 per cent increase in the number of automobiles in the business district.

The development of perimeter or fringe parking and the park-and-ride plan, whereby the drivers of vehicles park them in outlying areas and use an express transit service into the center of the city is another partial solution to the transit and traffic problem. The greater use of express busses with fares on a zoned basis and fewer stops per mile would also aid in solving the problem.

Establishment of a public transit "authority" has been suggested as a possible solution. Under such operation many of the special taxes paid by privately owned transit properties would not be levied. The authority would purchase the transit property and operate it.

Public officials have been negligent in giving consideration to the encouragement of greater utilization of transit facilities in order to relieve traffic congestion. A common problem which they face is that of congested traffic in the downtown areas which is driving business to outlying shopping centers. It is a curious fact, also, that a merchant may complain that a strip of curb in front of his store is reserved for a transit stop when such a stop picks up and discharges potential customers. According to surveys made in metropolitan areas, most city travel is by private passenger car, and the average automobile carries 1.7 persons. It would, therefore, take 29 automobiles to carry the 50 people who could easily ride in a transit vehicle. One person in a moving automobile takes up 500 feet of street space, and the same person in a moving transit vehicle uses only 70 feet. The obvious solution is greater utilization of public transit in order to relieve both the traffic problem and the transit problem.

PRIVATE AUTOMOBILES

The position of the transit industry today and the factor that will condition its future is the private automobile. It is understandable that the private automobile should be favored for recreational purposes, but surveys show that over half of car trips are for the purpose of transportation to work or for business. In some cities the decrease in transit passengers is matched by new car registrations in the county or city.

The cost of operating a 1952 low-priced car based on annual mileage of 10,000 miles is shown in the following tabulation:[20]

	Cost per Year	Cost per Mile
Fixed costs:		
Depreciation	$ 460.00	$0.0460
Extra depreciation allowance	....	......
Insurance	182.28	.0182
License fee and taxes	11.00	.0011
Interest on investment (at 3%)	69.00	.0069
Total fixed costs	$ 722.28	$0.0722
Operating costs:		
Gasoline	$ 190.00	$0.0190
Oil	10.00	.0010
Tires	40.00	.0040
Maintenance	70.00	.0070
Miscellaneous expenses	10.00	.0010
Total operating expenses	$ 320.00	$0.0320
Total car costs	$1042.28	$0.1042

If the car is sold or traded after being owned only a year, the depreciation costs will be higher and the cost per mile correspondingly higher. If the car is a higher-priced car and if it is not driven at least 10,000 miles a year, the cost per mile will also be higher.

To the majority, however, the computing of automobile costs includes only those expenditures for gasoline and oil; and, if the gas tank is full, many motorists feel that the trip by car costs them nothing. This unrealistic attitude has so permeated the entire population that, even though transportation facilities are available at a lower cost, the riding public is just not availing itself of the facilities.

The private automobile has far-reaching effects on all our lives.

---

[20] "How Much Does It Cost to Run Your Car?" *Changing Times* as condensed in *Reader's Digest*, October, 1953.

Car owners apparently are more than willing to make any sacrifices necessary to own the latest model vehicle possible, not only because of the convenience afforded by the modern automobile but also because of the pleasure derived from this ownership.

QUESTIONS AND PROBLEMS

1. What is mass transportation? What are the different kinds of equipment used in urban passenger transportation?
2. Trace the development of transit operations up to 1930.
3. What are the trends in transit equipment?
4. Enumerate the reasons for the adoption of busses in transit operations. What is the position of busses with respect to use?
5. List and explain some of the factors in transit operations.
6. "A basic difficulty of transit operations has been the rigidity of the fare structure." Explain.
7. How do you account for the different types of fares which are used in transit operations?
8. What effect has the changing pattern in the average length of ride had upon transit company operations? Would you favor a zone fare? Why or why not?
9. "Municipal operation of urban transit lines does not provide the solution to any transit problems, whether financial or otherwise." Comment.
10. Why is the private automobile the primary competitor of the urban transit systems?
11. "The obvious solution is greater utilization of public transit in order to relieve both the traffic problem and the transit problem." Would you agree? What solution would you suggest?
12. In view of the financial plight of transit companies, what are some possible solutions which can be undertaken by cities? Transit companies?

BIBLIOGRAPHY

BIBLIOGRAPHY

BOOKS

ASHBY, W. T., and Others. *The Motor Truck Red Book*. New York: Traffic Publishing Co., Inc., 1942.

BAUER, JOHN, and COSTELLO, PETER. *Transit Modernization and Street Traffic Control*. Chicago: Public Administration Service, 1950.

BROEHL, W. G., JR. *Trucks, Trouble, and Triumph*. New York: Prentice-Hall, Inc., 1954.

BURGESS, R. H., JR. *Freight Transportation Selling*. Washington, D.C.: Traffic Service Corporation, 1950.

BURLEIGH, M., and ADAMS, C. M. *Modern Bus Terminals and Post Houses*. Ypsilanti, Mich.: University Lithoprinters, Inc., 1941.

DAY, H. J. *Motor Carriers Accounting and Cost Control System*. Washington, D.C.: Traffic Service Corporation, 1949.

DEARING, C. L., and OWEN, W. *National Transportation Policy*. Washington, D.C.: Brookings Institution, 1949.

———. *Toll Roads and the Problem of Highway Modernization*. Washington, D.C.: Brookings Institution, 1951.

EDWARDS, F. K. *Principles of Motor Transportation*. New York: McGraw-Hill Book Co., Inc., 1933.

HEBDEN, N., and SMITH, W. S. *State-City Relationships in Highway Affairs*. New Haven, Conn.: Yale University Press, 1950.

HILL, S. E. *Teamsters and Transportation: Employee-Employer Relationships in New England*. Washington, D.C.: Public Affairs Press, 1942.

JUSTIN, CARTER A. *Selling Motor Truck Service*. Washington, D.C.: American Trucking Associations, Inc., 1950.

LABATUT and LANE (ed.). *Highways in Our National Life*. Princeton, N.J.: Princeton University Press, 1950.

LEE, S. J. *Automotive Transportation in Industry*. Chicago: Fleet Management Corp., 1950.

LINDHOLM, R. W. *Taxation of the Trucking Industry*. Columbus, Ohio: Ohio State University, 1951.

MASON, E. S. *The Street Railway in Massachusetts*. Cambridge, Mass.: Harvard University Press, 1932.

MASON, L. W. *Local Trucking.* New York: McGraw-Hill Book Co., Inc., 1951.

MILLER, J. A. *Fares, Please.* New York: D. Appleton-Century-Crofts Co., Inc., 1943.

MILLER, J. M. *Law of Freight Loss and Damage Claims.* Dubuque, Iowa: Wm. C. Brown & Co., 1953.

OPPENHEIM, S. C. *The National Transportation Policy and Inter-carrier Competitive Rates.* Harrisburg, Penn.: Evangelical Press, 1945.

OWEN, W. *Automotive Transportation.* Washington, D.C.: Brookings Institution, 1949.

RODDA, W. H. *Inland Marine and Transportation Insurance.* New York: Prentice-Hall, Inc., 1949.

SHIDLE, N. G. *Motor Vehicle Transportation in American Life.* Washington, D.C.: National Education Association, 1945.

STOCKER, H. E. *Motor Traffic Management.* Rev. ed. New York: Prentice-Hall, Inc., 1942.

TAFF, CHARLES A. *Operating Rights of Motor Carriers.* Dubuque, Iowa: Wm. C. Brown & Co., 1953.

TUCKER, H., and LEAGER, M. C. *Highway Economics.* Scranton, Penn.: International Textbook Co., 1942.

WAGNER, WARREN H. *A Legislative History of the Motor Carrier Act, 1935.* Denton, Md.: Roe Publishing Co., 1935.

MONOGRAPHS

ASSOCIATION OF AMERICAN RAILROADS. *Highway Motor Transportation.* Washington, D.C., 1945.

BERGE, STANLEY (ed.). *Motor Freight Management.* Chicago: Northwestern University, 1951.

BLACK, GUY. *Long-Haul Truck Transportation of California Fresh Fruits and Vegetables.* California Agricultural Experiment Station, University of California, 1955.

CRANDALL, BURTON B. *The Growth of the Intercity Bus Industry.* Syracuse, N.Y., 1954.

GLASCOW, C. C., JR., and GIFFORD, G. L. *An Analysis of Motor Carrier Tariffs.* Knoxville, Tenn.: Tennessee Press Association, University of Tennessee, 1952.

MCCARTY, J. F. *State Regulation and Taxation of Highway Carriers.* Berkeley, Calif.: Bureau of Public Administration, University of California Press, 1953.

———. *Highway Financing by the Toll System.* Berkeley, Calif.: Bureau of Public Administration, University of California Press, 1951.

MOSSMAN, FRANK H. (ed.). *Principles of Urban Transportation.* Cleveland, Ohio: Western Reserve University Press, 1951.

REGULAR COMMON CARRIER CONFERENCE. *Individual Home Study Course on Sales Training.* Washington, D.C., 1953.

TRANSPORTATION COMMITTEE ON PRACTICES AND PROCEDURES (National Traffic Committee, Regular Common Carrier Conference, Common Carrier Conference–Irregular Route). *Report of Survey: Recommendations for More Efficient Handling of Small Shipments.* Washington, D.C.: American Trucking Associations, Inc., 1954.

———. *Guide to Better Motor Carrier Operations.* Washington, D.C.: American Trucking Associations, Inc., 1954.

———. *Principles of Freight Terminal Operations.* Washington, D.C.: American Trucking Associations, Inc., 1954.

———. *Shipper-Motor Carrier Relations.* Washington, D.C.: American Trucking Associations, Inc., 1954.

WYETH, H. F. *The Motor Carrier Industry.* New York: Shields and Co., 1951.

GOVERNMENT PUBLICATIONS

BOARD OF INVESTIGATION AND RESEARCH. *Relative Economy and Fitness of the Carriers.* House Doc. No. 595, 78th Cong., 2d sess. Washington, D.C.: U.S. Government Printing Office, 1944.

———. *The National Traffic Pattern.* Sen. Doc. No. 83, 79th Cong., 1st sess. Washington, D.C.: U.S. Government Printing Office, 1945.

———. *Interstate Trade Barriers Affecting Motor-Vehicle Transportation.* Sen. Doc. No. 81, 79th Cong., 1st sess. Washington, D.C.: U.S. Government Printing Office, 1945.

———. *Carrier Taxation.* House Doc. No. 160, 79th Cong., 1st sess. Washington, D.C.: U.S. Government Printing Office, 1944.

———. *Federal Regulatory Restrictions upon Motor and Water Carriers.* House Doc. No. 637, 78th Cong., 2d sess. Washington, D.C.: U.S. Government Printing Office, 1944 (Summary report).

———. *Federal Regulatory Restrictions upon Motor and Water Carriers.* Sen. Doc. No. 78, 79th Cong., 1st sess., U.S. Government Printing Office, 1945.

———. *Technological Trends in Transportation.* Sen. Doc. No. 76, 79th Cong., 1st sess. Washington, D.C.: U.S. Government Printing Office, 1945.

———. *Public Aids to Domestic Transportation.* House Doc. No. 159, 79th Cong., 1st sess. Washington, D.C.: U.S. Government Printing Office, 1945.

———. *Comparison of Rail, Motor and Water Carrier Costs.* Sen. Doc. No. 84, 79th Cong., 1st sess. Washington, D.C.: U.S. Government Printing Office, 1945.

———. *Report on Rate-Making and Rate-Publishing Procedures of Railroad, Motor, and Water Carriers.* House Doc. No. 363, 78th

Cong., 1st sess. Washington, D.C.: U.S. Government Printing Office, 1944.

BUREAU OF PUBLIC ROADS. *Highway Statistics.* (Summary to 1945; annually since that time.) Washington, D.C.: U.S. Government Printing Office.

———. *Annual Reports* to the Congress. Washington, D.C.: U.S. Government Printing Office.

DEFENSE TRANSPORT ADMINISTRATION. *Report on Revenue Vehicles Owned and Operated by Class I Carriers of Property.* Washington, D.C., 1952.

———. *Automobile Transportation in Defense or War.* Washington, D.C.: U.S. Government Printing Office, 1951.

DEPARTMENT OF AGRICULTURE. *Interstate Barriers to Truck Transportation.* Washington, D.C., 1950.

———. *The Transportation and Handling of Grain by Motor Truck in the Southwest.* Washington, D.C., 1952.

———. *Transportation of Frozen Citrus Concentrate by Railroad and Motor Truck from Florida to Northern Markets.* Washington, D.C.: U.S. Government Printing Office, 1951.

———. *Trucks Haul Increased Share of Fruit and Vegetable Traffic.* Washington, D.C., 1953.

———. *Length of Haul to Leading Markets by Motortruck, 1941 and 1950.* Washington, D.C., 1953.

DEPARTMENT OF COMMERCE. *Domestic Transportation.* Washington, D.C.: October–November, 1945; February–March, 1946; June–July, 1946.

———. *An Evaluation of Motor Truck Transportation.* Washington, D.C.: May–August, 1948.

———. *Establishing and Operating a Trucking Business.* Washington, D.C.: U.S. Government Printing Office, 1946.

———. *Charges for Private Use of Federally-Provided Transportation Services and Facilities.* Washington, D.C., 1953.

———. Bureau of the Census, *Pilot Survey of Commodity Movements by Truck,* March–May, 1953. Washington, D.C., December, 1954.

FEDERAL CO-ORDINATOR OF TRANSPORTATION. *Public Aids to Transportation.* Vols. I and IV. Washington, D.C.: U.S. Government Printing Office, 1940.

HOUSE COMMITTEE ON INTERSTATE AND FOREIGN COMMERCE. *Federal Regulation of the Sizes and Weight of Motor Vehicles.* House Doc. No. 354, 77th Cong., 2d sess. Washington, D.C.: U.S. Government Printing Office, 1941.

———. *National Transportation Inquiry.* Parts 1 and 2. 80th Cong., 2d sess. Washington, D.C.: U.S. Government Printing Office, 1948.

———. *Agreements between Carriers.* 80th Cong., 1st sess. Washington, D.C.: U.S. Government Printing Office, 1947.

———. *Trip Leasing.* 83rd Cong., 1st sess. Washington, D.C.: U.S. Government Printing Office, 1953.

HOUSE COMMITTEE ON PUBLIC WORKS. *Highway Needs of the National Defense.* House Doc. No. 249, 81st Cong., 1st sess. Washington, D.C.: U.S. Government Printing Office, 1949.

———. *National Highway Study.* Parts I and II. 83rd Cong., 1st sess. Washington, D.C.: U.S. Government Printing Office, 1953.

HOUSE COMMITTEE ON ROADS. *Interregional Highways.* House Doc. No. 379, 78th Cong., 2d sess. Washington, D.C.: U.S. Government Printing Office, 1944.

INTERSTATE COMMERCE COMMISSION. *Annual Reports* to the Congress. Washington, D.C.: U.S. Government Printing Office.

———. *Monthly Comment on Transportation Statistics.* Washington, D.C.

———. *Some Aspects of Postwar Air and Surface Transportation.* Washington, D.C., 1945.

———. BUREAU OF ACCOUNTS AND COST FINDING. *Territorial Cost Scales and Operating Performance Factors in Middle Atlantic Territory.* Identification A and B. Washington, D.C., 1948.

———. BUREAU OF ACCOUNTS AND COST FINDING. *Territorial Studies of Motor Carrier Costs and Operating Performance Factors. Central Territory.* Parts I and II. Washington, D.C., 1949.

———. BUREAU OF ACCOUNTS AND COST FINDING. *Territorial Study Showing Development of Unit Costs, Operating Performance Factors, and Cost Scales.* Washington, D.C., 1950.

———. BUREAU OF ACCOUNTS AND COST FINDING. *Unit Costs, Performance Factors, Cost Scales and Traffic Data for Motor Common Carriers of General Freight in Southern Territory.* Washington, D.C., 1953.

———. BUREAU OF ACCOUNTS AND COST FINDING. *Simplified Procedure for Determining Cost of Handling Freight by Motor Carriers.* Washington, D.C., 1953.

———. BUREAU OF ACCOUNTS, COST FINDING, AND VALUATION. *Cost Study of Class I Motor Carriers of General Freight in the Middlewest Territory—Year 1953.* Washington, D.C., 1954.

———. BUREAU OF ACCOUNTS, COST FINDING, AND VALUATION. *Cost Study of Class I Motor Carriers of General Freight in the Southwest Territory—Year 1953.* Washington, D.C., 1954.

———. BUREAU OF TRANSPORT ECONOMICS AND STATISTICS. *Motor Operations of Class I Railroads.* Washington, D.C., 1953.

———. BUREAU OF TRANSPORT ECONOMICS AND STATISTICS. *Class I, II, and III Motor Carrier Revenues, Ton-Miles, and Passenger-Miles, 1939–51.* Washington, D.C., 1953.

———. BUREAU OF TRANSPORT ECONOMICS AND STATISTICS. *Historical Development of Transport Coordination and Integration in the United States.* Washington, D.C., 1950.

————. Bureau of Transport Economics and Statistics. *Statistics of Small Shipments.* Washington, D.C., 1953.

————. Bureau of Transport Economics and Statistics. *Practices of Motor Carriers of Property in the Division of Revenues on Joint Hauls.* Washington, D.C., 1945.

————. Bureau of Transport Economics and Statistics. *Territorial Studies of Motor Carrier Costs, Traffic, and Rate Structure. Western Trunk Line Territory.* Parts I and II. Washington, D.C., 1947.

————. Bureau of Transport Economics and Statistics. *Territorial Studies of Motor Carrier Costs, Traffic, and Rate Structure. Southern Intraterritorial.* Parts I and II. Washington, D.C., 1946, 1947.

————. Bureau of Transport Economics and Statistics. *Motor Operations by or for Class I Railroads, 1944.* Washington, D.C., 1948.

————. Bureau of Transport Economics and Statistics. *Operating Costs of Intercity Motor Carriers of Passengers.* Washington, D.C., 1945.

————. Bureau of Transport Economics and Statistics. *Statistics of Class I Motor Carriers.* (Annual.) Washington, D.C.: U.S. Government Printing Office.

————. Bureau of Transport Economics and Statistics. *Revenues, Ton-Miles, and Passenger-Miles of Class I, II, and III Motor Carriers, 1940, 1941, and 1944–1948.* Washington, D.C., 1949.

————. Bureau of Transport Economics and Statistics. *Explanation of the Development of Motor Carrier Costs with Statement as to Their Meaning and Significance.* Washington, D.C., 1946, and revised issues of 1949 and 1954.

————. Motor Carrier Cases, Vols. I–LXI. Washington, D.C.: U.S. Government Printing Office.

Joint Committee on the Economic Report. *Highways and the Nation's Economy.* 81st Cong., 2d sess. Washington, D.C.: U.S. Government Printing Office, 1950.

National Resources Planning Board. *Transportation and National Policy.* Washington, D.C.: U.S. Government Printing Office, 1942.

Office of Defense Transportation. *A Review of Highway Transport and Transit Industries during the War.* Washington, D.C., 1945.

————. *Civilian War Transport, 1941–1946.* Washington, D.C.: U.S. Government Printing Office, 1948.

————. *Report of the Federal Manager of Motor Carrier Transportation Systems and Properties.* Washington, D.C., 1947.

————. *Supplemental Report of the Federal Manager of Motor Carrier Transportation Systems and Properties.* (Prepared by Bureau of Transport Economics of the Interstate Commerce Commission.) Washington, D.C., 1946.

SECRETARY OF COMMERCE. *Issues Involved in a Unified and Co-ordinated Federal Program for Transportation.* Washington, D.C.: U.S. Government Printing Office, December 1, 1949.

SENATE COMMITTEE ON INTERSTATE AND FOREIGN COMMERCE. *Regulation of Rate Bureaus, Conferences, and Associations.* 80th Cong., 1st sess. Washington, D.C.: U.S. Government Printing Office, 1947.

———. *Regulation of Rate Bureaus, Conferences, and Associations.* 79th Cong., 2d sess. Washington, D.C.: U.S. Government Printing Office, 1946.

———. *Regulation of Rate Bureaus.* 78th Cong., 1st sess. Washington, D.C.: U.S. Government Printing Office, 1944.

———. *Study of Domestic Land and Water Transportation.* 81st Cong., 2d sess. Washington, D.C.: U.S. Government Printing Office, 1950.

———. *Domestic Land and Water Transportation.* 82d Cong., 2d sess. Washington, D.C.: U.S. Government Printing Office, 1952.

SENATE COMMITTEE ON PUBLIC WORKS. *Federal Aid Highway Act of 1950.* 81st Cong., 2d sess. Washington, D.C.: U.S. Government Printing Office, 1950.

———. *Federal Aid Highway Act of 1952.* 82d Cong., 2d sess. Washington, D.C.: U.S. Government Printing Office, 1952.

OTHER REPORTS

AMERICAN TRANSIT ASSOCIATION. *Transit Fact Book.* (Annual.) New York.

AMERICAN TRUCKING ASSOCIATIONS, INC. *Trends.* (Annual.) Washington, D.C.

———. *Financial and Operating Statistics, Class I Motor Carriers of Property.* (Annual.) Washington, D.C.

AUTOMOBILE MANUFACTURERS ASSOCIATION. *Automobile Facts and Figures.* (Annual.) Detroit, Mich.

———. *Motor Truck Facts.* (Biennial.) Detroit, Mich.

AUTOMOTIVE SAFETY FOUNDATION. *Highway Facts.* Washington, D.C., 1952.

NATIONAL ASSOCIATION OF MOTOR BUS OPERATORS. *Bus Facts.* (Annual.) Washington, D.C.

NATIONAL HIGHWAY USERS CONFERENCE. Many reports are issued by the Conference. Washington, D.C.

TRANSPORT RESEARCH, INC. *Manual of Highway Carriers, Class I Freight.* (Annual.) Washington, D.C.

PERIODICALS

The rapid developments which take place in commercial motor transportation are reported in the many periodicals in the field, some of which are footnoted in the text. *Public Roads,* published bimonthly by the

Bureau of Public Roads, is a valuable source of information. *Highway Research Abstracts,* published monthly, except August, by the Highway Research Board, Washington, D.C. is one of the many publications of the Board which are helpful. The reader is referred also to the following representative trade papers for current articles dealing with the freight aspects of commercial motor transportation:

American Cartagemen, published monthly by American Cartagemen Publishing Corp., Detroit.

Commercial Car Journal, published monthly by Chilton Company, Inc., Philadelphia.

Fleet Owner, published monthly by McGraw-Hill Publishing Co., New York.

Motor Transportation, published monthly by Motor Transportation, Inc., Seattle.

Power Wagon, published monthly by Motor Truck Publishing Company, Inc., Chicago.

Southern Motor Cargo, published monthly by Motor Cargo, Inc., Memphis.

The Petroleum Transporter, published bimonthly by the Petroleum Transportation Publishing Co., Inc., Washington, D.C.

Traffic World, published weekly by Traffic Service Corporation, Washington, D.C.

Transport Topics, published weekly by American Trucking Associations, Inc., Washington, D.C.

In the commercial motor passenger field are the following publications:

Bus Transportation, published monthly by McGraw-Hill Publishing Co., New York.

Mass Transportation, published monthly by Kenfield-Davis Publishing Company, Chicago.

Passenger Transportation, published weekly by American Transit Association, New York.

Index

INDEX

This book has been set on the Linotype in 11 point Baskerville leaded 2 points and 10 point Baskerville leaded 1 point. Chapter numbers and titles are in 18 point Spartan Medium italics. The size of the type page is 27 by 46½ picas.